# MANUAL OF
# EUROPEAN ENVIRONMENTAL LAW

# MANUAL OF
# EUROPEAN ENVIRONMENTAL LAW

by

ALEXANDRE KISS
Professor of Law
University Robert Schuman
Strasbourg, France

DINAH SHELTON
Professor of Law
Santa Clara University
Santa Clara, California

A PUBLICATION OF
THE STANDING CONFERENCE OF RECTORS, PRESIDENTS AND
VICE-CHANCELLORS OF THE EUROPEAN UNIVERSITIES

**C R E    COPERNICUS**

AND

## CAMBRIDGE
## GROTIUS PUBLICATIONS LIMITED
1993

*SALES &*
*ADMINISTRATION*

*GROTIUS PUBLICATIONS LTD*
*P.O. BOX 115, CAMBRIDGE CB3 9BP, ENGLAND*

British Library Cataloguing in Publication Data

Kiss, Alexandre
  Manual of European Environmental Law
  I. Title II. Shelton, Dinah
  341.762

  ISBN 1-85701-018-3 (Paperback)
  ISBN 1-85701-019-1 (Hardback)

©
GROTIUS PUBLICATIONS LIMITED
1993

Typeset in Monotype Baskerville by Carnegie Publishing Ltd., Maynard St., Preston
Printed in Great Britain by Gomer Press, Llandysul, Dyfed

# SUMMARY OF CONTENTS

# TABLE OF CONTENTS

## PART I   OVERVIEW

# PART II   SECTORAL PROTECTION

# PART III  TRANSSECTORAL ISSUES

# FOREWORD

The Standing Conference of Rectors, Presidents and Vice-Chancellors of the European Universities (CRE) is pleased to co-publish this Manual of European Environmental Law with Grotius Publications. Conceived as a teaching tool and reference work for lawyers and non-specialists alike, it is the first publication of the COPERNICUS programme (Co-operation Programme in Europe for Research on Nature and Industry through Co-ordinated University Studies). This programme was set up by the CRE in 1988 to promote environmental education and research in an east–west, interdisciplinary perspective. We hope that the Manual will receive wide circulation and be used in most of the universities of Europe and beyond, as well as by lawyers, political decision-makers and industrialists concerned with the ever-present problems of environmental law.

The idea of this publication was first tested at an international colloquium on Law and Environment hosted by the University of Angers in France (November 1991). The 'Angers Appeal', which concluded the meeting, was addressed to universities and research institutes throughout Europe. It recommended that the study of environmental law be systematically incorporated as a compulsory subject in different university curricula, and that research projects be developed in order to codify appropriate standards for the protection and conservation of the natural environment in all its forms. The present Manual should stimulate reflection and teaching in this field and help to raise awareness of the issues involved.

The CRE wishes to express its gratitude to the organizers and sponsors of the Angers colloquium, as well as to the participants from universities, international organizations and the private sector, all of whom gave of their time and expertise. Although many of the Angers papers – often considerably revised – have been included in this volume in the form of case studies, the arduous task of writing the main text, editing the contributions and compiling the source material has fallen to two co-authors, both of whom were present in Angers: Professor Alexandre Kiss of the University Robert Schuman, Strasbourg and Professor Dinah Shelton of Santa Clara University in the USA. The CRE is much indebted to them for their meticulous and inspired treatment of the wealth of available material.

Last but not least, the CRE wishes to thank the international organizations which have sponsored the writing of this book. Directorate-General XI of the Commission of the European Communities in Brussels has provided a generous grant to cover the preparation of the manuscript in both English and French; moreover, the Director of Legal Affairs, Dr Ludwig Krämer – who is also a contributor to the Manual – has given his personal support to the whole undertaking. UNESCO, through its Division of Higher Education and its Environmental Education Section, has also funded a large part of our collective efforts through its UNITWIN Programme, and we are particularly grateful to the Director General, Professor Federico Mayor, for his unfailing encouragement of COPERNICUS and for having written the Preface to this publication. The work of UNESCO in environmental education is exemplary, and the CRE is honoured to have been associated with it.

Professor Hinrich Seidel
President CRE

## CRE

The Conference of European Rectors (CRE) is the association of European universities. Its membership comprises some 500 universities or equivalent institutions of higher education in over 30 countries. It provides a forum for discussions on academic policy and the institutional development of universities, including their role within European society. As a non-governmental organization, it represents the universities' point of view in governmental and non-governmental circles concerned with higher education in Europe. CRE organizes bi-annual conferences, training seminars for newly appointed university heads, and other meetings on issues of particular interest to its members. It also runs a number of inter-university co-operation programmes.

## COPERNICUS

COPERNICUS (Co-operation Programme in Europe for Research on Nature and Industry through Co-ordinated University Studies) is a programme of CRE designed to bring together universities and other concerned sectors of society from all parts of Europe to promote a better understanding of the interaction between man and the environment and to collaborate on common environmental issues. The aims of the programme are: to incorporate an environmental perspective into all university education and to help develop teaching materials as necessary; to stimulate and co-ordinate integrated, multidisciplinary and collaborative research projects; and to disseminate the research and empirical findings widely to economic and political decision-makers. Priority areas for the time being are comparative environmental law, resource economics, public health, and environmental management. To encourage the bridging of former divisions between eastern and western Europe, COPERNICUS has set up transnational projects involving institutions from the Baltic and Danube regions. Future plans involve expanding the programme to other regions in Europe.

# PREFACE

UNESCO has been pleased to provide support for the publication of this Manual of European Environmental Law prepared by Professor Alexandre Kiss and Professor Dinah Shelton for the European Rectors' Conference (CRE).

This is an important outcome of Project COPERNICUS, which promotes collaboration between universities, industry and the public sector with specific reference to the fields of environmental law, economics and health. Through COPERNICUS, the CRE has made a major contribution to UNESCO's Project UNITWIN which seeks to reinforce university teaching and research in key domains related to sustainable development. UNITWIN, in turn, links up with other programmes to form part of UNESCO's contribution to the implementation of Agenda 21, drawn up by the United Nations Conference on Environment and Development (Rio de Janeiro 1992) to define the specific contribution of each UN specialized agency to the promotion of sustainable development.

Environmental problems have far-reaching social implications and their solution will call for radical changes in public awareness and attitudes as well as new legislative frameworks. It is for this reason that UNESCO places great emphasis on environmental education as an essential component of the curriculum at all educational levels. To this end, the International Environmental Education Programme (IEEP) was established by UNESCO and the United Nations Environment Programme (UNEP) in 1975 to promote the incorporation of environmental education, as an interdisciplinary topic, into policy-making, planning, curriculum design and teacher training within the Member States of UNESCO. Following on from the Earth Summit, environmental education – including the essential development dimension – is set to acquire even greater importance in UNESCO's programme.

Against this background the publication of this manual may be seen as most timely. It provides a thorough discussion of the wide range of issues coming within the purview of environmental law, contains a wealth of information on legislative practice and content within the European setting and is particularly instructive on the interrelationship between the national, regional and international dimensions. It should make a valuable contribution to a relatively new but fast-evolving university discipline and should at the same time prove a useful tool for the non-academic reader concerned directly or indirectly with environmental questions.

UNESCO thanks the authors for making their scholarship available in the form of this lucid and well-documented study.

Federico Mayor
Director-General UNESCO

# AUTHOR'S NOTE

The purpose of this book is to provide teaching materials and a reference work for University and professional courses in environmental law. It is hoped that the book will prove useful beyond the legal community and will support multi-disciplinary studies. Given this aim, we present an overview of all the main aspects of environmental laws in Europe.

Unlike the usual treatises, most chapters include case studies drawn from presentations delivered at a colloquium on Environmental Protection and the Law, held at Angers, France, in November 1991. Some papers have been updated and edited; in all cases, the texts represent the views of the contributors. They are, of course, not responsible for any expressions or errors appearing in the rest of the book.

For study and teaching purposes, primary documents are included after the textual materials, in all chapters except IV. It is impossible to include all the relevant documents, so selections have been made to illustrate the principal approaches and significant legal developments in the field. An effort has been made to select documents from national, Community and international law, to indicate the variety of approaches in as many countries as possible.

The chapters conclude with questions and problems for discussion, and a bibliography. The questions are drawn from current legal problems and are intended to provoke discussion and use of the texts provided.

Environmental needs and the laws that address them change very rapidly. It is therefore likely that some of the materials we include have been amended or replaced during the writing and publication of the book, in spite of efforts to incorporate the most recent information available. In one instance, we anticipate developments; we use the term European Community or EC throughout the text to refer to the present Communities.

We would like to thank CRE for initiating this project and for the constant support and help given by Alison de Puymège, Andris Barblon, and Peri Pamir. In addition, the book benefitted from the aid of Santa Clara University. We are especially grateful to Angeles de Leon, who typed innumerable drafts of the various chapters with equal parts good will and efficiency. We would like to acknowledge Tammy Brown, Anne Heindelle, and Mark Wolfe, who provided excellent student research on several subjects.

# CHRONOLOGICAL TABLE OF
# INTERNATIONAL AND EC DOCUMENTS

| | |
|---|---|
| 19 May 1900 | Convention for the Preservation of Wild Animals, Birds and Fish in Africa, 188 Parry 418; 10. |
| 19 March 1902 | Convention for the Protection of Birds Useful to Agriculture (Paris), 30 Martens (2d) 686; 10, 124. |
| 11 March 1941 | Arbitral Award, Trail Smelter Case, 3 *U.N.R.I.A.A.* 1911; 331, 338, 340. |
| 4 November 1950 | European Convention for the Protection of Human Rights and Freedoms (Rome), 213 *U.N.T.S.* 221; 43, 494, 511. |
| 18 April 1951 | Treaty Establishing the European Coal and Steel Community (Paris), 261 *U.N.T.S.* 140; 18. |
| 25 March 1957 | Treaty Establishing the European Economic Community (Rome), 298 *U.N.T.S.* 11; 18, 19, 35, 351, 353, 467. |
| 25 March 1957 | Treaty Establishing the European Atomic Energy Community (Euratom) (Rome), 298 *U.N.T.S.* 167; 18. |
| 20 March 1958 | Agreement Concerning the Adoption of Uniform Conditions of Approval and Reciprocal Recognition of Approval for Motor Vehicle Equipment and Parts (Geneva) 335 *U.N.T.S.* 211; 336, 351. |
| 29 July 1960 | Convention on Third Party Liability in the Field of Nuclear Energy (Paris), Kiss 159; 75, 408. |
| 29 April 1963 | Agreement Concerning the International Commission for the Protection of the Rhine against Pollution (Bern), Kiss, 176; 255. |
| 21 May 1963 | Vienna Convention on Civil Liability for Nuclear Damage, 2 *I.L.M.* 727 (1963); 75, 408. |
| 5 August 1963 | Treaty Banning Nuclear Weapon Tests in the Atmosphere, in Outer Space and Under Water (Moscow), Kiss 185; 278. |
| 23 September 1966 | Agreement Between Belgium and France Concerning Nuclear Accidents, *Moniteur belge*, 7 March 1967; 498. |
| 16 December 1966 | UN Covenant on Civil and Political Rights, 6 *I.L.M.* 368 (1967); 43. |
| 16 December 1966 | UN Covenant on Economic, Social and Cultural Rights, 6 *I.L.M.* 360 (1967); 43. |
| 27 June 1967 | EC Directive Relating to the Classification, Packaging and Labelling of Dangerous Substances, 67/548/EEC, O.J., L 196, 16 August 1967; 4, 396, 399, 400. |

# TABLE OF NATIONAL LAWS AND CASES

# LIST OF ABBREVIATIONS

| | |
|---|---|
| ACP | African, Caribbean and Pacific States |
| AFDI | Annuaire français de droit international |
| A.J.I.L. | American Journal of International Law |
| Am.J.Comp.L. | American Journal of Comparative Law |
| BAT | Best available technology |
| BATNEEC | Best available technology not involving excessive costs |
| BEP | Best environmental practice |
| BPEO | Best practical environmental option |
| CEFIC | European Chemical Industries Federation |
| CFC | Chlorofluorocarbon |
| CITES | Convention on International Trade in Endangered Species |
| Cmd | United Kingdom Command Papers |
| CMLR | Common Market Law Review |
| COM | Commission |
| Comp.L | Comparative Law |
| Conn. | Connecticut |
| CSCE | Conference on Security and Co-operation in Europe |
| CSFR | Czech and Slovak Federal Republic |
| Den. | Denver |
| DOE | Department of Environment |
| EC or EEC | European Economic Community |
| ECR | European Community Reports |
| EEZ | Exclusive economic zone |
| EIA | Environmental impact assessment |
| EMEP | Co-operative Programme for Monitoring and Evaluation of the Long-Range Transmission of Air Pollution in Europe |
| Env.L | Environmental Law |
| Envtl Pol. & L. | Environmental Policy and Law |
| EPA | Environmental Protection Agency |
| EQS | Environmental Quality Standard |
| ETS | European Treaty Series |
| EURATOM | European Atomic Energy Community |
| Eur.Ct.H.R. | European Court of Human Rights |
| Eur.Ct.J. | European Court of Justice |
| FAO | United Nations Food and Agricultural Organization |
| GA | General Assembly |

| | |
|---|---|
| GAO | General Administrative Order |
| GDR | German Democratic Republic |
| GEMS | Global Environment Monitoring System |
| GMO | Genetically modified organisms |
| HELCOM | Helsinki Commission |
| HL | Hunting Law |
| Hous. | Houston |
| IAEA | International Atomic Energy Agency |
| ICJ | International Court of Justice |
| ICSU | International Commission of Scientific Unions |
| ILM | International Legal Materials |
| ILO | International Labour Organization |
| IMC | Isolation, Monitoring, Control |
| INC | Intergovernmental Negotiating Committee |
| Int'l Env.L | International Environmental Law: Multilateral Agreements |
| Int'l. J | International Journal |
| Int'l. L. | International Law |
| IPC | Integrated Pollution Control |
| IPCC | Intergovernmental Panel on Climatic Change |
| IUCN | World Conservation Union (formerly International Union for the Conservation of Nature and Natural Resources) |
| J. | Journal |
| Kiss | *Selected Multilateral Treaties in the Field of the Environment* (UNEP, 1983) |
| L. | Law |
| LW | Law on Hydraulic Power |
| MARPOL | International Convention for the Prevention of Pollution by Ships |
| Md. | Maryland |
| Mich. | Michigan |
| NIH | National Institute of Health |
| Nat.Res. J. | Natural Resources Journal |
| NGO | Non-governmental Organization |
| NPD | Nature Protection Decree |
| NPL | Nature Protection Law |
| OECD | Organization for Economic Co-operation and Development |
| O.J. | Official Journal of the European Communities |
| OSCOM | Oslo Commission |
| PARCOM | Paris Commission |
| Parry | Parry, Consolidated Treaty Series |
| PCBs | Polychlorinated biphenyls |
| Q. | Quarterly |
| Res. | Resolution |
| SCA | Soil Clean-up Act |
| Solic. J. | Solicitor's Journal |
| SPA | Soil Protection Act |
| Stan. | Stanford |

| | |
|---|---|
| TCSP | Technical Commission on Soil Protection |
| Tex. | Texas |
| TIAS | US Treaties and Other International Instruments |
| U. | University |
| UES | Uniform Emission Standards |
| UK | United Kingdom of Great Britain and Northern Ireland |
| UKTS | UK Treaty Series |
| UN | United Nations Organization |
| UNCED | United Nations Conference on Environment and Development |
| UNCLOS | United Nations Convention on the Law of the Sea |
| UNECE | United Nations Economic Commission for Europe |
| UNEP | United Nations Environment Programme |
| UNESCO | United Nations Educational, Scientific and Cultural Organization |
| UNGA | United Nations General Assembly |
| UNIDO | United Nations International Development Organization |
| UNRIAA | United Nations Reports on Arbital Awards |
| UNTS | United Nations Treaty Series |
| US | United States |
| USC | US Code |
| USSR | Union of Soviet Socialist Republics |
| VOC | Volatile Organic Compounds |
| WHO | World Health Organization |
| WMO | World Meteorological Organization |
| WWF | Worldwide Fund for Nature (formerly World Wildlife Fund) |

# PART I

# OVERVIEW

CHAPTER I

# INTRODUCTION

European environmental law is a new legal discipline, but one already substantial and complex. Defining its scope is not easy, because it continues to evolve rapidly. In addition, the basic terms "environment", "law" and even "European" have multiple definitions and usages. Chapter I discusses some of the terminology and characteristic aspects of this increasingly important area of law, then reviews its history and legal framework.

## A. Terminology

### 1. *Environment*

The term environment can describe a limited area or almost infinite space and factors. In its largest physical sense the environment has been described as "the house created on earth for living things".[1] Webster's *Dictionary* begins with a general definition of environment as "the circumstances, objects, or conditions by which one is surrounded".[2] It goes on to provide a more precise meaning:

> the complex of physical, chemical, and biotic ,actors (as climate, soil, and living things) that act upon an organism or an ecological community and ultimately determine its form and survival

to which it adds "the aggregate of social and cultural conditions that influence the life of an individual or community". The last definition is very broad and brings urban problems such as traffic congestion, crime, and noise within the field of environmental protection.

Some legal definitions also are expansive. Section 1(1) of the supplementary provisions to the 1991 Bulgarian Environmental Protection Act defines environment as

> a complex of natural and anthropogenic factors and elements that are mutually inter-related and affect the ecological equilibrium and the quality of life, human health, the cultural and historical heritage and the landscape.

Similarly, Portuguese Basic Environmental Law 11/87 of 7 April 1987, applies to virtually all components of the natural and human environment. The first category,

---

[1] Barry Commoner, *The Closing Circle* 32 (1972). "Ecology", the study of the inter-relationship of all living things and their surroundings, is sometimes substituted for "environment".

[2] "Environment", *Webster's Ninth New Collegiate Dictionary*, 1983.

defined in article 6, includes air, light, water, soil and subsoil, flora and fauna. The human environment, listed in article 17, comprises the countryside, natural and cultural heritage, and different forms of pollution.

Environment may be defined more narrowly in relation to a particular legislative purpose. For example, section 1 of the British Environmental Protection Act 1990, defines environment in light of its aim of integrated pollution control:

> the environment consists of all, or any, of the following media, namely, the air, water and land; and the medium of air includes the air within buildings and the air within other natural or man-made structures above or below ground.

A legal text adopted by the Council of the European Economic Community provides an example of a general, though not all-inclusive definition:

> (1)(c) ' environment" means water, air and land and their inter-relationship as well as relationships between them and any living organism.[3]

It describes well the focus of most environmental law; however, the relationship between humans and the artificial environments they create, that is, urban and working environments, today is included in many comprehensive environmental laws and integrated environmental plans.

The definition of environment has several implications for environmental law. The dictionary definition, quoted above, notes that the environment determines the form and survival of an organism or community. Environmental law springs from this understanding, representing national, regional, and international efforts to ensure the continued viability of the planet and the sustainability of its myriad species. The various legal techniques utilized for this purpose are the subject of subsequent chapters.

The scope of laws also is affected by the definition of environment. Law and policy are responding to increasing environmental deterioration, produced by natural causes, such as volcanic eruptions, and by human intervention. Law cannot affect the natural processes that cause environmental changes. However, laws can and do regulate human behaviour, including human behaviour in response to natural disasters. In this regard, the 1991 Bulgarian Environmental Protection Act provides that all persons, the state and municipal authorities have the right to available information concerning the environment (article 9), including data about the results of activities that bring or may bring about pollution or damage to the environment (article 8). In addition, authorities and other persons must inform the population without delay of pollution or damage to the environment, including natural disasters (article 13).

## 2. *Pollution*

Humans cause environmental harm through pollution and through acts that destroy the ecological balance, such as eliminating certain species and clear-cutting

---

[3] Article 2, Council Directive of 27 June 1967, O.J. no. L 196, 16 June 1967 p. 1.

forests. Most definitions of pollution demonstrate the focus of environmental law on human conduct; a commonly accepted definition is

> … the introduction by man, directly or indirectly, of substances or energy into the environment resulting in deleterious effects of such a nature as to endanger human health, harm living resources and ecosystems, and impair or interfere with amenities and other legitimate uses of the environment.[4]

This definition clearly limits pollution to changes produced by human activities. By referring to "substances or energy" it includes not only solid, liquid or gaseous material, but also noise, vibrations, heat and radiation. On the other hand, not every introduction is deemed polluting, only those that reach a level sufficient to cause (1) danger, i.e. risk of, or (2) actual harm to humans, living resources and ecosystems. In addition, substances can be considered polluting or harmful if their introduction interferes with other uses of the environment, including aesthetic appreciation. Using this approach, the UK Environmental Protection Act 1990 defines pollution as the release into any environmental medium from any process of substances which are capable of causing harm to man or any other living organisms supported by the environment.[5] "Harm" is defined as injury to the health of living organisms or other interference with the ecological systems of which they form part and, in the case of man, includes offence caused to any of his senses or harm to his property.[6] In this regard there may be differing value judgments about the acceptable quality or quantity of matter introduced, reflected in various national laws.

It should be noted that a few texts define pollution without regard to whether it originates in human activities and irrespective of harm to the environment. For example, according to the Bulgarian Environmental Protection Act of October 1991 "pollution of the environment" means

> the change of its qualities as a result of the occurrence and introduction of physical, chemical or biological factors from a natural or anthropogenic source in the country or outside it, irrespective of whether they exceed or not the standards valid for the country.

It is through the concept of "damage to the environment" that the Bulgarian law focuses on harmful pollution, defining damage as "pollution that disturbs or may cause irreversible disturbance of the equilibrium of the ecosystems, exceeding the prescribed standards and requirements."

In sum, environment, pollution and other concepts fundamental to action in this field have several meanings. Those who draft legislation and those who must

---

[4] OECD Council Recommendation C(74) 224 of 14 November 1974. There are numerous other definitions in doctrine and legislation, from pollution as any alteration of the environment regardless of harm, to pollution as tangible damage resulting in provable monetary damages. The OECD definition represents a middle view and is most widely accepted.

[5] Environmental Protection Act, 1990 c. 43 Part I, sec. 1 (3).

[6] *Id.*, sec. 1 (4).

implement and comply with it, should have a clear understanding of the specific meaning they intend to afford these terms.

## 3. *Law*

The value judgments of a society often find expression in law. From small communities to all of humanity, different political groups translate their concerns and chosen means to address them into authoritative norms and procedures. Law is necessary and inevitable, though generally not sufficient in itself, to shape social behaviour toward agreed goals. It is based on the power of a designated authority to adopt, implement, and enforce rules and to create institutions.

Law must be distinguished from moral principles and religious belief, as well as from etiquette or rules of social conduct. The distinction is not easily described and there are numerous schools of jurisprudence to define law and establish its distinctive characteristics. The fact that gravity and other natural phenomena are referred to as "laws of nature" indicates one common perception of law as an immutable rule based on scientific evidence. Alternatively, some view law as distinct from courtesy or moral principles because laws impose sanctions for their breach while, for example, failure to write a thank you note for a gift does not result in arrest or other public sanctions. For others, the distinction does not exist or is, perhaps, irrelevant, because the violation of rules of a club or a private enterprise also may be sanctioned, without those rules being considered laws. Similarly, failure to write the thank you note referred to above may be punished by the giver withholding further presents.

In a practical sense law can be viewed as binding norms adopted by public authorities through procedures accepted as valid for their creation. The most common procedures are legislative, according to constitutional provisions, but other law-creating mechanisms exist, including executive decrees, the recognition of rules by judges (common law) or states (customary international law). As this indicates, law can be enacted at all levels of political organization: towns, cities, counties or parishes, departments, regions, states or *Länder* within a federal system, national governments, international regional organizations, and global institutions. The recognized means of adopting laws and thus the concept of what constitutes law may be different from one political level to the next as well as from one country to the next.

## 4. *Europe*

In a geographic sense, the continent of Europe is rather easily defined on three sides: the Atlantic Ocean in the west, the Arctic Sea in the north and the Mediterranean Sea in the south. The islands of Great Britain, Ireland, Iceland, Malta, Crete and Cyprus are included, although they are not physically attached to the continent. The eastern boundary is less obvious; indeed, there is no clear geographic delimitation, although the Ural Mountains are commonly referred to as a dividing line.

Within this broad region there are shared characteristics of religion, tradition, music, history and culture extending over much of the same area indicated by geography. Despite some ethnic conflicts, there is also a growing interdependence and recognized solidarity, demonstrated in the aftermath of the nuclear reactor accident at Chernobyl, when much of Europe was affected and responded with cooperation and parallel innovative measures of environmental protection.

Europe also may be defined in economic and political terms through existing legal and political institutions. The oldest of these is the United Nations Economic Commission for Europe (UNECE) which includes western, central, and eastern European countries, as well as Canada and the United States. The membership of the Conference on Security and Cooperation in Europe (CSCE, also known as the Helsinki process) is even broader, now including most of the former republics of the Soviet Union.[7] Eliminating the North American and easternmost states, the next largest organization is the Council of Europe, today consisting of twenty-nine European states, all except Albania, the Czech Republic, Romania, Slovakia, and most of the states that formerly comprised Yugoslavia and the Soviet Union.[8] In its narrowest terms, the emerging political unit of the twelve-member European Community (EC) could be used to define Europe. However, the common civilization and sense of solidarity deriving from history, geography, cultural, political and economic factors, argue for a larger Europe including western republics of the former Soviet Union. This is the Europe referred to in the title.

## B. Basic Characteristics

Environmental law has several characteristic aspects, apart from its definitional imprecision. First, rules of nature, found in biology, chemistry and physics, are basic to environmental law. Few legal disciplines require the same consideration of scientific knowledge. Most areas of law attempt to regulate variable and often unpredictable human interrelationships. In contrast, environmental law uses science to predict and regulate the consequences of human behaviour on natural phenomena.

The need for environmental law to take into consideration the "laws of nature" inevitably leads to an interdisciplinary approach to environmental problems. Lawmakers and jurists must rely on and utilize scientific expertise. Scientists themselves also must share knowledge. For example, in the area of global warming, atmospheric scientists, trained in meteorology and chemistry, produce climate change models, but must depend upon biologists and ecologists to analyze the impact of these changes on biotopes and ecological systems.

Scientific expertise is required not only to advise on the current state of knowledge, but to predict and assess risks in areas of scientific uncertainty; the latter is crucial

---

[7] As of February 1993, the member states of the CSCE are Albania, Armenia, Austria, Azerbaijan, Belarus, Belgium, Bulgaria, Canada, Czechoslovakia, Cyprus, Denmark, Estonia, Finland, France, Germany, Greece, Holy See, Hungary, Iceland, Ireland, Italy, Kazakhstan, Kirgistan, Latvia, Liechtenstein, Lithuania, Luxembourg, Malta, Moldova, Monaco, Netherlands, Norway, Poland, Portugal, Romania, Russia, San Marino, Spain, Sweden, Switzerland, Tajikistan, Turkey, Turkmenistan, the Ukraine, Uzbekistan, the United Kingdom, the United States and Yugoslavia.

[8] Of the independent states that were part of Yugoslavia and the USSR, only Lithuania and Slovenia have joined as of 15 May 1993.

because "solutions" to environmental concerns can in turn create new problems. In the past many enterprises constructed tall smokestacks to control industrial air pollution, based upon knowledge that air pollutants can be reduced by dispersion at high altitudes. Today it is recognized that the tall stack solution primarily served to transfer pollution from local venues to areas located at greater distances, producing long-range harm, especially from acid rain.

Inherent in the multidisciplinary approach is a need for integrated measures to avoid transferring pollution from one medium to another, e.g. cleaning up the air should not lead to increased water pollution. Because the components of the biosphere, that make up the totality of the environment, are interrelated, care must be taken to study causes, effects, objectives and policy options, to avoid simply diverting or even increasing environmental harm rather than eliminating it.

In addition to having complex, interrelated components, the environment is dynamic and constantly evolving. This characteristic requires that laws and policies be flexible, capable of rapid alteration to respond to new circumstances. At the same time, and perhaps paradoxically, the legal framework must look long-term, being concerned with maintaining life and the ecological balance in an unseen future.

Irreversibility of environmental harm is a third element that impacts upon decision-making. Legislators and other officials are forced to accept the fact that environmental harm can be permanent, as is the case, for example, with the extinction of species. This leads to the need to focus on preventive measures rather than traditional legal remedies for a breach of law. Indeed, prevention is essential even for remediable harm because rehabilitation and repair can be prohibitively expensive.

In sum, interdisciplinarity, dynamism, and irreversibility are basic to environmental regulation, being derived from characteristics of the environment itself. European environmental law, composed of national, regional and international norms regulating human activities that threaten continued environmental deterioration, reflects these characteristics, while incorporating varied national priorities and values.

## C. History of European Environmental Law

Due to the expansion of communications and knowledge and to technological change over the years, environmental measures have evolved from responding almost exclusively to local problems to addressing a large and increasing number of regional and global issues. Initial measures of what today would be recognized as environmental regulation, discussed in more detail below, sought to protect human health and safety through combating urban pollution of essential local resources such as drinking water and air. In addition, private law concepts of nuisance and other property torts expanded to protect owners from property damage caused by their neighbours' polluting activities. Later, more general regulations were enacted to protect commercially harvested living resources, such as forests and fish, from over-exploitation. In recent decades, scientists and the public increasingly have recognized the interdependence of all elements of the biosphere. As a result, immediate interests in physical and economic health and safety have become incorporated in a more global awareness of the need for measures to ensure environmental sustainability, thus aiming at what can be called a "common concern".

The first stage of environmental regulation aimed at protecting the health and safety of communities from the consequences of urbanization. Even in fifth century Rome, there were complaints that the Tiber river was seriously polluted by the filth of the city, as well as protests against odours emanating from various homes. One of the earliest known environmental measures is an ordinance adopted by Edward I in 1306 to prohibit the use of coal in open furnaces in London. Also in the fourteenth century, Charles VI forbade in Paris "bad-smelling and nauseating smoke".

These measures became more widespread with the Industrial Revolution. A Napoleonic decree of 15 October 1810, applicable in France, Belgium and the Netherlands, concerned factories and workshops that were unhealthy, dangerous, or emitted disturbing odours. Although the legislation of the three countries has subsequently diverged, there remain common basic principles and measures. These have served since 1810 to combat danger, damage and nuisances caused by polluting installations, by including a requirement for municipal authorization to create, operate or alter factories. Systems of licensing or of authorization also were enacted early in Luxembourg (1872) and Germany (1869). Other industrial air pollution measures linked to health and safety were adopted in England (1863) and Italy (1865, 1888).

Public law measures to combat local pollution were supplemented by the development of private law concepts of reasonable use of property and private nuisance. In fact, legal controls on property use are reported in urban centres of both ancient Greece and Rome. Regulating the conduct of neighbourhood activities also was a principal motivation of the Napoleonic decree of 1810. Later, concepts of nuisance and neighbourliness were adopted in international law to decide cases of transfrontier pollution.

From a different direction, states' concerns with protecting their economic resources led to both national and international measures to regulate the commercial exploitation of resources such as forests, game, fish, and fur seals. Pressure for such laws often came from those whose livelihood depended upon the continued availability of the resource. As early as 1734 Finland adopted a forestry law concerning the disappearance of some central pine forests due to over-cutting of trees for export. In Bohemia, edicts to protect the forest date back to the Middle Ages, and were the source of a forestry law in 1852. Similar legislation continued in force into this century: Switzerland enacted a forestry law in 1902 and, in 1930, Romania adopted its first law for the protection of natural monuments, which led to the creation of thirty-six nature reserves. However, all these early resource measures were limited; most plant and animal species, and especially migratory animals, were subject to taking, capture or killing by anyone.

It was only recently, particularly since the reconstruction following World War II, that international public opinion began to demonstrate concern over the general state of the environment, leading to broader measures to combat pollution of inland waters, oceans, air, and soil, and to protect biological diversity. State agencies and institutions were created to implement the adopted measures. In large part, this widespread movement developed in response to visible, sometimes catastrophic, environmental deterioration. The catalyst for many individuals and groups was the *Torrey Canyon* accident in 1967, the first of a series of major oil tanker spills. People also began rejecting a "throw-away" society, reacting to the increasing amounts of trash cluttering open spaces, streets and highways. This led to measures to combat the creation and dumping of wastes. Finally, the impact of the arrival of the nuclear age cannot be overlooked. The explosions at Hiroshima and Nagasaki led many, including scientists, to question for the first time the concept of "scientific progress" and the aims and consequences of modern development. Throughout the 1950s and l960s books such as Rachel Carson's *Silent Spring* and science fiction films such as *The Thing* stirred public concerns about the potentially deadly impact of human activities and led to pressure for broader measures of environmental protection.

In response, a few, mostly industrial, states adopted national legislation at the end of the 1960s. As the environmental movement continued to gather support, other states joined in, with the result that by the beginning of the 1990s, virtually all states of the world had adopted environmental legislation. Taken together, national laws, many based upon European or United States models, now total in the thousands.

Just as substantive concerns have evolved, so have the legal techniques that respond to them. Recent innovations aim to prevent environmental harm, rather than respond to damage already caused, calling for environmental impact assessment, public participation in environmental decision-making, and monitoring environmental conditions. All these techniques rely upon scientific and technical input for their effectiveness. Another movement seeks to elaborate in both constitutional and international texts a right to a safe and healthy environment. As the problems and priorities continue to shift, the norms, techniques and institutions necessarily will evolve with them.

Recently, business and industry have begun to recognize the importance of environmental issues. Economic investments increasingly are being directed towards environmental protection. This development is not an alternative to law, but rather a means of implementing existing legal texts and inspiring the creation of others. For example, insurance plays a role in preventing environmental damage. Within a general legal structure, insurance companies now often put conditions for and exercise surveillance over the activities they insure; the same is true of lending institutions in respect to their borrowers.[9]

International developments have paralleled those within states. The first multilateral environmental treaty was the Convention for the Preservation of Wild Animals, Birds and Fish in Africa.[10] According to its Preamble it was motivated by the desire to halt the massacre of diverse animal species which are useful or inoffensive to man. The Treaty encouraged the destruction of creatures deemed harmful to human interests, including lions, leopards, crocodiles and poisonous snakes. The 1902 Convention for the Protection of Birds Useful to Agriculture quickly followed. Its very title indicates the utilitarian economic approach of the period. During the same

---

[9] See Chapter III for a discussion of the various legal and market techniques used for environmental protection.

[10] 19 May 1900, 188 Parry 418.

decade, some international boundary water agreements contained provisions against water pollution, designed to protect states against harmful acts by their neighbours. The numbers of such provisions substantially expanded between and after the two World Wars.

Post-World War II environmental consciousness has had a major impact on international law. Several environmental measures for the protection of areas outside the territory of any state, such as the high seas, outer space, and Antarctica, date from the 1950s; even more were adopted between 1968 and 1972, after the *Torrey Canyon* disaster. However, the watershed event in international environmental law was the Stockholm Conference on the Human Environment in 1972 which summed up the awakened global conscience and marked the beginning of a truly ecological era. The Conference produced a Declaration of twenty-four principles, and an action plan. The Declaration has had major influence, being the first general text of international environmental law. Since that time, international organizations and the European Community have developed environmental programmes and normative enactments based on the seminal work at Stockholm.

During the past decade, international legal involvement has intensified with deepening awareness and knowledge of environmental problems. Some of the most significant concerns, such as climate change, depletion of the ozone layer, and diminishment of biological diversity, have been recognized as planetary issues. In 1983, the United Nations took the initiative with regard to global problems by establishing the Brundtland Commission and then publishing its report on critical environmental and development issues.[11] Subsequently, for the twentieth anniversary of the Stockholm Conference, the United Nations convened a global Conference on Environment and Development, held in Rio de Janeiro, from 3 to 14 June 1992.

The Conference, sometimes referred to as the "Earth Summit", brought together more than 170 countries to focus on the issue of environmentally sustainable development. At the end of the Conference, five major texts issued: (1) Agenda 21, a complex, nearly 800-page plan linking development and environmental action; (2) the Rio Declaration on Environment and Development, setting forth twenty-seven principles, some previously contained in the 1972 Stockholm Declaration, some containing new elements; (3) a Framework Convention on Climate Change; (4) a Convention on Biological Diversity; and (5) a non-binding Statement of Principles on Forests, that may be a step towards a legally binding international forestry convention.

The treaties and other documents of the Earth Summit primarily constitute an encouragement to further action, reflecting a global solidarity in the face of planetary environmental problems. In addition, the meeting marked a definitive fusion between environmental protection and the sustainable development of countries. Finally, and perhaps most importantly, the Conference texts emphasize the essential role and participation of non-governmental organizations in environmental protection. Linked to this, principle 10 of the Rio Declaration states that "each individual shall

---

[11] *Our Common Future*, World Commission on Environment and Development (1987).

have appropriate access to information concerning the environment that is held by public authorities, including information on hazardous materials and activities in their communities, and the opportunity to participate in decision-making processes". Thus, the path is widened for individual and group involvement in solving environmental and development concerns of the community, the state and the planet.

## D. The Legal Framework

Efforts to resolve environmental issues can involve a variety of techniques and institutions, such as education, advertising, media reports and grass roots mobilization of public opinion. Among the possible alternatives, law is the most common method utilized to confront this and other social problems.

Environmental law includes all rules derived from international treaties and custom, EC regulations and directives, national constitutions, legislation, municipal enactments, regulations adopted by national or local regulatory and administrative agencies, court decisions, and common law. As a branch of law, it overlaps with others, integrating concepts derived from tort and property law, utilizing principles of criminal law, and operating within the limits of constitutional law. It also requires consideration of the entire field of administrative law and practice, because environmental protection is largely regulated, implemented, and enforced by administrative bodies.

State law and policy regarding property, its ownership and use, particularly affect environmental law. A basic question posed in all legal systems is what objects or things may be owned, that is, are capable of appropriation. Views on this question differ over time and place. Until relatively recently, human beings could be owned by other human beings. Today, such ownership is condemned. Conversely, the high seas and outer space have long been deemed exempt from property claims or, based on another theory, seen as the common property of everyone. Today, national claims of sovereignty or exclusive use extend over large areas of the world's oceans. Wild plants and animals are held to belong to no one, but may be appropriated upon capture.

Property regimes regulate the ownership and use of land and other forms of property, balancing competing rights and interests, including environmental concerns. The balance may be struck quite differently from one state to another. In Sweden, for example, the

natural environment is open to everyone under a legal principle called the Right of Common Access (*Allmanratten*). This allows any person to camp, walk, or pick wildflowers and mushrooms on someone else's land, provided it is done at a prescribed distance from the owner's dwelling. In contrast, English laws of private property broadly protect owners against "trespass" by uninvited persons.

In nearly all European laws, property ownership or use may be restricted on the basis of the interests of neighbours or for the public interest. An important development has been the privatization of enterprises and land in formerly communist states. New codes of property have been elaborated to regulate, *inter alia*, the balance between private ownership and environmental protection. In the Czech Republic, privatization project contain an evaluation of the environmental obligations of the enterprise.

In most states, private property may be expropriated by the state for the creation of nature reserves or public trusts, or servitudes may be established, such as height restrictions on buildings, which restrict property use for the benefit of others. The concept of neighbourliness, linked to the tort of nuisance, serves to limit potentially harmful uses of property. European states vary in their approaches to these issues and the degree to which the rights of private property owners are subordinated to environmental concerns.

The following materials introduce the European legal framework and sources of law on the national, regional and international levels. They conclude with a discussion of the relationship between the different sources and levels of law-making.

## 1. *Sources of National Laws*

Within Europe there are numerous legal systems based on different legal traditions. Most European systems originate in Roman law, but some are based on German and Scandinavian traditions, still others are formed from common law. The states governed through these systems may be unitary or federal, centralized or decentralized, with written or unwritten constitutions. In spite of this variety, the major sources or means of creating law throughout the region have much in common.

### a. *Constitutions*

In general, constitutions establish the structure and hierarchy of legal norms. The constitution itself is usually the supreme law for the political community it governs, representing fundamental values recognized by the sovereign will of its founding members. In addition, the constitution normally delineates the relationship between the various kinds of law, between legislative norms or executive regulations, and between national and international law.

Constitutions proclaim the basic norms and fundamental guarantees of each society and determine the appropriate procedures for creating other legal norms. Most constitutions contain written bills of rights or charters of fundamental human rights and liberties.

The constitution also creates the basic institutions of government and regulates their functioning and their interaction. It establishes and describes the scope of governmental powers, including competing or complementary functions of the legislative, executive and judicial branches of the government. In a federal state the constitution adds a vertical dimension in regulating the fundamental relationship between the national government and the component units of the federation.

Within Europe, there are both unwritten and written constitutions. Some are recently rewritten, replaced or modified, like those of some central and eastern Europe, while others, like the largely unwritten British constitution, have existed and evolved over centuries. There are short, framework constitutions and long, detailed ones.

One global trend that has had an impact on Europe is the adoption of constitutional provisions concerning environmental protection. As discussed further below, most constitutions written or amended since 1970 have included a proclamation of individual environmental rights or a formulation of duties of the state. This trend is evident in the new constitutions prepared for central and eastern European countries. For example, article 72 of the Constitution of the Republic of Slovenia provides that "each person shall have the right in accordance with statute to a healthy environment in which to live".[12] The same article imposes responsibility on the state for environmental protection and foresees individual liability for environmental damage. A perhaps unique paragraph concludes the article: "the protection of animals from cruelty shall be regulated by statute". Article 73 of the Constitution requires each person to protect rare and precious natural areas, as well as structures and objects forming part of the national and cultural heritage. Both state and local government bodies are responsible for preserving the natural and cultural heritage.

### b. Legislation

Legislation, based upon democratic principles, is the expression of popular sovereignty represented by the legislative branch of government: i.e. the Parliament, Cortes, Bundestag, Stortning, or by direct democracy through initiatives or referenda. Many legislatures are composed of two chambers, both of which are involved in the process of adopting laws. Legislative procedures generally are outlined in the constitution, supplemented by laws and rules of procedure of the legislative branch. In some states the legislature alone enacts laws through majority vote; in others the executive or head of state must approve all bills passed by the legislature. In parliamentary systems, the government normally introduces laws, although a single member may have the right to present a private bill (e.g. Denmark). A further variation is found with regard to framework legislation (*loi cadre*) which needs additional implementing legislation before being applicable or enforceable.[13]

Legislation generally is easier to modify or repeal than are provisions of the constitution. In many states, the process for modification or repeal must be parallel or identical to that used to enact the law. In others, a legislative enactment effectively may be repealed through certain judicial decisions or through adherence to a treaty whose provisions supersede the law in question.

Not every text adopted by a legislature creates legislation. Legislatures may adopt resolutions of intent or declarations of policy without intending that these form part of the body of national law. If a text is intended as legislation, its provisions should be generally applicable, rather than addressed to a particular individual or company; the act must be published or publicly declared; and it should provide a clear indication of the behaviour required or prohibited by its provisions. It is not a

---

[12] The Constitution of the Republic of Slovenia (1991), translated by Sherrill O'Connor-Sraj, Garry Moore, edited by Miro Cerar, Janez Kranjc (1992).

[13] In some countries, such as Belgium and Spain, framework laws are implemented through series of Royal Decrees or Royal Orders rather than through supplementary legislation.

necessary condition that it provide sanctions for its breach. Legislation sometimes provides incentives for compliance rather than punishing violations. For example, government contracts may be made available to companies who meet air quality standards and withheld from companies that pollute.

Laws vary in scope with respect to the persons subject to them and the areas to which they apply. The primary basis of competence to enact and enforce legislation is territorial. Thus, properly enacted legislation generally applies to all persons within the boundaries and subject to the jurisdiction[14] of the state which has adopted the law and does not apply to persons within the territory of another state. For example, a law enacted by State A that prohibits individuals to hunt or capture wild birds would have no applicability to hunting activities in State B, but would apply to citizens of State B who live in or visit State A. Sometimes, however, legislation is addressed to all nationals of the enacting state without regard to their state of residence. These laws normally concern the fundamental duties of citizens, including military service, taxes, and the prohibition against treason. Finally, a state may seek to regulate the conduct of all persons wherever located, as for example, by a national law that makes it illegal for anyone anywhere to counterfeit the currency of the country.

Conflict can arise about the applicability of environmental laws outside the territory of the enacting state, due to different state environmental policies and the fact that environmental damage sometimes crosses political boundaries. A state that is particularly strict concerning pesticides may seek to prohibit its companies from establishing subsidiaries in other countries where regulation is more lax and foreign investment is sought, in order to avoid the "rebound" effect of importing pesticide-contaminated foods. Within Europe, the potential for such conflicts motivated many of the early environmental measures taken by the EC.

Another problem in environmental legislation is the existence of conflicting laws and policies within a single country. Environmental legislation often has been enacted in response to the problems of a particular environmental sector, without thoroughly considering the various other legal regimes affected by such laws. For example, measures to protect endangered species can affect or conflict with hunting regulations, land use policy, forest management, roads and transport, commercial regulation, or measures taken to protect other environmental sectors such as water and soil. The problem of fragmentation and conflicting laws is a current one and there is considerable need for a coherent, integrated approach to environmental codification.

### c. Executive Decrees

Some constitutions give power to the executive to initiate or enact laws through decree. In Italy, the government may issue ministerial decrees without parliamentary approval. The decrees have the force of law for sixty days during which time Parliament may approve them as legislation. Presidential decrees and decrees issued by the prime minister take this form. Similarly, in Spain, the executive may issue a

---

[14] "Subject to the jurisdiction" means that the law generally extends to ships, airplanes and outer space objects registered within the state, and to military operations and bases wherever located.

legislative royal decree (*real decreto legislativo*) which it sends to parliament for approval. This has been used to adopt EC environmental norms into the Spanish legal code.

In addition to constitutions that grant executive decree powers, legislative enactments may delegate authority to the executive to issue decrees. In this way, executive decrees may be used to establish the necessary regulatory scheme to complete framework legislation.

### d. Common Law

In common law countries, law traditionally emerges from the customs and usages of the community. Common law consists of principles deduced from these customs and usages, by the application of reason, a sense of justice and conscience. It is not based on legislative enactment. When conflict arises within the community, the issue is settled through litigation with the judge pronouncing the relevant law on the basis of precedent and practice. The role of the judge has been analogized to that of Isaac Newton, who did not invent the laws of gravity, but merely described them on the basis of scientific evidence before him. However, unlike the laws of gravity, rules of common law are not static and absolute. Rather, they are flexible and can be adapted to societal changes, leading to reinterpretation of the fundamental principles of common law by the courts. At the same time, being based on practices and usages of the community, ratified by reliance on judicial precedent, the common law operates through a relatively slow evolution. Such evolution does not always correspond to the needs of environmental protection, which may call for rapid response. Thus, statutory environmental law (legislation) also is found in common law countries.

Common law principles and norms have contributed to the development of environmental law. Tribunals deciding environmental cases often have based their decisions on common law torts. A tort is a legal wrong which can be the basis of a private action brought by an injured party.[15]

### e. Administrative Agency Rule-making

Whether the basic legal system is one of civil law or of common law, an increasing feature of all modern states is the growth of administrative agencies or bureaux with regulatory powers. These administrative bodies exist at all levels of government, from the local to the national, and generally are the part of government most in contact with the public. The legal powers of an administrative body are derived from the legislation which creates the institution and delegates to it certain functions and powers of rule(law)-making and implementation. For example, in Germany, federal administrative authorities are delegated responsibility for preparing legislative proposals, research, consultation and information. In addition there are state (*Länder*) regulatory agencies that function on the basis of general administrative law rules or specific provisions of various environmental laws.

---

[15] In contrast, a criminal act is an offence against the public, prosecuted by the state.

Agency law-making generally is limited to adding the necessary details of substance and procedure to a previously enacted legislative scheme. However, within its mandate, the rules, regulations and general orders promulgated by an administrative body pursuant to its delegated powers have the force of law. This role is extremely important in the environmental sector where changing conditions demand flexible and rapid action. In German environmental law, administrative ordinances may be adopted on the federal level to guide Länder in the exercise of discretionary powers and in interpreting federal law. Administrative rules also designate pollution standards, methods of measurement and pollution control instruments.

In some countries administrative "circulars" may be issued by authorities. These are of less juridical effect than rules but may have considerable impact on the application of the law. It should be noted that the Court of Justice of the European Community has rejected the use of such circulars to implement EC directives.[16] According to the Court, directives must be incorporated in a public manner which fully meets the requirements of legal certainty and transposes their obligations into binding national law.

Administrative agencies also interpret legislation through their role in implementing the law. In many countries, administrative tribunals exist which apply the relevant legislation and administrative regulations, using not only the text of the laws, but also legislative intent and precedent. In this regard, they may have some of the attributes of a common law judge.

### f. Regional or Local Law

A major difference in the governmental structure of states is the contrast between unitary and federal states. Germany and Austria with their Länder, Switzerland with its cantons, and the new Community of Independent States formed by some of the units of the former USSR, constitute European federal states. Belgium, Spain, and the United Kingdom of Great Britain (England, Scotland and Wales) and Northern Ireland decentralize through giving substantial autonomy to various regions, without being fully federal in nature.

The characteristic of federal states is a division of competence and jurisdiction between the national government and the governments of the component units. In Germany, legislative powers in the field of environmental law are divided under the Federal Constitution (*Grundgesetz*) between the Federation (*Bund*) and the sixteen states (*Länder*). The Bund and Länder have concurrent legislative powers in several areas of environmental law, including waste disposal, air and noise pollution control, consumer protection, and hazardous substances legislation. When federal law is adopted in these fields it pre-empts state law. In regard to nature protection, land use, and water resources management, the Bund has the right to enact framework laws which are supplemented and implemented at the level of the Länder. In addition, there are by-laws (*Satzungen*) adopted at municipal and regional levels, based on express

[16] Case 239/85, *Commission* v. *Belgium*, 1986 E.C.R. 3645, 51 C.M.L.R. 248 (1988) (holding a government circular to be inadequate to implement a Community toxic waste directive).

statutory authorization over matters such as local waste disposal bodies and discharge of water into waste water purification systems.

Conflicts can arise between component units of a federal state or between one or more of them and the national government. In such cases, the question may be deemed one for political solution or may be referred to the judiciary for decision.

Whether the state is unitary or federal, any particular question may be a matter for centralized action or may be subject to local or regional response. In particular, environmental issues can be dealt with under a national environmental protection act, such as the Portuguese Basic Environmental Law of 7 April 1987, or may be left to local initiative in a unitary state, or to regulation by federal units in a federal state. In Belgium, the three regions (Flemish, Walloon, and Brussels) have both legislative and executive powers over environmental questions, limited only by the obligation to comply with general norms established by the national government. In contrast, Italian environmental law is in practice the prerogative of the central government, although general legislative and executive power is shared between the national government and the 20 regions, 95 provinces and 7,991 communes.

Even if environmental norms are adopted at the national level, most countries decentralize implementation, that is, rely upon local application and enforcement of the norms. For example, Sweden and Denmark, unitary states, are committed to decentralized authority. Swedish debates over the question of how much authority to vest in the National Environmental Protection Board resulted in a compromise according to which the Board was given supervisory and coordinating roles, with the authority to prescribe precautionary measures and other pollution abatement measures. In addition, licensing of polluting industries is vested in a national quasi-judicial administrative agency, the Franchise Board for Environmental Protection. Large companies must apply directly for permits each time they change their production or manufacturing processes, build a new plant, or simply increase their capacity by expanding their operations or by introducing new technology.[17] Yet, actual control and enforcement is left principally to county administrations. In particular, county courts retain the function of levying fines and determining compensation for damages caused by non-compliance with the terms of an operating permit. In Germany, also, even where environmental legislation is enacted on the federal level, executive competence rests largely with the Länder and their administrative units.

## 2. The European Community

The legal framework of the European Community derives from a series of treaties: the 1951 Paris treaty instituting the European Coal and Steel Community; the 1957 European Atomic Energy Community (EURATOM) agreement; and the 1957 Treaty of Rome creating the European Economic Community (Common Market). To encourage further evolution, the three agreements called for periodic intergovernmental conferences, the first of which produced the 1986 Single European Act, the second resulted in the 1991 Maastricht Treaty on European Union.

---

[17] Smaller companies apply to the appropriate county administration for permits to operate.

Taken together these texts create institutions and authorize the adoption of further norms. Four institutions are particularly responsible for achieving the aims of the Community: the Council of Ministers, the European Commission, the European Parliament, and the Court of Justice. These bodies are assisted by the Economic and Social Committee, the Court of Auditors and the European Investment Bank.

According to article 189 of the Treaty of Rome, Community standards are adopted in the form of regulations, directives and recommendations. Only the first two are binding. The Commission has the sole right to initiate norms, but their adoption requires a decision of the Council after consultation with Parliament. The Treaty of Maastricht, article 138b, authorizes the majority of Parliament to request the Commission to submit a proposal on matters for which the Parliament considers Community action is necessary. In addition, the Parliament will have the power to veto certain environmental acts.

### a. Treaty Provisions

Because widespread concern with environmental matters arose after adoption of the first Community treaties, the issue of Community competence in the field was only definitively settled with the 1986 Single European Act. Before the Single European Act, measures concerning the environment were mainly based on article 100 of the Treaty of Rome, which relates to the approximation of national laws having a direct effect on the establishment or functioning of the Common Market. The provision of the Treaty which most closely relates to environmental matters is article 36, which states that the provisions of the Treaty "shall not preclude prohibitions or restrictions ... justified on grounds ... of the protections ... of health and life of humans, animals, or plants ..."

Environmental protection became part of Community policy in 1972 as a result of the Paris Conference of the Heads of States and Governments, held in conjunction with the Stockholm Conference on the Human Environment. The Paris meeting adopted a Declaration stating that

> Economic expansion is not an end in itself. Its firm aim should be to enable disparities in living conditions to be reduced. It must take place with the participation of all the social partners. It should result in an improvement in the quality of life as well as in standards of living. As befits the genius of Europe, particular attention will be given to intangible values and to protecting the environment, so that progress may really be put at the service of mankind.[18]

The Single European Act added Title VII to the Treaty, to define Community principles of action on the environment. As amended by the Treaty of Maastricht, the principles contained in article 130R are:

— preserve, protect, and improve the quality of the environment;

— contribute to the protection of the health of individuals;

[18] E.C. Commission, 6th General Report (1972), p. 8.

— ensure a prudent and rational utilization of natural resources; and

— promote, at the international level, measures to deal with regional or world-wide environmental problems.

Article 130R also states that community action is founded on a high level of protection, based on the precautionary principle and preventive action; on the rectification of damage at the source, and on the principle that the "polluter pays". Further, environmental protection requirements must be integrated into the definition and implementation of other Community policies. Member States may take more stringent provisional measures of environmental protection not based on economic reasons, subject to Community review. Community action is to be based upon available technical and scientific data, environmental conditions in the diverse regions, benefits and costs which can result from action or lack of action, and, finally, economic and social development of the Community as a whole and balanced development of its regions. An overriding principle is "subsidiarity": Community action on environmental matters is to be taken only when the objectives can be attained better through regional action than through measures taken by the individual member states.

### b. Regulations

Regulations are true Community law, binding in all their elements and directly applicable in all member states. A regulation establishes direct rights and imposes duties on private parties without interference of national law. Regulations generally can be adopted in the field of environmental protection only when the subject concerns external trade of the Community. For example, Regulation 348/81 establishes a common rule applicable to the importation of products derived from whales.

### c. Directives

Directives bind each state to achieve a given result but leave the means and methods to individual state control. The Council of Ministers usually adopts Directives on proposal from the Commission, including among the final articles a date or time, usually two years, within which Member States must implement the Directive in national law. The Directive is then notified to Member States. Almost all of the more than two hundred Community legislative texts concerning the environment, adopted since the 1960s, are in the form of directives. In *Francovich and Bonifaci* v. *Italy*,[19] the European Court of Justice held that a member state can be liable to individuals for damages caused by the state's failure to implement a Community directive. Although not involving an environmental directive, the judgment grants individuals the right to enforce, before their national courts, directives that have not been implemented, where the directive in question involves the granting of rights to

---

[19] Eur. Ct. J., Joined Cases C–6 and 9/90 (19 Nov. 1991).

individuals and there is a causal link between the failure to implement and the damage suffered by the individual.

### d. Action Programmes

The general framework of Community environmental policy is found in the five Action Programmes adopted to date.[20] The Council, when adopting the European Communities' First Action Programme on the Environment (1973–6), declared that the task of promoting harmonious development of economic activities and continued and balanced expansion,

> cannot now be imagined in the absence of an effective campaign to combat pollution and nuisance or of an improvement in the quality of life and the protection of the environment; the improvement in the quality of life and the protection of the natural environment are among the fundamental tasks of the Community.[21]

The objectives of Community environmental policy, as set forth in the first Action Programme are to improve the setting and quality of life, the surroundings and living conditions. To this end, the policy should:

— prevent, reduce and as far as possible eliminate pollution and nuisances;

— ensure sound management of and avoid any exploitation of resources or of nature which causes significant damage to the ecological balance;

— guide development in accordance with quality requirements, especially by improving working conditions and the settings of life;

— ensure that more account is taken of environmental aspects in town planning and land use;

— seek common solutions to environment problems with States outside the Community, particularly in international organizations.

More recent Programmes of Action focus on education, the need for increased public access to official environmental information, and the need for increased opportunities for individuals and groups to defend their rights or interests in administrative procedures.

The Programmes of Action are primarily aimed at the organization itself, rather than the member states. Each Programme aims to combat pollution and, recently, to integrate environmental considerations in all Community action as well as increase public access to official environmental information. While not legally binding,

---

[20] First Programme of Action on the Environment, O.J. 1973, No. C 112/1; Second Programme of Action, O.J. 1977, No. C 139/1; Third Programme of Action, O.J. 1983, No. C 46/1; Fourth Programme of Action (1987–92), O.J., 1987, No. C 328/1. A Fifth Action Plan, entitled *Towards Sustainability, A European Community Programme of Policy and Action in Relation to the Environment and Sustainable Development*, covers the years 1993–2000.

[21] First Action Programme, *id.*

Programmes of Action can assist in the development of law since the intended actions often imply the drafting of legal rules.

### e. Implementation

Implementation of Community norms by Member States involves adapting national legislation, administrative structures and procedures so that they conform to regulations and directives, and putting EC norms into practice. Where environmental quality standards are imposed, the state must ensure that the standards are met. Some directives also require Member States to submit reports to the Commission on specific aspects of the environment. The Court of Justice has emphasized the importance of prompt implementation of directives.[22]

The Commission, which supervises implementation of EC norms, has both formal and informal enforcement means at its disposal, including taking action before the European Court of Justice, which enforces European law. The Court's judicial precedents are important sources of direction on application and interpretation of the law.

Community law has had an enormous impact in Member States, where most environmental laws have been adopted in response to Community Regulations and Directives. Portuguese Decree Law No. 186/90 of 6 June 1990, for example, expressly refers to Community Directive 85/337/EEC as its source. In addition, Community law has had considerable influence in recent years on laws of non-member states, especially in central and eastern Europe. For example, the 1991 Bulgarian Environmental Protection Act provides that in cases of transboundary pollution, treaties and conventions to which Bulgaria is a party shall apply; it then adds: "[i]n the absence of such regulatory instruments shall be applied the requirements and standards of the European Community" (article 6). Other provisions in the Bulgarian Act, concerning environmental information and environmental impact statements, are based entirely on Community directives. In Western Europe, non-member Switzerland has adopted measures similar to the EC Seveso Directive on hazardous accidental pollution.

In spite of this impact, there remain delays and failures in implementing EC law. The Commission has begun numerous infringement procedures against Member States, particularly in regard to water quality.[23] The process of negotiating standards at the Community level means that directives often are the product of compromise and may be incompatible with various aspects of national law, requiring substantial domestic action. For instance, the Netherlands had to introduce new legislation, significantly changing its water management system, in order to comply with several Community water directives. The same Community negotiating process also may

---

[22] See e.g. Commission v. Italy, Case 52/75, 1976 E.C.R. 277, 284, Common Mkt. Rep. (CCH) 8345.

[23] Community complaints concerning environmental issues rose from nine in 1984 to 465 in 1989. Commission infringement actions increased from two to thirty-eight between 1984 and 1987. Most complaints and actions concern drinking water quality, environmental impact assessments, and the protection of wild birds.

result in broad or discretionary standards that limit environmental protection. This is the case with the Community bathing water directive. It contains a vague definition of the waters it regulates, with the result that every Member State applies different criteria in identifying bathing waters, often excluding poor quality sites based upon the high cost of their amelioration. Similarly, states are given complete discretion to designate waters covered by the freshwater fish and shellfish waters directives. In at least one state no waters have been designated for protection under the EC standards.

## 3. International Law

The process of creating international law is less certain and more varied than the procedures found in national legal systems or in the EC. Treaties and custom create binding norms, while other sources have a more indirect influence on the development and direction of the law.

### a. Treaties

Treaties are agreements governed by international law and concluded between states or between states and international organizations. Traditionally, treaties were negotiated and concluded at conferences convened and hosted by one State. This procedure is still used, but today nearly all multilateral treaties are drafted and adopted within the framework of an international organization such as the United Nations or the Council of Europe.

In general, treaties are legally binding only for the states and organizations which accept them through adoption, ratification or accession. Nearly all treaties are written, but need not be so to be legally binding. Treaties can be bilateral, between two states, or multilateral, between several or many states, and they can be called by one of numerous titles: treaty, convention, covenant, compact, agreement or protocol. The name generally is not significant insofar as the legal effect of the treaty is concerned; the crucial element is that the states involved intend for the document to be binding. In this regard, certain terms often are used to indicate non-binding policy or coordination of efforts: exchange of letters, memorandum of understanding.

The contents of treaties usually establish substantive rules and measures of implementation or supervision. In spite of the general variety of treaties, common provisions are found in the more than 1,000 agreements that touch upon environmental protection, that set them apart from other international agreements. Most characteristic are the establishment of flexible amendment procedures and action plans calling for further measures. Many environmental treaties are framework agreements requiring completion by additional international protocols. In addition, many treaties must be implemented within states parties through internal legislative measures. The latter are often referred to as "non-self-executing agreements".

### b. Custom

Another method of creating international law is through unwritten custom: the consistent behaviour of states over time, creating "evidence of a general practice accepted as law".[24] Custom is slow to form and often imprecise in content. Moreover, proof of the requisite constant and uniform behaviour and acceptance of the practice as law may be difficult. Thus, the increasing role played by codification of norms of customary law, meaning that customary rules are included in a treaty and thus transformed into written law.

### c. Other Sources

Other sources of international law formation include, first, reference to principles generally accepted by national legal systems throughout the world. With the proliferation of national texts concerning environmental protection, common principles are likely to be easier to find in coming years. Finally, international law also may be identified through studying judicial decisions and scholarly publications, international programmes of action or declarations of principles, and resolutions of international organizations.

## 4. Relationships between the Systems of Law

National, Community and international law can be seen as forming an interlocking web of relationships. However, from the perspective of an individual or company, it may be clearer to describe the structure as a pyramid, with the vast base of national laws, a smaller number of EEC norms, and a still more limited number of applicable international standards.

International law, originating both in treaty and in custom, generally regulates inter-state relations and imposes obligations on adhering states at the international level. In addition, the domestic legal systems of states may incorporate international law and make it binding internally. How this is done varies, as does the normative status given to international norms compared to state constitutional and legislative provisions. The main principle is that international law is binding upon states which are free to determine the best legal procedure to implement it.

Some constitutions explicitly provide that customary international law is automatically applicable as law within the state (e.g. article 25, Constitution of Germany: "The general rules of public international law are an integral part of federal law. They shall take precedence over the laws and shall directly create rights and duties for the inhabitants of the territory"). Other states may require an affirmative statement by the government that the particular customary rule has been accepted by the state before it will be given effect, or may require that the norm be transformed into written domestic law.

As for treaties, nearly all constitutions establish a procedure by which the state becomes a party to international agreements, generally through a process of signature followed by ratification and publication. Treaties so accepted usually become the law of the land, although in some cases, such as Great Britain, an additional Act of

---

[24] Article 38(1)(b), Statute of the International Court of Justice.

Parliament is necessary to transform the treaty into law applicable and enforceable within the state.

The domestic status of international law, or the hierarchy of laws that may be applied by a court, also vary. In some cases customary international law is deemed superior to conflicting state legislation (e.g. article 28(1), 1975 Constitution of Greece: "the generally recognized rules of international law ... are an integral part of Greek law and have an authority superior to any inconsistent legislative provision"). In other cases customary international law is given the same status as national law but superior to the state or local law (e.g. article 9, Constitution of Austria: "The generally recognized rules of international law shall be considered as component parts of the Federal Law").

The status of treaties in the hierarchy of domestic law differs from one state to another, although it is most common for ratified treaties to override inconsistent domestic laws. Thus, article 55 of the French constitution of 1958 provides that "treaties or agreements duly ratified or approved shall, upon their publication, have an authority superior to that of laws ..." The provision has been interpreted to include Community laws. A decision of the Conseil d'Etat, France's highest administrative tribunal, determined that European Community rules should supersede French law whenever created and that the French government cannot maintain regulations that are incompatible with the objectives of EC directives.

The Federal Tribunal of Switzerland also has held that an international agreement prevails over subsequent and inconsistent domestic law. In the Netherlands, article 66 of the Constitution provides that "legal regulations in force within the Kingdom shall not apply if this application should be incompatible with provisions ... of agreements entered into either before or after the enactment of the regulations".

As for Community law, the Court of Justice of the European Community has held in several decisions that subsequent domestic legislation of the member states cannot prevail when inconsistent with Community law and that judges of member states are under a duty not to give effect to such domestic legislation. The uniqueness of Community law lies in the fact that it is not only the Treaty, but legal texts adopted pursuant to the Treaty – EC directives and regulations – that are binding. Regulations directly apply in all respects, while directives are incorporated and applied through domestic law.

Given the numerous sources of law and levels of action, the question of coordination arises in order to avoid duplication or conflict. The Community recognized this quite early, noting that "in each different category of pollution, it is necessary to establish the level of action (local, regional, national, Community, international) that befits the type of pollution and the geographical zone to be protected ...[25]

---

[25] Principle 10, Programme of Action of the European Communities on the Environment, 22 November 1973 (O.J. no. C 112, 20.12.1973).

# E. Documents

*1. The Stockholm Declaration on the Human Environment,*
adopted 16 June 1972, U.N. Doc. A/CONF.48/14/rev.1
(U.N. Pub. E.73, IIA.14)(1973).

The United Nations Conference on the Human Environment,

...

   Proclaims that:

1.   Man is both creature and moulder of his environment, which gives him physical sustenance
     and affords him the opportunity for intellectual, moral, social and spiritual growth ... Both
     aspects of man's environment, the natural and the man-made, are essential to his well-being
     and to the enjoyment of basic human rights – even the right to life itself.

   ...

6.   A point has been reached in history when we must shape our actions throughout the world
     with a more prudent care for their environmental consequences. Through ignorance or
     indifference we can do massive and irreversible harm to the earthly environment on which
     our life and well-being depend ... To defend and improve the human environment for
     present and future generations has become an imperative goal for mankind – a goal to be
     pursued together with, and in harmony with, the established and fundamental goals of
     peace and of world-wide economic and social development.

7.   To achieve this environmental goal will demand the acceptance of responsibility by citizens
     and communities and by enterprises and institutions at every level, all sharing equitably in
     common efforts. Individuals in all walks of life as well as organizations in many fields, by
     their values and the sum of their actions, will shape the world environment of the future.
     Local and national governments will bear the greatest burden for large-scale environmental
     policy and action within their jurisdictions. International cooperation is also needed in
     order to raise resources to support the developing countries in carrying out their responsi-
     bilities in this field. A growing class of environmental problems, because they are regional
     or global in extent or because they affect the common international realm, will require
     extensive cooperation among nations and action by international organizations in the
     common interest. The Conference calls upon governments and peoples to exert common
     efforts for the preservation and improvement of the human environment, for the benefit of
     all the people and for their posterity.

## PRINCIPLES

States the common conviction that:

### Principle 1

Man has the fundamental right to freedom, equality and adequate conditions of life, in an
environment of a quality that permits a life of dignity and well-being, and he bears a solemn
responsibility to protect and improve the environment for present and future generations ...

### Principle 2

The natural resources of the earth including the air, water, land, flora and fauna and especially
representative samples of natural ecosystems must be safeguarded for the benefit of present and
future generations through careful planning or management, as appropriate.

### Principle 3

The capacity of the earth to produce vital renewable resources must be maintained and, wherever practicable, restored or improved.

### Principle 4

Man has a special responsibility to safeguard and wisely manage the heritage of wildlife and its habitat which are now gravely imperiled by a combination of adverse factors. Nature conservation including wildlife must therefore receive importance in planning for economic development.

### Principle 5

The non-renewable resources of the earth must be employed in such a way as to guard against the danger of their future exhaustion and to ensure the benefits from such employment are shared by all mankind.

### Principle 6

The discharge of toxic substances or of other substances and the release of heat, in such quantities or concentrations as to exceed the capacity of the environment to render them harmless, must be halted in order to ensure that serious or irreversible damage is not inflicted upon ecosystems ...

### Principle 7

States shall take all possible steps to prevent pollution of the seas by substances that are liable to create hazards to human health, to harm living resources and marine life, to damage amenities or to interfere with other legitimate uses of the sea.

...

### Principle 9

Environmental deficiencies generated by the conditions of underdevelopment and natural disasters pose grave problems and can best be remedied by accelerated development through the transfer of substantial quantities of financial and technological assistance as a supplement to the domestic effort of the developing countries and such timely assistance as may be required.

...

### Principle 13

In order to achieve a more rational management of resources and thus to improve the environment, States should adopt an integrated and coordinated approach to their development planning so as to ensure that development is compatible with the need to protect and improve the human environment for the benefit of their population.

...

### Principle 21

States have, in accordance with the Charter of the United Nations and the principles of international law, the sovereign right to exploit their own resources pursuant to their own environmental policies, and the responsibility to ensure that activities within their jurisdiction or control do not cause damage to the environment of other states or of areas beyond the limits of national jurisdiction.

### Principle 22

States shall cooperate to develop further the international law regarding liability and compensation for the victims of pollution and other environmental damage caused by activities within the jurisdiction or control of such States to areas beyond their jurisdiction.

...

## Principle 24

International matters concerning the protection and improvement of the environment should be handled in a cooperative spirit by all countries, big or small, on an equal footing. Cooperation through multilateral or bilateral arrangements or other appropriate means is essential to effectively control, prevent, reduce and eliminate adverse environmental effects resulting from activities conducted in all spheres, in such a way that due account is taken of the sovereignty and interests of all States.

...

## 2. The Rio Declaration on Environment and Development
adopted 14 June 1992 at Rio de Janeiro, A/CONF.151/5/Rev.1, 31 *I.L.M.* 874, (1992).

### Preamble

The United Nations Conference on Environment and Development,

Having met at Rio de Janeiro from 3 to 14 June 1992,

Reaffirming the Declaration of the United Nations Conference on the Human Environment, adopted at Stockholm on 16 June 1972, and seeking to build upon it,

With the goal of establishing a new and equitable global partnership through the creation of new levels of cooperation among States, key sectors of societies and people,

Working towards international agreements which respect the interests of all and protect the integrity of the global environmental and developmental system,

Recognizing the integral and interdependent nature of the Earth, our home,

Proclaims that:

### Principle 1

Human beings are at the centre of concerns for sustainable development. They are entitled to a healthy and productive life in harmony with nature.

### Principle 2

States have, in accordance with the Charter of the United Nations and the principles of international law, the sovereign right to exploit their own resources pursuant to their own environmental and developmental policies, and the responsibility to ensure that activities within their jurisdiction or control do not cause damage to the environment of other States or of areas beyond the limits of national jurisdiction.

### Principle 3

The right to development must be fulfilled so as to equitably meet developmental and environmental needs of present and future generations.

### Principle 4

In order to achieve sustainable development, environmental protection shall constitute an integral part of the development process and cannot be considered in isolation from it.

### Principle 5

All States and all people shall cooperate in the essential task of eradicating poverty as an indispensable requirement for sustainable development, in order to decrease the disparities in standards of living and better meet the needs of the majority of the people of the world.

### Principle 6

The special situation and needs of developing countries, particularly the least developed and those most environmentally vulnerable, shall be given special priority. International actions in the field of environment and development should also address the interests and needs of all countries.

### Principle 7

States shall cooperate in a spirit of global partnership to conserve, protect and restore the health and integrity of the Earth's ecosystem. In view of the different contributions to global environmental degradation, States have common but differentiated responsibilities. The developed countries acknowledge the responsibility that they bear in the international pursuit of sustainable development in view of the pressures their societies place on the global environment and of the technologies and financial resources they command.

### Principle 8

To achieve sustainable development and a higher quality of life for all people, States should reduce and eliminate unsustainable patterns of production and consumption and promote appropriate demographic policies.

### Principle 9

States should cooperate to strengthen endogenous capacity-building for sustainable development by improving scientific understanding through exchanges of scientific and technological knowledge, and by enhancing the development, adaptation, diffusion and transfer of technologies, including new and innovative technologies.

### Principle 10

Environmental issues are best handled with the participation of all concerned citizens, at the relevant level. At the national level, each individual shall have appropriate access to information concerning the environment that is held by public authorities, including information on hazardous materials and activities in their communities, and the opportunity to participate in decision-making processes. States shall facilitate and encourage public awareness and participation by making information widely available. Effective access to judicial and administrative proceedings, including redress and remedy, shall be provided.

### Principle 11

States shall enact effective environmental legislation. Environmental standards, management objectives and priorities should reflect the environmental and developmental context to which they apply. Standards applied by some countries may be inappropriate and of unwarranted economic and social cost to other countries, in particular developing countries.

### Principle 12

States should cooperate to promote a supportive and open international economic system that would lead to economic growth and sustainable development in all countries, to better address the problems of environmental degradation. Trade policy measures for environmental purposes should not constitute a means of arbitrary or unjustifiable discrimination or a disguised restriction on international trade. Unilateral actions to deal with environmental challenges outside the jurisdiction of the importing country should be avoided. Environmental measures addressing transboundary or global environmental problems should, as far as possible, be based on an international consensus.

### Principle 13

States shall develop national law regarding liability and compensation for the victims of pollution and other environmental damage. States shall also cooperate in an expeditious and more determined manner to develop further international law regarding liability and compensation for adverse effects of environmental damage caused by activities within their jurisdiction or control to areas beyond their jurisdiction.

## Principle 14

States should effectively cooperate to discourage or prevent the relocation and transfer to other States of any activities and substances that cause severe environmental degradation or are found to be harmful to human health.

## Principle 15

In order to protect the environment, the precautionary approach shall be widely applied by States according to their capabilities. Where there are threats of serious or irreversible damage, lack of full scientific certainty shall not be used as a reason for postponing cost-effective measures to prevent environmental degradation.

## Principle 16

National authorities should endeavour to promote the internalization of environmental costs and the use of economic instruments, taking into account the approach that the polluter should, in principle, bear the cost of pollution, with due regard to the public interest and without distorting international trade and investment.

## Principle 17

Environmental impact assessment, as a national instrument, shall be undertaken for proposed activities that are likely to have a significant adverse impact on the environment and are subject to a decision of a competent national authority.

## Principle 18

States shall immediately notify other States of any natural disasters or other emergencies that are likely to produce sudden harmful effects on the environment of those States. Every effort shall be made by the international community to help States so afflicted.

## Principle 19

States shall provide prior and timely notification and relevant information to potentially affected States on activities that may have a significant adverse transboundary environmental effect and shall consult with those States at an early stage and in good faith.

...

## Principle 26

States shall resolve all their environmental disputes peacefully and by appropriate means in accordance with the Charter of the United Nations.

## Principle 27

States and people shall cooperate in good faith and in a spirit of partnership in the fulfilment of the principles embodied in this Declaration and in the further development of international law in the field of sustainable development.

*3. Single European Act,*
29 June 1987, 1987 O.J. no. L 169, as amended by the Treaty on European
Union, Maastricht, 7 February 1992.[26]

### TITLE I: COMMON PROVISIONS
ARTICLE A

*By this Treaty, the High Contracting Parties establish among themselves a European Union, hereinafter called "the Union".*

### TITLE II : PROVISIONS AMENDING THE TREATY ESTABLISHING
### THE EUROPEAN ECONOMIC COMMUNITY
### WITH A VIEW TO ESTABLISHING THE EUROPEAN COMMUNITY
ARTICLE 3

*For the purposes set out in Article 2, the activities of the Community shall include, as provided in this Treaty and in accordance with the timetable set out therein:*

*(k) a policy in the sphere of the environment;*

ARTICLE 3b

*The Community shall act within the limits of the powers conferred upon it by this Treaty and of the objectives assigned to it therein.*

*In areas which do not fall within its exclusive competence, the Community shall take action, in accordance with the principle of subsidiarity, only if and in so far as the objectives of the proposed action cannot be sufficiently achieved by the Member States and can therefore, by reason of the scale or effects of the proposed action, be better achieved by the Community.*

*Any action by the Community shall not go beyond what is necessary to achieve the objectives of this Treaty.*

ARTICLE 25

A TITLE VII SHALL BE ADDED TO PART THREE OF THE EEC TREATY READING
AS FOLLOWS:

### TITLE VII: ENVIRONMENT
ARTICLE 130R

1.  ~~ACTION BY THE COMMUNITY RELATING TO THE ENVIRONMENT SHALL
    HAVE THE FOLLOWING OBJECTIVES~~: *Community policy on the environment shall contribute
    to pursuit of the following objectives:*
    — to preserve~~[ing]~~, protect~~[ing]~~ and improve~~[ing]~~ the quality of the environment;
    — ~~to contribute towards~~ protecting human health;
    — ~~to ensure a~~ prudent and rational utilization of natural resources;
    — promoting measures at international level to deal with regional or worldwide
      environmental problems.

2.  *Community policy on the environment shall aim at a high level of protection taking into account the diversity
    of situations in the various regions of the Community.* It shall be based *on the precautionary principle
    and* on the principles that preventive action should be taken, that environmental damage
    should as a priority be rectified at source and that the polluter should pay. Environmental

---

[26] Provisions to be added by the Treaty on European Union are in italics. Language removed from the
Single European Act is indicated by striking out the deleted words and phrases.

protection requirements [shall be a component of the Community's other policies] *must be integrated into the definition and implementation of other Community policies.*

In this context, harmonization measures answering these requirements shall include, where appropriate, a safeguard clause allowing Member States to take provisional measures, for non-economic environmental reasons, subject to a Community inspection procedure.

3. In preparing its [action relating to] *policy on the environment*, the Community shall take account of:

   — available scientific and technical data;
   — environmental conditions in the various regions of the Community;
   — the potential benefits and costs of action or lack of action;
   — the economic and social development of the Community as a whole and the balanced development of its regions.

4. THE COMMUNITY SHALL TAKE ACTION RELATING TO THE ENVIRONMENT TO THE EXTENT TO WHICH THE OBJECTIVES REFERRED TO IN PARAGRAPH 1 CAN BE ATTAINED BETTER AT COMMUNITY LEVEL THAN AT THE LEVEL OF THE INDIVIDUAL MEMBER STATES. WITHOUT PREJUDICE TO CERTAIN MEASURES OF A COMMUNITY NATURE, THE MEMBER STATES SHALL FINANCE AND IMPLEMENT THE OTHER MEASURES.

4. Within their respective spheres of competence, the Community and the Member States shall cooperate with third countries and with the [relevant] *competent* international organizations.

The arrangements for Community cooperation may be the subject of agreements between the Community and the third parties concerned, which shall be negotiated and concluded in accordance with Article 228.

The previous subparagraph shall be without prejudice to Member States' competence to negotiate in international bodies and to conclude international agreements.

ARTICLE 130s

1. The Council, acting [unanimously on a proposal from the Commission] *in accordance with the procedure referred to in Article 189c* and after consulting [the European Parliament] *the Economic and Social Committee,* shall decide what action is to be taken by the Community *in order to achieve the objectives referred to in Article 130r.*

2. *By way of derogation from the decision-making procedure provided for in paragraph 1 and without prejudice to Article 100a, the Council, acting unanimously on a proposal from the Commission and after consulting the European Parliament and the Economic and Social Committee, shall adopt:*
   — *provisions primarily of a fiscal nature;*
   — *measures concerning town and country planning, land use with the exception of waste management and measures of a general nature, and management of water resources;*
   — *measures significantly affecting a Member State's choice between different energy sources and the general structure of its energy supply.*

The Council may, under the conditions laid down in the preceding subparagraph, define those matters referred to in this paragraph on which decisions are to be taken by a qualified majority.

3. *In other areas, general action programmes setting out priority objectives to be attained shall be adopted by the Council, acting in accordance with the procedure referred to in Article 189b and after consulting the Economic and Social Committee.*

*The Council, acting under the terms of paragraph 1 or paragraph 2 according to the case, shall adopt the measures necessary for the implementation of these programmes.*

4.   *Without prejudice to certain measures of a Community nature, the Member States shall finance and implement the environment policy.*

5.   *Without prejudice to the principle that the polluter should pay, if a measure based on the provisions of paragraph 1 involves costs deemed disproportionate for the public authorities of a Member State, the Council shall, in the act adopting that measure, lay down appropriate provisions in the form of:*
     — *temporary derogations and / or*
     — *financial support from the Cohesion Fund to be set up no later than 31 December 1993 pursuant to Article 130d.*

ARTICLE 130T

*The protective measures adopted pursuant to Article 130s shall not prevent any Member State from maintaining or introducing more stringent protective measures. Such measures must be compatible with this Treaty. They shall be notified to the Commission.*

## Questions and Problems

1.   What is the "environment"? Which of the following raise environmental issues for a local region:
     a.   utilization of high speed trains
     b.   raising of livestock
     c.   construction or expansion of a mental institution
     d.   building a prison
     e.   use of motorized lawn-mowers or leaf-blowers
     f.   a new airport runway
     g.   a rodent control or elimination programme?

2.   To what extent do the definitions of pollution in national and Community law and the Stockholm Declaration involve detrimental change to the environment? How is detriment determined?

3.   What is the role of science in environmental law? How does scientific uncertainty impact on the development of legal norms?

4.   Should the focus of environmental regulation be on actual harm or risk of harm? Should the goal be prevention or remedy? Should potential irreversibility of damage play a role in decisions that are taken?

5.   Compare the Stockholm and Rio Declarations. Are there differences in approach and emphases in the two documents?

6.   To what extent do property laws affect the approaches to and content of environmental law?

7.   Has the development of Community action and law in the environmental field limited the scope of state sovereignty referred to in Principles 21 and 24 of the Stockholm Declaration?

8.   As you study the remaining chapters, consider:

a. to what extent the Stockholm Declaration predicted and influenced subsequent environmental developments and problems

b. the advantages and disadvantages of centralized/decentralized governance of environmental matters.

## Bibliography

Bentil, J. K., "Implementation of Common Market Environmental Protection Laws", 128 *Solic. J.* 393 (1984).

Birnie, P. and Boyle, A., *International Environmental Law* (1992).

Caldwell, L., *Between Two Worlds: Science, The Environmental Movement, and Policy Choice* (1992).

Haagsma, A., "The European Community's Environmental Policy: A Case-study in Federalism", 12 *Fordham Int'l L. J.* 311 (1989).

Haigh, N., *EEC Environmental Policy and Britain* (2nd ed., 1990).

Harris, B., "EEC Laws on Environmental Protection", 137 *New L. J.* 1958 (1987).

Johnson, S. P. and Corcelle, G., *The Environmental Policy of the European Communities* (1989).

Kiss, A. and Shelton, D., *International Environmental Law* (1991).

Kramer, L., *Focus on European Environmental Law* (1992).

Mitchell, J. K. (ed.) *Global Environmental Change: Human and Policy Dimensions* (1990).

OECD, *The State of the Environment* (1991).

Rehbinder, E., and Stewart, R. B., "Legal Integration in Federal Systems: European Community Environmental Law", 33 *Am. J. Comp. L.* 371 (1985).

Sohn, L., "The Stockholm Declaration on the Human Environment", 14 *Harv. Int'l L. J.* 423 (1973).

Vandermeersch, D., "The Single European Act and the Environmental Policy of the European Economic Community", 12 *Eur. L. Rev.* 87 (1987).

Wagenbaur, R., "The European Community's Policy on Implementation of Environmental Directives", 14 *Fordham Int'l L. J.* 455 (1990).

World Commission on Environment and Development, *Our Common Future* (1987).

## CHAPTER II

# FUNDAMENTAL CONCEPTS

## A. Aims

Environmental laws and policies are based upon a desire to achieve certain objectives through the measures adopted. In this regard, piecemeal and sometimes conflicting norms can reflect different views about the ultimate rationale for and aims of environmental protection. Some suggest that benefit to humans is the prime reason for respecting the environment. This utilitarian view is seen in early legal instruments which protected "useful" birds and animals and encouraged destruction of others. The European Community originally based environmental protection on a utilitarian approach, derived from the Treaty of Rome provision that affirms as a goal for Member States "the constant improvement of the living and working conditions of their peoples".

An alternative view sees intrinsic value in the environment, seeking to protect its components whether or not they are necessary to or exploitable by mankind. This is reflected in the slogan "Earth First". Accordingly, many current legal texts protect all endangered species of flora and fauna as part of the natural heritage, without distinction according to their immediate economic value to humanity.

Conflicts or divergences between the utilitarian and intrinsic value approaches to the environment may be limited by rejecting the idea that humans exist separate and apart from the environment. By acknowledging that the biosphere is composed of complexly interdependent elements, of which mankind is one part, this approach seeks to ensure the existence of each interdependent element through preservation of all sectors and ecosystems. The survivability of each part depends upon the survivability of the whole and vice versa. Perhaps reflecting this view, none of the texts that refer to conservation and transmission of the environment and its elements to future generations limits the reference to future human beings.

The aim of protecting the entire biosphere has an influence on the development of law in several ways. First, as already stated, it extends environmental protection beyond those elements deemed economically useful. Second, it leads to more integrated solutions as the interdependence of environmental sectors – air, soil, water, flora and fauna – is recognized. Thus, it avoids legislative measures that risk transferring harm from one environmental milieu to another by addressing only one sector or one problem, such as air or water pollution. Third, it recognizes that environmental interdependence is not limited by geographic boundaries and may require regional or, in a growing number of cases, global solutions to environmental problems.

# B. Principles

In attempting to ensure continuity of the biosphere and its components, environmental principles have been elaborated which are now common to national, regional and international law. The terminology is not always defined or used with precision, leading to some confusion and duplication. However, there are core meanings that allow each principle to be distinguished from the others. The legal principles reflect an overarching concept that environmental protection is a matter of public or common concern. Individual or local reactions like NIMBY ("Not in my back yard!") or YIMBY ("Yes, in my back yard!"), based on environmental purity or economic necessity, are not determinative, but may be factors in decision-making. Thus, in the Netherlands, the Council of Ministers agreed on 19 June 1992, to a Bill that gives the Minister of Public Health, Physical Planning and Environmental Affairs, and the provinces, more power to compel municipalities to cooperate in environmental decisions of broad interest or an urgent nature.

## 1. *Conservation*

One of the earliest terms used in environmental protection, conservation aims to maintain sustainable quantitative levels of environmmental resources. It requires management of renewable resources and avoidance of waste in regard to non-renewable natural resources. Conservation does not fully address environmental quality, being based upon the status quo and demanding only maintenance of the conditions necessary for continued resource existence. The World Conservation Strategy of IUCN, an action plan recommended to governments, demonstrates the conservation principle in establishing as its objectives: (1) maintaining essential ecological processes and systems supporting life; (2) preserving genetic diversity; and (3) achieving sustainable utilization of species and ecosystems.

When applied to exploited species of flora and fauna, conservation is often carried out through establishing "optimal sustainable yields", adopting hunting and fishing regulations, and creating reserves. Optimal sustainable yield signifies exploitation of a renewable natural resource without exceeding the limits which guarantee the renewal and thus the sustainability of the stock. In recent texts, "conservation" has been supplemented or replaced by reference to "sustainable development", assuring the on-going productivity of exploitable natural resources and conserving all species of fauna and flora. Sustainable use or development is often defined as a use which maintains and enhances the renewable natural resource base in a manner that meets the needs of the present generation without compromising the ability of future generations to meet their own needs from the same resource base.[1] Such a definition presumes both goals can be met, which is not always evident. For example, population growth and limits on the food production capacity of the environment can

---

[1] This definition of sustainable development was adopted by the Brundtland Commission in *Our Common Future*.

produce conflict between the short-term food needs of the present generation and the long-term development of sustainable agricultural practices.[2]

## 2. *Amelioration*

Improvement of environmental quality is one of the Community principles added by Single Act article 130r. Setting a more ambitious goal than conservation, amelioration requires positive action to improve the environment. The first EC programme of action devoted an entire chapter to improvement of the environment and quality of life, cited as a fundamental task of the Community.

## 3. *Precaution and Prevention*

According to the European Community, the best environment policy consists in preventing the creation of pollution or nuisances at their source, rather than subsequently trying to counteract their effects. Prevention implies assessment of risks to avoid harm and action based upon existing knowledge. However, the consequences of decisions and actions are not always fully known in advance; there is a significant problem of action in the face of uncertainty about economic and scientific conditions associated with environmental protection. Thus, in the 1980s, a more stringent "precautionary principle" (*Vorsorgeprinzip*) developed in environmental policy, to suggest that certain measures should be taken in the face of scientific uncertainty about the likelihood of harm or before the threshold of environmental risk is reached.

Uncertainty poses a legal problem because those drafting environmental protection laws try to base their proposals on knowledge of the environment, its state, the causes and degree of its deterioration and the remedies likely to prove effective. However, knowledge in all these areas is incomplete and subject to frequent revision. Instead of decisions based upon an objective evaluation of scientific facts, such as the dangerousness of a particular chemical, it is sometimes necessary to address problems more subjectively or intuitively and assess solutions based on partial knowledge and uncertainty about certain aspects, including the extent to which there is uncertainty and who are the knowledgable experts. For example, the consequences of polluting emissions are not always clearly established, nor is the likelihood of improvement through a reduction in emissions, particularly with regard to cumulative pollutants from diverse sources and pollutants that show their effects only after long periods of time.

Causality is an area of particular uncertainty, along with questions about the economic impact of environmental harm and the costs of anti-pollution measures. To avoid harm, causality is assumed in some cases of scientific uncertainty. Thus, a strong version of the precautionary principle reverses the normal burden of proof and requires an actor to prove in advance that his proposed action will *not* cause harm to the environment. Some States declare that measures must be taken "even when there exists no scientific proof in evidence of a causal link between the emissions and

---

[2] See FAO, *The State of Food and Agriculture*, 1989.

the effects"[3] or "if there are reasons to believe that damage or negative effects could be caused even if there is inadequate or inconclusive scientific evidence to prove the existence of a causal link between emissions and effects".[4] The precautionary principle thus signifies that measures of environmental protection should be taken in advance of any known harm.

The precautionary principle was first enunciated internationally by the OECD in a 1987 Ministerial Declaration of the Second International Conference on the Protection of the North Sea (London, 1987). Since then, it has been cited frequently in the context of marine pollution, climate change, dangerous wastes, and hazardous products. The Maastricht Treaty on European Union includes the precautionary principle in Article 130r. Principle 15 of the Rio Declaration calls for applying the precautionary principle, stating that "Where there are threats of serious or irreversible damage, lack of full scientific certainty shall not be used as a reason for postponing cost-effective measures to prevent environmental degradation."

While not fully defined, scientific uncertainty provides a basis for determining policy in the face of uncertainty about whether preventive measures are necessary. It proposes choosing the best strategy on the basis of impartial evaluation of known facts, through reasonable assumptions extrapolating from what is known, and through hypotheses which seek to predict what is not known based on probabilities derived from existing knowledge. The exact degree of scientific agreement required to make policy decisions will vary from one country to another and will partly depend on the potential gravity of harm and the degree of risk that the harm will actually occur. A small probability of catastrophic harm may call for measures more urgently than a high risk of minor consequences. Unfortunately, these issues also may be subject to scientific uncertainty. The question often asked is: what are the consequences of being wrong about the decision taken?

The Netherlands' legislation on protection of the soil and on dangerous substances offers an example of the precautionary principle. It provides that anyone who produces a substance, puts it at the disposition of another, utilizes or introduces it into the Netherlands, who knows or reasonably should know that by his action the substance can present a danger for humans or for the environment, has the duty to take all measures which could be reasonably demanded of him in order to limit, as much as possible, the danger.[5] Such measures can include prohibiting certain pollutants, emissions, discharges, or immersions; reducing other emissions; and managing hazardous wastes to avoid environmental risks.

The precautionary principle thus may assume that prevention is required, until activities or products are proven safe, based on the knowledge that many environmental processes and changes can be irreversible. In this regard, there is a danger that the measures taken eventually could prove to have been significantly more costly than the dangers averted. Taken to an extreme, the precautionary principle could

[3] Ministerial Declaration of the Third International Conference on the Protection of the North Sea, The Hague, March 1990.

[4] Nordic Council Conference on Marine Pollution, Final Document, Copenhagen, October 1989.

[5] M. J. Dreden, De Zorgplicht in de milieuwetgeving, *Milieu en recht,* 1989/2, Feb., p. 50.

lead to prohibiting the majority of economic developments, as almost all involve some risk of environmental harm. The problem in applying the precautionary principle is to balance the risk or probability of harm against the economic costs of the measures proposed and the likelihood that the measures will be effective in avoiding the harm; in order to justify the measures, their costs should be less than the projected cost of the environmental damage avoided. It must be noted that often opinions are very divergent among scientists and economists on both these points, particularly when it comes to measuring damages avoided and costs to future generations, e.g. possible increased cancer levels due to depletion of the ozone layer.

The need to balance risk and cost means there will be a combination of measures with different costs which will be implemented in a progressive fashion according to the gravity of risk or harm and based on the best available knowledge of the problem. The greater the risk, particularly of irreversible or serious harm to the environment, the more strict the precautionary measures that must be taken.

## 4. *Protection*

Protection can be seen as a general principle which includes, but goes further than some of the concepts described above. It includes both abstaining from harmful activities and taking affirmative measures to ensure that environmental deterioration does not occur. It has a wider scope than does conservation, which is generally limited in application to the field of natural resources. However, protection does not necessarily encompass the concept of amelioration.

Increasingly, the concept of protection results in comprehensive ecological planning and management, including substantive regulations, procedures, and institutions on a national scale. Sectoral conservation of resources is giving way to integrated, system-oriented ecological policies that take into account the interdependence of environmental elements within ecosystems.

## 5. *Polluter Pays*

The polluter pays principle was developed as a method of allocating the costs of pollution control. At an international level, the OECD member countries agreed in 1972 that subsidies should not be provided to cover pollution control costs; these costs instead should be borne by polluters who could generally pass them on to consumers. In other words, the cost of pollution control should be reflected in the cost of goods and services which cause pollution in production and/or consumption. The objectives are (1) to require that the generators of pollution bear the costs of measures taken to ensure that the environment is in an acceptable state, and (2) to avoid distortion of international trade or unfair competitive advantage for the industry of one country over that of another. Both the European Community Single European Act and Maastricht Treaty express the view that the cost of preventing and eliminating nuisances must in principle be borne by the polluter.

The polluter pays principle also can be applied in a direct way as a form of pollution tax or penalty. For example, Turkish law establishes an environmental pollution prevention fund based in part upon taxes from sales and inspections of motor vehicles; fees imposed on Turkish-registered ships and airline tickets and cargo; shares collected from enterprises determined to be causing pollution; and all fines imposed according to the environmental protection law. Further, a 1988 amendment provides that the expenditures required for preventing, limiting or combating pollution shall in principle be met by the polluter. Thus, if the polluter fails to take the necessary action to stop, eliminate or reduce pollution, and measures must be taken by the public sector or the authorities, the resulting expenditures will be collected from the polluter. The latter may escape responsibility if it can be shown that all necessary measures were taken to prevent the pollution.

Similarly, the 1991 Bulgarian Environmental Protection Act provides in article 3 that persons polluting the environment and using natural resources shall pay charges at rates set by the Council of Ministers for the contamination and resource use. The funds collected are deposited to the account of the municipality on whose territory the pollutant or the user are located; 50 per cent of the funds are to be used for municipal environmental protection; 40 per cent for regional inspectorate for environmental protection and 10 percent for the national environmental protection fund.

## 6. Other Principles

Based on EC norms and Programmes of Action, and other texts of national and international law, additional principles can be identified. In some cases these are subsidiary principles necessary to implement those already discussed.

For example, in taking precautionary or preventive measures, legal texts may require reliance on the best available technology (BAT), the best available technology not entailing excessive costs (BATNEEC), the best environmental practices (BEP) or the best practicable environmental option (BPEO).

Best available technology is defined in both national and international texts. In Irish legislation the best available technology is that technology generally accessible which is the most effective in preventing, minimizing or rendering harmless pollution emissions. The UNECE Convention on the Protection and Use of Transboundary Watercourses and International Lakes, adopted 17 March 1992, defines BAT as the latest stage of development of processes, facilities or methods of operation concerning the practical suitability of a particular measure for limiting discharges, emissions and waste.

Assessing whether something is the best available technology requires comparative assessment of processes, facilities and methods of operation recently and successfully tried; technological and scientific advances; economic feasibility; time limits; the nature and volume of discharges; and low- and non-waste technology. As the UNECE text notes, "it therefore follows that what is best available technology for a particular process will change with time in the light of technological advances, economic and social factors, as well as in the light of changes in scientific knowledge and understanding".[6]

---

[6]  Annex I, article 2.

BATNEEC adds an explicit cost/benefit analysis to the notion of best available technology. "Not entailing excessive cost" implies that the costs should not be excessive in relation to the environmental protection to be achieved. The concept originates in Community law, and has been adopted in both Ireland and the United Kingdom. The Irish Environmental Protection Agency has the power to prescribe standards based on BATNEEC, embracing both the process adopted and how that process is operated – including staff numbers and working methods, training, supervision and operating procedures.

Evaluating the "best environmental practices" and the "best practicable environmental options" requires integrated, multi-factor analysis. The UNECE Watercourses Convention calls for consideration of the environmental hazard of the product throughout its life cycle (production, use, disposal), substitution of less polluting processes or substances, scale of use, potential environmental benefit or penalty of substitute materials or activities; advances and changes in scientific knowledge and understanding, time limits for implementation, and social and economic implications.[7]

The United Kingdom in April 1987 created a new unified pollution inspectorate in order to achieve greater integration of pollution control through selecting the "best practicable environmental option" (BPEO). The revision came after a Royal Commission concluded that action regarding industrial pollutants should be chosen to cause the least environmental damage overall, employing knowledge of industrial processes and techniques.[8] BPEO requires identification of the least environmentally damaging manner for discharge of pollutants and, further, demands use of processes be based upon the best available technology not entailing excessive cost (BATNEEC).

BPEO policies generally also require that measures avoid transferring pollution from one medium to another, i.e. from air to water, or across boundaries. In this regard, the German Land of Hesse has an integrated environmental permit process that requires those discharging wastes and pollutants containing certain heavy metals to take into account the cross-media impacts of the measures they select to avoid waste and control pollution. More generally, Turkish legislation provides that "on principle, the measures to be taken to protect the environment and to prevent pollution are to be determined and implemented as an integrated whole".

Finally, because some environmental harm cannot be avoided, there are principles that seek to limit and reduce adverse consequences as fully as possible and to avoid side effects. These require that those who cause damage to ecosystems and ecological processes rehabilitate and restore them as fully as practicable.

[7] Annex II, article 2.
[8] Fifth Report of the Royal Commission on Environmental Pollution (1980).

## C. The Right to Environment

The constitutions of many countries today, including virtually every constitution adopted or revised since 1970, either state the principle that an environment of a specified quality constitutes a human right or impose environmental duties upon the state. However, the texts generally do not simply state that everyone has a "right to environment". In virtually every case, explanatory or qualifying language is included to specify the type of environment that is sought: decent, healthful, natural, clean, ecologically balanced, safe. The standards seem to range from the minimum necessary to sustain life, to absolute purity. Thus, rather than a right to environment, there is a right to [a certain quality of] environment.

Within Europe, article 45, para. 1 of the 1978 Spanish Constitution speaks of the right to enjoy an "environment suitable for the development of the person". Article 66 of the Portuguese Constitution provides that "all have the right to a human, healthy and ecologically balanced human environment and the duty to protect it". The article goes on to require the state, through its agencies and popular initiatives, to take various measures to prevent pollution and assure conservation of nature. The Polish, Slovenian, and Turkish Constitutions similarly provide both for environmental rights and duties.

In contrast, the Greek, Albanian, and Bulgarian Constitutions, as well as the 1991 Constitution of the Russian Federation speak only of the duty of the state to protect the environment. All but the Greek impose the same duty on citizens or on "everyone".

In 1989 Hungary amended its Constitution to add that "the Hungarian Republic recognizes and enforces the right to a healthy environment for everyone". (Article 18 of Act XXXI, 1989). In addition, environmental protection is linked to the right to health in article 70/D, Chapter XII:

(1) People living in the territory of the Hungarian Republic have the right to the physical and mental health of the highest possible level.

(2) This right is ensured in the Hungarian Republic by the organization of the labour security system, public health institutions and medical care as well as by protecting the man-made and natural environment.

Romania's 1991 Constitution contains similar language in article 22.

At the international level, in the two decades since the Stockholm Conference, one of the most widely quoted provisions of the final Stockholm Declaration has been Principle 1. It provides:

Man has the fundamental right to freedom, equality and adequate conditions of life, in an environment of a quality that permits a life of dignity and well-being, and he bears a solemn responsibility to protect and improve the environment for present and future generations ...

While this formulation stops well short of proclaiming a right to environment, it links human rights and environmental protection. It appears to view human rights as a fundamental goal and environmental protection as an essential means to achieve the "adequate conditions" for a "life of dignity and well-being" that are guaranteed.

The links between human rights and the environment may be viewed as deriving from the fact that human health and existence, legally protected as the right to health and the right to life, are dependent upon environmental conditions. Some scholars conclude that this link requires recognition of a right to environment as an independent human right. Others promote the idea of a right to environment as a means of accomplishing environmental protection, as a prerequisite to fully ensuring the right to life.

Since Stockholm, a growing number of international texts have included references to environmental rights[9] or a right to an environment of a certain – or uncertain – quality. This trend has engendered considerable discussion and controversy over whether a right to environment or specific environmental rights do or should exist. Although the 1950 European Convention on Human Rights does not contain a right to environment, case law of the European Commission and Court of Human Rights indicates that environmental deterioration can lead to violations of human rights that are recognized by the Convention, including the right to privacy and family life, and the right to property.[10] This also may be the case with the United Nations Covenants on Civil and Political, and Economic, Social and Cultural Rights.

European Community texts on environmental protection encompass three specific rights: the right to environmental information, the right to public participation, and the right to access to remedies for environmental harm or adverse administrative decisions. Directives on both water and air pollution contain public rights to information. For example, Directive 1176/160, on bathing water quality, states that "public interest in the environment and in the improvement of its quality is increasing; the public should therefore receive objective information on the quality of bathing water".[11] The duty to provide information also is elaborated in connection with mandatory environmental assessment projects, according to Directive 85/337.

On 7 June 1990, the European Community adopted a Directive on Freedom of Access to Information on the Environment.[12] Its aim is to ensure freedom of access to and dissemination of information on the environment by public authorities. The latter are required to make available information relating to the environment to any person upon request without the person having to prove an interest. Exceptions are provided to protect commercial and industrial confidentiality and personal data. If

---

[9] The term "environmental rights" is used to designate human rights that are protected specifically in the context of environmental protection. These include freedom of association, the right of access to information, the right to participation in government, and due process rights.

[10] See e.g. *Powell and Rayner*, Judgment of 21 February 1990, Eur.Ct.H.R. Ser. A, vol. 172; *The Skarby Case*, Judgment of 28 June 1990, Eur.Ct.H.R. Ser. A, vol. 180–B; *The Fredin Case*, Judgment of 18 February 1991, Eur.Ct.H.R. Ser. A, vol. 192; *Oerlemans* v. *Netherlands*, Judgment of 27 November 1991, Eur.Ct.H.R. Ser. A, vol. 219.

[11] Directive 76/160, O.J. 1976 no. L 31/1.

[12] 90/313/EEC, O.J. no. L 158, 23 June 1990. Detailed discussion of this Directive and other Community texts concerning information and public participation can be found in Chapter VIII.

a request for information is refused, the applicant may seek a judicial or administrative review of the decision.

Among national laws, chapter two of the Bulgarian Environmental Protection Act of 1991 guarantees all persons and state and municipal authorities the right of access to available information concerning the state of the environment, with judicial recourse in case the information is not provided. This information shall be collected, from corporate and physical persons producing goods and services, by the Ministry of Environment, the Ministry of Health and the Ministry of Agriculture and Food Industry. These authorities must furnish and announce the information through the mass media or other means. All authorities and private entities are obligated to inform the population without delay when pollution or damage to the environment occur, including natural disasters, industrial accidents and fires. They also must provide information about changes in the environment and requirements for the health and safety of the population.

The issue of the need for or desirability of a right to environment continues to engender debate. Those who favour it emphasize that human rights and human beings cannot exist in the absence of a safe and healthy environment. Opponents focus on the vague nature of the "right" and the problems of enforcement. In national, Community and international law, the trend seems to be toward a middle position guaranteeing environmental rights rather than a right to environment.

## D. Documents

*1. The Environment Law of Turkey,*
Law No. 2872 of 9 August 1983.

Article 3: The general principles regarding environment protection and prevention of environmental pollution are as follows:

(a) Protecting the environment and preventing environmental pollution are the duty of individuals and legal entities as well as of all citizens, and these are required to comply with the measures to be taken and the principles laid down in reference to these matters.

(b) Formulation and implementation of the decisions and measures regarding environment protection and pollution shall be based on the principle of protecting the health of human beings and of all living things and of making short and long term assessments by taking into account the positive and negative effects on development efforts as well as the costs and benefits of the measures to be taken.

(c) Institutions authorized to make decisions and evaluate projects concerning the use of land and resources shall pursue the objective of protecting and not polluting the environment, at the same time taking care not to affect development efforts adversely.

(d) In economic activities and in the choice of production methods, the most suitable technology and methods shall be selected and implemented with the purpose of preventing and limiting environmental problems.

(e) (Amended on 3 March 1988 by Article 1 of Law no. 3416) The expenditures required for preventing, limiting or combating pollution shall in principle be met by the polluter. The expenditures required to be made by public sector companies or corporations if the polluter fails to take the necessary measures to stop, eliminate or reduce pollution, or if such measures have to be taken directly by the authorities, will be collected from the polluter under the provisions of Law no. 6183 Concerning Procedures for Collecting Public Debts. However, if polluters can prove that they took all the measures necessary for preventing the said pollution, they may be exempted from the responsibility for meeting the expenditures made for prevention or limitation of pollution.

...

(g)   In principle, the measures to be taken to protect the environment and to prevent pollution are to be determined and implemented as an integrated whole.


## 2. Constitutional Provisions

*Constitution of Bulgaria*, 1991, chapter II, art. 31:

The State bodies and enterprises, the cooperatives and public organizations, as well as every citizen, are duty-bound to protect and preserve nature and natural resources, the water, air and soil, as well as the cultural monuments.

*Constitution of Greece*, 1975, part II, art. 24:

1.   The protection of the natural and cultural environment constitutes a duty of the State. The State is bound to adopt special preventive or repressive measures for the preservation of the environment.

*Constitution of Poland*, 1989, chapter VIII, art. 71:

Citizens of the Republic of Poland shall have the right to benefit from the natural environment and it shall be their duty to protect it.

*Constitution of Portugal*, 1982, part I, section III, chapter II, art. 66:

1.   Everyone shall have the right to healthy and ecologically balanced human environment and the duty to defend it.

2.   It shall be the duty of the State, acting through appropriate bodies and having recourse to or providing support for popular initiatives, to:

  (a)   Prevent and control pollution, its effects and harmful forms of erosion;

  (b)   Order and promote regional planning aimed at achieving a proper location of activities, a balanced social and economic development, and resulting in biologically balanced landscapes;

  (c)   Create and develop natural reserves and parks and recreation areas and classify and protect landscapes and sites so as to ensure the conservation of nature and the preservation of cultural assets of historical or artistic interest;

  (d)   Promote the rational use of natural resources, safeguarding their capacity for renewal and ecological stability.

*Constitution of Spain*, 1978, chapter III, art. 45:

Everyone has the right to enjoy an environment suitable for the development of the person as well as the duty to preserve it.

*Constitution of Turkey*, 1982, Chapter VIII (a), art. 56:

Everyone has the right to live in a healthy, balanced environment.

It is the duty of the State and the citizens to improve the natural environment, and to prevent environmental pollution.

## Questions and Problems

1. What is the difference between prevention, precaution, protection, conservation, and amelioration?

2. Under the polluter pays principle, who bears the costs of installing anti-pollution technology and of cleaning up a river polluted by a paper mill?
   — the owners
   — those involved in the operation of the mill
   — consumers of paper
   — taxpayers
   — local government

3. Is the right to environment an enforceable right? What is its content and meaning? Compare the constitutional provisions above.

4. A new biotechnology company with limited capital is in the process of developing a freeze-resistant tomato. There are no known risks associated with the genetic experiments being done. The laboratory is located in a complex that is generally accessible. As security, the company has identification cards for its employees and keeps its doors locked during and after working hours. The directors of the company have learned that they can obtain additional security for about 500,000 ECU, including barred windows, computer-coded entry cards and stronger, more tamper-proof locks. It is estimated that it could take 2 million ECU for state-of-the-art security that would keep the laboratory virtually sealed off from the outside. What should the directors do? Suppose, instead, that the laboratory is involved in breeding European honey bees with highly aggressive, but disease-resistant, exogenous bees?

5. Should dams be constructed to withstand the strongest earthquakes and floods likely to occur within one hundred years? Five hundred years? One thousand years? What if the costs of the additional safety would raise costs of hydroelectric power to five times the current rates? Ten times? Should a dam be prohibited if the costs are excessive?

## Bibliography

Alfredson, G. and Ovsiouk, "Human Rights and the Environment", 60 *Nordic J. Int'l L.* 19 (1991).

*Environnement et Droits de L'homme* 79 (P. Kromarek, ed. 1987).

Gibson, J., "The Right to a Clean Environment", 54 *Saskatchewan L. Rev.* 5 (1990).

Gormley, W. P., "The Right to a Safe Environment", 28 *Indian J. Int'l L.* 1 (1988).

Gormley, W. P., "The Right of Individuals to be Guaranteed a Pure, Clean and Decent Environment: Future Programmes of the Council of Europe", 1975 *Legal Issues In Eur. Integration* 23.

Gormley, W. P., *Human Rights and the Environment: The Need for International Cooperation* (1976).

Gray, C. Boyden and Rivkin, D. B., "A 'No Regrets' Environmental Policy", 83 *Foreign Policy* 47 (1991).

Gundling, L., "The Status in International Law of the Principle of Precautionary Action", 5 *Int'l J. Estuarine & Coastal L.* 23 (1990).

Handl, G., "Human Rights and Protection of the Environment: A Mildly 'Revisionist' View", in *Human Rights and Environmental Protection* (Cançado Trindade, ed. 1992).

Hodkova, I., "Is there a Right to a Healthy Environment in the International Legal Order?", 7 *Conn. J. Int'l L.* 65 (1991).

Shelton, D., "Human Rights, Environmental Rights, and the Right to Environment", 28 *Stan. J. Int'l L.* 103 (1991).

Steiger, M., "The Fundamental Right to a Decent Environment", in *Trends in Environmental Policy And Law* 5 (M. Bothe ed. 1980).

Thorme, M., "Establishing Environment as a Human Right", 19 *Den. J. Int'l L. & Pol'y* 302 (1991).

Uibopuu, M., "The Internationally Guaranteed Right of an Individual to a Clean Environment", 1 *Comp. L.Y.B.* 101 (1977).

## CHAPTER III

# TECHNIQUES OF ENVIRONMENTAL LAW

Various inter-related techniques have developed to further the aims and apply the basic principles of environmental law. Usually, States enact and implement several of them, based upon particular threats to the environment, national and local conditions, traditions and cultural norms, and the economic situation specific to each country. Some techniques have achieved broad acceptance in national, regional and international law. These are discussed in detail in this and following chapters.

In general, environmental laws are complex and fragmented. Detailed knowledge is necessary to comply with all the regulations applicable to any particular project. In fact, diversity and dispersion of norms have been hallmarks of environmental law. However, a trend toward codification and comprehensive environmental planning is serving to integrate formerly disparate laws.

Initially, in response to specific threats of environmental pollution and degradation, many countries enacted legislation to curb industrial effluents and nuisances potentially harmful to a particular sector of the environment, such as air or water. More recently, comprehensive "anti-pollution" laws have been added to continued sectoral legislation. The UK Environmental Protection Act 1990 establishes a system of Integrated Pollution Control. The Secretary of State designates by regulations those industrial processes that have the potential for significant release of harmful substances. The processes are subject to centralized regulation of all discharges into the environment. In addition, the pollutants they emit are considered in their entirety before deciding what discharges and what levels of discharges are allowed.

As a supplement to or substitute for anti-pollution laws, some states have enacted comprehensive codes regarding conservation and management of the environment and natural resources of the country. Codification involves more than the reproduction and restatement of applicable statutory texts; instead it constitutes a systematic consolidation and revision of the law, a major legislative effort. It also tries to regulate the two major branches of environmental law: pollution on the one hand, and protection of nature on the other. Sweden adopted a comprehensive code in 1988, updating and strengthening environmental protection.

In the codification effort, umbrella or framework legislation may be adopted, laying down basic legal principles without attempting to include all relevant statutory provisions. Normally, such legislation declares national environmental goals and policies. It may include institutional arrangements designating the competent governmental authorities or commissions and common procedural principles for environmental decision-making, such as environmental impact assessment, licensing and enforcement, applicable to all sectors. In 1987, Portugal adopted a framework law, the *Lei de Bases do Ambiente*. The text divides the environment into sectors (air, water, soil, flora and fauna), and establishes prohibitions, duties, guidelines, and definitions for each. Subsequent Portuguese environmental law completes the framework legislation or incorporates new Community directives into it.

The list of environmental laws and regulations in Europe is particularly long because EC rule-making must be added to national and local norms. To illustrate, an enterprise that seeks to build a new industrial plant containing an incinerator for its industrial waste products must prepare an impact assessment under EC Directive 85/337/EEC, Annex I (Environmental Impact Assessment), in addition to complying with any local zoning or other regulations. Its industrial activity will bring it within Directives 82/501/EEC (major accident hazards of industrial activities) and 87/216/EEC (Seveso). As an industrial facility it will require prior authorization according to article 3 of Directive 84/360/EEC (combating air pollution from industrial plants). If it discharges any dangerous substances into adjacent waters, it will be regulated by Directive 76/464/EEC (pollution of the aquatic environment by dangerous substances) and if it fails to incinerate all of its wastes, Directive 78/319/EEC (toxic and dangerous wastes) will apply.

The plans for the plant become much more difficult if the site is near an estuary containing bathing waters (Directive 76/160/EEC) and/or shellfish waters (Directive 79/923/EEC) or if it contains important wetlands (Directive 79/409/EEC). In addition, if any part of the waters provides a source of drinking water, it is further protected (Directive 75/440/EEC) as is any aquifer underneath the site (Directive 80/68/EEC). As this example indicates, Community norms regulate many aspects of environmental law and provide a unifying factor in European law.

Keeping in mind these general comments, we turn now to a review of the various techniques of environmental law and their characteristics in national, Community, and international law.

## A. Preventive Measures

Preventive measures aim to avoid harm and reduce or eliminate the risk of harm. As such, they concern pollution or other environmental damage that is foreseeable through the normal operations of an activity or the use of a product, as well as measures that should be taken to mitigate or prevent harm in case of accidental damage.

### 1. *Regulation*

#### a. *Standard-setting*

Four categories of standards may be distinguished according to the subjects they regulate. First, *quality standards* fix the maximum allowable level of pollution in an environmental sector or target during normal periods. A quality standard may set the level of mercury permissible in rivers, the level of sulphur dioxide in the air, or the noise level of airplanes in the proximity of residential areas. Quality standards often vary according to the particular utilization of the environmental sector. For example, different water quality standards may be set for drinking water, agricultural waters, and waters used for bathing and fishing. Quality standards also can vary in geographic scope, covering national or regional zones, or a particular source, such as a river or lake. However, each quality standard establishes base norms against which compliance or deviance are measured.

*Emission standards* specify the quantity or concentration of pollutants that can be emitted in discharges from a specific source. Often the environmental sector of the discharge is a variant factor: groundwater, air, soil. For example, the Danish Parliament has fixed for 1995 a maximum limit of 125,000 tons for the emission of sulphur dioxide into the air from all power plants.[1]

Emission standards also may vary according to the number of polluters and the capacity of the sector to absorb pollutants. Different standards may be imposed in response to particular climatic conditions, for example persistent fog or inversion layers.

As a general rule, emission standards apply to fixed installations, such as factories or homes; mobile sources of pollution are more often regulated by product standards. Emission standards establish obligations of result, leaving to the polluter the free choice of means to conform to the norm. The UK Environmental Protection Act 1990, for example, provides that the Secretary of State may establish limits for the total amount, or the total amount in any period, of any particular substance that may be released into the environment in, or in any area within, the United Kingdom. Based on these limits, quotas may be allocated to persons carrying on processes involving release of the substances. Sweden regulates the total emissions of all substances from each plant or factory through a system of permits and inspection, requiring use of the best practicable means to achieve environmental protection. This system controls polluting emissions to air, water and land in an integrated package.

*Process standards* establish specifications applicable to fixed installations, such as requiring a particular factory production procedure. In contrast to emission standards, process standards impose certain means of production and generally do not allow the polluter to choose other methods to reduce emissions. Often, these norms require the installation of purification or filtration systems. Process standards also are used to regulate the operations of hazardous activities where there are risks of accidents. For example, according to Community Directive 82/501/EEC, known as the Seveso Directive, EC member states must take measures to require all manufacturers engaged in listed activities to prove to the competent authority at any time that they have identified existing major accident hazards, adopted appropriate safety measures, and provided persons working on the site with sufficient information, training and equipment in order to ensure their safety. Further, manufacturers should notify the appropriate authorities of information relating to dangerous substances listed in an annex to the Directive, if the substances are employed or produced in one form or another at some stage during the manufacturing process. Owners or

---

[1] Compared to 212,000 tons in 1980.

operators must prepare emergency plans and assistance to respond to consequences outside the installation and inform potential victims of the emergency measures to be taken in case of accident.

*Product standards* may fix: (1) the physical or chemical composition of items such as pharmaceuticals or detergents, (2) the handling, presentation and packaging of products, particularly those which are toxic, or (3) the levels of pollutants the product can emit during its use, e.g. automobile emission standards. For economic reasons, these uniform rules aimed at preserving human health or other components of the environment are usually adopted for an entire industry.

Product standards can take numerous forms. Danish legislation regulates the sulphur content of fuels. Another product standard may list substances whose presence is forbidden in certain products; for example, mercury in pesticides. In general, new source standards are drafted to reflect the best available pollution control technology, in some cases requiring a percentage reduction of pollutants emitted in comparison with older sources.

Product standards generally are based on normal uses of the product. However, many of the labelling requirements are intended to avoid accidental environmental harm through misuse, spills, or improper disposal of the product.

### b. Restrictions and Prohibitions

If an activity, product or process presents a risk of environmental harm, regulations other than standards can be imposed to reduce or eliminate the harm. When the likelihood of risk is too great, the measure may call for a total product or process ban. The numbers and types of restrictions are almost unlimited. However, there are certain ones that are commonly used.

*Listing* restricted or banned products, processes or activities is a technique often used in environmental regulation. It permits individualizing situations and gives the regulation some flexibility by permitting easy modification and adaptation. Lists also avoid too much technical detail being included in the basic legislative or regulatory text. The use of lists is very common in regard to pollution by dumping of wastes, discharge of hazardous substances during normal operations, and the protection of wild flora and fauna, especially endangered species.

The French law on classified installations uses lists to regulate polluting activities. The law covers stationary installations operated or owned by any natural or legal person, public or private, that may threaten any danger or nuisance to neighbourhood amenities, public health and safety, agriculture, conservation, nature, the environment, or sites or monuments. Installations included on the list (nomenclature des installations classées) are subject to prior authorization or declaration of their activities, depending on the risk of danger or nuisance they pose.

There are two categories of listed installations, Type A and Type D. Prior to beginning activities, Type A installations must be authorized by the relevant Prefect. The procedure includes one month of public inquiry and can result in technical standards being prescribed for the installation. Type D installations must declare their operations and are subject to general standards for the category of installation. In addition, the

Prefect may impose, on his own or a third party's initiative, special standards where the general standards are insufficient to provide adequate environmental protection.

Lists also are used to protect endangered species. Those species threatened with extinction often appear on lists that prohibit taking, trade and other harmful activities. The 1979 EC Directive on the Conservation of Wild Birds provides a rather complete example of the technique of lists for the protection of all species of birds living in the wild on the European territory of member states.

In some cases the listed categories would be too numerous and too complex for effective implementation. In such cases, the law may establish lists of exceptions rather than inclusions. For example, a Luxembourg law of 1 August 1988, specifies projects *not* requiring an environmental impact statement.

*Zoning* was originally aimed at protecting private residential areas and dwellings, by prohibiting the construction of industrial and similar installations in residential zones. Today, land use controls play a major role in environmental law for both urban and rural areas. Zoning provides a means to distribute activities harmful to the environment in order to limit potential damage. Different legal rules may apply from zone to zone for more effective protection.

Generally, once a zoning scheme for the relevant land and water areas is approved by the state or local government, special procedures must be used to obtain exceptions. The land use classification specified in a general plan is presumed applicable until the plan expires. Using this technique, areas that are important for environmental purposes can be zoned for uses compatible with those purposes. Activities such as heavy industry that generate pollution and degrade resources can be restricted to certain areas specified in the plan. They also can be required to meet certain design standards to avoid or minimize environmental threats to human health and critical resources such as water.

Environmental factors may be considered in overall regional planning procedures, such as classifying a city, a region or the entire territory of a country into broad land use categories such as residential, industrial, agricultural, forest, or nature conservation, as in Ireland and France. Designated areas may be given special legal protection for purposes such as health care or nature conservation, including national parks, reserves, and sanctuaries.

Land use planning and zoning regulations are normally expressed in negative terms, as prohibitions or restrictions on any undesirable utilization or change in utilization of the area. Modern planning also may encourage and promote land uses that are considered beneficial or compatible with environmental objectives.

Because of the evolution of environmental protection schemes and the numerous levels of government involved, land use regulations can become extremely complex. For example, in Denmark there are estimated to be about 50 planning systems which have more or less direct importance to land use, with a number of different legal means of control.[2] The overall system of land use planning and regulation is controlled through numerous, often-amended statutes.

---

[2] O. Christiansen, "Comprehensive Physical Planning in Denmark", in *Planning Law in Western Europe* (J. F. Garner and N. P. Gravells, eds., 1986).

In the United Kingdom, all development proposals since 1947 have required a grant of planning permission from the local authority. Today, grants must be based on and in accordance with development plans prepared by local authorities, with policy guidance from the Secretary of State for the Environment. Development plans must include a policy on "the conservation of natural beauty and amenity of land", but this is only one of the considerations that go into the plans. A great deal of discretion is afforded decision-makers.

*Trade and taking prohibitions* and *restrictions*, both temporary (suspensions) and permanent, are commonly utilized for the protection of wild flora and fauna. For example, the 1973 Convention on International Trade in Endangered Species of Wild Fauna and Flora (CITES) uses trade restrictions and prohibitions as means of protecting endangered species. The Convention lists in a first appendix all species threatened with extinction that are or may be affected by trade. Trade in these species is virtually prohibited, requiring prior grant and presentation of export and import permits issued under stringent conditions.[3] Two additional appendices list those species which may become threatened with extinction unless trade is regulated. The EC, a contracting party to CITES, has issued regulations banning the importation of cetacean and fur seal products.

Trade regulations also are used to prohibit or regulate the transport and dumping of toxic and dangerous wastes. The Basel Convention of 1989 regulates the transfer of toxic or dangerous wastes and particularly requires informed consent of the countries concerned prior to any transfer. EC Directives establish similar standards in this field.

Finally, other regulatory measures may establish labelling requirements to indicate contents and permissible uses of products. In a positive sense, the "green label" is increasingly used to identify environmentally safe products. Labelling is discussed further in the context of legislative and market incentives to environmental protection.

## 2. Licensing

The most widely used technique to prevent environmental harm is government authorization through permits, certifications, or licences. Each activity or establishment considered environmentally hazardous is defined or listed and made subject to formal licensing procedures. In the United Kingdom, it is unlawful to carry out a process listed as polluting or potentially harmful without an authorization from the enforcing authority. In some air pollution cases, the authority is a local agent; in other situations it is the central Inspectorate of Pollution.

Some licensing systems have been adopted in conformity with international texts. For example, the explanatory memorandum to the German Emissions Control Act of 15 March 1974 refers to Resolution (68)4 of the Committee of Ministers of the Council of Europe concerning air pollution control. The Oslo Convention of 15 February 1972 for the Prevention of Marine Pollution by Dumping from Ships and

---

[3] For a detailed discussion of CITES, see Chapter V.

Aircraft envisages a system of permits, as do the Paris Convention for the Prevention of Marine Pollution from Land-Based Sources of 4 June 1974, and the Bonn Convention of 3 December 1976 on Protection of the Rhine against Chemical Pollution. The European Community is a party to the latter two Conventions.

Whether based on international treaties or not, all European countries derive their licensing systems from one or more legal instruments. In some countries, such as the United Kingdom, a general environmental protection law includes among its preventive measures a licensing system for certain categories of installations. This is also the case in Germany, Denmark and the Netherlands. Alternatively, a law may establish a licensing or authorization system for installations causing pollution or nuisances (classified installations) without addressing broader issues of environmental protection. Such laws exist in France, Luxembourg and Belgium. Finally, various texts may contain detailed licensing rules dating from different periods and thus reflecting different approaches, as in Ireland and Italy. Whatever the approach, major new construction is subject to licensing in virtually every country.

In addition to laws containing general licensing measures, it is common to find norms that regulate directly or indirectly only specific aspects of environmental protection, such as air pollution, drinking water, noise, chemicals, and taking of wildlife. In this regard, hazardous installations such as nuclear plants, mines, natural gas or petroleum works are likely to have more stringent licensing requirements.

### a. Licensing Goals

For much of Europe, the permit process originated in a Napoleonic decree of 1810, whose aim was to protect the immediate area surrounding a project. Based on this and the prior approval provisions of its Nuisance Act, the Netherlands has regulated all activities that carry some threat to the local environment. The Act requires a permit granted by the local authority for any operation that might cause danger, damage, or nuisance. Similarly, in Belgium, an authority issuing a licence to a company is required to ascertain that persons living in the company's vicinity will not be exposed to disturbances exceeding those to which the locale is normally subjected.

More recent legislation expresses broader goals. For example, the German Emissions Control Act of 1974 requires that any licensed installation be constructed and operated in such a manner as to avoid serious nuisance to the environment or any major danger, inconvenience or disturbance to the community or the surrounding area. The aim is to protect "human beings, fauna and flora and all other things against any damage to the environment insofar as such damage may be caused by installations subject to licensing, and to ensure protection against any significant danger, inconvenience or disturbance ..." The Act also seeks to prevent the occurrence of any damage to the environment. Similarly, the Netherlands has adopted a series of sectoral environmental protection statutes that establish general licensing schemes: the Surface Waters Pollution Act 1969, the Air Pollution Act 1970, the Sea Water Pollution Act 1975, the Chemical Waste Act 1976, the Waste Substances Act 1977, the Noise Nuisance Act 1979, and the Soil Protection Act 1987.

The requirements of each law were standardized with the adoption of the Environmental Health General Provisions Act 1979.

Most licensing controls are not designed to eliminate all pollution or risk, but rather to control serious pollution and to reduce its levels as much as possible. Licences represent a middle ground between unregulated industrial practices and absolute prohibitions. They can provide an alternative to zoning as a means to site installations and allow experimentation through the granting of temporary licences. Where environmentally hazardous products are present, such as industrial chemicals, pesticides or pharmaceuticals, authorizations may be required at each step for the manufacture, use, marketing, importation or exportation of the product.

### b. Scope of Controls

The requirement that installations acquire a licence is often given broad application. For example, in the Netherlands, a Royal Decree of 31 December 1969 states that

> as extensive a scope as possible shall be ascribed to the concept of an 'installation' with the result that almost all human activities liable to cause serious damage or nuisance outside the limits within which they are exercised may be regarded as an 'installation' under the Nuisances Act.

The 1952 Nuisances Act specifies that the term "installation" should be construed as covering any place used for given activities, even in the absence of any construction (section 1(2)). Belgian legislation refers to "works, factories, workshops, stores, warehouses, open quarries, machinery, equipment, etc.".

Most laws on licensing make no distinction between profit-making and non-profit enterprises, except as to public bodies. In particular, military operations are generally exempt. It should be noted that Community Directive 85/337 on environmental assessment applies to public as well as private projects, except for those relating to national defence. In the United Kingdom, licensing systems do not apply to acts of the Crown unless specific rules exist to that effect.

Retroactivity becomes a problem when licensing regimes are instituted: are installations constructed and operating prior to initiation of the system obliged to obtain a licence? While in principle laws are not given retroactive effect, it has been argued that exemption for existing installations grants them a *de facto* subsidy. In response, some laws have been made explicitly retroactive, e.g. the Irish Local Government (Water Pollution) Act of 1977. It seems that the trend favours requiring licensing for the continued operation of pre-existing facilities.

An essential condition for initial and continuing authorization is compliance with certain environmental standards; the British Environmental Protection Act, for example, imposes environmental conditions on the grant of all authorizations. These conditions are reviewed at least once every four years and require, for example, use of the best available techniques not entailing excessive cost (BATNEEC); compliance with obligations under Community law or other international obligations relating to environmental protection; compliance with limits or requirements and achievement of quality standards or objectives prescribed by legislation; imposition of emission limits; and a requirement of advance notification of any proposed change in the operations of the activity or process.[4]

Conditions often are based upon environmental impact assessments whose preparation may be incorporated into the licensing process and which form part of the decision for or against issuing the licence. In many cases, particularly in regard to chemicals and pharmaceuticals, elaborate testing procedures according to accepted laboratory practices serve the same purpose and may replace environmental impact assessments.

### c. Procedures

Most licensing systems operate on the basis of a list, or an inventory of activities necessitating a licence, because of their foreseeable potential harm to the environment. These lists may constitute part of the law (usually an appendix), as in Denmark, Ireland, and the United Kingdom. They also may be contained in a supplementary legal instrument, such as an implementing decree (France) or regulation (Germany). Initial control consists of an examination of the installations and an assessment of the foreseeable results of their operations; licensed activities generally also are subject to measures of on-going special supervision.

The existence of several different licensing systems may result in similar functions being confided to different bodies in respect to the same installation. In practice, several licences may be required for a single project. For example, the Netherlands Nuisances Act of 1952 was followed by other specific regulations concerning surface water and air pollution control, each of which set up a new licensing system supplementing the earlier controls. In some cases, e.g. France, multiple licence applications may be merged. Provision then is made for a more detailed investigation, incorporating the procedures of the different licensing systems. A single administrative act incorporates all measures required under the various laws. In other countries, such as Denmark and Netherlands, separate applications must be submitted, and there are separate decision-making procedures.

Where several independent procedures exist and must be followed, it is possible that a licence may be issued to conduct activities, but the same company can be refused a permit to construct the proposed buildings in which the activity is to take place, or vice versa. In order to avoid such problems, priorities may be established or coordination mandated between the different agencies.

The decision-making process for granting a licence may be exercised by central authorities, regional or local bodies. The decision should be based on information supplied by the applicant, including a description of the planned activities, sometimes accompanied by maps and plans of the installation and its surroundings, a study of accident risks, and a description of possible anti-pollution or anti-nuisance measures. In many cases, an environmental impact assessment will form part of the application procedure. There may be publicity, including the display of notices and/or

---

[4] Environmental Protection Act 1990, ch. 43, sec. 7.

publication in the press, followed by public hearings and expert testimony. In general, the costs of the procedure are borne by the public authorities, but in certain cases, costs are payable by the applicant (France, Ireland, and Luxembourg).

Community Directive 85/337/EEC now plays a significant role in licensing procedures in Europe. It provides in article 6 that any demand for authorization of a public or private project which could have an effect on the environment, as well as information received on this subject, should be made public. States also should ensure that opportunity is given to concerned members of the public to express an opinion before the project is approved. States members should establish the means to provide this information and allow consultation. The particular characteristics of the projects or sites concerned may determine what sector of the public is affected, control the location where the information can be consulted and establish the particular methods of information (poster, newspapers, displays). States also may determine the manner according to which the public should be consulted, whether it is by written submission, public inquiry or other, and fix the appropriate time limits for the various stages of the procedure.

Once the inquiry is closed, the authority may grant a licence, if appropriate with conditions, give partial or temporary authorization, or refuse a licence entirely. If the licence is refused, there may be grounds for appeal to a judicial body for review of the decision. In most cases, there are both time limits and restrictions on who make take the appeal.

## 3. *Environmental Impact Assessment (EIA)*

First introduced in the United States in 1969, EIA is a procedure to ensure that adequate and early information is obtained on likely environmental consequences of development projects and on possible alternatives and measures to mitigate harm. It is generally a prerequisite to decisions to undertake or to authorize designated construction, processes or activities. The EIA procedure requires that a developer or business owner submit a written document to a designated agency or decision-making body, describing the future environmental impact of the intended action. The procedure may be integrated into licensing schemes or land use planning. Legislative measures mandating environmental impact statements commonly set forth a list of activities to which the requirement applies; a designation of who has to prepare it and pay for it; the procedure to be followed; the contents of the report; and the consequences which follow upon its submission.

Directive 85/337/EEC of 27 June 1985, obliged Member States to have national EIA legislation by July 1988. Most Member States have complied and some non-Member European States have developed legislation based on the EC Directive. The Directive has a very broad scope, requiring assessment, prior to consent being given, of the effects of those public and private projects likely to have significant impact on the environment due to the nature, size or location of the project. Assessment must be made of both the direct and indirect effects of a project on (1) human beings, fauna and flora; (2) soil, water, air, climate, and landscape; (3) the interactions between the factors mentioned in (1) and (2), and (4) material assets and the cultural heritage.

Member States retain power to exempt a specific project from the assessment requirement in exceptional cases, but must inform the Commission.

The Directive (Annex I) and some national laws, such as the Bulgarian Environmental Protection Act of October 1991, list classes of projects that require impact assessments, assuming that they risk substantial environmental impact. The Directive also lists in Annex II the classes of projects subject to an assessment procedure if national law deems it necessary. In accordance with the Directive, the British Town and Country Planning (Assessment of Environmental Effects) Regulations of 1988 list mandatory assessment projects in Schedule 1. The Schedule includes applications involving crude oil refineries, thermal and nuclear power stations, radioactive waste, iron and steel smelting, asbestos extraction, chemical installations, construction of motorways, long-distance railways, airports with runways of 2,100 metres or more in length, trading ports, inland waterways and waste disposal installations and operations. Swiss legislation goes further and requires assessment of the impact on the land of military manoeuvres.

An increasing number of national laws require preparation of an impact statement for any proposed activity that is likely to affect the environment significantly. For example, the British Regulations cited above demand that proposed developments, beyond the listed categories, be accompanied by an impact statement if they are likely to have significant effects on the environment by virtue of factors such as the nature of the development, its size or its location. Circular 15/88 gives further guidance, stating that assessment will be required primarily in three situations: (1) when there are major projects of more than local importance; (2) occasionally when projects on a smaller scale are proposed for particularly sensitive or vulnerable locations; and (3) in a small number of cases, when projects present unusually complex and potentially adverse environmental effects, and expert and detailed analysis of those effects would be desirable and relevant to the issue of whether or not the development should be permitted.

The British statute establishes criteria and thresholds, and lists categories of projects to which the requirement may apply: agriculture, mining and energy, metal processing, glass-making, and industries relating to chemicals, food, textiles, leather, wood, paper, and rubber, together with industrial and urban development projects. All applicants for planning permission for major projects within these categories must consider whether their planning application is subject to environmental assessment and needs to be accompanied by an environmental statement. In addition, applicants may request an opinion from the local planning authority on the need for a project assessment. Whether or not an opinion is requested, there are possible appeals to the Secretary of State if the authority decides in favour of assessment, fails to give an opinion, or decides assessment is required of unassessed projects submitted without an advance opinion, or where the planning application is refused.

Most environmental impact assessments must include, at a minimum, a description of the proposed activity; a description of the potentially affected environment, including specific information necessary for identifying and assessing the environmental effects of the proposed activity; a description of the practical alternatives including the option of no action; an assessment of the likely or potential environmental impacts of the proposed activity and alternatives, including the direct, indirect, cumulative, short-term and long-term effects; an identification and a description of measures available to mitigate adverse environmental impacts of the proposed activity and alternatives, and an assessment of those measures; and an indication of gaps in knowledge and uncertainties that may be encountered in compiling the required information. Community Directive 85/337/EEC specifies this information in its annex III.[5]

Once the impact statement is prepared, it is examined by an agency or neutral body, in general after hearings with public participation. Public participation is assured by many laws; including the Bulgarian Environmental Protection Act of October 1991, which provides in article 20 that all concerned physical and juridical persons have the right to take part in the discussion of the results of an environmental assessment.

Generally, on the basis of expert and public opinions, if it is determined that the activity or project would cause serious and irreparable damage to the quality of the environment, the agency is directed to refuse authorization or approval. If the project or activity can be modified to eliminate or compensate for the negative effects, it may be approved subject to such modification or control.

In international law, environmental impact assessment is required in a transboundary context under the provisions of a treaty signed at Espoo, Finland, 25 February 1991.[6] The treaty includes the general elements found in domestic environmental assessment plans and provides a model for further legislation. It requires that states parties establish an environmental impact assessment procedure with regard to listed activities that are likely to cause significant adverse transboundary impact. Impact is defined to mean any effect caused by a proposed activity on the environment, including human health and safety, flora, fauna, soil, air, water, climate, landscape and historical monuments or other physical structures or the interaction among these factors; it also includes effects on cultural heritage or socioeconomic conditions resulting from alterations to those factors.

The list of activities subject to the EIA requirement includes crude oil refineries, thermal and nuclear power stations, treatment, storage and disposal of radioactive waste, smelting, asbestos factories, chemical installations, road and rail construction, oil and gas pipelines, ports, toxic and dangerous waste disposal, large dams and reservoirs, ground-water abstraction, pulp and paper manufacturing, major mining, offshore oil production, storage of petroleum and chemicals, and major deforestation. In determining the significance of the activity to the environment, criteria are provided in the treaty: size, location, and effects, including those giving rise to serious effects on humans or on valued species or organisms, those which threaten the existing or potential use of an affected area and those causing additional loading which cannot be sustained by the carrying capacity of the environment.

---

[5] Schedule 3 of the British Town and Country Planning (Assessment of Environmental Effects) Regulations 1988 requires the same information demanded by the Directive.

[6] All European states except Malta and Turkey have signed the treaty.

The Espoo Convention sets out in detail the procedural and substantive requirements of an environmental impact assessment. First, any proposed, listed activity likely to cause significant adverse transboundary impact shall be notified to any potentially affected Party as early as possible. The latter has the right to participate in the environmental impact assessment procedure if it wishes. Significantly, the public in the affected area also has the right to be informed of and to participate in the assessment procedure, even though it takes place in another country.

The environmental impact assessment documentation submitted by the originator must contain a description of the proposed activity and its purpose; a statement of the reasonable alternatives including a no-action alternative; information on the environment likely to be significantly affected and alternative sites; the potential environmental impact of the proposed activity and its alternatives and an estimation of its significance; mitigation measures to keep adverse environmental impact to a minimum; an explicit indication of predictive methods and underlying assumptions as well as the relevant environmental data used; an identification of gaps in knowledge and uncertainties encountered in compiling the required information; where appropriate, an outline for monitoring and management programs and plans for post-project analysis, and a non-technical summary, including a visual presentation.

Consultations and decisions about the proposed activity must take into account the outcome of the environmental impact assessment, including possible alternatives to the proposed activity and measures to mitigate significant adverse impacts. Moreover, any party can request a determination whether a post-project analysis should be carried out based on the environmental impact assessment. Such analyses must include surveillance of the activity and determination of the extent of adverse transboundary impact. This includes monitoring compliance with the conditions of approval of the activity and the effectiveness of mitigation measures, as well as verification of past predictions in order to utilize the results in regard to future activities of the same type.

The proliferation and breadth of environmental impact assessment procedures reflect their important contribution to environmental protection. By insisting on investigation and communication of environmental risks to those likely to be affected, EIAs ensure a degree of informed decision-making.

## B. Implementation Measures

The implementation, as well as the formulation, of environmental laws and policies must be based on the collection of reliable information and on its continuous assessment. The techniques adopted in environmental laws to ensure this are surveillance, reporting, and monitoring.

Surveillance is the acquisition of data, mainly a scientific activity, on which further action such as monitoring may be based. For example, EC Directive 82/883/EEC establishes procedures for surveillance and monitoring of environments affected by titanium dioxide waste. The Directive is concerned with obtaining information on physical, chemical, biological and ecological conditions. Its provisions on surveillance include taking samples of the affected environments, such as water samples. It can be done by individual enterprises, by associations or by local or national authorities. Once the information is gathered, it must be assembled, organized and analyzed by an appropriate agency or institution to which the information is sent. It is common to find environmental laws requiring reporting by enterprises or state institutions. Nearly all EC Directives on polluting operations require reports to be filed with state agencies and the Community.

Monitoring is the continuous assessment of information, comparing it to mandated parameters. If necessary, the monitoring organ can intervene based on the reports and other means of surveillance that make it possible to assess the effectiveness of legislation or action taken. Monitoring provides constant feedback for decision-making, from long-term protection to rapid guidance in emergency situations. The British Environmental Protection Act 1990, requires national authorities (Her Majesty's Inspectorate of Pollution) and local authorities to monitor developments and technology and techniques for preventing or reducing pollution of the environment due to releases into the air, water and land from the prescribed industrial processes.

The EC Titanium Dioxide Directive provides a specific example of monitoring on the regional level. After samples are taken, they are analyzed, compared to specified parameters, and also compared to samples taken from a zone deemed to be unaffected by titanium dioxide discharges. The Directive establishes common reference methods of measurement in order to permit comparable analyses of the physical, chemical, biological and ecological characteristics of the environments monitored. Each report on the implementation of the Directive that Member States forward to the Commission must contain details of the surveillance and monitoring operations carried out by national or local bodies, including a description of the sampling point, the sampling methods, the results of measuring the parameters whose determination is mandatory, the methods of measurement and analysis used and, where appropriate, their limits of detection, accuracy and precision, and changes in the frequency of sampling and analysis. The effectiveness of surveillance and monitoring of the environments affected must itself be monitored and assessed.

Some countries have centralized their surveillance, monitoring and assessment in a single governmental agency. Others rely on a network of decentralized institutions, coordinated by a national commission or an agency. In Germany, ambient air quality is monitored by two networks. The first, more comprehensive one, is run by the state (Länder) authorities who have primary responsibility for monitoring ambient air quality according to standards established by the federal government in the Federal Emission Protection Act and other ordinances and decrees. The Federal Environment Agency controls the second system, which analyzes the causes of environmental damage and assesses long-range transboundary air pollution, particularly the deposit of air pollutants. The Agency operates a measuring network of stations throughout the country to monitor levels of sulphur dioxide, nitrogen oxide, chlorine, carbon monoxide and suspended particulates, including lead and cadmium, as well as meteorological conditions.

A monitoring network also may include both government-sponsored and non-governmental academic and research institutes and laboratories. Many countries have established a system of controlled self-monitoring by industries, whereby polluting industrial establishments are required to monitor their waste discharges and submit regular reports to the competent environmental agency. The agency spot-checks the information received, by field inspections and by analyses or tests performed in its own laboratories.

Sweden, for example, requires that all applications for permits be accompanied by a document stipulating how the company is to monitor its discharges. The document must contain fairly specific information about the parameters to monitor, the methodology of monitoring, and where and when to carry out monitoring. This information can be incorporated into the conditions under which the permit is granted. Alternatively, another document, the "checking permit", can stipulate how the data are to be reported and to which particular authority. Large companies may be required to take measurements on a daily basis or even more frequently. The results are reported monthly to the county authorities. External control is provided through compulsory inspections carried out annually by independent consultants.

The environmental audit or independent review, sometimes referred to as the eco-audit, has come to serve two purposes. First, it is a legislative control mechanism of growing popularity. Second, it is a device of importance to business in sales, acquisitions and other transactions involving assets, where the risk of liability for environmental non-compliance can be a crucial element in negotiations and contracts.

With increasingly complex technology, company structures and environmental regulations, it is sometimes difficult for management and authorities to remain fully informed about the environmental consequences of company operations. This can result in hidden problems, leading to accidents as well as to violation of environmental laws and regulations. Environmental auditing is the systematic investigation of the procedures and work methods of a company or institution, as they are relevant to its environmental responsibilities. Primarily a management tool, it is designed to determine to what degree these procedures and methods are consistent with legal regulations and generally accepted practices.

Audits can be part of the legal–administrative procedure for decision-making or part of the role of the judiciary. There can be parliamentary commissions of inquiry or monitoring by non-governmental environmental organizations, which play an important review role. Often research is undertaken by independent experts in the field. Environmental audits add an element of external quality control to the administrative system.

In March 1992 a proposed Community regulation on eco-auditing was published.[7] Intended to apply from 1 July 1994, it will have immediate and direct effect in the member states without the necessity of national enabling legislation. The Regulation refers to the use of environmental auditing techniques, within the framework of environmental protection systems, as a means to evaluate environmental performances in a systematic, periodic and objective way, and provide information

[7] EC Regulation (Com (91) 459 final (O.J. no. 92/C/76/02 of 27 March 1992).

on environmental performance to the public (article 1). The Preamble explicitly states that environmental auditing can provide an effective management tool to improve environmental performances of companies and a supplement to the normal obligations of management.

As set forth in the Regulation, the audit is voluntary for industrial activities. Enterprises that choose to participate in the programme must abide by the procedures established in or pursuant to the Regulation. These include the methods and subjects of the audit. Companies also agree to implement measures that appear necessary in light of the audit and to allow verification of the audit by designated environmental audit verifiers.

The standardized procedures for eco-auditing include an environmental statement that must provide specific information, set forth in article 8. This information includes:

— a description of the company's activities relevant from the environmental point of view;

— an assessment of all significant environmental issues relating to its activities;

— a summary of quantitative data;

— a presentation of the company's environmental policy and programme, including the company's specific objectives and activities concerning improved protection of the environment in a given site, and general information on measures aimed at achieving such objectives and deadlines established for such measures;

— an evaluation of the environmental performance of the company's protection system, which is a coordinated set of measures established, implemented, revised and updated by a company; and

— a deadline for producing the next statement.

Articles 7–8 of the Regulation establish qualifications, terms of reference, and procedures for designating Accredited Environmental Verifiers, who will have the function of reviewing audits and establishing standardized conditions and reports.

Apart from its function as a regulatory mechanism, environmental audits form a growing part of business transactions. Purchasers of businesses may seek to have environmental representations and warranties, or a determination of whether they will be assuming liabilities for environmental damage. This can involve physical inspection of property and assets, including any disposal site used in the processes carried out on the property; examination of documents, including all operating licences and permissions; and physical and scientific analysis of processes, by-products, and waste streams. Specific investigation usually is made for any signs of past environmental misconduct that would lead to a claim for liability for environmental damage in the future. The results of the audit can govern the nature and extent of protection built into the contract covering acquisition of the company or asset.

## C. Enforcement and Remedial Measures

In spite of all preventive measures, environmental harm does occur, sometimes through intentional or negligent conduct, sometimes through accident. In order to deter wrongful conduct and remedy violations that do take place, the law must determine appropriate enforcement actions and remedies. As such, it has to address such questions as the degree or amount and kind of harm that may lead to legal action, who is entitled to instigate the action, before what forum or tribunal, and what appropriate orders, sanctions, or compensation may be foreseen. The procedures may include civil actions, administrative remedies, and criminal prosecution.

### 1. The Nature of Responsibility or Liability

The concept of remedial action generally implies that damage or harm has occurred to something. However, the breach of a statutory obligation, without measurable harm, can result in sanctions or remedies, just as infraction of speeding laws can result in a traffic citation and fine even if no accident occurs. Thus, public liability can be based on a risk of future harm. The Bulgarian Environmental Protection Act of 1991 provides for both types of sanctions. Article 29 states that persons found guilty of harming others by pollution or damage to the environment shall be bound to remedy the damage. In addition, article 35 provides that the Minister of Environment shall issue punishment decrees for violation of the Act.

The concept of harm to the environment is often viewed as a property concept, where economic value is placed on the lost or damaged object. This may include market value, loss of income, and damage to moral, aesthetic and scientific interests. Under German tort law, any natural or legal person is liable for environmental damages to the extent that they constitute an injury to the life, body, health, freedom, property or other right, such as the right to operate and establish a business, of another person if the injury is unlawful and was caused wilfully or negligently.

The economic approach poses problems for protection of species of wild fauna and flora that are not exploited and thus have no market value, as well as for ecosystems or landscapes the economic value of which cannot be assessed. Evaluating the economic value of the intangible aspects of the environment, such as biological diversity, balanced ecosystems, etc., is difficult. The situation is similar for areas that are under common ownership, and even more for those areas that are for common use but not capable of ownership, such as the high seas and outer space.

Measurement or evaluation of harm for the purpose of damage awards also involves important questions of the threshold or *de minimis* level of harm, proximity of harm, especially for long-term, long-distance, multiple-authored actions and, finally, the possible irreversibility of the harm caused. The last issue is something that is thus far largely ignored in law.

## 2. The Scope of Responsibility

In most cases anyone harming the environment may be held liable to those injured or may be subject to criminal or administrative sanctions sought by the state. Liability is most often imposed on the principal owner or manager of a polluting enterprise. In France, directors and managers of classified installations may incur criminal liability for violations of approved operating procedures or standards. In Germany the operator (*Inhaber*) of the installation is responsible; this is the person having actual and legal power over the installation, including those acting pursuant to a lease agreement.

The Netherlands' Soil Sanitation Act indicates the potentially broad scope of liability. Civil liability may be imposed on anyone who contaminates soil; the seller of contaminated land (real estate) or its owner, even if the pollution was committed prior to his ownership; the owner of the company whose process created the contaminants; the carrier who transports the contaminants; and the manager of the company who caused the contamination. The government may clean up sites with serious soil pollution and then recover the cleanup costs from those responsible.

In all cases where someone is alleged to be responsible for environmental harm, there is a problem of proof: it is necessary to show a causal link between the acts of the person or company sought to be held liable and the harm that has occurred. This can be difficult when there are multiple sources, a cumulative effect or diffuse pollution, especially over time, or where the action is indirect. The degree of required proximity between the causes and harm must also be decided. For example, should a lender be liable for environmental damage caused by a borrower's use of the funds? If the lender's control of the borrower's activities is very direct, a claim might be pursued in some countries because the causal link would be deemed sufficiently strong.

In Germany, a Federal Supreme Court judgment has eased the plaintiff's burden of proof. If the plaintiff proves that his health or property has been damaged by emissions generated by the defendant, the defendant must prove that the emissions were immaterial or in accordance with local customs and that he has taken and observed all reasonable and economically feasible pollution control measures. In addition, the 1991 German Liability Act (*Gesetz über die Umwelthaftung/UmweltHG*) establishes a complex system of presumptions of cause, and exemptions or exclusions from such presumptions. There is a general presumption of cause that applies, if taking into account the circumstances of each particular case, an installation is found to have been capable of causing the ensuing damage. The presumption of cause does not apply if the installation has operated in accordance with permits and conditions imposed under administrative law. Compliance is presumed if proper control measures were implemented, such as use of safety equipment and regular inspections. Avoidance of presumed liability can be a strong incentive to increased compliance with preventive measures. The German Liability Act provides the injured party with a right to information from operators of installations and from environmental authorities.

In most countries, persons can be held liable for their intentional or negligent acts that cause harm. In addition, some laws hold persons liable for all consequences of their actions, even those that are accidental. This is known as strict or no-fault liability. As an example of the latter, the German Federal Water Management Act (*Wasserhaushaltsgesetz–WHG*) provides that anybody who adds or discharges substances into water or otherwise affects water in such a manner as to alter its physical, chemical or biological properties, is required to compensate for any damage arising to another person, without regard to whether the discharge was the result of a purposeful act or omission or not. Only *force majeure* (natural disaster, war, "Act of God", etc.) excuses liability. Turkish legislation also provides that

> polluters of the environment and those who cause damage to the environment are responsible, regardless of degree of fault, for the damage arising from the pollution and destruction they cause.

Without being explicitly based on a strict liability regime, the French criminal courts often give more weight to the threat posed to the neighbourhood and the amount of pollution caused by the activity than to the intent of the directors and managers.

Traditionally, strict liability was limited to the operators of particularly hazardous activities, such as nuclear power installations. However, the application of this concept is growing. In the German Environmental Liability Act that entered into force on 1 January 1991, owners of numerous environmentally relevant installations are strictly liable for damages caused by environmental effects resulting from installation emissions. The installation can be any one of some one hundred types listed in an annex to the Act. The Annex includes virtually all installations requiring a permit under the Federal Pollution Control Act (e.g. furnaces, gas turbines, cooling towers, chemical and pharmaceutical installations, paint shops, storage facilities for hazardous substances, and installations governed by the Waste Disposal Act). Damages are deemed to have been caused by an environmental effect if they result from substances, vibrations, noise, pressure or other actions emitted into the ground, air or water.

## 3. *Enforcement Actions*

Normally, civil actions are commenced by those who have suffered harm to themselves or their property. They seek to halt further damage and repair that which has been done. As noted in the prior section, remedies can be sought only if the damage results from the breach and damages is not too remote from the wrongful action. This rule affects who may bring claims. Enforcement of public laws is generally a matter for state authorities, who institute administrative or criminal proceedings. In some cases breach of a public statutory duty also may be the basis of a civil action for damages against the wrongdoer. This is true in France, but the person bringing the civil action must have a particular interest in the matter. Some national laws, however, permit consumers or others with no direct injury to sue. In Bulgaria, the law allows anyone to bring claims. First, those who are injured may bring a claim for damages; they also may seek to stop the damage and eliminate the consequences of pollution. The latter kind of claim, seeking to end harmful pollution and eliminate its effects, also may be lodged by municipal authorities, as well as by "associations of citizens with an ideal purpose and by every citizen".

### a. Civil Liability

In most countries, an individual who has suffered damage may bring a civil suit against the installation that caused the harm, based on concepts of tort, or a legal wrong. The tort of nuisance is the most frequent action, especially in common law. It claims an unreasonable, unwarrantable or unlawful use by a person of his own real or personal property, or improper, indecent, or unlawful personal conduct, which is wrong because it injures the right of another or the public, and produces significant annoyance, inconvenience, discomfort or hurt. Deciding a case of nuisance requires balancing the general right of a property owner to use his or her property, with consideration of the harm caused another, analyzing the reasonableness of use of the property. Thus, the type of act, the place and circumstances involved are important variable factors in determining whether conduct such as playing loud music constitutes a nuisance.

There are many bases for liability other than nuisance, including trespass, strict liability for ultra-hazardous activities, and negligence. In France, the most common ground for holding polluting enterprises civilly liable is similar to nuisance; it is the notion of abnormal harm to the neighbourhood (*inconvenient anormal de voisinage*). Claims brought on this basis are subject to strict liability; thus the plaintiff need not prove the defendant's negligence to establish liability, nor may the defendant escape liability by showing compliance with all government regulations.

Negligence, a common tort action in Ireland and the United Kingdom, requires a showing that the defendant owed plaintiff a duty of care, the duty was breached, and there were resulting proximate damages. Similarly, a provision of Italian tort law, article 2043, establishes that any fraudulent, malicious or negligent act that causes unjustified injury or harm to another results in an obligation to pay damages. Damages can be sought for impairment of health and, according to recent cases, for aesthetic and biological harm.

In Ireland and the United Kingdom, trespass is the action brought for an unpermitted, volitional entry onto someone's land, either by a person or something sent by a person. Somewhat different is the action that may be brought based on the nineteenth century case of *Rylands* v. *Fletcher*. In this case, the English courts held that the owner of property from which a substance or thing escaped was strictly liable to his neighbour who suffered damage as a result. The principle in the case is now extended to environmental pollutants produced on one property and causing harm on another. A similar principle is codified in Italian Civil Code section 2051 (liabilities arising from property in custody).

With another law akin to trespass, Germany permits any owner of land to prohibit the intrusion of gases, vapours, smells, smoke, soot, heat, noises, shocks and similar interferences emanating from another piece of land if such emissions are material (not insignificant), not in compliance with local customs (*nichtortsublich*) and if pollution control measures are economically feasible for the polluter. If control measures are not feasible and the neighbour has to tolerate emissions that prejudice the use of, or income from, his property, a claim for financial compensation arises. A similar provision exists in article 844 of the Italian Civil Code.[8]

Another possibility exists in regard to Italian Civil Code article 2050 which requires a plaintiff to prove injury, cause and that the activity was dangerous. Defendants are then liable unless they can prove that they adopted all possible measures, including the best available technology, to avoid the injury or damage. Going further, some laws may impose liability regardless of the preventive measures taken by the defendant. Strict liability for dangerous or ultra-hazardous activities is common among European legal systems.

Environmental protection is leading to the creation of new torts, as well as use of the traditional ones. In Italy, law 349/86 holds liable any person who, by intentionally or negligently violating a law or provision adopted in accordance with a law (such as a permit), affects or causes harm to the environment. Damages are paid to the Italian government. Case law indicates that the conduct causing the harm must be intentional or negligent. Damages may be allocated not only on the basis of actual proof of harm, but also according to the degree of culpability of the wrongdoer, the expenses required to restore the prior situation and the profits earned by the wrongdoer. Compensation may be obtained for the suffering of the population as a whole and damage to the environment in the broad sense. Any government authority may file a complaint and certain national environmental associations, designated by the state according to the law, may become *amicus curiae*[9] or subsequently intervene as a party to the proceedings. Individual citizens cannot bring such actions.

### b. Administrative Procedures

Administrative procedures include injunctions, fines, and refusal, suspension, revocation, or modification of permits. Proceedings usually can be initiated either by the authorities, concerned individuals or companies, or by associations. In some states, including France, administrative procedures are the primary quasi-judicial means of enforcing environmental laws.

According to the French regulations on classified installations, if an installation operator fails to file the requisite declaration or apply for the necessary authorization prior to use, or fails to give notification of specified events, the Prefect, who represents the state in a *departement* (county), may demand that the legal requirements be fulfilled within a specified period of time. In the interim, the Prefect may suspend the activities of the installation. The Prefect also may order operations terminated in cases of serious and persistent harm to the environment.

---

[8] The owner of adjacent land can prevent smoke, heat, fumes, smell or similar invasions if they exceed normal tolerability. The court must balance ownership versus production rights and take into account the priority of a given use.

[9] This term refers to individuals or organizations who are not parties to law suits, but who, generally with the court's permission, submit briefs or information as "friends of the court".

If an operating classified installation fails to comply with regulatory standards applicable to it, such as emission controls, the Prefect at his discretion may either (1) order the installation to be shut down pending measures to comply with the standards; (2) order the operator to pay into an escrow account the amount necessary to modify the activity so that it can comply with applicable standards; or (3) carry out the necessary work to bring an installation into compliance and charge the operator the costs. French administrative courts, as courts of first resort, and the Council of State (Conseil d'Etat), on appeal, may review administrative decisions, except for criminal matters or specifically delegated subjects within the competence of ordinary judicial authorities. A similar system is in operation in Turkey.

In Italy the main enforcement tool is suspension or revocation of the required permits issued by local governments, thus shutting down non-complying production facilities. Regions and municipalities may release and revoke licences for violations of measures concerning air pollution control, waste handling activity and waste water discharge. In this connection they have extensive access, inspection and verification powers. In addition, any mayor has the power to issue injunctions or other orders in circumstances of clear and immediate danger.

Environmental laws also may permit agencies to impose fines on violators. Ireland's Planning Code establishes sanctions ranging from fines to Enforcement Orders requiring the immediate cessation of an illegal use or the pulling down or removing of an illegal structure. In water and air pollution legislation, the licensing authority has power to review the conditions of the licence at regular intervals, with the residual power to close down a plant in serious circumstances. In Bulgaria, too, administrative fines may be imposed for all offences, other than negligible breaches, that do not constitute a crime. Fines can be both individual and corporate and are substantially increased for repeated misconduct. Nonetheless fines alone are sometimes criticized as being ineffective sanctions, in effect permitting large, wealthy polluters to pay for the "right" to pollute. Yet, where substantial in amount, they can be a significant deterrent.

### c. Penal Law

The function of penal law is to protect the most important values of society, by creating and enforcing penalties, including those involving deprivation of liberty. Increasingly, national law is imposing criminal liability on those who pollute and perform other acts damaging to the environment. For example, section 107 of the British Water Act provides that a person commits an offence if he causes or knowingly permits any poisonous, noxious or polluting matter or any solid matter to enter any controlled [protected] waters. A 1990 amendment to the Czech criminal code enacted the new offence of "endangering the environment" which can be prosecuted for either intentional or negligent acts. Law 17/1192 Coll adds that everyone is obliged to prevent environmental pollution and minimize the unfavourable impact of his or her activity. Knowledge of the consequences of resource exploitation is presumed. Everyone who learns of a threat to the environment or environmental damage is obliged to take the measures possible to eliminate the threat and to report the situation to state authorities.

In most states, not only the company, but also directors and other senior managers may be held responsible. Normally, a company will be guilty of an offence if the offence-relevant conduct involves instructions or other acts of a 'directing mind' of the company. Conversely, the director's position as a directing mind will not always produce criminal liability on his part, but may do so. The British Environmental Protection Act 1990 provides that

> When an offence under this Act which has been committed by a body corporate is proved to have been committed with the consent or connivance of, or to be attributable to any neglect on the part of, any director, manager, secretary or other similar officer of the body corporate or any person who was purporting to act in any such capacity, he as well as the body corporate shall be guilty of that offence and be liable to be proceeded against and punished accordingly.

In some countries, such as the Netherlands, criminal proceedings may be brought against the responsible company/corporation itself, the person who ordered the action to be performed and the person actually charged with executing the criminal act. In Italy, criminal sanctions apply to the legal representatives of a company, i.e. the chairman and/or managing director. Sometimes higher level employees actually in charge of technical matters and environmental compliance may be implicated, but criminal responsibility generally is imposed only if they have broad managerial powers.

Liability may be primary, accomplice, or conspiracy. An example of primary liability is given in the Water Act above. In many countries, accomplice liability is imposed on those who give help, support or assistance to a person committing an offence, or who incite, encourage, or counsel such a person. The lesser offence of conspiracy involves a decision by two or more parties to perpetrate an unlawful act.

There are elements of environmental offences that distinguish them from other areas of criminal law. Most criminal law is based upon a direct individual relationship between a perpetrator and a victim who has been harmed. Environmental protection can involve perpetrators and victims who can be identified only statistically, where harm results from barely measurable multiple causes. Two possibilities exist. The first is to assume the requisite danger or harm to public interests traditionally protected by penal law, such as life, health and property. The other is to develop new offences against the environment, protecting independent natural elements without requiring an element of provable harm to specific victims. Both approaches can be found in existing provisions of penal law.

Italian criminal law is quite specific in designating offences to the applicable environmental sectors. For example, it is a criminal offence to poison drinking water; to pollute and harm water set aside for protected uses; and to not execute an order of the public authority adopted to protect water bodies for public health. Case law establishes that negligence can be enough to impose liability. More broadly, Spain criminalizes violations of environmental laws or regulations, as well as acts that cause or produce, directly or indirectly, emissions or dumping of any kind, to the atmosphere, the soil or land or sea water, seriously endanger the health of persons, or could seriously endanger conditions of animal life, forests, natural spaces or crops (Penal Code Article 347).

Penal sanctions can range from fines for petty offences to imprisonment for more serious offences. The Irish Environmental Protection Agency Bill 1990 suggests maximum penalties that include a large fine and/or twelve months in prison. Some laws, like the British, also provide that convictions for certain environmental offences can lead to revocation of the permit to continue the same line of work or denial of a permit for other relevant employment. In France, the criminal court (*la juridiction pénale*) also may close the operation and grant the accused time to bring it into compliance with applicable standards.

In Spanish law, punishment consists of imprisonment or fines (between Pta 175,000 and 5,000,000). The maximum penalty is imposed if the industry operates clandestinely, or if it disobeys express orders from an administrative authority regarding the correction or suspension of a contaminating activity. The same is true if it supplies untrue information regarding its environmental impact or hampers inspection by the administration. In all these cases, the court has the power to temporarily or permanently close the establishment, and ask the government to intervene to safeguard the rights of workers on the site.

The Czech environmental protection act, Article 27, provides that everyone who by damaging the environment or by other criminal activity causes ecological damage is obliged to restore the natural functions of the damaged ecosystem or its parts. If restoration is not possible or not reasonable, substitute compensation is required. These sanctions are in addition to the provisions of the criminal code that establish a punishment of up to eight years imprisonment for intentional endangering of the environment or five years for negligent endangerment.

## 4. *Remedies*

Normal civil remedies are compensatory, usually money damages, and injunctive, ordering that the activity cease and repairs be made. Thus, in Bulgaria, persons may lodge a claim and ask that damage be halted and that the consequences of the pollution be eliminated. In French civil actions, the defendant may be found liable in money damages, and/or the court may require the installation to eliminate the damage through improving its operations. Penalties can be imposed if the improvements are not made in a timely way. Moreover, the court may modify the standards applicable to the classified installation, but such modifications must relate to the damaging activity, must be technically feasible and must not be less stringent than the applicable Prefect's standards.

Portugal's Decree Law No. 186/90 provides a range of remedies including fines, confiscating machinery and tools, closing the installation, prohibiting the exercise of a profession or activity, and depriving a company or individual of the right of public competition. There also exists an obligation to restore the environment, which will be undertaken by the state and charged to the company if the latter fails to carry out its duty.

Other sanctions may include a denial of government contracts or blacklisting of harmful products. Lending institutions may refuse loans or other benefits to projects failing to meet environmental standards or those scheduled for establishment in areas not attaining quality objectives. For example, the European Investment Bank may reject projects for areas not attaining EC air quality objectives.

In Germany statutory liability limits apply to damages for injury to health, life or property. With regard to ecological damages, i.e. to nature and landscape, the Liability Act requires that the party liable pay for restoration measures such as re-cultivating lands or reintroducing endangered species affected by the installation. For certain listed ultra-hazardous installations, liability insurance is mandatory. The importance and impact of liability insurance is analyzed further below.

In general, the measure of damages for environmental harm presents particular problems for the civil litigant. The *Amoco Cadiz* case reflects this. After the tanker ran aground on 16 March 1976, spilling nearly 230,000 tons of oil along the coast of Brittany, multiple lawsuits were filed in the United States by the French government, various French administrative departments, towns, businesses, associations, individuals, and the insurers of the cargo. The alleged damages included the costs of cleanup, estimated at 450 million French francs, damage to fish and shellfish of 140 million, and losses caused by the reduction in tourism, of more than 400 million. In addition, the claimants sought $2.2 billion damages for general environmental harm. The Court awarded $85.2 million. The award for the costs of cleanup included compensation for the time public employees, including elected officials and the military, took from their regular duties or put in overtime to assist, as well as travel costs, food and lodging for volunteers, and the costs of material and equipment purchased for the cleanup. Coastline and harbour restoration costs were included but not a claim for damage to the quality of life (lost enjoyment). Individual claims for loss of income were approved, but no damages for injury to the biomass. The Court found this claim complex, attenuated, speculative and based on a chain of assumptions. The Court further held that no one could claim compensation for injury to the environment. However, the French government was allowed the expenses incurred to reintroduce species that suffered from the pollution and its consequences.

## 5. *Remedies for Transfrontier Environmental Harm*

The liability regimes just discussed primarily apply when the actor and the harm lie within a single state. The issues become more complicated when harm occurs across state boundaries. Traditionally, such harm is included in the notion of state responsibility for acts contrary to international law. Under this doctrine, states may be held liable for pollution that causes demonstrable damage to persons or property in another state.

The principle of state responsibility for environmental harm is contained in various international texts and some national laws. Principle 21 of the Stockholm Declaration, repeated in Principle 2 of the Rio Declaration, provides that states have the responsibility to ensure that activities under their jurisdiction or control do not cause damage to the environment of other states or to areas beyond national jurisdiction. A bilateral boundary treaty between the Netherlands and Germany signed 8 April 1960, provides in article 63(1) that each of the contracting parties is obliged to protect its boundary waters against pollution and will be responsible to the other for damage caused by a violation of this duty.

On the national level, the 1991 Bulgarian Environmental Protection Act provides that persons found guilty of harming others by pollution or damage to the environment shall be bound to remedy the damage. Article 31 refers specifically to the elimination of the harmful effects of transboundary environmental pollution and calls for implementation of remedies on the basis of a treaty or, in the absence of one, general rules of international law.

In spite of widespread acceptance of the principle of state responsibility for transboundary harm, very few international liability claims have been presented. In addition to all the normal problems of environmental litigation, including determining the degree of fault or legal basis necessary to impose responsibility, inter-state procedures are lengthy and problems of proof are exacerbated when more than one state and long distances are involved. There is also a general issue concerning the extent to which states are accountable for the actions of private parties under their jurisdiction or control. Most activities causing environmental harm are those of private persons, particularly companies, and often these activities are legal where they occur. The general rule seems to be that the state whose territory serves to support the activities causing environmental damage elsewhere or under whose control it occurs is responsible for the resulting harm. Even if it is necessary to show an act or omission by state agents, this will normally be present due to widespread requirements of environmental impact assessments and licensing.

In spite of uncertainty in implementing international inter-state responsibility, it remains necessary to compensate victims of transfrontier pollution. The increasingly accepted solution is to settle the issue on the inter-personal level within states as part of private law, rather than through public international law. In such cases, an inhabitant of one state who suffers damage due to pollution originating in another state can file a civil action against the polluter. Of course the same fundamental litigation problems remain: establishing causation, identifying the polluter, and proving damage. In addition three new problems are added: jurisdiction, choice of law and execution of judgments.

Jurisdiction to judge a case can exist in the state of the victim or the state of the polluter. Some states have entered into treaties to settle the transfrontier jurisdictional issues. Within Europe, national law generally favours jurisdiction in the defendant's domicile because the accused is then able to defend itself in local tribunals, the evidence of harmful activity is more readily available, witnesses more easily may be called, and execution of a judgment in favour of the plaintiff will be enforced more easily. However, it can be argued that the victim should have the benefit of local courts, and that evidence of damage will be more readily available in the victim's forum. In addition, the victim should not have to bear the additional costs of litigating in a foreign country.

In 1968, the Member States of the European Community adopted a Convention concerning Jurisdiction and the Enforcement of Judgments in Civil and Commercial

Matters. The treaty narrowed the issues but failed to settle the jurisdictional question. Article 3 provides that a defendant may be sued in the courts of the place where the harmful event occurs. National courts reached conflicting results on the issue of whether the harm occurs where the wrongful act is committed or where the injury is suffered. However, the European Court of Justice delivered a judgment in 1976 in which it stated that article 3 is ambiguous, thus leaving the choice of forum to the injured party.

Choice of law is an issue determined by the court of jurisdiction. Generally, tribunals apply their own local law, but the principle of non-discrimination requires that the plaintiff's complaint be judged according to rules at least as favourable as those that would apply in the state where the activities took place. Finally, the complex issue of recognition of judgments is governed for some states by article 31 of the 1968 EC Convention, which provides that decisions rendered in one contracting state may be executed in another on request of any interested party. For states not party to the treaty, recognition will largely depend on local law and public policy.

## 6. *European Convention on Civil Liability*

The Council of Europe adopted in June 1993 a draft Convention on Civil Liability for Damages Resulting from the Exercise of Activities Dangerous for the Environment. It establishes general standards for indemnification of those injured by hazardous activities and products. Based on the "polluter pays" principle and building upon earlier agreements on civil liability damage caused by nuclear substances and the transportation of dangerous merchandise, the Convention eases the burden of proof on persons seeking reparations and broadly imposes responsibility. Within Contracting States it applies to all persons, companies and all agencies exercising control over dangerous activities. The place of the harm is irrelevant for liability if the activity or event takes place on the territory of a contracting state. However, if the damage occurs in a non-contracting state, the Convention permits reservations to be filed demanding reciprocity of remedies.

Dangerous activities and dangerous substances are within the scope of the Convention, with special attention given to genetically modified organisms. The quality of dangerousness is largely based upon assessment of the risk of harm to man, the environment or property.[10] Nuclear damage is excluded if the incident is regulated by the Paris Convention on Civil Liability of 1960 or by the Vienna Convention of 1963 with its amendments, or by national legislation at least as favourable to the plaintiffs as the Conventions. Workplace accidents covered by social security and auto accidents, in places inaccessible to the public as well as assimilated to other activities within the installation, also are excluded. The Convention will apply to all incidents occurring after its entry into force. For waste disposal sites, generally only damage occurring after the Convention enters into force will be covered.

Damages may be recovered for deaths, bodily harm, and injury to property other than that found on the site or within the installation where the dangerous activity has

[10] See below, Chapter VI.

taken place. In addition, recovery can be had for environmental harm, limited to the costs of reasonable measures taken to restore or rehabilitate the environment to its prior state. For this purpose, environment is broadly defined to include biotic and abiotic natural resources, such as air, water, soil, fauna and flora, the interaction between them, cultural property and characteristic aspects of the countryside. Finally, recovery is possible for the costs of mitigating measures and any losses or damage caused by such measures after an incident or event when the loss or damage derives or results from dangerous elements contained in dangerous substances, dangerous genetically modified organisms or dangerous micro-organisms, or results from radiation or wastes. The maximum amount of liability may be fixed by local law, which should also insist upon adequate insurance coverage taking into account the risks associated with the activity.

Articles 6 to 12 set out the basic principles of responsibility. First, anyone who is in control of a dangerous activity is responsible for damage caused by that activity.[11] The problem of multiple or long-term sources is confronted by placing the burden of proof on the various persons who were in control of the activity or activities to prove they were not responsible. Joint responsibility may be imposed over all those in control when damage results from slow or continuous contamination or multiple sources. For waste disposal sites, the person in control at the moment the damage occurs is responsible. In cases where the activity has ceased when the damage occurs, the last person in control will be liable unless he can show that the causative event took place before he was in control.

Liability is not imposed if damage occurs as a result of armed conflict, a natural disaster, an intentional act of a third party, a state command, "pollution of a level acceptable having regard to the relevant local circumstances", or if the activity was taken for the benefit of the person damaged, to the extent it was reasonable for the latter to be exposed to the risks of the dangerous activity, or if the injured party was at fault.

From the perspective of the plaintiff, there are several favourable provisions. Article 10 provides that a judge, in examining the proof of causality in any case falling within the terms of the Convention, should take into account the probable risk of damage inherent in the dangerous activity in question. Moreover, the statute of limitations is rather long. According to article 18, actions should be brought within five years of the date on which the plaintiff knew or reasonably should have known of the damage and of the identity of the person in control. No action may be brought more than thirty years after the causative event or the last in a series of causative events. For waste disposal sites, the final date is thirty years from the closure of the site. Article 20 permits the action to be filed either in the courts of a state party where the damage occurred, where the dangerous activity took place, or where the defendant has their permanent residence.

---

[11] States parties may reserve to the basic principle of liability, to the extent of allowing the defendant to escape liability if it can show that the state of scientific and technical knowledge at the moment of the incident was insufficient to indicate the dangerous properties of the substance or the organism.

Injunctive relief may be sought by environmental associations in the courts where the dangerous activity takes place, on conditions set by national or local law. States may declare at signature, ratification, or accession that this possibility will be open to non-governmental organizations based in other states parties. Environmental groups may demand prohibition of any illegal dangerous activity threatening serious environmental harm as well as injunctions against the person in control of dangerous activity, in order to require preventive or remedial actions be taken. Where remedial action is sought, the courts of the state where the action should be taken also have jurisdiction over the case. Public authorities have the right to intervene when environmental groups bring actions.

All judgments rendered by a tribunal with jurisdiction are entitled to be recognized in other states parties unless contrary to public order, the defendant was not properly notified of the action in time to prepare a defence, or if the decision is irreconcilable with a decision rendered between the same parties (*res judicata*).

## D. Economic and Market Devices for Environmental Protection

Apart from the range of direct regulatory measures discussed above, legislators may enact various economic incentives and disincentives intended to affect conduct towards the environment. Often such measures aim to include the cost of environmental damage, as well as the cost of raw materials, production, marketing, etc. in the price of a product. Even the concept of "product" changes, as the consumption of fresh air and clean water becomes priced and polluters pay, through charges or taxes, for causing deterioration to these resources.

Economic measures may include provision of funds for environmentally clean or progressive investment, deposit schemes for containers, subsidies, emission charges, product charges, exemption fees, administrative fees to supervise environmental protection, non-compliance fees, and tradable emission quotas. Some common types of charges are pure incentives to change behaviour, others are revenue-producing to finance policy programmes.

### 1. *Taxation*

— Effluent charges

Charges that are levied according to the quantity and/or quality of discharge of polluting substances into the environment.

— Product charges

Charges levied on products that are polluting in the manufacturing or in the consumption phase or that are obsolete and for which a disposal system is introduced.

— Tax differentiation

As a practical matter, tax differentiation may subsidize a relatively clean product by introducing a product charge on a polluting substitute. The differentiation results in more favourable prices for clean products.

— User charges

Payments, either at a uniform rate or based on amounts involved, for the costs of collective treatment of wastes.

— Administrative charges

Control and authorization fees, paid-for authority services, such as the registration of chemicals or for implementation and enforcement of certain regulations.

Taxes on polluting industries or products are a common mechanism used to induce environmental improvement. Though opposed by industry, most European countries have enacted some form of environmental tax or other fiscal incentives. This is in line with the generally accepted "polluter pays" principle. Both the United Nations and the OECD favour greater use of environmental taxes and charges.

Environmental levies are imposed in the Netherlands, particularly under the Surface Waters Pollution Act, which provides for a levy on discharges into waterways. The levies help finance the costs of administering environmental legislation. Industrial plants that suffer a loss because of measures taken under an environmental act also may be compensated from these levies.

In France, in accordance with the polluter pays principle, several taxes are imposed, based either on discharges into the environment of various pollutants or on reimbursement of clean-up costs borne by the municipality. Taxes also are paid on the volume of water used and waste water discharged into running waters, the emission of sulphur-based chemicals, nitrogen oxides or hydrochloric acid, and the use of lubricants.

The Swedish government has made economic instruments a key element in its Environmental Bill of 1991. There are charges related to nitrogen oxide and taxes on pesticides, as well as levies on sulphur and carbon dioxide. In 1973 a tax on drink containers was introduced, designed to give returnable cans and bottles an advantage over throw-away containers. There is now a highly developed system of deposits on returnable packaging and some 85 per cent of all aluminum cans are recycled each year. In addition to bottles, levies are imposed on cadmium and mercury batteries.

Since 1984 sales in Sweden of artificial fertilizers and pesticides have included environmental charges of 10 and 5 per cent of the sales price respectively. The money is designated for environmental research and nature conservation projects. In addition, domestic aircraft must pay just under $2 for every kilogram of hydrocarbons utilized. After the programme began, the main domestic carrier began a programme to replace the engine combustion chambers on its twenty planes to cut hydrocarbon emissions by 90 per cent and nitrogen oxides by 10 to 15 per cent. Finally, because road transport is responsible for over 50 per cent of air pollution emissions in Sweden, a combination of economic instruments has been enacted to favour cars with lower petrol consumption and to reduce the total volume of traffic on the roads. First, an energy tax is levied on motor fuel, heating oil and fuel oil, with amounts differentiated according to three environmental categories, depending on the sulphur and aromatic hydrocarbon content of these fuels. There is a tax differential in favour of unleaded petrol, a reduced sales tax on cars with catalytic converters, and heavier taxation of company cars.

## 2. Loans

In some countries, such as France, government financial assistance and incentives, taking the form of low-interest loans, aid the construction and operation of more environmentally safe installations and recycling systems. The Clean Air Mutual Fund imposes a special tax based on the amount of sulphur dioxide emitted on combustion facilities that have more than 50 megawatt capacity or emissions exceeding 2,500 tons. These funds are available to help finance pollution control equipment at such plants. In other circumstances, financial aid may be granted for the purchase of efficient heating systems or anti-pollution devices, recycling units to permit treatment of waste water before its discharge or construction of oil waste treatment installations. In addition, bank lending policies may include environmental behaviour as a factor in assessing the credit-worthiness of a concern.

## 3. Insurance

Not only governments, but investors may put pressure on companies to act in an environmentally sound way and insurance companies may exercise influence to avoid high payouts for environmental accidents.

The laws and practices governing insurance coverage of pollution-related claims vary from one jurisdiction to another. However, a general principle is that insurance covers fortuitous events only. Therefore, if damage results from pollution caused by deliberate acts or omissions of the insured, there will usually be no coverage. For example, a common policy in the Netherlands provides:

> The insurance shall not cover the liability for damage resulting from actions or omissions in defiance of any State regulation with regard to the environment, if such action or omission occurred by order of or with the approval of the policyholder or any of the insureds mentioned in the schedule.
>
> If the policyholder or the insured meant in the previous paragraph is a body corporate, the policyholder or insured shall, for the purpose of this exclusion, be considered to be a member of the board of management as well as any staff member employed by the policy holder or insured charged by the management with the special responsibility of observing the above regulations.[12]

In addition, liability policies usually cover only damage resulting from a discrete occurrence or accident. Thus, if damage arises gradually, for example, through cumulative pollution, insurance may not cover the harm. The German *Allgemeine Versicherungsbedingungen für die Haftpflichtversicherung* cover bodily injury from environmental impairment without any restriction but excludes property damage that results from gradual harm. The Dutch General Liability policy was amended to make clear that it does not cover pollution caused by the gradual corrosion of underground tanks

---

[12] MAS Policy, quoted in John H. Wasink, "Environmental Liability Insurance in Europe and the United States, An Introduction" in *Environmental Liability Law Quarterly*, 3/89, p. 71.

and barrels. Like other policies, it now excludes "liability for damage in connection with environmental impairment, unless such impairment is a sudden and unexpected occurrence, and this occurrence is not the direct effect of a gradual process".

Disputes over the application of exceptions, especially over broad interpretations of "accidental pollution" clauses, led to the introduction of pollution exclusion in the 1980s, completely eliminating coverage for pollution, whether or not the source was sudden and accidental. As an alternative, the insurance industry began offering, on a limited basis, Environmental Impairment Liability (EIL) coverage at premiums several times higher than the average policy. Coverage is narrowly drawn, often excluding the cleanup of hazardous waste dump sites and including only gradual escape of pollutants from the insured's own property. In addition, policies typically cover tangible property loss or damage, but exclude such consequences as loss of use of a facility caused by toxic air pollution in the area. Several environmental regulatory programmes require insurance coverage as a precondition to licensing or issuance of required permits. In some cases, letters of credit, trust funds or solvency tests may be substituted for insurance.

Most recently, insurance companies in several countries have formed pools (France, Italy, and the Netherlands). These pools underwrite new, relatively unknown pollution risks under a controlled regime of environmental legislation. Unlike earlier policies, there is a tendency to extend coverage to gradual pollution risk. The MAS pool of the Netherlands includes the following clause:

> The insurance covers the liability for bodily injury or material damage as a consequence of environmental impairment taking place directly from the location(s) mentioned in the schedule, provided the claim for indemnification of damage and expenses has been received by the insurer during the period of insurance.

The MAS policy also provides extended coverage for loss of economic use of property not physically damaged and for clean-up costs and measures taken to mitigate harm taken by or on behalf of the insured and for which the insured would have civil liability. Generally, there is no coverage for expenses incurred for the restoration and reconstruction of the insured's operating equipment or installation grounds.

## 4. Grants and Subsidies

Environmental funds, which have been created in several countries, often directly fund environmental protection. In Turkey an environmental fund has been established to prevent environmental pollution and improve the environment. The Fund's use is allocated through the Environmental General Directorate of the Prime Ministry and is legislatively restricted to projects of research, cleaning up the environment, education and training, purchasing technology and projects, organizing project competitions, assistance in the form of credit to legal entities setting up purification plants, reforestation, studies, and, as of a 1988 amendment, the purchase, maintenance and repair of all equipment to be used in preventing environmental pollution or in improving the environment, and all plants and enterprises to be set up for the manufacture of such equipment. Another provision of the Environment Act, article 29, provides that "activities concerned with the prevention and elimination of pollution shall be encouraged by incentives" to be established in special regulations. In Sweden, too, a wide range of grants is available to fund measures that are not yet legally required, to encourage implementation of new standards. For example, there are grant schemes for farmers who farm without chemical pesticides or artificial fertilizers.

Among European countries, Austria spends the largest proportion of its national budget – nearly 2 per cent – on environmental protection. Rather than tax polluting enterprises, it uses financial incentives to encourage them to reduce their polluting activities. It has created funds for the environment which, together with a regulation on hydraulic works from 1959, constitute the major national instruments of environmental protection. More than 9,500 plans involving water management were financially supported between 1957 and 1985. Virtually all industrial processes involving water usage are encouraged by credits from the fund, which finances 80 per cent of the project at 2 per cent for 20 years. Other aspects or measures are financed at 3 per cent for 15 years. Numerous measures of credit also are in place to encourage clean, environmentally safe technology and research.

Another form of economic incentive has been proposed by Denmark, an "environmental bonus." This programme would reward workers for environmental economies involving reduction of the consumption of resources and pollution of water, air, and soil.

## 5. *Negotiable Permits*

Germany has begun cautiously to apply a system of negotiable permits, sometimes referred to as "bubbles". The total amount of pollution permissible within an area is fixed by authorities. This is the "bubble". Each company is required to obtain an emission permit from local authorities. Companies investing in processes which reduce pollution may exchange or sell their permits to other companies located in the same geographic area.

## 6. *Deposits*

Another market mechanism is mandatory deposits on glass or plastic containers to encourage their return or recycling. In Denmark, the government issued a decree in 1984 limiting the importation and sale of beverages whose packaging was not approved; it also initiated a deposit-return system. The European Court of Justice on 20 September 1988 found that the Danish regulation was, on balance, disproportionate to the objective sought. The interest in environmental protection had to be weighed with the principle of free competition and free circulation of goods. Now, in general, Community member states must notify and obtain authorization from the European Commission, pursuant to articles 92 and 93 of the Treaty of Rome, for various forms of aid to encourage technological investment to protect the environment.

## 7. Labelling

The "ecolabel" is a recent, increasingly popular incentive to environmental protection. It is part of a gradual trend away from "end of the pipe" reactive solutions, which can be extremely costly, toward identifying and avoiding environmental problems before they occur. The new approach requires manufacturers to examine the entire life-cycle of products – production, distribution, use and disposal – with the aim of minimizing environmental degradation at all stages in all media: air, water and soil.

Environmental labelling programmes constitute an economic instrument promoting pro-environmental purchasing on the side of the public and a precautionary approach on the side of industry. Labelling requirements themselves are not new; they have been used to detail the nutritional content of foods, the proper use and hazards of cleaning products, and the dangers of cigarettes. However, broader environmental concerns have only recently resulted in adaptation of labels to promote environmentally "friendly" products.

Environmental labelling involves a public or private body granting labels to inform consumers about products deemed to be less destructive of the environment than similar competitive products, based on a holistic, overall judgment of the product's environmental quality. As such, it excludes "negative" labels which warn of particular dangers, and specific matters such as the use of recycled materials.

Germany issued the first environmental label in 1978 (der blaue Engel). Its programme now has over 3,600 labelled products in 64 product categories. Norway, Sweden, and Finland, within the Nordic Council programme, Austria, Portugal, and France announced labelling programmes beginning in 1991, with Netherlands studying the issue. All programmes are based upon committee determination or suggestions to a government minister of product categories that should be eligible for labelling, based on the principle that the label should potentially effect a significant reduction in environmental damage. Once the product category has been selected, the types and degrees of environmental damage caused by the products in the category are examined. The product scope is defined, and criteria are established in cooperation with expert working groups. Manufacturers voluntarily submit products for consideration, agree to contractual conditions, and pay a fee for use of the label for a period of years. Initial criteria may be expanded if the industry as a whole improves its environmental performance.

Labelling programmes are very difficult to administer due to the need to comprehensively assess the entire life-cycle of the product, provide financing and establish product categories and criteria. However, their use continues to spread. The EC adopted Regulation 880/92 on 23 March 1992[13] to create a Community system for awarding the ecology label, based on voluntary participation of manufacturers. The determination of product groups and ecological criteria will be ensured by the Commission, assisted by a committee composed of representatives from the Member

[13] O.J. no. L 99/1 of 11 April 1992.

States. Initially, the regulation will not apply to food, beverages and pharmaceutical products.

In conclusion, like all forms of environmental regulation, economic incentives must be studied to evaluate their effectiveness in protecting the environment. Effectiveness requires analysis of the changes in producer and/or consumer behaviour and the costs of the measures taken. Some procedures may have only small effect while being administratively cumbersome, thus failing to meet the requirements of efficiency or effectiveness. On the other hand, efforts at environmental protection can provide a degree of economic growth. In Ireland, it was estimated in 1991 that the environmental technology sector is growing at a rate of 7.5 per cent a year. These variables in turn require that the many institutions and agencies concerned with environmental protection introduce new measures according to their respective functions and procedures.

# E. Documents

*1*. Turkey, *The Environment Law*,
Law no. 2872 of 9 August 1983.

...

Article 10: Firms, corporations and businesses which may pave the way to environmental problems as a result of the activities they plan to carry out shall prepare an "Environmental Impact Assessment Report". In this report, the manner of treatment of the discharge and waste that may cause environmental pollution as well as the measures to be taken in this regard shall be specified by keeping in mind all possible effects on the environment.

Principles regarding which type of projects will require an "environmental impact assessment report", the points to be included in it, and which authorities will approve it shall be stipulated by special regulations.

Article 11: Firms, corporations and businesses, establishment of which is being planned, shall be required to set up, either independently or jointly, the purification plants or systems stipulated in the current regulations. Until such purification plants or systems are set up and put in working order, operating and usage licences shall not be granted to firms, corporations or businesses.

Any firm, corporation or business which receives permission to operate and begins operations is required to inform in advance the highest official of the local administration of plans to modify its activities or enlarge its facilities. The official shall immediately inform the Environment General Directorate of the Prime Ministry and the relevant Ministry.

Business concerns, which are responsible for purification, removal or treatment of discharge and waste of all kinds, shall also take precautions to ensure that no damage is inflicted on the environment through these measures.

The necessary technical methods to be implemented in introducing discharge and waste directly or indirectly into the receptor area shall be stipulated by special regulations, keeping in mind the nature of the receptor area and the possible ways of utilizing it.

...

Article 15: To firms, corporations and businesses that violate the prohibitions contained in this law, or fail to meet the requirements stipulated by law, the highest official of the local administration shall grant a sufficient period of time (principles governing which shall be set down in a special regulation) to rectify such illegal activities and fulfil the requirements stipulated in the law.

Within this period no further penalty shall be imposed for violating the law or failing to meet a requirement.

The activities of firms, corporations and businesses that fail to do these things within the period granted shall be terminated either temporarily or permanently and either partially or completely, depending on the nature and kind of the prohibition or on the requirement that was not fulfilled.

Article 16: In cases when environmental pollution poses a threat to public health, the Ministry of Health and Social Welfare, either on its own or at the request of the Environment General Directorate of the Prime Ministry, shall decide temporarily to terminate, either partially or completely, the activities causing this pollution, and shall request the highest official of the local administration to implement this decision.

...

Article 28: (Amended on 3 March 1988 by Article 8 of law no. 3516) Polluters of the environment and those who cause damage to the environment are responsible, regardless of degree of fault, for the damage arising from the pollution and destruction they cause.

Article 29: Activities concerned with the prevention and elimination of pollution shall be encouraged by incentives. For this purpose new principles shall be introduced to the incentive system determined at the beginning of every year by taking into consideration the views of the Environment General Directorate of the Prime Ministry.

The principles relating to incentive measures shall be made explicit in special regulations. If individuals and legal entities that commit the acts leading to the fines specified in this law fail to fulfil their obligations within the time period granted, they may not benefit from incentives contained in this Article, and any incentives previously granted in their favour shall be suspended.


## 2. United Kingdom, *Environmental Protection Act 1990.*

### Part I

6.  (1)  No person shall carry on a prescribed process after the date prescribed or determined for that description of process by or under regulations under section 2(1) above (but subject to any transitional provision made by the regulations) except under an authorization granted by the enforcing authority and in accordance with the conditions to which it is subject.

    (2)  An application for an authorization shall be made to the enforcing authority in accordance with Part I of Schedule 1 to this Act and shall be accompanied by the fee prescribed under section 8(2) below.

    (3)  Where an application is duly made to the enforcing authority, the authority shall either grant the authorization subject to the conditions required or authorized to be imposed by section 7 below or refuse the application.

    (4)  An application shall not be granted unless the enforcing authority considers that the applicant will be able to carry on the process so as to comply with the conditions which would be included in the authorization.

...

7. (1) There shall be included in an authorization

   (a) subject to paragraph (b) below, such specific conditions as the enforcing authority considers appropriate, when taken with the general condition implied by subsection (4) below, for achieving the objectives specified in subsection (2) below.

   (b) such conditions as are specified in directions given by the Secretary of State under subsection (3) below; and

   (c) such other conditions (if any) as appear to the enforcing authority to be appropriate;

   but no conditions shall be imposed for the purpose only of securing the health of persons at work (within the meaning of Part I of the Health and Safety at Work etc. Act 1974).

   (2) Those objectives are:

   (a) ensuring that, in carrying on a prescribed process, the best available techniques not entailing excessive cost will be used:

      (i) for preventing the release of substances prescribed for any environmental medium into that medium or, where that is not practicable by such means, for reducing the release of such substances to a minimum and for rendering harmless any such substances which are so released; and

      (ii) for rendering harmless any other substances which might cause harm if released into any environmental medium.

   (b) compliance with any directions by the Secretary of State given for the implementation of any obligations of the United Kingdom under Community Treaties or international law relating to environmental protection;

   (c) compliance with any limits or requirements and achievement of any quality standards or quality objectives prescribed by the Secretary of State under any of the relevant enactments.

   ...

   (3) Except as respects the general condition implied by subsection (4) below, the Secretary of State may give directions to the enforcing authorities as to the conditions which are, or are not, to be included in all authorizations, in authorizations of any specified description or in any particular authorization.

   (4) ... [T]here is implied in every authorization a general condition that, in carrying on the process to which the authorization applies, the person carrying it on must use the best available techniques not entailing excessive cost:

   (a) for preventing the release of substances prescribed for any environmental medium into that medium or, where that is not practicable by such means, for reducing the release of such substances to a minimum and for rendering harmless any such substances which are so released; and

   (b) for rendering harmless any other substances which might cause harm if released into any environmental medium.

   ...

(8)   An authorization for carrying on a prescribed process may, without prejudice to the generality of subsection (1) above, include conditions:

    (a)   imposing limits on the amount or composition of any substance produced by or utilized in the process in any period; and

    (b)   requiring advance notification of any proposed change in the manner of carrying on the process.

...

(10)  References to the best available techniques not entailing excessive cost, in relation to a process, include (in addition to references to any technical means and technology) references to the number, qualifications, training and supervision of persons employed in the process and the design, construction, lay-out and maintenance of the buildings in which it is carried on.


## 3. Council Directive 85/337/EEC of 27 June 1985 on the Assessment of the Effects of Certain Public and Private Projects on the Environment, O.J. no. L 175 of 5 July 1985.

The Council of the European Communities,
   ...
   whereas the 1973 and 1977 action programmes of the European Communities on the environment, as well as the 1983 action programme ... stress that the best environmental policy consists in preventing the creation of pollution or nuisances at source, rather than subsequently trying to counteract their effects; whereas they affirm the need to take effects on the environment into account at the earliest possible stage in all the technical planning and decision-making processes;
   ...
has adopted this directive :

### Article 1

1.   This directive shall apply to the assessment of the environmental effects of those public and private projects which are likely to have significant effects on the environment.

2.   For the purposes of this directive :
       'project' means :
— the execution of construction works or of other installations or schemes,
— other interventions in the natural surroundings and landscape including those involving the extraction of mineral resources;
       'developer' means :
— the applicant for authorization for a private project or the public authority which initiates a project;
       'development consent' means :
— the decision of the competent authority or authorities which entitles the developer to proceed with the project.

3.   The competent authority or authorities shall be that or those which the Member States designate as responsible for performing the duties arising from this directive.

4.   Projects serving national defence purposes are not covered by this directive.

5. This directive shall not apply to projects the details of which are adopted by a specific act of national legislation, since the objectives of this directive, including that of supplying information, are achieved through the legislative process.

### Article 2

1. Member States shall adopt all measures necessary to ensure that, before consent is given, projects likely to have significant effects on the environment by virtue *inter alia*, of their nature, size or location are made subject to an assessment with regard to their effects. These projects are defined in article 4.

2. The environmental impact assessment may be integrated into the existing procedures for consent to projects in the Member States, or, failing this, into other procedures or into procedures to be established to comply with the aims of this directive.

3. Member States may, in exceptional cases, exempt a specific project in whole or in part from the provisions laid down in this directive. In this event, the Member States shall :

   (a) consider whether another form of assessment would be appropriate and whether the information thus collected should be made available to the public;

   (b) make available to the public concerned the information relating to the exemption and the reasons for granting it;

   (c) inform the Commission, prior to granting consent, of the reasons justifying the exemption granted, and provide it with the information made available, where appropriate, to their own nationals.

The Commission shall immediately forward the documents received to the other Member States. The Commission shall report annually to the Council on the application of this paragraph.

### Article 3

The environmental impact assessment will identify, describe and assess in an appropriate manner, in the light of each individual case and in accordance with the articles 4 to 11, the direct and indirect effects of a project on the following factors:
— human beings, fauna and flora,
— soil, water, air, climate and the landscape,
— the inter-action between the factors mentioned in the first and second indents,
— material assets and the cultural heritage.

### Article 4

1. Subject to article 2 (3), projects of the classes listed in annex I shall be made subject to an assessment in accordance with articles 5 to 10.

2. Projects of the classes listed in annex II shall be made subject to an assessment, in accordance with articles 5 to 10, where member states consider that their characteristics so require. To this end Member States may *inter alia* specify certain types of projects as being subject to an assessment or may establish the criteria and/or thresholds necessary to determine which of the projects of the classes listed in annex II are to be subject to an assessment in accordance with articles 5 to 10.

### Article 5

1. In the case of projects which, pursuant to article 4, must be subjected to an environmental impact assessment in accordance with articles 5 to 10, Member States shall adopt the

necessary measures to ensure that the developer supplies in an appropriate form the information specified in annex III inasmuch as :

(a) the Member States consider that the information is relevant to a given stage of the consent procedure and to the specific characteristics of a particular project or type of project and of the environmental features likely to be affected;

(b) the Member States consider that a developer may reasonably be required to compile this information having regard *inter alia* to current knowledge and methods of assessment.

2. The information to be provided by the developer in accordance with paragraph 1 shall include at least :
   — a description of the project comprising information on the site, design and size of the project,
   — a description of the measures envisaged in order to avoid, reduce and, if possible, remedy significant adverse effects,
   — the data required to identify and assess the main effects which the project is likely to have on the environment,
   — a non-technical summary of the information mentioned in indents 1 to 3.

3. Where they consider it necessary, Member States shall ensure that any authorities with relevant information in their possession make this information available to the developer.

Article 6

1. Member States shall take the measures necessary to ensure that the authorities likely to be concerned by the project by reason of their specific environmental responsibilities are given an opportunity to express their opinion on the request for development consent. Member States shall designate the authorities to be consulted for this purpose in general terms or in each case when the request for consent is made. The information gathered pursuant to article 5 shall be forwarded to these authorities. Detailed arrangements for consultation shall be laid down by the Member States.

2. Member States shall ensure that :
   — any request for development consent and any information gathered pursuant to article 5 are made available to the public,
   — the public concerned is given the opportunity to express an opinion before the project is initiated.

3. The detailed arrangements for such information and consultation shall be determined by the Member States, which may in particular, depending on the particular characteristics of the projects or sites concerned :
   — determine the public concerned,
   — specify the places where the information can be consulted,
   — specify the way in which the public may be informed, for example by bill-posting within a certain radius, publication in local newspapers, organization of exhibitions with plans, drawings, tables, graphs, models,
   — determine the manner in which the public is to be consulted, for example, by written submissions, by public enquiry,
   — fix appropriate time limits for the various stages of the procedure in order to ensure that a decision is taken within a reasonable period.

## Article 7

Where a Member State is aware that a project is likely to have significant effects on the environment in another Member State or where a Member State likely to be significantly affected so requests, the Member State in whose territory the project is intended to be carried out shall forward the information gathered pursuant to article 5 to the other Member State at the same time as it makes it available to its own nationals. Such information shall serve as a basis for any consultations necessary in the framework of the bilateral relations between two Member States on a reciprocal and equivalent basis.

## Article 8

Information gathered pursuant to articles 5, 6 and 7 must be taken into consideration in the development consent procedure.

## Article 9

When a decision has been taken, the competent authority or authorities shall inform the public concerned of :

— the content of the decision and any conditions attached thereto,
— the reasons and considerations on which the decision is based where the member states' legislation so provides.

The detailed arrangements for such information shall be determined by the Member States. If another Member State has been informed pursuant to article 7, it will also be informed of the decision in question.

## Article 10

The provisions of this directive shall not affect the obligation on the competent authorities to respect the limitations imposed by national regulations and administrative provisions and accepted legal practices with regard to industrial and commercial secrecy and the safeguarding of the public interest.

Where article 7 applies, the transmission of information to another Member State and the reception of information by another Member State shall be subject to the limitations in force in the member state in which the project is proposed.

## Article 11

1. The Member States and the Commission shall exchange information on the experience gained in applying this directive.

2. In particular, Member States shall inform the Commission of any criteria and/or thresholds adopted for the selection of the projects in question, in accordance with article 4 (2), or of the types of projects concerned which, pursuant to article 4 (2), are subject to assessment in accordance with articles 5 to 10.

3. Five years after notification of this directive, the Commission shall send the European Parliament and the Council a report on its application and effectiveness. The report shall be based on the aforementioned exchange of information.

4. On the basis of this exchange of information, the Commission shall submit to the Council additional proposals, should this be necessary, with a view to this directive's being applied in a sufficiently coordinated manner.

## Article 12

1. Member States shall take the measures necessary to comply with this directive within three years of its notification.

2.   Member States shall communicate to the Commission the texts of the provisions of national law which they adopt in the field covered by this directive.

### Article 13

The provisions of this directive shall not affect the right of Member States to lay down stricter rules regarding scope and procedure when assessing environmental effects.

...

### Annex III

Information referred to in article 5 (1)

1.   Description of the project, including in particular :
     — a description of the physical characteristics of the whole project and the land-use requirements during the construction and operational phases,
     — a description of the main characteristics of the production processes, for instance, nature and quantity of the materials used,
     — an estimate, by type and quantity, of expected residues and emissions (water, air and soil pollution, noise, vibration, light, heat, radiation, etc.) resulting from the operation of the proposed project.

2.   Where appropriate, an outline of the main alternatives studied by the developer and an indication of the main reasons for his choice, taking into account the environmental effects.

3.   A description of the aspects of the environment likely to be significantly affected by the proposed project, including, in particular, population, fauna, flora, soil, water, air, climatic factors, material assets, including the architectural and archaeological heritage, landscape and the inter-relationship between the above factors.

4.   A description[14] of the likely significant effects of the proposed project on the environment resulting from :
     — the existence of the project,
     — the use of natural resources,
     — the emission of pollutants, the creation of nuisances and the elimination of waste; and the description by the developer of the forecasting methods used to assess the effects on the environment.

5.   A description of the measures envisaged to prevent, reduce and where possible offset any significant adverse effects on the environment.

6.   A non-technical summary of the information provided under the above headings.

7.   An indication of any difficulties (technical deficiencies or lack of know-how) encountered by the developer in compiling the required information.

---

[14] This description should cover the direct effects and any indirect, secondary, cumulative, short-, medium- and long-term, permanent and temporary, positive and negative effects of the project.

## 4. Convention on Environmental Impact Assessment in a Transboundary Context (Espoo, 25 February 1991), 30 I.L.M. 800 (1991).

The Parties to this Convention,

Mindful of the need and importance to develop anticipatory policies and of preventing, mitigating and monitoring significant adverse environmental impact in general and more specifically in a transboundary context,

Conscious of the need to give explicit consideration to environmental factors at an early stage in the decision-making process by applying environmental impact assessment, at all appropriate administrative levels, as a necessary tool to improve the quality of information presented to decision makers so that environmentally sound decisions can be made paying careful attention to minimizing significant adverse impact, particularly in a transboundary context,

Have agreed as follows:

### Article 1 DEFINITIONS

For the purposes of this Convention,

...

(vi) "Environmental impact assessment" means a national procedure for evaluating the likely impact of a proposed activity on the environment;

(vii) "Impact" means any effect caused by a proposed activity on the environment including human health and safety, flora, fauna, soil, air, water, climate, landscape and historical monuments or other physical structures or the interaction among these factors; it also includes effects on cultural heritage or socio-economic conditions resulting from alterations to those factors;

...

### Article 2 GENERAL PROVISIONS

1. The Parties shall, either individually or jointly, take all appropriate and effective measures to prevent, reduce and control significant adverse transboundary environmental impact from proposed activities.

2. Each Party shall take the necessary legal, administrative or other measures to implement the provisions of this Convention, including, with respect to proposed activities listed in Appendix I that are likely to cause significant adverse transboundary impact, the establishment of an environmental impact assessment procedure that permits public participation and preparation of the environmental impact assessment documentation described in Appendix II.

...

6. The Party of origin shall provide, in accordance with the provisions of this Convention, an opportunity to the public in the areas likely to be affected to participate in relevant environmental impact assessment procedures regarding proposed activities and shall ensure that the opportunity provided to the public of the affected Party is equivalent to that provided to the public of the Party of origin.

### Article 3 NOTIFICATION

1. For a proposed activity listed in Appendix I that is likely to cause a significant adverse transboundary impact, the Party of origin shall, for the purposes of ensuring adequate and effective consultations under Article 5, notify any Party which it considers may be an

affected Party as early as possible and no later than when informing its own public about that proposed activity.

2.  This notification shall contain, *inter alia:*

    (a)  Information on the proposed activity, including any available information on its possible transboundary impact;

    (b)  The nature of the possible decisions; and

    (c)  An indication of a reasonable time within which a response under paragraph 3 of this Article is required, taking into account the nature of the proposed activity; and may include the information set out in paragraph 5 of this Article.

3.  The affected Party shall respond to the Party of origin within the time specified in the notification, acknowledging receipt of the notification, and shall indicate whether it intends to participate in the environmental impact assessment procedure.

...

6.  An affected Party shall, at the request of the Party of origin, provide the latter with reasonably obtainable information relating to the potentially affected environment under the jurisdiction of the affected party, where such information is necessary for the preparation of the environmental impact assessment documentation. The information shall be furnished promptly and, as appropriate, through a joint body where one exists ...

7.  When a Party considers that it would be affected by a significant adverse transboundary impact of a proposed activity listed in Appendix I, and when no notification has taken place in accordance with paragraph 1 of this Article, the concerned Parties shall, at the request of the affected Party, exchange sufficient information for the purposes of holding discussions on whether there is likely to be a significant adverse transboundary impact.

8.  The concerned Parties shall ensure that the public of the affected Party in the areas likely to be affected be informed of, and be provided with possibilities for making comments or objections on, the proposed activity, and for the transmittal of these comments or objections to the competent authority of the Party of origin, either directly to this authority or, where appropriate, through the Party of origin.

...

## Article 5 CONSULTATIONS ON THE BASIS OF THE ENVIRONMENTAL IMPACT ASSESSMENT DOCUMENTATION

The Party of origin shall, after completion of the environmental impact assessment documentation, without undue delay enter into consultations with the affected Party concerning, *inter alia*, the potential transboundary impact of the proposed activity and measures to reduce or eliminate its impact ...

## Article 6 FINAL DECISION

1.  The Parties shall ensure that, in the final decision on the proposed activity, due account is taken of the outcome of the environmental impact assessment, including the environmental impact assessment documentation, as well as the comments thereon received pursuant to Article 3, paragraph 8 and Article 4, paragraph 2, and the outcome of the consultations as referred to in Article 5 ...

## Article 7 POST-PROJECT ANALYSIS

1.  The concerned Parties, at the request of any such Party, shall determine whether, and if so to what extent, a post-project analysis shall be carried out, taking into account the likely

significant adverse transboundary impact of the activity for which an environmental impact assessment has been undertaken pursuant to this Convention. Any post-project analysis undertaken shall include, in particular, the surveillance of the activity and the determination of any adverse transboundary impact. Such surveillance and determination may be undertaken with a view to achieving the objectives listed in Appendix V.

2.  When, as a result of post-project analysis, the Party of origin or the affected Party has reasonable grounds for concluding that there is a significant adverse transboundary impact or factors have been discovered which may result in such an impact, it shall immediately inform the other Party. The concerned Parties shall then consult on necessary measures to reduce or eliminate the impact.

## Appendix II CONTENT OF THE ENVIRONMENTAL IMPACT ASSESSMENT DOCUMENTATION

Information to be included in the environmental impact assessment documentation shall, as a minimum, contain, in accordance with Article 4:

(a)  A description of the proposed activity and its purpose;

(b)  A description, where appropriate, of reasonable alternatives (for example, locational or technological) to the proposed activity and also the no-action alternative;

(c)  A description of the environment likely to be significantly affected by the proposed activity and its alternatives;

(d)  A description of the potential environmental impact of the proposed activity and its alternatives and an estimation of its significance;

(e)  A description of mitigation measures to keep adverse environmental impact to a minimum;

(f)  An explicit indication of predictive methods and underlying assumptions as well as the relevant environmental data used;

(g)  An identification of gaps in knowledge and uncertainties encountered in compiling the required information;

(h)  Where appropriate, an outline for monitoring and management programmes and any plans for post-project analysis; and

(i)  A non-technical summary including a visual presentation as appropriate (maps, graphs, etc.).

...

## Appendix V   POST-PROJECT ANALYSIS

Objectives include:

(a)  Monitoring compliance with the conditions as set out in the authorization or approval of the activity and the effectiveness of mitigation measures;

(b)  Review of an impact for proper management and in order to cope with uncertainties;

(c)  Verification of past predictions in order to transfer experience to future activities of the same type.

*5. Council Regulation 880/92/EEC of 23 March 1992 on a Community Eco-label Award Scheme, 1992* O.J. no. L 99/1 of 11 April 1992.

THE COUNCIL OF THE EUROPEAN COMMUNITIES,

...

Whereas there is increased public interest in information about products with reduced environmental impact;

Whereas some Member States have already an award scheme for such products and several other Member States are considering the setting up of such a scheme;

Whereas a system to award an eco-label for products with reduced environmental impact will highlight more benign alternatives and therefore provide consumers and users with guidance;

Whereas such guidance can best be achieved by establishing uniform criteria for the award scheme to apply throughout the Community;

...

Has adopted this Regulation:

Article 1 : Objectives

This Regulation establishes a Community eco-label award scheme which is intended to:
- promote the design, production, marketing and use of products which have a reduced environmental impact during their entire life cycle, and
- provide consumers with better information on the environmental impact of products, without, however, compromising product or workers' safety or significantly affecting the properties which make a product fit for use.

Article 2 : Scope

This Regulation shall not apply to food, drink or pharmaceuticals.

Article 3 : Definitions

For the purpose of this Regulation:

(a) 'substance' means chemical elements and their compounds as defined in Article 2 of Council Directive 67/548/EEC of 27 June 1967 on the approximation of the laws, regulations and administrative provisions relating to the classification, packaging and labelling of dangerous substances;

(b) 'preparation' means mixtures or solutions as defined in Article 2 of Council Directive 67/548/EEC;

(c) 'product group' means products which serve similar purposes and which have equivalence of use;

(d) 'cradle to grave' means the life cycle of a product from manufacturing, including the choice of raw materials, distribution, consumption and use to disposal after use.

Article 4 : General principles

1. The eco-label can be awarded to products which meet the objectives set out in Article 1 and which are in conformity with Community health, safety and environmental requirements.

2. The eco-label shall in no case be awarded:

   (a) to products which are substances or preparations classified as dangerous in accordance with Directives 67/548/EEC and 88/379/EEC. The label may be awarded to products containing a substance or preparation classified as dangerous in accordance with that Directive in so far as the products meet the objectives set out in Article 1;

(b)  to products manufactured by processes which are likely to harm significantly man and/or the environment.

3.  Products imported into the Community, for which the award of an eco-label in accordance with this Regulation has been requested, must at least meet the same strict criteria as products manufactured in the Community.

## Article 5 : Product groups and ecological criteria

1.  The conditions for awarding the label shall be defined by product groups. Product groups, the specific ecological criteria for each group and their respective periods of validity shall be established in accordance with the procedure laid down in Article 7 following the consultation procedure provided for in Article 6.

2.  The Commission shall begin these procedures at the request of the competent body or bodies referred to in Article 9, or on its own initiative. A competent body may act on its own initiative or at the request of any interested organization or individual; in the latter case it shall decide whether such a request is appropriate. Before submitting a request to the Commission the competent body shall conduct appropriate consultation of interest groups and inform the Commission of the results thereof.

3.  Each product group shall be defined in such a way as to ensure that all competing products which serve similar purposes and which have equivalence of use are included in the same group.

4.  The specific ecological criteria for each product group shall be established using a 'cradle-to-grave' approach based on the objectives set out in Article 1, the general principles set out in Article 4 and the parameters of the indicative assessment matrix shown in Annex I. The criteria must be precise, clear and objective so as to ensure uniformity of application by the competent bodies. They must ensure a high level of environmental protection, be based as far as possible on the use of clean technology and, where appropriate, reflect the desirability of maximizing product life. Should it prove necessary to adapt the indicative assessment matrix to technical progress, such adaptation shall be made in accordance with the procedure laid down in Article 7.

5.  The period of validity of product groups shall be about three years. The period of validity of a criterion may not exceed the period of validity of the product groups to which it relates.

## Article 6: Consultation of interest groups

1.  With a view to the definition of the product groups and the specific ecological criteria referred to in Article 5 and before submitting a draft to the Committee referred to in Article 7, the Commission shall consult the principal interest groups who shall meet for this purpose within a consultation forum. In so doing, the Commission shall take account of the results of national consultations.

2.  The forum should involve at least the Community-level representatives of the following interest groups:
— industry,
— commerce,
— consumer organizations,
— environmental organizations.

Each of them may be represented by having a maximum of three seats. The participating interest groups should ensure appropriate representation according to the product groups concerned and having regard to the need to ensure continuity in the work of the consultation forum.

...

### Article 7 : Committee

1. The Commission shall be assisted by a committee composed of the representatives of the Member States and chaired by the representative of the Commission.

2. The representative of the Commission shall submit to the committee a draft of the measures to be taken. The committee shall deliver its opinion on the draft within a time limit which the chairman may lay down according to the urgency of the matter. The opinion shall be delivered by the majority laid down in Article 148 (2) of the Treaty in the case of decisions which the Council is required to adopt on a proposal from the Commission. The votes of the representatives of the Member States within the committee shall be weighted in the manner set out in that Article. The chairman shall not vote.

3. The Commission shall adopt the measures envisaged if they are in accordance with the opinion of the committee.

4. If the measures envisaged are not in accordance with the opinion of the committee, or if no opinion is delivered, the Commission shall, without delay, submit to the Council a proposal relating to the measures to be taken. The Council shall act by a qualified majority.

5. If the Council has not acted within three months from the date of referral to it, the proposed measures shall be adopted by the Commission.

### Article 8 : The eco-label

...

3. The decision to award a label to individual products which fulfil the criteria referred to in Articles 4 and 5 shall be taken by the competent bodies referred to in Article 9 in accordance with the procedure laid down in Article 10.

4. In accordance with the procedure laid down in Article 7, the Commission shall decide on a case-by-case basis whether it is possible to state on the label the principal reasons for awarding the eco-label and establish rules for this purpose.

5. The label shall be awarded for a fixed production period which may in no circumstances exceed the period of validity of the criteria. Where the criteria relating to products are extended without change, the validity of the label may be extended for the same period.

6. The eco-label shall under no circumstances be used before the conclusion of a contract covering the conditions of use as provided for in Article 12.

### Article 9 : Designation of competent bodies

1. Within six months from the entry into force of this Regulation each Member State shall designate the body or bodies, hereinafter referred to as the 'competent body (bodies)', responsible for carrying out the tasks provided for in this Regulation, particularly in Article 10, and shall inform the Commission thereof.

2. The Member States shall ensure that the composition of the competent bodies is such as to guarantee their independence and neutrality and that the competent bodies apply the provisions of this Regulation in a consistent manner.

### Article 10 : Applications for the award of an eco-label

1. Manufacturers or importers in the Community may apply for the award of an eco-label only to the competent body or bodies designated by the Member State in which the product is manufactured or first marketed or into which the product is imported from a third country.

...

3. After the product assessment, the competent body shall decide whether to award a label. If it decides that a label should be awarded, it shall notify the Commission of its decision and enclose the full results of the assessment together with a summary thereof.

...

5. If the competent body decides to award a label to a product already rejected by the competent body of another Member State, it shall draw the Commission's attention to this fact when notifying its decision under paragraph 3. The Commission shall in all such cases take a decision on the proposed award in accordance with the procedure laid down in Article 7.

...

7. If an application for the award of an eco-label is rejected, the competent body shall immediately inform the Commission and advise the applicant of the reasons for the rejection.

8. On receiving an application for a label, the competent body may conclude that the product does not fall within a product group for which criteria have already been agreed. In these cases, the competent body shall decide if a proposal for the establishment of a new product group should be forwarded to the Commission for adoption in line with the procedures laid down in Articles 6 and 7.

...

### Article 11 : Costs and fees

1. Every application for the award of a label shall be subject to the payment of the costs of processing the application.

2. The conditions governing the use of the label shall include payment of a fee by the applicant for the use of the label.

3. The sums referred to in paragraphs 1 and 2 shall be fixed by the competent bodies referred to in Article 9 and may vary from Member State to Member State. Indicative guidelines for this purpose shall be established in accordance with the procedure laid down in Article 7.

### Article 12 : Terms of use

1. The competent body shall conclude a contract, covering the terms of use of the label, with each applicant. To this end a standard contract shall be adopted in accordance with the procedure laid down in Article 7.

2. The terms of use shall also include provisions for withdrawing the authorization to use the label.

### Article 13 : Confidentiality

Competent bodies, the Commission and all other persons concerned may not disclose to third parties information to which they have gained access in the course of assessing a product with

a view to the award of the label. Once a decision has been taken to award the label, however, the following information may not in any circumstances be kept confidential:
- — the name of the product,
- — the manufacturer or importer of the product,
- — the reasons and relevant information for awarding the label.

...

### Article 15 : Information

Each Member State shall ensure that consumers and undertakings are informed by appropriate means of the following:

(a)   the objectives of the eco-label award scheme;

(b)   the product groups which have been selected;

(c)   the ecological criteria for each product group;

(d)   the procedures to be followed for applying for a label;

(e)   the competent body or bodies in the Member State.

### Article 16 : Advertising

1.   References to the eco-label in advertising may not be made until a label has been awarded and then only in relation to the specific product for which it was awarded.

2.   Any false or misleading advertising or the use of any label or logo which leads to confusion with the Community eco-label introduced by this Regulation is hereby prohibited.

...

### Annex I   Indicative Assessment Matrix

| Environmental fields | Product life-cycle |
|---|---|
| Pre-production | Production |
| Distribution (including packaging) | Utilization |
| Disposal | Waste relevance |
| Soil pollution and degradation | Water contamination |
| Air contamination | Noise |
| Consumption of energy | Effects on eco-systems |
| Consumption of natural resources | |

## Questions and Problems

1. What type of standards (e.g. emission, quality, product, process) are best for controlling:
   - — air pollution in a city
   - — long-range air pollution
   - — pollution of a drinking-water reservoir
   - — accidental marine pollution
   - — pollution of underground water?

2. Should prohibitions be enacted based upon (1) provable future damage, (2) statistical likelihood of harm, (3) risk?

3. Can environmental trade restrictions and prohibitions and eco-labelling be reconciled with international and Community norms limiting or eliminating trade barriers?

4. Who should establish the goals and scope of licensing? Should the public play a role?

5. How much control over activities that might harm the environment is possible through a licensing or permit process?

6. At what level should licences and permits be granted?
    — national government
    — regional authorities
    — local administration?

7. Who prepares an environmental impact assessment and who pays for it?

8. According to the Community directive on environmental impact assessments, how much participation and influence does the public have during the process? Compare the directive to the Turkish legislation and the Espoo Convention on this point.

9. What are the advantages and disadvantages to leaving environmental protection to market mechanisms such as consumer preferences, insurance policies, and audits during the sale of assets?

10. Should environmental audits be prepared by the company, an independent private or public body, or the licensing authority?

11. What should be the scope of an environmental audit? Should the results be published?

12. Assume a particular pesticide has contaminated the grain used to feed chickens. The result is that the eggs are tainted and must be destroyed. If the cause can be demonstrated, who, if anyone, is liable? Whose claims, if any, should be allowed:
    — the owners of the chickens
    — sellers of contaminated grain
    — consumers who must pay more for eggs?

13. In the case described in question 12, what should be the form of responsibility: civil damages, administrative sanctions, or criminal penalties? Should the remedies be considered as alternatives or is it possible to use more than one?

14. In your view, what enforcement means are the most effective
    — fines
    — prison sentences
    — closure of an establishment
    — monetary compensation to those harmed by environmental damage?

15. Does compliance with the terms of a licence or permit exclude the possibility of civil liability for environmental harm? If so, should the licensing authority have any liability?

16. Evaluate the effectiveness of the following fiscal measures:
— tax reductions for manufacture, sale and use of ecologically-sound products
— imposition of surcharges on products and processes that harm the environment.

17. Are ecological loans, subsidies and tax reductions compatible with EEC principles of eliminating market distortions? *See Commission* v. *Belgium*, case C-2/90, 9 July 1992; *Danish Bottle Case*, ECR 4607 (1988).

## Bibliography

Gross, A. C. and N. E. Scott, "Comparative Environmental Legislation and Action", 29 *Int'l & Comp. L.Q.* 619 (1980).

Hager, G., "Waste Control under German Law: Liability and Preventive Measures", 25 *Hous. L. Rev.* 963 (1988).

Lutz, R. E., "Laws of Environmental Management: A Comparative Study", 24 *Am. J. Comp. L.* 447 (1976).

Mayda, J., "Penal Protection of the Environment", 26 *Am. J. Comp. L.* 471 (1978) (supp).

*Milieu Aansprakelijkheid (Environmental Liability Law Quarterly)*, March 1989 (symposium issue on liability insurance).

Prieur, M., "Environmental Regulations and Foreign Trade Aspects", 3 *Fl. Int'l L.J.* 85 (1987).

Prieur, M., "Les études d'impact et le contrôle du juge administratif en France", *Revue Juridique de l'environnement* 1991.

Tarlocki, A. D. and P. Tarak, "An Overview of 'Comparative Environmental Law' ", 13 *Den. J. Int'l L. & Pol.* 85 (1983).

*UNEP, Environmental Auditing* (Report of United Nations Environment Programme) (1989).

Waite, A., "Criminal and Civil Liability of Company Directors", 3 *Land Manag. & Envt'l L. Rep.* 74 (3/1991).

Zalob, D. S., "Approaches to Enforcement of Environmental Law: An International Perspective", 3 *Hastings Int'l & Comp. L. Rev.* 299 (1980).

## CHAPTER IV

# INSTITUTIONS AND AGENCIES

Implementation of the legal techniques discussed in Chapter III requires the creation and functioning of appropriate institutions nationally, regionally, and internationally. In recent years, the numbers and kinds of organs with jurisdiction to act in this field have multiplied, due to the dispersion and variety of environmental regulations.

## A. National Institutions

Environmental tasks can be centralized or distributed among state, regional and local bodies. Nearly all states that have recognized the need for environmental protection have placed jurisdiction over major policy issues in a national governmental authority. In some cases responsibility is given to organs with broad jurisdiction, that handle environmental matters in the context of other issues; there are also specialized agencies, such as forestry and water ministries, and full environmental agencies or ministries with general or plenary authority over the subject. In addition, judicial or quasi-judicial bodies often enforce environmental regulations, including Community and international norms.

In many cases, governmental organs are assisted by expert consultative bodies, including scientists and representatives of the public, whose role may include elaborating general policy or responding to precise questions.

The essential characteristics of all environmental agencies or organs are coordination of environmental policy and action. Specific functions can include

— decision-making or inter-departmental coordination

— setting policy

— management of resources

— planning

— licensing

— surveillance and monitoring

— reporting

— direct action

Hungary has both general and specialized agencies. In 1988, it created a Ministry of Environmental Protection and Water Management, combining two formerly separate organs, the National Office for Water Management and the National Bureau for Environmental Protection. In addition, the Ministry of Agriculture is responsible for the protection of arable land, forests, and household animals; the Ministry of Industry for the protection of mineral resources and energy questions; the Ministry of Interior for household wastes; and the Ministry of Health (now Welfare Ministry) for questions concerning human health. In 1990 the government established the Ministry of Environmental Protection and Area Planning; water pollution remains within its jurisdiction, but water use has been given to the Ministry of Housing, Telecommunication and Traffic. Many states besides Hungary (e.g. Ireland, Italy, Turkey, Bulgaria) divide authority between a Ministry or Department of the Environment with primary responsibility, and other specialized agencies concerned with specific topics.

In Ireland, the central Environmental Protection Agency provides access to the results of environmental monitoring, assists with preparation of environmental impact statements, and, in a system of integrated pollution control, may issue a single all-inclusive licence. The Department of the Marine also has an important role regarding marine environment issues.

The primary task of Italy's Ministry of the Environment is to ensure that environmental conditions "consistent with the fundamental interests of the population" and with the "quality of life" are promoted, maintained or restored. It acts also to safeguard nature conservation and protection, and to "defend any natural resources against pollution". As such, it directs and coordinates, monitors and proposes or issues national guidelines. Other administrative organs also are concerned with environmental questions, including the Ministries of Health and of the Sea. However, the Environment Ministry determines general criteria and technical norms, standards, characteristics and limits in several areas of environmental protection, including water pollution and air pollution control and waste disposal. The Ministry has express power to issue temporary protective orders in case of non-compliance by local authorities and to use the police and other security forces to prevent and repress environmental violations. The Turkish Environmental General Directorate, created in 1984 by Decree law 222, has similar comprehensive functions and powers.

In some cases the creation of a national authority has been coupled with a continued or even an enhanced degree of decentralization over implementation of policy. For example, in Denmark there is a department concerned with protection of the environment, the conservation of nature, extraction of natural resources, and comprehensive planning. In addition 14 counties (*Amter*) and 276 municipalities play a large role in implementing the laws.

France also has decentralized implementation. The Minister of Environment defines French policy on environmental issues on behalf of and under the authority of the Prime Minister. However, the principal authorities responsible for applying most laws of environmental protection, in particular for classified installations, are the Prefects (*Préfets*), the local representatives of the French State. The Prefect is supported by a team of *inspecteurs des installations classées* who devise technical standards for use by classified installations and ensure implementation of the standards. City mayors also have a role in granting building licences and permits for the discharge of waste into city sewer systems.

In addition to these policy and enforcement bodies, France has had inter-departmental advisory groups such as the High Committee for the Environment, the Inter-ministerial Committee for the Quality of Life, and the National Nature Conservation Council. Formerly independent administrative agencies for water, air quality and waste recycling and disposal have been merged in a new central agency, the *Agence de l'environnement et de la maitrise de l'énergie*, created by a law enacted 22 December 1990. In addition, since 1 January 1991, regional environmental branches (*services extérieurs*), under the direct authority of the Minister of the Environment, have been entrusted the task of locally implementing government directives.

Local authorities in other countries sometimes are delegated or take on unique or extensive powers. In Ireland, the thirty local authorities provide water supplies, drainage, planning, and control environmental assessment and licensing for effluent discharges and air emissions. Under the 1990 Local Government (Water Pollution) (Amendment) Act, local authorities and courts are empowered to require polluters to carry out and bear expenses of remedial measures and have flexible powers to review and amend licences.

In Italy, the Provinces are often entrusted with enforcement and record-keeping roles. Municipalities also monitor compliance, often through health agencies. One unusual aspect of the Italian structure is that the large cities have a special environment section of the first instance courts, with exclusive competence over environmental criminal matters. Both central and local authorities are required to inform the police or the public prosecutor of such matters.

Federal States usually divide both law-making and implementation authority horizontally, among agencies at the same level of government, and vertically, between national and state levels. For example, in Germany, due to the distribution of executive powers, different federal administrative authorities are concerned with environmental protection, including the Federal Minister for the Environment, the Federal Environmental Office and the Federal Health Office. Federal authorities prepare legislative proposals and undertake research, consultation and information, generally with regard to air and noise pollution, dangerous substances, nuclear energy and federal land use planning. Based on the Federal Emission Control Act, emission standards have been established for about two hundred substances and eighty processes. The federal government also has set effluent standards under the Federal Water Resources Management Act covering a variety of substances for about fifty processes.

Vertically, German environmental regulation authority is divided between federal and state governments. On the level of the Länder, general administrative law rules or specific provisions of various environmental laws establish various environmental and health/industrial safety regulatory agencies. Most Länder environmental agencies are organized into three tiers (Superior State Authority, Upper State Authority and Lower State Authority). The Superior State Authorities are the Ministers of Environmental Affairs who, with the Federal Minister of the Environment, draft environmental laws and ordinances supervising execution of environmental laws and take decisions in important individual cases. Upper State Authorities are generally district administrations in charge of the supervision of the Lower Environmental

Authorities, those parts of county or city administrations responsible for the execution and implementation of environmental laws on the local level. The Länder may regulate water pollution, nature protection, and country planning, if the federal government has not set general principles through framework laws, and implement federal law in all areas where it has acted.

Austria, also a federal state, adopted a constitutional amendment in 1983 specifying federal competence to take measures to combat dangerous environmental pollution resulting from the violation of emission standards.

The situation is complex in Belgium where constitutional amendments adopted in 1970 devolved legislative and executive powers to three regions and to three communities (Flanders, Wallonia, Brussels; Flemish, French, German). Each region and community has legislative power vested in a council, whose acts have the same force and value as national acts. In some matters the regions have exclusive jurisdiction, attributed to them in 1980 and 1988. Residuary matters belong to the national state. Jurisdiction over environmental matters, including policies to combat air, water and noise pollution, was largely but not entirely transferred to the regions in the 1980 Institutions Reform Act. The national authority retains jurisdiction to set minimum requirements, such as quality, product and emission standards. The regions must respect these standards, but can adopt more restrictive measures. Both local and national norms are superseded by general and sector standards set by the European Community. Environmental impact statements are done for either the regional or national authority, depending on whether the particular project falls within the jurisdiction of the regions or the national state, i.e. who licenses the project. Nuclear power stations, construction of long-distance railway lines, and airports with runways longer than 2,100 metres must be approved by the national government.

In contrast, the UK has taken a centralized approach combining a number of pollution control functions in a unified inspectorate within the Department of the Environment. The objects are to achieve integrated control based on selecting the best practicable environmental options and to avoid cross-media pollution.

## B. European Community

The treaties that created and transformed the European Community establish four major organs: the Council of Ministers, the European Commission, the European Parliament, and the Court of Justice. In general, norms are adopted by the Council upon proposal by the Commission and after consultation with the European Parliament. In some cases, the Economic and Social Council also must be consulted.

The Council is the only institution that directly represents the governments of the Member States. Each government has one seat on the Council and is represented by its Foreign Minister for major decisions, but it may send any of its specialized Ministers according to the subject matter of the meeting, e.g. the Minister of Environment for environmental matters. The Council adopts regulations and directives after submission of a proposal by the Commission and the requisite consultations. The Council acts either upon unanimous or weighted majority vote.

The Commission has seventeen members chosen by agreement of the governments of the Member States. There are one or two members from each of them. Commissioners act in the Community's interest and not on behalf of their individual States. The Commission is appointed by unanimous agreement of the Member States for a four-year renewable term and can only be removed by vote of censure from the European Parliament.

The two principal functions of the Commission are to propose Community policy to implement the Treaties and to provide for the administration of the Community. In regard to the first activity, the Commission prepares, discusses and adopts preliminary drafts of proposed standards for submission to the Council. In addition, article 155 of the Treaty of Rome provides that the Commission must "ensure that the provisions of the Treaty and the measures taken by the institutions pursuant thereto are applied". The latter authority is exclusive and may not be delegated to any other organ or institution.

In supervising implementation of Community obligations, the Commission acts where it finds a Treaty infringement, first by sending a formal notice, then by delivering a "reasoned opinion". Subsequently, if further action is needed, the Commission may bring a judicial proceeding against the involved Member State or entity or take other measures. For example, in January 1992, the president of the Commission warned Italy that its slow incorporation of EC rules could result in sanctions being taken by other Member States, including a refusal to lift border restrictions at the beginning of 1993. According to the Commission, Italy had incorporated into national law only 65 of 137 EC Directives.

The 518 Members of the European Parliament are directly elected by the peoples of the Member States of the Community and serve for a period of five years. Members of Parliament do not sit by nationality, but according to political party affiliation. The Parliament participates in the formulation of EC law and the Community budget as well as in monitoring the activities of the European Commission and Council. Parliament's main influence on legislation lies in its right to be consulted, its right to move amendments and its power to delay legislation by withholding its opinion until the Commission responds to its proposed amendments. The Maastricht Treaty on European Union establishes decision-making procedures that will give significant new powers to the Parliament. When the Council has transmitted to Parliament its Common or interim Position and Parliament initially rejects or amends it, the Council must convene a "Conciliation Committee" to negotiate a compromise. Within specified time limits, the Council representatives and the Parliamentary representatives must attempt to negotiate a common position. Once achieved, the Council and Parliament vote on the Committee proposal, by qualified and absolute majorities, respectively. Unless approved by both, the proposal lapses. If the Committee fails to achieve a common proposal, the Council may go forward with its draft unless the Parliament rejects it by absolute majority.

Once a regulation or directive is adopted, the Court of Justice ensures correct interpretation and application of its provisions. The Court is composed of thirteen Judges and six Advocates-General, the former organized in four Chambers of three Judges and two Chambers composed of six judges. There is one Judge sitting for each

Member State, with the thirteenth member nominated by one of the large Member States in rotation. The Advocates-General also are nominated by Member States. The Judges and Advocates-General serve six year, renewable terms.

The Court has jurisdiction to settle disputes within the Community and to award damages. It may review the validity of acts of the Council or the Commission and give judgment on actions by Member States, the Council, or the Commission when it is alleged that there has been legal incompetence, errors of substantial form, infringement of the Treaties or abuse of power. Any individual or company may appeal a Decision addressed to it, or an act which, although in the form of a Regulation or Decision addressed to another person, is of direct and individual concern.

The Single European Act established a Court of First Instance, set up in 1988 in part to relieve the increasing caseload of the Court of Justice. The Court consists of twelve judges nominated by Member States. Its jurisdiction extends only to staff complaints and actions brought under competition law by natural and legal persons (companies). Actions brought by Member States or Community institutions and questions referred by national courts do not fall within its competence. Appeals may be taken to the Court of Justice on points of law only.

In addition to the major Community organs, the Economic and Social Committee established by the Treaty of Rome acts as a consultative body to ensure the involvement of all economic and social groups in the development of the European Community. The Council and Commission are required to consult the Committee on a number of subjects, including the environment. The ESC is composed of 189 members representing employers, workers, and various interest groups from agriculture, transportation, the professions and consumers. Members are appointed by the Council for a term of four years on proposal of the Member States' governments.

Finally, the Council has created a European Environmental Agency, by Regulation adopted 7 May 1990. Its main objective is to provide technical and scientific support to the Community and Member States regarding environmental protection. The Agency will be directed by a management board consisting of one representative from each Member State and two representatives from the Commission. In addition, the European Parliament will designate two "scientific personalities" to the board. The Agency will begin functioning when the site for its headquarters is chosen by the Council. In the meantime, the Commission has been asked to establish a transitional task force to identify priorities for the Agency's work.

Unlike other organs of the Community, the Agency is open to countries not members of the Community, who share the environmental concerns of the Member States. Particular emphasis is placed upon air quality and atmospheric emissions; water quality, pollutants and water resources; the state of the soil; protection of flora and fauna; land use and natural resources; waste management; noise emissions; hazardous chemical substances; and coastal protection.

# C. International Institutions

Like all international organizations, those concerned with the environment are inter-governmental in character. They are established by treaty signed by the original states creating the organization. Other states may join according to the provisions of the agreement. Examples of such treaties are the Charter of the United Nations, the Statute of the Council of Europe and the Treaty of Rome, creating the European Economic Community.

Within international organizations, member states generally are represented by governments and individual delegates are bound by government instructions regarding the policies they support or oppose. However, international organizations often create subsidiary bodies composed of independent experts who participate in their individual capacities and who are barred from accepting governmental instructions.

Most international organizations have a plenary body, for example, a conference of states parties or a General Assembly, such as is found in the United Nations. These bodies generally have no legislative powers, but may make recommendations or discuss matters within their competence; such recommendations are binding upon the organization itself as well as its organs. In some cases, the recommendations can have substantial influence on the direction and development of the law, in particular leading to the formation of customary international law. This is especially seen when international bodies adopt declarations of principles, e.g. the 1968 European Water Charter.

It is exceptional to find an "executive organ" such as the United Nations Security Council or the Council of OECD, that can take decisions binding on member states. Equally rare are judicial bodies with compulsory jurisdiction to decide disputes between or among member states.

In addition to these major organs, subsidiary bodies are quite common and, indeed, necessary. They are delegated competence over specialized subjects, and may undertake fact-finding or discussions of problems that arise in the field of their authority. Sometimes, they initiate projects for new treaties or make recommendations. Some of these, such as the United Nations Commission on Environment and Development and the Committee on Cultural Cooperation of the Council of Europe, are governmental in nature. Others, such as the United Nations Environment Programme, are staffed by independent members of the United Nations secretariat.

International organizations utilize a wide variety of voting procedures, although the most common arrangement affords each state one vote. Sometimes a simple majority is required to adopt measures. In other cases super-majorities or even unanimity may be demanded for action to be taken. Some organizations have weighted voting, according to the size, population, or contributions of each state. In recent years, even organizations based on majority voting procedures have often preferred to act on the basis of consensus rather than votes.

The budgets of international organizations normally are adopted by the plenary body and are based on contributions from member states. Very few international organizations have the ability directly to control revenues through fees imposed on the private sector. Such taxing power is generally reserved to member states.

Because of the inter-governmental nature of most international organizations, the role of non-governmental bodies and individuals may be strictly limited. However, some organizations, such as the Council of Europe and the United Nations, have a registry system for accrediting non-governmental organizations (NGOs) to participate in meetings and to submit documents. NGOs can be very influential and their role in environmental matters is growing as a result of the UNCED meeting in Rio. In the field of the environment, international organizations share many structural and functional aspects, and often carry on overlapping activities.

*Research* is particularly important to the activities of international organizations. Although they rarely carry out their own scientific research, they often study comparative or international law prior to drafting new international instruments. Member states usually make the major scientific contributions while the international organization undertakes the role of coordinating the tasks delegated and disseminating the results. In some cases, financial assistance may be given by the organization, as in the European Community, or research contracts may be concluded with experts or research groups.

*Exchange of information* is another important task of international organizations. National and international studies and projects and the results of research in such fields as the environment are shared among member states. In some cases, the organization prepares a synthesis of the information received.

*Regulatory functions* are often exercised through drafting new norms, either by recommendations or decisions, treaties or other international standards. Sometimes regulation may continue after a treaty is adopted, when the text creates an organ of supervision. In such cases, the organ is often given responsibility for elaborating rules for application of the treaty or for modifying existing norms.

*Supervising implementation* of international norms generally does not extend to coercive action. More frequently, states parties submit reports to designated international bodies on the national implementation of international standards. In some cases, fact-finding or other investigations may occur with resulting recommendations to individual member states.

*Management of natural resources* is rare, but sometimes found in environmental treaties. For example, the Commission established by the Interim Convention on the Conservation of North-Pacific Fur Seals has power to recommend to states parties appropriate measures concerning the size, sex, and age composition of the seals taken each year.

Each international organization is limited in its activities by the competence conferred on it by its constituting treaty. Thus, the World Health Organization can address environmental problems that touch upon human health and the International Labor Organization can concern itself with environment of the workplace. In addition, some organizations have a geographic limitation, being restricted to a particular region or sub-region.

Global organizations have a particular role to play with regard to environmental problems that affect the entire biosphere. These issues are generally addressed by the United Nations and its specialized agencies, such as UNESCO, the Food and Agriculture Organization (FAO), the World Meteorological Organization (WMO).

Since the 1950s, the United Nations has been active in questions concerning the environment, through its Economic Commission for Europe. More generally, United Nations efforts began in 1968, when the General Assembly recommended convening the Stockholm Conference on the Human Environment. Following a recommendation of the Conference, held in 1972, the United Nations created the United Nations Environment Programme (UNEP).

UNEP has a Governing Council of fifty-eight members which meets and reports periodically to the General Assembly through the UN Economic and Social Council. The role of UNEP is primarily that of a catalyst for action by other institutions. Environmental problems are considered and programmes elaborated, but implementation is undertaken by the United Nations as a whole with the aid, if appropriate, of regional governmental and non-governmental organizations as well as individual states. A UN Environment Fund may contribute part of the cost of a programme or operation.

Particular actions of UNEP involve assessment of the global environment, through continuous monitoring, research, exchange of information and examination of data. Under the heading "Earthwatch" UNEP coordinates national installations and services largely through the Global Environment Monitoring System (GEMS). INFOTERRA is an international information system on the environment that puts national and international establishments in contact with experts, linking some 6,000 cooperating institutions, with information supplied by 129 countries and 13 United Nations organs. Finally, UNEP has created a Geneva-based International Register of Potentially Toxic Chemicals, based on a network of correspondents covering 111 countries. This data bank acts to exchange information on some 500 substances, their physical and chemical characteristics, methods of utilization, their concentrations in the environment and effects or toxicity for man and the environment. A legal list contains information on national and international regulations and recommendations.

UNEP also has elaborated a programme of regional seas and has considered the management of water resources, desertification, shared natural resources, and protection of the ozone layer. UNEP's efforts to develop international environmental law have had a marked influence on governments both in regard to legislation adopted and in their attitudes toward environmental problems. Finally, UNEP has been instrumental in the adoption of treaties, such as the Basel Convention on Toxic Waste.

In November 1992, the General Assembly authorized creation of a Commission on Sustainable Development.[1] The Commission's primary task is coordinating and supervising implementation of the results of the Rio Conference, especially the integration of environment and development issues. It reviews state reports and reports from other inter-governmental and non-governmental organizations. The Commission, modelled after the UN Human Rights Commission, consists of representatives of fifty-three States elected by the Economic and Social Council from among Member States of the United Nations and its specialized agencies. As

[1] A/C.2/47/L.61, 27 November 1992.

recommended by the Rio Conference and the General Assembly, the contributions and participation of non-governmental organizations are particularly emphasized.

The other organs of the United Nations increasingly concerned with environmental issues are the Human Rights Commission and the Sub-Commission on Prevention of Discrimination and Protection of Minorities. In 1988 the Sub-Commission first considered the relationship between the environment and human rights, taking up the issue of the movement of toxic and dangerous products and wastes. It adopted a resolution referring to the right of all peoples to life and the right of future generations to enjoy their environmental heritage. It called for a ban on the export of toxic and dangerous wastes and a global convention on that subject. During its 1989 session, the Sub-Commission added the topic of human rights and the environment to its agenda, adopting a resolution to undertake a study of the environment and its relation to human rights. It appointed a Special Rapporteur who has since then been preparing reports on the topic. These actions have been approved by the Human Rights Commission.

United Nations specialized agencies also have taken action in the environmental field. The mandate of the United Nations Education, Science and Cultural Organization (UNESCO) led it to create in 1970 a study on the interactions between man and the environment. This resulted in the designation and creation of some seventy biosphere reserves by 1987, serving to conserve and utilize resources, including characteristic examples of ecosystems and human habitats. In addition, UNESCO is at the origin of the Ramsar Convention on Wetlands of International Importance and the World Cultural and Natural Heritage Convention.

The United Nations Food and Agriculture Organization (FAO) is concerned with conservation of natural resources in the context of its mission to promote agriculture, better soil and water management, improved yields of crops and livestock and development of agricultural research. FAO supports research and monitoring, legal and technical assistance, and has participated in drafting numerous international texts.

The World Health Organization (WHO) obviously is concerned with environmental impacts on human health. Like FAO, it publishes manuals and guides, collects and disseminates information, furnishes technical assistance and organizes courses and seminars, establishes centres of information, conducts research and monitors particular pollutants harmful to health. Similar functions are carried out in the field of meteorology by the World Meteorological Organization.

Further specific topics related to the environment are within the competence of the International Atomic Energy Agency (IAEA) and the International Labor Organization (ILO). Both these organizations are engaged in standard-setting. The IAEA establishes norms designed to protect health and reduce to a minimum the dangers to which persons and property are exposed from radiation, including norms of nuclear safety and codes of proper procedure. The ILO in turn assists countries in improving their working environment. In addition to standard-setting, ILO promotes and supports efforts at international, regional and national levels to reduce occupational accidents and diseases.

On the regional level, in Europe the Council of Europe and the Organization for Economic Cooperation and Development (OECD) have been concerned with environmental protection. The broad mandate of the Council of Europe permits it to address all questions except those of national defence. However, it may adopt only recommendations and draft conventions which are then submitted for adoption to the Member States. Nature conservation has been a principal focus of its environmental work and it has approved numerous recommendations and agreements concerning various aspects of this subject. In addition, it has held hundreds of meetings and ministerial conferences over the past twenty years to promote transnational cooperation.

The OECD was founded to administer the Marshall Plan in Europe after the Second World War. Transformed in the 1960s, it has the power to take decisions which are binding for all member states who participate in their adoption. It also may address recommendations to member states. While not binding, these reflect the general views and intentions of the governments that vote in favour of them. Since 1970 OECD has had a Committee on the Environment to help define policies in regard to environmental problems. OECD formulated the first legal definition of pollution and enunciated basic standards applicable to transfrontier pollution. It has been one of the principal organizations in developing fundamental norms of international environmental law.

The numerous tasks involved in environmental protection necessitate a cooperative approach among the national, regional and international institutions. There is a certain degree of overlap and problems for which the institutional competence is not always clear. However, action at all levels is necessary to ensure progress in developing environmental law.

# PART II

# SECTORAL PROTECTION

CHAPTER V

# BIODIVERSITY AND THE
# PROTECTION OF NATURE

## A. Overview

All human activities, including environmental laws, have an impact on biological diversity. In recent centuries, the impact has been largely negative, with increased exploitation, pollution, and population growth leading to destruction and loss of habitat. It is estimated that in less than two hundred years, 128 species of birds and 95 species of mammals have disappeared from the globe. In some regions, over half the endemic species have become extinct since 1950. In others, large proportions of the remaining species have declining populations: in the Netherlands, one-quarter of all mammal species, more than 50 per cent of all butterfly and freshwater fish species, plus two-thirds of the amphibian and all the reptile species reflect this trend. In France, more than 30 per cent of the species of flora are declining. Through Europe, large mammals, including the wolf, bear, lynx, and other wildcats, face particular hostility and threats from competing land users, especially farmers and hunters.

The problem of biodiversity is particularly acute in parts of central and eastern Europe. In Bulgaria, for example, among ranging birds and reproducing species of other vertebrates, 21.1 per cent are considered threatened, including nearly a quarter of all birds and flora and more than a quarter of all reptiles. Mammals are increasingly threatened. Romania also presents a serious case: although it has only 2 per cent of the surface area of Europe, it contains about 40 per cent of all European plant species. Many of these, as well as wild fauna, are in danger of disappearing.

The threats to biodiversity are many; the most important are contamination and disturbance of habitat due to economic development, urbanization, fires, erosion, agricultural monoculturization, and other human interventions. Particular problems stem from industrial pollution and drainage of rivers and water basins. In response to growing recognition of a crisis, environmental law has made the protection of all species from human-induced destruction one of its principal goals. Within Europe, the Council of Europe stimulated national action by declaring 1970 the European Year of Nature. It also helped to conclude the 1979 Bern Convention on the Conservation of European Wildlife and Natural Habitats.

Protection of selected species of wild fauna became generalized, both nationally and internationally, in the nineteenth century. Taking action earlier, France regulated fishing for trout from the mid-seventeenth century, adding other species of fish in the nineteenth century. Most early regulations remain in force, although they have been harmonized with recent measures, such as the 29 June 1984 French law on freshwater fish and the management of water basins. The purpose of fishing and similar protective regulations is to conserve species for further exploitation, recognizing that competing uses of water – transport, discharge of wastes, and energy production – have an impact on the viability of the living resources.

Increased attention has been devoted recently to the role of species in the ecosystem in which they appear, and to the particular threats that face them. This has produced a shift from regulatory measures that presume exploitation, to generalized provisions that prohibit most takings and address harm resulting from changes to habitats, and from oil spills, pesticides and other forms of pollution. Problems of urban ecology also are included in some nature protection legislation. In addition to measures against pollution, numerous laws, internationally, regionally and nationally, seek directly to protect plants and animals, and their habitats, from destruction. Taking this approach, the European Community recently adopted a directive on the conservation of natural habitats and of wild fauna and flora (Council Directive 92/43 of 21 May 1992).

The trend towards an ecosystem approach has led to calls for a comprehensive plan to protect biological diversity. The United Nations Conference on the Environment and Development took steps in this direction by opening for signature a Convention on Biological Diversity.[1] Efforts are likely to continue to achieve generalized agreement on a framework of further national, regional and international obligations.

At present, most states have general Nature Protection Acts, often supplemented by – and sometimes in conflict with – hunting and fishing regulations, forestry laws, park and nature reserve legislation, and agricultural policies. In France, protecting wildlife species dependent on a single watercourse could fall within the competence of the administrative departments concerned with agriculture and forests, with equipment or with maritime and navigation matters, as well as within the jurisdiction of police enforcing laws on fish, on water, and on classified installations.

Many states are attempting to unify disparate provisions within comprehensive, more stringent codes focusing on integrated nature protection, recognizing that water systems in particular need coordinated approaches. In the Austrian Burgenland, a Nature Protection Act of November 1990 aims at protecting the diversity of indigenous plant and animal species and their natural habitats. The maintenance of wetlands and other habitats is directly emphasized. Many federal states, like Austria, enact measures regarding the taking of plants or animals at the state or local level and regulate trade in plants and animals, particularly endangered species, on a national basis.

Most nature protection legislation is based on techniques of licensing, limitations, and prohibitions. However, new laws containing economic measures, including subventions and financial support, can be found. In some cases more far-reaching proposals have been adopted. The French law of 10 July 1976 on the protection of

---

[1] Convention on Biological Diversity, adopted 22 May 1992, opened for signature 5 June 1992.

fauna and flora, codified in the rural code in 1989 (art. L and R. 200–1 *et seq.*), proclaims as a general principle in article 9 that each animal, both wild and domestic, is *un être sensible* (a being capable of feelings). According to Michel Prieur this permits recognition of an animal as a new subject of law.[2]

On an international level, many global and regional texts contain rules protecting wildlife[3] and there are numerous treaties that aim to conserve a single species (whales, seals, migratory birds), or to protect all species through a particular means (trade restrictions, habitat conservation). In general these rules are formulated to protect individual members of a species, rather than the species itself. In addition, several declarations affirm that plants and animals constitute a global heritage. Finally, the UN Convention on Biological Diversity aims to protect the genetic pool of all species, using techniques similar to those found in national legislation.

## 1. Protection of Specimens and Species of Flora and Fauna

### a. Hunting and Fishing Regulations

Many countries, especially northern ones, distinguish species according to whether or not the animal is classified as game, or whether the plant is subject to commercial exploitation. Most hunting acts attempt to maintain or conserve species by setting conditions under which certain species of plants or animals may be taken. Finland's Hunting Act (1962), for example, lists game species and contains detailed provisions on hunting seasons, the requirements for hunting, and prohibited means of taking. A Fishery Act (1982) regulates fishing on the principle of productive use of fishing waters. In Norway, too, fishing legislation is based on regulation of the catch for sustainable use, while the Wildlife Act 1981 is based on the principle of protection.

The fishing law of Portugal is typical of European legislation; it provides the time, seasons and hours during which fishing is prohibited; the minimum size for taking the fish of certain species; the prohibited means and methods of fishing; and measures to protect the free circulation of fish. It also prohibits sale, transport, keeping and consuming the fish of certain species during the period fishing is prohibited. The administrative authority can prohibit fishing of endangered species entirely or par-tially. All the provisions contain penal sanctions and foresee civil liability.

National laws generally take one of two different approaches to hunting and fishing. In some countries, hunting is permitted unless limited or prohibited. In other countries, such as Sweden, all hunting is prohibited unless specifically authorized. In Norway, game species are designated by the King, primarily on the basis of existing "surpluses" of the species, their value as a resource, tradition, and the amount of

---

[2] Michel Prieur, *Droit de l'Environnement* (2nd ed.), p. 268.

[3] There are also several instruments that protect domestic or captive animals, including pets. *See,* for example, the European Convention for the Protection of Pet Animals (Strasbourg, 13 November 1987), *Int'l Env. L.* 987:84; European Convention for the Protection of Vertebrate Animals Used for Experimental and Other Scientific Purposes (Strasbourg, 18 March 1986), *Int'l Env. L.* 986:21.

damage caused by the animals. The list of game species and hunting seasons is reconsidered every three years.

The degree of protection varies considerably according to the scope of the law. The Swedish Hunting Act (1987:259) prohibits catching or killing all wild animals and birds, tracking or pursuing them, as well as interfering with nests or taking or destroying birds' eggs.

In many countries, exceptions to hunting regulations permit killing wildlife causing damage, even endangered species. In Norway, everyone is entitled to kill a predator (bear, wolf, wolverine, lynx, and three species of eagle) if it is deemed necessary in order to remove a present and serious threat of injury to persons or where there is danger of a direct attack on cattle or domesticated reindeer. There have been criminal proceedings involving application of this exception, which was sought by sheep-holders and farmers opposed to protection for predatory mammals. In Sweden, too, "protective hunting" of predators is permitted, except, since 1990, for wolves. In Iceland, legislation concerning the Arctic fox, the only indigenous terrestrial mammal in the country, continued in 1991 to permit the fox's destruction.

Most hunting and fishing is regulated by licence. In some countries, a licence for hunters is issued only after the applicant passes an examination on weapons and species. Authorization to hunt is always accompanied by regulations, such as limits on the season for hunting, and prohibition of certain hunting methods, e.g. recorded animal calls to lure animals into the open or fishing with explosives. Sometimes hunters are required to provide food for animals during particularly harsh winter months (Austria). In some cases, hunters must maintain records of the animals killed and plans of those sought to be killed. Fishing regulations usually establish the minimum size of the fish that can be taken. In Austria, hunters must engage controllers, qualified persons who have passed examinations, to ensure that the Hunting Acts are upheld.

Some legislation imposes a duty of conservation on hunters and those fishing. Such laws sometimes have been interpreted to apply only to targeted game species. As a result, problems have arisen where efforts to conserve fish stocks have led fishermen to shoot cormorants and herons. In addition, although most countries allow landowners to control hunting on their property, this is not always the case (Switzerland, France).

Numerous national and some international provisions prohibit certain means of killing or capturing specimens of wildlife. These generally prohibit non-selective means of killing and capture and those capable of causing local disappearance of species. The Bern Convention on the Conservation of European Wildlife and Natural Habitats includes a special Appendix listing hunting means prohibited for mammals (snares, live animal decoys, tape recorders, electrical devices, explosives, nets, traps, poison, etc.) and for birds (snares, limes, hooks, explosives, nets, traps, poisons). There are wide variations in national practice: Hungary prohibits poison bait, the Czech Republic adds iron traps, but permits poison gas to reduce the fox population in areas infected with rabies. Germany and Switzerland have federal prohibitions on most methods listed in the Bern Convention. Finland permits the use of strychnine.

### b. Prohibitions on the Taking of Native Species

Apart from game species, more general protective measures may apply to all species. European countries that are parties to the Bern Convention on Protection of European Wildlife and Natural Habitats, discussed below, have enacted restrictions against injury to, and destruction or taking of, some or all wild plants and animals. In France, species deemed to belong to the national biological heritage are protected from every form of taking or harmful action. The species are listed in a regulation, based on the opinion of the national council for nature protection, by the minister charged with nature protection together with the Minister of Agriculture or the minister of fishing. For game animals, the opinion of the national hunting council also must be sought. Protective measures include prohibiting the unlicensed destruction or capture, as well as mutilation, domestication, transport, sale or purchase of protected animals.

Every European country today has a law on the protection of wild flora, although in some cases the only legal instrument is forest legislation. The laws vary in strictness and methods, but most contain restrictions and prohibitions. Active measures of protection increasingly are used, including permits and licensing. Agriculture and forest exploitation may be regulated, with crop rotation and land management provisions providing for hedges, uncultivated slopes, or ponds. Norway permits the King to prohibit development, construction, traffic, and other activities threatening to wildlife.

The large majority of texts concerning flora prohibit or limit direct taking: cutting, picking, and pulling out, as well as transport and trade. Many also prohibit destruction, without defining the term or indicating if it encompasses unintended acts as well as acts of deliberate vandalism. The United Kingdom's Wildlife and Countryside Act of 1981 is specific, stating that destruction of a protected plant is lawful when "it is the incidental result of a lawful operation and could not reasonably be avoided".

Measures protecting floral habitats remain rare. In the Italian region of Piedmont, the regional government may prohibit agricultural activities temporarily, to preserve plant species in need of special protection. Walls are protected in Denmark when two species of fern are found growing on them. In Norway, the Nature Protection Act of 1970 has been applied to protect mistletoe, and a 1976 order prohibits felling the trees on which it grows. More generally, the Hungarian Decree on Nature Conservation of 1982 provides that if species cannot be otherwise safeguarded, the particular habitat of the species shall be placed under legal protection.

Although there are great differences in the species protected from one country to the next, many states protect well-known and sought after examples which, though not currently endangered, could become so due to their popularity. This is the situation in Switzerland, Austria, Italy and the Netherlands. Other states limit protection to endangered species and still a third group, including Hungary and Greece, protects both categories, with different regulations applicable to each. Great Britain generally prohibits taking of wild plants, with an exception for the owners and agents of private property on which such plants are found. Separate rules apply to Northern Ireland which has its own list of protected species. Increasingly, the regulations applicable to wild flora are being applied to mushrooms with the result that collecting wild mushrooms is prohibited in several cantons of Switzerland and regions of Italy. In other areas, the number of days for mushroom-picking is limited as well as the total weight of the mushrooms that can be taken and transported in a single day.

Some laws are very general and comprehensive: in Austria, most Länder prohibit wanton disturbance, injury or killing of wild animals and the destruction of wild plants. The laws cover all organisms except those regulated by hunting and fishing acts. The trend is toward more stringent protection through habitat-specific legislation.

Finland's Nature Conservation Act (1923) is a framework law; it entitles authorities to pass the necessary decrees to give species the protection they need, although some birds and mammals are directly protected by the Act. Further, in natural parks and other conservation areas killing or harming any kind of animal is generally forbidden. Similar to Finland, Sweden links its protection of fauna through both the Nature Conservation Act and the hunting and fishing regulations, with the former protecting species not defined as game. Section 14 of the Act allows specific endangered species of fauna or flora to be declared protected throughout Sweden or in parts of it. However, only certain activities are banned. For example, the law prohibits picking certain flora, but there is no rule to halt destruction through housing construction or road development. In Switzerland and parts of Italy, the focus is on commercialization of plant use. All taking of plants for commercial use is prohibited without authorization.

Some laws focus on mammals, birds and fish. Norway has separate laws for terrestrial fauna, covered by the Wildlife Act 1981 and sea-fish and freshwater fish, regulated by Acts of 1983 and 1964 respectively. No general legislation protects marine mammals, insects, crustaceans, reptiles, and flora, although endangered species of the latter are protected under the Nature Conservation Act 1970. The Wildlife Act is a management act, pursuant to which any catching, hunting, killing or injuring of mammals, birds, amphibians and reptiles is prohibited unless authorized. The Act permits harvesting for the benefit of agriculture and outdoor recreation.

Some countries extend protection to species of insects. In Belgium the law protects several moths, butterflies, the praying mantis, and other insect species. In certain parts of France, the collection of all butterflies and day-flying moths is prohibited, while Germany protects some three hundred species.

### c. Endangered Species

Endangered species benefit from the most stringent protective measures of international, regional and national law. The Convention on International Trade in Endangered Species of Wild Fauna and Flora, 1973 (CITES), attempts to safeguard endangered species through regulating international trade, one of the principal activities leading to the taking of wild plants and animals.[4]

---

[4] It is estimated that towards the end of the 1960s, five to ten million crocodile skins were traded on the international market. In 1972, Kenyan ivory exports reached 150 tons.

CITES is based on international cooperation between importing, transit, and exporting states. The Convention lists animals according to three different categories. The first appendix contains all species threatened with extinction that are or may be affected by trade, such as the tiger, leopard, whale, and many types of parrots. Trade in either an animal or plant of a listed species, or any readily recognizable part or derivative of it, may be authorized only in exceptional circumstances set forth in the Treaty. Where such circumstances exist, export of any listed Appendix I specimen requires prior grant and presentation of an export permit. Importing states also have a duty to require import permits, which can only be issued after an opinion of a Scientific Authority that the import is for purposes that are not detrimental to the survival of the species and that any living specimen will be suitably housed and cared for. In addition the imported specimen may not be used for primarily commercial purposes. Re-exportation requires a permit confirming that the specimen was properly imported, that the transportation will be safe, and that an import permit has been issued by the new state of importation.

Appendix II lists those species not currently threatened with extinction, but which may become so, and species upon which they are dependent. Trade in any specimen of these species is governed by CITES article IV regulations, whose requirements are less strict than those governing threatened species. Permits are still required, however, and must be based upon an opinion of a Scientific Authority that the export will not be detrimental to the survival of the species. The Scientific Authority may advise the Management Authority to limit the grant of export permits in order to maintain the level of the species population above levels that would endanger it. Import of an Appendix II specimen requires only prior presentation of an export permit or re-export certificate. It is not prohibited to bring in animals for commercial purposes. Import permits for marine animals can be based upon annual quotas established on advice of the Scientific Authority in consultation with other national or international scientific authorities.

Appendix III lists those species that one state party identifies as being subject to regulation within its jurisdiction to prevent or restrict exploitation, and for which it needs the cooperation of other parties to control trade. CITES article V provides that export of a specimen of any species from a state that has included that species in Appendix III requires the prior grant and presentation of an export permit. Permits are issued on conditions virtually identical to those required for Appendix II animals. Importation of an Appendix III specimen requires presentation of a certificate of origin and, if the specimen comes from a state that listed the species, an export permit. Appendix III has not been widely used by states; with only a dozen listing approximately 150 species (compared to 30,000 species of orchids alone in Appendix II and nearly one thousand species contained in Appendix I).

To carry out the obligations contained in CITES, each state party must designate one or more scientific authorities and management authorities to give the required opinions and issue permits and certificates. Enforcement is through measures taken by each state to penalize prohibited trade and to confiscate or return to the state of export any specimens illegally imported, with specific protection for living specimens. Supervision of state implementation is through a system of state reports to the

Secretariat established by CITES. In addition to the Secretariat, CITES provides for a Conference of State Parties that meets every two years to examine progress in the restoration and conservation of protected species. The Conference amends the Appendices, including transferring a species from one list to another. Such changes must be approved by a two-third majority of parties present and voting at the Conference.

Virtually every European state implements CITES and has adopted its own legislation identifying and protecting indigenous endangered species. In addition, the European Community is a party to CITES and has issued conforming directives and regulations.[5]

### d. Protection of Migratory Species

Quite a few international, mostly bilateral, agreements exist for the protection of migratory species. On the global level, the Bonn Convention of 23 June 1979 on the Conservation of Migratory Species of Wild Animals seeks to protect migratory species from depredations in all states through which they transit and in which they spend part of their lives. Based on a recognition that wild animals are an irreplaceable part of the earth's natural system that must be conserved for the good of mankind, the Convention defines migratory species as the entire population or any geographically separate part of the population of a species of wild animal that habitually and predictably crosses one or more national jurisdictional boundary. This includes birds, land and sea mammals, reptiles and fish. An important concept in the treaty is that of "conservation status", the sum of the influences acting on a migratory species that might affect its long-term distribution and abundance. This status is considered favourable when the population data indicate: (1) that the species is maintaining itself on a long-term basis as a viable component of its ecosystem; (2) the range of the species is neither currently being reduced nor likely to be reduced long-term; (3) there is and likely will remain sufficient habitat to maintain the population on a long-term basis; and (4) the distribution and abundance are at or near historic coverage and levels to the extent consistent with wise wildlife management.

Conservation status serves as the criterion for determining the applicable rules of the Convention. States parties must pay special attention to migratory species whose conservation status is unfavourable and take steps to conserve such species and their habitats. Endangered species, listed in Convention Appendix I, are accorded immediate protection by range states. The latter are required to conserve and where possible restore the habitats of the species; eliminate, prevent or minimize impediments to their migration; prevent, reduce, or control factors endangering them; and prohibit the taking of animals belonging to such species.

Appendix II lists migratory species that have an unfavourable conservation status and need international agreements for their conservation and management; states parties are encouraged to enter into such agreements. The Convention provides the basic elements of and guidelines for agreements.

---

[5] Regulation 3636/82 (2 December 1982), O.J. no. L 384, 31 December 1982, modified O.J. no. 367, 28 December 1983, p. 1, 2.

The Convention establishes a Conference of States Parties, as the decision-making organ of the Convention. It meets once every three years and monitors the conservation status of migratory species, makes recommendations to parties for improving the conservation status of species, reviews the progress being made under agreements, and recommends convening meetings of range states in order to improve the conservation status of a migratory species for which there is no agreement. A scientific council and secretariat assist in carrying out the aims of the Convention.

### e. Limitations on the Introduction of Exotic Species

Widespread destruction of native species can occur through the introduction of exotic species against which local ones have little or no protection. Consequently, legislation in many countries prohibits the release or introduction of non-native species, or requires special permission to introduce them. In other cases, such as Norway, the law prohibits the introduction of exotic fauna, but does not regulate the introduction of new plant species except for some limited bans inserted into regulations governing protected areas.

In maritime states, particularly in nordic countries where the economy is partly based on fishing, the fishing acts generally prohibit the introduction of fish not previously occurring in the waters in question.

Recent international agreements include provisions on exotic species. The Protocol on Mediterranean Specially Protected Areas, discussed further below, suggests in article 7 that States Parties prohibit the introduction of exotic species into the designated protected areas. Similarly, the Bern Convention on the Conservation of European Wildlife and Natural Habitats requires States Parties to encourage the introduction of native species of wild flora and fauna and strictly to control the introduction of non-native species.

### f. Measures Directed Toward the Preservation of One or Several Species

Numerous national and international measures aim to protect specific animal species, such as whales, seals and birds. So far there are no provisions addressing particular plant species, apart from the listing of endangered plants in CITES appendices.

The Community has adopted several measures protecting specific species. EC Regulation 348/81 prohibits the importation or sale of products of cetaceans (whales and some other marine mammals) in application of the International Convention for the Regulation of Whaling. Directive 83/129 concerns the importation into Member States of furs of young seals and derivative products. Member States are required by the directive to take or maintain all necessary measures to ensure that the white furs of young harp seals and blue furs of capuchon as well as objects made from these furs are not imported for commercial purposes into their territories. However, the directive does not apply to products derived from traditional hunting practices by indigenous populations. Seals also are protected by a 1957 bilateral convention between Norway and the former Soviet Union.

Birds are protected by sometimes overlapping conventions and also by an EC directive. These legal instruments sometimes require the creation of protected zones. In addition, it is clear that birds are the principal object of the 1979 Bonn Convention on the Protection of Migratory Species.

One of the first international environmental agreements, the 1902 Paris Convention for the Protection of Birds Useful to Agriculture, contained several precedential measures, in spite of its utilitarian approach. In particular, it forbade taking nests and eggs and capturing and destroying clutches. It also prohibited placing and using traps, cages, nets, and other means designed to capture or destroy birds *en masse*. Importing, transiting, transporting, and selling nests, eggs and the young of protected species were banned, as was all hunting, capture, and sale between 1 March and 15 September of each year. However, the Convention provided numerous exceptions and derogations. A second International Convention for the Protection of Birds, adopted in 1950, is more in conformity with modern ecological practices. Several European states that did not accept the earlier agreement are parties to the 1950 text. The treaty removes the designation of certain species as "nonuseful" and extends the list of prohibited methods of killing and capture, including, for example, the use of spring traps and motor vehicles during hunting. Also, states can no longer offer rewards for the killing or capture of birds. With minor exceptions, all birds are protected during their breeding periods and all migratory birds during their transit. Three other innovations appear: states parties agree to regulate trade in protected birds; they support the creation of land or water reserves; and they agree to study and adopt the proper means to prevent the destruction of birds by waste oil and other water pollution, by lighthouses, electric cables, insecticides, poisons, or any other means. The most original feature in the Convention mirrors the usual method of lists by enumerating those birds that *can* be taken within the territory of each state party. It is understood that any bird that does not appear on the list is protected. The method has practical advantages for enforcement through the identification of species, because the number of species that can be hunted or captured is far less numerous than the number of those that must be protected.

There are two types of exceptions. First, certain states, such as the Netherlands and Sweden, are granted specific exceptions.[6] Second, all states may derogate in cases of massive damage to agriculture, to game or to fish, and destruction of birds is permitted when bird populations threaten other species whose conservation is desirable. Similarly, measures of exception can be accorded in the interests of science and education, as well as to restock and reproduce game birds and falcons. Finally, each state has the possibility of establishing a list of bird species permissible to be kept in captivity by individuals.

The 1979 EC Directive on the Conservation of Wild Birds covers all species of birds living in the wild on the European territory of states members, as well as bird nests, their eggs and their habitats. All necessary measures must be taken to maintain or adapt bird population levels corresponding to ecological, scientific, and cultural

---

6  The prohibition on harvesting eggs does not apply to lapwing eggs in the Netherlands.

requirements, taking account of economic and recreational factors. The general protective regime includes the same measures as the international conventions referred to above, but also adds that a sufficient diversity and area of habitats must be provided, particularly through the establishment of protected areas. A rather complex system of lists is used. Annex I species – now numbering nearly 150 – must be the object of special conservation measures, primarily concerning their habitats, which must be classified as special protected areas. The same measures must be applied to regularly migrating species not listed in Annex I. Member states must pay particular attention to the protection of wetlands of international importance, in apparent reference to the Ramsar Convention discussed below. For Annex I species the Directive also prohibits the sale, transport, keeping for sale and offering for sale of live or dead birds and of any readily recognizable parts or derivatives thereof.

A second annex is divided into two parts. The first lists those species that can be hunted in the geographical area to which the Directive applies. Species in the second part of the annex may be hunted only in those states that are specifically mentioned. Such hunting must comply with principles of "wise use and ecologically balanced control of the species of birds concerned". Finally, a third Annex enumerates bird species for which sale, transport, holding and offering for sale are permitted or can be authorized provided that the birds have been legally killed or captured or otherwise legally acquired.

The Directive authorizes certain exceptions supervised by the Commission. In no case may a state make exceptions from the provisions concerned with protection of habitats or the maintenance of bird populations at required levels. States may take measures stricter than those provided by the Directive. In either case, periodic reports on national measures taken to implement the Directive must be submitted to the Commission.

### g. Measures Relating to the Transportation of Animals

The 1968 European Convention on the Protection of Animals in International Transport requires that all animals should have sufficient space and should in principle be able to lie down; they should have air; and a veterinarian may prescribe periods of rest and feeding. All suffering must be avoided or minimized in case of strike or when reasons of *force majeure* prevent the normal functioning of transport. In addition, different provisions apply to the different means of transport. Community Directive 77/489, adopted in 1977, is based on the Convention and contains virtually identical provisions.

### h. Gene Banks

Gene banks are the most recent means adopted to protect genetic diversity, particularly of plants. In several countries, the germplasm of plants, mostly crops, have been collected and stored since the 1970s. Difficult legal issues over safety of the material, ownership, development of national laws restricting availability of the germplasm, and intellectual property rights over development of new strains, led the

United Nations Food and Agriculture Organization to propose a Global System for the Conservation and Utilization of Plant Genetic Resources. The system, in place since 1983, aims to ensure the safe conservation, and promote the unrestricted availability and sustainable utilization, of plant genetic resources for present and future generations, by providing a flexible framework for sharing the benefits and burdens. The system covers the conservation (*ex situ* and *in situ*) and utilization of plant genetic resources at molecular, population, species and ecosystem levels. It is based upon a framework, the International Undertaking; an inter-governmental Commission; and the International Fund for Plant Genetic Resources.

As of the end of 1991, 128 countries were participating in the system. The Commission discusses matters related to plant genetic resources and monitors the implementation of the principles contained in the Undertaking, a non-binding agreement concerning exploration, collection, conservation, evaluation, utilization and availability of plant genetic resources. The Commission has drafted an International Code of Conduct for Plant Germplasm Collecting and Transfer, and has begun preparation of a code of conduct for biotechnology.

The Undertaking is based upon the principle that plant genetic resources, as part of the heritage of mankind, should be conserved for future generations, subject to the overriding sovereign rights of nations over their genetic resources. The Fund is intended to support projects on the conservation and sustainable development of plant genetic resources. In operation, the system has faced difficult issues of national sovereignty over plant genetic resources, and rights of farmers and breeders, without fully resolving the debate.

## 2. *Protection of Habitats and Ecosystems*

Anti-pollution measures, such as the Community directive on pollution of the aquatic environment by dangerous substances, can have a direct effect on the protection of wild flora and fauna. Such norms may explicitly state their environmental goal to be nature protection: e.g. EC Directive 78/659 concerns "the quality of fresh waters needing protection or improvement in order to support fish life". It establishes water quality standards for two types of waters: salmonid (those supporting salmon, trout, grayling and whitefish, for example) and cyprinid waters (those supporting, for example, cyprinids and pike, perch or eel). States have five years to conform to the designated values. Monitoring through sampling and testing is required, according to the requirements of the directive. Boundary waters are controlled and tested through consultation between the riparian states. Certain exceptions are permitted for particular geographical and climatic conditions and amendments may be made by a designated Community scientific and technical committee. A similar directive governs shellfish water quality.[7]

In addition to anti-pollution measures, various types of property "set-aside" or conservation measures seek to protect plants and animals. Community Directive

---

[7] Directive on the Quality Required of Shellfish Waters, 79/923/EEC, O.J. no. L 281 (10 November 1979) p. 47.

92/43 on the conservation of natural habitats and of wild fauna and flora specifically aims to protect biodiversity by conserving natural habitats.[8] It calls for a coherent European ecological network of special conservation areas, called Natura 2000. Each Member State must contribute to the creation of Natura 2000 in proportion to the representation within its territory of natural habitat types and the habitats of species listed in annexes to the directive.

The first nature reserve in Europe, the forest of Bialoweza, was established in the fourteenth century by King Jagello of Poland, in order to preserve the aurochs (the European bison) and the tarpan (wild horse), species already threatened with extinction. Other nature reserves were established in the nineteenth century, and the first European national parks were established in Sweden in 1909. By 1990, some 1,400 protected areas were recorded across the European continent (minus Russia), amounting to some 36.5 million hectares.

### a. Protected Areas

Creation of public sites and protected areas is a common technique for protecting wild flora and fauna, although originally public parks were designed primarily to protect scenic areas for recreational purposes. Now, such sites are particularly important in countries like Norway where there is no general legislation on protection of flora. Protected areas also have been important in France, where legislation aimed at protecting wild flora and fauna developed relatively late. Only in 1976 was a general principle of nature protection enunciated. Now, flora and fauna are deemed to represent a "national biological heritage".

In international law, the UNESCO Convention for the Protection of the World Cultural and Natural Heritage (Paris, 1972), and the Ramsar Convention on Wetlands of International Importance (Ramsar, Iran, 1971) are both based on site protection. Each state party to the UNESCO Convention is obliged to identify and delineate the different natural areas situated on its territory that are of outstanding interest and need to be preserved as part of the world heritage of mankind as a whole. For these, an international system of protection is provided, based upon national legislation of the country where the site is located; international obligations of identification, protection, conservation, presentation and transmission to future generations of the heritage of the state; and, finally, international assistance and cooperation to preserve and conserve world heritage sites.

An international Committee, known as the World Heritage Committee, establishes and publishes a World Heritage List of sites forming part of the global cultural and natural heritage, and a list of World Heritage in Danger. The latter includes property threatened by serious and specific dangers, such as the threat of disappearance caused by accelerated deterioration, large-scale public or private projects or rapid urban or tourist development projects. The Committee receives and studies requests by states parties for international assistance for protection, conservation,

---

[8] Directive on the Conservation of Natural Habitats of Wild Fauna and Flora, 92/43/EEC, O.J. no. L 206 (22 July 1992), p. 7.

presentation or rehabilitation of any property included or potentially suitable for inclusion on one of the lists. Assistance can include studies, provision of experts, technicians and skilled labourers, training of staff and specialists, supply of equipment, low-interest or interest-free loans, and, in exceptional cases and for special reasons, non-repayment grants. Generally, only part of the cost is borne by the international community. Financial support is provided through an international trust fund derived from various sources. States parties have mandatory contributions and there are voluntary contributions or gifts from states, inter-governmental and non-governmental organizations, public or private bodies, and individuals.

The Ramsar Convention was the first treaty based on the idea that the habitat of endangered species should be the focus of protection. Although originally intended to protect the habitat of waterfowl, the Convention has taken on additional importance as it has become recognized that wetlands are among the most productive sources of ecological support on earth, acting as habitat for myriad species and as flood control regions. Wetlands are defined in the Convention as being areas of marsh, fen, peatland or water, whether natural or artificial, permanent or temporary, with water that is static or flowing, fresh, brackish or salt, including areas of marine water whose depth does not exceed six metres at low tide. Waterfowl are defined as birds ecologically dependent on wetlands.

Each state party to the Convention must designate at least one suitable wetland within its boundary for inclusion in a List of Wetlands of International Importance. The list is maintained by a non-governmental organization, the World Conservation Union (IUCN). The boundaries of each wetland are precisely established; they may incorporate riparian and coastal zones adjacent to the wetland, and islands or bodies of marine water of importance as waterfowl habitats. In ascribing wetlands on the list, States Parties accept responsibilities of conservation, management and wise use of migratory stocks of waterfowl. States also must formulate and implement their planning to promote conservation of the wetlands included on the list. Promotion of conservation includes establishing nature reserves and providing adequately for their wardening.

Where a wetland extends across the territories of two or more states or where there is a shared water system, states must consult with each other about implementing their Convention obligations. They must endeavour to coordinate and support present and future policies and regulations concerning conservation of wetlands and their flora and fauna.

International action includes advisory conferences on the conservation of wetlands, where non-governmental experts and organizations may participate, and where recommendations to state parties may be adopted by majority vote. To date, more than 320 wetlands have been inscribed on the list, over 80 per cent of which are in Europe, western Asia and north Africa.

The World Heritage Convention and the Ramsar Convention both establish general obligations and performance standards, leaving it to each state party to enact and apply its own legislation according to its own needs and priorities. Neither agreement defines any type of protected area or requires adoption of any particular kind of protective measure. In contrast, there are several regional texts containing more specific obligations.

A 1982 protocol to the Barcelona Convention for the Protection of the Mediterranean Sea against Pollution (16 February 1976) expressly aims at the creation of specially protected marine areas between the Strait of Gibraltar and the meridional limit of the Dardanelles in order to safeguard particular sites presenting a biological and ecological value or of particular importance by reason of their scientific, aesthetic, historic, archaeological, cultural or educational interest. The Protocol generally applies to the territorial waters of the states parties, but also may include internal waters and wetlands or coastal areas designated by states parties. The essential obligation of contracting states is to create protected areas and to take the necessary action to ensure their protection and, if necessary, restoration. States must protect the genetic diversity of species as well as satisfactory levels of their populations, their breeding grounds and their habitats, representative examples of ecosystems and ecological processes. The Convention provides a non-exhaustive list of measures that can be taken to ensure the protection of the designated areas – including prohibiting dumping, and regulating the passage of vessels, fishing, hunting, exploration, exploitation, and archaeological activity. It also recommends that buffer zones be created around the areas.

The fact that boundaries often bisect natural areas, habitats and ecosystems has led to the creation of "twin" transboundary parks in Europe. The first such arrangement resulted from a 1925 treaty, the Krakow Protocol, between Poland and Czechoslovakia. It resulted in the creation of three border parks whose directors collaborate on promotion of tourism and shared information and research. Similarly, since 1972, the Gran Paradiso National Park in the Italian Alps has been paired with the Vanoise National Park in France, nearly tripling the protected area and providing year-round protection to the ibex. A similar rationale underlies the Waddenzee National Park, which covers all the natural range of seals along the tidal flats of Denmark, Germany and the Netherlands. In 1987, the three coastal states entered into an administrative agreement on a common secretariat that sets out the duties of its parties to cooperate in research and management of the Waddenzee ecosystem as a whole. Similarly, Spain and France coordinate signposts, visitor centres and tourist information for the French Pyrénées Occidentales National Park and the Spanish Ordesa National Park. In total, there are twenty-four paired parks involving twenty countries, with further efforts underway, including tripartite consideration of a park around Mont Blanc, the highest peak in the Alps.

On the national level, various kinds of protected sites are established by law. These set aside areas where specific land use restrictions are established for conservation purposes. In some countries, only the national legislature can establish a national park (Finland, Spain, and Sweden). The laws of other countries permit areas to be established pursuant to regulation. In Norway, for example, the Nature Protection Act sets up minimum requirements framed in general terms. If they are fulfilled, a protected area is created by specific regulations. Sweden and most federal states, including Switzerland, Germany and Austria, divide authority between the national and local governments in designating sites. In Sweden, the national government establishes national parks, identifies wetland areas, and establishes certain protected areas in accordance with the Environmental Protection Act; the County Board or municipality establishes nature reserves, natural monuments and nature conservation areas.

Protected sites may be created through acquiring public ownership of land, giving the state the capacity as landowner to prohibit or restrict access and activities. Alternatively, the police power of the state may be used to regulate human activities on both publicly and privately owned land. Common law countries tend to prefer the approach of public ownership and strongly protect owners of private property. In contrast, most civil law countries utilize police powers to regulate and conserve nature. Most laws establish the conditions under which compensation must be paid to the landowner of property that falls within a newly created protected area. In Norway, for example, land taken for a nature reserve or natural monument must be compensated because further use of the land is prohibited, whereas land included in national parks or protected landscape areas is not compensated, because the owner generally may continue to inhabit and use the land.

Legislation creating protected areas generally describes the various categories of areas, with clear indications of their boundaries, and specifying the restrictions and prohibitions imposed with respect to each of them. The law usually also designates or creates the management authority or authorities and establishes enforcement measures and penalties.

Legislative regulation of activities generally either prohibits all activities unless specifically authorized, or lists prohibited activities. In the latter case, laws often state that the list is non-exhaustive and that all other activities are prohibited that would undermine or cause detriment to the protection of the area. Some activities may be specifically permitted; in addition it is not uncommon for the law to delegate discretion to the management authority to allow variance or exemptions from the restrictions imposed. In particular, the authority may permit access to restricted areas for purposes of scientific research. In Catalonia, for example, the law of 30 March 1988 concerning Aigues Tortes National Park, allows a permit to be granted for prohibited activities, in exceptional cases for reasons of public interest, provided that it has been expressly shown that there is no other viable solution, and provided mitigating measures are taken. In general, authorized exceptions should require an environmental impact assessment. In Greece, the 1986 Environmental Protection Act provides that decrees creating protected areas may require EIAs in respect of activities that otherwise would be exempt from them. A Directive of the EC on the protection of natural habitats makes EIAs mandatory for a wide range of projects when these are undertaken in Special Areas of Conservation or areas pertinent to the directive on the conservation of wild birds.

Many laws provide for the establishment of buffer zones around, but constituting an integral part of, protected areas. They create a transition between the protected area of prohibited activities and the outside world. Special controls govern the buffer zone. For example, in Spain, construction is generally prohibited around national parks. Spain also creates zones around the buffers. In these "zones of influence" special measures, such as prohibiting the use of pesticides, may be taken for the protection of waters flowing into the protected area. Similarly, the Swedish Water Act calls for denying permits for proposed activities upstream of a national park or nature reserve when the activity will result in damage to the protected area.

Some laws go further and establish general principles for the protection of parks and reserves against outside activities. The German Nature Protection Act of 1976 provides that all actions that may lead to the destruction of, or cause damage to, or induce changes in a nature reserve, a national park or natural monument shall be prohibited pending more specific provisions to be adopted.

The number of sites and amount of protected land varies enormously. In France, 95 per cent of the territory is not built up, but the overwhelming amount is cultivated or exploited. Natural sites account for approximately 10 per cent of the open spaces, but number about 7,500. Approximately 9.1 per cent of the total area of Iceland is found in 72 protected sites, while in Norway the figure is about 5.6 per cent. Danish law is perhaps the most complete. Nearly all natural or semi-natural sites existing in the country are protected by law and authorization is required for all activities, including agriculture. Although authorizations are often granted, the existence of the law tends to discourage applications clearly incompatible with the concept of protection. In addition, the authorizations often are accompanied by restrictions or conditions aimed at preventing serious harm to the environment. Since 1985, an EC regulation on improving agricultural efficiency permits EC member states to provide financial assistance to farmers in areas designated as "environmentally sensitive" who practice agricultural methods compatible with preserving the natural environment. Great Britain has implemented the regulation, designating the appropriate zones and concluding agreements with farmers, who seem generally supportive of the policy.

## b. Types of Protected Areas

Traditionally, protected areas have been referred to as nature parks or nature reserves, although legislation and treaties today often use other names. Efforts at harmonizing the use of terminology have been generally unsuccessful. However, all protected areas share some of the same characteristics: prohibiting or limiting human activities, or even denying human access in order to remain uninhabited and, as much as possible, undisturbed. In addition, certain activities may be regulated regardless of the designation of the area where the activity is planned; for example, in some states construction of all ski lifts, buildings, parking lots, and depots must have prior permits; garbage may be deposited only in designated places, and tents, trailers, or camping cars may be placed only in camping sites.

There are five common types of protected area:

1. Nature reserves (*Naturschutzgebiete*) are generally subject to the strictest regulation. These are areas of special beauty or unique features, or are the habitats of rare or endangered flora or fauna. Their primary purpose is to protect the habitats of wild flora and fauna. They are placed under state control and their boundaries may not be altered except by legislation. Within such reserves it is strictly forbidden to hunt, fish, or exploit any of the resources or to perform any act likely to harm or disturb the fauna or flora. It is likewise prohibited to alter the

configuration of the soil or pollute the water. All human presence, including overflight, requires prior permission of the competent national authority. France has created 104 nature reserves under the authority of article 16 of the 1976 Nature Protection Act, as well as numerous other kinds of reserves: hunting, fishing, protection of biotopes, private, national parks, and regional nature parks. There also are areas in "permanent state of alert".

2.  National parks are the oldest form of protected area. Hiking and recreation areas, such as those established under the Recreation Act of Finland, are similar in nature. Parks are placed under state control and in most cases can have their boundaries changed only by legislation. They are areas set aside exclusively for the propagation, protection, conservation and management of vegetation and wild animals, as well as for the protection of sites and landscape. France has seven national parks, mostly found in mountainous regions, more easily protected due to lack of accessibility and the relatively limited population. However, the public is admitted for recreational purposes and fishing or hunting may be permitted.

3.  Game preserves or sanctuaries are established for the conservation, management and propagation of wild animal life and the protection and management of its habitat. Hunting and capturing animals is regulated by the reserve authorities. Other human activities, including settlement, are controlled or prohibited. In Cyprus, regulations enacted in July 1989 under the Fisheries Law provide protection to the main turtle beaches as a turtle preserve. Two species of marine turtle found to be declining in numbers use the beaches as breeding grounds. Boats and fishing are prohibited in the area and the public is not allowed on the beaches at night. No vehicles, sunbeds or umbrellas are permitted. Similarly, under the Nature Protection Act of 1976, French prefets may issue orders for the preservation of areas that are the habitat of listed protected species of animals or plants (*arrêtes de protection de biotope*). These orders may prohibit or restrict any activity that is liable to affect the habitats concerned. More than 150 such orders have been issued so far.

    Sanctuaries often are created by administrative regulation, due to the need for rapid action. In addition to the examples of France and Cyprus, Norway provides in its Nature Conservation Act that biotope reserves and bird sanctuaries can be created in places of major importance to flora or fauna, without fulfilling the legal requirements of the four main types of protected area (national parks, protected landscape areas, nature reserves and national monuments).

4.  Natural monuments (*Naturdenkmaeler*) are zones of particular scenic beauty or historical or cultural value. They may be trees, waterfalls, rock formations or fossils. In the Netherlands, natural monuments can be designated by administrative order on both public and private land under the Nature Conservation Act of 1967. Damaging a natural monument is illegal but private landowners may apply for a permit to conduct prohibited activities.

5.  Wilderness reserves (*Naturparks*) are a relatively new designation for certain protected areas. A wilderness may be defined as a large roadless area of

undisturbed vegetation where most human activities are prohibited. Wildernesses generally remain open for hiking and camping, without having developed campsites. Hunting and fishing are permitted in some areas. Permits are usually required for entry or for overnight camping. In Finland, the Wilderness Act of 1991 designated a total area of about 1.5 million hectares of land (4.4 per cent of the country) as wilderness areas, most of it in Lapland. Mining and permanent roads are prohibited as is the construction of buildings other than for traditional uses by indigenous persons. In Italy, mountains about the 1,600-metre line are protected from quarrying, building and road construction.

In addition to the five traditional types of reserves, the United Kingdom has a category of "sites of special scientific interest". They may be the subject of Nature Conservation Orders to protect them for twelve months. When such sites are identified by the Nature Conservancy Councils for England and Scotland or the Countryside Council for Wales, notification is given to the Minister competent for the region concerned and to the owner or occupier of the land, specifying what activities or operations are likely to damage the fauna, flora or other features sought to be conserved. Any proposed activity needing a permit will require consultation with the Nature Conservancy Council.

Certain types of habitats and landscapes may be specifically protected without being designated a protected site. As with the protection of animals, early regulation often was based on sustainable use of natural resources. For example, a Danish Royal Decree issued in 1805 imposed a duty on owners of forests to maintain, improve and conserve them. The impetus was a need to provide timber for naval purposes. Today, forests are recognized as crucial for regulation of water, prevention of erosion and provision of habitats for wild fauna. As a result, the laws of many countries are undergoing reform, to stress conservation as well as timber production. A 1985 amendment to the United Kingdom Forest Act mandates that the Forestry Commission seek to achieve a reasonable balance between timber production and nature conservation. Both Swedish and Spanish law contain similar provisions.

Recent legislation also tends to provide protection to natural forests by prohibiting clear cutting of indigenous woodlands. Other laws permit cutting, but require replanting with native species. As early as 1902, the Swiss Forest Act established that the forest area of the country could not be diminished, that any clearing of forests or wooded areas requires a permit and either afforestation or reforestation of an equivalent area. A 1991 revised Act provides explicitly for the preservation of forests as a natural environment. Any clearing will be granted only for exceptional, important reasons; financial considerations are an insufficient reason. Clear-cutting is prohibited, as is the use of pesticides. The law applies to both public and private lands.

The Forest Zones Protection Act of Finland is perhaps the most comprehensive law on forests. It seeks to prevent the erosion of northern forest areas by protecting the zones where each species of tree grows. Should the protection lead to a lack of household wood, the state must compensate the homeowners. The same Act foresees the establishment of protected forest zones in the Finnish archipelago, along the shoreline and in all places where the forest has remained a shelter for settlement, agriculture, and habitats against wind and erosion. The protected forests are delimited independently of ownership and no compensation is due. Third, the Act forbids cutting wood close to the waterline of lakes, rivers, and the sea, if the trees provide spawning grounds for fish. No exceptions are provided to the ban on cutting.

## 3. Comprehensive and Integrated Protection

Increasingly, efforts to protect wild fauna and flora are using a comprehensive approach that combines most of the methods described above and tends to general protection of biotopes (flowing bodies of water, wetlands, dry, unfertilized grasslands) under the heading "integrated protection of nature". In international law, the UN Convention on Biological Diversity, opened for signature 5 June 1992, provides an example. The Convention seeks to protect biological diversity and sustainable development through principles of management, elaboration of conservation strategies, creation of protected zones, and monitoring. It treats the problem of the introduction of exotic species and issues arising from biotechnology.

Earlier regional agreements also adopt this approach. The Convention on the Conservation of European Wildlife and Natural Habitats (Bern, 19 September 1979), reflects many modern concepts of nature conservation. It refers to wild flora and fauna as a natural heritage of intrinsic value that must be preserved and handed on to future generations and emphasizes the importance of conserving natural habitats as one of the essential elements of conservation. The Convention also stresses the need for states to cooperate in conserving species and habitats where the problems posed are transfrontier in nature. All states parties are obliged to take measures to maintain populations of wild flora and fauna at a level which corresponds to "ecological, scientific and cultural requirements, while taking account of economic and recreational requirements and the needs of sub-species, varieties or forms at risk locally" (article 2). Particular attention must be paid to endangered and vulnerable species and habitats. Similarly, special protection is given to fragile habitats, listed in two appendices, and to those of migratory species, including areas of wintering, staging, feeding, breeding or moulting.

Chapter III of the Convention is devoted to the protection of species. It underlines the importance of conserving flora and lists in Appendix I those species strictly protected, for which article 5 prohibits picking, collecting, cutting, or uprooting. Prohibition of sale or possession is left to the discretion of the contracting parties. A second Appendix lists wild animals that are protected by article 6, which prohibits deliberate capture and killing, damage to or destruction of breeding or resting sites, deliberate disturbance during particularly vulnerable times (breeding, rearing, hibernation), the deliberate destruction or taking or possession of eggs from the wild, even if empty, and the possession of and internal trade in these animals, alive or dead, and any recognizable part or derivative of them. Special provisions regarding migratory species add a duty on range contracting parties to coordinate their efforts to protect these species and to coordinate their protective measures, such as those establishing closed seasons.

A third Appendix to the Convention protects vulnerable species whose exploitation is regulated through national laws which should include closed seasons, temporary or local prohibition of exploitation, and restrictions on trade in specimens. Indiscriminate means of capture and killing and means capable of causing local disappearance or disturbance are forbidden.

Contracting parties may adopt stricter conservation measures than those provided under the Convention, but also may make exceptions to the provisions for reasons of public health and security, air safety or other overriding public interests, to prevent serious damage to crops, livestock, forests, fisheries, water and other property, for purposes of research and education, repopulation, reintroduction and breeding, and for the taking, keeping or "judicious exploitation" of certain wild animals and plants. Contracting parties must submit biannual reports on the exceptions they invoke to a standing committee composed of representatives of the contracting parties, including the EC. The standing committee is generally responsible for monitoring the treaty's application, making recommendations to contracting parties on measures to be taken for its implementation, sometimes following information received from individuals or NGOs. It also may propose the conclusion with third states of agreements that would enhance the effective conservation of species or groups of species, and keeps under review the Convention and its appendices, to examine whether modifications are necessary.

Towards the end of November 1991, the European states containing parts of the Alpine region, together with the European Community, adopted a comprehensive Convention on Protection of the Alps.[9] Article 2 establishes the general obligations of contracting parties. They are to maintain a comprehensive policy of protection and preservation of the Alps, equitably considering the interests of all Alpine states and the Community in using resources wisely and exploiting them in a sustainable way. The principles of prevention, cooperation, and polluter-pays are to be respected, with particular emphasis on expanding transfrontier cooperation in the interest of the Alps.

The comprehensive nature of the Convention and its concern with integrated protection are reflected in the listing of subjects regarding which states are to take appropriate measures: population and culture; regional management; air quality; soil preservation; regulating waters; protection of nature and preservation of scenery; mountain agriculture; mountain forestry; leisure and tourism; transportation; energy; and waste (article 2[2]). Particular goals or objectives are stated for each of these domains. For example, measures regarding air quality are to be taken "with a view towards obtaining a drastic reduction of polluting emissions and their harms in the Alpine region, including transboundary pollution affecting the region, in such a way as to arrive at a rate that is not harmful to humans, flora or fauna" (article 2[2][c]).

For each of the listed subjects, the parties also agree to cooperate in and harmonize research and scientific study, establish shared or complementary systematic

<hr />

[9] Convention on the Protection of the Alps, done at Salzburg, 7 November 1991, 31 I.L.M. 767 (1992). The signing states were Austria, France, Germany, Italy, Liechtenstein, Switzerland and Yugoslavia. The European Community also signed. The status of the former Yugoslavia, Slovenia and Croatia is not discussed.

monitoring, and collaborate in legal, scientific, economic and technical fields. A Conference of the Contracting Parties is established to meet regularly to discuss common issues and means of cooperation, as well as to consider reports from states parties on implementing measures they have taken. The Conference also may adopt amendments, protocols, annexes and financial measures.

A Permanent Committee, composed of delegations of the Contracting Parties, is established as the Convention's executive organ. Among its powers, the Committee will determine the participation of non-governmental organizations, analyze information in state reports, collect relevant information, monitor compliance with decisions of the Conference, examine draft protocols, and propose measures and recommendations to the Conference. Although comprehensive, the Convention is clearly designed as a framework Convention with the intention that further measures be adopted through protocols and annexes.

### 4. Implementation

The effectiveness of measures for the protection of nature remains difficult to assess. Efforts by CITES to protect the elephant and some other endangered species appear to have met with success in the short term.[10] On the other hand, studies by the European Community in regard to its Directive on the Conservation of Wild Birds are not encouraging. In a 1991 report, the Community noted that no state has implemented the directive through a single legislative or regulatory act, in part because nature protection is often regionalized or decentralized (Germany, Belgium, Spain, Italy and the United Kingdom). Even in France, annual norms concerning hunting are taken in part at the departmental level.

Hunting regulations, dating from earlier periods, have not always been adapted to the requirements of the Community directive on birds, in part due to pressure from hunting and fishing associations. As a result, the Commission has opened procedures for partial non-conformity with the directive against the majority of member states. Germany and the Netherlands have been subject to two judgments of the Court of Justice for incompatibility of several provisions of their national legislation. Thus far, the necessary modifications have not been made. In total, the Commission has opened some twenty procedures against hunting rules and practices which in its view fail to conform to the requirements of the directive.

Failure to comply with the bird directive constitutes the most important problem of compliance among EC environmental measures. The directive foresees that states members designate habitats for particularly threatened bird species and that they take inside these habitats specific conservation measures. The habitats as a whole should combine to form a coherent European resource, susceptible to assure the conservation and survival of birds. Since 1979, only about six hundred habitats have been designated, while the Commission estimates that twice that number are needed. According to the Commission, only Belgium and Denmark have fully fulfilled their obligations on this particular point.

10 See Kiss and Shelton, *International Environmental Law* (1991) pp. 262–3.

Complaints to the Commission generally concern two situations: either an insufficient number of designated zones or the destruction of habitat due to an economic activity (agricultural, industrial, urban, tourist, etc.). The balance of economic interests and environmental requirements is presented in nearly every case. Finally, the reports required to be filed by states members on application of the directive are found to be so general that they permit virtually no control or verification of whether the terms of the directive have been respected.

With increasing regulation aimed at protecting biological diversity, attention must be given to determining whether the legal techniques that have been developed are adequate and effective to achieve the desired goal. It seems likely that there will be different answers in regard to different situations. Techniques that work in one case may prove ineffective in another. Continued evaluation and monitoring are necessary to this determination.

## 5. *Biotechnology*

Developments in biotechnology have provoked a growing number of questions concerning the impact of genetic alterations on biological diversity. The 1992 UN Convention on Biological Diversity defines biotechnology to include any technological application that utilizes biological systems, living organisms, or derivations of them, to create or modify products or processes to a specific use. One of the most controversial subjects concerning this science is the potential hazard associated with the handling and introduction into the environment of genetically modified organisms (GMOs).

The need to promote biosafety has centred on two related issues: first, the handling of GMOs at the laboratory level, in order to protect workers and prevent the accidental liberation of such organisms into the surrounding ecosystem ("contained use"); second, the need for regulatory systems to govern the deliberate release of GMOs into the environment, either for testing purposes or on a commercial scale.

Genetic engineering has reached the point where living organisms can be adapted in the laboratory. Of course, many genetically modified organisms (GMOs) are not intended to stay in the laboratory. For example, research is being carried out to introduce herbicide resistance into virtually all major crops as a means of making it easier to control weeds. In addition, because of the noxious effects of long-term pesticide use, genetic engineering of micro-organisms has developed as an alternative strategy to improve pest control. Some one hundred fungus species and many bacterium species are known to have insecticidal effects. Research is being carried out to improve these effects. However, current technology generally is limited to the transfer of single genes coded to develop specific resistance traits (e.g. colour). A narrow resistance pattern could increase crop vulnerability as pests develop means to overcome the uniform trait, thus further reducing biodiversity.[11]

[11] Of course, breeding for specific traits has long been widely practised in agriculture for both livestock and plants, as well as by owners and breeders of dogs and cats. Biotechnology enlarges the possible scope and rapidity with which particular traits can be introduced.

Finally, the area that has received the most publicity involves the use of biotechnology to raise crop yields, including broadening the germplasm basis from which new genetic combinations can be created and improving and speeding up the propagation of plants. The most widely used and commercially successful application of plant biotechnology is the rapid and large-scale multiplication of plants through clones produced in tissue culture. The technique is currently used to mass-produce ornamental, fruit, vegetable, medicinal plant and tree species. A substantial number of scientists urge caution in releasing genetically engineered organisms, because of the possibility that such organisms might have an unfavourable impact upon the environment and because considerable scientific uncertainty exists about the scope and degree of environmental risk. There is fear that the GMOs, as living organisms, could evolve into destructive pathogens. Moreover, genetically altered genes may naturally transfer to wild-grown relatives, with unforeseeable consequences. Particular concern is expressed about GMOs released in or close to a centre of genetic diversity of that crop. Mass production of identical plant materials introduces greater danger of genetic destruction because all specimens are equally vulnerable to a single disease or pest. No resistant varieties remain as alternative sources. The widespread use of cloned crops or artificial seeds to replace sexually reproducing crops will thus likely increase crop vulnerability.

Finally, the release of genetically modified micro-organisms (bacteria and fungi) could pose particular problems. Very little is known about microbial communities; few have been named or studied. However, current research indicates that natural genetic transfer between different micro-organisms is relatively frequent, making it conceivable that engineered species could transfer throughout the microbial world in unforeseeable ways.

Other scientists see biotechnology as permitting them to pursue plant breeding efforts, with favourable impact on food supplies, international trade in agricultural products, the environment and existing plant resources. However, the commercial nature of many of these potential benefits provides another source of conflict, more directly related to economic development. This concerns who should have access to, control of, and benefits from genetic resources.

In the past twenty years, genetic manipulation has come under strong regulation and control. The first national guidelines for biosafety dealt primarily with contained use. More recently, efforts have been made to regulate the deliberate release of GMOs into the environment, based on concern that the modified organisms could cause unforeseeable ecological damage. Most developed countries have established, or are establishing, national regulatory guidelines for safety in handling recombinant DNA at the experimental stage. In addition, guidelines for the deliberate release of GMOs into the environment during field testing, based on OECD recommendations, also exist in several countries. The first standards were Guidelines for Research Involving Recombinant DNA Molecules, adopted in 1976 by the United States National Institute of Health. The Guidelines created a national Recombinant DNA Advisory Committee with specified minimum memberships of scientists and persons knowledgeable in law, standards of professional conduct and practice, public attitudes, the environment, public health, occupational health, and related fields. Each institution conducting GMO research was required to organize an Institutional Biosafety Committee, whose members would have the capability to assess the safety of recombinant DNA research activities and any potential risk to public health or the environment. At least two members of the Committee had to be independent of the institution. Certain deliberate releases required the approval of both the committees mentioned, as well as the National Institute of Health. The rules are binding on all institutions receiving NIH funding.

A similar approach was adopted by the UK, which created an Advisory Committee on Genetic Manipulation. The Committee issued voluntary guidelines for free release in 1986 and has established a subcommittee to review other releases. The Environmental Protection Act 1990, part VI, adds new regulations concerning genetically modified organisms. France and Germany also have committees that must be consulted before a release, but their guidelines are not yet developed.

While drawing on common principles, national regulations differ in several respects and reflect varying levels of public concern over the potential risks of biotechnology. In large part the controls represent application of the precautionary principle, because the risks to health and the environment are not yet known.

The European Community issued directives in 1990 providing a lengthy series of control procedures both for laboratory research and for release of GMOs. The first Council directive[12] enunciates principles of good microbiological practice for operations concerning micro-organisms inside laboratories. The exposure of the work place and the environment to all physical, chemical or biological agents should be maintained at the lowest possible level; measures of technical control at the source should be taken, measurement means and control instruments should be tested and maintained in good state and measures of confinement should be regularly reviewed by the user. The latter should proceed with laboratory uses only after prior assessment from the point of view of risks that these could present for human health and the environment. A register of work completed should be maintained and presented on demand to competent authorities. In case of accident, the authority should be immediately informed and the state where the accident takes place should take the appropriate emergency measures and alert any other state which could be affected by the accident, as well as the European Commission. The latter should also receive, at the end of each year, a synthesis report on laboratory uses.

The second EC directive,[13] adopted the same day, concerns the voluntary release of genetically modified organisms into the environment. It also applies to the market entry of products consisting of such organisms or containing them, that are intended to be voluntarily released. Member states should take all appropriate measures to avoid negative effects that could result from such operations for human health or for the environment. Any person who intends to proceed to the release of such micro-organisms must send a notification to the competent authority accompanied by a technical file containing necessary information as well as an evaluation of the

---

[12] Council Directive 90/219/EEC of 23 April 1990, O.J. no. L 117, 8 May 1990.
[13] Council Directive 90/220/EEC of 23 April 1990, O.J. no. L 117, 8 May 1990.

foreseeable risks and a declaration evaluating the impact on health and on the environment. Any operation of release requires the prior written consent of the competent authority. The latter should also give its consent to any placing of GMOs on the market. If the opinion is favourable, the file is sent to the Commission, which, in turn, informs all the competent authorities in member states and decides if placing the product on the market is permitted.

Efforts to implement the directives in France are contained in a bill introduced in the National Assembly on 25 May 1992. It requires a prior public investigation before certain research projects can go forward using GMOs. A strong debate ensued between those who favour the amendment as a democratic means for the public to be informed about genetic engineering and some scientists who object to the measure as putting the brakes on medical progress and innovation. Objection centres on the requirement of public discussion regarding laboratory activities. The French law would provide that any use of GMOs for research, development or teaching in a public or private institution and any placing for sale of products derived from them requires prior approval. Any change in the conditions of use requires a second approval. Conditions are based upon the risks posed by the organisms. Type I, deemed to pose no risk, requires no special precautions, while other organisms can be employed only in strictly regulated conditions of confinement and decontamination. Most controversial is the proposed prior assessment of all laboratories that have not used GMOs previously. The assessment would be based upon a report prepared by the laboratory and would be made available to the public for a period of one month. Scientists object that this threatens their research.

At the international level, there are, as yet, no internationally-accepted biosafety standards. However, efforts are underway, due to concern that GMOs released in one country could multiply and transfer their genes to plants in other countries. In addition, countries with weak legislation could become testing sites for experiments forbidden elsewhere, presenting health and environmental hazards.

Since 1985, an informal *ad hoc* working group on safety in biotechnology, composed of UNEP, WHO, UNIDO, and FAO, has reviewed the current situation regarding biosafety, particularly in the laboratory and during research. It has not yet made specific recommendations. The FAO Commission on Plant Genetic Resources also is involved in this issue. At its Third Session, in April 1989, it requested FAO to draft a Code of Conduct for Biotechnology, as it affects the conservation and use of plant genetic resources, in cooperation with other relevant international organizations. The development of the Code of Conduct, endorsed in principle, is on the FAO agenda for 1993.

The UN Convention on Biological Diversity contains few obligations in regard to biotechnology safety. Pursuant to article 19(3), the parties will examine whether it is useful, perhaps by protocol, to take measures and establish procedures, including prior informed consent, concerning the transfer, retention and utilization in complete security of any modified living organism resulting from biotechnology that risks having unfavourable effects on the conservation and sustainable use of biological diversity. Article 19(4) requires each state party to communicate, or to have communicated by private parties, all information concerning the utilization or safety measures necessary or imposed by the state in regard to the manipulation of GMOs, as well as all available information on the potentially harmful impact of specific organisms to be introduced into another state party.

Finally, it should be recalled that the Council of Europe Convention on Civil Liability for Damages Resulting from the Exercise of Activities Dangerous for the Environment specifically covers damage caused by genetically modified organisms.[14]

## B. Case Studies

### 1. Jean Gottesmann, *Nature Conservation Legislation in Switzerland: Protected Species and Areas*

"Protection of species" refers to preserving endangered species from extinction by appropriate remedial action, including law. Objects of protection are species of plant and animal life, important in preserving the balance of nature and/or which provide especially favourable conditions for biological communities. The goal is therefore to protect whole species and biological communities rather than individual plants and animals.

Swiss law protects not only species themselves, but also biotopes (habitats), the homogeneous living spaces required for the survival of specific species of plants and animals. Article 24(6) of the Swiss Federal Constitution contains various regulations designed to protect biotopes, with paragraph 4 providing the basis for enforcement measures. In addition, an article concerning nature conservation and the preservation of areas of natural beauty was adopted into the Federal Constitution on 27 May 1962. Implementing the Constitution, the Nature Protection Law (NPL, in force 1 January 1967) imposes a general obligation on the Federal government to conserve nature and preserve areas of natural beauty and a specific obligation to designate biotopes of national importance and specify goals to be set in their protection (Art. 18a NPL). The Cantons are required to protect areas of regional and local importance having the character of biotopes (Art. 18b NPL). Other specific protection is provided under Art. 21 of the NPL (shoreline vegetation) and Art. 24(6) para. 5 of the Federal Constitution (moors and moor landscapes of particular beauty and national importance).

The NPL covers nature protection in general in a broad manner and does not provide a complete legal codification. Other fields of law have regulations deemed of equal importance. This division into various legal fields raises problems of interpretation. The following summary is intended as a guide to the different regulations in force.

---

[14] See *supra*, Chapter III.

### a. Flora and Fauna

— *Protected species*

The Federal Constitution, article 24(6) para. 4, authorizes the Federal Government to adopt regulations for the protection of flora and fauna. The Federal Legislature has used this authority on behalf of species by establishing standards in four areas. Art. 18, para. 1 of the NPL prescribes measures to prevent the extinction of indigenous plant and animal life through the conservation of adequate living spaces (biotopes) and other means. Due allowance is made for the interests of agriculture and forestry. Under art. 20 of the NPL, the Federal Council may forbid, either totally or in part, the selling, buying or destruction of rare plants. The Council is also authorized to take all necessary precautions in order to protect certain threatened or otherwise protection-worthy animal species. Each canton may, within its own territory, prohibit the destruction of other species. The cantonal authority can make exceptions in determined areas to permit collecting and digging out protected plants and capturing animals for scientific, educational and medical purposes.

The nature protection decree (NPD), which was revised on 16 January 1991 and entered into force on 1 February 1991, for the first time contains explicit measures implementing the Bern Convention of 19 September 1979 on the Conservation of European Wildlife in their Natural Habitats. Unauthorized persons are forbidden to pick, dig out, tear out, carry off, offer for sale, sell, buy or destroy, especially through technical means, some fifty species of plants growing naturally.[15] Forty-nine species of animals are protected, in addition to the animals mentioned in the Federal Hunting Law (HL) of June 1986.[16] In order to prevent the extinction of protected animals and plants, Art. 13 of the NPD provides that measures to conserve their biotopes should involve an adapted type of agricultural and forestry activity. Together with regulations for the protection of species (Art. 20 NPD) and for ecological/biological compensation (Art. 15 NPD), these measures provide for the continuation of flora and fauna in their natural environment.

The ecological compensation measures (Art. 18b(2) NPL) are designed in particular to connect isolated biotopes with one another, if necessary through the creation of new biotopes. The law is also intended to promote diversity of species and, as much as possible, the natural and careful exploitation of the soil; to introduce nature into built-up and settled areas; to integrate it with them as much as possible, and to enhance the beauty of the landscape. The Federal Office for Environment, Forests and the Landscape (BUWAL) publishes "Red Lists" of endangered and rare plant and animal species.[17]

The Federal Law on hunting and the protection of mammals and birds of June 1986 (HL) is intended to preserve the diversity of species and the biotopes of

---

[15] Art. 20, para. 1, and the list contained in appendix 2 to the NPD.
[16] Art. 20, para. 2, and the corresponding list in appendix 3 of the NPD.
[17] Art. 14, para. 3, NPD.

indigenous and migratory mammals and birds in their natural environment.[18] The Act covers birds, beasts of prey, ungulates, rabbits and hares, beavers, ground hogs and squirrels.[19] Art. 5(1) sets forth twenty-eight species which may be hunted together with the open and closed season for each. Eleven species of wild duck are protected while seven species may be hunted throughout the year.[20]

Finally, there is the Bern Convention of 19 September 1979 on Conservation of European Wildlife and Natural Habitats, which came into force for Switzerland on 1 June 1982. Amendments to the Convention's appendices II and III, adopted 11 December 1987, entered into force in Switzerland on 12 March 1988. The Convention contains regulations which are indirectly and directly applicable. To the latter category belong the three appendices listing protected species. These regulations have the force of domestic law.

### — Hunting

Article 25 of the Federal Constitution vests competence in the federal authorities to issue regulations on fishing and hunting, particularly for the conservation of large game animals such as deer and the protection of seeds useful to agriculture and forestry. The rule assigns competence which needs to be implemented through local legislation. The cantons may establish their own regulations, provided the Federal Government has not acted in this respect.

The Federal Government has made use of its powers to specify the prerogatives of the cantons with regard to hunting regulations. Originally, control of local hunting rights belonged to magistrates and feudal landowners. This authority was transferred to the cantonal authorities and now is guaranteed by the Federal Constitution.[21]

The cantons determine the conditions for issuance of the hunting permit or shooting licence, decide the hunting system to be adopted (i.e. ground/tenant hunting or patent hunting), delimit the game preserve and guarantee adequate surveillance.[22] The cantons have the legal obligation to enforce federal law in this respect. Hunting permits are issued by the cantonal authorities subject to the passing of an examination.[23] As already mentioned, Art. 5 of the HL states the open and closed seasons for each species which may be hunted. The cantons can release into the wild animals which may be hunted, as long as they are given an adequate and appropriate living space and sufficient care. Animals which cause great damage or threaten the diversity of indigenous species may not be released. The Federal Council determines the animal species considered suitable for release.[24] Article 8 of a hunting decree designates thirteen species which may not be released. Articles 1 and 2 of the same

---

[18] Art. 1(1) HL.
[19] Art. 2 HL.
[20] Art. 5(2) and 5(3) HL.
[21] Art. 31(2).
[22] Art. 3(2) HL.
[23] Art. 4 HL.
[24] Art. 6 HL.

decree specify the auxiliary means which may and may not be used in hunting. Finally, it should be mentioned that in Switzerland, in contrast to some other countries, hunting rights are not based on permission granted by the landowner.

### — Fishing

The competence of the federal authority to issue fishing regulations also is stated in Art. 25 of the Federal Constitution. The federal law on fishing (FL) of 14 December 1973 regulates the catch and protection of species of fish, crabs and aquatic life in public and private waters.[25] Its aim is to conserve, improve and restore fishing waters, protect them from damage and improve the composition of fish stocks through the protection of highly valued fish species.[26] The cantons have authority under art. 6 FL to grant fishing rights (but without any special privileges) and to determine fishing conditions, e.g. fishing on permit, tenant rights, fishing free-of-charge. The cantons regulate the right to set foot and walk on the shore.[27] The federal authority determines which instruments and methods may be used to catch fish as well as how fishing equipment must be used and which devices and what procedures may be used to take crabs.[28] The federal authority regulates the conservation of fish and crabs[29] as well as the protection of their living spaces.[30] Fishing surveillance is the responsibility of the cantons.[31] Unlike hunting, fishing does not allow entry onto other people's property except for access to the fishing area. Therefore federal legislation regulates the right of access only in the periphery,[32] leaving the rest to the cantons. Regulation of the right of access plays only a small part in cantonal legislation.

### b. Protected Areas

### — Protection of designated areas and reserves

At the national level, Switzerland has a National Park in the Engadine and the Münster valley, in the canton of Grisons.[33] This national nature reserve, with an area of about 170 sq km, protects nature from all human interference and leaves flora and fauna to develop naturally. Art. 1 of the Law on National Parks permits interference only when necessary for administration of the reserve.

Within the cantons and communes, there are approximately fifty forest reservations of about 1,200 hectares as well as many nature reserves, protected either by civil

---

[25] Art. 1(1) FL.
[26] Art. 2 FL.
[27] Art. 7 FL.
[28] Arts. 8, 10(1) and 11 FL.
[29] Arts. 13–21 FL.
[30] Arts. 22–26 FL.
[31] Art. 29 FL.
[32] Art. 7 FL.
[33] The federal law establishing the Park is based on Art. 24(6), paras. 3 and 4, of the Federal Constitution, concerning conservation and protection of areas of natural beauty.

law contracts and servitudes or by Government decrees. Conservation of nature and the protection of areas of beauty is reserved to the cantons by Art. 24(6) para. 1 of the Federal Constitution.

### — Protection of biotopes

Until now, the protection of biotopes could be considered synonymous with the protection of species. However, there is the question of protecting certain types of biotope which are in danger of extinction or in marked retrogression, and which have particular ecological value. In this context, the word "biotope" is synonymous with "ecosystem". Legally, the notion encompasses plant and animal life together with their living spaces and the system of which they are a part.[34]

In Switzerland the protection of biotopes dates from 1 April 1902, when a federal law was passed prohibiting the reduction of the forested area of Switzerland.[35] A Government "forest decree" of 1 October 1965, concerning federal supervision of the forest police, provides that the regional distribution of Swiss forests must be preserved. The regulations mentioned are based on Art. 24(1) of the Federal Constitution, which vests responsibility for supervising the forest police in the federal government.

The entry into force of the NPL established the basis for the protection of natural living spaces of indigenous flora and fauna.[36] Since 1 January 1985, special protection measures apply to shore and marsh areas as well as moors, "exceptional" (rare) forest species, hedges, scrub, dry turf and other areas which play a compensatory role in the balance of nature or provide particularly favourable conditions for biological communities.[37] It is prohibited to remove, cover or damage shore vegetation in any way.[38] Moors and moor landscapes of exceptional beauty and national importance are protected. No construction or soil modification is permitted, except where required to protect the area and the hitherto existing agricultural exploitability.[39]

Since 1 February 1988 the Federal Council is responsible for indicating the biotopes of national importance, based on recommendations of the cantons. It determines the location of the biotopes and establishes goals for their protection.[40] The cantons are responsible for taking measures to protect and maintain the designated biotopes. They take timely action to ensure that the measures are implemented.[41] They are also responsible for the protection and maintenance of biotopes designated to be of regional or local importance (Art. 18b, para. 1 NPL). Likewise, they are responsible for ensuring ecological compensation with scrub growth, isolated

---

[34] Arts. 13–22 NPD.

[35] Art. 31(1) of the Federal Law on federal responsibility for forest surveillance, hereafter referred to as the "forest law".

[36] Art. 1(d) NPL.

[37] Art. 18(1) bis NPL.

[38] Art. 27 NPL.

[39] Art. 24(6), para. 5, of the Federal Constitution – the "Rothenthurm Initiative".

[40] Art. 18a, para. 1, NPL.

[41] Art. 18a, para. 2, NPL.

clumps of trees, hedges, shore tillering (formation of fresh shoots) and other natural and site-compatible vegetation.[42] The Federal fishing law contains additional regulations to protect biotopes.[43]

Among other things, the purpose of the federal hunting law is to maintain and protect the living space of indigenous and migratory mammals and birds and to protect endangered species of animals.[44] The Federal Council, based on recommendations of the cantons, designates protected sites for waterbirds and migratory birds of international and national importance. It also designates those areas in which hunting is prohibited according to a decree on areas in which hunting is prohibited, dated 18 August 1981. The cantons may designate additional areas and bird reservations from which hunting is banned. Conforming to the Ramsar Convention, which came into force in Switzerland on 16 May 1976, appropriate wetlands are designated for inclusion in the list of wetlands of international importance.

The Swiss federal law on territorial planning of 22 June 1979 makes it necessary to designate protected areas for brooks, rivers, lakes and shores as well as living spaces for flora and fauna for which protection is necessary.[45] On 1 February 1991, the inventory of raised bogs of national importance, including transitional moors, became effective.

### — Protection of the landscape

The Federal government has been responsible since 27 May 1962, for the care of the landscape, preserving it intact where the public interest predominates over other considerations.[46] Classification includes designating objects of national, regional and local importance.[47]

Based on recommendations from the cantons, the Federal Council draws up inventories of objects of national importance.[48] For this purpose it can use existing inventories drawn up by Government institutions and private nature conservation associations. Inclusion on an inventory signifies that an object deserves particular attention and full protection, or, in any case, the greatest possible care.[49] Exceptions are allowed only for equal or overriding interests of national importance.[50]

The Federal Law on the use of hydraulic power (LW) of 22 December 1916

---

[42] Art. 18b, para. 2, NPL.

[43] Art. 22: protection of natural shores and the stock of plants; Art. 23: protection of food animals for fish: Art. 24; obligations of persons receiving permission to take action of a technical nature; and Art. 25; preventive measures that must be taken in connection with new installations.

[44] Art. 1, para. 1 (a) and (b) HL.

[45] Art. 17, paras. 1(a) and (d).

[46] Art. 24(6), para. 1 of the Federal Constitution. This principle is also contained in Art. 1(a) and Art. 3(1) NPL.

[47] Art. 4 NPL.

[48] The federal inventory of landscapes and natural monuments (FLN) came into force on 21 November 1977 (Art. 3 FLND) and contains to date 120 objects of protection.

[49] Art. 6(1) NPL.

[50] Art. 6(2) NPL.

establishes the principle that natural aesthetic assets must be cared for and preserved intact and undiminished where the public interest predominates. Hydraulic installations must be carried out in such a way as to minimize disturbance to the landscape.[51]

Under Art. 17, para. 1(b) of the NPL, it is necessary to designate areas of protection for especially beautiful sites and landscapes of natural or cultural value. Since 12 December 1987, moor landscapes have also been objects of protection. The same strict regulations apply to moor biotopes (see protection of biotopes, pp. 145–6).

### c. Issues and Policies

#### — Recent developments

The NPL, in general, has turned out to be too weak to accomplish its assigned goal. In particular it has not corresponded to ecological realities although existing shortcomings have been partly overcome in recent years. The powers of the Government were considerably strengthened by inclusion of Article 24(6) on environmental protection in the Federal Constitution and the passage of an additional environmental protection law and implementing decrees. On 6 December 1987 the so-called Rothenthurm Initiative (people's initiative for the protection of moors) was adopted by referendum against the opposition of the Federal Government and Parliament. Included as Article 24(6) para. 5 in the Federal Constitution, it explicitly protects moors and moor landscapes. The Constitutional amendment was invoked to prevent the creation of an army post in the moor country of Rothenthurm, canton of Schwyz.

An important revision in the NPL, reinforcing the protection accorded to biotopes, was adopted on 1 February 1988. Originally this was a counter-proposal of Parliament to the Rothenthurm Initiative. Since 1 February 1991 new biotope protection regulations have been in force implementing the (revised) NPD and the Law on the protection of raised bogs and transitional moors of national importance.

#### — Trends

Switzerland is expected to soon have a law protecting heavily watered meadows of national importance included in the inventory. The next step will be a law protecting fens of national importance and a law protecting moor landscapes of national importance (all included in the inventory). Finally, a further revision of the NPL and a new federal forest law are in preparation. These measures will considerably strengthen existing legislation and have consequences for territorial planning.

#### — Public opinion and the media

The developments referred to above reflect increased public awareness of the importance of nature conservation and protection of wildlife. The surprising success of the Rothenthurm Initiative has triggered considerable activity and new legislation.

---

[51] Art. 22 LW.

Media-sponsored public opinion polls show that environmental protection in the broadest sense is of primary concern in people's minds.

### — Implementation of international agreements

On 19 June 1975 the Swiss Federal Assembly approved the 1972 UNESCO Convention on protection of the world's natural and cultural heritage and the 1971 Ramsar Convention, which protects wetlands of international importance. It authorized the Federal Council to ratify the two agreements. On 19 August 1981 the Federal Council issued a very detailed regulation on the protection of species, in execution of CITES. On 16 June 1975 the Federal Department of Political Economy issued a control decree and on 20 October 1980 a decree regulating standards for scientific equipment. Both of these measures implement the Convention on the protection of species. As previously mentioned, the revised NPD, in force since 1 February 1991, executes the Bern Convention of 9 September 1979.

### — Delay in execution

As a federal state, Switzerland leaves nature conservation and protection of areas of beauty to the cantons. The Federal Government supports this activity through large subsidies, in proportion to the financial means and requirements of the respective cantons.[52] The cantons are responsible in practice for the execution of Federal laws and decrees.[53] As a result there is danger of differing interpretations of federal laws by the cantons. In recognition of this, the Confederation for the first time has introduced a unified regulation for execution of federal laws and decrees.[54] Under this regulation, the Federal Department of Internal Affairs executes the NPL as long as no other federal authorities are competent to do so. The fact is that execution of the NPL has been lax among both federal and cantonal authorities, due to a lack of personnel and financial means (in an affluent country like Switzerland!) and a lack of will and determination on the part of the responsible authorities. If Switzerland is to be a "model" in respect of environmental preservation, a great deal of work remains to be done in the near future at all levels.

## 2. A. N. van der Zande and A. R. Wolters, *Nature Conservation in the Netherlands*

The Netherlands is a small, densely populated country straddling the estuaries of two large rivers, the Rhine and the Meuse. By the time these rivers reach the Netherlands they are carrying large amounts of pollutants and poisonous substances. Furthermore, the high degree of industrialization and urbanization and the intensiveness of Dutch agriculture impose a heavy burden on nature and the environment. Every square metre of land has been claimed: space is scarce in the Netherlands.

[52] Arts. 4–12 NPD.
[53] Art. 17(1) and Art. 26(1) NPD.
[54] Art. 23(1) NPD, in force 1 February 1991.

In the late 1980s many reports warned of the alarming state of the Dutch environment. The most comprehensive of these was "Concern for Tomorrow", which laid the basis for the National Environmental Policy Plan of 1989. In addition, Queen Beatrix marked a turning point in Dutch thinking about the environment and nature conservation, when, in her celebrated Christmas speech of 1988 she underlined the special responsibility of the present generation and proposed that attention be paid to the "Rights of Nature".

At the end of 1989 the Dutch government published three ambitious "green" plans: The National Environmental Policy Plan, the Nature Policy Plan and the Third National Policy Document on Water Management. National debate about these plans was so intense that it caused the Cabinet to fall, and a new government coalition was formed. In 1990 the government made clear its determination to stand by the proposals in all three plans by adopting them as official government policy.

Current Dutch legislation on nature conservation cannot be understood without knowing the background and the main goals of the Nature Policy plan of the Netherlands. Two concepts are central in any nature conservation policy: area protection and species protection. Each population of a species lives in a certain area, therefore it is important to clarify the intensifying relationship between the legislation protecting areas and the legislation protecting species. In addition, nature conservation policy is an aspect of policy on environmental protection and is dependent on that policy. "Nature" in the Netherlands is part of a European and global ecological system. Dutch nature conservation must therefore be embedded in an international framework. The Netherlands has always been active in international nature conservation conventions and treaties and intends to increase its involvement still more.

The priority issues for future nature conservation legislation need to be identified now. The present situation is quite fluid and many problems require attention. However, it seems that the two problems on which an international forum could most profitably focus are the dilemma between internationalization and devolution, and the challenge of rehabilitating and developing nature ("creative nature conservation") via nature conservation legislation.

Nature conservation and legislation on nature conservation are undergoing a process of "internationalization". Yet concomitantly there are strong pressures in the Netherlands to devolve responsibility for implementing nature conservation policy to regional authorities. A comparable process can be seen in Germany (in the relationship between the federal government and the Länder) and in Belgium. In the UK the Nature Conservancy Council has been split into several regional units. The situation described above gives rise to a dilemma and creates a need to redefine the position of the national authority.

The second challenge facing the Netherlands is the rehabilitation of areas that have value for nature conservation and the creation of "new" nature conservation areas. This so-called nature development policy is examined below, in light of the need for new legislative tools to implement the policy.

### a. The Dutch Nature Policy Plan

The first attempts to conserve nature in the Netherlands were made in 1906, when the Society for the Preservation of Nature in the Netherlands started to purchase and manage valuable and threatened areas. The approach of protecting nature by acquiring the ownership of land also was followed by the National Forest Service. Since World War II the national government has subsidized the purchase of land for nature conservation and management. The protection of areas by legislation also dates from that time. The first system was of *meldings gebieden* (areas in which any threats to nature conservation had to be reported to the President of the National Plan). This system was incorporated into the Physical Planning Act of 1960, which gave local authorities responsibility for handling threats to nature conservation. The authorities had to ensure that local plans adequately protected areas and landscape features deemed important for nature conservation.

The Nature Conservation Act became operational in 1968, after more than forty years of preparation, study and discussion. In the 1970s various areas were designated Protected Nature Monuments or State Nature Monuments under the provisions of this Act. In the 1960s nature conservation efforts were broadened to embrace the countryside as a whole, where the intensification of agriculture was causing a dramatic loss of ecological values (i.e. habitats and species). New means were needed to combat this problem. Three were developed in 1975 and were published in the Memorandum on Agriculture, Nature Conservation and Landscape Protection:

— management agreements between the authorities and individual farmers, for the protection of nature values such as meadow birds;

— the purchase of agricultural land having the highest and most vulnerable nature values;

— maintenance agreements between the authorities and individual farmers and landowners, for the protection of small landscape elements and edges of fields (hedges, turf walls, etc.).

In the mid-1980s it became clear that despite all the efforts at conservation, nature was still deteriorating rapidly in the Netherlands. The extinction of the otter (*Lutra lutra*), a typical Dutch wetland species, was symbolic of the dramatic situation.

An analysis of the successes and failures of Dutch attempts to conserve nature reveals two factors as responsible for the deterioration of nature. The first is the state of the physical environment. Even the largest nature reserves in the country cannot escape the impact of acid deposits, eutrophication, contamination and dehydration caused by a systematic lowering of water tables for agriculture. Internal management cannot compensate for these externally generated changes in the ecosystem. The second factor is the loss and fragmentation of areas of value for nature conservation. The 600,000 ha of land deemed to be of value for nature conservation at the beginning of the century have shrunk to 160,000 ha. The remaining area comprises numerous very small reserves, separated by insurmountable barriers such as roads, canals and urban areas. Many populations of plants and animals will die out in these fragmented habitats if no appropriate measures are taken.

The Dutch government has decided to take two steps to redress the situation:

1. to improve the environment drastically so that by 2010 an acceptable quality is attained for people, plants and animals. The measures needed to achieve this are set out in the national Environmental Policy Plan and the Third National Policy Document on Water Management;

2. to enlarge the fragmented, too small nature reserves (and areas of value for nature conservation) and link them in a national ecological network. This national ecological network and the measures needed to realize it are presented in the Nature Policy Plan.

Clearly, protection alone, though important, is not sufficient to achieve the ecological network. Existing nature reserves can be enlarged and new reserves created only if land can be withdrawn from other forms of land use and favourable ecological conditions can be created for wild flora and fauna. In the Netherlands this new approach is called nature development policy.

Traditionally, land already exhibiting its value as a natural area or wildlife habitat has been acquired for nature conservation. What is new in the current nature development policy is the interest in land which has little or no current value in terms of its "naturalness" or habitat value, but which has a high potential value, for example because of its location in the regional ecohydrological system. Extreme examples can be found in the Netherlands in the area east of the coastal dunes, where bulbs are cultivated intensively and therefore there is little "nature" to conserve. But calcareous groundwater flows out from the dunes, and this makes the area very promising for nature development. The national ecological network consists of core areas, nature development areas and ecological corridors. The sustainability of the network should be guaranteed by the measures made available to implement environmental policy. A buffering policy also will be necessary, to cope with external influences at local and regional levels.

The goals of the Nature Policy Plan will be reached using a variety of means: legislation, recommendations, financial incentives and publicity. It is important not to focus on a single legislative instrument when trying to achieve a goal. Protecting an area by giving it a certain legal status is only one way of creating the conditions and situations necessary for nature conservation. Other means, such as giving grants for certain types of management, or entering into management contracts with specific groups of users, may be more effective or successful. In any case, the effect of the various types of policy instruments at the government's disposal should be evaluated regularly, to establish the optimal mix.

The Nature Policy Plan will be realized by using the following instruments:

— the Nature Conservation Act will be used in a planned and systematic way, in order to protect the relevant parts of the core areas;

— the purchase of land by government and conservation agencies in the core areas and in areas earmarked for nature development will be stimulated;

— a network of National Parks in the core areas will be implemented;

— management agreements between the authorities and individual farmers whose land falls within the network will be given a new stimulus;

— the protection of flora and fauna will receive a new stimulus through species protection plans;

— unorthodox methods of nature conservation such as sponsoring, partnership projects between the public and private sectors and contracts with target groups will be stimulated;

— education and research will be stimulated.

New legislative instruments will have to be created for nature development. The legal status of the policy plan itself will have to be confirmed and plans will have to be prepared annually for its implementation. Areas will have to be allocated for nature development projects.

### b. The Protection of Areas

Protecting areas by owning and managing them is currently (1991) an extremely important part of nature conservation. On 31 December 1990 private nature conservation organizations in the Netherlands were managing 102,000 ha of nature reserves and woodland and 22,200 ha of farmland. The National Forest Service (the government agency responsible for managing nature areas and woodland) was managing 79,000 ha of nature areas, woodlands reserves and farmland.

Statutory protection under the 1968 Nature Conservation Act had an unsteady beginning and was mainly used for urgent situations requiring immediate protection. Only since the mid-1980s has statutory protection been more planned, with the aim of successively designating certain types of habitats. As of 15 October 1991, 231,473 ha had been designated for nature conservation, 150,000 ha of which are in the Dutch part of the Wadden Sea.

The tasks listed in the Nature Policy Plan have clarified the policy framework within which the Nature Conservancy Act operates. The 1992–7 Programme for Nature and Landscape incorporates a medium-term scheme under which more than one hundred areas will be designated for conservation during the five year period. The accent is on habitats of international significance.

This more planned approach makes it easier to harmonize nature conservation with other government policies.

In the mid-1980s a drastic revision of the Nature Conservation Act began. The most important changes envisaged are:

— combining the two categories of area protection;

— switching from lists that only indicate forbidden practices (which required permits) to complete lists that include all such practices;

— clarifying the authority of the central government and of the twelve provinces to designate areas for nature conservation;

— extending the scope of the Act to cover phenomena of cultural and historical value by creating a new conservation category of protection called "protected landscape".

The revision will also accord legal status to the Nature Policy Plan and to the programmes for implementing that Plan. This will be done in order to give the Plan the necessary legal status for its implementation. One important topic being studied but that has not yet been incorporated in the proposal for changes is the obligation to provide compensation in the case of unavoidable damage to a nature monument. Obligatory compensation has been incorporated in the Dutch Forestry Act. However, an important difference between that Act and the Nature Conservation Act is that the Forestry Act gives generic protection to all woodland, whereas the Nature Conservation Act only protects specifically designated areas. Moreover, the underlying philosophy of the Nature Policy Plan is that obligatory compensation must be incorporated in the laws and regulations that control damage to nature, such as the legislation on roads and on excavations.

The problem of external influences on nature has many points in common with the problem of harmonizing the protection of areas and the protection of the environment. This topic is addressed later, as is the problem of allocating responsibility between central government and the provinces.

The intended extension of the Act's scope to cover cultural and historical elements is controversial and raises the question of the extent to which patterns of historical geography can be or already are sufficiently protected by the system of town and country planning (known as "physical planning") operational in the Netherlands. The Physical Planning Act was revised in 1985. It now allows for the land use or zoning plan for an area to include a description of the main features of the historical patterns that are deemed to be quintessential to the area. These patterns thus receive greater attention than previously.

A problem arises because so much Dutch legislation is available to designate areas. A given area can be accorded a special status under several laws: a nature area rich in woodland can be designated as such in a land use plan; it can be designated a protected nature area under the Nature Conservation Act; it is protected by the Forestry Act and the Estates Act of 1928; it can be part of a National Park; and it can be designated as a wetland of international importance under the Ramsar Convention or a special area for conservation under the EC Bird-Directive. The justification for this approach is that the multiple designations form a complementary set of specific aspects of conservation occurring in only one piece of legislation. But the corollary of this argument is that there is much overlap in conservation regimes and the man in the street increasingly is confronted with red tape, perhaps needing several permits to carry out one action. Therefore there is strong pressure in the Netherlands to integrate conservation regimes and to simplify the issue of permits. Conservationists, though, are worried that this process will reduce the effectiveness and stringency of nature conservation.

### c. Protection of Species

In the Netherlands the protection of species has long been provided for in numerous pieces of legislation:

a.  species that are hunted for sport are protected under the Hunting Act;

b.  birds are protected under the Bird Act;

c.  seriously threatened species are covered in the section of the Nature Conservancy Act dealing with species;

d.  the international trade in endangered exotic species is regulated on the basis of the Act on the Protection of Exotic Species and related legislation;

e.  the legislation on fishery covers species that are fished;

f.  pests are covered by the veterinary and plant protection legislation.

Furthermore, until the 1970s the animal or plant was central in nature conservation rather than the quality of the habitat. The proposed Flora and Fauna Act, which appeared in draft late in 1987, attempts to integrate the legislation listed above under a, b, c and d. It is intended to harmonize conservation regimes, the procedures followed in the case of damage, etc. It includes two new aspects: (1) protection of small-scale habitat elements, and (2) regulation of the introduction or reintroduction of species.

Whether there should be a general obligation to care for wild plants and animals is a moot point (as is, to a lesser extent, the obligation to care for nature areas). Such an obligation would institute a mechanism to enable action to be taken against acts that are not specifically forbidden but that have a negative impact on plants and animals. The survival of populations rather than of individuals is a crucial principle in the new legislation. "Wise use" is the motto chosen for this legislation in the Nature Policy Plan.

The Nature Policy plan also makes clear how habitat conservation is to be regulated in a more general sense. A three-pronged approach is proposed for the species, with the highest priority being those on the "Red Lists":

1.  The policy for the national ecological network takes into account the conservation of priority species;

2.  Additional areas may be accorded protection under the Nature Conservancy Act, to benefit species having an important part of their habitat outside the national ecological network;

3.  Under the Flora and Fauna Act smaller elements and structures in the landscape that are important to priority species can also be designated as protected habitats (including badger sets, buildings where bats roost, etc.).

The policy required for managing these priority species is twofold: first, stimulating the necessary regulations via the management plans of the National Forestry Service and subsidized non-governmental organizations; second, giving grants to the general public, farmers, etc., preferably on the basis of plans to protect certain species (e.g. the partridge).

### d. The Relation between Nature areas and Environmental Policy

The preceding paragraphs have made several references to the complex relationship between environmental legislation and nature conservation legislation. There are three important needs:

— conserving the abiotic situation in a protected area;
— safeguarding a protected area against external environmental influences;
— establishing environmental policy norms on the basis of the vulnerability of nature areas and species.

The following aspects are important. More and more protected nature areas are being included in environmental legislation, thereby becoming subject to a certain conservation regime under that particular legislation. This legislation may specifically prohibit certain acts in the designated area, even though they were already forbidden (or could be forbidden) because the area is designated a protected area under the Nature Conservancy Act. Clearly, this gives rise to a complicated situation, and one may ask whether such a double or sometimes even triple system is desirable. If not, the question becomes which legislation or regime must yield. The citizen's desire for a simple integrated system does not necessarily coincide with the interests of conservation.

The situation is even more complex as regards giving areas the necessary protection against influences from "elsewhere". Clearly, carbon dioxide and acid rain operate on such a large scale that their effects cannot be legally regulated from an individual, protected area. But there are local and regional influences that require and allow for a more area-specific approach. This again raises the question of whether the protection should be assured through the Nature Conservation Act or environmental legislation, or both. The Netherlands has opted for both and is attempting to achieve formal legal fine-tuning between both regimes.

Environmental norms are a topic of a very different order and there is not space to do them justice here. In general, the question is to what extent it is desirable to work with one generic national environmental norm rather than with a differentiated set that also includes specific (more stringent) norms directed at ecological values (general environmental quality and exceptional environmental quality). Dutch policy on the environment opts for the least possible differentiation and the most well-defined general environmental quality that also safeguards ecological values (especially those that are vulnerable). But Dutch policy on nature assumes that it is desirable to achieve an exceptional environmental quality for a certain number of types of areas and of species.

Nature-oriented environmental norms will therefore be an important issue in the future.

### e. Dutch Nature Policy and International Policy on Nature

The Netherlands has always been active in international nature conservation, particularly regarding the protection of whales, Antarctica, wetlands, coastal zones and seas, rainforests, the Western Palearctic flyway and, more recently, nature conservation in Central and Eastern Europe. The Netherlands also contributes actively to international treaties like the Ramsar Convention.

Despite this acknowledged and valuable role in international nature policy, the Netherlands has been criticized about its application of international regulations at home. The designation of protected zones under the EC Bird Directive is a case in point.

In 1985 the Dutch government presented a policy document in the Lower House of Parliament relating to the designation and use of areas as wetlands of international importance. The designation policy contained in this document is also the guiding principle for the implementation of other similar international conservation regimes. The crucial principle is that the Dutch government will not designate an area under international law until:

a. the areas have been safeguarded using means available in national legislation (purchase of land, or designation as a protected nature monument);

b. those responsible for the administration of these areas agree about the conservation regime.

Moreover, it is argued that giving international protection to areas that satisfy these criteria must be seen as a recognition of their international value, rather than as imposing an additional or more stringent conservation regime on them. After all, designation as a protected or state nature monument results in a more stringent protection than any international designation. Despite this tenable position the Dutch government decided within a short period to designate twenty more areas, including the Wadden Sea, as special areas of conservation under the EC Bird Directive.

An alternative to the present approach would be to incorporate each of the individual international conservation regimes into Dutch legislation on nature conservation, thereby making them directly binding for the users of these areas. Such an approach is followed in the regulations on agriculture. In the Dutch situation this alternative would have many disadvantages for the aims of nature conservation, creating a proliferation of regulations and little extra protection.

### f. Internationalization and Devolution

In the Netherlands devolution has been in progress for ten years. The principles behind the policy of devolving authority from the central government to the regional authorities (provinces) and, thence, to local authorities are that:

— decision-making should be as near to the citizen as possible;

— the higher tier should perform only those tasks that the lower tier cannot perform;

— because of their scale and type, some tasks can be done more efficiently by a higher (or lower) tier of government.

The devolution of nature conservation has been discussed between the national and provincial governments for almost ten years but was recently intensified. On the other hand the number and power of supranational authorities with nature policies is growing. The Bird Directive and the Habitat Directive are notable examples of this process of internationalization of nature conservation authority within the EC. Both trends influence the authority exerted by the central government.

In the Nature Policy Plan the tasks of the central government are defined in terms of national or international values and responsibilities. The priority habitat types in the national ecological network and the priority species include all those habitats and species that are regarded as having national or international importance. Consequently, the areas and species that are of national or international importance and that require national responsibility must be determined when discussing how tasks should be allocated between the central government and the provinces. The principle suggested here is that the onus is on the central government to prove that a provincial authority cannot do the job adequately. Another principle that was chosen in the case of the Wadden Sea is that the central government is responsible for protecting the area as such, but the three cooperating provinces can be made responsible for the management phase, including issuing (or refusing) the permits for most of the acts that are potentially harmful to the area. In a Europe that is changing, economically and politically, it is important to keep in mind that the question of which authority should impose the protection of nature is less important than protection itself. Nevertheless, it is expected that the question raised above will become more and more important in the near future.

### g. Nature Development as a Challenge

Nature development policy is an increasingly important element in the Netherlands. Many questions arise about the best way to carry out projects involving this new and exciting approach to nature conservation. It is not merely a question of buying the land and financing the necessary measures. In a country like the Netherlands at least a handful of permits is needed to be able to carry out nature development projects. The systems of requiring permits under various laws have also been developed to secure proper procedures so that ecological values and landscapes can be accorded due importance. Now, permits will have to be acquired for nature conservation, the aims of which are in complete contrast with the aims of parties wishing to build houses, roads, or recreational facilities.

In fact, nature development requires a shift in the land use designations contained in the land use plans for urban and rural areas. Some farmers and other land users will oppose nature development projects. There must be a proper procedure for designating nature development areas satisfactorily and rapidly. A two-track system has been chosen in the Netherlands:

— the areas of the national ecological network designated for nature development will be incorporated in the physical planning documents at national, provincial and local level;

— areas designated for nature development will be described accurately on large scale maps, which will be used when purchasing land.

The central government and the twelve Dutch provinces have reached agreement about the planning process, including the financial arrangement to reimburse the provinces for their share of the work. The process of designating areas for nature development is regulated by a ministry directive in which the provinces play a major role, though they must work within the limits of the national plan. There is much debate about whether land for nature development projects should be acquired via voluntary sales or whether land should be acquired by other means (compulsory purchase). In the most complex situations the government uses the Land Development Act to implement nature development projects. This Act, which was drawn up to facilitate land consolidation schemes, has provisions for an exchange of land ownership to enable works to be carried out without the permission of all the individual owners.

It is still too early to assess the merits of the approach described above, as the processes of decision making about individual projects have only recently started. But it has interesting implications and has aroused much enthusiasm among decision makers. The future will show whether it is possible to "create" new nature in a densely populated country like the Netherlands. Nature conservation legislation will certainly receive a strong stimulus from this challenge.

## 3. Antti Haapanen, *Nature Protection in Finland*

Finland is a rich industrialized country which is highly dependent on renewable natural resources. The modern industry has been constructed largely since the Second World War. Forest industries are prevalent, although energy-consuming and requiring great amounts of clean water. Some decades ago hydroelectric power plants played a major role in energy production. Finland has taken major steps in recent years to safeguard its natural heritage.

### a. Protection of Areas

The Nature Conservation Act dates from 1923 and is one of the oldest nature conservation acts in the world. The principles regarding establishment of national parks and other nature reserves are still almost the same as seventy years ago. Special acts are needed to establish national parks or nature reserves larger than 500 hectares. Smaller nature reserves can be established by decrees issued by the president of Finland. These regulations concern state-owned areas. A nature reserve on privately owned areas, including areas owned by local authorities or companies, can be established by a decision of the County Board, i.e., the provincial government. These decisions are made, in principle, forever and are binding on all future owners, even the state. The decision may only be revoked if the nature reserve loses its value as a natural area or if it greatly hampers a project with major common interest. State expropriation of areas for nature conservation has in recent years been used in about ten cases annually.

In 1981 the Nature Conservation Act was amended so that the owner can be compensated for economic losses he or she may have when a nature reserve is established. The compensation is paid once. An agreement between the owner and the nature conservation authorities must be reached before a decision on the nature reserve can be made.

Implementation of the Nature Conservation Act started immediately after it entered into force in 1923. However, it was only in the late 1960s that many nature reserves were established. At the present time there are about 850 nature reserves, mostly on private properties, and 28 national parks (Table 5.1). They cover about 4 per cent of the Finnish territory.

In the late 1960s, nature conservation authorities started systematic planning. The plans aim at safeguarding such unique areas as national parks or different sites like peatlands, eutrophic wetlands, especially rich forest sites, archipelagos in the Baltic Sea or in inland waters. The Council of State has made so-called decisions in principle. These decisions bind all government sectors and indicate to private owners the areas which will be set aside as nature reserves.

It is the task of the nature conservation authorities to carry through the nature conservation plans. So far, about 100,000 hectares of land areas have been bought for nature conservation purposes and the owners of 12,000 hectares have been compensated for their economic losses at a cost of about 1,300 million French francs. To preserve those areas which still need protection will cost some 1,400 million French francs. Shoreline areas are especially expensive.

A special Wild River Act entered into force in 1987. The construction of new hydroelectric power plants is forbidden on the fifty-three rivers or parts of rivers mentioned in the Act. Two similar special Acts concern two other rivers. In addition, two big rivers – one on the Finnish–Swedish border and the other on the Finnish–Norwegian border – are in practice protected. The compensation payable under the Wild Rivers Acts is estimated to cost the government about 300 million French francs.

The Wilderness Act entered into force in 1991. One and a half million hectares on twelve different areas of state-owned land will be kept roadless in northernmost Finland. These areas are used for reindeer-herding and outdoor recreation. Forestry is fairly limited in these areas.

### b. Protection of Species

The Nature Conservation Act applies to the conservation of wild species as well as protected sites. The protection of rare species has long traditions in Finland.

In 1991 an amendment to the Nature Conservation Act entered into force. It states that the Council of State shall decide on those species which are endangered (section 16b) and on those species which are especially protected. The nature conservation authorities have to make special conservation plans for these species. If a land owner is informed that such a species lives on his or her land, the owner must inform the County Board if he or she seeks to change the land use in a way that may be harmful for that particular species. The authorities can then begin negotiations with the owner to guarantee the site. In certain cases the Nature Conservation Act (section 18, subsection 2) can be invoked to forbid such a land use for two years.

Implementation of the new amendment will begin in the coming years. It is already obvious that habitat protection and management is an essential task in the preservation of viable populations of endangered species. Forty per cent of these species require special types of forest sites, in many cases virgin forest areas. Many species occur in man-made habitats produced by old types of land use.

### c. Conclusions

The Finnish experience demonstrates that effective legislation is a prerequisite for the conservation of the Natural Heritage. However, in addition to that, competent officials devoted to the task, public support and political will are as badly needed.

Table 5.1 Legally protected areas in Finland. Situation on 1 April 1991

|  | Number | Land (ha) | Water | Total area |
|---|---|---|---|---|
| National Parks | 27 | 670 528 | 31 450 | 701 978 |
| Strict nature reserves | 19 | 148 764 | 2 925 | 151 789 |
| Peatland protection areas | 173 | 396 807 | 7 253 | 404 060 |
| Wilderness areas | 12 | 1 377 842 | 110 075 | 1 487 917 |
| Protected areas on private land | 884 | 18 579 | 40 283 | 58 862 |
| Protected areas on state-owned land | 28 | 30 729 | 6 149 | 36 878 |
| Total | 1 143 | 2 643 249 | 198 136 | 2 841 385 |

National parks and nature reserves cover 4.0 per cent of the Finnish territory. When wilderness areas are taken into account these areas cover 8.4 per cent.

## C. Documents

*1. Convention on the Conservation of European Wildlife and Natural Habitats*
(Bern, 19 September 1979). E.T.S. 104.

The Member States of the Council of Europe and other signatories hereto,
...
*Recognizing* that wild flora and fauna constitute a natural heritage of aesthetic, scientific, cultural, recreational, economic and intrinsic value that needs to be preserved and handed on to future generations;
*Recognizing* the essential role played by wild flora and fauna in maintaining biological balances;

*Noting* that the numerous species of wild flora and fauna are being seriously depleted and that some of them are threatened with extinction;

*Aware* that the conservation of natural habitats is a vital component of the protection and conservation of wild flora and fauna;

*Recognizing* that the conservation of wild flora and fauna should be taken into consideration by the governments in their national goals and programmes, and that international cooperation should be established to protect migratory species in particular;

...

*Have agreed as follows:*

### Article 1

1. The aims of this Convention are to conserve wild flora and fauna and their natural habitats, especially those species and habitats whose conservation requires the cooperation of several States, and to promote such cooperation.

2. Particular emphasis is given to endangered and vulnerable species, including endangered and vulnerable migratory species.

### Article 2

The Contracting Parties shall take requisite measures to maintain the population of wild flora and fauna at, or adapt it to, a level which corresponds in particular to ecological, scientific and cultural requirements, and the needs of subspecies, varieties or forms at risk locally.

### Article 3

1. Each Contracting Party shall take steps to promote national policies for the conservation of wild flora, wild fauna and natural habitats, with particular attention to endangered and vulnerable species, especially endemic ones, and endangered habitats, in accordance with the provisions of this Convention.

2. Each Contracting Party undertakes, in its planning and development policies and in its measures against pollution, to have regard to the conservation of wild flora and fauna.

3. Each Contracting party shall promote education and disseminate general information on the need to conserve species of wild flora and fauna and their habitats.

### Article 4

1. Each Contracting Party shall take appropriate and necessary legislative and administrative measures to ensure the conservation of the habitats of the wild flora and fauna species, especially those specified in the Appendices I and II, and the conservation of endangered natural habitats.

2. The Contracting Parties in their planning and development policies shall have regard to the conservation requirements of the areas protected under the preceding paragraph, so as to avoid or minimize as far as possible any deterioration of such areas.

3. The Contracting parties undertake to give special attention to the protection of areas that are of importance for the migratory species specified in Appendices II and III and which are appropriately situated in relation to migration routes, as wintering, staging, feeding, breeding or moulting areas.

4. The Contracting Parties undertake to coordinate as appropriate their efforts for the protection of the natural habitats referred to in this Article when these are situated in frontier areas.

## Article 5

Each Contracting Party shall take appropriate and necessary legislative and administrative measures to ensure the special protection of the wild flora species specified in Appendix I. Deliberate picking, collecting, cutting or uprooting of such plants shall be prohibited. Each Contracting Party shall, as appropriate, prohibit possession or sale of these species.

## Article 6

Each Contracting Party shall take appropriate and necessary legislative and administrative measures to ensure the special protection of the wild fauna species specified in Appendix II. The following will in particular be prohibited for these species:

a. all forms of deliberate capture and keeping and deliberate killing;

b. the deliberate damage to or destruction of breeding or resting sites;

c. the deliberate disturbance of wild fauna, particularly during the period of breeding, rearing and hibernation, insofar as disturbance would be significant in relation to the objectives of this Convention;

d. the deliberate destruction or taking of eggs from the wild or keeping these eggs even if empty;

e. the possession of and internal trade in these animals, alive or dead, including stuffed animals and any readily recognizable part or derivative thereof, where this would contribute to the effectiveness of the provisions of this Article.

## Article 7

1. Each Contracting Party shall take appropriate and necessary legislative and administrative measures to ensure the protection of the wild fauna species specified in Appendix III.

2. Any exploitation of wild fauna specified in Appendix III shall be regulated in order to keep the populations out of danger, taking into account the requirements of Article 2.

3. Measures to be taken shall include:

    a. closed seasons and/or other procedures regulating the exploitation;

    b. the temporary or local prohibition of exploitation, as appropriate, in order to restore satisfactory population levels;

    c. the regulation as appropriate of sale, keeping for sale, transport for sale or offering for sale of live and dead wild animals.

## Article 8

In respect of the capture or killing of wild fauna species specified in Appendix III and in cases where, in accordance with Article 9, exceptions are applied to species specified in Appendix II, Contracting Parties shall prohibit the use of all indiscriminate means of capture and killing and the use of all means capable of causing local disappearance of, or serious disturbance to, populations of a species, and in particular, the means specified in Appendix IV.

## Article 9

1. Each Contracting Party may make exceptions from the provisions of Articles 4, 5, 6, 7, and from the prohibition of the use of means mentioned in Article 8 provided that there is no other satisfactory solution and that the exception will not be detrimental to the survival of the population concerned:

    — for the protection of flora and fauna;

— to prevent serious damage to crops, livestock, forests, fisheries, water and other forms of property;

— in the interests of public health and safety, air safety or other overriding public interests;

— for the purposes of research and education, of repopulation, of reintroduction and for the necessary breeding;

— to permit, under strictly supervised conditions, on a selective basis and to a limited extent, the taking, keeping or other judicious exploitation of certain wild animals and plants in small numbers.

2.   The Contracting Parties shall report every two years to the Standing Committee on the exceptions made under the preceding paragraph. These reports must specify:

— the populations which are or have been subject to the exceptions and, when practical, the number of specimens involved;

— the means authorized for the killing or capture;

— the conditions of risk and the circumstances of time and place under which such exceptions were granted;

— the authority empowered to declare that these conditions have been fulfilled, and to take decisions in respect of the means that may be used, their limits and the persons instructed to carry them out;

— the controls involved.

...

## 2. Council Directive 92/43/EEC of 21 May 1992
## on the Conservation of Natural Habitats and of Wild Fauna and Flora,
## O.J. No. L 206 of 22 July 1992.

...

[Article 1]
For the purpose of this Directive:

(a)   conservation means a series of measures required to maintain or restore the natural habitats and the populations of species of wild fauna and flora at a favourable status as defined in (e) and (i);

(b)   natural habitats means terrestrial or aquatic areas distinguished by geographic, abiotic and biotic features, whether entirely natural or semi-natural;

(c)   natural habitat types of Community interest means those which, within the territory referred to in Article 2:

(i)   are in danger of disappearance in their natural range; or

(ii)   have a small natural range following their regression or by reason of their intrinsically restricted area; or

(iii)   present outstanding examples of typical characteristics of one or more of the five following biogeographical regions: Alpine, Atlantic, Continental, Macaronesian and Mediterranean ...

(d)   priority natural habitat types means natural habitat types in danger of disappearance, which are present on the territory referred to in Article 2 and for the conservation of which the Community has particular responsibility in view of the proportion of their natural range which falls within the territory referred to in Article 2; ...

(e) conservation status of a natural habitat means the sum of the influences acting on a natural habitat and its typical species that may affect its long-term natural distribution, structure and functions as well as the long-term survival of its typical species within the territory referred to in Article 2.

The conservative status of a natural habitat will be taken as 'favourable' when:
— its natural range and areas it covers within that range are stable or increasing, and
— the specific structure and functions which are necessary for its long-term maintenance exist and are likely to continue to exist for the foreseeable future, and
— the conservation status of its typical species is favourable as defined in (i);

(f) habitat of a species means an environment defined by specific abiotic and biotic factors, in which the species lives at any stage of its biological cycle;

(g) species of Community interest means species which, within the territory referred to in Article 2, are:

(i) endangered, except those species whose natural range is marginal in that territory and which are not endangered or vulnerable in the western palearctic region; or

(ii) vulnerable, i.e. believed likely to move into the endangered category in the near future if the causal factors continue operating; or

(iii) rare, i.e. with small populations that are not at present endangered or vulnerable, but are at risk. The species are located within restricted geographical areas or are thinly scattered over a more extensive range; or

(iv) endemic and requiring particular attention by reason of the specific nature of their habitat and/or the potential impact of their exploitation on their habitat and/or the potential impact of their exploitation on their conservation status.

...

(h) priority species means species referred to in (g) (i) for the conservation of which the Community has particular responsibility in view of the proportion of their natural range which falls within the territory referred to in Article 2; ...

(i) conservation status of a species means the sum of the influences acting on the species concerned that may affect the long-term distribution and abundance of its populations within the territory referred to in Article 2; The conservation status will be taken as 'favourable' when:
— population dynamics data on the species concerned indicate that it is maintaining itself on a long-term basis as a viable component of its natural habitats, and
— the natural range of the species is neither being reduced nor is likely to be reduced for the foreseeable future, and
— there is, and will probably continue to be, a sufficiently large habitat to maintain its populations on a long-term basis;

(j) site means a geographically defined area whose extent is clearly delineated;

(k) site of Community importance means a site which, in the biogeographical region or regions to which it belongs, contributes significantly to the maintenance or restoration at a favourable conservation status of a natural habitat type in Annex I or of a species in Annex II and may also contribute significantly to the coherence of Natura 2000 referred to in Article 3, and/or contributes significantly to the maintenance of biological diversity within the biogeographic region or regions concerned. For animal species ranging over wide areas, sites of Community importance shall correspond to the places within the natural range of such species which present the physical or biological factors essential to their life and reproduction;

(l) special area of conservation means a site of Community importance designated by the Member States through a statutory, administrative and/or contractual act where the necessary conservation measures are applied for the maintenance or restoration, at a favourable conservation status, of the natural habitats and/or the populations of the species for which the site is designated;

(m) specimen means any animal or plant, whether alive or dead, of the species listed in Annex IV and Annex V, any part or derivative thereof, as well as any other goods which appear, from an accompanying document, the packaging or a mark or label, or from any other circumstances, to be parts or derivatives of animals or plants of those species;

...

## Article 2

1. The aim of this Directive shall be to contribute towards ensuring bio-diversity through the conservation of natural habitats and of wild fauna and flora in the European territory of the Member States to which the Treaty applies.

2. Measures taken pursuant to this Directive shall be designed to maintain or restore, at favourable conservation status, natural habitats and species of wild fauna and flora of Community interest.

3. Measures taken pursuant to this Directive shall take account of economic, social and cultural requirements and regional and local characteristics.

## Article 3

1. A coherent European ecological network of special areas of conservation shall be set up under the title Natura 2000. This network, composed of sites hosting the natural habitat types listed in Annex I and habitats of the species listed in Annex II, shall enable the natural habitat types and the species' habitats concerned to be maintained or, where appropriate, restored at a favourable conservation status in their natural range. The Natura 2000 network shall include the special protection areas classified by the Member States pursuant to Directive 79/409/EEC.

2. Each Member State shall contribute to the creation of Natura 2000 in proportion to the representation within its territory of the natural habitat types and the habitats of species referred to in paragraph 1. To that effect each Member State shall designate, in accordance with Article 4, sites as special areas of conservation taking account of the objectives set out in paragraph 1.

3. Where they consider it necessary, Member States shall endeavour to improve the ecological coherence of Natura 2000 by maintaining, and where appropriate developing, features of the landscape which are of major importance for wild fauna and flora, as referred to in Article 10.

## Article 4

1. On the basis of the criteria set out in Annex III (Stage 1) and relevant scientific information, each Member State shall propose a list of sites indicating which natural habitat types in Annex I and which species in Annex II that are native to its territory the sites host. For animal species ranging over wide areas these sites shall correspond to the places within the

natural range of such species which present the physical or biological factors essential to their life and reproduction. For aquatic species which range over wide areas, such sites will be proposed only where there is a clearly identifiable area representing the physical and biological factors essential to their life and reproduction. Where appropriate, Member States shall propose adaptation of the list in the light of the results of the surveillance referred to in Article 11. The list shall be transmitted to the Commission, within three years of the notification of this Directive, together with information on each site. That information shall include a map of the site, its name, location, extent and the data resulting from application of the criteria specified in Annex III (Stage 1) provided in a format established by the Commission in accordance with the procedure laid down in Article 21.

2.   On the basis of the criteria set out in Annex III (Stage 2) and in the framework both of each of the five biogeographical regions referred to in Article 1 (c) (iii) and of the whole of the territory referred to in Article 2 (1), the Commission shall establish, in agreement with each Member State, a draft list of sites of Community importance drawn from the Member States' lists identifying those which lost one or more priority natural habitat types or priority species. Member States whose sites hosting one or more priority natural habitat types and priority species represent more than 5 per cent of their national territory may, in agreement with the Commission, request that the criteria listed in Annex III (Stage 2) be applied more flexibly in selecting all the sites of Community importance in their territory. The list of sites selected as sites of Community importance, identifying those which host one or more priority natural habitat types or priority species, shall be adopted by the Commission in accordance with the procedure laid down in Article 21.

...

4.   Once a site of Community importance has been adopted in accordance with the procedure laid down in paragraph 2, the Member State concerned shall designate that site as a special area of conservation as soon as possible and within six years at most, establishing priorities in the light of the importance of the sites for the maintenance or restoration, at a favourable conservation status, of a natural habitat type in Annex I or a species in Annex II and for the coherence of Natura 2000, and in the light of the threats of degradation or destruction to which those sites are exposed.

5.   As soon as a site is placed on the list referred to in the third subparagraph of paragraph 2 it shall be subject to Article 6 (2), (3) and (4).

## Article 5

1.   In exceptional cases where the Commission finds that a national list as referred to in Article 4 (1) fails to mention a site hosting a priority natural habitat type or priority species which, on the basis of relevant and reliable scientific information, it considers to be essential for the maintenance of that priority natural habitat type or for the survival of that priority species, a bilateral consultation procedure shall be initiated between that Member State and the Commission for the purpose of comparing the scientific data used by each.

2.   If, on expiry of a consultation period not exceeding six months, the dispute remains unresolved, the Commission shall forward to the Council a proposal relating to the selection of the site as a site of Community importance.

...

## Article 6

1.   For special areas of conservation, Member States shall establish the necessary conservation measures involving, if need be, appropriate management plans specifically designed for the

sites or integrated into other development plans, and appropriate statutory, administrative or contractual measures which correspond to the ecological requirements of the natural habitat types in Annex I and the species in Annex II present on the sites.

2.  Member States shall take appropriate steps to avoid, in the special areas of conservation, the deterioration of natural habitats and the habitats of species as well as disturbance of the species for which the areas have been designated, in so far as such disturbance could be significant in relation to the objectives of this Directive.

3.  Any plan or project not directly connected with or necessary to the management of the site but likely to have a significant effect thereon, either individually or in combination with other plans or projects, shall be subject to appropriate assessment of its implications for the site in view of the site's conservation objectives. In the light of the conclusions of the assessment of the implications for the site and subject to the provisions of paragraph 4, the competent national authorities shall agree to the plan or project only after having ascertained that it will not adversely affect the integrity of the site concerned and, if appropriate, after having obtained the opinion of the general public.

4.  If, in spite of a negative assessment of the implications for the site and in the absence of alternative solutions, a plan or project must nevertheless be carried out for imperative reasons of overriding public interest, including those of a social or economic nature, the Member State shall take all compensatory measures necessary to ensure that the overall coherence of Natura 2000 is protected. It shall inform the Commission of the compensatory measures adopted. Where the site concerned hosts a priority natural habitat type and/or a priority species, the only considerations which may be raised are those relating to human health or public safety, to beneficial consequences of primary importance for the environment or, further to an opinion from the Commission, to other imperative reasons of overriding public interest.

...

Article 8

1.  In parallel with their proposals for sites eligible for designation as special areas of conservation, hosting priority natural habitat types and/or priority species, the Member States shall send, as appropriate, to the Commission their estimates relating to the Community co-financing which they consider necessary to allow them to meet their obligations pursuant to Article 6 (1).

2.  In agreement with each of the Member States concerned, the Commission shall identify, for sites of Community importance for which co-financing is sought, those measures essential for the maintenance or re-establishment at a favourable conservation status of the priority natural habitat types and priority species on the sites concerned, as well as the total costs arising from those measures.

3.  The Commission, in agreement with the Member States concerned, shall assess the financing, including co-financing, required for the operation of the measures referred to in paragraph 2, taking into account, amongst other things, the concentration on the Member State's territory of priority natural habitat types and/or priority species and the relative burdens which the required measures entail.

4.  According to the assessment referred to in paragraphs 2 and 3, the Commission shall adopt, having regard to the available sources of funding under the relevant Community instruments and according to the procedure set out in Article 21, a prioritized action framework

of measures involving co-financing to be taken when the site has been designated under Article 4 (4).

...

## Article 10

Member States shall endeavour, where they consider it necessary, in their land-use planning and development policies and, in particular, with a view to improving the ecological coherence of the Natura 2000 network, to encourage the management of features of the landscape which are of major importance for wild fauna and flora. Such features are those which, by virtue of their linear and continuous structure (such as rivers with their banks or the traditional systems for marking field boundaries) or their function as stepping stones (such as ponds or small woods), are essential for the migration, dispersal and genetic exchange of wild species.

## Article 11

Member States shall undertake surveillance of the conservation status of the natural habitats and species referred to in Article 2 with particular regard to priority natural habitat types and priority species.

## Article 12

1.  Member States shall take the requisite measures to establish a system of strict protection for the animal species listed in Annex IV (a) in their natural range, prohibiting:

    (a)   all forms of deliberate capture or killing of specimens of these species in the wild;

    (b)   deliberate disturbance of these species, particularly during the period of breeding, rearing, hibernation and migration;

    (c)   deliberate destruction or taking of eggs from the wild;

    (d)   deterioration or destruction of breeding sites or resting places.

2.  For these species, Member States shall prohibit the keeping, transport and sale or exchange, and offering for sale or exchange, of specimens taken from the wild, except for those taken legally before this Directive is implemented.

3.  The prohibition referred to in paragraph 1 (a) and (b) and paragraph 2 shall apply to all stages of life of the animals to which this Article applies.

4.  Member States shall establish a system to monitor the incidental capture and killing of the animal species listed in Annex IV (a). In the light of the information gathered, Member States shall take further research or conservation measures as required to ensure that incidental capture and killing does not have a significant negative impact on the species concerned.

## Article 13

1.  Member States shall take the requisite measures to establish a system of strict protection for the plant species listed in Annex IV (b), prohibiting:

    (a)   the deliberate picking, collecting, cutting, uprooting or destruction of such plants in their natural range in the wild;

    (b)   the keeping, transport and sale or exchange and offering for sale or exchange of specimens of such species taken in the wild, except for those taken legally before this Directive is implemented.

2.  The prohibitions referred to in paragraph 1 (a) and (b) shall apply to all stages of the biological cycle of the plants to which this Article applies.

## Article 14

1.  If, in the light of the surveillance provided for in Article 11, Member States deem it necessary, they shall take measures to ensure that the taking in the wild of specimens of species of wild fauna and flora listed in Annex V as well as their exploitation is compatible with their being maintained at a favourable conservation status.

2.  Where such measures are deemed necessary, they shall include continuation of the surveillance provided for in Article 11. Such measures may also include in particular:
    — regulations regarding access to certain property,
    — temporary or local prohibition of the taking of specimens in the wild and exploitation of certain populations,
    — regulation of the periods and/or methods of taking specimens,
    — application, when specimens are taken, of hunting and fishing rules which take account of the conservation of such populations,
    — establishment of a system of licences for taking specimens or of quotas,
    — regulation of the purchase, sale, offering for sale, keeping for sale or transport for sale of specimens,
    — breeding in captivity of animal species as well as artificial propagation of plant species, under strictly controlled conditions, with a view to reducing the taking of specimens of the wild,
    — assessment of the effect of the measures adopted.

## Article 15

In respect of the capture or killing of species of wild fauna listed in Annex V (a) and in cases where, in accordance with Article 16, derogations are applied to the taking, capture or killing of species listed in Annex IV (a), Member States shall prohibit the use of all indiscriminate means capable of causing local disappearance of, or serious disturbance to, populations of such species, and in particular:

(a) use of the means of capture and killing listed in Annex VI (a);

(b) any form of capture and killing from the modes of transport referred to in Annex VI (b).

## Article 16

1.  Provided that there is no satisfactory alternative and the derogation is not detrimental to the maintenance of the populations of the species concerned at a favourable conservation status in their natural range, Member States may derogate from the provisions of Articles 12, 13, 14 and 15 (a) and (b):

    (a) in the interest of protecting wild fauna and flora and conserving natural habitats;

    (b) to prevent serious damage, in particular to crops, livestock, forests, fisheries and water and other types of property;

    (c) in the interests of public health and public safety, or for other imperative reasons of overriding public interest, including those of a social or economic nature and beneficial consequences of primary importance for the environment;

    (d) for the purpose of research and education, of repopulating and re-introducing these species and for the breeding operations necessary for these purposes, including the artificial propagation of plants;

    (e) to allow, under strictly supervised conditions, on a selective basis and to a limited extent, the taking or keeping of certain specimens of the species listed in Annex IV in limited numbers specified by the competent national authorities.

2.  Member States shall forward to the Commission every two years a report in accordance with the format established by the Committee on the derogations applied under paragraph 1. The Commission shall give its opinion on these derogations within a maximum time limit of 12 months following receipt of the report and shall give an account to the Committee.

3.  The reports shall specify:

    (a)  the species which are subject to the derogations and the reason for the derogation, including the nature of the risk, with, if appropriate, a reference to alternatives rejected and scientific data used;

    (b)  the means, devices or methods authorized for the capture or killing of animal species and the reasons for their use;

    (c)  the circumstances of when and where such derogations are granted;

    (d)  the authority empowered to declare and check that the required conditions obtain and to decide what means, devices or methods may be used, within what limits and by what agencies, and which persons are to carry out the task;

    (e)  the supervisory measures used and the results obtained.

    ...

## Article 18

1.  Member States and the Commission shall encourage the necessary research and scientific work having regard to the objectives set out in Article 2 and the obligation referred to in Article 11. They shall exchange information for the purposes of proper coordination of research carried out at Member State and at the Community level.

2.  Particular attention shall be paid to scientific work necessary for the implementation of Articles 4 and 10, and transboundary cooperative research between Member States shall be encouraged.

    ...

## Article 22

In implementing the provisions of this Directive, Member States shall:

(a)  study the desirability of re-introducing species in Annex IV that are native to their territory where this might contribute to their conservation, provided that an investigation, also taking into account experience in other Member States or elsewhere, has established that such re-introduction contributes effectively to re-establishing these species at a favourable conservation status and that it takes place only after proper consultation of the public concerned;

(b)  ensure that the deliberate introduction into the wild of any species which is not native to their territory is regulated so as not to prejudice natural habitats within their natural range or the wild native fauna and flora and, if they consider it necessary, prohibit such introduction. The results of the assessment undertaken shall be forwarded to the committee for information;

(c)  promote education and general information on the need to protect species of wild fauna and flora and to conserve their habitats and natural habitats.

## 3. United Kingdom, *Environmental Protection Act 1990*.

### Part VI
### Genetically Modified Organisms

106. (1)  This Part has effect for the purpose of preventing or minimizing any damage to the environment which may arise from the escape or release from human control of genetically modified organisms.

(2)  In this Part the term "organism" means any acellular, unicellular or multicellular entity (in any form), other than humans or human embryos; and, unless the context otherwise requires, the term also includes any article or substance consisting of or including biological matter.

...

(4)  For the purposes of this Part an organism is "genetically modified" if any of the genes or other genetic material in the organism

(a)  have been modified by means of an artificial technique prescribed in regulations by the Secretary of State, or

(b)  are inherited or otherwise derived, through any number of replications, from genes or other genetic material (from any source) which were so modified.

...

107. (1)  The following provisions have effect for the interpretation of this Part

(2)  The "environment" consists of land, air and water or any of those media.

(3)  "Damage to the environment" is caused by the presence in the environment of genetically modified organisms which have (or of a single such organism which has) escaped or been released from a person's control and are (or is) capable of causing harm to the living organisms supported by the environment.

...

(5)  Genetically modified organisms present in the environment are capable of causing harm if:

(a)  they are individually capable, or are present in numbers such that together they are capable of causing harm; or

(b)  they are able to produce descendants which will be capable, or which will be present in numbers such that together they will be capable, of causing harm; and a single organism is capable of causing harm either if it is itself capable of causing harm or if it is able to produce descendants which will be so capable.

(6)  "Harm" means harm to the health of humans or other living organisms or other interference with the ecological systems of which they form part and, in the case of man, includes offence caused to any of his senses or harm to his property.

...

(9)  Organisms of any description are under the "control" of a person where he keeps them contained by any system of physical, chemical or biological barriers (or combination of such barriers) used for either or both of the following purposes, namely:

(a) for ensuring that the organisms do not enter the environment or produce descendants which are not so contained; or

(b) for ensuring that any of the organisms which do enter the environment or any descendants of the organisms which are not so contained, are harmless.

(10) An organism under a person's control is "released" if he deliberately causes or permits it to cease to be under his control or the control of any other person and to enter the environment; and such an organism "escapes" if, otherwise than by being released, it ceases to be under his control or that of any other person and enters the environment.

...

108. (1) Subject to subsections (2) and (7) below, no person shall import or acquire, release or market any genetically modified organisms unless, before doing that act

(a) he has carried out an assessment of any risks there are (by reference to the nature of the organisms and the manner in which he intends to keep them after their importation or acquisition or, as the case may be, to release or market them) of damage to the environment being caused as a result of doing that act; and

b) in such cases and circumstances as may be prescribed, he has given the Secretary of State such notice of his intention of doing that act and such information as may be prescribed.

...

(3) Subject to subsections (4) and (7) below, a person who is keeping genetically modified organisms shall, in such cases or circumstances and at such times or intervals as may be prescribed

(a) carry out an assessment of any risks there are of damage to the environment being caused as a result of his continuing to keep them;

(b) give the Secretary of State notice of the fact that he is keeping the organisms and such information as may be prescribed.

...

(5) It shall be the duty of a person who carries out an assessment ... to keep, for the prescribed period, such a record of the assessment as may be prescribed.

(6) A person required ... to give notice to the Secretary of State shall give the Secretary of State such further information as the Secretary of State may by notice in writing require.

(7) Regulations under this section may provide for exemptions, or for the granting by the Secretary of State of exemptions to particular persons or classes of person, from the requirements of subsection (1) or (3) above in such cases or circumstances, and to such extent, as may be prescribed.

(8) The Secretary of State may at any time

(a) give directions to a person falling within subsection (1) above requiring that person to apply for a consent before doing the act in question; or

(b) give directions to a person falling within subsection (3) above requiring that person, before such date as may be specified in the direction, to apply for a consent authorizing him to continue keeping the organisms in question; and a person given directions ... shall ... be subject to section 111 in place of the requirements of this section.

(9) Regulations under this section may

(a) prescribe the manner in which assessments under subsection (1) or (3) above are to be carried out and the matters which must be investigated and assessed;

(b) prescribe minimum periods of notice between the giving of a notice under subsection (1)(b) above and the doing of the act in question;

(c) make provision allowing the Secretary of State to shorten or to extend any such period;

(d) prescribe maximum intervals at which assessments under subsection (3)(a) above must be carried out; and the regulations may make different provision for different cases and different circumstances.

...

109. ...

(2) A person who proposes to import or acquire genetically modified organisms

(a) shall take all reasonable steps to identify, by reference to the nature of the organisms and the manner in which he intends to keep them (including any precautions to be taken against their escaping or causing damage to the environment), what risks there are of damage to the environment being caused as a result of their importation or acquisition; and

(b) shall not import or acquire the organisms if it appears that, despite any precautions which can be taken, there is a risk of damage to the environment being caused as a result of their importation or acquisition.

(3) A person who is keeping genetically modified organisms

(a) shall take all reasonable steps to keep himself informed of any damage to the environment which may have been caused as a result of his keeping the organisms and to identify what risks there are of damage to the environment being caused as a result of his continuing to keep them;

(b) shall cease keeping the organisms if, despite any additional precautions which can be taken, it appears, at any time, that there is a risk of damage to the environment being caused as a result of his continuing to keep them; and

(c) shall use the best available techniques not entailing excessive cost for keeping the organisms under his control and for preventing any damage to the environment being caused as a result of his continuing to keep the organisms;

and where a person is required by paragraph (b) above to cease keeping the organisms he shall dispose of them as safely and as quickly as practicable and paragraph (c) above shall continue to apply until he has done so.

(4) A person who proposes to release genetically modified organisms

(a) shall take all reasonable steps to keep himself informed, by reference to the nature of the organisms and the extent and manner of the release (including any precautions to be taken against their causing damage to the environment), what risks there are of damage to the environment being caused as a result of their being released;

...

(c)  ... shall use the best available techniques not entailing excessive cost for preventing any damage to the environment being caused as a result of their being released; and this subsection applies, with the necessary modifications, to a person proposing to market organisms as it applies to a person proposing to release organisms.

...

110. (1)  The Secretary of State may serve a notice under this section (a "prohibition notice") on any person he has reason to believe

(a)  is proposing to import or acquire, release or market any genetically modified organisms; or

(b)  is keeping any such organisms;

if he is of the opinion that doing any such act in relation to those organisms or continuing to keep them, as the case may be, would involve a risk of causing damage to the environment.

(2)  A prohibition notice may prohibit a person from doing an act mentioned in subsection (1)(a) above in relation to any genetically modified organisms or from continuing to keep them; and the prohibition may apply in all cases or circumstances or in such cases or circumstances as may be specified in the notice.

(3)  A prohibition notice shall

(a)  state that the Secretary of State is ... of the opinion mentioned in subsection (1) above;

(b)  specify what is, or is to be, prohibited by the notice; and

(c)  ... specify the date on which the prohibition is to take effect;

and a notice may be served on a person notwithstanding that he may have a consent authorizing any act which is, or is to be, prohibited by the notice.

(4)  Where a person is prohibited by a prohibition notice from continuing to keep any genetically modified organism, he shall dispose of them as quickly and safely as practicable or, if the notice so provides, as may be specified in the notice.

(5)  The Secretary of State may at any time withdraw a prohibition notice served on any person by notice given to that person.

111. (1)  Subject to [exceptions provided by regulations], no person shall import or acquire, release or market any genetically modified organisms ... except in pursuance of a consent granted by the Secretary of State and in accordance with any limitations and conditions to which the consent is subject.

(2)  Subject to [exceptions provided by regulations], no person who has imported or acquired any genetically modified organisms (whether under a consent or not) shall continue to keep the organisms ... except in pursuance of a consent granted by the Secretary of State and in accordance with any limitations or conditions to which the consent is subject.

(3)  Any person who is required under subsection (2) above to cease keeping any genetically modified organisms shall dispose of them as quickly and safely as practicable.

(4) An application for a consent must contain such information and be made and advertised in such manner as may be prescribed.

...

(8) Where an application for a consent is duly made to him, the Secretary of State may grant the consent subject to such limitations and conditions as may be imposed under section 112 below or he may refuse the application.

...

(10) The Secretary of State may at any time, by notice given to the holder of a consent, revoke the consent or vary the consent (whether by attaching new limitations and conditions or by revoking or varying any limitations and conditions to which it is at that time subject).

112. (1) The Secretary of State may include in a consent such limitations and conditions as he may think fit ...

(3) Subject to [limited exceptions], there is implied in every consent for the importation or acquisition of genetically modified organisms a general condition that the holder of the consent shall

   (a) take all reasonable steps to keep himself informed (by reference to the nature of the organisms and the manner in which he intends to keep them after their importation or acquisition) of any risks there are of damage to the environment being caused as a result of their importation or acquisition; and

   (b) if at any time it appears that any such risks are more serious than were apparent when the consent was granted, notify the Secretary of State forthwith.

(4) Subject to [limited exceptions], there is implied in every consent for keeping genetically modified organisms a general condition that the holder of the consent shall

   (a) take all reasonable steps to keep himself informed of any damage to the environment which may have been caused as a result of his keeping the organisms and of any risks there are of such damage being caused as a result of his continuing to keep them;

   (b) if at any time it appears that any such risks are more serious than were apparent when the consent was granted, notify the Secretary of State forthwith; and

   (c) use the best available techniques not entailing excessive cost for keeping the organisms under his control and for preventing any damage to the environment being caused as a result of his continuing to keep them.

(5) [The same implied conditions apply to release or marketing].

...

(7) There shall be implied in every consent for keeping, releasing or marketing genetically modified organisms of any description a general condition that the holder of the consent:

   (a) shall take all reasonable steps to keep himself informed of developments in the techniques which may be available in his case for preventing damage to the environment being caused as a result of the doing of the act authorized by the consent in relation to organisms of that description; and

   (b) if it appears at any time that any better techniques are available to him than is required by any condition included in the consent ... shall notify the Secretary of State of that fact forthwith.

...

114. (1)  The Secretary of State may appoint as inspectors, for carrying this Part into effect, such number of persons appearing to him to be qualified for the purpose as he may consider necessary.

...

(3)  The powers of an inspector are

(a)  at any reasonable time (or, in a situation in which in his opinion there is an immediate risk of damage to the environment, at any time)

(i)  to enter premises which he has reason to believe it is necessary for him to enter and to take with him any person duly authorised by the Secretary of State and, if the inspector has reasonable cause to apprehend any serious obstruction in the execution of his duty, a constable; and

(ii)  to take with him any equipment or materials required for any purpose for which the power of entry is being exercised;

(b)  to carry out such tests and inspections (and to make such recordings), as may in any circumstances be necessary;

(c)  to direct that any, or any part of, premises which he has power to enter, or anything in or on such premises, shall be left undisturbed (whether generally or in particular respects) for so long as is reasonable necessary for the purpose of any test or inspection;

(d)  to take samples of any organisms, articles or substances found in or on any premises which he has power to enter, and of the air, water or land in, on, or in the vicinity of, the premises;

(e)  in the case of anything found in or on any premises which he has power to enter, which appears to him to contain or to have contained genetically modified organisms which have caused or are likely to cause damage to the environment, to cause it to be dismantled or subjected to any process or test (but not so as to damage or destroy it unless this is necessary);

(f)  in the case of anything ... found on premises ... which appears to be a genetically modified organism ... to take possession of it and detain it for so long as is necessary for all or any of the following purposes, namely

(i)  to examine it and do to it anything which he has power to do under [paragraph e];

(ii)  to ensure that it is not tampered with before his examination of it is completed; and

(iii)  to ensure that it is available for use as evidence in any proceedings for an offence under section 118 below;

(g)  to require any person whom he has reasonable cause to believe to be able to give any information relevant to any test or inspection ... to answer ... such questions as the inspector thinks fit to ask and to sign a declaration of the truth of his answers;

(h) to require the production of, or ... the furnishing of extracts from, any records which are required to be kept under this Part ... and take copies of, or of any entry in, the records;

(i) to require any person to afford him such facilities and assistance with respect to any matters or things within that person's control or in relation to which that person has responsibilities as are necessary to enable the inspector to exercise any of the powers conferred upon him by this section;

(j) any other power for the purpose mentioned in subsection (1) above which is conferred by regulations made by the Secretary of State.

...

116. (1) For the purposes of the discharge of his functions under this Part, the Secretary of State may, by notice in writing served on any person who appears to him [involved or about to be involved with genetically modified organisms], require that person to furnish such relevant information available to him as is specified in the notice, in such form and within such period following service of the notice as is so specified.

...

117. (1) Where, in the case of anything found by him on any premises which he has power to enter, an inspector has reason to believe that it is a genetically modified organism or that it consists of or includes genetically modified organisms and that, in the circumstances in which he finds it, it is a cause of imminent danger of damage to the environment, he may seize it and cause it to be rendered harmless (whether by destruction, by bringing it under proper control or otherwise).

...

118. [Offences]

119. (1) In any proceedings for ... offences ... it shall be for the accused to prove that there was no better available technique not entailing excessive cost than was in fact used to satisfy the condition or to comply with that section.

...

120. (1) Where a person is convicted of any offence ... in respect of any matters which appear to the court to be matters which it is in his power to remedy, the court may, in addition to or instead of imposing any punishment, order him, within such time as may be fixed by the order, to take such steps as may be specified in the order for remedying those matters.

...

## Questions and Problems

1. Discuss the advantages and disadvantages of placing responsibility for wildlife protection with:
   — national authorities;
   — regional or local bodies;
   — private persons or associations;
   — international bodies.

2. What economic incentives could be used to protect endangered species?

3. Is the "polluter pays" principle applicable to wildlife protection?

4. What difference would it make if the focus of wildlife law was the protection of individual specimens rather than species?

5. Should legal instruments list species that may be taken or those that cannot be exploited?

6. Is there such a thing as "species integrity"? How would such a concept affect biotechnology?

7. Should activities involving genetically modified organisms be submitted to prior authorization? Should an EIA be required? Are either or both requirements contained,in the UK law? What other protections are included in the legislation?

8. Are reparations possible for the destruction of an endangered species?

9. What is "wise use"?

10. Do all living species have intrinsic value and require protection? Consider elephants, dolphins, wolves, snakes, parasites, viruses.

11. How can nature be protected outside specially designated areas?

12. Can protected areas be safeguarded against harmful external factors?

13. Evaluate the merits of a programme for hunters to compensate farmers for harm done to crops by wild game. Should the fee for a licence include an amount for this purpose?

14. Community Directive 79/409 relates to the conservation of all species of wild birds in the territory of Member States. Article 6 provides that Member States shall prohibit the sale of live or dead wild birds, except for listed species. Article 14 permits Member States to take stricter protective measures. The Vogelwet (Bird Law) of the Netherlands (31 December 1936) protects all birds living in the wild in Europe, except for birds listed in the Hunting Law. It prohibits the importation and sale of live or dead birds and provides sanctions.

The red grouse is a bird living mainly in the British Isles, where it is hunted and sold. It is not a species listed as endangered on any international list; it is listed under the Bird Directive as a species exempt from the Directive's protections. There are no red grouse in the Netherlands and the bird is not listed in the Dutch Hunting Law.

In December 1984, inspectors enforcing the Vogelwet found three red grouse in a poultry and game shop in the Hague. The owners of the shop were prosecuted and convicted under the Vogelwet. On appeal, the Court sought a preliminary ruling from the European Court of Justice on the compatibility of the Vogelwet with Article 36 of the EEC treaty, which permits trade restrictions for the protection of the health and life of animals. How should the Court rule? *See* Eur. Ct.J., *Gourmetterie van den Burg BV*, Case 169/89, 23 May 1990.

## Bibliography

Batchelor, A., "The Preservation of Wildlife Habitat in Ecosystems: Toward a New Direction under International Law to Prevent Species' Extinction", 3 *Fl. Int'l L.J.* 307 (1988).

de Klemm, C., "Conservation of Species: The Need for a New Approach", 9 *Envt'l Pol'y & L.* 117 (1982).

de Klemm, C., "Migratory Species in International Law", 29 *Nat. Res. J.* 935 (1989).

European Parliament, *Nature Conservation*, Environment, Public Health and Consumer Protection Series No. 17 (1991).

FAO, Commission on Plant Genetic Resources, *Report on the Fourth Session* (Rome, 1991), FAO CPGR/91/REP.

FAO, *Global System for the Conservation and Utilization of Plant Genetic Resources, Progress Report* (1991), FAO C91/24 (October, 1991).

Favre, D., *International Trade in Endangered Species* (1989).

Lyster, S., *International Wildlife Law* (1985).

Lyster, S., "The Convention on the Conservation of Migratory Species of Wild Animals", 29 *Nat. Res. J.* 979 (1989).

Memorandum on the Implementation of the Wetlands Convention, 1985. Ministry of Agriculture and Fisheries, The Hague.

Nature Policy Plan of the Netherlands, 1990. Ministry of Agriculture, Nature Management and Fisheries, The Hague.

Norton, B., *The Preservation of Species* (1986).

Prieur, M. (ed.), *Forêts et Environnement en Droit Comparé et en Droit International* (1985).

Wilson, E., *Biological Diversity* (1988).

Wolters, A. R., "Top-down approach in protecting wetlands: a Dutch experience", in *People's Role in Wetland Management: Proceedings of the International Conference on Wetlands* (1989), 623–635. Centre for Environmental Studies.

Wolters, A. R. & A. N. van der Zande, 1990. Nieuwe ontwikkelingen en uitdagingen in het natuurbeschermingsrecht (New developments and challenges in nature conservation law). *Milieu en Recht* 7/8: 306–18.

## CHAPTER VI

# PROTECTION OF THE SOIL

## A. Overview

Soil is the part of the earth between its surface and bedrock. It contains the nutrients necessary for maintenance of plant life and it acts to filter out pollutants before they reach subterranean water sources or enter the food chain. Soil also helps to avoid flooding by absorbing considerable amounts of water. Nearly all soil constitutes a habitat for flora and fauna and in this way contributes to biodiversity. In addition to its natural roles, soil is a primary resource for construction, physical support for structures, and of historical evidence on the origins of humans, plants and other animals, and the earth. Soil naturally erodes and degrades, but it is increasingly threatened by excess demands on all the roles it plays. Overuse of soil depletes the nutrients and leads to erosion and desertification; the filtration system breaks down when too many chemicals in quantities too great are passed through soil. When its characteristics are altered, its ability to prevent flooding diminishes.

Erosion is a principal threat to the soil, affecting about 20 per cent of European soils. It occurs naturally due to flooding, the natural flow of water, and strong winds. Cataclysmic events like earthquakes, forest fires, and volcanoes also change the configuration of soil and can lead to considerable erosion. However, the principal cause of erosion today is incorrect management of forests and agricultural lands, principally through intensive and environmentally unsound cutting and farming methods.

Contamination of heavy metals and organic toxic substances, including fertilizers and pesticides, is a particularly serious problem in many parts of the European Community. Under certain conditions, these pollutants may be suddenly released. Moderate to high accumulation of cadmium occurs in 40 per cent of European agricultural soils; in 15 per cent of the lands the concentration poses high ecological risks.

Industrial waste has become a major source of soil contamination, and radioactive contamination also must be considered. The accident at the nuclear power plant in Chernobyl contaminated 20 per cent of the farmland and nearly 15 per cent of the forests of Belarus. Less dramatic, but more widespread, an estimated 28 per cent of the wastes from European oil refineries are disposed of through landfill.

Natural acidification is a slow process of decay over thousands of years. This acidification is greatly increased by sulphuric acid, ammonia and nitric acid coming from atmospheric pollution, as well as ammonia derived from animal wastes. These deposits lead to a reduction in the fertility of the soil. In many instances, such soil degradation is irreversible, at least in the short and medium term. As of 1991, acidification of European soils due to deposits of sulphur and nitrogen compounds, including ammonia, exceeded the critical acid loads for sensitive ecosystems in 73 per cent of the total European area, with substantial excesses in 10 per cent of Europe.[1]

Finally, soil is removed for construction of houses, roads, bridges, etc. In central Europe, soil removal has become a major problem, with irreversible losses.

Cumulating these causes, human-induced soil degradation has significant environmental consequences. A study initiated by UNEP in 1987 and produced by the International Soil Reference and Information Centre in the Netherlands found that 15 per cent of the global land is deteriorated, of which 60 per cent is moderately or seriously affected. Water erosion is responsible for approximately half and wind for one-quarter of the degraded surface area. Chemical and physical deterioration currently affect 240 million and 80 million hectares, respectively.

Legal protection for soil is rather recent, although some forestry laws protected trees at least in part to avoid erosion and consequent flooding. Part of the neglect has been due to a general perception of soil as a renewable resource in regard to its primary uses for food and energy production. Until the twentieth century, agricultural production was a closed environmental cycle that used almost no fossil fuels or artificial pesticides, and there was minimal loss or degradation. Today, erosion and the contamination of soil – which in turn lead to water pollution, famine, and loss of biodiversity – are cause for grave alarm. However, unlike air, water, and flora and fauna, there are few laws directly addressing soil pollution. The Netherlands was the first state in Europe to have specific legislation on soil protection. Soil clean-up regulations date from 1983, after the public became aware of toxic sites in the country. Broader measures were enacted in 1987 with the Soil Protection Act. The policies of the act are, first, to protect the functions of the soil through conservation and restoration, and, second, to regulate pollution sources, from traffic to animal waste. Both require establishment of soil quality standards, something not yet generally developed. The law is a framework law, with full implementation through a General Administrative Order. The Act itself provides that every citizen has the duty to prevent all soil-threatening actions and report such actions to the appropriate authorities. In 1991 the Netherlands adopted a voluntary system to clean up polluted soils on operating industrial sites. A private foundation set up by industry implements the cleanup initiative, although there is some government funding. Companies bear the cost of cleanup of their own property, but pay no costs for cleanup of other sites.

In addition to the Soil Protection Act, many other Dutch laws affect soil quality: the Waste Disposal Act, Nuisance Act, Chemical Waste Act, Pesticides Act, Nature Conservation Act, Air Pollution Act, Fertilizers Act, and Acts relating to Ground and Surface Waters. Similar dual efforts at protecting the soil directly and through regulation of pollution sources is found in a few other states and at the international level.

National legislation generally includes provisions on the soil in the general law on the environment (Switzerland, Portugal), or specifically regulates certain soil functions in separate legislation. As an example of the latter, Cyprus' soil protection

---

[1] Netherlands National Institute of Public Health and Environmental Protection, "The Environment in Europe: A Global Perspective" 26 March 1992, pp. 14–15.

legislation[2] concerns only the conservation of the solid surface of the soil. It is thus exclusively concerned with erosion and landslides. The law establishes a management system for fragile soil and calls for soil conservation on the basis of national plans. Malta adopted a similar law, 28 June 1973 on the protection of fertile soil.

Iceland began combating erosion in 1895, because of the country's particularly serious problems. By 1907 a national agency for the conservation of soil was established. Further legislation on soil conservation was adopted in 1965, integrating soil protection with protection of flora.

In some cases a partially integrated approach may be taken. In 1989, the Italian legislature approved the first law on soil protection,[3] linking it with water protection. Italy cites erosion as its major environmental problem, much of it resulting from flooding. The cities of Venice and Florence have suffered serious damage and destruction in recent years.

Another approach is taken in the United Kingdom, which couples legislative protection with common law tort actions establishing liability for soil contamination. In Germany, Baden-Wuertemberg adopted the first German soil protection law in July 1991, intended to prevent soil contamination and foster cleanup. It integrates soil and land use issues into state and municipal planning processes. On the federal level, to stimulate economic progress and investment in the states of the former GDR, the German Parliament exempted investors from liability or responsibility for clean-up of the some 25,000 contaminated sites in the eastern region.

Clean-up of contaminated soil has become a major environmental problem throughout Europe. Although there is little soil protection legislation, laws to protect groundwater from contamination impact on this field. Authorities may demand clean-up of abandoned and active contaminated sites if pollution levels are such that the groundwater table is threatened. Few sales of large industrial property are made today without prior soil investigation, risk analysis and related conditions being considered or included in the sales contract. This applies in particular to chemical plants, gas works and petroleum industry installations. The trend is toward estab-lishing requirements to protect the ground and soil even where groundwater is not threatened. In addition, the legislation of some countries requires, as a licensing condition, that abandoned plants be dismantled within a certain time after operations cease. Restoration to pre-plant conditions may be required.

On the international level, the Committee of Ministers of the Council of Europe adopted the European Soil Charter in 1972 and the United Nations Food and Agriculture Organization proclaimed a World Soil Charter in 1981. A year later, UNEP declared a World Soils Policy, recognizing that soil is a finite resource on which increasing demands are placed. Source-based action includes measures to control the shipment and disposal of hazardous wastes.

The Soil Charters both contain non-binding guidelines for action and basic princi-ples. They focus on the need for land-use policies that create incentives for people to participate in soil conservation. These policies require technical, institutional and

---

[2]  28 April 1952, completed 28 July 1967.
[3]  18 May 1989, modified no. 85 of 20–26 February 1990.

legal frameworks. In order to ensure optimum land use, a country's land resources should be assessed in terms of their suitability at different levels of inputs for different types of land use, including agriculture, grazing and forestry. Land having the potential for a wide range of uses should be kept in flexible forms of use so that future options for other potential uses are not denied. Utilization of land for non-agricultural purposes should be organized in such a way as to avoid, as much as possible, the occupation or permanent degradation of good quality soils.

Within the European Community, a 1985 directive[4] supported financial action by member states to encourage environmentally sound farming practices. It revised several established policies on farm investment, forestry and farm woodlands, and training and use of new technology. In particular, with regard to environmentally sensitive areas, member states were authorized to pay farmers to retain environmentally compatible practices and abstain from intensifying production. Denmark, Germany and the United Kingdom all have identified such areas and made arrangement with farmers. The EC budget contributes twenty-five per cent of the costs of such measures.

Recent Community regulations call for the withdrawal of farmland from agricultural production in order to reduce production by 20 per cent, leaving withdrawn land fallow, with the possibility of rotation, afforested or non-agricultural use. Remaining production should be monitored in order to ensure that further intensification does not occur.

Use of pesticides and fertilizers is regulated in virtually all countries, with certain products banned from sale or use. At a world-wide level, the FAO has elaborated a Code of Conduct on the distribution and use of pesticides. This subject is treated in a later chapter, as these products can cause harm to all environmental sectors.

Mining and industrial activities are regulated to the extent they impact on soil viability. For example, the use of impermeable surfaces to prevent spillage or leaks from storage is sometimes mandated, particularly in loading and unloading areas, beneath process plants and above-ground storage tanks. The latter can be required to have overfill detectors and high level alarms that automatically shut down operations if there is spillage. Inventory controls indicate losses through leakage. Legal standards also may require that all pipelines be made of anti-corrosive materials.

In general, it appears that soil is receiving increasing attention as a fundamental sector of the environment requiring complex special measures of protection against loss of its functions in ecosystems. As yet, however, there has not been the development of soil quality standards to the extent that water quality standards appear in national and regional texts.

[4] Directive 797/85/EEC.

# B. Case Studies

## 1. Michel Prieur, *Legal Protection for Soil*

Soil was for many years largely ignored by environmental law. However, since the European Soil Charter of the Council of Europe (30 May 1972), national environmental policy-makers have given particular attention to the functions and rapid deterioration of soil. Some national laws in Europe have begun to integrate soil into their general environmental laws or in specific laws, while awaiting a European treaty on soil protection.[5] These reflections have led to formulating new approaches to better incorporate soil protection in future environmental law.

### *Functions of the Soil and Sources of its Deterioration*

It is possible to distinguish six related not always complementary soil functions in a given zone. Three functions are primarily ecological and three are related more to human activities.

The three ecological functions are:

— The production of biomass: this function is at the base of human and animal life because it assures the provision of food, renewable energy and primary substances such as minerals. From this point of view, the soil is a physical foundation for the system. It is also a nutritional base, a reservoir of substances (water, air, and nutrients) necessary to the growth of vegetation. Due to the expanded use of fossil fuels and minerals during the second half of this century, problems of environmental pollution have appeared and the two other ecological functions of the soil have become increasingly important.

— Soil acts to filter, absorb, and transform pollution, protecting the environment in general and groundwaters and the food chain more specifically. The porous nature of soil makes it capable of stocking large quantities of water. In absorbing rainwater and controlling its progressive transportation to underground or surface waters, soil plays an important role in balancing water resources and protecting the countryside against erosion and destruction. In addition, thanks to the ability of clay to absorb chemical molecules and organic matter, soil plays a filtration and absorption role which protects groundwaters and the food chain from chemical pollution. In the same way, flora and fauna of the soil assure to some extent the transformation of organic toxic substances.

   The filtration, absorption and transformation capacities of the soil are limited. These limits are defined on one hand by physical, chemical and biological characteristics and on the other hand by the quality and quantity of pollutants.

— Biological habitat and genetic reservoir: the third ecological function of soil

---

[5] M. Prieur, "Feasibility Study of National and European Actions to Undertake for Soil Protection", Sixth European Ministerial Conference on the Environment. Brussels, 11–12 October 1990.

comes from the fact that it constitutes an important biological habitat for numerous organisms of flora and fauna which should be protected against extinction. This preservation of the genetic heritage is one of the most important factors for the survival of humanity.

The three functions directly linked to human activities are:

— Physical support: The soil is the spacial foundation for the installation of technical and industrial structures and the establishment of socio-economic activities. The soil also serves as physical support for the construction of buildings and factories, for transportation infrastructures and circulation, as well as for activities needing space, such as sports, recreation, waste dumps, etc. In several European countries, there already exists a very large competition between the functions of physical support and that of biomass production, above all agriculture.

— Source of primary substances: soil is a direct source of primary matter like water, argile, sand, gravel, and minerals, used in order to achieve socio-economic goals.

— Cultural heritage: the soil constitutes a cultural patrimony containing paleontological and archaeological treasures, unique sources of information which should be protected as historical evidence of the earth and of human cultures.

To conclude, it is necessary to insist on the fact that each of these six functions plays a fundamental role in the protection and conservation of soil. The constant of spacial variation in the place accorded to each of them and the competition that exists between them is of extreme importance in guiding conservation policy and rational management of this resource.

Natural soil loss occurs through erosion, sedimentation and acidification. Soil erosion by natural means is caused by floods and extreme superficial runoff due to heavy rainfall, as well as by strong winds. Neotectonic movements and earthquakes that result in landslides or movement can also cause erosion and sedimentation. In addition, volcanic eruptions can lead to sedimentation through deposit of ash or lava.

Soil degeneration and damage caused by periodic natural disasters is generally aggravated and accelerated by human action. For example, deforestation, strip mining, and paving over the earth lead to greater runoff. Overfarming and other poor agricultural practices accelerate erosion when strong winds or rains arrive.

Natural acidification of soil is an extremely slow process that in the tropics, for example, has taken hundreds of thousands of years. The natural process has been strongly increased by human behaviour. Human activities that affect the soil are both direct and indirect, through the atmosphere. Diffuse sources primarily come from air pollution, due to excessive utilization of fossil fuels and other primary elements by industrial processes, motor vehicles, and energy production. These pollutants lead to three types of soil degeneration problems.

First, deposits of sulphuric acid, ammonia and nitric acid coming from sulphur dioxide and nitrogen oxide in the air, as well as deposits of ammonia from animal waste products, pollute the soil. In excess, these deposits lead to a reduction of soil fertility and increase the mobility of heavy metals. They can lead to water pollution in both surface and underground waters, and a non-reversible degradation of important resources, such as the forests of central Europe and Scandinavia.

Pollution also results from the accumulation of toxic substances, principally heavy metals (for example lead, cadmium, copper, zinc, and nickel) and toxic organic substances (for example, PCB, KCB, HCH, PCDT). The behaviour of organic toxins in the soil is little known. Soil is also contaminated by radioactive substances.

Apart from these diffuse pollution sources, soil degradation occurs through physical and chemical changes introduced by human activities. The category of physical changes includes grading for road and building construction and excavations for the extraction of primary substances. In several European countries these influences already have reached a disquieting level. The problems need to be regulated through planning and rational utilization of the soil.

Soil erosion is a serious threat not only for soils of the Mediterranean region, but also for northern Europe. Erosion is provoked by clearing and/or by poor agricultural, forest and technical practices. Erosion results also from forest fires caused or aided by human acts, a considerable menace in southern Europe.

Unsound agricultural practices lead to soil depletion; this has resulted in serious soil deterioration in all zones of intensive growing in Europe.

Chemical changes come from dumping industrial and household wastes and sewage sludge, utilization of fertilizers and phyto-sanitary products. These can lead to pollution by heavy metals, pollution of groundwaters by nitrates, and contamination of both the soil and groundwaters by pesticides and herbicides, leading to accelerated loss of biological resources of the soil.

It is necessary to emphasize that there are numerous interactions between the diffuse and specific influences on the soil. These influences are synergistic, confronting earth scientists and managers with problems of growing magnitude.

For centuries, the soil was considered exclusively as a source of food, renewable energy and primary substances. This attitude is explained by constant economic growth coupled with a fear of large famines. But, until the last century, there was little pollution of the environment, leaving the ecological functions of the soil – filtration, absorption, transformation and preservation of genetic resources and cultural objects – unaffected. Moreover, the disappearance of soil due to urbanization, industrial development, recreation, waste disposal and mineral extraction, remained limited.

The situation radically changed in the middle of the last century. On the one hand, an overconsumption of land began, resulting from an increase in the development of human settlements and infrastructures. The soil disappeared under a concrete layer. On the other hand, this overconsumption caused both direct and indirect pollution, for example along roads and by factories. These in turn caused the ecological functions of the soil to be threatened or no longer utilized correctly.

In sum, it can be said that for centuries the soil conserved all its ecological, technical, industrial and socio-economic functions, thanks to its physical, chemical and biological characteristics. Today, symptoms constantly appear that indicate that these functions are severely tested by diffuse and specific attacks which increasingly threaten our pedological system.

On the base of current knowledge and in ranking the problems according to their urgency, it is possible to distinguish harm from reversible dangers. Reversible means that the effects can be repaired by nature or by technical or biological measures, making the damages "reparable". Non-reversible harm is that which it is impossible to remedy or that which is reparable only in the very long term (for example, over one hundred years).

Applying this distinction, it appears that the following phenomena are not reversible:

— loss of soil through excavation and by extraction of materials, mineral exploitation and erosion, except in limited cases;

— contamination and pollution by heavy metals coming from atmospheric pollution and products utilized in agriculture, as well as by radioactive elements;

— advanced acidification, involving the degradation of constituents of the soil.

Reversible damage includes:

— soil pollution from organic compounds, coming from air pollution or agricultural sources, and which, in the medium or long term, is degradable through chemical or biochemical means;

— the compacting, sliding, and other deterioration in the structure of the soil.

### Comparison of National Laws

Some elements of a legal model for soil protection can be drawn from a comparative study of the policies and positive laws of European countries, keeping in mind that soil receives generally less attention than other fundamental elements of the biosphere. Of course, the contrasting characteristics of different states (such as the level of industrialization, amount of forest cover, population density, geology, climate conditions, presence or absence of coasts, etc.) influence the gravity of the different problems and the legal responses to them. However these particularities are subsidiary to concerns of transfrontier pollution and to European solidarity.

All European States have adopted norms and conduct policies with direct or indirect effect on soil protection. Most often these measures are enacted in response to crises or urgent and serious problems and do not reflect long-term visions of rational, economic and prudent management of a fragile good. One can speak of "catastrophe visibility" as a major factor producing policies and standards. It is also clear that the measures adopted are frequently insufficient to protect the soil.

Harm caused by humans, of the greatest concern, can be categorized as follows:

— effects of intensive and high-producing agricultural techniques;

— effects of industrialization and global enrichment;

— effects of urbanization of developed societies.

These external variables, all expressions of "modernity" are coupled with internal variables in ecosystems. In addition, most pollutants move easily from water to soil, then to water, from air to the soil, etc. The external and internal variables combine to produce harm in two ways: homeopathic and slow or accidental.

The possible legal measures to protect soil are numerous: a specific law aimed at the integral and varied functions of the soil; specific laws concerning only one or certain soil functions; specific provision on the soil integrated in a general law on the environment, or integrated in diverse sectoral laws; utilization of contractual instruments or financial incentives. It seems today that the legal measures in force concerning soil protection are more often of an indirect than a direct type.

For agriculture, the large majority of states have adopted legislation and regulations which balance the effects of intensified agriculture on the soil. The utilization of chemical or animal fertilizers, sewage sludge, pesticides, and herbicides is often limited, usually in connection with water quality standards.

Other, non-agricultural uses of soil are regulated by legal provisions concerning:

— soil degradation provoked by certain industrial activities;

— mining activities;

— maintenance of public health;

— the management of household and industrial wastes, of variable toxicity, and more generally of effluents;

— the protection of open spaces, including areas that are fragile, unique, or of a historical character;

— urban planning of dedicated uses for different zones.

No doubt these provisions have an effect, though sometimes only indirect, on the protection of soil.

The often broad character of the contents of environmental impact assessments required by European national laws generally allows inclusion of effects of projected operations on the soil. However, this depends on many factors and it does not seem that the soil is considered as seriously as other elements. A narrowly drawn impact study can raise problems especially for planning or agricultural work.

In some cases, fiscal incentives are used, as well as the elaboration of technical recommendations and information programmes in regard to real or potential polluters. In addition, European policies such as leaving arable lands fallow or taking into account the "polluter pays" principle can have an incentive effect on soil protection.

From the abundance of texts and their relative similarity, it appears that :

— much has been done in a reactive manner in a climate of urgency;

— a piecemeal approach to soil protection has resulted in dividing management of the subject among multiple agencies;

— there are doubts about the effectiveness of certain legal provisions;

— the experience of states with highly polluted or deteriorated soil only modestly influences preventive measures in less polluted states.

### A Better Soil Protection Policy

The bases of action should be established in advance, before envisaging the technical means, or adopting legal measures. The soil as a precious and finite good should be seen as part of the common heritage to be preserved for future generations; as such, real property ownership cannot block a policy of soil protection, but should be considered as a social function. This suggests that the conservation and restoration of the soil is in the general interest.

It is necessary to take preventive action to guarantee the quality and diversity of the soil for all future uses, some of which are impossible to foresee today.

Administrative authorities should permit soil use based on the principle of reversibility and the decontamination of polluted soil in the general interest. As part of the precious and limited collective heritage, the soil, whatever its use may be, should be governed by the principle of sustainable use.

The soil should be treated with equal importance and intensity as other fundamental elements of life, such as air or water, the interdependence of all being evident.

All the functions of the soil should be integrated in equal legitimacy: however, the major importance, if not exclusive value, historically attached to productive soil functions should today be balanced by a priority preoccupation with the environmental aspects of the soil.

It is necessary that states establish scientific and technical organizations and assign them tasks of

— soil analysis and control;

— cleanup of contaminated sites;

— analysis of processes of contamination;

— undertaking methods of restoration and prevention.

These "observers" should be coordinated at the European level, and the body of their analyses, studies, results, propositions, should be made accessible to the public, and directly utilizable in impact studies.

In addition to fixing and harmonizing anti-pollution standards, the establishment of a framework soil law, governed by unified rules seems a necessity for the integrated management and protection of the soil. However, its utility depends on arriving at scientific criteria permitting classification of soils (fertility, contamination ...).

The opportunity for campaigns of information and recommendations in regard to agents whose activities represent a threat to the integrity of the soil should be explored.

If an exclusive and exhaustive soil law is not adopted, it then becomes useful for each sectoral law to consider the necessary link of that sector to the soil, including explicit provisions imposing environmental consideration of the soil. This policy should also cover agricultural policy, industry, transport, urban development and land use. All legal instruments relating to the management of space should include a section on soil and soil quality, to which the technical organs mentioned above can contribute their competence.

Environmental impact assessment procedures should be extended to agricultural activities. Like the best available technology requirement imposed upon industry, agriculture should conform to a rule of using the best agricultural practices, taking into account the soil and ecosystems. In addition, the law should imperatively and expressly specify that the soil is among the elements to consider systematically in assessing the consequences of projected installations or activities.

Given the gravity of threats to the soil from abandoned dumps and contaminated industrial sites, the Community should envisage a common and harmonious action to restore sites, identify those responsible, foresee financing on the base of the polluter pays principle, and organize strict preventive procedures including an eventual obligation of insurance to guarantee the future restoration of the sites.

A tax for excessive uses or dumping of harmful matter on the soil should be imposed to limit abuses and permit the financing of soil restoration operations.

In conclusion, it should be noted that the Community has taken a number of sectoral actions aimed at protecting soils, which contribute to establishing a defence strategy:

— Directive 86/278 of 12 June 1986 on sewage sludge used in agriculture;

— Directive 80/68 of 17 December 1979 on the protection of groundwaters against pollution caused by certain dangerous substances;

— Regulation 2092/91 of 24 June 1991, regulating biological agriculture;

— Directive 91/676 of 12 December 1991 on combating soil pollution from nitrates;

— Directive 91/156 of 16 March 1991 on the control of wastes; and

— Regulation 2328/91 of 15 July 1991 concerning the improvement of the efficiency of agricultural structures.

## 2. H. Hacourt, *Council of Europe Activities Relating to Soil Protection*

### *Work of the Council of Europe*

Many national and international organizations, both governmental or non-governmental, have looked into or are still considering the problems of soil conservation. In the Council of Europe problems of soil protection are a priority activity in its programme of work.

The Parliamentary Assembly and the Standing Conference of Local and Regional Powers in Europe have long been working in this field. These two bodies of the Council of Europe have produced recommendations on concrete measures that consider the soil a natural resource like the air, water, habitats, etc. and thus aim to preserve the quality of its physical, chemical and biological properties.

On an inter-governmental level, the Committee of Ministers of the Council of Europe, in 1972, adopted the "European Soil Charter". Unfortunately, it remains topical, perhaps even being more topical now than in 1972 because environmental problems, particularly those relating to natural resources, are more acute today, mainly owing to the break-neck development of industrial society in Europe.

Other activities undertaken in the Council of Europe have a more or less direct bearing on soil conservation problems. Two activities are described here by way of example:

— Building on directives of the European Communities that ask Member States to reduce farmland areas in order to cut food stocks, the Council of Europe is endeavouring to define principles to govern the recovery of these abandoned farmlands for conservation purposes. The aim of this activity is to re-establish as many natural environments as possible, the best way of saving the wild species of fast disappearing flora and fauna.

— In 1990, the 6th European Ministerial Conference on the Environment adopted the European Conservation Strategy. In its sectoral aspects, the Strategy devotes one of its points to soil and defines a series of principles. The final principle states its aim to: "strengthen the legal foundations and their application on a national scale and draft, if necessary, a European legal instrument for soil protection".

Finally, the above-mentioned European Ministerial Conference on the Environment, and the Conference of Ministers responsible for land planning and development reviewed the problems of soil conservation; they sent the Committee of Ministers of the Council of Europe resolutions seeking, on the one hand, to explore the possibility of drafting a suitable convention on soil protection and, on the other hand, to apply certain principles in developing a rational land-use policy. Indeed, the urbanization of land should be better regulated by national, regional and local development plans aimed in principle at economical, reversible use.

### Draft European Convention for Soil Protection

In most states, soil protection *per se* does not appear in national legislation; it is merely included in legislation on environmental protection in general which is very often sectoral.

The report of the Belgian delegation at the 6th European Ministerial Conference on the Environment pointed out five different ways of legally protecting soil:

1. draft a specific law covering all the functions of the soil. That is the most innovative approach.
2. draft specific rules covering only certain functions of the soil;
3. draft specific rules within general environmental legislation;
4. incorporate soil protection in sectoral environmental laws;
5. allow privileged use of contractual instruments or incentives.

On an international level, one must distinguish between two kinds of instrument:

1. texts containing principles of soil protection among norms covering the environment as a whole. This is found in the Plan of Action (recommendations 19 to 23) adopted by the Stockholm Conference in June 1972, the Final Act of the Helsinki Conference in August 1975, the World Charter for Nature

proclaimed by the United Nations General Assembly in October 1982, the 1987 Report of the Global Environment and Development Commission;

2. texts devoted especially to soil protection: the 1972 European Soil Charter of the Council of Europe, the World Soil Charter proclaimed by the FAO in 1981, and several recommendations of the Parliamentary Assembly and the Standing Conference of Local and Regional Powers in Europe.

At the 6th European Ministerial Conference on the Environment (Brussels, October 1990), the Ministers of the Environment took up a recommendation from the preceding conference (Lisbon, June 1987) which had asked "to study the possibility of drafting an appropriate Convention on soil protection". In Brussels, the Ministers recommended

that the Committee of Ministers of the Council of Europe take action, starting with a Recommendation, to implement a concrete programme of work comprising a series of initiatives to protect the soil, leading, if appropriate in the light of the experience gained, to the drafting of a framework convention in 1993 and possible additional protocols providing legal security for the future.

The current activities of the Council of Europe relating to soil derive from the above-mentioned text formulated at the Ministerial Conference. At present, action is focused on the recommendation and programme of work is underway, bearing in mind the possibility of drafting a Convention.

It is worth specifying that a draft Convention has not yet been written and that the decision to draft it will only be taken by the Committee of Ministers of the Council of Europe on the basis of earlier work. No one at this stage can predict the decision of the Council of Ministers or the acceptance of a Convention by the governments of Member States. Some reticence already exists.

Should a positive decision be made, what shape should this Convention take and what should it contain? In the opinion of the Ministers of the Environment, the European Convention should be a framework Convention based on the technique adopted for the Geneva Convention (1979) on long-range transboundary air pollution.

The European Convention might include commitments of principle, a framework for cooperation among the contracting parties with a view to setting up research programmes, and intensified exchanges of information and mutual assistance. Subsequently, the European Convention might be supplemented by additional protocols spelling out the scope of certain points.

One can envisage the following main chapters:

1. A preamble referring to the urgency of international action, the activities of the international organizations, in particular the Council of Europe, the enactment of specific national legislation in certain member states of the Council of Europe.

   The preamble might also describe the causes of soil degradation, the seriousness of the damage (reversible and irreversible), and the need for coordinated action in the field of information, research and monitoring with a view to soil protection.

2. The first chapter would contain general provisions, including, *inter alia*, the

definition of soil, its ecological functions and the functions linked to human activities.

3.  The second chapter would set out the general principles:

    — fundamental principles: e.g. the soil is a common heritage and a non-renewable natural resource; its protection should systematically be taken into consideration in all other policies: agricultural, forestry, industrial, urbanism, and transport;

    — principles of soil management: e.g. the soil should be managed in an economical way and its use should be limited by the priority given to maintaining unpolluted agricultural land;

    — functional principles: consideration of multifunctionality through the harmonization of ground use and the rule of reversibility insofar as eventual changes in land-use are concerned.

4.  The third chapter would ask the contracting parties to undertake research and exchange information, to carry out evaluations and scientific observations and to cooperate with each other on problems relating to soil degradation. The instruments might include:

    — joint research in several fields;

    — exchanges of legal, scientific and socio-economic information;

    — soil observatories: their creation and functions as well as a coordinated observatory network.

5.  The fourth chapter could define specific action to protect the soil in order to ensure proper conservation. These specific activities might be spelled out, supplemented and amended by the protocols to the convention.

6.  The fifth chapter would set up a liaison body responsible for implementation and follow-up of the Convention; this body might in turn create working parties to prepare studies on specific issues.

7.  The sixth chapter would set up a permanent secretariat.

8.  The seventh chapter would set out the final provisions usual in any convention: settlement of disputes, signature, ratification, acceptance and approval, adhesion, entry into force, denunciation and the depositary.

There would then be the protocols and annexes that the contracting parties decide to add.

There are four arguments in favour of the Convention:

1.  The Convention would constitute a single instrument covering the various problems of soil pollution, thereby enabling States better to organize international cooperation to monitor trends in soil degradation and improve coordination of their national policies;

2.  The Convention would not force States that did not so wish to participate in its activities; only the contracting parties would be concerned by these activities, thereby also ensuring a solid financial base;

3.  The Convention would enable States that do not belong to the Council of Europe to participate in its activities along with the other States;

4.  The Convention would lend continuity to the networks of cooperation that might be set up.

There are also four arguments against the Convention:

1.  Soil protection is a very complex issue that is intertwined with other problems like the irrational use of pesticides, fertilizers, waste storage, etc. Similarly, in the more specific case of soil pollution, it can be indirect or, in some instances, direct;

2.  The complexity of the problems might make it difficult to incorporate all the issues raised by soil protection in a single text; likewise, the system of additional protocols might slow the incorporation of Convention standards in national legislation;

3.  A Convention might not provide the requisite flexibility to respond to the different circumstances in the field of pollution within and among countries;

4.  A Convention calls for the creation of operating mechanisms; funds are required to cover the functioning of a Secretariat.

The foregoing is the current line of action of the Council of Europe. Will it bear tangible results? It will be up to the governments of member States to decide. In any event, our feeling is that a Convention would be a useful instrument to rationalize soil protection efforts in Europe.

## 3. Alberto Lucarelli, *Soil Protection in Italy*

In 1989 the Italian parliament promulgated law 183/89 for the protection of the soil and water catchment basins. The law had, for many years, passed back and forth between the two Chambers in a long and tortuous approval procedure.[6]

In fact, the proposal for an organic law on the protection of the soil dates back to 1966. In order to protect the territory from damage caused by overflowing watercourses, administrative bodies already existed *ad hoc*.[7] After the tragic floods of 1966 and when the Arno overflowed in Florence, the Commissione de Marchi was established in 1967. It formulated proposals for a proper policy for soil protection, identifying four main points:

a)  a basin or group of catchment basins as the basis for any action;

b)  the basin authority as a central authority;

c)  a finalized basin plan for the purification of the water sources;

---

[6] The bill, which on parliamentary initiative was presented to the Camera dei Deputati (Chamber of Deputies) by On. Botta *et al* on 22 July 1987, was approved only on 11 May 1989. For the preparatory work on L. 183/89, *see* legislature n. 293, May 1989, Territorial and Communications Department, Chamber of Deputies, study service.

[7] For the Po, the Po authority instituted L. 12.7.1956 n. 735; for Venice, the water authorities instituted L.5.5.1907 n. 57.

d) the restructuring of existing governing bodies, i.e. the Ministry of Public Works and the Ministry of Agriculture.

The law of 18 May 1989 was modified by L. no. 253 of 7 August 1990[8] after certain regulations were pronounced unconstitutional by the Constitutional Court.[9] In final form it assures, according to art. 1,

... the protection of the soil, the purification of the water sources, the fulfillment and management of the water heritage for the use of sensible economic and social development, the protection of environmental aspects related to them.

The main points of the law govern:

1. the central agencies of the state (arts. 4–9) and the inter-relationships between them, the regions and the local institutions.

2. the catchment basins which divide up the entire national territory, classified into eleven national relief basins (art.14) and eighteen interregional (art.15) and regional (art.16) ones

3. the basin authority (art.12) operating the national relief catchment basins.

4. basin plans (arts. 17–20) drawn up by the basin authority governing actions and regulations directed towards the conservation, protection and utilization of the soil, as well as the proper use of the water source in the basin.

The law attributes a central role to the state bodies, as evident from art. 4(2) col. 1 which gives the Prime Minister key functions. The Prime Minister has, by decree, and with the prior deliberation of the Cabinet, the power to approve the following:

a) decisions concerning the methods and criteria, even technical, to carry out the realization, planning, programming, fulfillment, examining and checking of the basin plans and of the intervention and management programmes.

b) acts related to delimiting the national and inter-regional relief basins.

c) plans for the national relief basins.

d) the national intervention programme.

e) acts directed towards providing a substitute in the case of persistent inactivity by those assigned functions by law, if it concerns duties which must be carried out within essential boundaries, with respect to the obligations assumed or the nature of the intervention.

f) every other act of direction and coordination governed by the present law. Art. 2 provides for collecting, formulating, archiving, researching and studying the elements and the general conditions of or risks to the physical environment; drawing and up-dating of topical maps of the territory; evaluating and studying the results of implementing the plans, programmes and work projects provided

---

[8] Disposizioni integrative alla L. 18 maggio 1989, n. 193, recante norme per il riassetto organizzativo e funzionale della difese del suolo, in Gass. Uff. n. 205 of 3 September 1990.

[9] Judgment no. 85 of 20–26 February 1990. See P. Mantini, "La legge per la difesa del suolo e la gestione delle acque", in *Lezioni di Diritto Pubblico dell'Ambiente* (1991), pp. 205 ss.

for under the law; and putting into effect the initiatives necessary to fulfill the aim of art. 1. Planning, programming and implementation are considered in art. 3 and implemented in the organization, conservation and the reclamation of soil in the catchment basins; in the protection and systemization of the water supplies, flood control and regulation of the mining industries, the strengthening of unstable areas, the protection of the coasts, the containing of subsidence of the soil, the purification of surface and underground water supplies; the sensible utilization of water resources, both surface and underground, as well as several other minor projects.

According to art. 4, the Prime Minister may, by decree, approve national relief basin plans after deliberation of the Cabinet, hearings before the National Committee for the protection of the soil (incorporated in art. 6) and subject to the opinion of the Consiglio Superiore of Public Works. The language of the article evidences legislative intent to attribute to the Cabinet the duty of directing and coordinating the core problems of soil protection.

Furthermore, law n.183/89 should be read in close reference to law n. 400/88[10] which defines in detail Prime Minister's office. Together the laws create a model of collaboration and general integration of the duties of the Prime Minister with the other central bodies of the public administration.

The innovative aspect of the law is the choice of the Ministry of Public Works as the key agency (art. 5). This Ministry is attributed executive and organizational powers, as well as those of planning and coordinating projects. Under the direction of this Ministry, a national committee for the protection of the soil, a predominantly technical–scientific body, has been set up (art. 6). Its primary responsibilities are the adoption of national basin plans and the drawing-up and presentation of proposals, opinions and observations to implement the duties contained in art. 4.

The first critical comment to be made about law 183/89 concerns the assignment of environmental protection functions to the Ministry of Public Works. It is difficult to understand why the legislature limited, or relegated to a secondary role, the new Ministry of the Environment. Its institutional duties[11] include assuring, within a concise framework, the promotion, conservation and improvement of environmental conditions, as well as the conservation and use of the national heritage and the protection of natural resources from pollution. In addition, the Ministry of the Environment is assigned functions relating to reform of the Administration of Public Works,[12] and functions in relation to the organization of the national territory and

---

[10] For the law see Suppl. ord. G.U.R.I., n. 214 of 12.9.1988. For a comment see S. Labriola, "Il governo della Republica, organi e poteri, commentario alla L. 23.8.1988 n. 40, Rimini 1989; AA.VV., La Legge sulla Presidenza del Consiglio, in il Foro Italiano, June 1989, V. 373–384.

[11] Art. 1 L.349/86. On the law of the Ministry of the Environment in general, see P. Maddalena, IL Ministro dell'Ambiente in Comuni d'Italia, 1987, 767; A. Gustapane, Alcune osservazioni sulla recente istituzione del Ministero dell'ambiente, in Sanità pubblica, 1987, p. 143; E. Picozza, L'ambiente allo Stato, in Corr. giur., 1987, p. 1044; A. Postiglione, Una svolta per il diritto all'ambiente: la legge 8 luglio 1986, n. 349 i Riv. giur. amb., 1986, p. 251; S. Labriola, Ministero dell'Ambiente, in Studi parlamentari di politica costituzionale, 1986, fasc. 2–3–10; F. Salvia, Il Ministerio dell'Ambiente, La Nuova Italia, Roma 1989.

[12] Art. 2, col. 1, L. 349/86.

the protection of soil, as well as the national planning of the destination of the water resources (arts. 90/91 of the same decree).[13] In spite of this, the only powers assigned by law 183/89 to the Ministry of the Environment are those incorporated in art. 5(3) which confers upon it administrative functions regarding pollution control and the disposal of wastes in the national and inter-regional relief basins. In our opinion, the lack of a central authority for all state environmental protection could become the cause of a conflict between the Ministry of the Environment's responsibility for general environmental protection and the predominant duty of the Ministry of Public Works to protect soil and water resources. Such a division would lead to difficulties in following a consistent environmental policy, resulting in fragmentary and isolated intervention having little effect on the conservation and purification measures needed to counteract harm from pollution. In order to avoid such conflict, a member of parliament has proposed to create a single Ministry of the Territory.[14] The contradictions and problems of law 183/89 highlight the urgent need for such a Ministry, which could redefine and incorporate the functions presently performed by the Ministries of the Environment and Public Works, of 'Beni Ambientali e Culturali' and Civil Protection.

The main uncertainties which emerge from the law under examination concern the lack of precise coordination and the need to unite in one Ministry the functions which are currently distributed among various administrations. Nonetheless, the regulations in question constitute the first organic attempt at a serious policy for the protection of soil and water resources. Italy now has an eco-environmental policy which moves away from the emergency response approach characterizing recent legislation. This legislative reform has also put substantial financial resources at the disposition of the government. A fund of 2,400 billion lira, created by the three-year plan for soil protection, together with other resources made available by the Ministry of the Environment for the safeguarding of the environment and the purification of water resources, represent considerable financial support. This will help further the objectives of the law, in particular fulfillment of the basin plans. These plans, discussed in detail below, will create the means by which to plan and control the national territory. With new and efficient legislation and with suitable financial resources, the ability of the government and its institutions to carry out their duties will be put to the test.

Art. 10 of law 183/89 governs the duties of the regions. They perform the functions delegated to them and those specifically related to water and land management. They are also entrusted with a primary role in the formulation, adoption and activation of the catchment basin plans at the regional level. Inter-regional plans require their approval (art. 10(1)(d)). With regard to regional and inter-regional basins, the regions

---

13 Col. 1 of art. 81 of the DPR 616/77. The DPR n. 617 has delegated to the regions, on the basis of col. 2 of art. 18 of the Constitution, a series of administrative functions already state responsibility. The delegation concerns administrative functions related to town-planning, use of the territory including the environment and the protection of nature.

14 The proposal to set up a Ministry of the Territory was announced in the sitting of 28 July 1988 by On. Kassim Serafini, a member of the enviro-territorial working Commission.

approve and execute intervention projects (art. 10 col. 1 lett. e). However, regional authority concerning national relief catchment basins is limited. The regions collabo-rate in the surveying and formulation of the project plans (art. 10(1)(b)) and draw up proposals for the formation of programmes, studies and projects (art. 10(1)(c) They are also present, even if subordinate to the state bodies, in the institutional and technical committees of the basin authorities which, according to art. 12 (e) and (g) adopt and control the realization of the basin plans.

Therefore the power of the regions in the above-mentioned plans is placed in a subordinate position in relation to the central body of public administration. Finally, it must be noted that the 1990 amendment to 183/89 provides that basic principles of action concerning direction and coordination, approved by the decree of the Prime Minister after deliberation of the Cabinet, must be submitted beforehand to the permanent Conference on relations between the State, the regions and the auto-nomous provinces of Trento and Bolzano. This modification, resulting from the judgment of the Constitutional Court n. 85 of 20–26 February 1990, is intended to push the government to consider more seriously regional needs in the formulation of direction and coordination. The expression used by the legislature is ambiguous, as it does not specify the legal status of the opinion of the State–regional conference.

In article 10 the legislature did not intend to create a rigid separation between the duties of the State and those of the regions. The law, without always achieving its goal, aims to create a system of cooperation between the regions and the various central administrations involved in achieving common aims such as the safeguarding of the territory.

Of particular interest is art. 1(5) which affirms that "the provisions of the current law constitute fundamental rules of socio-economic reform of the republic as well as basic principles, within the meaning of art. 117 of the Constitution". It should be immediately specified that the nature of the socio-economic reform in this law is not determined merely by legislative intent, but derives from the object of the law in its socio-political motivation, its objectives and its contents. Present doctrine considers state laws on socio-economic reform of equal stature to the legal framework govern-ing matters of regional legislative functions. The law, and in particular the basin plans, thus control those local norms on the organization of the territory, such as regulations on town planning, which art. 117(2) reserves to the regional authority. In sum, the autonomous territories are confronted with regulations that govern as a framework law; insofar as the national norms only fix general principles, the regions may make their own laws. National guidelines cannot invade the regional authority with particular detailed rules.

In this view it should be noted that the regulations in question, and in particular those governing the basin plans, are not limited to establishing principles, but regulate in detail all matters which have an effect on the territory. This could raise doubts as to the constitutional legitimacy of the law. However, it is hard to imagine how a key law could govern all the aspects of the territory and respect the limits of art. 117 of the Constitution, by leaving regions the responsibility for urban matters. Among the rules that could generate conflict between the State and the regions is art. 4, which requires that the Prime Minister approve the basin plans. The problem lies in determining how the Prime Minister can assume duties which are really the concern of the regions. The provisions of art. 14 (national relief basins) and art. 17 (value, purpose and content of the basin plans) are governed by the detailed nature of the plans. It seems, therefore, unfounded to state that all the regulations of law must have a basic socio-economic reform value, as art. 4(v). In the text there are essential rules of procedure which should not be considered at the same level as the basic principles of the juridical system.

In conclusion, the law in question alters the constitutional principle of art. 117 and limits the level of regional autonomy, undermining their authority. This tendency could lead to transferring responsibility for town-planning to the State, with the risk of inciting new conflicts between the State and the regional autonomies.

The law, in part 2, entitled "limits, means, interventions, resources" indicates the limits of application of the regulations. Art. 13 states that the whole national territory, including the smaller islands, is divided into national, inter-regional and regional relief basins. Art. 1(III)(d) gives the first definition of a catchment basin:

> the place from where river or melted waters from snow and glaciers, flowing down to the surface, collect in a particular water-course, either directly, or by means of tributaries. It can also be an area which has become flooded by water from the very same water source, including all territories with outlets to sea and those with a coastline; if a territory becomes flooded by water from more than one water source, it is considered as belonging to the catchment basin with the higher surface of rainwater.

National relief basins are explained in art. 14, inter-regional in art. 15 and the regional in art. 16(II). As far as the national catchment basins are concerned, they are the responsibility of the basin authority (art. 12) which is made up of the following bodies: Institutional Committee, Technical Committee, Secretary General and Technical Secretary. The first of these is predominantly political, presided over by the Ministry of Public Works or Ministry of the Environment. The main duties of the Institutional Committee are to establish criteria and methods of formulating basin plans, deciding on times and formalities and to promote the necessary measures to guarantee their realization.

The Technical Committee has a consultative role within the Institutional Committee, making use of the Technical Secretary. The Committee, presided over by the Secretary General, consists of civil servants belonging to the State, and those of the regions which form part of the Institutional Committee. The Minister of Public Works has been appointed head of the Technical Committee. This Committee, so as to have a purely technical function, is closely bound to the political powers. This undoubtedly represents a negative aspect of the law. A body that has to carry out a technical–consultative role would function better with fewer restraints imposed by the political power.

Both the administrative body of the basin authority and the Secretary General are chosen from the Technical Committee or from experts with a suitable qualification. The Secretary General is nominated by the Institutional Committee with the agreement of the Ministry of Public Works and the Ministry of the Environment. The tasks of the administration are to fulfill the duties necessary for the smooth running of the basin authority, to supervise the duties of the Institutional Committee, and to oversee relations with state and regional administrations and local institutions, guaranteeing fulfillment of the directives. Finally, the Technical Secretary is composed of employees of public works and the staff assigned by the relevant state and regional administrations.

The establishment of the basin authority is the result of considerable planning and reflection on the part of the Senate which proposed this body. As the centre of policy and implementation, the basin authority should have had, particularly in the political Institutional Committee, a more flexible structure to carry out its duties without too many bureaucratic obstacles. As it is, the authority is composed of four Ministries, namely those of Public Works, the Environment, Agriculture and Forestry, and "Boni Culturali e Ambientali", as well as the regions of the territories concerned. Such a tightly bureaucratic organization should be balanced by a flexible agent such as the Secretary General, who, in this state-controlled structure, could accomplish the task of delegated administrator, ensuring direct and efficient intervention.

It is hoped that the basin authority, following the experience of other European countries,[15] will manage, in the near future, to achieve the main objective for which it was set up: the establishment of a national basin plan. The basin plans, if well structured and approved, could set governing regulations, resulting in the conservation, protection, and utilization of the soil as well as the correct use of the basin waters. The basin plan regulates all the activities related to the protection of the soil from pollution, floods, and the utilization of the soil for agriculture, forestry, industry and mining and all forms of protection and use of the water sources. Given the general nature of the basin plan, this could be linked to the territorial land use plan, which operates on a much wider territorial scale and which establishes the directives the administrations should adopt. The territorial plan of coordination is provided for in arts. 5 and 6 of the general town-planning law n. 1150 of 1942, before DPR 1972/8 delegated powers to the regions by ordinary statute.

The hazy legislative definition of these plans (art. 5 III Col.E.U) means that, to date, they have been adopted by only a few regions. The plans, according to art. 5(1) act "to orient and coordinate urban duties carried out in specific parts of the territory", establishing the directives to follow in the particular territory, in relation to specific public interests such as the landscape, archaeology, art and protection of the soil. In conclusion it is maintained that the basin plan, being of a general nature which can be related to territorial plans of coordination, may be considered as something new. They not only have town-planning objectives, but the local agents receiving direction from the provisions contained in the basin plans are the administrative authorities holding territorial

---

[15] For France, see L. 16.12.1964, n. 1245 and successive decrees; For Germany, see law on the use of the water sources, of 27 June 1957, amended in 1990; for the United Kingdom, see the Water Reorganization Bill of 1973, previously the River Authorities, set up by the law of 1963. For the United States, see the Clean Water Act of 1977. With regard to foreign models, cf. the close examination of G. Cordini, op. cit., pp. 439ss.; Le Recueil de législation sanitaire, 1974, vol. XXV, N. 3, p. 689, 1978, vol. XXIV, pp. 412–13; G. Notarbartolo; Il governo dei fiumi in Francia, in AA. VV., La difesa del suolo e la politica delle acque, Milano, 1990, pp. 155ss.; R. Macrory, La gestione dei bacini idrografici in Inghilterra e nel Galles, idem, pp. 193ss.

powers of planning and economic development, taking into account the private sector (Art. 17(4) and (6) of L. 183/89). In contrast, receivers of the regulations in the territorial plans of coordination are the administrative authorities of urban planning.

Art. 17(4) places the basin plan at the top of the system of planning, which merges with the existing regional plans wherever possible. It otherwise imposes on the relevant authorities the obligation of adjusting their methods of town planning within twelve months. This provision raises several problems related to changing regional plans approved by regional authorities to the national basin plans approved by D.P.C.M. The state acts which approve national basin plans have a directive function in regional duties.[16] The plans must implement the state duties provided for by art. 81(1) DPR 616/77).

According to the Constitutional Court[17] there is power to restrain and direct the legislative power and that of regional administration not only regarding legislative acts, but also administrative acts of direction and coordination. The Court, in judgment n. 150 of 1982 held that state direction and coordination should be brought back to the rule of state law, from which it draws its own basis and its capacity to limit the legislative power of the regions. The Court also stated that direction and coordination should conform to the criteria which restrain and direct the government's choices in relation to the needs of the whole state.

The prevalence of the basin plan in the regional programmes, approved by law, is justified by needs of a precise nature pursued in 183/89. Having established the principle of preference of the state administrative act of direction and coordination over the legislative power of the regions, problems could arise if the national basin plan does not limit itself to the above-stated functions, but if its provisions become more detailed. Interference of the national relief basin plan in more detailed regional programmes could lead to possible conflict between state and regional autonomies.

In accordance with the decision of the Constitutional Court,[18] the national basin plan should contain only general directives, leaving ample space for adapting to regional concerns. It is worth mentioning again that the rules governing the basin plans are not limited only to the establishing of principles and directives, but also govern, with substantially detailed rules of procedure, all the aspects which affect the territory. If too detailed and therefore unconstitutional, the basin plan loses its directive function with regard to regional planning.

In conclusion, L.183/89 does not propose any solution to the problem of division between the State and the regional (or provincial) autonomies in governing the territory. The setting-up of new authorities could generate further conflict, not only of a state–regional nature, but also between state bodies. The creation of a new method of territorial-urban planning would make the relationship between the State and the regional autonomies even more strained, resulting in each defending its own actions and duties. This situation goes against the Constitution of 1948 and the legislation of 1972 and 1977 which dealt with the total transfer of urban matters to

---

[16] See art. 17 1. n. 281 of 1970; art. 2 1. n. 382/1975 and art. 4 DPR 616/77.

[17] See C. Cost. n. 150 of 1982, n. 64 of 1987, n. 195 of 1986, n. 177 of 1986.

[18] Judgment of the Constitutional Court, n. 340 of 15.12.1983, n. 340 in Cons. Stato, 1983, II, p. 1459.

the regions. Some reason for the current law can be found in the inactivity of the regions, which, assigned duties in the 1970s, have not proved themselves capable of carrying them out. The inability and inertia of the regions in finding means of planning in order to govern their own territory has led to the State taking alternative means. It has consequently decided to intervene directly in the governing of the territory, and has not confined itself only to its functions of direction and coordination.

## 4. Malcolm Forster, *Liability for Contaminated Land in the United Kingdom*

### a. General principles of liability for environmental harm in English law

English law makes no special provision for liability for environmental degradation.[19] Therefore, liability for damage arising from contaminated land is governed by the general principles of the common law of tort. The actions which are of most immediate relevance in this context are:

— the tort of nuisance;
— the action under the rule in *Rylands* v. *Fletcher*;
— the tort of negligence;
— the action in trespass.

### The tort of nuisance

Actionable nuisance takes one of two forms, private nuisance and public nuisance (the latter is also capable of being a crime as well as a tort).

*Private nuisance* consists in an unlawful interference by the defendant with the plaintiff's use and enjoyment of his land, or of some right enjoyed by him over land or connected with it. The action is widely used in pollution cases, which provide some of the best-known examples of its operation.[20] It is of clear application to pollution from contaminated land.

There are, however, several limitation on the usefulness of the action. First, it is clear that it is in essence a proprietary remedy, in that the plaintiff must show that he has an interest in land which has been affected by the conduct complained of.[21]

Second, it is not every trifling interference with such land which will ground the action. Nuisance will only arise if the interference with the plaintiff's land or his enjoyment of it is unreasonable in all the circumstances.[22] In years past, there may

---

[19] With the exception of the special regime for damage caused by contamination arising from oil carried by ships, introduced under the Merchant Shipping (Oil Pollution) Act 1970. This regime merely reflects the provisions of the CLC and Fund Conventions.

[20] See, for example, *Halsey* v. *Esso Petroleum [1961]* 1 W.L.R.683 (noise and air pollution); *Young & Co.* v. *Bankier Distillery Ltd [1893]* A. C. 691 (water pollution).

[21] *Malone* v. *Laskey* [1907] 2 K.B.141.

[22] See, for example, *Andreae* v. *Selfridge & Co Ltd [1938] Ch.1* – no nuisance when building works, although admittedly annoying for the plaintiff, were carried on with reasonable skill in a manner calculated to reduce noise to a minimum.

have been some difficulty in persuading the court that environmental concerns should weigh particularly heavily in coming to this conclusion, and the requirement of unreasonableness still poses some problems for the plaintiff. An important sub-category of this problem is the extent to which regard may be had to the nature of the area in which the land is situated. Thus, in a famous sentence, a judge once remarked that something which would not be a nuisance in a low-income district might well be so in an exclusive residential neighbourhood.[23] Although this is a powerful element in determining whether a nuisance exists[24] it might be thought that serious pollution from a contaminated site would now ground liability in most areas. Furthermore, the locality issue should be kept in perspective – arguments about the polluted state of the area will not avail a defendant if the plaintiff is claiming, not mere interference with his enjoyment of the land, but actual physical damage to it,[25] as will usually be the case in land contamination actions. Even in highly polluted areas a nuisance can still be established if the necessary elements are present.[26]

On occasions, problems can be caused by defendants who claim statutory authority for the activities which give rise to the complaint. Recent cases have established that statutory authority can be a complete answer to an action in nuisance, provided the defendant can show that the activities complained of are either expressly authorized by the statute or are an inevitable consequence of those activities so that Parliament must have intended to cloak them with impunity also.[27]

A recent case where a similar issue was considered is *Gillingham Borough Council* v. *Medway (Chatham) Dock Co. Ltd (1991)*. In this case a former naval dockyard at Chatham was given planning permission to operate as a commercial port. Access to the port was limited to two residential roads and heavy traffic was experienced for 24 hours a day. It was known when planning permission was granted that this would be a consequence, but it was considered that the economic benefit of having a commercial port outweighed the environmental disadvantages. Nevertheless, the local authority later commenced a court action alleging that the use of the residential roads by HGVs was a public nuisance for which the company operating the port was responsible. It sought an injunction to prevent it. In its defence, the company pleaded that no public nuisance could arise from a lawful act and that the grant of planning permission had made their activity lawful.

The case came before Buckley J. and he considered that the grant of planning permission was analogous to statutory authority. Statutory authority can be a defence to a nuisance action and he found that here the grant of planning permission acted in the same way. The planning system acts as a delegation of Parliament's authority to planning authorities to strike a balance between community and individual

---

[23] "What would be a nuisance in Belgrave Square would not necessarily be one in Bermondsey" – *Sturges* v. *Bridgman (1879)* 11 Ch. D. 852 at 857.

[24] And perhaps more influential still when the judge comes to decide what remedy shall be awarded if a nuisance is found to exist.

[25] *St Helens Smelting Co.* v. *Tipping (1865)* 11 H.L.C 642.

[26] See, for example, *Rushmer* v. *Polsue & Alfieri Ltd [1907]* A.C. 121.

[27] *Allen* v. *Gulf Oil Refining Ltd [1981]* A.C. 1001

interests and has elaborate provisions for objections to be heard and appeals to be made. A grant of planning permission is not a licence to commit nuisances, but an authorization to change the character of the neighbourhood, and that could lead to activity previously unlawful losing that quality. Whether or not the use of the highway constituted a nuisance had to be judged by the character of the locality as the nuisance was based on allegations of impairment to the use and enjoyment of property. The character of the locality had changed with the grant of planning permission and the annoyance complained of resulted from the consented works which benefited from the same sort of immunity from suit as those authorized by statute. A nuisance has to be considered in the light of its existing environment, not one existing in the past.

Normally, the person who causes the nuisance is liable for it, but the owner or occupier of the land from which the nuisance arises may be liable (even if he does not cause the nuisance himself) if he has given express or implied consent for the activities causing the nuisance.[28] Of particular relevance to contaminated land issues are cases which have held that a landowner may adopt a nuisance of which he has notice[29] and that he may also be liable for nuisance which began before he owned or occupied the site, if he knew or ought reasonable to have been aware of them.

*Public nuisance* is an unlawful act which materially affects the life, health or property or the reasonable comfort and convenience of a class of Her Majesty's subjects who are affected by it. Actions for public nuisance are brought by the Attorney-General and, although they have been used in environment-related cases,[30] they are of little practical importance.

### The rule in Rylands v. Fletcher

In the case which gave it its name,[31] the rule was formulated thus:

> … the person who for his own purposes brings on his lands and collects and keeps there anything likely to do mischief if it escapes, must keep it at his peril and, if he does not do so, is *prima facie* answerable for all the damage which is the natural consequence of its escape.[32]

If liability exists under this rule, that liability does not depend on fault, but is strict.[33]

Before there can be liability, there must be an escape, so there will be no liability for contamination of the site *per se*, unless there is evidence of pollution leaching into watercourses or adjoining land.

Furthermore, the use concerned must be "non-natural". This requirement, added to Blackburn J.'s formulation by the House of Lords, has added an element of uncertainty, as some courts have taken the view that "natural" here means "ordinary"

---

[28] *Tetley* v. *Chitty [1986]* 1 All E.R. 663

[29] *Sedleigh-Denfield* v. *O'Callaghan [1940]* A.C. 880.

[30] E. G. *Attorney-General* v. *P.Y.A. Quarries Ltd [1957]* Q.B. 169 (noise, dust and fumes from blasting).

[31] *Rylands* v. *Fletcher (1868)* L.R. 3 H.L. 330.

[32] The words are those of Blackburn J. in the Court of Exchequer Chamber, see (1866) L.R. 1 Ex. 265, approved in the House of Lords.

[33] There are some defences, for example Act of God and sabotage.

or "not exceptional". Nonetheless, it may well be that deposit of polluting material on land is within the rule.[34]

The *Rylands* v. *Fletcher* doctrine has recently been considered in an important new case dealing with land contamination: the case of *Cambridge Water Company Limited v. Eastern Counties Leatherwork plc*, decided by the Court of Appeal on 19 November 1992. In that case a drinking water borehole had been contaminated by a solvent spilled at the Respondent's leather works. At first instance the court had held that the use of the land for leather treatment was not a "non-natural" use of the land and therefore disallowed the claim for compensation made by the Water Company whose use of the borehole had been interfered with. In the Court of Appeal the appeal brought by the Water Company was successful. The Court queried whether the "non-natural" test was correct and in any event stated that anyone who interferes with a "natural right" must pay compensation to the owner of the right. The abstraction of water in a condition which it is naturally found in strata was regarded as a natural right and therefore the pollution caused by the solvent was a risk that had to be borne by the person who caused it, i.e. the leather company.

### The tort of negligence

Over the past decades, the action for negligence has expanded enormously at the expense of many of the other tort actions. A plaintiff must be able to demonstrate:

— that a duty of care is owed to him by the defendant;

— that the defendant is or has been in breach of that duty; and

— that the damage of which he complains is the foreseeable consequence of that breach of duty.

Until quite recently, negligence has not made substantial inroads into practice in the environmental field, as the necessity to establish fault on the part of the defendant made it less attractive that an action under *Rylands* v. *Fletcher*, for example. In addition, there has been some uncertainty over the scope of foreseeable damage.

In recent years, however, there have been more examples of successful negligence actions in the environmental field. Cases concerning unnecessary exposure of industrial workers to noise[35] and the poisoning of a neighbour's bees by insecticide sprayed on agricultural land[36] provide convenient examples. In another case, of potentially extremely wide application, a public authority responsible for the control of river pollution was found liable in negligence for failing to warn lower riparian owners of pollution which was damaging to crops.[37] Clearly, where a landowner has dangerous substances or wastes on his land, a much higher standard of care will apply to him than would be the case if his operations were entirely innocuous. It might even be

---

[34] A Canadian court has held that landfill operations in which methane gas developed were covered by the rule. *Gersten* v. *Municipality of Metropolitan Toronto* (1973) 41 DLR (3d) 641.

[35] *Thompson* v. *Smiths Ship Repairers (North Shields) Ltd [1984]* 1 W.B. 405

[36] *Tuton* v. *A. D. Walter Ltd [1985]* 3 w. l. r. 797.

[37] *Scott–Whithead* v. *National Coal Board (1987)* 53 P. & C.R. 263.

that, in a proper case, where the defendant's land was the only known source of a particular pollutant in the district, the plaintiff may be able to employ the doctrine of *res ipsa loquitur* to shift the burden of proof to his opponent.

Although negligence has some advantages over other torts (it does not require the plaintiff to have an interest in land, for example), it is often simpler to try and establish that the defendant's activities constitute a nuisance. Furthermore, there is some ground for thinking that the courts (and especially the House of Lords) are beginning to take a restrictive view of what kinds of damage are foreseeable,[38] which may prove a particularly important brake on developments in the environmental area.

### An action in trespass

Trespass to land (which is also, as its name suggests, a purely proprietary remedy), requires that the defendant's unlawful act has caused direct physical interference with the land. The leading case in the environmental field[39] concerned the discharge of sewage into a river in such a manner that it settled on the land of the plaintiff.

Although trespass is normally pleaded in connection with a physical entry of a person or thing onto the land of the plaintiff, in theory the action is broad enough to include seepage or leaking of dangerous material from adjoining or other land.

A major advantage of using the trespass action is that trespass, unlike nuisance, is actionable *per se* and does not require the plaintiff to prove that he has suffered any damage in addition to the fact of the trespass itself.

### b. The position of subsequent purchasers of contaminated land in English law

The application of these general principles of English common law to contaminated land take on another dimension when they are read together with the rules of land law concerning the obligations (or lack of them) imposed on the vendor of a piece of land to disclose the extent of his knowledge about that land and its past history.

### The caveat emptor rule in conveyancing

The law and practice of conveyancing in England has hitherto placed only a very limited duty of disclosure upon the seller of land. While he must not actively mislead his purchaser, he is under no duty to inform that purchaser of any defect in the land itself. It is the business of the purchaser, by diligent enquiry, to satisfy himself that the land he is purchasing is not subject to any liabilities other than those of which he is aware and which he is willing to undertake. Should it subsequently transpire that

---

[38] See, for example, *D. & F. Estates* v. *Church Commissioners [1988]* 3 W.L.R. 368; *Yeun Kun Yeu* v. *Attorney-General of Hong Kong [1988]* A.C. 177.

[39] *Jones* v. *Llanwrst Urban District Council [1911]* 1 Ch. 193.

the land is subject to additional liabilities, he will not (in the absence of fraud or misrepresentation) have any legal redress against the vendor.

This principle applies throughout the English law of contract.[40]

> Ordinarily, the failure to disclose a material fact which might influence the mind of a prudent contractor does not give the right to avoid the contract ... [This view] can be supported on the ground that it is of paramount importance that contracts should be observed, and that if parties honestly comply with the essential of the formation of contracts – i.e. agree in the same terms on the same subject-matter – they are bound and must rely upon the stipulation of the contract for protection from the effect of facts unknown to them.[41]

Nonetheless, the harshness of this rule has been modified in a number of cases, although only a few have any likely application in the case of contaminated land:

— There is a duty of full disclosure if the contract is a contract uberrimae fidei, such as a contract of insurance. A contract for the sale of land, however, is not such a contract.

— A vendor may not keep silent when to do so would cause a positive representation made by him or on his behalf to be distorted by his silence. So, if the land is misdescribed in the sale particulars, the vendor must correct the error. It would not, however, seem that this "corrective" duty extends to actively informing the purchaser of defects of which the contract or particulars say nothing.

— It is normal practice, prior to concluding the contract, for the purchaser to send to the vendor "preliminary enquiries", which may relate to the title to the land, its present use, planning consents granted in respect of it, etc.[42] The vendor must reply accurately to these enquiries and must not mislead the purchaser. On the other hand, he is not obliged to volunteer any additional information unless it is directly asked for, perhaps in a supplementary enquiry. Indeed, it is not uncommon for the vendor to reply that the matters enquired about are not within his knowledge and to direct the purchaser to rely not upon the vendor's answers, but on his own enquiries. Furthermore, it would seem that the vendor does not have to answer very broadly-worded enquiries – e.g. "Does the vendor know of any facts which might influence a prudent purchaser in his purchase of the property?"

— There is some authority for saying that a vendor may not conceal physical defects in the property of which he has knowledge,[43] but these cases relate to

---

[40] Although it has undergone some modification in respect of certain consumer sales, these modifications do not extend to the sale of land.

[41] Per Lord Atkin, in *Bell* v. *Lever Brothers Ltd.* *[1932]* A.C. 161, at p. 227.

[42] Other enquiries are addressed to the local authorities in whose districts the land lies. These relate to information, including environmental information, held in the public registers, but they would not necessarily reveal to the purchaser a full history of the uses to which the site has been put in the past.

[43] This may sound in the tort of deceit, leading to rescission of the contract and/or damages to the purchaser.

defects in buildings (such as cracks in walls which are concealed behind wallpaper, etc.) of a kind intrinsically different to land contamination.[44]

In 1988, the Conveyancing Standing committee of the Law Commission considered a number of possible modifications to the present law. These included:

— implied conditions in the contract that the property was sound, except for matters specifically brought to the purchaser's attention or, if the purchaser had carried out an inspection, any matters which that examination ought to have revealed;

— a proposal that the vendor should be obliged to provide the purchaser with a survey report on the property;

— that the vendor should be obliged to provide purchasers in advance with answers to "standard" searches and enquiries;

— the institution of a system of conditional contracts.

In the end, the Standing Committee proposed that the "unjustifiably ramshackle" *caveat emptor* rule should be replaced by:

... a positive duty to disclose *all* material facts about the property he is selling, provided that he is aware of those facts or ought reasonably to be aware of them. To this significant extent, the *caveat emptor* rule should be reversed.[45]

This proposal brought forth howls of protest from the professions involved in the sale of land and, in 1989, despite its dogged reiteration of its view that the *caveat emptor* principle promoted an adversarial atmosphere in the sale of land which was undesirable and unhelpful, it had to admit that change would be hard to achieve, if only because it would be hard to frame adequately the extent of a duty of disclosure. Buyers' views of what amounts to a substantial defect differ widely.

Finally, the Committee rather lamely concluded that what was required was an atmosphere of co-operation between parties to a land sale, in which, amongst other things, sellers realized that buyers require (and have a right to) certain information, which should be made available to them and

... our approach is therefore to set up and encourage voluntary arrangements under which standard basic information is volunteered to buyers without causing procedural delays, and buyers themselves are encouraged to pursue other matters of individual concern.[46]

---

[44] It is clear, however, that where the defect in the property exists as a result of the activities of the vendor himself, he may be liable in negligence to a purchaser for damage caused to him by the negligent creation of the hazard. Hitherto, cases have concerned defects in houses (e.g. defective heating systems installed by an amateur) rather than extending to uses of the site which may give rise to substantial liabilities to third parties.

[45] *Caveat Emptor in Sales of Land*, A Consultation Paper from the Conveyancing Standing Committee of the Law Commission. 1988.

[46] *Let The Buyer Be Well Informed*, Recommendations of the Conveyancing Standing Committee of the Law Commission, December 1989.

Such a timorous conclusion did not satisfy many observers, including the House of Commons Environment committee (see below), and the matter may yet be reviewed, at least in connection with contaminated land.

### c. The impact of environmental liability rules and the caveat emptor doctrine in the field of commercial acquisitions

The inter-relation of the general rules of environmental liability and the operation of the *caveat emptor* doctrine in conveyancing have produced very striking results in the commercial law field, among others. By way of example, potential liability for land contamination has had enormous impact in the field of major corporate acquisitions.

As mentioned above, it is possible for a purchaser of land to be held liable for environmental torts arising from activities which took place prior to his acquisition of the land. By virtue of the *caveat emptor* principle, it is also incumbent on the purchaser to satisfy himself as to the possible presence of features of the land which may give rise to liabilities of this sort.

As a result, the practice of corporate lawyers addressing a major acquisition, in cases where the company being acquired has significant assets in the form of holdings of land, has changed to accommodate concerns over land contamination. Enquiries about possible environmental liabilities are now made at the earliest possible stage in the negotiations. These enquiries may take many forms, ranging from careful examination of the registers of consents, etc. maintained by the planning and pollution control agencies, through scanning of newspapers and trade journals (for indications of past pollution incidents) to on-site investigations. These latter may include sampling of soil, water, etc. on and around the site, surveys and inspections by suitably qualified inspectors acting for the proposed purchaser and interviews with members of the staff of the company to be acquired, in order to learn about the pollution performance of the company. Enquiries of this sort, of course, are precisely the sort of direct and specific enquiry before contract which fall within the exception to the *caveat emptor* rule mentioned above. Enquiries may not be confined only to environmental matters, but may, for example, extend to the financial resources available to the vendor for possible clean-up liability.

Once this information has been received and analyzed, it is then used as an important (sometimes the most influential element) in deciding upon the purchaser company's bid strategy. The simplest response to a discovery of a potential liability would be to reduce the purchase-price of the company to reflect that liability. Although this is a simple response, it is not always satisfactory, if only because the extent of the costs involved may not be foreseeable with any accuracy (and sometimes because the scale of liability is too large).

Another possibility is to proceed with the acquisition, but seek an indemnity from the vendor for certain kinds of liability. While this has some attractions, it is clearly dependent on the credit-worthiness of the vendor. Another problem is that, if the purchaser intends to continue the same kind of operations on the site, it may be difficult in the future to allocate damage between the activities of the vendor and the purchaser.

An increasingly frequent response is for the purchaser only to acquire certain assets of the vendor company and not others. So, liabilities may be left with the vendor, or perhaps the share-capital of the vendor company may not be acquired along with its assets, leaving a separate defendant for future actions. Another alternative is to require that the vendor take certain steps to remedy the potential pollution problem as one of the terms of the acquisition contract, in effect providing the purchaser with a "cleaned-up" site prior to completion of the purchase. Although this looks initially unattractive to the vendor, in fact it may be preferable to tackle the problem at once, sell the site outright to a satisfied purchaser and be free of any future liability in respect of it.

Environmental liabilities (particularly from contaminated land) are now taken so seriously in the United Kingdom that there have been cases in which a purchaser has abandoned a major corporate acquisition, because it was not given satisfactory answers to pre-contract enquiries on this matter.

### d. Public law provisions relating to the allocation of clean-up costs for contaminated land

English law contains no equivalent of the United States Comprehensive Environmental Response, Compensation and Liability Act.[47]

Many of the issues involved in clean-up or restoration of contaminated land are dealt with (insofar as they are dealt with) under the provisions of the Town and Country Planning Act 1990. This Act contains the framework for the development control system on which land use planning is based. Any building, mining or engineering operations to be undertaken on land, or any material change in the use of that land, requires a grant of planning permission. Local planning authorities may refuse planning permission if they think that there is substantial danger of land contamination.[48]

Planning permission is usually made subject to conditions, and it is these conditions which are used as the major vehicles for addressing liability problems related to land contamination. The Department of the Environment has instructed local planning authorities that they should use their power to impose conditions on industrial development and waste disposal sites, in order to ensure that the operations sanctioned by the planning consent do not expose subsequent users of the site to dangers arising from the presence of contaminants. Furthermore, it has made it plain that contaminated sites may require remedial action to be taken before any subsequent development can take place. It should be noted that, at present, it may still happen that such clean-up operations may be required as a condition attached to the permission for the *subsequent* development (particularly if the dangers of contamination were not realized when the previous development commenced), so these may represent a major limitation on the commercial attractiveness of the site to subsequent purchasers.

[47] 42 U.S.C. 9603, the so-called "Superfund" legislation.
[48] See DOE Circular 21/87.

It should be noted that planning conditions are subject to strict rules as to their content, in that they must be imposed for a recognized planning purpose, they must relate to the development in question and they must be reasonable in all the circumstances. In many cases, these conditions will not present too much difficulty in the case of land contamination, but, if there should be any question on the matter, it is open to the authority and the developer to enter into an agreement under section 106 of the 1971 Act, which would enable the local authority to secure action beyond that which would be permitted under the provisions of the Act imposing conditions on the planning consent.[49]

Other forms of provision for clean-up in the public law are somewhat sectoral. Thus, under the Environmental Protection Act 1990, a holder of a waste management licence will not be able to surrender that licence until the site in respect of which it is issued has been certified by the authority as being environmentally safe.[50] Furthermore, the Act contains provisions which enable the local authority to require occupiers of land to remove from the land waste which has been deposited on it. If the authority forms the view that the waste presents a threat of pollution to land, air or water or of harm to human health, the authority itself may take action to remove it and bill the occupier for its costs.[51] There is a similar power in respect of closed landfill sites.[52]

### e. Registers of land which have been subjected to a potentially contaminating use

On 1 April 1992, local authorities started work compiling registers of land which may be contaminated. Section 143 of the Environmental Protection Act 1990 imposes a duty on authorities to compile and maintain registers of land which is or has been put to a "contaminative use". It should be noticed that "contamination" is not synonymous with "pollution". Contamination merely denotes the presence of certain substances, without making any judgment as to whether or not they are harmful.

A Department of the Environment Working Party came to the conclusion that it would be impracticable to compile a register of land which was actually contaminated, as this would involve enormous public costs (for soil sampling, etc.), would be very time-consuming and would not address the technical difficulties which exist in judging whether or not a clean-up operation has effectively removed all traces of contamination.

The types of use deemed contaminative are set out in regulations. The registers do not cover land which has been contaminated by other means, for example by unauthorized dumping of waste, accidental spillages or activities on adjacent land.

Registration may well cause a reduction in site-value and, in extreme cases, may render land unsaleable. The government is taking the view that entry on the register

---

[49] This power has recently been amended by the Planning and Compensation Act 1991, which will in some circumstances permit the applicant for planning permission voluntarily to offer to enter unilaterally into a planning obligation of a type similar to that more usually arising by agreement under section 106 of the 1990 Act – see section 12, 1991 Act.

[50] See section 39.

[51] Section 59.

[52] Section 61.

may cause "blight and alarm", but that it is better if everyone is aware of the possibility of contamination. It believes that such alarm can be reduced to a certain extent by clear information and prompt response to queries.

Local authorities will have a duty to correct inaccuracies on the register, but sites which are cleaned up will not be removed from the register thereafter, as they will still have been subject to the contaminative use.

## 5. F.A.M. de Haan and S.E.A.T.M. van der Zee, *Soil Protection: The Dutch Case*

### Introduction

Global public awareness about soil pollution arose with the Love Canal affair in the USA in 1978. A similar Dutch situation arose with the discovery of severe contamination under a housing estate in the village of Lekkerkerk in 1990. A governmental decision was made for a clean-up operation of this site and at the same time the Provincial Authorities were requested to make inventories of possible comparable situations. This revealed several thousand locations where the soil, according to the knowledge of that time, was supposed to be severely polluted. Under the growing pressure of public opinion, regulations for remediation of the most threatening situations were developed in a relatively short time period, as set down in the Soil Clean-up (Interim) Act (SCA) of 1983. This law thus had a curative nature and was meant as a temporary measure.

In the meantime, general legislation for soil protection was under development, fitting in the framework of the emerging policy for overall environmental protection. This led to the Soil Protection Act (SPA) of January 1987. The SPA is primarily preventive, aiming at preservation of good soil quality and at prevention of further impairment of soil. At the time of termination of the SCA, which will coincide with a revision of the SPA, the SCA will be incorporated, also in revised version, in the SPA and the latter then will cover preventive aspects of soil quality as well as the curative aspects.

Before discussing both laws in somewhat greater detail, a few remarks are made about some points of departure in soil protection policy in the Netherlands.

### a. Soil protection policy

As mentioned by Moen and Brugman (1987) the central concept of Dutch environmental policy is the concept of being "guests in our own environment", also indicated as "good stewardship". This concept implies a right and a duty. The right is to use our environment for our own purposes and well-being, but under certain restrictions coming from the duty to pass over a liveable environment to future generations. This concept has the same basis as sustainability, the term serving as a guideline in the Brundtland Report (World Commission on Environment and Development, 1987). In the National Environmental Policy Plan, sustainability was elaborated further for specific Dutch environmental conditions. Practical implementation of it faced a large number of concerns, not only social or sociological, but also scientific (in regard to whether the aim can be realized).

In order to pursue the goal of sustainability, a two-track policy may be followed: (1) effect-oriented; and (2) source-oriented. This is also true for general environmental protection, but the discussion here is limited to soil protection.

The effect-oriented policy implies the preservation of those properties of soil which are essential for the various soil functions. In connection with this the concept of so-called "multifunctionality of soil" was introduced. Because of the usually excessive social implications of soil protection, this term has led to numerous discussions and misunderstandings, unintentional and intentional. Maintenance and restoration of soil multifunctionality must be considered as the efficacy of ethic principles for human handling. For soil this implies that the various possibilities for use are kept open or repaired. Effects of present use of soil which might prevent another soil use must be reparable and thus eliminated within a reasonable time period.

Instead of applying the multifunctionality concept one may also consider the different, specific functions of soil. The most important ones are:

— the bearing function, for instance as playground for children and for building houses;

— the planned growth and crop production function, covering natural vegetation and crops for animal and human consumption well; in relation to crop production quantity aspects like yield play a role as well as quality aspects, because health of the consumers can easily be influenced by plant composition;

— the filtering function for groundwater and surface water;

— the ecological function, especially the role of the soil ecosystem in cycling elements like carbon and nitrogen.

Protection of soil functions requires the availability of standards for soil quality. Derivation of such standards is far from trivial because of the complexity of the soil system and the numerous chemical compounds that have to be taken into consideration. In the Netherlands reference values for heavy metals have been derived, pertaining to "non-heavily contaminated" situations. Although this constitutes a very important first step in soil quality assessment, there remains much to be done to arrive at scientifically sound soil quality standards. This makes it necessary to have a source-oriented policy in addition to an effect-oriented one.

When considering sources of soil pollution, a distinction can be made between so-called diffuse sources and point sources. Examples of the first category are emissions into the air by industries and traffic, leading to widespread soil contamination in the neighbourhood. The degree of contamination then usually decreases with the distance to the source. Especially when various sources are present, slightly spread over or concentrated in a certain area, it is usually hard to determine the exact contribution of each source to the soil contamination. Similarly, the application to soil of excessive amounts of animal manures resulting from intensive animal husbandry must be considered a diffuse source for soil pollution; such applications sometimes occur over large areas as is the case in specific parts of the Netherlands and certain regions of other Western European countries as well. The policy for protecting soil against pollution from diffuse sources is based on the concept that long-term preservation of soil quality requires an equilibrium between input and output of substances. This is only possible for non-accumulating or non-persistent substances. The limiting conditions for the output are then given by the acceptable concentrations in groundwater and in the crops. The approach, followed in protecting soil and groundwater against pollution by excessive manuring, is discussed later.

Examples of point sources for soil pollution are waste disposal sites, storage tanks and discharge of liquid wastes (e.g. septic tanks). In these cases the so-called IMC (isolation, monitoring, control) criteria are applied, especially in the construction of new storage or disposal sites. IMC criteria may be specified for each point source under consideration. In these specifications, risk analysis of possible failure plays an important role.

An important principle in Dutch environmental policy is that of "the polluter pays". This principle plays a role not only in the prevention of pollution but also in remedial actions. The first draft of the Soil Clean-up Interim Act attempted to recover the costs of the clean-up operation by charging taxes to, for example, the industry responsible for the pollution. This principle, however, caused much discussion and commotion, including in Parliament. It was felt unfair that a present-day owner was burdened with the legacy of a predecessor when ownership of the polluted area had changed. As far as possible the principle is still applied in cost recovery. A key discussion concerns whether the polluter could or should have been aware of the adverse effects of his behaviour at the time of pollution. This has led to much jurisprudence in this area.

Environmental policy in the Netherlands, including soil protection policy, is laid down in Environmental Programmes. These are published by the Government under the auspices of three departments: the Ministry of Public Health, Physical Planning and Environment; the Ministry of Agriculture, Nature Conservation and Fisheries; and the Ministry of Transport and Water Management.

### b. The Soil Clean-up Act (SCA)

A central point in the SCA is the soil clean-up programme, assessed each year by the provinces. The provincial authorities use information gathered by their own inventories, by communities or by individual citizens. A priority scheme is established based on the (supposed) gravity of the situations. If during a certain year a new location is discovered, it can be included in the programme after consultation with the community, the environmental inspectorate and the ministry. Before the programme is implemented, it is subject to a ministerial judgment, which takes two aspects into account: whether the site can be considered for clean-up, and whether a financial contribution towards costs will be given by the government. If both criteria are met, execution of the programme may start. The operation can be performed under the responsibility of the provincial authorities in consultation with the relevant community, or under the responsibility of the community itself on its own request. The practical execution is done by specialized companies.

Criteria for the necessity for clean-up are "a severe threat to public health and/or to the environment". Here a major problem arises with regard to a quantitative risk assessment based on substances-contents in soil. As was stated in a recent report to the C.E.C on Soil Quality Assessment:

Ideally, a quantitative evaluation of soil quality as a basis for risk assessment requires complete information about transfer factors (between contaminated soil and: air-water-plants-soil-organisms – human beings) and about dose-effect relationships for the exposure of the organism under consideration:

— for all components that can cause malfunctioning or disfunctioning of soil

— for all different soil types and soil properties that are found

— and for all combinations of the different variables (e.g. pH, redox potential, accompanying substances) that control compound behaviour in the soils system.

Because this is an impossible task at the present stage of knowledge, a number of limitations and restrictions had to be made.

In the first draft of the Guideline for Soil Remediation accompanying the SCA, signal values were given in order to estimate the severity of the situation. These are the so-called A-B-C values with the following meaning:

A-value:    background; no expected problems

B-value:    indication of need for further investigation

C-value:    a level of contamination that requires further action in view of possible serious effects.

Although it was clearly stressed that these values were of preliminary nature only and should be used carefully, in practice they tended to be applied as rigid, soundly based criteria which supposedly allowed a quantitative risk evaluation of the sites involved. This single-value interpretation of soil quality has led to much, sometimes unnecessary, commotion and, in many cases, to damage and economic losses. The first complete and quantitative elaboration of human exposure to soil pollution has been given by Van Wijnen (1990), using a multimedia exposure model. As mentioned earlier, the guidelines of the revised SCA give new reference values for heavy metals in soil, in which the content is considered in relation to the clay content and the organic matter content of the soil. "Severe threat to the environment" is a phrase that is still awaiting further scientific foundation.

The second criterion of the ministerial judgment concerns the financial contribution. It is taken as a general point of departure that the national government and the local governments, especially communities, share the costs. This principle has been followed from the very beginning of soil clean-up programmes, because the problems were judged too severe to search for the polluter of each site, and, once identified, to convince him of the duty to finance the remedial action. In the division of costs among the different contributing authorities, a threshold fee was introduced. This fee is dependent on the number of citizens in the community, and amounts for each individual site to 10 Dutch guilders per head, with a maximum of 200,000 Dutch guilders per location. Of the costs exceeding the threshold value, 10 per cent must be paid by the community and 90 per cent is paid by the national government. Special regulations are made for communities of low financial strength (which are for other reasons already under governmental financial supervision). As mentioned earlier, an identified originator of the pollution can be prosecuted by the national governmental counsel for redress of costs. Although experience with such prosecution is still limited, a number of cases have resulted in mutual agreement about paying the costs. So far, the total number of summons amounts to 122, in which a total of some 700 million Dutch guilders is claimed.

Of course the SCA contains a number of articles dedicated to specific subjects. For practical reasons these are omitted. Regular revisions of the SCA permit it to be adjusted on the basis of experience gained.

The amount of money involved in the clean-up operation from the governmental side was 288 million Dutch guilders in 1990. This will supposedly increase to 365 million Dutch guilders by 1994. In addition a contribution by so-called third parties (especially industrial companies that became new owners of polluted sites) is expected to jump from 130 million Dutch guilders in 1991 to 255 million Dutch guilders in 1994. In such cases the clean-up is supervised by the government. The present user of soil can also attempt to recover the costs from the polluter or the person(s) who sold the contaminated ground. It is expected that total costs for soil clean-up in the Netherlands will amount to some 50 billion Dutch guilders.

### d. The Soil Protection Act (SPA)

Introduction of the SPA was preceded by preparations lasting more than 15 years. In 1971 a first draft in relation to soil pollution was offered to the Second Chamber of Parliament. Discussion of this led in 1976 to a motion, sustained by the full parliament, that a general act should be developed aiming at testing all possible soil-threatening actions. A considerable speeding-up of the procedure resulted from discoveries of (supposedly) severe soil pollution situations and from the commitment to perform the EC guideline for the protection of groundwater, and so in December 1980 a bill on soil protection was offered to the Second Chamber. After much discussion and amendments (in which also the First Chamber played an important role) the bill finally passed parliament, resulting in the introduction of the SPA on 1 January 1987.

The SPA remains a framework law which provides very general regulations only. Practical implementation is achieved by means of so-called General Administrative Order (GAO). The purpose of the law is to offer an outline for measures and regulations in order to protect the properties of soil which constitute the conditions for proper soil functioning. This goal is indicated as the "general protection level". Because measures at this level are sometimes insufficient to protect specific soil functions, a "special protection level" is maintained as well. This allows, for instance, the assignment of "soil protection areas" where far-reaching regulations can be applied in order to preserve the soil.

Of course many laws are related in one way or another to soil. Examples are the

Waste Disposal Act, Nuisance Act, Chemical Waste Act, Pesticides Act, Nature Conservation Act, Air Pollution Act. Fertilizers Act, Groundwater Act, Surface Water Pollution Act, etc. As is determined in the SPA, in all situations related to soil quality, the SPA has priority over the other laws and regulations.

The SPA contains an article about the "duty of care", indicating that every citizen has the duty to prevent all soil-threatening actions and even the duty to report such actions to the relevant authorities as soon as they come to his knowledge. This article was included to emphasize the personal responsibility of each individual and has as such a somewhat philosophical nature. It also has interesting juridical aspects with respect to administrative law, civil law and penal law.

The institution of advisory committees for the relevant ministries is regulated in the SPA. First there is a Technical Commission on Soil Protection (TCSP) which is composed of persons nominated by the Minister of Public Health, Physical Planning and Environment. The following specialties are represented in the TCSP: human health, (eco)toxicology, waste treatment and disposal, hydrology, soil science, and the science of sediments. TCSP provides the ministers with advice, either on request or on its own initiative. Such advice is published in official reports. So far, some 25 opinions have been given about subjects such as groundwater protection, use of animal manure, use of pesticides, use of organic fertilizers like compost and sewage sludge, discharge of liquid wastes, and tests of IMC criteria. The TCSP takes only technical aspects of soil protection into consideration and is an advisory committee on a national level.

The provinces have their own advisory committees which treat specific provincial problems. These provincial committees account for technical aspects and social aspects as well. Members include representatives of the provincial inspectorate for the environment, the directorate of agriculture and nature conservation, and the directorate of water management. The provincial committees may also ask the TCSP for advice.

Special articles of the SPA focus on risk liability, financial bail, and taking action in case of incidents and accidents.

As mentioned before, practical implementation of the SPA is achieved by GAOs. So far the following have been issued:

— Decree on discharges;

— Decree on storage and disposal;

— Decree on storage of oil products;

— Decree on use of animal manure;

— Decree on use of other organic fertilizers;

— Decree on building materials.

In the following section the decree on use of animal manures is described in more detail by way of example.

## d. GAO: Decree on Use of Animal Manures

This GAO became operational on 1 April 1987 and was introduced at the level of general soil protection policy.

During recent decades an extreme growth of intensive animal husbandry has occurred in the Netherlands. For a number of reasons this expansion took place in several specific areas, where sandy soils prevail. The result was a strong imbalance between minerals that are imported in the country in the form of feed and raw materials for feed production, and minerals exported by dairy and animal products. The minerals that end up in manure and animal slurries are far exceeding the amounts needed for proper crop fertilization. Because of the high transport costs of the slurries, the excess of minerals is brought onto the soil in the areas where they are produced, thus threatening the quality of soil, ground water and surface water. The most threatening constituents of the manure are:

— nitrogen: in the form of ammonia it makes a contribution to soil acidification; in the form of nitrate it is easily leached to the ground water, making this water unsuitable for drinking water purposes;

— phosphorus: after saturation of the phosphate retention capacity of soil phosphate will leach to groundwater and surface water, and contribute to eutrophication; furthermore surface run-off/erosion contribute to enhance phosphorus levels in surface waters;

— heavy metals, especially cadmium, copper and zinc: these may induce plant toxicity, toxicity for components of the soil ecosystem, and contribute to undesirable composition of crops and vegetables, with respect to human and animal consumption.

Standards for the use of animal manure were based on the phosphate content. A differentiation was made between application rates for grassland, silage corn and arable land. The final goal is set at an application rate which balances the uptake of phosphate by crops, which is on the average 70 kg $PO_4$ per hectare per year. This is again in accordance with the principle that addition of substances to soil should not exceed the (acceptable) removal by crops and by leaching. Because of the excessive availability of manures, this goal can be reached only after a certain time period, during which the application rates are decreased by steps. Table 6.1 gives the application rates for the various soil uses and different phases.

Table 6.1. Application rates for animal manure, expressed as kg P205 ha/yr

| Period | Grassland | Sillage com | Arable land |
| --- | --- | --- | --- |
| 1.5.87–1.1.91 | 250 | 350 | 125 |
| 1.1.91–1.1.95 | 200 | 250 | 125 |
| 1.1.95 | 175 | 175 | 125 |
| 2000 | final rate | final rate | final rate |

An exception clause was introduced for those soils which are to be considered as phosphate-saturated. Here, the final rate was made applicable from the moment the GAO became effective. Assessment of (the degree of) phosphate saturation of soil can be obtained by means of soil analysis according to the "Protocol of phosphate-saturated soils", which was developed by financial support of the Ministry of Public Health, Physical Planning, and Environment.

It must be emphasized that the phosphate standards for manure application do not safeguard the soil and ground water from contamination and pollution with other substances like nitrogen and heavy metals. Unfortunately, this had to be accepted under the pressure of the circumstances and because of the large proportions of the problem. One of the opinions of the TCSP (1986) points out this on-going pollution in a quantitative manner.

In order to quantify the manure problem properly both nationally and on the farm level, manure accounting was made mandatory on both levels. Manure accounting at the farm level also provides a tool for control.

To avoid leaching and washing away of manure substances as much as possible, the use of manure has to be strongly restricted during autumn and winter. Thus, regulations about time and way of application are also given. During certain time periods use of manure is completely prohibited.

A revision of the GAO is at present in preparation. The most important adjustments are:

— sharpening the application rates for silage corn during the second phase (1991–5) according to (in kg $PO_4$/ha/year): per 1991: 250; per 1993: 200; per 1994: 150; for phase 3 (1-1-95) the standard will be 125 instead of 175;

— prescriptions for means of application in order to reduce ammonia losses to the atmosphere; this can be achieved by injection of the slurry or by ploughing directly after application. It must be realized that more efficient application of the manure leads to enhanced leaching of nitrogen. Also, nests of birds may be destroyed when injection on meadows is done in spring. Recently the TCSP (1990) has suggested additional regulations in order to avoid this problem;

— extension of the period of prohibition of manure application;

— adjustment of the procedure for selection of phosphate-saturated soils.

Of course such sharpening of regulations strongly enhances the problems in the areas involved. On the other hand it puts more pressure on finding solutions for the problem, for instance by the development of technologies treating the slurries and exporting the resulting products, or by decreasing the number of animals.

### e. Compatibility of Standards

As was indicated in previous sections the implementation of the various regulations is closely related to standards for good soil quality. Compliance with the C-value that may not be exceeded is considered an indication that soil quality is acceptable. This assessment is debatable in view of the time dependency of contamination and the necessity to protect other sectors (air, surface and groundwater) besides the soil.

Quality standards should be based on sustainable use of the various resources. This involves the anticipation of possible adverse effects in the future. Contamination is a time-dependent process, because contaminants are mobile. Hence, they may not comprise a problem at their current position, but may become a problem after displacement. To prevent unfavourable developments, quality standards should be formulated such that adverse effects are also unlikely after displacement. This implies chain control: standards have to protect the weakest compartment and consequently standards for different compartments need to be compatible.

At this moment it appears this is not the case. Pesticides, for example, may not occur in groundwater in excess of 0.1 per cent of the applied amount at the soil surface. The only reason that such high applications are tolerated is that transformation of pesticides occurs while they reside in the unsaturated soil. By the time they leach into groundwater, the pesticide concentrations are expected to be below 0.1 mg m.$^3$ due to decay. Whether this is indeed the case depends on soil type, the pesticide under consideration, etc. When our anticipation based on scientific knowledge fails, the tolerance regarding concentrations in soil has a high price. Concerning 1, 2-dichloropropane, forbidden as a by-product of a pesticide in 1980, a slug is still moving to groundwater. Transformations appear to be slow and contamination is expected of drinking water wells in East Netherlands until 2100. A peak concentration is expected about the year 2030 of five hundred to one thousand times the current level considered acceptable in ground water.

A second example concerns heavy metals. It is well known that manure and fertilizer contain heavy metals. For instance, pig manure may have large Cu-concentrations, and phosphate fertilizer may contain much cadmium. The same is the case for natural precipitation as is shown in Table 6.2. In this table also the profound input rates due to the use of sewage sludge are visible. Sewage sludge contains large amounts of all heavy metals. We now consider different crops, as indicated in general terms in Table 6.2. For realistic Dutch crop rotation schemes, fertilization was assumed to be exactly in agreement with the NPK-requirements of the crops. However, the source of these elements (N,P,K) was varied. In one scheme the requirements were met by fertilizer. In another scheme, manure or sludge was applied until one of N, P, or K requirements (e.g. N) were met. The remaining demand of the two other elements (e.g., P and K) was fulfilled with commercial fertilizer. Because the heavy metal contents of manure, sludge, and fertilizer are reasonably well known, the input of Table 6.2 could be calculated. The input by precipitation are average values for the Netherlands.

To quantify the leaching rate and the uptake rate is a problem, as it requires quantifying a sorption equation, as was done by Boekhold et al (1990), and a relationship between plant uptake rate and the solution concentration. However, one can easily assess the acceptable removal rates, when it is assumed that: (1) groundwater recharge quality remains equal to the current mean groundwater quality, and (2) removal by crops is exactly in agreement with crop quality standards. Whereas (1) defines the "stand-still" principle for ground water, (2) is related with uptake for the case crop quality is just acceptable. For the Dutch situation these removal rates are also shown in Table 6.2, and may be considered maximum permissible removal rates.

It is observed that emission rates are larger than removal rates in many cases. This implies that on average, for the Netherlands, heavy metal accumulation will occur until a steady state is reached. At this steady state, input equals removal and the total content in soil is constant. Then one may expect, for the cases of Table 6.2 where input is larger than removal, that either crop quality or ground water recharge quality (or both) become sub-standard. It may take a long time to reach steady state, but quality standards also may be exceeded relatively fast, depending on the soil and environmental conditions. Anyway, this example shows that current standards should be obeyed also over the long term. This implies that the quality standards for air (represented by atmospheric deposition in the example), soil, groundwater as well as surface water, should in principle be consistent.

Table 6.2. Calculated input and removal rates (in mg/m² year). Removal rates are in agreement with current Dutch standards for crop quality, and stand-still principle for groundwater quality. (After Ferdinandus *et al.*, 1989.)

|  | Cd | Cu | Pb | Zn |
|---|---|---|---|---|
| **Input** | | | | |
| Agricultural crops— | | | | |
| commercial fertilizer (cf) | 0.55 | 1.7 | 4.7 | 15.5 |
| sewage sludge + cf | 0.84 | 91.0 | 55.0 | 250.0 |
| cattle manure + cf | 0.38 | 6.0 | 6.2 | 21.0 |
| pigs' manure + cf | 0.15 | 15.5 | 4.6 | 60.5 |
| Horticultural crops (cf) | 1.35–1.6 | 3.6–4.3 | 5.5–7.5 | 27.5–330 |
| Precipitation | 0.2 | 3.2 | 13.0 | 20.0 |
| **Removal** | | | | |
| Agricultural crops for— | | | | |
| human consumption | 0.30–0.25 | 3.6–11.0 | 0.1–.05 | 36.0–110 |
| animal fodder | 0.15–0.75 | 3.6–13.5 | 7.0–31.0 | 36.0–75.0 |
| Horticultural crops | 0.43–0.85 | 3.7–7.5 | 1.7–4.5 | 37.0–75.0 |
| Ground water recharge | 0.1 | 1.3 | 1.3 | 7.5 |

In developing a methodology for sound standards based on mass balances, the concept of "discrepancy factor" (Fd) may be useful. One may define Fd as the ratio of the input rate (by emission, application, etc.) over the removal rate (in agreement with a good product and environmental quality, by harvesting, transformations, leaching, etc.). Given a particular yield and composition, leaching flux in agreement with good ground water quality, etc., Fd may be calculated. When Fd exceeds one, a surplus is applied and production is non-sustainable. Because Fd (phosphate) is larger than Fd (nitrogen) for manure applications, manure regulations in the Netherlands are expressed in $P_2O_5$-equivalents.

## f. Perspectives

Currently, awareness is growing that environmental (including soil) protection is not only a governmental responsibility. Instead, industry and the public have their own responsibility. An instrument that comes into perspective in the Netherlands to aid in preventing contamination at its source is the Environmental Management System (EMS). Originally started as an experiment, the Ministry of Public Health, Physical Planning and Environment incorporated it into its policies in 1989. By 1995, 1,200 companies will have to develop an EMS voluntarily or face enforcement. An EMS is based on the concept of integrated protection, and it is described as: all provisions (technical organization, administrative, etc.) within a company or organization, aimed at gaining insight into controlling, and where possible at limiting adverse influences of a company's activities on the environment. EMSs are designed to:

— assure compliance with local, regional, national and international environmental laws and regulations;

— establish and make known internal policies and procedures needed to achieve the organization's environmental objectives;

— identify and manage company risks resulting from environmental risks;

— identify the level of resources and staff appropriate to the company's environmental risks and objectives, ensuring their availability when and where needed.

Introduction, in obligatory ways, of such management systems within the member states of the European Community would be a very important step towards international adjustment of environmental policy, also with respect to soil protection.

Legislation in relation to soil protection should also be developed at the international level. This requires, in the first place, agreement on standardization of soil quality. Therefore research aimed at development of soil quality standards remains one of the most urgent topics in order to sustain such legislation. At the same time the source-oriented policy deserves increasing attention as soil protection will profit from internationally agreed rules for the addition to soil of threatening substances.

# C. Documents

*1.* Bulgaria, *Ownership and use of Farm Land Act,*
No. 17 / 03/01/1991, amended No. 74 / 10/09/1191.

Article 2

Farm land, for the purposes of this Act, shall be all land, set aside for farming, that:

1. is not within the building development boundaries of settlements;

2. is not included as part of the forest reserve;

3. is not built-up by: industries or other economic enterprises, recreation or health establishments, religious denominations or other public organizations; nor is within courtyards,
nor under warehouses auxiliary to such buildings as the above;

4. is not under open mining, energy, irrigation, transportation or other public utilities; nor is
adjacent to such utilities.

...

Article 4

1. Proprietors shall use farm land for its proper use.

2. Proprietors shall be free to determine a manner of using farm land. Proprietors shall use
land in a manner such as is not detrimental to soils and in compliance with sanitation, fire
safety and environmental protection standards.

3. Buildings and installations may be erected on farm land such as are related to farm land
use by procedure and on terms as provided by the Territorial and Urban Development
Act.

*2.* Council of Europe, *European Soil Charter,*
Res. (72)19, 30 May 1972.

The Committee of Ministers of the Council of Europe,
adopts and proclaims the principles of the European Soil Charter ...

1. Soil is one of humanity's most precious assets. It allows plants, animals and man to live on
the earth's surface.

   Soil is a living and dynamic medium which supports plant and animal life. It is vital to
man's existence as a source of good and raw materials. It is a fundamental part of the
biosphere and, together with vegetation and climate, helps to regulate the circulation and
affects the quality of water.

   Soil is an entity in itself. As it contains traces of the evolution of the earth and its living
creatures, and is the basic element of the landscape, its scientific and cultural interest must
be taken into consideration.

2. Soil is a limited resource which is easily destroyed.

   Soil is a thin layer covering part of the earth's surface. Its use is limited by climate and
topography. It forms slowly by physical, physico-chemical, and biological processes but it

can be quickly destroyed by careless action. Its productive capacity can be improved by careful management over years or decades but once it is diminished or destroyed reconstitution of the soil may take centuries.

3. Industrial society uses land for agriculture as well as for industrial and other purposes. A regional planning policy must be conceived in terms of the properties of the soil and the needs of today's and tomorrow's society.

Soil may be put to many uses and it is generally exploited according to economic and social necessity. But the use made of it must depend on its properties, its fertility and the socio-economic services which it is capable of providing for the world of today and tomorrow. These properties thus govern the suitability of land for farming, forestry and other uses. Destruction of soil, in particular for purely economic reasons based on considerations of short-term yield, must be avoided.

Marginal lands raise special problems and special opportunities for soil conservation because, properly managed, they have great potential as nature reserves, re-afforestation areas, protection zones against soil erosion and avalanches, reservoirs and regulators of water systems and as recreation zones.

4. Farmers and foresters must apply methods that preserve the quality of the soil.

Machinery and modern techniques permit considerable increases in yields, but, if used indiscriminately, they may disrupt the natural balance of the soil, altering its physical, chemical and biological characteristics. The destruction of organic matter in the soil by inappropriate methods of cultivation and the misuse of heavy machinery are important factors in impairing soil structure and hence the yield of arable crops. The soil structure of grassland may be similarly damaged by intensive stocking.

Forestry should put appropriate emphasis on methods for improved exploitation which will prevent soil deterioration.

Methods of tillage and harvesting should conserve and improve the properties of the soil. The introduction of new techniques on a wide scale should be undertaken only after its possible disadvantages have been studied.

5. Soil must be protected against erosion.

Soil is exposed to the weather; it is eroded by water, wind, snow and ice. Careless human activity speeds up the process of erosion by damaging the soil's structure and its normal resistance to erosive action.

In all situations, suitable physical and biological methods must be applied to protect the soil against accelerated erosion. Special measures must be taken in areas liable to floods and avalanches.

6. Soil must be protected against pollution.

Certain chemical fertilizers and pesticides, used without discernment or control, may accumulate in cultivated land and may thus contribute to the pollution of soil, groundwater, water courses, and air.

If industry or agriculture discharges toxic residues or organic wastes that could endanger the land and water, those responsible must provide for adequate treatment of water or the disposal of wastes in suitable places, as well as for the restoration of the dumping areas after use.

7. Urban development must be planned so that it causes as little damage as possible to adjoining areas.

Towns obliterate the soil upon which they stand and effect neighbouring areas as a result of providing the infrastructure necessary to urban life (roads, water supplies, etc.) and by producing growing quantities of waste which must be disposed of.

Urban development must be concentrated and so planned that it avoids as far as possible taking over good soil and harming or polluting soil in farmland and forest, in nature reserves and recreational areas.

8. In civil engineering projects, the effects on adjacent land must be assessed during planning, so that adequate protective measures can be reckoned in the cost.

Operations such as the building of dams, bridges, roads, canals, factories, or houses may have a more or less permanent influence on surrounding land, both close at hand and at a distance. Often they alter natural drainage and watertables.

Such repercussions must be assessed so that suitable measures are taken to counteract damage.

Costs of measures to protect the surrounding area must be calculated at the planning stage and, if the installation is temporary, costs of restoration must be included in the budget.

9. An inventory of soil resources is indispensable.

For effective land planning and management and to permit the establishment of a genuine policy of conservation and improvement, the properties of the different types of soil, their capabilities and distribution, must be known. Each country must make an inventory, as detailed as necessary, of its soil resources.

Soil maps, supplemented as appropriate by special maps on land-use, geology, real and potential hydrogeology of soils, soil capability, vegetation, hydrology, and the like, are necessary for this purpose. The production of such maps by specialized agencies working together is a basic necessity in each country. These maps should be prepared in such a way as to permit comparison at international level.

10. Further research and interdisciplinary collaboration are required to ensure wise use and conservation of the soil.

...

11. Soil conservation must be taught at all levels and be kept to an ever-increasing extent in the public eye.

...

12. Governments and those in authority must purposefully plan and administer soil resources.

Soil is an essential but limited resource. Therefore, its use must be planned rationally, which means that the competent planning authorities must not only consider immediate needs but also ensure long-term conservation of the soil while increasing or at least maintaining its productive capacity.

A proper policy of soil conservation is therefore needed, which implies an appropriate administrative structure necessarily centralized, and properly coordinated at the regional level. Appropriate legislation is also required to allow the planned apportionment of land for different uses in regional and national development, to control techniques of land-use which might cause deterioration or pollution of the environment, to protect the soil against the inroads of natural and human hazards and where necessary to restore it.

States which accept the principles set out above should undertake to devote the necessary funds to their implementation and promote a genuine soil conservation policy.

## Questions and Problems

1. What are the best legislative techniques for soil protection:
   — specific regulations concerning the different uses
   — a general legal text (law, EEC directive, treaty)
   — an integrated approach including other environmental sectors and the various forms of pollution?

2. How can economic incentives be used for soil conservation?

3. What is the role of agriculture in soil depletion and deterioration?

4. What are the best forestry practices for assuring soil conservation?

5. Can national legislation in a European state assure the conservation of its soil or is international action necessary?

6. How should an environmental management system created by companies be integrated into national environmental protection?

7. Compare legislation on soil protection in Italy and the Netherlands.

8. Draft a European Convention on Soil Protection.

## Bibliography

Blum, W., *Problèmes de conservation du sol*, 1988, Collection Sauvegarde de la nature, Council of Europe.

Blum, W., *La pollution des sols par les métaux lourds*, Information document of the 6th European Ministerial Conference on the Environment, Council of Europe.

Boekhold, A. E., S. E. A. T. M. van der Zee and F. A. M. de Haan, "Prediction of cadmium accumulation in a heterogeneous soil using a scaled sorption model", Model Care 90, IAHS Publ. 195, pp. 211–20 (1990).

Boekhold, A. E. and S. E. A. T. M. van der Zee, "Long-term effects of soil heterogeneity on cadmium behavior in soil", 7 *J. Contam. Hydrol.* 371–90 (1991).

Council European Communities, Council Directive of 15 July 1980 relating to the quality of water intended for human consumption. O.J. no. L 229, 30 August 1980, 11–29.

De Boo, W., A closer look at cadmium in agriculture, (in Dutch), Meststoffen 1, pp. 36–9 (1988).

De Haan, F. A. M., A. C. M. Bourg, P. C. Brooks, W. Verstraete, S. P. McGrath, W. H. van Riemsdijk, S. E. A. T. M. van der Zee and J. V. Giraldez, *Soil Quality Report: State of the Art Report on Soil Quality*, (1989).

De Haan, F. A. M., "Agronomic and environmental implications of soil enrichment with mineral elements originating from animal slurries", Proc. Am. Feed Industry Assoc. Nutr. Symposium, St. Louis, pp. 6–14 (1990).

Edelman, Th., 1984. Achtergrondgehalten van stoffen in de bodem, Reeks Bodembescherming 34, Staatuitgeverij, 's-Gravenhage, 49 pp. (in Dutch).

Environmental Programme of the Netherlands 1986–90 (in Dutch), Staatsuitgeverij, 's-Gravenhage (1990).

European Conservation Strategy, 1990, 6th European Ministerial Conference on the Environment, Council of Europe.

Ferdinandus, H. N. M., Berekening van zware metalen balansen voor de bodem. Rapport Technische Commissie Bodembescherming, A89/01–R, Leidschendam, (in Dutch) (1989).

Ferdinandus, H. N. M., Th. M. Lexmond and F. A.M. de Haan, Heavy metal balance sheets for the sustainability of current agricultural practices (in Dutch). 4 *Milieu* 48–54 (1989).

Fournier, F., Les aspects de la Conservation des sols, 1972, Collection Sauvegarde de la nature, Council of Europe.

Gravesteijn, L. J. J., "Contaminated industrial sites in the Netherlands" in F. Arendt, M. Hinsenveld and W. J. v.d. Brink (eds.), 1 *Contaminated Soil '90,* 17–18 (1990).

Hacourt, H., "Approaches qualitative et quantitative", NATUROPA No. 65 (1990).

Hosman, A. P. M., Wet Bodembescherming (in Dutch); Handboek voor Milieubeheer, deel Bodembescherming; Samson, Alphen a/d/ Rijn, p. K1000-1-29 (1987).

Keuzenkamp, K. W., H. G. von Meijenfeldt and J. M. Roels, "Soil Protection policy in the Netherlands, the second decade", in F. Arendt, M. Hinsenveld and W. J. v.d. Brink (eds.). 1 *Contaminated Soil '90,* 3–10 (1990).

Lamé, J.P.A., Interimwet bodemsanering (in Dutch); Handboek voor Milieubeheer, deel Bodembescherming; Samsom, Alphen a/d Rijn, p. K2000-1-21 (1987)

Lexmond, Th. M., W. H. van Riemsdijk and F.A.M. de Haan, Onderzoek naar fosfaat en koper in de bodem in het bijzonder in gebieden met intensieve veehouderij. Reeks Bodembescherming 9, Staatuitgeverij,'s-Gravenhage, 159 pp (in Dutch) (1982).

Lexmond, Th. M. and Th. Edelman, Huidige achtergrondwaarden van het gehalte aan een aantal zware metalen en arseen in grond. Handboek voor Milieubeheer, deel Bodemberscherming, Samsom, Alphen a/d Rijn, D4110-1-32 (1987).

Moen, J. E. T. and W. J. K. Brugman, "Soil Protection Programmes and Strategies in other Community Member States: examples from Netherlands" in H. Barth and P. L. L'Hermite (eds.), *Scientific Basis for Soil Protection in the European Community* pp. 429–36 (1987).

National Environmental Policy Plan, Staten General, Second Chamberkj, 21137 (1989).

Report presented by the Belgian delegation. Feasibility study on national and/or European action to be undertaken in the field of soil protection, 6th Ministerial Conference on the Environment, Council of Europe.

Technical Commission on Soil Protection, Advies gebruik dierlijke meststoffen, VTCB A86/01, Leidschendam, 30pp (in Dutch) (1986).

Technical Commission on Soil Protection, Advies wijziging besluit gebruik dierlijke meststoffen, TCB A90/03, Leidschendam, 19pp (in Dutch) (1990).

Van der Zee, S.E.A.T.M., "Transport of reactive contaminants in heterogeneous soil systems", Ph.D Thesis, Agricultural Universith Wageningen, 283 pp. (1988).

Van der Zee, S. E. A. T. M., H. N. M. Ferdinandus, A.E. Boekhold and F.A.M. de Haan, "Long-term effects of fertilization and diffuse deposition of heavy metals on soil and crop quality", in Van Beusichem, M. L. (ed.) *Plant Nutrition, Physicology and Applications*, p 323–6 (1990).

Van der Zee, S.E.A.T.M., and F.A.M. de Haan, Soil and groundwater quality indicators. Proceedings J.R.C., Ispra (in press).

Von Meijenfeldt, H. G., and E. C. M. Schippers, "The bill is presented; Motives behind the recovery of soil clean-up costs in the Netherlands", in F. Arendt, M. Hinsenveld and W. J. v. d. Brink (eds.), *Contaminated Soil '90*, Vol. I, pp. 11–16 (1990).

## CHAPTER VII

# FRESHWATERS

## A. Overview

Continental or freshwaters are essential to all life on land. However, only 2.7 per cent of the earth's water is freshwater and a large proportion of this limited quantity is frozen in glacial ice caps at the two poles and on high mountains. At the same time, the demand for water continues to increase with population growth, improved living standards, and the extension of water-utilizing industries such as mining and metal processing, agriculture,[1] cement production, and wood processing. On average a European consumes about 800 m² of water per year, approximately 70 times more than a Ghanian, but less than each inhabitant of the United States, whose consumption exceeds 3,000 m² annually. Urban concentrations, in particular, pose considerable problems for the provision of water as well as for the removal of water once it is used. The problems are likely to increase in the coming years with limits on available water becoming a greater factor in development.

Water goes through a constantly repeating cycle and does not disappear. However, once utilized, freshwater is generally discarded with its waste contents. The latter can impact on the water cycle, and contaminate rivers, lakes, underground water sources, the oceans and the atmosphere. Thus, freshwater pollution problems cannot be isolated from those of other sectors of the environment. Marine chemical pollution, for example, derives in large part from freshwater contamination. In addition, the protection and management of water resources are closely linked to those of soil; pollution, soil erosion, and the disappearance of ground cover, particularly forests, can have grave repercussions on water.

The problem of protecting freshwater cannot be understood without taking into account the many uses of water. Water quality is partly a function of the utilizations foreseen rather than a matter of establishing uniform absolute measures. One can schematically classify uses according to the degree of purity required by the needs of certain industries, by production of drinks and food, drinking water, water used in refrigeration circuits, water used for irrigation, etc. The European Water Charter, adopted in 1968 by the Council of Europe, proclaims that water quality should be preserved at levels adapted to the use which is foreseen and, in particular, should satisfy the needs of public health.

In certain cases water can be reused or recycled. It also can be regenerated if the

---

[1] Approximately 73 per cent of water consumption throughout the world is agricultural.

pollution is not excessive. The European Water Charter declares that when used water is returned to the natural milieu, it should not compromise further uses, public or private, that might be made of it. Obviously these conditions necessitate regulation and management of water resources.

Law must take into account other factors as well. First, the notion of a hydrographic basin or collection basin is particularly important. Within an area marked by watershed lines, the basin collects all waters into a river or lake that consequently risks receiving all pollution originating in the area. Therefore, to be effective, regulations aimed at combating pollution should be directed at the entire basin. Unfortunately, this is not always done, especially when basins include the territories of more than one state.

A second factor important to regulation is the difference between surface and underground waters. The first have a certain capacity for regeneration, although it can be significantly less for lakes than for rivers and other moving bodies of water. In contrast, underground water sources are the slowest to renew and have limited capacity for regeneration. In addition to their natural vulnerability, they often constitute the primary source of drinking water; in the Community they represent 75 per cent overall, but 88 per cent in Italy and 98 per cent in Denmark. For these reasons groundwater generally needs stronger legal protection than surface waters.

Third, the legal treatment of pollution is complicated by differences between identifiable "point" sources and "diffuse" pollution coming from many sources, each of which is separately responsible for possibly insignificant amounts of pollution. Small, often continuous, discharges of wastes and utilization of pesticides in agricultural activities are examples of diffuse pollution.

Finally, it is difficult to separate the quantitative from the qualitative aspects of protecting water sources, that is, regulation from management. Increasingly, legal regulation is by integrated water management, considering the entire water cycle, aquatic and land ecosystems, human activities and socio-economic factors. The principal mechanism is planned uses. An international conference on water and the environment, which took place 26–31 January 1992 in Dublin, favoured water management at the lowest effective governmental level, involving the concerned populace. However, decentralization of management presumes the existence of national authorities, even international ones, that can define the objectives, the priorities, and, when necessary, establish norms for a water system.

In fact, there are numerous examples of integrated management among European countries. The 1986 German basic water law contains numerous prescriptions for planning, including preparation of "management plans" and "framework plans" at the level of hydrographic basins or regions, to guide governmental decisions concerning development, conservation and utilization of water resources. These plans are coordinated with land use planning for national and regional development objectives. They involve not only specialized water services but other governmental departments, such as those in charge of regulating other resources (e.g. mining) or responsibility for protection of the countryside.

Similarly, planning plays an important role in the Netherlands, in managing and protecting both underground water sources (law of 22 May 1981) and surface waters (law of 24 June 1981). The Dutch law of 14 June 1989 on water resource management foresees a system of planning at different levels – state, provinces and local authorities – coordinated with the national environment plan.

Numerous examples could be cited for other countries: Norway (1985 law on planning and construction), Italy (law 183 of 18 May 1989 reorganizing and restructuring the conservation of soil, articles 17 and 21), Spain (law no. 29/1985 on water, title III), France (law 92–3 of 3 January 1992 on water, chapter I). It can be said that the management of water resources is a generalized duty of public authority. Management involves both the protection of the environment – particularly the battle against pollution – and the entire utilization of water resources. The concept of the basin here plays a major role.

## 1. The Protection of Freshwaters in International Law: Transfrontier Pollution

Freshwater protection cannot be separated from other aspects of international environmental law. In particular, principles of transfrontier pollution are applicable, i.e. those international norms concerning pollution whose origin is within one country but whose effects are felt within another. In addition specific rules govern international rivers and lakes.

Norms on transfrontier pollution largely originate in customary international law, although some were first formulated by international institutions, such as the United Nations Programme for the Environment (UNEP) or the Organization of Economic Cooperation and Development (OECD). The fundamental, often reiterated principle on transfrontier pollution is contained in the 1972 Stockholm Declaration on the Human Environment: States have an obligation to ensure that activities within the limits of their jurisdiction do not cause damage to the environment of other states. Various texts adopted at the 1992 Rio Conference on Environment and Development confirmed this principle.

Other international principles also have emerged or are in process of emerging: the obligation urgently to notify states potentially affected of any event that might cause sudden harmful effects to their environment and, if necessary, the obligation to provide aid; the obligation to inform a foreign state of projects or activities capable of having measurable effects on the environment and to consult before approving the project; the right to equality of access to procedures and remedies that are afforded for any person, whatever their state of residence, who is or risks being affected by environmental deterioration, and finally, equal application of national legislation, no matter where environmental damage occurs. These principles should be supplemented by those relating to polluter liability and perhaps the provisions of the Espoo Convention of 25 February 1991 on environmental impact assessment in a transboundary context, discussed above.

Particular standards applicable to international rivers and lakes have been fragmentary and disperse until quite recently; rules normally were adopted by riparian states for a particular lake, a river or even a single section of a river. Thus, conventional norms protect the Rhine against pollution only between Lake Constance and the mouth of the river; the elements of its hydrographic basin appear only in a fragmentary fashion in several provisions of a treaty of 3 December 1976 on protection against chemical pollution.

The Council of Europe adopted in 1968 the European Water Charter, already cited, which proclaims major principles applicable to the protection and management of water. However, the same organization had no success in its efforts, dating from 1974, to adopt a European Convention for the Protection of International Watercourses. Only on 17 March 1992 was a treaty adopted in a different framework on the protection and utilization of transfrontier rivers and international lakes in Europe.

Each party to the Convention, signed by twenty-two European countries and the Community, under the auspices of the UN Economic Commission for Europe, agrees to prevent, control and reduce water pollution coming from all sources, especially from dangerous substances. They also agree to establish reasonable and equitable uses for transfrontier waters, in regard to activities that risk or could risk transfrontier impact. The Convention foresees the application of the precautionary principle and the polluter pays principle. It announces the need to safeguard the capacity of future generations to satisfy their own needs. On the technical level, the Convention foresees the application of measures such as obtaining prior authorization for any discharge of used waters, monitoring of discharges, prohibiting use of dangerous substances, the developing water quality objectives and criteria as well as environmental impact assessment in regard to water management. If the norms are implemented they will constitute the synthesis of principles of transfrontier pollution and specific rules protecting freshwaters.

The UNECE also adopted a 1980 Declaration of Policy on Prevention and Control of Water Pollution, including Transboundary Pollution; Principles Regarding Cooperation in the Field of Transboundary Waters; and a 1990 Code of Conduct on Accidental Pollution of Transboundary Inland Waters.

Global action is even more recent. In 1992, the United Nations International Law Commission finalized a code on non-navigational uses of international watercourses.[2] The text is a draft framework agreement providing a reference for states that have no specific treaties or agreements on waters shared with neighbouring states. The draft convention codifies recognized principles: (a) no State has the right to cause appreciable damage to another State; (b) each State has a right to an equitable share in the uses of the waters of an international river, lake or other source; and (c) each State is under a duty to negotiate in good faith a solution to any conflict of water-related interests with neighbouring States. Exchange of data and information, prior notification of planned measures, and consultation are part of the basic duty.

## 2. Means and Methods to Protect Water Against Pollution

Community environmental law plays a particularly important role in protecting freshwater against pollution. Of course, not all European states are members of the Community. Nonetheless, it is useful to treat Community law together with national

---

[2] Comments on the code were due from governments on 1 January 1993. The draft will have a second reading by the Commission before being sent to the General Assembly for adoption.

laws of member and non-member states; even Member States may implement Community directives in different ways.

In this field, as others, the applicable norms should be considered together with other measures of environmental protection, especially procedures that seek to prevent environmental deterioration by licensing, preparing impact studies, providing for public information and participation, regulating industry functioning, monitoring, and establishing remedies in case of breach of regulations including damages and sanctions. These procedures govern activities that exclusively or primarily affect freshwater, especially when they impact on water quality.

In France, an industrial plant that produces or stocks dangerous substances and discharges polluting material into water or air must prepare an impact statement covering all the consequences of its activities on the environment, including effects on water. The impact statement is submitted to public inquiry, before a permit to construct or authorization to function is obtained. The licence can be granted on conditions, including measures to be taken to protect water. Particular measures of security can be prescribed if it is a matter of an installation that carries with it risk of major accidents, thus bringing it under the Community "Seveso Directive".[3] Regular monitoring must then be exercised over the functioning of the plant. Legal remedies – administrative, civil and penal – can be invoked against it for breach of applicable standards regarding the environment in general or specific norms regarding the protection of water. The latter are integrated into overall standards: thus norms prescribed by Community directives should be applied and all discharges, trickles, jets, direct or indirect deposits of water or matter, and more generally any act capable of altering water quality on the surface or underground must have a licence from the prefect of the department.[4]

The procedure just described applies, in general outline, in several countries (Belgium, Luxembourg, Netherlands, United Kingdom). It also can be applied to protect other sectors, such as marine waters or air. The following materials concern means and methods specific to freshwaters.

### a. Regulating Discharges into Water

One technique, corresponding to air pollution emission standards, prohibits certain discharges, and regulates or licences others. The most important legal instrument in this regard is Community Directive 76/464 of 4 May 1976[5] relating to pollution caused by certain dangerous substances discharged into the Community aquatic environment. It makes a distinction between two categories of dangerous substances. The first category, detailed in Annex I, includes carcinogens, organohalogenes, organophosphorus and compounds, mercury and its compounds, cadmium and its compounds, persistent oils and synthetic substances. Any discharge liable to contain any of the substances figuring on this "black list" requires prior

---

[3] See below at pp. 405–6, 442.

[4] French decree no. 75–218 of 23 February 1975 and application ordinance of 13 May 1975.

[5] O.J. no. L 129, 18 May 1976.

authorization by the competent authority of the state concerned. The latter must adopt norms establishing maximum quantities of these substances in discharges, but only within the limit values set by the Community based on toxicity, persistence, and bioaccumulation.

In contrast to pollution caused by substances appearing on the "black list", the second, Annex II, category is composed of matter that must be reduced rather than eliminated. The list consists of approximately twenty metals and their compounds (zinc, lead, arsenic, etc.), biocides and their derivatives, substances having a deleterious effect on the taste and/or smell of products for human consumption, as well as certain organic compounds of silicon. The discharge of such substances requires prior authorizations based on established emission standards. However, states should also establish programmes to reduce water pollution by Annex II substances; these norms should be set with reference to quality objectives in accordance with Council directives.

Implementation of the directive is considerably more difficult than it might appear. First, the number of "substances and families of substances" enumerated in Annex I is approximately 1,500; however, the ecotoxicological consequences are known for only about ten per cent of them. Research in progress should improve knowledge in this field and already has led to the adoption of directives supplementing that of 1976, to control mercury discharges,[6] cadmium discharges,[7] and hexachlorocyclohexane.[8]

Most Community Member States have adopted emission standards, some before enactment of the Community directives. Standards were set in England and Wales in 1951 and are maintained in part 3 of the 1989 water law. Spain adopts the same method in law no. 29 of 2 August 1985, art. 93 and royal decree no. 849 of 11 April 1986, art. 251(a). In France it appears in a decree of 25 February 1975 and its regulations of application. Similarly, Italian law no. 319 of 10 May 1976, as modified, in article 9 and annexes A and C, establishes emission standards. National standards of Member States must conform to Community directives, as must the methods by which they are applied.[9]

Emission standards and discharge licences can be combined with a system of charges. In Spain, the law calls for imposition of charges on all who obtain a licence to emit, calculated on the basis of the discharge authorized.[10]

Several international treaties similarly adopt the system of controlling emissions, with black lists for prohibited substances and grey lists for those whose discharge

6  Directive 82/176 of 22 March 1982, O.J. no. L 74, 27 March 1982.

7  Directive 83/513 of 26 September 1983, O.J. no. L 291, 24 October 1983.

8  Directive 84/491 of 9 October 1984, O.J. no. L 274 of 17 October 1984.

9  In the United Kingdom, application of directive 82/176 of 22 March 1982, concerning limit values and quality objectives for mercury discharges, created political problems. British tradition is decentralized and informal, calling for negotiations with the industries in question, rather than imposing strict and uniform rules. See, L. D. Guruswamy, I. Papps and D. J. Storey, "The Development and Impact of an EEC Directive: the Control of Discharges of Mercury to the Aquatic Environment", *J. Common Market Studies*, vol. XXII no. 1, Sept. 1983.

10  Article 105 and royal decree no. 849 of 11 April 1986, articles 289 ff.

should be reduced. In particular, the Bonn Convention on Protection of the Rhine against Chemical Pollution, adopted 3 December 1976, follows closely the model of Community Directive 76/464, adopted several months earlier. Similarly, two treaties concerning pollution of the sea from land-based sources – including rivers – apply the system of regulating emissions; the Paris Convention of 4 June 1974, concerning the North East Atlantic and the Arctic, and the Protocol of Athens of 17 May 1980, supplementing the Barcelona Convention for the Protection of the Mediterranean Sea against Pollution.

### b. Determining water quality standards

A second method of regulating freshwaters is based on establishing the admissible level of given pollutants in a specific aquatic milieu, rather than setting emission limits for each source of pollution. This method is used by the United Kingdom, in part because of the fact that its rivers are short and rapid, discharging pollutants into the sea rather rapidly. Establishing water quality objectives is a method particularly adapted to combating diffuse source pollution. In contrast, when point sources can be identified, it is easier to prohibit pollution at its origin in order to protect water quality. In this case, emission standards are used.

In most cases, the two methods can be combined. Community Directive 76/464 of 4 May 1976, discussed above, takes this approach to combating pollution caused by the discharge of dangerous substances. In addition to establishing emission standards, the directive calls for fixing water quality standards for black list sub- stances, in function of the toxicity, persistence and accumulation of these substances in living organisms and sediments (article 6, para. 2). For the grey list, member States should establish programmes to reduce discharges, fixing their own water quality objectives conforming to Community directives (article 7, para. 3).

Water quality standards have been used by the Community in a variety of fields where it is necessary to take into account the intended use of the waters. The texts are characterized by their aim of protecting human health, and by their technical details. Specific directives have been adopted for:

— the quality required of surface waters intended for abstraction of drinking water, Directive 75/440 of 16 June 1975, O.J. no. L 194, 25 July 1975;

— water quality intended for human consumption, Directive 80/778 of 15 July 1980, O.J. no. L 299, 30 August 1980;

— water quality of bathing waters, Directive 76/160 of 8 December 1975, O.J. no. L 31, 5 February 1976;

— water needing protection or improvement in order to support fish life, Direc- tive 78/659 of 18 July 1978, O.J. no. L 222, 14 August 1978;

— water quality required of shellfish waters, Directive 79/923 of 30 October 1979, O.J. no. L 281, 10 November 1979.

Unfortunately, the transposition of these directives into national law in member states has not gone smoothly. The Commission has initiated complaint procedures against nearly every member state for failure to abide by the requirements of the bathing water Directive. The most frequent violation seems to be failure generally to apply the directive, outside a limited number of areas, and failure to take the required number of samples or analyses. As a result, the quality standards established in the directive have not been obtained.

Similarly, effective application of the drinking water directive is lacking. In 1990, the Commission opened or continued procedures against the majority of member states due either to unauthorized express derogations from provisions of the directive, or to exceeding maximum authorized concentrations.[11]

### c. Special Measures to Protect Groundwaters

A Community directive defines groundwater as "all water which is below the surface of the ground in the saturation zone and in direct contact with the ground or subsoil".[12] Pollution of groundwater can be caused by direct discharge, or by indirect percolation of pollutants through the ground or subsoil. Agricultural activities, including the use of fertilizers or pesticides, and dumping of garbage or other wastes containing polluting substances play an important role in this regard. Laws to protect groundwater, whose deterioration is virtually irreversible, must consider these factors.

Community legislation has led in this field. In the majority of Community Member States, there were few, if any, specific measures protecting groundwater against pollution. Instead, States relied upon their general legislation concerning the environment (Denmark, Spain, Greece, Ireland, Italy, United Kingdom). The case of Germany is typical: protection of groundwater was within general water legislation (federal law on the management of water, 1957, 1976, 1986), as well as laws governing charges on used waters (federal law of 1976, 1984, 1987 and 1987), the reduction and elimination of wastes (federal law of 1986) and the regulation of drinking water. Only Luxembourg and the Netherlands had special laws to protect groundwater. In the latter country, a 1981 groundwater law protected sensitive zones and established norms for the utilization of groundtable water. Laws on soil are also important in protecting groundwater. In this regard, the Netherlands has adopted several laws: the 1981 law on chemical wastes, the 1982 soil clean-up law, and the 1986 law on soil protection. One particular measure limits the utilization of organic fertilizer to the equivalent of 175 kilograms of phosphate per hectare.

The Community intervened in this field for the first time through Directive 76/464 on protection of the Community aquatic milieu. Several years later, the Council adopted Directive 80/68, cited above, specifically concerning groundwater. It applies methods analogous to the earlier Directive in establishing two lists containing essentially the same families and groups of substances, and establishing a system of prior authorization for emissions. However, the particular characteristics of groundwater necessitated the introduction of a distinction between direct and

---

[11] Commission of the European Communities, Eighth Annual Report to the European Parliament on Application of Community Law, 31 July 1991, COM(91) 321 final, pp. 76–7.

[12] Council Directive 80/68 of 17 December 1979 concerning the protection of groundwater against pollution caused by certain dangerous substances, O.J. no. L 20, 26 January 1980.

indirect pollution. Direct discharge of substances appearing on list I must be prevented and the introduction of substances on list II limited. For indirect pollution, authorities must conduct an investigation prior to any disposal that might lead to indirect discharge. The decision to permit or prohibit the activity depends upon the results of the investigation. Whether a discharge is direct or indirect, all permits must specify the place and method of discharge, the precautions to be taken, the maximum admissible quantity of a substance in an effluent, monitoring arrangements for the discharge, and, if necessary, measures for monitoring groundwater and its quality. Member States must supply the Commission of the Community at its request and on a case by case basis, all necessary information on the investigations it conducts, the results obtained, the details of permits granted, the results of monitoring and inspection operations, and the results of inventories.

Although Directive 80/68 does not speak of it, another important groundwater protection measure is the creation of protective perimeters around groundwater catchment areas, especially areas that are sources of drinking water. Certain activities can be prohibited or limited in these areas, as provided in article 13 of the French water law of 3 January 1992.

In some cases, groundwaters are polluted by accident, through broken pipes, leaking reservoirs or cisterns, or traffic accidents involving vehicles carrying polluting substances. To counter these, precautionary measures can require waterproof pavement where vehicles are loaded and unloaded, monitoring and regular inspection of pipelines and pumping stations, and establishment of emergency plans. In large part, industries can assure these operations and establish professional guidelines, but Community norms concerning major industrial risks also play a significant role.

## 3. Special Protection for Watercourses or Sites

Besides the creation of protected perimeters, States can enact measures aimed at the construction and functioning of hydro-electric plants. Such measures may lead to conflicts between energy producers and the affected population as has been the case in Norway where numerous watercourses are entirely or partly protected by Parliamentary decision against any construction or works. In Finland, a special law protects cascades and rapids, imposing a special permit process for the construction of hydro-electric plants. The law also lists rivers for which no permit can be issued. Finally, lakes and rivers situated in zones of ecological protection benefit from the general protection accorded these zones.

## 4. Protection and Integrated Planning

The recent French water law, promulgated 3 January 1992, provides a good example of water management and integrated protection. It follows Community directive 76/464 in making no distinction between freshwaters and waters of the territorial sea. However, contrary to Community norms, it treats together and in the same manner surface and groundwater. It states that water forms part of the common heritage of the nation and that water protection, management and development as a usable resource, respecting natural equilibria, are matters of general interest (article 1). The objective of the law is to assure the sustainable management of water resources, preserving aquatic ecosystems, sites and wetlands, protecting against all deterioration of the quality of surface and ground waters, and enhancing the value of, developing and protecting water resources. The latter should be allocated in a manner satisfactory to the requirements of health, safe drinking water for the population, agriculture, fishing, industry, energy production, transport, tourism and leisure. (article 2).

The law builds upon several administrative structures existing in France. Utilizing a pragmatic method, law 64/1245 of 16 December 1964 created six financially autonomous water agencies. Each agency is administered by an administrative council composed of eight representatives from each of the following groups: territories (regions, cities, villages), consumers, the state, as well as a representative of employers. These constitute a kind of "water parliament", which can establish and collect a "tax" or charge on pollution emissions. The charges are imposed on any person, public or private, physical or moral, who emits pollution. Clients of a water distribution service pay the charge as part of their water bill. The funds collected are used to assist groups and individuals to obtain anti-pollution equipment, including treatment plants. It is a practical application of the polluter-pays principle combined with the principle of solidarity, in the regional framework of a hydrographic basin.

Using the basin concept, the law of 3 January 1992 foresees the preparation of water management master plans. The master plan, prepared with participation from the local water commissions, is put before the public for observations for two months (articles 3–5).

Although water resource management is thus organized on a community basis, the government defines quality norms, the measures necessary to preserve and restore this quality, norms dividing water for different uses and adopts necessary prescriptions and prohibitions. Article 8 (4) states that the sale or distribution of substances likely to cause deterioration of water quality can be prohibited or regulated. The third aspect of the law is the licensing of all installations, works and activities of a non-household nature that use surface or ground waters, whether restored or not, that risk causing a modification of the level or run-off of water, as well as those that emit, discharge or deposit directly or indirectly, continuously or sporadically, polluting and even non-polluting matter. A nomenclature for these installations and activities is established according to the dangers that they present and the degree of harm they pose to water resources and aquatic ecosystems. This list is not exhaustive. A licence is accorded after a public inquiry. The licence can be withdrawn or modified in the interest of public health and in case of a major threat to the aquatic milieu. Existing installations and activities have three years to conform to these requirements. The law states that installations submitted to licensing according to the general regime of classified installations for environmental protection (law of 19 July 1976) should also respect these provisions (articles 10 and 11). Finally, as has been noted, protective perimeters can be established if a catchment or reservoir does not have sufficient natural protection to assure water quality (article 13, para. I). Inside these perimeters all activities and installations that might directly or indirectly threaten water quality can be forbidden (article 14, paragraph I).

The law creates procedures permitting challenges to claimed violations of its provisions, as well as administrative and penal sanctions. Finally, two chapters set out the means of local intervention in water management, including clean-up and distribution.

The drought years that have passed through Europe since the middle of the 1980s underline even further the need to maintain the link between qualitative and quantitative protection of water and rational management of this resource.

# B. Case Studies

## 1. Stefano Burchi, *Recent Trends in the Law and Administration of Freshwater Resources in Western Europe*

Current western European legislation or legislative information on freshwater resources is complex and diverse; however, there are themes which recur, with fairly consistent treatment in law. These may point to present and future directions of water resource management law and administration. Some of the themes are relatively novel when compared to earlier laws, while others are familiar. Among the former are the prominent role of formal planning processes and instruments in water resources decision-making, and the interplay between water and land-based natural resources. Other recurrent themes are the fading role of private waters and vested water rights; the cautious mobility of water rights from less to more economically efficient uses of water; integration and regionalization of water administration, particularly along river basin lines; and the recourse to regulatory and financial mechanisms for the prevention and control of pollution from point-sources.

### a. Water Resources Planning

Water resources planning is increasingly and consistently finding formal recognition in legislation as a mechanism for sound short- and long-term water resources decision-making.

Spain's 1985 Water Act and attendant implementing regulations offer convincing evidence of the central role assigned to water resources planning in the overall legal framework for the management of a country's water resources. The Spanish law provides an elaborate set of rules outlining the topology of plans (there shall be a River Basin Plan and national Hydrological Plan), the contents of the plans, the process of forming, approving, and revising the different plans, and the effects of approved plans. In particular, water resources planning is to be coordinated with other sectoral planning exercises, most notably in the fields of agriculture, energy, and land use, and such coordination is to be effected at the level of the National Hydrological Plan. The participation of the general public in the process of forming the River Basin Plans is expressly provided for by making the draft of the general outlines of such Plans available to the public on request, for comment. River Basin

Plans are subject to mandatory revision every eight years following their approval. Water Plans are binding on the Government, and, subject to certain qualifications, they are also restrictive of land use planning determinations.

In Germany, 1986 amendments to the Federal Water Act provide for two different kinds of planning instruments, at the river basin or regional level, to guide and orient all governmental decision-making with regard to water resources management. Coordination of water planning with land use planning and regional development objectives is mandatory. Certain water plans have binding effect on all Government agencies in charge of natural resources management.

In Holland, comprehensive legislation for water resources management enacted in 1989 mandates the formation of different interrelated water planning instruments at State, provincial, and local levels, covering essentially surface water resources management relating to both quantity and quality. Groundwater management plans are provided for by separate groundwater management legislation enacted in 1981.

In Italy, river basin plans have been mandated by a fundamental 1989 law inaugurating a river basin approach to certain limited aspects of water resources management in that country. River basin plans are, at least theoretically, very ambitious in scope, spanning from conservation to development, from water alloca- tion to water pollution control, from the control of harmful effects of water to forestry, fisheries, and mining development, from coastal zone management to the control of soil contamination. River basin plans must be coordinated with other general development plans and with land use plans, and have a binding effect. Separate water pollution control plans were mandated by 1976 water pollution control legislation, but implementation is far behind schedule.

### b. Controlling Water Pollution from Diffuse Sources

Recent water legislation reflects the increasing awareness of the interdependence of land and water resources, and of relevant management mechanisms and processes. Traditionally, such interdependence was reflected in laws governing the development of irrigated agriculture, often in combination with land redistribution goals. However, attention is shifting towards the impact of land use activities on the quality of water resources, not only on the surface, but also and more importantly, underground.

The protection of sources of water, especially drinking water, tends to be effected in legislation through zoning designated perimeters in which potentially contamin- ating human activities are prohibited or restricted. A recent example of this is the United Kingdom 1989 Water Act. Also, the zoning of the areas surrounding estab- lishes sources of public water supplies is mandated by the new French water law. Holland's 1986 Soil Protection Act provides that Provincial Governments are to lay down rules restricting land uses in designated groundwater catchment areas.

Concern for the impact of pesticides and fertilizers employed in agriculture on the quality of surface and underground waters is reflected in the most recent pollution control legislation. Under the United Kingdom 1989 Water Act, for example, the Government has authority to designate Nitrate Sensitive Areas in which special measures apply to abate nitrate leaching into waters resulting from the use of fertilizers. These measures may be compulsory or voluntary, they may involve absolute standards or a process of negotiation, and farmers may be compensated for the losses stemming from a Designation Order. It depends on the terms of each specific Order. In the Netherlands, the 1987 Regulations severely restrict the application of animal manure to the soil with regard to the quantities and timing of applications, based upon the nature and designated use of the soil. A Community directive, enacted in June 1991 seeks to protect inland, coastal, and marine waters from nitrate pollution of agricultural origin. The Directive provides for the designation by Member States of Nitrate Sensitive Areas, and for restrictions in such Areas of the quantities, rates and timing of applications of livestock manure and chemical fertilizers, and as the nitrogen contents of municipal sewage effluent. A time frame for compliance is provided. Outside the designated Areas, the same measures are positively recommended for adoption by Member States as part of so-called rules of good agricultural practice.

The land-water interface is further compellingly borne out in other recent statutes which address specific water quality concerns resulting from exposure to land uses, or, vice versa, concern for the quality of the soil as a result of water-related activities. For example, under Italy's 1982 waste disposal control legislation, the siting of waste disposal dumps is subject to strict licensing and monitoring requirements with a view to protecting land and water resources from the risks of contamination. Similarly, legislation was adopted in 1981 in Switzerland to restrict the siting, construction and operation of designated installations handling liquid substances which may adversely affect water resources. To this end, the Cantons are to zone their respective territories into four different classes of water protection areas, each calling for standard restrictions of varying severity. The Netherlands' 1986 Soil Protection Act's provisions on the control of soil degradation view instead a number of water-related activities – notably, the discharging of wastewater into the soil, the abstraction of groundwater, and land drainage – as a source of hazard to the productivity and stability of the soil. As a result, these activities are scheduled for regulatory restrictions, and the responsible persons will be held liable for the damages resulting from soil degradation.

### c. Control of Pollution of Water Resources from Point Sources

Licensing of waste discharges into or near water bodies has undoubtedly become central to the prevention and abatement of water pollution from point sources, and tends as a result to replace everywhere the simple – but largely ineffective – system of prohibiting all waste discharges. In the United Kingdom, for example, a system of prior administrative "consents" to discharge trade and sewerage effluent into waters is in effect. Standards of effluent quality are negotiated on a case by case basis with each polluter, and are tailored to achieve pre-determined ambient water quality objectives. The 1989 statute has introduced for the first time the requirement that these ambient water quality objectives be achieved within a given time frame.

In Italy and Spain, on the other hand, the waste discharge permit systems inaugurated by the respective laws in 1976 and 1985 are based on uniform, nationwide, effluent quality standards. In Italy, the system is complemented by a time frame for implementation. In Spain, no time limits are set.

Increasingly, licensing and permit requirements are complemented by charging systems designed to penalize the dischargers of waste into waters. This system has long been in effect in France, and has been adopted also by Italy and Spain. In France and Spain the waste discharge fee is paid by all dischargers as long as the discharge continues. In Italy, the fee is payable only temporarily, as long as dischargers do not comply with the prescribed effluent quality standards. Britain's 1989 Water Act foresees a system of waste discharge payments for direct discharges into rivers and coastal waters.

Complementary to more specific water pollution control mechanisms is the legal requirement that a minimum flow be maintained in a watercourse. Minimum flow requirements can be laid down for the protection of fish habitats, such as with France's 1984 Inland Fisheries Law. Britain's 1989 Water Act reflects a variety of concerns, including, in particular, safeguarding the scenic and amenity values of watercourses, and the attainment of ambient water quality objectives. An additional complementary instrument is the legal requirement that the impact of proposed water withdrawals on, *inter alia*, the quality, flow and volume of the system be assessed prior to the granting of a licence or permit. A mandatory requirement to this effect appears in the French Water Law.

### d. The State of "Private" Waters and Vested Water Rights

The legal status of water as a commodity privately owned by individuals is on a continuing decline. The most significant recent example of this trend is the 1985 Spanish water law, which placed all waters above and underground in the State public domain as state property. Greece's 1987 legislation on waters dedicates all water resources to serving the interests of society as a whole. The French Water Law brings waters formerly outside the public domain within the scope of the law's water resources management mechanisms and controls.

In those countries where water resources are in the public domain, the government retains authority to grant water use rights subject to terms and conditions, including modification or evocation of the rights by the government under given circumstances, and subject to compensation if the modification or revocation is not due to the fault of the right holder. Spain's 1985 Water law establishes a system of administrative water rights.

A delicate problem which arises whenever the government seeks to assert its role as owner or guardian of the resource, and regulator of its uses on behalf of the public, is the fate of existing or vested water rights, both actual, i.e., in progress at the moment the change takes effect, and potential. In particular, this problem confronts policy-makers and legislators during a transition from systems of water rights based on private property values (notably, when the right to use surface or groundwater accrues from ownership of the land along a stream – riparianism – or above an aquifer) to systems based on administrative grants of user rights. While any legislature may change the rules of water use, it is widely felt that any changes should not cause undue hardship to "existing" users, i.e., those users entitled to use water on the basis of pre-existing laws or customs. Retroactive application of legislation could be deemed a taking of property, giving rise to compensation for expropriation.

Particularly relevant, in this regard, are the experience of the United Kingdom in switching from a private-property system of surface and underground water rights to an administrative permit system, and the experience of Spain in reclassifying all water resources as public domain subject to administrative grants of water rights. England and Wales imposed a system of administrative water use licences on riparian rights in the 1963 Water Act. A water use licence can be obtained only if one owns or possesses riparian land. At the same time, a riparian owner no longer can draw water from a stream or from under his land free from government control, except for minor, largely domestic, uses. There was no court challenge to this reform. Spain's 1985 Water Act protected vested rights in groundwater by offering relevant holders the option of either recording their rights with the Government and preserving them free from government interference for fifty years, or not recording their rights and risking loss of them to competing users. The option was made available only for a limited transition period. The law was challenged in court by vested rights holders who claimed that they had been substantially deprived of constitutionally protected property rights. The challenge was rejected by Spain's Constitutional Court in a November 1988 judgment, which held that the special regime of vested water rights is a legitimate interference with constitutionally protected property rights, on the grounds of (a) the subordination of rights in natural resources in general to the "general interest" enshrined in the Constitution, and (b) the reasonableness of the restrictions in light of the general interest.

### e. Transferability of Water Rights

The transfer of water rights, i.e., their exchanging hands and use through government agency or market mechanisms, is practiced subject to considerable restrictions. By and large, these stem from the prevailing view that a grant of water attaches to a particular use, and, in the case of irrigation rights, to a particular piece of land, and that, as a result, it cannot be disposed of separately from the use or the land to which it is attached. The general trend is to allow some flexibility in this domain, subject to prior government approval of a transfer. Far less flexibility exists in the domain of irrigation water rights, which tend to attach to the land they serve. The issue of water rights mobility is particularly relevant in arid countries. The Spanish 1985 Water Act allows water rights to change hands and use, subject to the prior consent of the Government and to the conformity of the proposed change with the provisions of river basin plans in effect.

### f. Integration and Regionalization of Government Water Administration

There is significant evidence that functional integration of the government water resources administration is a goal that is being consistently pursued in developing and developed countries alike. What varies is the depth of integration sought, and the level of government at which integration is pursued.

In Finland, integration of the government water administration has reached from the liquid to the atmospheric phase of the hydrologic cycle. The former National Board of Waters, since 1986 renamed National Board of Waters and the Environment, is now responsible for air pollution control as part of its expanded water management mandate. In Ireland, overall responsibility for the management of water resources is consolidated in the Environment Ministry.

Integration of water management functions at river basin level is reflected in recent Spanish legislation. In that country, the river basin orientation dating from 1926 was confirmed in the 1985 law. The *Confederaciones Hidrograficas* perform a number of water management functions ranging from river basin planning to allocating water for different uses, and from water quality control to constructing and operating water development projects. In an effort at achieving sustained integration, the former *Comisarias de Aguas* have been merged in the *Confederaciones Hidrograficas* together with their original operational functions. A distinctive train of the *Confederaciones* is the representation of users in their internal organizational and decision-making structure on an equal footing with the government representatives. An advisory National Water Council with membership drawn from the Central Government, the Autonomous Communities governments, and the *Confederaciones* ensures the overall consistency of water administration in the country as a whole.

In the United Kingdom, the high point of integration of water management functions was reached in 1973, when almost all water management functions, from utility services to river basin operation, and from regulation of water use to pollution control, were combined in ten Regional Water Authorities operating at the level of groups of river basins in England and Wales. Under the 1989 Water Act, however, the water utility function of the Water Authorities has been separated from the rest of the water management functions, and will be carried out by private companies under government licence in the former Water Authorities areas. The public and regulatory functions of the Water Authorities have been transferred to a new National Rivers Authority (NRA) of government appointees. As a result, the NRA still concentrates in its hands a gamut of water management functions reflecting a partial integration policy. What has radically changed is the level of control which has shifted from river basin to the central government.

Regionalization, i.e., bringing government water administration closer to the regional levels of government, has characterized the recent history of water administration in countries like France, Italy, Spain, Belgium, Greece, Portugal and the United Kingdom. In most cases, but not all, regionalization has been based on the river basin or groups of river basins as a unit of government.

In Belgium, a system of regional governments was instituted in 1980 and has brought about a fragmentation of water policy and management into three separate regional components. The water administration of the country is now carved into three administrations each independent of the other. As a result, the river basin approach has suffered a serious setback.

In Spain, the *Confederaciones Hidrograficas* which pre-existed the system of regional autonomy inaugurated by the 1978 Constitution were reconciled with the Autonomous Communities by the 1985 basic Water Act by directing that the government water administration of all basins exceeding the ambit of any one Autonomous Community would continue to be arranged along river basin lines, with all corresponding water management functions. The government water administration of all other river basins, and the relevant water management functions, would fall in the sphere of competence of the Community concerned. Some Communities challenged this division of labour on the same grounds as their Italian counterparts, but the Spanish Constitutional Court by and large upheld the 1985 law in a November 1988 judgment. The Court found the law respectful of the constitutionally established role of the Autonomous Communities and the various Charters of the appellant Communities.

Timid but significant steps towards a regionalization of water administration along river basin lines, have been taken by Greece and Portugal. In Greece, the 1987 legislation on water resources has instituted regional water commissions at river basin levels, with membership drawn from the regional governments concerned, central government ministries, the local governments and irrigation users' groups. The task of the commissions is to advise the national Interministerial Water Commission on all projects for the development of basin water resources. In Portugal, a Commission for the management of the Ave River was created in 1986; other actions await a comprehensive water law.

### g. Management of Transboundary Water Resources

In addition to the multilateral treaties adopted under the auspices of the United Nations Economic Commission for Europe, various treaties of more limited coverage are found within Europe. Recent examples include the Convention on the International Commission for the Protection of the Elbe, done at Magdeburg, 8 October 1990, signed by Germany, Czechoslovakia, and the Community. It creates a Commission, with broad-ranging powers to foster active cooperation among Member States. The eight Danubian countries also have pledged, at a meeting held in Budapest in February 1991 to develop a Convention for the protection and use of the Danube River, modelled after the ECE-sponsored Espoo Convention.

## 2. Ludwig Krämer, *Freshwaters and Community Law*

The objective of the Community environmental policy is to protect, preserve and improve the quality of the environment in the Community "ecosystem", to contribute to political, economic and social integration, and thus to protect the environment within the Community to the extent that the Community has a role to play. Community environmental policy and national policies of Member States are interdependent, complementary and cumulative. Their common objective is the best possible environmental protection.

The Community is not a State; its policy cannot be compared to that of national environmental policy because the Community does not have general competence and is limited to pursuing the objectives assigned to it by Community treaties. Community legislative texts are not adopted by an elected Parliament but by the

Council of Ministers which, in environmental matters, decides in nearly all cases by unanimity. The Community has multiple public opinions: press, radio and television are national and inform the public in the different Member States about environmental matters, not in the Community interest, but in the national interest.

To these general differences aspects specific to the environment must be added: only a minority of Member States have a national environmental policy that is substantial and coherent. National consciousness of ecological problems and the value of active policies in this field vary considerably from one Member State to another. The implementation of Community measures is carried out by Member States who do not all agree on the importance of effective application of environmental legislation adopted at the regional, national or Community level.

In the first Community Action Programme, the protection of freshwaters and marine waters was a priority matter. The approach chosen by the Community involved a double strategy, on one hand to establish water quality objectives and on the other, to set norms limiting water pollution.

Quality standards set the parameters an environmental milieu should meet at a given moment, to be compatible with the usage that is envisaged for it. Such objectives thus require that the utilization of waters be determined.

The water quality objectives for drinking water,[13] fishing[14] and shellfish waters[15] leave to Member States the designation of waters to which the provisions of the directives are applicable. In each directive, the parameters have been determined, for which value limits are fixed. There are mandatory limits and recommended limits. Member States are obliged to undertake clean-up programmes to attain the objectives of the directives sometimes within five years (fishing waters), six years (shellfish waters) or ten years (surface waters).

Implementation of the directives has been more than difficult. Several Member States have not identified fishing or shellfish waters in order to escape application of the directives. A judgment of the Court of Justice in 1988 declared such practices incompatible with Community law. Other Member States have identified only waters which already met the requirements of the directives, thus avoiding the necessity of elaborating and implementing clean-up programmes. The programmes raised the most difficulties. Most Member States have not adopted them[16] and the programmes which have been adopted do not all conform to the environmental requirements of the directives. Thus, the principal objective of the directives to ensure respect for the values of the directives through the programmes and permanent clean-up and gradually to improve the quality of freshwaters has not bee attained.

The directive on the quality of bathing waters[17] is constructed along similar lines.

[13] Directive 75/440 of 16 June 1975, O.J. no. L 194, 25 July 1975.

[14] Directive 78/659 of 18 July 1978, O.J. no. L 222, 14 Aug. 1978.

[15] Directive 79/923 of 30 Oct. 1979, O.J. no. L 281, 10 Nov. 1979.

[16] This led to a condemnation of Germany by the Court of Justice in 1991 for non-respect of Directive 75/440; France escaped a similar condemnation in 1991, having presented during the judicial procedure and for the first time, mandatory programmes, sixteen years after adoption of the directive.

[17] Directive 76/160 of 8 Dec. 1975, O.J. no. L 31, of 5 Feb. 1976.

It sets nineteen parameters and, for the majority of them, mandatory and recommended standards. Member States have a period of ten years to conform their bathing waters to the requirements of the Directive. Apart from this, the directive is distinguished from preceding directives in two aspects: it objectively determines what is a bathing water – either water where bathing is expressly authorized, or water where bathing is not forbidden and where it is normally practiced by a large number of bathers – and foresees regular publication of relative values concerning implementation of the direct. The Commission is thus able to exercise a considerable pressure on Member States when bathing waters have not been identified and thus not regularly evaluated by Member States in spite of a large number of frequent bathers. The development of tourism and public awareness on these questions have contributed to pushing Member States to regularly monitor their waters and to take clean-up measures in case of necessity. The directive is still far from being fully applied throughout the Community. However, efforts are being made, in spite of a certain north–south split.

The directive applies to all bathing waters, with the greatest impact on the more numerous bathing waters of coastal zones. Member States continue to designate few inland waters and instead of cleaning up inland waters, the directive has had its greatest effect in demonstrating the poor quality of these waters and of gradually reducing the frequency of their use for bathing.

The directives relating to the quality of drinking water[18] and underground waters[19] are integrated in the general Community water policy and the division of labour between the Community and Member States. The directive on drinking water fixes, for undesirable substances, concentrations not to be exceeded, giving Member States five years to take clean-up measures. The directive requires only the specified result of respecting the maximum concentrations authorized by the directive. Thus, Member States have the option of purifying water before its delivery to the consumer rather than halting pollution at its sources. It seems that the majority of Member States produce drinking water by purification to meet the standards of the directive, instead of acting to prevent pollution.

The directive on the protection of underground waters against pollution contains neither quality objectives, nor emission standards. On the other hand, it imposes precise obligations on Member States as far as direct or indirect dumping of dangerous substances in underground waters is concerned and permits artificial enriching of the waters only if pollution of them is excluded. The directive foresees, among others, measures designed to avoid pollution of underground waters by the discharge of wastes.

The Community sought a different approach in regard to discharge of dangerous substances in the aquatic milieu, without always finding a consensus on the policy to follow. The views of Britain diverged from those of other Member States. The UK felt that in the final analysis, it is the degree to which the substance pollutes the environment that is important. Consequently, in their view it is only necessary to fix

---

[18] Directive 80/778 of 15 July 1980, O.J. no. L 229, 30 Aug. 1980.
[19] Directive 80/68 of 17 Dec. 1979, O.J. no. L 20, 26 Jan. 1980.

quality standards and monitor compliance with them. In contrast, other Member States felt that the discharge in the water of dangerous substances – those harmful to humans and/or the environment due to their toxicity, permanence or bioaccumulation – should be minimized, to the extent possible. Consequently, it was necessary to fix maximum emission limits for these substances. The UK argued that such an approach aimed to harmonize natural geographic differences within the Community: in the UK, there are short, rapid rivers, close to the sea, which makes possible the discharge of dangerous substances because the substances are rapidly carried to the ocean where they are dispersed and eliminated. Slow and long continental rivers require a different approach.

The compromise arrived at[20] divides dangerous substances into two groups. The first group contains substances that are particularly dangerous due to their toxicity, persistence or bioaccumulation. The second group contains the other dangerous substances. Substances in the first group are to be regulated by specific Community legislation, which determines the emission levels that cannot be exceeded (the "continental" approach) and, at the same time, the quality objectives to respect (British approach). Discharge permits must be drafted for enterprises in a way that the emission norms are respected or the quality objectives achieved.

Any substance on the first list that has not been regulated by the Community should be treated as a list II substance. For these substances, the Member States agree to establish programmes to reduce pollution and fix quality standards. The Commission established a list of some 1,600 dangerous substances discharged into water. From this list, it has selected 129 substances to treat in a priority fashion. By the end of 1991, 17 of these substances were regulated by the Community. No Member State has transmitted a programme to the Commission on list II substances nor had they set quality standards for these substances. The effort of the Commission to establish quality objectives for one of these substances, chrome, failed for lack of unanimity on the Council. Similarly, the project of adopting rules for list I substances by qualified majority of the Council had not always succeeded.

To these legislative difficulties should be added the problems of fixing values, of the comparability of emission standards with quality objectives, of monitoring respect for given provisions and permits granted, of measurement methods, etc. Overall, the contribution of Community provisions to the reduction of pollution of freshwater is limited. A general revision of the approach concerning dangerous substances, announced in the Fourth Action Programme on the Environment (1987), has not yet been finalized.

Recently, the Community has begun elaborating other norms aimed at reducing contamination of freshwaters. Thus, directive 91/271 relating to the treatment of urban waste waters[21] requires Member States to equip all towns of more than 2,000 inhabitants with waste water collection systems to be installed between 1998 and 2005. The costs of implementing this directive are estimated to be nearly 60 million ECU. Another directive, adopted at the end of 1991, seeks to reduce nitrates in water

[20] Directive 76/464 of 4 May 1976, O.J. no. L 129, 18 May 1976. See *supra* p. 235.
[21] Directive 91/271, O.J. no. L 135, p. 40.

by imposing a limitation on the number of animals per hectare in areas where the nitrate concentration in the water reaches a critical level.[22] In this manner, methods of agricultural production are adapted to the absorption capacity of the environment.

Finally, the Commission is considering elaboration of a directive fixing an ecological water quality. The directive could constitute a framework for management, improvement in water quality and reduction of pollution in all Community waters.

A general analysis of Community environmental provisions on freshwaters and their implementation leads to the following observations:

Community directives give national, regional and local administrations the possibilities of managing their freshwaters, of reducing their pollution and improving their quality. Since all the directives, without exception, permit Member States to introduce or maintain more protective environmental provisions, national evolution leading to better environmental protection is not hampered.

The majority of directives foresee elaboration and implementation of management and clean-up programmes for water. However, in numerous regions of the Community such programmes have not been drafted. Thus, the objective of the directives, the environmental management of waters, is only partially realized. Member States that pursue an active national policy of environmental water management see measurable improvement in water quality. In Member States where such policies are less actively pursued, Community enacted limits are not sufficient to prevent deterioration.

This situation is in part due to the fact that the Commission of the Communities lacks human, financial and technical means to coordinate plans and programmes, to manage, in common with Member States, freshwater resources, to monitor clean-up measures envisaged or solicit adoption and implementation of such measures. In particular, the Commission is unable to coordinate different national actions, to orient them towards the objectives according to common principles, and to contribute to an integrated management of waters and water resources. Its activity is limited above all to elaborating new legislative texts and discussing these in the Community legislative process.

The freshwaters of the Community seem not to suffer too much from illegal discharge of undesirable substances, but rather from too many authorized, legal discharges. It is striking to note the degree to which information on the state of waters and on the authorized and actual discharges are unknown or, at least, not made public. The Court of Justice has found that the protection of the environment is an important objective of general interest:[23] permits to discharge substances in the natural milieu and in particular in water are generally negotiated and accorded between the administration and enterprises, as if these two social groups could dispose freely of the environment, a common good. Transparency and complete information about what is discharged in the natural milieu should be the norm and constitute a minimum requirement. However, anyone trying to obtain precise details on pollutants found in the Tage, the Ebre, the Rhone, the Meuse or even the Rhine, quickly discovers that commercial–administrative secrecy is the norm, not transparency.

[22] Proposal for directive. O.J. 1989 no. C 54, p. 4.
[23] Court of Justice, Case 302/86 (1988), p. 4607.

Community directives have not succeeded in modifying this state of events in a significant fashion.

In general, it is as important to know what an installation, public or private, places in the natural milieu, as it is when a product or a substance is placed in circulation or on the market. In such cases, recourse to commercial–administrative secrecy is not possible. Just as the number of cars entering the market from a factory cannot be held secret, the quantities of mercury, of cadmium or heavy metals that the factory discharges into water must not be hidden from the public. A parallel interpretation is necessary if one wishes to protect effectively the general interest in the environment.

The Community is far from having an inventory of emissions in water and of the most important sources of these emissions. It also lacks an inventory of the most important technologies or the best available technologies to reduce pollution to the extent possible and the investments which promote these technologies. Methods permitting benefits to all the Community from procedures of useful clean-up and, more generally, environmental know-how, are also largely absent. Moreover, the reports on implementation of the different directives as well as on other measures adopted by Member States are insufficient, even non-existent in certain cases, and do not make it possible to determine what approaches are efficient or inefficient, nor why they are such. Finally, the Community directives do not impose on Member States, at least with the necessary precision, an obligation to reduce water pollution permanently and do not require factories and other polluting installations to take measures in this regard.

## 3. Harald Rossmann, *The Austrian Legal Framework to Reduce Pollution of the Danube*

During the reconstruction of functioning economic structures in Europe after World War II, the main water-management goal was to make the best use of water resources to meet growing industrial, agricultural and domestic needs. One consequence was that rivers and other aquatic systems often were regarded as natural reservoirs for the collection of waste and dangerous remnants of explosively growing prosperity.

The Danube River was affected by this development. Although the Danube does not originate in Austria, and the international character of the Danube is part of the problem, this point should not be overemphasized.

As far as international measures are concerned, the Danube Convention, resulting from the Belgrade Conference in 1948, includes almost no provisions to stop or reduce water pollution effectively. What measures do exist internationally generally result from efforts of international organizations, such as the United Nations and its Economic Commission for Europe, to outline basic standards for water protection and water management. ECE recommendations include important measures to improve the quality of the waters of the Danube.[24] In addition, there are international

---

[24] For example, Declaration of a policy of preventive measures and control of water pollution (1980); Resolutions concerning the international cooperation on international waterways (1982, 1984, 1986); Principles of cooperation on international waterways (1987); Resolutions on waste-water management (1988, 1990); Concept concerning responsibilities and liabilities in case of transgressing water pollution (1990).

norms on harm resulting from industrial accidents. Finally, at the international level, mention must be made of the Final Act of the CSCE and the Declaration of the Danube States on protecting the waters of the Danube from pollution (1985).

National legal and administrative action against pollution of the Danube has been taken in Austria. According to the federal system established by the Austrian Constitution,[25] legislative and administrative competence is divided between the Federation and the nine Austrian states. Article 10[1]Z.10 B-VG allocates legislative functions over water management to the Federation. Executive powers are divided and allocated among the federal ministers of agriculture and forestry, the state governors, and, at the lowest level, the district authorities of the states. However, as far as the Danube river is concerned, competence rests with the federal government.

Norms governing the protection of water resources are part of the Water Management Act, 1959, amended in 1990 (Wasserrechtsgesetz – WRG). From 1959 to 1990, legal provisions to reduce dangerous, toxic or otherwise harmful components of waste water and to improve the quality of rivers incorporated the following basic measures:

— any action that might influence water quality was subject to administrative procedures controlled by the relevant water authorities. These aimed to exclude or at least minimize negative effects on water resources;

— permission to act required conformity to principles of water conservation and had to be justified in the public interest;

— general emission limits recommended by the supreme water authority for specified components of waste water could not be exceeded. More stringent rules had to be applied if the level or kind of pollution did not allow even the limited emissions;

— harm to water quality gradually had to adapt to the development of water conservation and technical standards;

— illegal waste water disposal was not only subject to penal law, but also administrative action to enforce restitution or compensation;

— for the long-term improvement of aquatic systems, the federal minister for agriculture and forestry could issue valid general regulations defining mandatory quality standards for such aquatic systems, thus prohibiting any activities that could endanger the determined goal.

In 1977, ministerial regulations were issued to improve the water quality of the Danube. These define the standard to be achieved, applying a system of classification. The regulations also include special standards for applying the Water Management Act when permitting deliveries of waste water into the Danube River and limitations with regard to the consistency of waste water and its temperature. The Danube regulations not only concern the Danube River but also its drainage area. Consequently, application by the water authorities should make it possible to achieve the defined goal within approximately twenty years.

---

[25] Bundesverfassungsgesetz–B–VG.

Amendments to the Water Management Act in 1990 completely revised and refined the general principles of water protection, enabling an integrative evaluation of activities influencing aquatic systems, considering the total ecological situation. This refined concept of water management demanded reorganization of operative means. At present, the legal framework provides a highly differentiated system of determined goals and the tools for their realization, including:

— a detailed concept of administrative permits;

— general planning instruments;

— general or individual restoration concepts in order to adapt plants to the latest technical standards;

— a concept of all-over research and control instruments;

— a general limitation of emissions, linked to systematic reduction of water pollution;

— a general system of intervention to influence the quality of aquatic systems up to and including the withdrawal of valid permits.

The amended Water Management Act will be the basis of a new regulation by the federal minister of agriculture and forestry defining class II quality as the goal to achieve with regard to all rivers in Austria, the Danube included. This quality standard is intended to generally regulate waste water attributes like consistency, temperature and other characteristics. If a river or part of it does not meet these quality standards, a system of precautions has to be tailored to achieve the determined goal. Finally, all plants that have ever emitted waste water must be adapted within ten years to the latest scientific and technical standards or be taken out of action.

## 4. Meinhard Schröder, *The Rhine*

The Rhine is the most important waterway of Western Europe. At the same time, because the Rhine basin is densely populated and highly industrialized, its waters serve the most varied purposes: e.g. the production of drinking water for human consumption, fishing, the direct and indirect supply of freshwater for agricultural lands, recreation and, last but not least, the production of water for industrial use.[26] It is evident that pollution of the Rhine can seriously impair these uses, if not render them impossible. For this reason, measures against pollution became an urgent and permanent task from the moment Rhine water quality began deteriorating.

Since the end of the 1940s, environmental problems of the Rhine waters have been attributed to three major sources:

First, there are pollutants (e.g. heavy metals and phosphorus) from effluent of the chemical industry, especially in the Swiss and German areas. Added to this are pollutants from municipal discharges as well as agricultural effluent (phosphates, nitrates, pesticides).

---

[26] See, for example, Art. 1(2) of the 1976 Convention for the Protection of the Rhine against Chemical Pollution.

Second, salinization of the Rhine is caused by chlorides. Salt is brought into the river, especially by the Alsatian potassium mines, with particular consequences for the Netherlands, where the Rhine is the main freshwater reservoir for the production of drinking water and the irrigation of agricultural lands.

Third, thermal pollution of the waters of the Rhine results from their use as cooling water for power stations.

Pollution by industrial accidents, resulting from concurring uses of the Rhine waters, must be added to these "normal" causes of pollution. Such incidents lead to a sudden discharge of harmful substances in high concentrations, made clear most recently after the accident in the Sandoz chemical plant (Basel, Switzerland).

All riparian states pollute the Rhine. Typically pollution also affects all riparian states, even though downstream states suffer more intensively and with varied results depending upon their uses of the water. As with all watercourses, pollution of the tributaries adds to the deterioration of Rhine waters. This must be taken into account when protection measures are taken.

### a. Legal Instruments

Given the fact that the sources and effects of Rhine pollution can be found in all riparian states and that the Rhine in its function as waterway is subject to international regimes, protection measures have been taken as part of transfrontier cooperation. From the beginning this included special international conventions, because customary international law on water is relatively young and its overly-general character only partly responds to the special environmental problems of a given river. So far, there are no principal differences in regulating the Rhine compared to other international rivers, where other special provisions and practices were settled. On the other hand, all riparian states except Switzerland are Member States of the European Community (EC). With the development of a European environmental law including a law relating to water, questions have been raised about the scope of EC competence regarding the protection of the Rhine and about how to coordinate international and European protection standards. Although a 1972 Community attempt failed to create a European Environmental Agency concerning the Rhine, which would have only involved the Member States indirectly, the EC did considerably influence the development of protection measures for the Rhine.

The legal instruments to protect Rhine waters against pollution are partly organizational and partly substantive in character. Today, they constitute a package of complementary measures that have reduced the environmental impairment of the Rhine since the middle of the 1970s.

In 1950, the International Commission for the Protection of the Rhine against Pollution was established. Its structure and tasks were elaborated in a convention signed in 1963 by the governments of the Federal Republic of Germany, France, Luxembourg, the Netherlands, and Switzerland. The participation of Luxembourg is based on its responsibility for pollutants introduced into the Rhine by the Moselle. The Commission has exclusive functions of investigation, recommendation, and, regarding legal instruments, preparation. Initially, the Commission was composed only of delegations of the governments of the member states and consulted experts of the respective delegations. After the EEC adhered to the Convention in 1976, the Commission was extended to include an EEC delegation. The Commission decides all questions unanimously. In the course of this, each delegation has one vote and the EEC, within its competence, takes the place of its member states. The work is carried out by working groups with the aid of independent experts and institutions. Commission investigations are implemented by national organs of the Member States on the basis of a decision of the Commission. The costs of the Commission are distributed by special arrangement; the costs of protection measures agreed on for the Rhine are decided separately.

As important as the impulses and recommendations of the Commission have been and still are, the Commission itself has not achieved any results of significance in the struggle against Rhine pollution. Besides the principle of unanimity this was and is caused particularly by the fact that the Commission is dependant on the willingness of the riparian states to cooperate concerning the implementation of its decisions. Obviously this willingness has to exist on a political level. This was recently evidenced by the Conferences of the Ministers of the Member States of the Rhine Commission, which take place regularly. Up to now, eleven conferences have been held and they have finally made considerable progress in the fight against pollution of the Rhine waters.

In 1976 the riparian states of the Rhine concluded a Convention for the Protection of the Rhine against Chemical Pollution, which entered into force in 1979. The Convention has been accepted by the EEC. With good reasons it incorporated essential elements of the EEC's Directive 76/464 on Pollution Caused by Certain Dangerous Substances Discharged into the Aquatic Environment. The Directive itself applies to the Rhine. By conforming the Convention and the Directive, States Parties avoided the application of different rules or higher standards to the Rhine than for other waters of the EEC. The Convention is a first step towards prohibiting the discharge of certain dangerous substances and to reducing the discharge of other substances. However, emission standards are so far not envisaged because they would be unrealistic, considering the Rhine as an industrially and commercially used river.

The Convention has a framework character and its objectives can be realized only if concrete measures are taken on the international level as well as on the national level. Specific means include national inventories of the discharges of pollutants, laying down emission standards proposed by the Commission, national regulations and programmes to reduce the discharge of grey list substances, national measuring stations to control discharges, and international information policies regarding accidents and the experiences gained from them.[27] In any case, annual reports of the Commission declare that the chemical pollution of the Rhine may have been reduced considerably since 1976. This success, however, was presumably reached not only because of the Convention but also due to related measures of national and European

---

[27] Article 11 of the Convention obliged riparian states to inform about chemical accidents and the experience thus gained. On the basis of this article, the Commission elaborated and continues the International Warning and Alarm Plan Regarding the Rhine.

Community law, which promotes environmentally favourable industry and the construction of purification plants.

Less favourable results have been reached until now by the Convention on the Protection of the Rhine against Pollution by Chlorides, concluded in 1976, in force since 1985. The objective of the Convention is gradually to reduce the discharge of chloride ions into the Rhine by at least 60 kg/s on annual average. The main responsibility regarding the reduction of the chloride load is borne by France because of its potassium mines. Nevertheless the other riparian states contribute, bearing some of the rising costs. The French obligation to install an injection system in the subsoil of Alsace in order to reduce discharges from Alsatian potassium mines has to date been fulfilled only in small part. Considerable opposition within France, especially within the Alsatian population, as well as disputes between France and the Netherlands concerning the apportionment of the costs have repeatedly led to a change of planning and a prolongation of the time period within which France must meet its obligations. This also explains why the Convention entered into force only in 1985. In 1987, France raised again the question of injecting the chlorides into the Alsatian subsoil. After long discussions, a new plan was elaborated, abandoning the idea of injection in favour of temporary stocking of the salts. On 25 October 1991, an additional protocol to the Chloride Convention was signed. As a guideline for the chloride concentration in the Rhine, a limit value of 200 mg/l at the German–Netherlands border was established. Alsacian salts are being stocked depending on whether the concentration exceeds this value or remains below it. It was agreed that the chloride stocks should be introduced into the Rhine in an environmentally compatible manner, not affecting the validity of the guidelines. Furthermore, the Netherlands accepted to introduce salty polder-water into mud flats rather than into the Ijsselmeer, so that the Ijsselmeer-water can be used for the production of drinking water. The costs for both measures are divided between the contracting parties according to their previous portions. In addition, all contracting parties are obligated to prevent an increase of the amounts of discharged chloride within the Rhine basin.

Under the impact of the 1986 chemical accident of Sandoz, preventing risks to the environment has attained a special priority. The most important instrument in this respect is the Action Programme Rhine[28] adopted at the 8th Ministerial Conference in October 1987. One objective of this "declaration of intention" is to increase the fish population up to the year 2000 and to guarantee the use of the Rhine waters for the production of drinking water. In a three-phase plan, inventories of pollutants and discharges will be made, common technical standards will be formulated and controlling instruments established.

Measures against thermal pollution of the Rhine, particularly the once-considered conclusion of a convention, are not planned at present. Thermal pollution of the Rhine does not appear to the Commission to be an urgent problem, perhaps due to the reduced construction of power plants.

Inland navigation on the Rhine is subject to the international regime of the

[28] Summary in Annual Report of the Commission, 1987, p. 76 *et seq.*

Revised Convention on the Navigation of the Rhine (Mannheim Convention) of 1868. This Convention is the basis for the work of the Central Rhine Commission in Strasbourg, with representatives from Belgium, Germany, France, Great Britain, the Netherlands and Switzerland. In 1970, the Central Rhine Commission issued a Ordinance Concerning the Carriage of Dangerous Goods by the Rhine; it entered into force in 1971. According to the ordinance, certain goods are no longer allowed to be transported on the Rhine; others can be carried only according to established security provisions.

### b. State Practice

In the past, riparian states seldom made public statements about the obligations imposed by international law on the protection of neighbouring territories. State responsibility has been not asserted, nor arbitration invoked, as provided by the Rhine Conventions. One reason for that may be that all riparian states not only are affected by pollution of the Rhine, but also contribute to it. Obviously, in this situation, they prefer more flexible negotiations like those of the Ministerial Conferences and the (confidential) consultations within the Commission. Against this background, it may be understandable that "declarations of intention" have been recently favoured over the more or less rigid Convention regulations.

### c. Judicial Decisions

Remarkable judgments have been issued by national courts regarding the effects of salinity of the Rhine on its use for Dutch agriculture and the supply of drinking water. In an action for damages caused to Dutch plaintiffs by MDPA, Dutch courts held that the 1976 Chloride Convention would be irrelevant for damage claims under civil law. Discharges permitted by the Convention would not automatically be justified as to Dutch inhabitants; as agreement under international law, the Convention would have no constitutive effect on civil law.[29] Similarly, public international law was not considered authoritative. On the other hand, the Tribunal Administratif of Strasbourg assumed that the Convention restricts the discretion of the authorities responsible for discharges from the moment it is signed. The responsible authorities also would have to consider the interests of foreign neighbours, protected by public international law.[30] The Conseil d'Etat, however, set the decision aside and spoke in support of the Harmon Doctrine.[31]

---

[29] Arrondissementsrechtsbank Rotterdam, decision of 8 January 1979 and of 16 December 1983, in RabelsZ 49 (1985) 741 et seq.; Hof Den Haag, decision of 19 September 1986 in RabelsZ 51 (1987) 491 et seq; Hoge Raad, decision of 23 September 1988 in RabelsZ 53 (1989) 699 et seq.

[30] Decision of 27 June 1983, Revue Juridique de l'Environnement 1983, 346 et seq.

[31] Decision of 18 April 1986, Revue Juridique de l'Environnement, 1986, 296, note 307. The Harmon Doctrine, named after the nineteenth-century United States Attorney General, asserts absolute sovereignty and denies responsibility for pollution damage caused other states. See Kiss and Shelton, International Environmental Law, pp. 119–20.

*d. Evaluation*

It is indisputable that the ecological situation of the Rhine has improved noticeably since the 1970s. Whether or not the river was highly or excessively loaded in 1972, today it is moderately loaded. Without doubt, this favourable trend is due to the work of the Rhine Commission and the common efforts of the riparian states. However, developments in European law on water pollution control and environmentally favourable production processes may have contributed. Further, there is a positive shift of emphasis taking place, from the approach of reducing pollutants to the approach of preventing them, like that described in the Action Plan Rhine. The concept of the Plan could become a model for the renovation of other rivers with similar pollution problems. As for the Rhine, it remains to be seen how far the concept will be implemented. Binding agreements do not exist, partly the goals may be too high. Problems which need special attention are the discharges by agriculture and in the atmosphere, as well as the not yet reliable measuring and valuation of organic micropollution. Accident prevention could be supported by the introduction of strict liability in all riparian state legislation relating to water, as already proposed by the German delegation. This would make easier judicial decisions on liability. The transparency of important ecological data concerning the Rhine will be improved by the EEC's Directive on Freedom of Access to Information on the Environment of 7 June 1990. However, public authorities' rash assertions of no danger to the environment after discharges due to industrial accidents are counterproductive.

The work of the Rhine Commission seems to be evaluated quite positively in Europe. The renewal of other rivers is often based on the approach of the Rhine renovation. This is shown clearly by the Convention on the International Commission for the Protection of the River Elbe between the governments of the Federal Republic of Germany and the Czechoslovak Federal Republic, as well as the EEC, signed in Magdeburg in 1990.

# C. Documents

*1. Convention on the Protection and Use of Transboundary Watercourses and International Lakes,*
Helsinki, 17 March 1992.

The Parties to this Convention,

...

Conscious of the role of the United Nations Economic Commission for Europe in promoting international cooperation for the prevention, control and reduction of transboundary water pollution and sustainable use of transboundary waters, and in this regard recalling the ECE Declaration of Policy on Prevention and Control of Water Pollution, including Transboundary Pollution; the ECE Declaration of Policy on the Rational Use of Water; the ECE Principles Regarding Cooperation in the Field of Transboundary Waters; the ECE Charter on Groundwater Management; and the Code of Conduct on Accidental Pollution of Transboundary Inland Waters,

Have agreed as follows:

## Article 1 DEFINITIONS

For the purposes of this Convention,

1.  "Transboundary waters" means any surface or ground waters which mark, cross or are located on boundaries between two or more States; wherever transboundary waters flow directly into the sea, these transboundary waters end at a straight line across their respective mouths between points on the low-water line of their banks;

2.  "Transboundary impact" means any significant adverse effect on the environment resulting from a change in the conditions of transboundary waters caused by a human activity, the physical origin of which is situated wholly or in part within an area under the jurisdiction of a Party, within an area under the jurisdiction of another Party. Such effects on the environment include effects on human health and safety, flora, fauna, soil, air, water, climate, landscape and historical monuments or other physical structures or the interaction among these factors; they also include effects on the cultural heritage or socio-economic conditions resulting from alterations to those factors;

...

6.  "Hazardous substances" means substances which are toxic, carcinogenic, mutagenic, teratogenic or bio-accumulative, especially when they are persistent;

7.  "Best available technology" (the definition is contained in annex I to this Convention).

## PART I

## PROVISIONS RELATING TO ALL PARTIES

### Article 2 GENERAL PROVISIONS

1.  The Parties shall take all appropriate measures to prevent, control and reduce any transboundary impact.

2.  The Parties shall, in particular, take all appropriate measures:

    (a)  To prevent, control and reduce pollution of waters causing or likely to cause transboundary impact;

    (b)  To ensure that transboundary waters are used with the aim of ecologically sound and rational water management, conservation of water resources and environmental protection;

    (c)  To ensure that transboundary waters are used in a reasonable and equitable way, taking into particular account their transboundary character, in the case of activities which cause or are likely to cause transboundary impact;

    (d)  To ensure conservation and, where necessary, restoration of ecosystems.

3.  Measures for the prevention, control and reduction of water pollution shall be taken, where possible, at source.

4.  These measures shall not directly or indirectly result in a transfer of pollution to other parts of the environment.

5.  In taking the measures referred to in paragraphs 1 and 2 of this article, the Parties shall be guided by the following principles:

(a) The precautionary principle, by virtue of which action to avoid the potential transboundary impact of the release of hazardous substances shall not be postponed on the ground that scientific research has not fully proved a causal link between those substances, on the one hand, and the potential transboundary impact, on the other hand;

(b) The polluter-pays principle, by virtue of which costs of pollution prevention, control and reduction measures shall be borne by the polluter;

(c) Water resources shall be managed so that the needs of the present generation are met without compromising the ability of future generations to meet their own needs.

6. The Riparian Parties shall cooperate on the basis of equality and reciprocity, in particular through bilateral and multilateral agreements, in order to develop harmonized policies, programmes and strategies covering the relevant catchment areas, or parts thereof, aimed at the prevention, control and reduction of transboundary impact and aimed at the protection of the environment of transboundary waters or the environment influenced by such waters, including the marine environment.

7. The application of this Convention shall not lead to the deterioration of environmental conditions nor lead to increased transboundary impact.

8. The provisions of this Convention shall not affect the right of Parties individually or jointly to adopt and implement more stringent measures than those set down in this Convention.

## Article 3 PREVENTION, CONTROL AND REDUCTION

1. To prevent, control and reduce transboundary impact, the Parties shall develop, adopt, implement and, as far as possible, render compatible relevant legal, administrative, economic, financial and technical measures, in order to ensure, *inter alia*, that:

(a) The emission of pollutants is prevented, controlled and reduced at source through the application of, *inter alia*, low- and non-waste technology;

(b) Transboundary waters are protected against pollution from point sources through the prior licensing of waste-water discharges by the competent national authorities, and that the authorized discharges are monitored and controlled;

(c) Limits for waste-water discharges stated in permits are based on the best available technology for discharges of hazardous substances;

(d) Stricter requirements, even leading to prohibition in individual cases, are imposed when the quality of the receiving water or the ecosystem so requires;

(e) At least biological treatment or equivalent processes are applied to municipal waste water, where necessary in a step-by-step approach;

(f) Appropriate measures are taken, such as the application of the best available technology, in order to reduce nutrient inputs from industrial and municipal sources;

(g) Appropriate measures and best environmental practices are developed and implemented for the reduction of inputs of nutrients and hazardous substances from diffuse sources, especially where the main sources are from agriculture (guidelines for developing best environmental practices are given in annex II to this Convention);

(h) Environmental impact assessment and other means of assessment are applied;

(i) Sustainable water-resources management, including the application of the ecosystems approach, is promoted;

(j)   Contingency planning is developed;

(k)   Additional specific measures are taken to prevent the pollution of groundwaters;

(l)   The risk of accidental pollution is minimized.

2.   To this end, each Party shall set emission limits for discharges from point sources into surface waters based on the best available technology, which are specifically applicable to individual industrial sectors or industries from which hazardous substances derive. The appropriate measures mentioned in paragraph 1 of this article to prevent, control and reduce the input of hazardous substances from point and diffuse sources into waters, may, *inter alia*, include total or partial prohibition of the production or use of such substances. Existing lists of such industrial sectors or industries and of such hazardous substances in international conventions or regulations, which are applicable in the area covered by this Convention, shall be taken into account.

3.   In addition, each Party shall define, where appropriate, water-quality objectives and adopt water-quality criteria for the purpose of preventing, controlling and reducing transboundary impact. General guidance for developing such objectives and criteria is given in annex III to this Convention. When necessary, the Parties shall endeavour to update this annex.

## Article 4 MONITORING

The Parties shall establish programmes for monitoring the conditions of transboundary waters.

## Article 5 RESEARCH AND DEVELOPMENT

The Parties shall cooperate in the conduct of research into and development of effective techniques for the prevention, control and reduction of transboundary impact. To this effect, the Parties shall, on a bilateral and/or multilateral basis, taking into account research activities pursued in relevant international forums, endeavour to initiate or intensify specific research programmes, where necessary, aimed, *inter alia*, at:

(a)   Methods for the assessment of the toxicity of hazardous substances and the noxiousness of pollutants;

(b)   Improved knowledge on the occurrence, distribution and environmental effects of pollutants and the processes involved;

(c)   The development and application of environmentally sound technologies, production and consumption patterns;

(d)   The phasing out and/or substitution of substances likely to have transboundary impact;

(e)   Environmentally sound methods of disposal of hazardous substances;

(f)   Special methods for improving the conditions of transboundary waters;

(g)   The development of environmentally sound water-construction works and water-regulation techniques;

(h)   The physical and financial assessment of damage resulting from transboundary impact.

The results of these research programmes shall be exchanged among the Parties in accordance with article 6 of this Convention.

## Article 6 EXCHANGE OF INFORMATION

The Parties shall provide for the widest exchange of information, as early as possible, on issues covered by the provisions of this Convention.

## Article 7 RESPONSIBILITY AND LIABILITY

The Parties shall support appropriate international efforts to elaborate rules, criteria and procedures in the field of responsibility and liability.

## Article 8 PROTECTION OF INFORMATION

The provisions of this Convention shall not affect the rights or the obligations of Parties in accordance with their national legal systems and applicable supranational regulations to protect information related to industrial and commercial secrecy, including intellectual property, or national security.

## PART II

## PROVISIONS RELATING TO RIPARIAN PARTIES

## Article 9 BILATERAL AND MULTILATERAL COOPERATION

1.  The Riparian Parties shall on the basis of equality and reciprocity enter into bilateral or multilateral agreements or other arrangements, where these do not yet exist, or adapt existing ones, where necessary to eliminate the contradictions with the basic principles of this Convention, in order to define their mutual relations and conduct regarding the prevention, control and reduction of transboundary impact. The Riparian Parties shall specify the catchment area, or part(s) thereof, subject to cooperation. These agreements or arrangements shall embrace relevant issues covered by this Convention, as well as any other issues on which the Riparian Parties may deem it necessary to cooperate.

2.  The agreements or arrangements mentioned in paragraph 1 of this article shall provide for the establishment of joint bodies. The tasks of these joint bodies shall be, *inter alia*, and without prejudice to relevant existing agreements or arrangements, the following:

    (a) To collect, compile and evaluate data in order to identify pollution sources likely to cause transboundary impact;

    (b) To elaborate joint monitoring programmes concerning water quality and quantity;

    (c) To draw up inventories and exchange information on the pollution sources mentioned in paragraph 2 (a) of this article;

    (d) To elaborate emission limits for waste water and evaluate the effectiveness of control programmes;

    (e) To elaborate joint water-quality objectives and criteria having regard to the provisions of article 3, paragraph 3 of this Convention, and to propose relevant measures for maintaining and, where necessary, improving the existing water quality;

    (f) To develop concerted action programmes for the reduction of pollution loads from both point sources (e.g., municipal and industrial sources) and diffuse sources (particularly from agriculture);

    (g) To establish warning and alarm procedures;

    (h) To serve as a forum for the exchange of information on existing and planned uses of water and related installations that are likely to cause transboundary impact;

    (i) To promote cooperation and exchange of information on the best available technology in accordance with the provisions of article 13 of this Convention, as well as to encourage cooperation in scientific research programmes;

(j)   To participate in the implementation of environmental impact assessments relating to transboundary waters, in accordance with appropriate international regulations.

3.   In cases where a coastal State, being Party to this Convention, is directly and significantly affected by transboundary impact, the Riparian Parties can, if they all so agree, invite that coastal State to be involved in an appropriate manner in the activities of multilateral joint bodies established by Parties riparian to such transboundary waters.

4.   Joint bodies according to this Convention shall invite joint bodies, established by coastal States for the protection of the marine environment directly affected by transboundary impact, to cooperate in order to harmonize their work and to prevent, control and reduce the transboundary impact.

5.   Where two or more joint bodies exist in the same catchment area, they shall endeavour to coordinate their activities in order to strengthen the prevention, control and reduction of transboundary impact within that catchment area.

## Article 10 CONSULTATIONS

Consultations shall be held between the Riparian Parties on the basis of reciprocity, good faith and good-neighbourliness, at the request of any such Party. Such consultations shall aim at cooperation regarding the issues covered by the provisions of this Convention. Any such consultations shall be conducted through a joint body established under article 9 of this Convention, where one exists.

## Article 11 JOINT MONITORING AND ASSESSMENT

1.   In the framework of general cooperation mentioned in article 9 of this Convention, or specific arrangements, the Riparian Parties shall establish and implement joint programmes for monitoring the conditions of transboundary waters, including floods and ice drifts, as well as transboundary impact.

2.   The Riparian Parties shall agree upon pollution parameters and pollutants whose discharges and concentration in transboundary waters shall be regularly monitored.

3.   The Riparian Parties shall, at regular intervals, carry out joint or coordinated assessments of the conditions of transboundary waters and the effectiveness of measures taken for the prevention, control and reduction of transboundary impact. The results of these assessments shall be made available to the public in accordance with the provisions set out in article 16 of this Convention.

4.   For these purposes, the Riparian Parties shall harmonize rules for the setting up and operation of monitoring programmes, measurement systems, devices, analytical techniques, data processing and evaluation procedures, and methods for the registration of pollutants discharged.

...

## Article 13 EXCHANGE OF INFORMATION BETWEEN RIPARIAN PARTIES

1.   The Riparian Parties shall, within the framework of relevant agreements or other arrangements according to article 9 of this Convention, exchange reasonably available data, *inter alia*, on:

(a)   Environmental conditions of transboundary waters;

(b)   Experience gained in the application and operation of best available technology and results of research and development;

(c)   Emission and monitoring data;

(d) Measures taken and planned to be taken to prevent, control and reduce transboundary impact;

(e) Permits or regulations for waste-water discharges issued by the competent authority or appropriate body.

2. In order to harmonize emission limits, the Riparian Parties shall undertake the exchange of information on their national regulations.

3. If a Riparian Party is requested by another Riparian Party to provide data or information that is not available, the former shall endeavour to comply with the request but may condition its compliance upon the payment, by the requesting Party, of reasonable charges for collecting and, where appropriate, processing such data or information.

4. For the purposes of the implementation of this Convention, the Riparian Parties shall facilitate the exchange of best available technology, particularly through the promotion of: the commercial exchange of available technology; direct industrial contacts and cooperation, including joint ventures; the exchange of information and experience; and the provision of technical assistance. The Riparian Parties shall also undertake joint training programmes and the organization of relevant seminars and meetings.

### Article 14 WARNING AND ALARM SYSTEMS

The Riparian Parties shall without delay inform each other about any critical situation that may have transboundary impact. The Riparian Parties shall set up, where appropriate, and operate coordinated or joint communication, warning and alarm systems with the aim of obtaining and transmitting information. These systems shall operate on the basis of compatible data transmission and treatment procedures and facilities to be agreed upon by the Riparian Parties. The Riparian Parties shall inform each other about competent authorities or points of contact designated for this purpose.

...

### Article 16 PUBLIC INFORMATION

1. The Riparian Parties shall ensure that information on the conditions of transboundary waters, measures taken or planned to be taken to prevent, control and reduce transboundary impact, and the effectiveness of those measures, is made available to the public. For this purpose, the Riparian Parties shall ensure that the following information is made available to the public:

(a) Water-quality objectives;

(b) Permits issued and the conditions required to be met;

(c) Results of water and effluent sampling carried out for the purposes of monitoring and assessment, as well as results of checking compliance with the water-quality objectives or the permit conditions.

2. The Riparian Parties shall ensure that this information shall be available to the public at all reasonable times for inspection free of charge, and shall provide members of the public with reasonable facilities for obtaining from the Riparian Parties, on payment of reasonable charges, copies of such information.

### ANNEX I
### DEFINITION OF THE TERM "BEST AVAILABLE TECHNOLOGY"

1. The term "best available technology" is taken to mean the latest stage of development of processes, facilities or methods of operation which indicate the practical suitability of a

particular measure for limiting discharges, emissions and waste. In determining whether a set of processes, facilities and methods of operation constitute the best available technology in general or individual cases, special consideration is given to:

(a)  Comparable processes, facilities or methods of operation which have recently been successfully tried out;

(b)  Technological advances and changes in scientific knowledge and understanding;

(c)  The economic feasibility of such technology;

(d)  Time limits for installation in both new and existing plants;

(e)  The nature and volume of the discharges and effluents concerned;

(f)  Low- and non-waste technology.

2.  It therefore follows that what is "best available technology" for a particular process will change with time in the light of technological advances, economic and social factors, as well as in the light of changes in scientific knowledge and understanding.

## ANNEX II
## GUIDELINES FOR DEVELOPING
## BEST ENVIRONMENTAL PRACTICES

1.  In selecting for individual cases the most appropriate combination of measures which may constitute the best environmental practice, the following graduated range of measures should be considered:

(a)  Provision of information and education to the public and to users about the environmental consequences of the choice of particular activities and products, their use and ultimate disposal;

(b)  The development and application of codes of good environmental practice which cover all aspects of the product's life;

(c)  Labels informing users of environmental risks related to a product, its use and ultimate disposal;

(d)  Collection and disposal systems available to the public;

(e)  Recycling, recovery and reuse;

(f)  Application of economic instruments to activities, products or groups of products;

(g)  A system of licensing, which involves a range of restrictions or a ban.

2.  In determining what combination of measures constitute best environmental practices, in general or in individual cases, particular consideration should be given to:

(a)  The environmental hazard of:

(i) The product;

(ii) The product's production;

(iii) The product's use;

(iv) The product's ultimate disposal;

(b)  Substitution by less polluting processes or substances;

(c)  Scale of use;

(d)  Potential environmental benefit or penalty of substitute materials or activities;

(e) Advances and changes in scientific knowledge and understanding;

(f) Time limits for implementation;

(g) Social and economic implications.

3. It therefore follows that best environmental practices for a particular source will change with time in the light of technological advances, economic and social factors, as well as in the light of changes in scientific knowledge and understanding.

ANNEX III
GUIDELINES FOR DEVELOPING
WATER-QUALITY OBJECTIVES AND CRITERIA

Water-quality objectives and criteria shall:

(a) Take into account the aim of maintaining and, where necessary, improving the existing water quality;

(b) Aim at the reduction of average pollution loads (in particular hazardous substances) to a certain degree within a certain period of time;

(c) Take into account specific water-quality requirements (raw water for drinking-water purposes, irrigation, etc.);

(d) Take into account specific requirements regarding sensitive and specially protected waters and their environment, e.g. lakes and groundwater resources;

(e) Be based on the application of ecological classification methods and chemical indices for the medium- and long-term review of water-quality maintenance and improvement;

(f) Take into account the degree to which objectives are reached and the additional protective measures, based on emission limits, which may be required in individual cases.

*2. Council Decision 90/160/EEC of 22 March 1990 concerning the Conclusion of the Agreement between the Federal Republic of Germany and the European Economic Community, on the one hand, and the Republic of Austria, on the other, on Cooperation on Management of Water Resources in the Danube Basin,* O.J. No. L 090, of 5 April 1990 p. 18.

The Council of the European Communities,
has decided as follows:

Article 1

The agreement between the Federal Republic of Germany and the European Economic Community, on the one hand, and the Republic of Austria, on the other, on cooperation on management of water resources in the Danube basin is hereby approved on behalf of the European Economic Community.

The text of the agreement is attached to this decision.

*Agreement between the Federal Republic of Germany and the European Economic Community, on the one hand, and the Republic of Austria, on the other, on cooperation on management of water resources in the Danube Basin*

The contracting parties,

desirous of increasing cooperation on management of water rescurces, in particular the protection of the aquatic environment and the regulation of discharges, anxious to take adequate account of the contracting parties' mutual interest concerning the management of water resources,

concerned to improve as far as possible the quality of the waters in the Danube basin forming a common frontier between the Republic of Austria and the Federal Republic of Germany,

have agreed as follows :

## Article 1

1. The contracting parties shall cooperate on water management, in particular, in carrying out water management tasks and implementing the water laws in the German and Austrian Danube basin.

2. Such cooperation shall take the form in particular of,

    (a)  exchange of experience,

    (b)  exchange of information on water management regulations and measures,

    (c)  exchange of experts,

    (d)  exchange of publications, regulations and guidelines,

    (e)  participation in scientific and specialist meetings,

    (f)  consideration of projects on the territory of the Federal Republic of Germany or the Republic of Austria which might substantially influence the proper management of water resources on the territory of the other state,

    (g)  consultations in the standing committee on management of water resources (article 7).

3. The agreement shall not apply to questions concerning fisheries and shipping; the treatment of questions concerning the protection of the aquatic environment against pollution shall not, however, be thereby excluded.

## Article 2

1. The contracting parties shall notify each other in good time of major projects on the territory of the Federal Republic of Germany or the Republic of Austria or where such projects might substantially influence the proper management of water resources on the territory of the other state.

2. The maintenance and achievement of proper management of water resources within the meaning of this agreement shall cover projects relating to :

    (a)  protection of the aquatic environment including the groundwater, in particular the prevention of pollution, and the discharge of waste water and heat;

    (b)  the maintenance and extension of watercourses which might lead to a change in the river flow, in particular the regulation and flow and damming control of watercourses, defence against high water and ice and interference with the water flow through installations in or on watercourses;

    (c)  the utilization of the aquatic environment including the groundwaters, in particular the use of water power and the diversion and abstraction of water;

    (d)  hydrography.

3. Notification pursuant to paragraph 1 shall be made directly between the relevant authorities and departments insofar as the effects remain restricted to their area of competence, or through the standing committee on management of water resources.

4. The contracting parties shall inform each other of the bodies responsible for notifying the standing committee on management of water resources and of the relevant authorities and departments.

### Article 3

1. The contracting parties shall take the necessary measures within their respective legal systems to ensure that projects on stretches of water forming the frontier shall not have a substantial adverse effect on the condition of water resources on the territory of the Federal Republic of Germany or the Republic of Austria. They shall hold consultations with the aim of reaching mutual agreement, insofar as one party invokes these effects within a period of three months of notification by adducing serious grounds.

2. In the case of projects on all other waters which might have a substantial adverse effect on the condition of water resources on the territory of the other state, the contracting parties shall, at the request of the party concerned, discuss the possibilities of preventing such effects before the projects are carried out.

### Article 4

1. In the case of projects on stretches of water forming the frontier which are carried out on the territories of the Federal Republic of Germany and the Republic of Austria, the competent authorities in each case shall decide on that part of the work to be carried out on their territory; in this connection they shall coordinate the timing of the necessary procedures and the substance of the decisions to be adopted.

2. In the case of projects on stretches of water forming the frontier which are to be carried out on the territory of only the Federal Republic of Germany or the Republic of Austria but which could have an adverse effect on the rights and interests of the other state, for example with regard to the water system and condition of the water, the competent authorities of the other state shall be given the opportunity in good time to submit their opinion, in particular on the substance and on the conditions and obligations laid down in the public interest.

3. Where a matter within paragraph 1 or 2 is communicated by one of the contracting parties to the standing committee on management of water resources, the competent authorities may not take their decision until the matter has been dealt with by that committee, unless a delay would lead to a dangerous situation.

### Article 5

The competent authorities shall carry out control measurements of the quality of the waters, jointly where this is expedient, in areas where the waters form or cross the frontier between the Federal Republic of Germany and the Republic of Austria.

### Article 6

The competent authorities shall coordinate their alarm, intervention and notification plans for averting dangers from high water and ice, for measures following accidents with harmful substances and in the event of critical conditions of the aquatic environment and shall, where necessary, draw up harmonized guidelines.

### Article 7

1. A standing committee on management of water resources shall be set up. Its duty shall be to contribute to the solution of questions arising from the application of this agreement through joint consultations. For this purpose it may address to the contracting parties recommendations drawn up by agreement.

2. The composition, procedures and specific powers of the aforementioned standing committee shall be governed by the statute in annex 1, which is an integral part of this agreement.

3. Recommendations pursuant to the third sentence of paragraph 1 may relate in particular to :

(a) minimum requirements in respect of discharges to the aquatic environment,

(b) measures to improve a critical condition of the aquatic environment which is due to influences from the territory of the Federal Republic of Germany or the Republic of Austria, insofar as these influences extend to the territory of the other state,

(c) other appropriate measures to protect the aquatic environment, including water quality objectives,

(d) analyses and methods to establish the type and extent of pollution of the aquatic environment and the evaluation of the analysis results.

...

*Declaration by the Federal Republic of Germany and the European Economic Community on the agreement on cooperation on management of water resources in the Danube basin between the Federal Republic of Germany and the European Economic Community on the one hand and the Republic of Austria on the other.*

The present areas of competence of the European Economic Community within the scope of the agreement are specified in the legal instruments of the European Economic Community listed in the annex to this declaration. Any changes in these areas of competence shall be communicated to the Republic of Austria in writing through diplomatic channels by the Federal Republic of Germany and the European Economic Community jointly.

Annex

Measures taken by the Council of the European Communities regarding water management.

1. Council Directive 75/440/EEC of 16 June 1975 concerning the quality required of surface water intended for the abstraction of drinking water in the member states (O.J. no. L 194, 25. 7. 1975, p. 26)

2. Council Directive 76/160/EEC of 8 December 1975 concerning the quality of bathing water (O.J. no. L 31, 5. 2. 1976, p. 1)

3. Council Directive 76/464/EEC of 4 May 1976 on pollution caused by certain dangerous substances discharged into the aquatic environment of the Community (O.J. no. L 129, 18. 5. 1976, p. 23)

4. Council Decision 77/795/EEC of 12 December 1977 establishing a common procedure for the exchange of information on the quality of surface freshwater in the community (O.J. no. L 334, 24. 12. 1977, p. 29)

5. Council Directive 78/176/EEC of 20 February 1978 on waste from the titanium dioxide industry (O.J. no. L 54, 25. 2. 1978, p. 19)

6. Council Directive 78/659/EEC of 18 July 1978 on the quality of freshwaters needing protection or improvement in order to support fish life (O.J. no. L 222, 14. 8. 1978, p. 1)

7. Council Directive 79/869/EEC of 9 October 1979 concerning the methods of measurement and frequencies of sampling and analysis of surface water intended for the abstraction of drinking water in the member states (O.J. no. L 271, 29. 10. 1979, p. 44)

8. Council Directive 80/68/EEC of 17 December 1979 on the protection of groundwater against pollution caused by certain dangerous substances (O.J. no. L 20, 26. 1. 1980, p. 43)

9. Council Directive 80/778/EEC of 15 July 1980 relating to the quality of water intended for human consumption (O.J. no. L 229, 30. 8. 1980, p. 11)

10. Council Directive 82/176/EEC of 22 March 1982 on limit values and quality objectives for mercury discharges by the chlor-alkali electrolysis industry (O.J. no. L 81, 27. 3. 1982, p. 29)

11. Council Directive 82/883/EEC of 3 December 1982 on procedures for the surveillance and monitoring of environments concerned by waste from the titanium dioxide industry (O.J. no. L 378, 31. 12. 1982, p. 1)

12. Council Directive 83/513/EEC of 26 September 1983 on limit values and quality objectives for cadmium discharges (O.J. no. L 291, 24. 10. 1983, p. 1)

13. Council Directive 84/156/EEC of 8 March 1984 on limit values and quality objectives for mercury discharges by sectors other than the chlor-alkali electrolysis industry (O.J. no. L 74, 17. 3. 1984, p. 49)

14. Council Directive 84/491/EEC of 9 October 1984 on limit values and quality objectives for discharges of hexachlorocyclohexane (O.J. no. L 274, 17. 10. 1984, p. 11)

15. Council Directive 86/280/EEC of 12 June 1986 on limit values and quality objectives for discharges of certain dangerous substances (O.J. no. L 181, 7 July 1986)

*3. Council Directive 76/464/EEC of 4 May 1976 on Pollution caused by Certain Dangerous Substances Discharged into the Aquatic Environment of the Community* O.J. No. L 181, 4 July 1986.

The Council of the European Communities,
has adopted this directive:

Article 1

1. Subject to article 8, this directive shall apply to:
   — inland surface water;
   — territorial waters;
   — internal coastal waters;
   — ground water.

2. For the purposes of this directive:

   ...

   (c) "fresh-water limit" means the place in the watercourse where, at low tide and in a period of low fresh-water flow, there is an appreciable increase in salinity due to the presence of sea-water;

   (d) "discharge" means the introduction into the waters referred to in paragraph i of any substances in list i or list ii of the annex, with the exception of :
       — discharges of dredgings,
       — operational discharges from ships in territorial waters,
       — dumping from ships in territorial waters;

   (e) "pollution" means the discharge by man, directly or indirectly, of substances or energy into the aquatic environment, the results of which are such as to cause hazards to human health, harm to living resources and to aquatic ecosystems, damage to amenities or interference with other legitimate uses of water.

### Article 2

Member States shall take the appropriate steps to eliminate pollution of the waters referred to in article 1 by the dangerous substances in the families and groups of substances in list i of the annex and to reduce pollution of the said waters by the dangerous substances in the families and groups of substances in list ii of the annex, in accordance with this directive, the provisions of which represent only a first step towards this goal.

### Article 3

With regard to the substances belonging to the families and groups of substances in list i, hereinafter called "substances within list i":

1.  All discharges into the waters referred to in article 1 which are liable to contain any such substance shall require prior authorization by the competent authority of the Member State concerned;

2.  The authorization shall lay down emission standards with regard to discharges of any such substance into the waters referred to in article 1 and, where this is necessary for the implementation of this directive, to discharges of any such substance into sewers;

3.  In the case of existing discharges of any such substance into the waters referred to in article 1, the dischargers must comply with the conditions laid down in the authorization within the period stipulated therein. This period may not exceed the limits laid down in accordance with article 6 (4);

4.  Authorizations may be granted for a limited period only. They may be renewed, taking into account any charges in the limit values referred to in article 6.

### Article 4

1.  Member States shall apply a system of zero-emission to discharges into ground water of substances within list i.

    ...

### Article 5

1.  The emission standards laid down in the authorizations granted pursuant to article 3 shall determine:

    (a)  the maximum concentration of a substance permissible in a discharge. In the case of dilution the limit value provided for in article 6 (1) (a) shall be divided by the dilution factor;

    (b)  the maximum quantity of a substance permissible in a discharge during one or more specified periods of time. This quantity may, if necessary, also be expressed as a unit of weight of the pollutant per unit of the characteristic element of the polluting activity (e.g. unit of weight per unit of raw material or per product unit).

2.  For each authorization, the competent authority of the Member State concerned may, if necessary, impose more stringent emission standards than those resulting from the application of the limit values laid down by the Council pursuant to article 6, taking into account in particular the toxicity, persistence, and bioaccumulation of the substance concerned in the environment into which it is discharged.

3.  If the discharger states that he is unable to comply with the required emission standards,

or if this situation is evident to the competent authority in the Member State concerned, authorization shall be refused.

4. Should the emission standards not be complied with, the competent authority in the Member State concerned shall take all appropriate steps to ensure that the conditions of authorization are fulfilled and, if necessary, that the discharge is prohibited.

### Article 6

1. The Council, acting on a proposal from the Commission, shall lay down the limit values which the emission standards must not exceed for the various dangerous substances included in the families and groups of substances within list i. These limit values shall be determined by:

(a) the maximum concentration of a substance permissible in a discharge, and

(b) where appropriate, the maximum quantity of such a substance expressed as a unit of weight of the pollutant per unit of the characteristic element of the polluting activity (e.g. unit of weight per unit of raw material or per product unit).

Where appropriate, limit values applicable to industrial effluents shall be established according to sector and type of product. The limit values applicable to the substances within list i shall be laid down mainly on the basis of:

— toxicity,
— persistence,
— bioaccumulation,

taking into account the best technical means available.

2. The Council, acting on a proposal from the Commission, shall lay down quality objectives for the substances within list i.

These objectives shall be laid down principally on the basis of the toxicity, persistence and accumulation of the said substances in living organisms and in sediment, as indicated by the latest conclusive scientific data, taking into account the difference in characteristics between salt-water and freshwater.

3. The limit values established in accordance with paragraph 1 shall apply except in the cases where a Member State can prove to the Commission, in accordance with a monitoring procedure set up by the Council on a proposal from the Commission, that the quality objectives established in accordance with paragraph 2, or more severe community quality objectives, are being met and continuously maintained throughout the area which might be affected by the discharges because of the action taken, among others, by that Member State. The Commission shall report to the Council the instances where it has had recourse to the quality objectives method. Every five years the Council shall review, on the basis of a Commission proposal and in accordance with article 148 of the treaty, the instances where the said method has been applied.

4. For those substances included in the families and groups of substances referred to in paragraph 1, the deadlines referred to in point 3 of article 3 shall be laid down by the Council in accordance with article 12, taking into account the features of the industrial sectors concerned and, where appropriate, the types of products.

### Article 7

1. In order to reduce pollution of the waters referred to in article 1 by the substances within list ii, Member States shall establish programmes in the implementation of which they shall apply in particular the methods referred to in paras. 2 and 3.

2.   All discharges into the waters referred to in article 1 which are liable to contain any of the substances within list ii shall require prior authorization by the competent authority in the Member State concerned, in which emission standards shall be laid down. Such standards shall be based on the quality objectives, which shall be fixed as provided for in paragraph 3.

3.   The programmes referred to in paragraph 1 shall include quality objectives for water; these shall be laid down in accordance with Council directives, where they exist.

4.   The programmes may also include specific provisions governing the composition and use of substances or groups of substances and products and shall take into account the latest economically feasible technical developments.

5.   The programmes shall set deadlines for their implementation.

6.   Summaries of the programmes and the results of their implementation shall be communicated to the Commission.

7.   The Commission, together with the Member States, shall arrange for regular comparisons of the programmes in order to ensure sufficient coordination in their implementation. If it sees fit, it shall submit relevant proposals to the Council to this end.

    ...

### Article 13

1.   For the purposes of this directive, Member States shall supply the Commission, at its request to be submitted in each case, with all the necessary information, and in particular :
    — details of authorizations granted pursuant to article 3 and article 7 (2),
    — the results of the inventory provided for in article 11,
    — the results of monitoring by the national network,
    — additional information on the programmes referred to in article 7.

2.   Information acquired as a result of the application of this article shall be used only for the purpose for which it was requested.

3.   The Commission and the competent authorities of the Member States, their officials and other servants shall not disclose information acquired by them pursuant to this directive and of a kind covered by the obligation of professional secrecy.

4.   The provisions of paragraphs 2 and 3 shall not prevent publication of general information or surveys which do not contain information relating to particular undertakings or associations of undertakings.

## Questions and Problems

1. Do all the riparian states of an international watercourse have the same rights and duties?

2. Discuss the necessity of adopting specific rules for the protection of groundwater.

3. Discuss the application of the polluter-pays principle to water administration and management.

4. Is there a hierarchy in the uses of water?

5. Should the consumption of water in Europe be reduced? By what means?

6. What standards should be used for preventing the different types of water pollution?

7. Discuss the usefulness of regionalization in water administration and management.

8. What is the relationship between EC legislation on freshwater and rules enacted by other international bodies?

9. To what extent do EC norms affect non-Member States?

10. What is the scope of the "professional secrecy" exception to the obligation for States to provide information, in article 13(3) of Directive 76/464 and article 8 of the Helsinki Convention?

11. Are the measures for the protection of the Rhine a model for other watercourses?

# Bibliography

Berber, F., *Die Rechtsquellen des Internationalen Wasserrechts* (1955).

Beurle, G., *Die Osterreichische und die Europaische Donau* (1957).

Beyerlin, U., *Rhine*, in *Landworterbuch Des Umweltrechts, Bd. II* (Kimmenich/v. Lersner/Storm eds. (1988).

Bucksch, R., *Reschtsprobleme bei der Internationalen Zusammenarbeit auf dem Gebiet des Gewasserschutzes* (1957).

Bucksch, R., "Fragen des Internationalen Wasserrechts", in *Berichte und Informationen* (1958).

Burchi, S., "Current Developments and Trends in the Law and Administration of Water Resources: A Comparative State-of-the-Art Appraisal", 3 *J. Envt'l L.* 69 (1991).

Gilbaud, J., *La Pêche et le Droit* (3rd ed., 1988).

Grabmayr, P., *Internationale Wasserwirtschaftliche und Rechtliche Zusammenarbeit an der Donau, Wasser- und Energiewirtschaft* (1973).

Gurnswamy, L. D., J. Papps and D. J. Story, "The Development and Impact of an EEC Directive: The Control of Discharges of Mercury to the Aquatic Environment", 22 *J. Com. Mkt. Studies* 71 (1983).

Hinteregger, G., "Die Internationale Trinkwasserdekade der Vereinten Nationen und regionale Aspeckte der internationalen Wasserwirtschaft", in *Internationale Wasserwirtschaft* (1990).

Institut pour une Politique Europeenne de l'Environnement (IPEE), *Etude des institutions relative à l'eau dans les pays de la Communaute Europeenne* (1990).

Kiss, A., *Droit International de l'Environnement* (1989), pp. 189 *et seq.*

_____, *La Protection du Rhin contre la pollution: état actuel de la question*, AFDI 1977, 861 *et seq.*

_____, *La Pollution du Rhin: Suite (et fin?)* AFDI 1983, 773 *et seq.*

_____, *Tchernobâle ou la pollution accidentielle du Rhin par les produits chimiques*, AFDI 1987, 719 *et seq.*

Lammers, I. G., *Pollution of International Watercourses* (1984).

Linneroth, J., "The Danube River Basin: Negotiating Settlements to Transboundary Environmental Issues", 30 *Nat. Res. J.* 629 (1990).

Oberleitner, F., "Osterreich und die internationale Wasserwirtschaft", in *Internationale Wasserwirtschaft* (1990).

Rossmann, H., *Kommentar Zum Wasserrechtsgesetz* (1990).

United Nations Economic Commission for Europe (UNECE), *Policies for Integrated Water Management*, E/ECE/1084 (1985).

## CHAPTER VIII

# PROTECTION OF THE MARINE ENVIRONMENT

## A. Overview

Action to protect the marine environment must take into account its natural characteristics and the variety of human uses of marine waters. While the former are virtually unchanging, the latter evolve sometimes rapidly.

The marine environment of the planet has some common aspects: the waters are salt, the seas all connect, and ocean currents are everywhere. The marine environment is also characterized by great diversity. The waters of closed or semi-closed seas, like the Mediterranean or the Baltic, renew themselves much more slowly than the Atlantic or Pacific Oceans and are thus more susceptible to pollution.

Socio-economic factors are also diverse, including population density, concentration of economic activities along the coastline, intensity of maritime traffic, existence of oil refineries, and levels of tourism. It is estimated that the population along the Mediterranean coast increases by nearly one hundred million persons during the summer months each year.

Deterioration of the marine environment demands legal responses with some universal aspects and others that are individualized, according to the different regional and local problems. In numerous cases regional or even global cooperation is required, even where the issue appears to be a local question like the cleanliness of several kilometres of coastland. The problem of French beaches polluted by sources in Spain is only one example where collaboration between countries is necessary.

Against these background characteristics, human uses of marine waters have considerably evolved throughout history, usually accompanied by increased environmental problems.

For millennia, the sea has been used as a means of transport. During this time, ships have increased in size and sophistication, especially since the invention of the steam engine. In the twentieth century, the arrival of supertankers has had considerable impact on the marine environment, particularly in case of accident.

The purpose of marine transportation has also evolved. Where ocean liners once moved millions of persons across the seas, air transport now serves. Marine vessels instead provide recreation and tourist cruises. At the same time, the transportation of products like oil has reached an enormous level, increasing the risk of environmental deterioration. According to 1990 estimates, 568,000 tons of oil are spilled into the marine environment each year as a result of ship movements.[1]

Most military activities on the seas are in the category of navigation. Atmospheric nuclear testing on the high seas, another military use, is prohibited by the Moscow Convention of 5 August 1963, to which the most states are parties. In fact, this Convention can be considered the most widely accepted international instrument in the broad field of environmental protection.

Fishing, another traditional use of the sea, also has been considerably transformed due to unprecedented expansion. Formerly small-scale coastal fishing is now an industry that impacts upon biological resources in the farthest and most inhospitable ocean reaches. It is estimated that the limits of sustainable exploitation of biological resources of the sea, that is, catches compatible with their continued reproduction, is close to being reached. Of course, pollution such as "black tides" resulting from oil spills also has a negative impact on biological resources of the sea.

New uses of the oceans have been added to these expanded traditional activities. A French government guideline for utilizing the "maritime public domain" (that part of the marine area belonging to the state) enumerated these other uses in 1972: aquaculture, shellfish farming, pleasure boating, and mining.[2] Unfortunately, dumping of wastes can be added, particularly massive dumping of industrial wastes on land and in the sea. In 1988 alone, industrial facilities discharged 1.7 million tons of liquid wastes and 2 million tons of solid wastes into the North Sea.[3] In addition, enormous quantities of agricultural pollutants like nitrates and phosphorus were transported by rivers and air to the North Sea.[4]

The causes of marine pollution are diverse. Some are voluntary, like dumping wastes into the sea when land-based disposal is deemed too expensive or difficult, or cleaning oil tanker hulls on the high seas followed by discharge of the oily residue into the ocean waters. Pollution also can be accidental, resulting from tanker groundings or loss of containers of toxic or dangerous products. Some factors that do not appear directly linked to pollution can still have a harmful effect. The tanker *Amoco Cadiz* went aground along the Breton coast on 16 March 1978, due to a combination of different causes: inadequate construction of the ship, lack of essential maintenance, insufficient training of the crew, and lack of action by coastal authorities. Rules relating to navigational safety, to the recruitment of personnel, and to the condition of ships, thus can have an impact on the incidence of marine pollution.

Legal instruments generally distinguish five categories of marine pollution:

— vessel-based pollution coming from normal utilization of the oceans, including accidents;

— deliberate and large dumping of wastes, mostly industrial;

---

[1]  G. Peet, *Operational Discharges from Ships*, AID Environment, Amsterdam, 1992, p. 1.

[2]  M. Prieur, *Droit de l'Environnement*, Dalloz, 2nd ed., 1991, p. 355.

[3]  Commission of the European Communities, *Europe 2000*, Luxembourg, 1991, p. 123.

[4]  RIVM, The Environment in Europe: A Global Perspective, Bilthoven (Netherlands), 1992, pp. 92–3.

— land-based pollution whether coming from direct discharges into the ocean or carried into it by rivers;

— pollution resulting from the exploration or exploitation of the seabed; and,

— pollution transported by air.

The last category is assimilated to air pollution in general, with the exception of the incineration of wastes at sea. Obviously, legal techniques to protect the marine environment should be adapted to the different situations, taking into account the consequences of pollution as well as its origin.

Before detailing the norms applicable to different aspects of marine environmental protection, it is useful to recall the general legal regime governing the sea, then to outline the specific applicable norms.

## 1. General Legal Regime

As with all areas of European environmental law, the rules existing in this domain must be examined on three different levels: international law, Community law, and national law. The relationship between the three can be visualized as a pyramid, with Community law integrating international law and national legislation conforming to both.

International law plays a larger role in regulating the marine environment than it does in other areas of environmental law. A large part of marine waters lies outside all national jurisdiction and is thus governed only by international regulations.[5] It is therefore useful to recall some of the fundamental principles of international law of the sea, in order better to understand norms that specifically concern protection of the marine environment.

At least since the beginning of the sixteenth century and arguably since the beginning of international law, ocean waters have been divided into zones falling within the sovereignty or jurisdiction of states and zones exempt from state appropriation. The rather complex legal situation is now codified in a global convention adopted by the large majority of states of the world: the 1982 United Nations Convention on the Law of the Sea (UNCLOS).

From the legal point of view, UNCLOS distinguishes five categories of marine spaces; of course, neither marine waters nor marine pollution divides according to these artificial legal frontiers.

a) The "internal waters" consist of ports, harbours and bays whose openings do not exceed forty kilometres. These waters are assimilated to land territory and maintained under the exclusive sovereignty of the coastal state.

b) A zone of up to twenty kilometres can be declared by the coastal state to be a "territorial sea". This zone is under sovereign control of the coastal state, but foreign ships have the right of innocent passage, that is, passage that does not harm defined interests of the coastal state. These interests include the

---

[5] For internal matters on board ships, the international law rule is that the national law of the state where the ship is registered and whose flag it flies governs.

environment, meaning the coastal state can legislate and apply its norms to protect the marine environment of the territorial sea.

c) The sea and sea-bed belong to the coastal state to the outer limits of the continental plateau, in other words to the beginning of the deep seabed. This area is of interest due to the mineral resources it may contain: oil and polymetallic nodules, but certain animal and vegetable species living on the sea bed may also be important.

d) Beginning in the early 1970s, a new zone of coastal state competence was claimed, largely for conservation reasons. UNCLOS recognizes the claims in establishing an "exclusive economic zone" (EEZ). This maritime area extends between the territorial sea and a line situated 360 kilometres from the coast. Within the EEZ, the coastal state has sole rights to exploit the marine living resources. In addition, the zone generally overlaps with the continental shelf, giving the coastal state exclusive jurisdiction also over mineral resources. Where the natural continental shelf is not as extensive as the EEZ, the Law of the Sea Convention permits the coastal state to extend the former to coincide with the latter. The coastal state also has the right and the duty to assure environmental protection within the EEZ, but it must respect the freedom of navigation of foreign ships.

e) The high seas are those waters that remain outside the designated zones. Conforming to traditional norms, they are governed by the principle of freedom of use by all states for purposes of navigation, fishing, exploitation of non-living resources, positioning of submarine cables, and military activities. In all cases there is some duty to monitor ships flying the state's flag. Also, the state that accords a ship the right to carry its flag, analogous to granting it nationality, is obliged to assure that the captain of the ship respects the norms of international law protecting the marine environment.

## 2. Standards Protecting the Marine Environment

### a. International Law

A large number of international treaties aim to protect the marine environment. With some oversimplification, they can be presented as a tree whose trunk is UNCLOS. The Convention establishes the major principles governing the subject and also acts as a framework treaty to be completed by the adoption of more precise obligations. The latter represent the branches of the tree, including international regional and global conventions concerning, for example, the dumping of wastes or pollution of the sea by vessels.

Regional conventions often are drafted to form a "system" comprised of several treaties: a framework treaty establishing principles of cooperation, accompanied or followed by protocols on precise subjects, and a plan of action aimed at assuring economic cooperation in light of regional development. The United Nations Environment Programme has elaborated such systems for eight "regional seas", beginning with the Mediterranean. The regional sea programme for the Mediterranean consists of a principal framework Convention, adopted in Barcelona 16 February 1976, and two protocols adopted the same day, one concerning vessel dumping operations, the other relating to cooperation in regard to combating pollution of the Mediterranean Sea by oil and other harmful substances in cases of emergency. Two other protocols have followed. The first, signed in Athens 17 May 1980, seeks to protect the Mediterranean against land-based pollution. The second, adopted in Geneva on 3 April 1982, concerns Mediterranean specially protected areas. An action plan, called the Blue Plan, establishes norms of cooperation for the development of certain Mediterranean countries.

A similar regional system covers the Baltic Sea. In 1974, the then seven Baltic littoral states signed in Helsinki a Convention on the protection of the Baltic marine environment. The instrument was later revised, in response to new knowledge of the environment and political changes in the region. On 9 April 1992, it was replaced by another Helsinki convention, adopted by the now twelve Baltic littoral states as well as the European Community. Russia and the three Baltic states of Latvia, Estonia and Lithuania are parties, while the German Democratic Republic is included in Germany. The treaty also indicates that non-littoral states can affect the deterioration of ocean waters; thus Czechoslovakia and the Ukraine have accepted to be signatories. In contrast to the 1974 Convention, its aim is to eliminate pollution entirely, not merely to reduce it (article 3, para. 1).

Among other innovations the Convention proclaims the precautionary principle as well as the best environmental practice and the best available technology. Other legal principles that have been analyzed earlier are found in international maritime conventions, as well as in Community directives and national laws: impact studies, licensing schemes, and lists of substances that cannot be dumped.

### b. Community Standards

Community law generally does not make a distinction between the sea and other aquatic milieu, regulating pollution of them without distinction. Some twenty directives thus apply to marine pollution. The most important among them is Directive 76/464 of 4 May 1976, relating to pollution caused by certain dangerous substances discharged into the aquatic environment of the Community.[6] It expressly states in its first article that it applies not only to internal freshwaters, but also to internal and territorial marine waters. A few instruments apply by their nature essentially to the marine environment, such as Directive 79/923 on the quality required of shellfish waters.[7] Other texts concern both inland waters and the marine environment, without expressly mentioning either: Directive 76/160 concerning the quality of bathing waters[8] and other directives prohibiting or regulating the discharge of specific chemical substances into any aquatic environment.[9] The titles of the different

---

[6] O.J. no. L 129, 18 May 1976.

[7] O.J. no. L 281 of 10 November 1979.

[8] 8 December 1975; O.J. no. L 31, 5 February 1976.

[9] For example, industrial wastes containing titanium dioxide, 78/176/EEC, 20 February 1978, O.J. no. L 54 of 25 February 1978; Discharges of hexachlorocyclohexane, 84/491/EEC of 9 October 1984, O.J. no. L 274, 17 October 1984.

directives indicate that some of them apply emission standards while others establish water quality objectives. Directive 76/464 utilizes both methods.

It should be added that the Community is a contracting party to all the major conventions protecting the marine environment within its jurisdiction, both global instruments and regional ones. In particular, the Community takes an active part in programmes aimed at protecting the Mediterranean and Baltic Seas.

### c. National Legislation

National laws are like Community laws in their relationship to international law. They generally reproduce the text of signed and ratified conventions, completing them if necessary with sanctions and penalties that only state authorities can adopt. Thus, French laws of 5 July 1983 and 31 May 1990, penalize violations of the MARPOL Convention concerning vessel-source pollution. National legislators also must attempt to apply Community directives and decide on the particular type of legal instrument and measures necessary to do so.[10]

There are few national legislative texts exclusively concerned with protecting the marine environment in general. Among the few, a Danish law of 1980 protects the marine environment of the Danish territorial sea, applying to all vessels, including foreign vessels, and prohibiting any discharge of oil, of chemical substances, or of wastes in quantity.

The absence of specific texts does not mean an absence of norms; they are found either in general instruments concerning environmental protection. In national laws, provisions generally aimed at combating pollution are normally applicable to the sea. In addition, the special procedures of environmental protection – licensing, impact studies – are utilized (see, for example, the Turkish law on the environment, 9 August 1983; Bulgarian law on environmental protection, 18 October 1991). Finally, rules of compensation applicable in case of environmental damage can be invoked for damage to the marine environment.[11]

In some countries, the general water law applies to the territorial sea. The French water law of 3 January 1992, states that its scope extends to marine waters within territorial limits. For the territorial sea, general rules to preserve water quality will be established by decree, setting both water quality standards and the measures necessary to restore and preserve this quality. The rules will also provide for prohibiting or regulating discharges, for direct or indirect deposits of water or matter, for monitoring of exploratory and commercial drilling. The law is enforced by penalties: its violation can be punished by either or both a fine of 200FF to 500,000FF and/or imprisonment of two months to two years. The implementing decrees will necessarily incorporate international and Community norms.

National legislation plays the most important role in protecting the coastline. Special laws exist on this subject in most maritime states, including Spain (law of 28

---

[10] For example, Portuguese law No 74/90 of 7 March 1990 relating to protection of the aquatic environment incorporates essentially all the Community standards adopted in this field.

[11] See, for example, section 3, Swedish law no 1986/225 on environmental damage.

July 1988), France (law of 3 January 1986), and those of Scandinavia. The French law calls for preservation of land and marine areas necessary to maintain biological equilibria. Special measures, taken in the interest of cleanliness of the beaches and coastal zones, forbid any direct or indirect discharge, deposit or seepage susceptible of affecting beaches and coastal areas frequented by the public. Liquid wastes should be collected for treatment at an appropriate plant. If that cannot be done, they should be collected and discharged in conditions regulated by the préfet after an opinion by the departmental safety council. Finally, within this "marine public domain" belonging to the state, both natural reserves and national parks can be created.

### 3. Particular Rules Concerning Specific Problems

From the above review, it is clear that most rules on the marine environment are found in international treaties. Many specific norms regulate the different sources of marine pollution. They also, however, address problems arising from accidental pollution and questions of reparation of damage.

#### a. Vessel Source Pollution

The general framework for international regulation of vessel source pollution is contained in UNCLOS articles 194(3)(b), 211 and 217–21. These provisions make no distinction between voluntary and accidental pollution. States should take measures to assure the safety of operations at sea, prevent dumping – accidental or intentional – and regulate the design, construction, equipment and operation of ships. Other provisions concern navigation and designation of maritime routes. In addition, states are asked to adopt norms to prevent, reduce and control pollution, both for flag ships and for foreign ships that enter their ports, territorial seas and their exclusive economic zones. In other words, the State is responsible for protecting the marine environment in zones extending 360 kilometres from its coastline.

These principles are detailed by a convention of global scope and by some regional conventions such as the 1992 Baltic Sea treaty. The global convention, called MARPOL (short for "marine pollution"), was adopted 2 November 1973, prior to UNCLOS. MARPOL does not define pollution,[12] but it lists the types of vessel emissions that can cause it: any release from a ship including escape, disposal, spilling, leaking, pumping, emitting or emptying (article 2 para. 3). Conforming to general practice, the Convention excludes from its coverage non-commercial government ships, including military vessels of all kinds.

The obligations of the contracting parties are detailed in easily modified annexes to the MARPOL Convention. In this way, the technical details are kept current, a consistent problem in environmental law. The obligations of states parties also are defined by different regulations for each polluting substance: oil (annex I), noxious liquids in bulk (annex II), harmful substances carried in packaged forms or freight

---

[12] This definition is found in the Law of the Sea Convention, art. 1(4).

containers, portable tanks or road and rail tank wagons (annex III), sewage (annex IV), and garbage (annex V). The general principle is one of prohibiting all discharge, but strictly defined exceptions exist for certain cases and certain specific zones, as well as for vessels that do not exceed a specified tonnage.

With one exception, the regional seas conventions limit themselves to proclaiming the principle that states parties should combat vessel source pollution, it being understood that the subject is regulated by the MARPOL Convention. The exception is the Baltic Sea Convention which announced, as of 1974, its own rules concerning vessel source pollution. The revised Helsinki Convention of 9 April 1992, also seeks to prevent vessel source pollution of the Baltic, but refers in large part to MARPOL (article 8 and annex IV). For the discharge of used waters by ships, the Helsinki agreement adopts some rules inspired by Marpol, but establishes a stricter control over their implementation.

### b. Atmospheric Pollution

This form of marine pollution has received relatively little attention. As a whole the general rules concerning air pollution apply to the marine environment as well as to land. In addition, UNCLOS has two specific provisions on the problem.

According to articles 212 and 222, States shall adopt international treaties as well as laws and regulations in order to prevent, reduce and control atmospheric pollution and shall ensure application of the norms thus adopted. Certain regional seas treaties announce similar principles, but without entering into details on preventing this form of pollution.

Incineration of wastes on board ships at sea poses particular problems. The practice is established on the North Sea as a way of eliminating certain chemical substances, primarily those containing organohalogens. Long-standing measures regulate incineration. In most cases, prior authorization of the flag state is required, but the coastal state must authorize incineration within waters under its jurisdiction.[13] Incineration at sea is completely prohibited on the Baltic Sea (article 10, 1992 Helsinki Convention).

### c. Dumping of Wastes

According to the definition contained in UNCLOS, dumping means any deliberate disposal of wastes or other matter from vessels, aircraft, platforms or other man-made structures at sea. Dumping does not include the disposal of wastes or other matter arising from the normal operations of vessels, aircraft, platforms or other man-made structures at sea or placement of matter for a purpose other than disposal (article 1, para. 5). Such operations fall into the scope of the MARPOL convention.

Dumping of toxic wastes into the sea, as with the "boues rouges",[14] has provoked

---

[13] Code of Practice, then Protocol of 2 March 1983 to the Oslo Convention of 15 February 1972 on dumping of wastes at sea.

[14] Titanium oxide coming from chemical industries or radioactive wastes.

sometimes very strong reactions. While use of the sea as a universal "garbage can" is a strong temptation for those seeking to reduce the sometimes high costs of eliminating industrial wastes; it often risks irreversible harm. Wastes dumped in the ocean are normally not recoverable, unlike wastes on the ground or even underground which can usually be cleaned up.

UNCLOS, article 210, provides that states shall adopt laws and regulations to prevent, reduce and control pollution of the marine environment by dumping. In particular, no dumping shall take place without the permission of the competent authorities of states. For the territorial sea, the exclusive economic zone and the continental shelf, the coastal state should deliver the authorization and regulate and control dumping, but the flag state is equally competent, as is the state on whose territory or offshore terminal the wastes are loaded.

Here again, as with vessel-source pollution, international regulations were already in place before the adoption of general principles. A global convention, adopted on 29 December 1972, prohibits all dumping of wastes containing substances listed on an annex to the convention, widely known as the "black list". It includes such substances as organohalogenic compounds, mercury and its compounds, and persistent plastics. The dumping of wastes containing substances on a second annex, the "grey list" is permitted only with a prior specific permit issued by the competent authorities. These are products containing significant amounts of, among other things, lead, arsenic, copper, zinc, cyanides, fluorides, pesticides and their by-products. Finally, a general permit is necessary for dumping any other waste. In addition, the Convention details the conditions under which dumping can be effectuated, based upon the characteristics of the matter, those of the dumping site, and the method of dumping.

All regional treaties reaffirm the need to control dumping of wastes at sea and some, like the Barcelona Convention of 16 February 1976 for the protection of the Mediterranean Sea against pollution, attach a protocol specifically on this issue. The method utilized is always the same: special permits are required for listed substances, with all other matter requiring a general permits. However, from one convention to another, the listed items are not the same. Some instruments are stricter and include additional substances omitted from another convention. The Baltic Sea Conventions forbid all dumping of wastes, except that of matter dredged from the sea bottom, and this operation requires a special permit. Finally, a relatively old convention entirely concerned with regulating the dumping of wastes, the Oslo Convention of 15 February 1972, applies to the north-east Atlantic and part of the Arctic Oceans.

In sum, apart from the global London Convention, special international norms apply to European waters; they protect the Baltic, the North Sea and Atlantic, as well as the Mediterranean. Although the methods adopted in these instruments are the same, they prohibit or regulate different types of wastes.

### d. Pollution Resulting from the Exploration and Exploitation of the Seabed

This form of pollution has been most difficult to regulate, largely for historical reasons. The world oil crisis of the 1970s led governments to encourage petroleum production, including in the North Sea. UNCLOS and regional seas agreements contain only a general principle that states should regulate the subject. Some detailed norms exist in non-binding texts, including the "conclusions" addressed to states by the United Nations Environment Programme.

The UNEP conclusions recommend that States establish permit systems based on prior impact assessments and statements of the ecological consequences of exploitation, a monitoring system in the interest of the environment, procedures of information, and consultation between states when damage could result from operations outside the limits of national jurisdiction. They also recommend that states establish security measures to apply to the operations, prior measures to remedy emergency situations, and provide for international responsibility and compensation for victims. Finally, the removal of installations after use is counselled. Most maritime states have adopted legislation utilizing standards. France applies its rules governing mining to the exploration and exploitation of the continental shelf. These have a licensing system, based on impact studies, public hearings and an opinion by a specially created commission (law of 16 July 1976).

For environmental protection against the exploration and exploitation of minerals of the deep seabed outside the jurisdiction of any state, UNCLOS establishes a unique new legal regime, declaring that the minerals constitute the common heritage of mankind. The treaty attempts to create a complex system for exploitation and monitoring. However, most of the major industrialized countries have not accepted it. In the interim, identical national laws have been introduced in the United States, Germany, France, and the United Kingdom. The laws generally provide the conditions for authorization to be accorded to explore and exploit the mineral resources of the seabed. The request must be accompanied by an environmental impact statement and a work plan indicating the measures to protect and monitor the marine environment. Before commencing work, the exploiter must make a declaration accompanying the work programme and join to it the impact notice for the exploratory efforts and an impact statement for the exploitation efforts. The work can be prohibited or submitted to particular conditions, if it might compromise the integrity of the marine environment. The obligations imposed on the licence-holder include assuring protection of the marine environment, conservation of the mineral deposits, and the security of property and persons. During the work, the permit holder can be required at any moment to take measures demanded in case of a serious breach of obligations aimed at protecting marine flora and fauna. If the measures are not taken, the permit can be withdrawn.

### e. Land-based Pollution

Land-based pollution can be defined as pollution of maritime zones due to discharges by coastal establishments, such as houses, towns, or industrial plants, or pollution coming from any other source situated on land or artificial structures, including pollution transported by rivers into the sea, or run-off from agricultural fields.

Regulation of land-based pollution sources first appeared in international law in 1974 in response to considerable increase in the population density of coastal regions.

For example,the population of Mediterranean littoral states jumped from 212 million in 1950, to pass 356 million in 1985. In 2025, it is expected to achieve 500 million. To these numbers must be added the seasonal increases due to tourism. Along the Mediterranean coast, a number of large cities do not treat their sewage (Istanbul, eight million inhabitants) or treat it only partially (Barcelona, Naples, Rome, Genoa). The situation is worse on the south coast. In most cases, the problem is financial; for a city containing between 20,000 and 200,000 inhabitants, the cost of a basic sewage treatment plant is approximately $150 per person. A more sophisticated system could cost $500 per person.

The diversity of origins of land-based pollution complicates the legal solutions. Countries that have no access to the sea, like Switzerland or Slovakia, can still contribute to marine pollution by discharging substances into rivers within their territory, even far from the mouth of the river. This adds to the difficult task of the international legislator who seeks to combat land-based pollution. Every European country contains part of at least one hydrographic basin whose principal rivers discharge into the Baltic, the North Sea, the Atlantic, the Mediterranean or the Black Sea. In sum, controlling land-based pollution requires controlling every significant source of pollution in Europe.

It is obvious that this problem necessitates cooperation among all polluting states. However, due to regional economic, social, and cultural differences – there is little in common on those point between the Persian Gulf, West Africa, the Caribbean and the European seas – international regulation is geographically based. Projects aimed at elaborating a global convention have not proceeded further than the adoption of guidelines by a committee of experts in 1985.

UNCLOS, article 194(3) speaks of land-based pollution using the formula applied to other sources of pollution: states should take the necessary measures to limit, as much as possible, the release of toxic, harmful or noxious substances, especially those which are persistent, from land-based sources. All regional seas conventions are based upon this principle, but the obligations that result from it are detailed in only some of them. For Europe, three texts are relevant: the Paris Convention of 4 June 1974 applicable to the north-east Atlantic and a part of the Arctic; the Athens Protocol of 17 May 1980 completing the Barcelona Convention of 1976 on protection of the Mediterranean, and the Helsinki Convention of 9 April 1992 on protection of the Baltic sea. The legislative instrument used to combat land-based pollution is different in the three cases. The first dedicates an entire treaty to the problem; the second has a protocol integrating into the convention framework specific applicable rules; in the third case provisions regarding land-based pollution were inserted in a more general treaty.

The two first instruments call for elaboration of programmes and the adoption of specific measures to eliminate, if necessary by stages, land-based pollution caused by listed substances (Paris Convention, annex A, part I; Athens Protocol, annex I. The latter list is more inclusive than that of the Paris Convention). A second category of substances can be discharged with a special licence issued by the appropriate authorities. Here again, the Athens Protocol is stricter than the Paris Convention. An interesting contribution of the Athens Protocol is that it provides for the elaboration and adoption of guidelines to deal with pipelines for coastal outfalls and sewage treatment. The Protocol also speaks of the control and progressive replacement of products, installations and industrial and other processes causing significant pollution of the marine environment (article 7).

The Protocol adds that these guidelines, standards or common criteria should take into account local ecological, geographical and physical characteristics, the economic capacity of the parties and their development needs. Obviously, some of these factors could be invoked abusively and render the Protocol ineffective. However, several provisions require precise types of cooperation, principally to assist developing countries (article 10).

The 1992 Baltic Convention, which replaces the 1974 treaty, is different. It utilizes modern concepts such as the best environmental practice and the best available technology. It states that measures should be taken by the Contracting Parties throughout the water basin discharging into the Baltic. The measures required include a licensing system for any direct or indirect introduction of harmful substances within the Baltic zone, unless it is a matter of negligible quantities (article 6). Annex III details the criteria and the measures concerning the prevention of land-based pollution, especially for sewage, industrial waste water, and waters containing dangerous substances. The Convention extends its coverage to pollution caused by aquaculture and that coming from diffuse sources, including agriculture.

### f. Accidental Pollution

A series of accidents has demonstrated the need to establish rules and procedures for shipping accidents that spill oil, gasoline or other substances that can harm the marine environment. In Europe, the French, English and Greek coasts have been particularly affected by "black seas". The *Torrey Canyon* disaster in 1967 spilled 110,000 tons of oil into the sea and the *Amoco Cadiz* lost 220,000 tons. International cooperation is obviously indispensable: the *Amoco Cadiz* was a ship built in Spain, belonged to an American company, flew a Liberian flag, was en route from the Middle East to Rotterdam, and had an Italian captain and a crew composed of several nationalities, mostly from South East Asia. Salvage was attempted by a German company; most damage occurred in France.

The seas around Europe are particularly exposed due to the number of oil tankers and intensity of other maritime traffic, increasing the risk of collision. International instruments calling for regional collaboration to prevent accidental pollution are particularly important. Generally, cooperation is a governing principle of international agreements of this type.[15] In addition to cooperation, emergency plans must be elaborated; their preparation and execution fall upon national authorities of the contracting states.

A distinction must be made between two types of action: those prior to an accident and those undertaken when the polluting accident occurs. The first measures are

---

[15] UNCLOS articles 198, 199, 204, and 211, para. 7; Helsinki Convention on the Baltic Sea (annex VII); Bonn Accord of 9 June 1969 and 13 September 1983 on the North Sea; Barcelona Protocol of 16 February 1976 on the Mediterranean.

indispensable to organize the second type of action. The first category includes the organization of emergency alerts and transmission of information (instructions given to ship captains and pilots); communication of information on national texts in force and on administrative structures or other bodies that can intervene; information on national emergency plans and on the personnel and materials available for common action; and organization and maintenance of means of communication. In certain cases, especially for the North Sea, systematic surveillance has been organized to limit pollution and to give especially rapid notification. Finally, regional aid centres can be established. One exists for the Mediterranean on Malta, but until now it has not had to intervene in a case of major pollution.

When an emergency occurs, the first task is to inform those who can be affected by it and who can usefully intervene. Assistance itself can take several variations: salvage of the ship, sending personnel and material to combat spills, sealing off tears in the hull, cleaning beaches, saving sea birds and animals, etc. As a whole, the principal points governed by legal norms regulate the transfrontier movement of personnel, products and equipment (passports, visas, customs), monitoring and control, establishment of methods and sites for the disposal of polluting substances, and financing assistance.

### g) Responsibility and Reparations for Harm caused by Marine Environmental Pollution

The norms of responsibility in cases of environmental harm are discussed elsewhere. They apply, of course, to marine environmental pollution and are generally regulated by the domestic law of the different states. However, when the polluter and the victim come from different states, specific legal rules have been adopted in order to resolve problems posed either by the type of environmental harm or by the fact that the national laws of the affected persons are in competition.

An international convention on civil responsibility for oil pollution damage was adopted in 1969 in Brussels. It has been modified several times and its scope extended to damage caused by other substances. In order to resolve the problem of identifying the polluter, the convention decided that whatever the facts, the owner of the vessel is responsible for the damage. His responsibility is presumed even in the absence of any fault. To avoid any discussion about the competent tribunal, the Convention states that the victims can bring the case before their national courts. Logically, it follows that the judgment rendered by the court should be enforceable in other contracting states. On the other hand, the liability of the owner is limited; a ceiling is set taking into account different categories of vessels. In cases where this amount is not sufficient to satisfy all the damages, an international insurance fund has been created; it can pay at least a part of the difference between the damages paid by the owner and the amount of the damages. Analogous provisions have been adopted for damage caused by the exploration or exploitation of mineral resources on the sea bed (London Convention of 1 May 1977).

These norms, and the solutions that they introduce in law – designation of liability, no-fault liability, limited liability, insurance funds – could become general approaches in environmental law.

# B. Case Studies

## 1. Tullio Scovazzi, *International Law and the Protection of the Marine Environment*

"States have the obligation to protect and preserve the marine environment." The wording of Art. 192 of the 1982 United Nations Convention on the Law of the Sea (UNCLOS) is simple. However, the provisions that follow in Part XII of the treaty, devoted to the "protection and preservation of the marine environment", as well as the provisions embodied in other international treaties, are far from being simple. By their number, technicality,[16] and complexity, they signal the difficult, though indispensable endeavour of protecting the sea. In analyzing this effort, several different factors must be taken into consideration: natural, political, economic and legal.

### a. *Natural Factors*

The marine environment can be viewed as a unitary milieu in which many of its natural characteristics interplay and interfere according to natural phenomena that current scientific knowledge cannot fully explain. According to the preamble of UNCLOS, "the problems of ocean space are closely interrelated and need to be considered as a whole". While the individual, numberless elements which compose the whole may be irrelevant, any impairment of the essential ecological processes of the sea and its life support systems must be prevented and avoided. The underlying unity of the oceans requires a unitary management regime.

Marine pollution may occur everywhere and is harmful wherever it occurs. All areas of the sea are subject to measures of protection. This can be inferred from the broad definition given in UNCLOS Art. 1(4):

> Pollution of the marine environment means the introduction by man, directly or indirectly, of substances or energy into the marine environment, including estuaries, which results or is likely to result in such deleterious effects as harm to living resources and marine life, hazards to human health, hindrance to marine activities, including fishing and other legitimate uses of the sea, impairment of quality for use of sea water and reduction in amenities.

Consequently, States shall take, individually or jointly as appropriate, all measures that are necessary to prevent, reduce and control pollution of the marine environment from any source (UNCLOS, art. 194). Corollaries to this obligation are the duty of States not to act so as to transfer, directly or indirectly, damage or hazards from one area to another or to transform one type of pollution into another (art. 195); and the duty to prevent, reduce and control "the intentional or accidental introduction

---

[16] For example, how to determine the capacity of the segregated ballast tank in order for the ship to operate safely on ballast voyages without recourse to using oil tanks for water ballast, is established by Annex I, Regulation 13 of the 1973/1978 Convention for the Prevention of Pollution from Ships.

of species, alien or new, to a particular part of the marine environment, which may cause significant and harmful changes thereto" (art. 196, para. 1).

The need to consider the sea as a unitary system does not exclude recognition of special situations which deserve particular attention. The effects of pollution are more severe in coastal waters and semi-enclosed seas than elsewhere. The characteristics of many regional seas make forms of regional management almost unavoidable and international cooperation should develop, as appropriate, on a regional basis.

Special measures are to be taken "to protect and preserve rare or fragile ecosystems as well as the habitat of depleted, threatened or endangered species and other forms of marine life" (art. 194, para. 4). Coastal states may adopt special and non-discriminatory measures with regard to pollution from vessels in ice-covered areas, where particularly severe climatic conditions and the presence of ice covering such areas for most of the year create obstructions or exceptional hazards to navigation, and pollution of the marine environment could cause major harm to or irreversible disturbance of the ecological balance (art. 234).

States bordering on enclosed or semi-enclosed seas "shall endeavour, directly or through an appropriate regional organization ... to coordinate the implementation of their rights and duties with respect to the protection and preservation of the marine environment" (art. 123 a). The Mediterranean, the Baltic, the Black Sea, the Red Sea and the Gulf Zone are considered as special zones according to the MARPOL Convention for the prevention of pollution from ships (London, 1973–8).

Environmental protection today is broadly envisaged. The balance of life on earth proceeds from the so-called global commons: the oceans, the atmosphere, Antarctica. According to the report "Our Common Future", referred to as the Brundtland Report, the oceans, covering over 70 per cent of the planet's surface, "play a critical role in its life-support systems, in moderating its climate, and in sustaining animals and plants, including minute, oxygen-producing phytoplankton".[17]

From an economic and social point of view, the goal of reaching an environmentally sound and sustainable development is linked to the preservation of the marine environment. For this reason the UN General Assembly has listed "the protection of the oceans and all kinds of seas, including enclosed and semi-enclosed seas, and of coastal areas and the protection, rational use and development of their living resources" among the environmental issues of major concern in maintaining the quality of the Earth's environment and especially in achieving environmentally sound and sustainable development in all countries.

### b. Political and Economic Factors

Protecting the marine environment, like other spaces and resources, must take into account the different uses that individuals and States make of the seas. Protection and preservation do not mean restoration to a pristine condition. "States have the sovereign right to exploit their natural resources pursuant to their environmental

---

[17] UN Doc. A/42/427 of 4 August 1987, p. 258.

policies and in accordance with their duty to protect and preserve the marine environment" (UNCLOS art. 193). ·

Different activities that can take place at sea correspond to different forms of marine pollution, each having its own peculiarities. UNCLOS lists the various sources of pollution. A balance must be struck between the ability or right to engage in a specific activity and the concurrent obligation to not substantially impair the marine environment. Both qualitative and quantitative aspects figure in this difficult exercise.

The disposal of a drum of waste into the sea is not likely to result in any substantial consequence. But the deliberate choice to use the sea and seabed as receptacles of large-scale hazardous wastes is likely to cause an irreparable alteration of the quality of the marine environment.

Fishing is a lawful activity which provides an indispensable food source. However, fishing beyond the natural reproductive pace of a species is destructive. The use of large-scale pelagic driftnets, which can exceed thirty miles in length, is an indiscriminate and wasteful fishing method, catching targeted and non-targeted fish, marine mammals and seabirds.

Navigation is an activity whose expected benefits outweigh potential harm to the marine environment. But supertankers, nuclear-powered ships and ships carrying dangerous substances cause risks which must be carefully assessed in order to prevent accidents or to combat the effects of accidents that do occur.

Military manoeuvres and other military uses of the sea are included in the freedom of the high seas, provided that they are not inconsistent with the principles of international law embodied in the Charter of the United Nations. It remains open to discussion how and to what extent this sensitive manifestation of high seas freedom may be reconciled with preservation of the marine environment.

The harmonization of potentially conflicting uses of the sea is primarily accomplished through the use of recommended or mandated procedures. The question to be tackled may be either bilateral (e.g. what special precautions the nuclear-powered ship of State A must observe while passing through the territorial waters of State B), regional (e.g. can dumping of waste be allowed in a semi-enclosed sea like the Mediterranean?) or global (e.g. how must salvage of ships in distress be regulated in order to meet the increased concern for the protection of the environment?). Each party has an interest in a specific and *per se* lawful use of the sea; all should cooperate in order to discuss and overcome possible conflicts and to draft and implement the appropriate provisions. This is especially true when one of the interests at stake is that of the international community in protecting the environment.

> States shall cooperate on a global basis and, as appropriate, on a regional basis, directly or through competent international organizations, in formulating and elaborating international rules, standards and recommended practices and procedures ..., for the protection and preservation of the marine environment, taking into account characteristic regional features. (UNCLOS art. 197).

The obligation to cooperate, far from being limited to the marine environment, is a fundamental aspect of present international environmental law. While presenting several facets, the obligation to cooperate corresponds to a general duty to act in good faith in taking into account the situation of other interested States. As stated by the International Court of Justice,

the parties are under an obligation to enter into negotiations with a view to arriving at an agreement, and not merely to go through a formal process of negotiation … they are under an obligation so to conduct themselves that the negotiations are meaningful, which will not be the case when either of them insists upon its own position without contemplating any modification of it.[18]

Harmonization of conflicting interests may result, in certain cases, in not proceeding with a specific activity, if serious environmental concerns exist. According to the World Charter for Nature, "activities which are likely to cause irreversible damage to nature shall be avoided" and

activities which are likely to pose a significant risk to nature shall be preceded by an exhaustive examination: their proponents shall demonstrate that expected benefits outweigh potential damage to nature, and where potential adverse effects are not fully understood, the activities should not proceed (art. 11, a, b).

An interesting example in this regard is the Antarctic Treaty Protocol on Environmental Protection (Madrid, 1991). It prohibits any activity relating to mineral resources, other than scientific research (art 6). Most mineral activities would have taken place on the continental shelf around Antarctica.

### c. Legal Factors

The already complex picture resulting from the interplay of natural, economic and political factors is further affected by the existence of a legal framework for the oceans. According to international law, the sea is not a unitary whole. There are marine zones subject to the sovereignty of coastal States (internal waters and territorial sea), marine zones beyond the limits of national jurisdiction (the high seas and the seabed and subsoil thereof), and marine zones of a *sui generis* nature where the specific rights of the coastal State co-exist with the specific rights of other States (the exclusive economic zone which can extend up to 200 n.m. from the coastline). Under the traditional law of the sea, coastal States could not extend their claims beyond a territorial sea of limited width (not more than twelve nautical miles) and marine activities were governed by the combination of both the territorial criterion (the coastal State has jurisdiction within its own territorial sea) and the flag criterion (on the high seas, the flag State has jurisdiction with respect to ships flying its flag).

The existing legal situation proved largely inadequate to meet the increasing concerns for protection of the marine environment. The 1967 *Torrey Canyon* accident provoked the United Kingdom to intervene on a foreign ship on the high seas, in order to combat the consequences of a maritime casualty endangering the sea and coastlines from oil pollution. Instead of being considered a violation of the freedom

---

[18] *North Sea Continental Shelf Case*, 1969 I.C.J., *Reports of Judgments, Advisory Opinions and Orders*, p. 47.

of the high seas, the British action prompted the adoption of the Convention relating to intervention on the high seas in cases of oil pollution casualties (Brussels, 1969). In 1970 Canada adopted the Arctic Waters Pollution Prevention Act, whose application extends to one hundred nautical miles from the nearest land. Despite initial protests from the United States, the jurisdiction of the coastal State with regard to the protection and preservation of the marine environment within its exclusive economic zone is today generally accepted (see UNCLOS art. 56(1b)).

The new regime does not solve all problems relating to the marine environment. While coastal States have jurisdiction within their exclusive economic zones, other States still enjoy "other internationally lawful uses of the sea" related to freedoms of navigation, overflight and of laying submarine cables and pipelines (art. 58(1)). It is evident that a State cannot claim freedom to dump wastes in foreign economic zones, but it is uncertain to what extent coastal States may interfere with the navigation of foreign ships by adopting laws and regulations for the prevention of pollution from vessels. UNCLOS allows such laws and regulations, provided that they conform and give effect to generally accepted international rules and standards established through the competent international organization or general diplomatic conference (art. 211, para. 5).

### d. The Role of Treaty Law in the Protection of the Marine Environment

By their nature, international customary rules are broad and their contents limited to rather vague obligations to preserve the environment and cooperate in this purpose. Such rules, binding on every State, need to be specified and elaborated in treaties. It may be important to ascertain that a State is under a customary obligation to ensure that ships flying its flag do not pollute. It is more useful to know that the instantaneous rate of discharge of oil from tankers must not exceed 60 litres per nautical mile and that the total quantity of oil discharged at sea must not exceed 1/15,000 of the total quantity of the cargo of which the residue formed a part (Regulation 9, para. 1 of Annex I, MARPOL).

States have thus far concluded a considerable number of treaties dealing with the marine environment. Given the principle that special rules derogate from general rules, the general/special relationship is based either on the object of the treaties (*rationae materiae*) or on their sphere of territorial application (*ratione loci*).

The only universal treaty, from the point of view of both the object and territorial application, is UNCLOS. Part XII of this Convention "is the first comprehensive codification of the principles of marine pollution articulated at the 1972 United Nations Conference on the Human Environment".[19] It is expressly designed to operate as an "umbrella" for further global, regional and national actions. Part XII expressly recognizes and mandates regional approaches. However, the obligations

---

[19] *Law of the Sea -- Protection and Preservation of the Marine Environment, Report of the Secretary-General*, UN Doc. A/44/461 of 18 September 1989, p. 5.

imposed by special conventions must be consistent with the general principles and objectives of the UNCLOS (art. 237).

The Convention for the Prevention of Pollution from Ships (MARPOL, London 1973, amended in 1978) is an example of a treaty of universal territorial application concerning a specific kind of marine pollution. MARPOL is intended to achieve the complete elimination of intentional pollution of the marine environment by oil and other harmful substances and the minimization of accidental discharge of such substances. The parties undertake to give effect to the provisions of MARPOL and of those annexes to which they are bound. MARPOL has progressively promoted the adoption of technical innovations, such as reception facilities at ports and loading terminals or segregated ballast oil tankers.

Another important treaty of the same category is the Convention on the prevention of marine pollution by dumping of wastes and other matter (London, 1972).

Several treaties of universal scope have the objective of preventing accidents at sea or of limiting their harmful consequences. Relevant examples are the above-mentioned Convention relating to intervention on the high seas in cases of oil pollution casualties (Brussels, 1969), its protocol (London, 1973) and the recent Convention on oil pollution preparedness, response and cooperation (London, 1990). A new convention on salvage was opened for signature in 1989, "noting that substantial developments, in particular the increased concern for the protection of the environment, have demonstrated the need to review the international rules contained" in the 1910 Convention on assistance and salvage at sea. The 1989 salvage convention provides that the reward for salvors shall be fixed taking into account, *inter alia*, "the skill and efforts of the salvors in preventing or minimizing damage to the environment" (art. 13, para. 1b).

Two treaties aim to ensure adequate compensation for persons who suffer damage resulting from the escape or discharge of oil from ships.[20] However, two serious oil pollution casualties caused by oil tankers, the *Amoco Cadiz* and *Patmos*, showed that the international system of compensation, while appropriate for the majority of casualties, may present shortcomings in regard to the limitation of liability and the exclusion of compensation for so-called ecological damage.

The mere fact that there are multilateral conventions that apply on a global basis is not sufficient to ensure widespread compliance with their provisions. Like any other international treaty, environmental conventions are subject to ratification or ad-hesion by states which are in principle free to decide not to become parties. In addition to examining the treaty provisions, it is useful to look at the tables of ratifications and the list of reservations to ascertain the effective acceptance of the conventions. The records of the MARPOL and London Dumping Convention seem satisfactory; the first is in force for 52 states, the combined merchant fleets of which

---

[20] The Convention on Civil Liability for Oil Pollution Damage (Brussels 1969, amended in 1984 and the Convention on the Establishment of an International Fund for Compensation for Oil Pollution Damage (Brussels, 1971).

constitute approximately 88 per cent of the gross tonnage of the world's merchant fleet, and the second is in force for 63 States.

Among regional treaties, some are especially intended to prevent a particular kind of pollution within a wide area. For example, the Convention on the Prevention of Marine Pollution from Land-Based Sources (Paris, 1974) covers the Atlantic and Arctic Oceans north of lat. 36 degrees north, east of long. 42 degrees west and west of long. 51 degrees east, excluding the Baltic and Mediterranean.

In other cases, regional treaties, often sponsored by UNEP, are adopted in the form of framework conventions providing general undertakings supplemented by protocols. The Convention for the Protection of the Mediterranean Sea against Pollution (Barcelona, 1976) allows the parties to enter into sub-regional agreements, either bilateral or multilateral, provided that such agreements are consistent with the convention and conform to international law. A few sub-regional agreements have been signed for certain Mediterranean seas, like the Adriatic (agreement between Italy and Yugoslavia, signed in 1974), the Ionian (agreement between Greece and Italy, signed in 1979), and the Ligurian sea (agreement between Italy, France and Monaco, signed in 1976).

The foregoing review of international legal instruments shows that there exists an articulated network for the protection of the marine environment in which, nonetheless, there remain gaps to be filled and duplications to be eliminated. Perhaps because of its marked international relevance, the field of marine environment has been the object of more conventional regulation than any other branch of environmental law. Strengthening and improving the international regime of environmental protection is based upon treaty law and might proceed along two parallel directions.

First, the normative coverage could be widened by the inclusion of some areas in which further international action is required, as, for example, marine pollution from seabed activities, from land-based sources, and from the atmosphere. Questions of responsibility and liability arising from any kind of marine pollution (and not only from oil pollution casualties) need particular attention.

Second, the problem of non-compliance or lack of effectiveness could be addressed through a number of legal devices: using incentives to attract new parties, bridging the gap between signature and entry into force through provisional application or declarations of voluntary compliance, providing procedures for updating treaties quickly, using instruments which also contain commitments of a non-binding nature, and strengthening the role of international institutions to develop rules set forth in framework conventions.

### e. The Action of the European Economic Community

When signing UNCLOS in 1984, the EEC made a list of Community texts applicable for the protection and preservation of the marine environment and directly related to subjects covered by the Convention. The majority of such texts concern discharges of industrial wastes at sea and reflects the objective of harmonizing the laws of Member States in order to eliminate distortions to competition within the European market.[21] The EEC has subsequently improved its action with regard to accidents at sea by Council Decision 86/85 of 6 March 1986 establishing a Community information system for the control and reduction of pollution caused by the spillage of hydrocarbons and other harmful substances at sea.

The EEC is a party, together with all or some Member States, to multilateral conventions for the protection of the marine environment. The participation of the EEC in international negotiations and agreements is an important factor in promoting the environmental objectives of the Community.

The extent to which the EEC is able to present itself as a unitary body in the international arena depends on political factors within the Community. For the time being, the EEC has improved its environmental role at a slow, but continuous, pace. This may confirm that the existence of a Community environmental policy is a relevant instrument for enhancing the quality of a global environment, seas and oceans included.

## 2. Said Mahmoudi, *The Baltic and the North Sea*

### a. *General Remarks*

The Baltic Sea[22] and the North Sea[23] are semi-enclosed seas.[24] The major source of pollution in both seas is land-based.[25] The most polluted areas are the coastal zones. The Baltic Sea has exceptional hydrographical and ecological characteristics which make its living resources very sensitive to changes in the environment. The

---

[21] Such texts are: 1981 Decisions establishing a Community information system for the control and reduction of pollution caused by hydrocarbons discharged at sea; 1976 Directive on pollution caused by certain dangerous substances discharged into the aquatic environment of the Community; 1975 Directive on the disposal of waste oils; 1978 Directive on waste from the titanium dioxide industry; 1979 Directive on the quality required of shellfish waters; 1982 Directive on limit values and quality objectives for mercury discharges by the chlor-alkali electrolysis industry; 1983 Directive on limit values and quality objectives for cadmium discharges; 1984 Directive on limit values and quality objectives for mercury discharges by sectors other than the chlor-alkali electrolysis industry.

[22] As far as the protection of environment is concerned, the Baltic Sea is defined in the 1974 Helsinki Convention (*infra*) as: "The Baltic Sea proper with the Gulf of Bothnia, the Gulf of Finland and entrance to the Baltic Sea bounded by the parallel of the Skaw in the Skagerrak at 7 degrees 44' 8" N".

[23] The North Sea, according to the definition of the Bonn Agreement (*infra*) comprises: "North Sea proper southwards of latitude 61 degrees N, together with: a) the Skagerrak, the southern limit of which is determined east of Skaw by the latitude 57 degrees 44' 00" 8N; b) the English Channel and its approaches eastwards of a line drawn fifty nautical miles to the west of a line joining the Scilly Isles and Ushant".

[24] Article 122 of the 1982 Law of the Sea Convention defines enclosed or semi-enclosed seas as: "a gulf, basin or sea surrounded by two or more States and connected to another sea or the ocean by a narrow outlet or consisting entirely or primarily of the territorial sea and exclusive economic zones of one or more coastal States".

[25] For a detailed account of the facts relating to the ecological situation of the Baltic Sea, see *Second Periodic Assessment of the State of the Marine Environment of the Baltic Sea, 1984–8: General Conclusions*, Helsinki, Helsinki Commission, 1990; see also "Status of the Baltic Sea – A Sea in Transition", Ambio, Special Report no. 7, September 1990. For the North Sea, see *Interim Report on the Quality Status of the North Sea*, February 1990, presented to the Third International Conference on the Protection of the North Sea. (*infra*).

North Sea, except for shallow coastal areas, is not sensitive to the same degree. The coastal states bordering the North Sea are advanced industrialized countries[26] in contrast to those surrounding the Baltic Sea which have distinctly different levels of industrial development and economic strength.[27] In addition, the North Sea is surrounded by the EC members – except for Sweden and Norway – and the protection of the marine environment is influenced by EC law whereas in the Baltic Sea area only Germany and Denmark are the EC members.

The pollution and ecological imbalance of the Baltic and the North Sea stem from different sources. The share of the contribution of each source varies in different sections and during different periods of time. The main sources of concern at present in both marine areas are: (1), input of hazardous substances; (2), input of nutrients; (3), dumping of dredged materials; (4), input of pollutants via the atmosphere; and (5), vessel source pollution. The primary source of pollution may be different for each country. In Denmark, a major agricultural country with very little heavy industry, the environmental priority is the problem of nutrient discharge and eutrophication. Industrial wastes are under controlled management. In the UK, on the contrary, inputs of nutrients to the North Sea are believed not to contribute directly or indirectly to marine eutrophication, but input of hazardous substances is the major source of concern.

National laws and regulations of the coastal states with respect to the protection of the Baltic and the North Sea have different degrees of stringency. Their primary objective is very often to tackle problems of localized geographic significance. National laws are generally framework laws, leaving detailed regulations to the discretion of administrative authorities. More importantly, the enforcement of the laws is not effected with the same rigour owing to various administrative policies and practices in different countries. The reason lies to a great extent in different industrial bases, economic possibilities and geographical and natural situations. In Germany, for example, the federal government has only a framework competence with respect to water pollution control. The detailed policies are determined and enforced by the states (Länder).[28] In France, on the other hand, both law-making and enforcement are centralized. Local units of government have no real power with respect to the environment.[29] This centralization is also found, at least to some extent, in the Netherlands.[30] Sweden and the U.K. are different:[31] government policy has been to delegate to the local or regional bodies the actual power for administration and enforcement of environmental laws.

In addition to the variations in law-making and enforcement systems, the content

---

[26] Belgium, Denmark, Federal Republic of Germany, France, the Netherlands, Norway, Sweden and the United Kingdom.

[27] Denmark, Estonia, Finland, Germany, Latvia, Lithuania, Poland, the Russian Republic and Sweden.

[28] E.Rehbinder, "The Federal Republic of Germany", in T. Smith and P. Kromarek (eds.), *Understanding US and European Environmental Law, A Practitioner Guide*, Graham and Trotman, London, 1989, pp. 8–20, at p. 8.

[29] C. Huglo, "France", *ibid.*, pp. 20–31, at p. 24.

[30] T. Drupsteen & P. Gilhuis, "The Netherlands", *ibid.*, pp. 47–58, at p. 54.

[31] R. Macrory, "The United Kingdom", *ibid.*, pp. 31–44, at pp. 32–3.

of the laws differs considerably depending on a number of factors. In the UK, for example, the geographical conditions such as fast-flowing rivers have favoured the use of natural mechanism as a means of dispersal of emissions.[32] Besides, the government has preferred to carry out environmental policy by voluntary or other non-legal measures wherever practicable. In Sweden, in contrast, the sensitivity of the water in the rivers, estuaries and the coastal areas has necessitated the adoption of relatively stringent regulations.

Another illustration of the difference in the marine environmental policies of the Baltic and the North Sea countries is the choice between Uniform Emission Standard (UES) and Environmental Quality Standard (EQS) for regulating the reduction or prohibition of harmful inputs into the seas. Some coastal states of the Baltic and the North Sea base their regulations mainly on one or the other of these approaches. Belgium and Sweden, for example, have chosen UES and the United Kingdom and Finland EQS. The more common practice is to combine both methods as is the case in Denmark, the Netherlands and the European Community.

Much of the environmental legislation of the North Sea states stems from EC directives. The European Community, both as a supranational organization with legislative and enforcement powers and as a contracting party to some regional conventions for the protection of the North Sea and the Baltic, can certainly play a crucial role in coordination and harmonization of the relevant national laws and regulations.

In addition to national laws and EC legislation, there are several regional or global conventions which either specifically or generally deal with the protection of the marine environment in the Baltic and the North Sea. The purpose of these conventions is to establish uniform practice and draw up uniform programmes for the states parties. They usually function as appropriate vehicles to deal with large-scale problems relevant to the whole marine environment in a specific area, and very often establish an institutional organ for the purpose of facilitating the implementation of the convention. These organs normally lack central control mechanisms, and supervision is limited to periodic reports submitted by member states. Unlike the EC, these organs may not bind a contracting party unwillingly.

The protection of the Baltic Sea is regulated by one comprehensive regional convention – the 1974 Convention on the Protection of the Marine Environment of the Baltic Sea Area (Helsinki). The Convention has a holistic approach dealing with all forms of marine pollution. Its institutional organ is the Baltic Marine Environment Protection Commission (HELCOM).

A piecemeal approach has been employed for the protection of the North Sea, subjecting each pollution source to the provisions of a separate convention. In this respect mention should be made of the following conventions: (1), 1972 Convention for the Prevention of Marine Pollution by Dumping from Ships and Aircraft (Oslo) – with its two amending protocols from 1983 and 1989 and the related organ, the

---

[32] J. Gibson and R. Churchill, "Problems of Implementation of the North Sea Declarations: A Case Study of the United Kingdom", D. Freeston & T. Ijlstra (eds.), *The North Sea: Perspectives on Regional Environmental Co-operation*, Graham & Trotman, London, 1990, pp. 47–65, at p. 52; Macrory, *op.cit.*, p.37.

Oslo Commission (OSCOM); (2), 1974 Convention for the Prevention of Marine Pollution from Land-Based Sources (Paris) – with its amending protocol from 1986 and related organ, the Paris Commission (PARCOM); (3), 1982 Memorandum of Understanding on Port State Control (Paris); and (4), 1983 Agreement for Co-operation in Dealing with Pollution of the North Sea by Oil and Other Harmful Substances (Bonn).

In addition to these regional instruments, there are two international conventions with global application, namely, the 1972 Convention on Prevention of Marine Pollution by Dumping of Wastes and Other Matters (London), and the 1973 Convention for the Prevention of Pollution by Ships as modified by the protocol from 1978 – MARPOL 73/78. The objective of these documents, both regional and global, is to *prevent* marine pollution. The only exception is the Bonn Agreement which is designed to cope with the *result* of a pollution incident.

In the following, the existing regional legal frameworks for the protection of environment in the Baltic and the North Sea will briefly be touched upon.

### b. The Baltic Sea

The Baltic Sea states can be roughly put into two distinct groups: those with economic and technological possibilities to promote effectively the protection of the Baltic Sea against pollution, and the others with economic problems and in need of many basic technologies. The corollary of such a gap is a conspicuous difference in the enforcement of existing environmental regulations with ensuing serious ecological problems off the coasts of the Baltic nations, Poland and eastern Germany. The 1974 Helsinki Convention, which entered into force in 1980, is a broad legal framework to provide for cooperation and assistance on a regional inter-governmental level.

The Helsinki Convention regulates the prevention of marine pollution in the Baltic Sea area in a comprehensive manner. The original membership of the Convention consisted of all States surrounding the Baltic Sea. After the disintegration of the Soviet Union, the Russian Republic took over its place. Out of the three newly independent States of Latvia, Estonia and Lithuania, only Estonia had acceded to the Convention by 1991. All the parties to the Convention are members of its institutional organ, the HELCOM. Decisions of the HELCOM are adopted unanimously.[33] Its primary function is to keep the implementation of the Convention under continuous observation.[34] The Convention contains separate provisions relating to land-based pollution,[35] vessel source pollution, dumping,[36] pollution caused by spillage of oil and other harmful substances, and pollution caused by the exploration and exploitation of the sea-bed and subsoil. While the Helsinki Convention itself embodies general principles and basic rules, six annexes elaborate detailed regulations in each case. The Helsinki Convention does not provide for any common control standard with respect to the

[33] Article 12(5).

[34] Article 13(a).

[35] The definition of land-based pollution in article 2 of the Helsinki Convention is different from the one in the Paris Convention in that it includes even airborne pollution.

[36] According to article 9, dumping of all harmful substances is prohibited. The only exception is dredged spoils, which may be dumped after special permit from the appropriate national authority.

land-based inputs. However, the contracting parties are obliged, according to article 6, to endeavour to establish common criteria for issuing permits for discharges. It has been agreed that a combined UES and EQS approach should be used for national control of discharges.

The continued severe condition of the Baltic Sea, particularly the problem of eutrophication and pollution from ships, led the heads of the governments of the states bordering the Baltic Sea to meet in a conference in Ronneby, Sweden in November 1990. The main theme and principal objective of the conference was the ecological restoration of the Baltic.[37] In order to attain this objective, it was decided *first*, that on the basis of national reports, a joint comprehensive programme for decisive reduction of emissions be prepared; *second*, that an *ad hoc* task force within the Helsinki Commission be set up to prepare the said programme. The most innovative move was to engage four international financial institutions[38] in the work of the task force in order to prepare investment projects for cleaning up an area stretching from eastern Germany to St Petersburg.

Intensive work on revising the Helsinki Convention after the Ronneby Conference led to the adoption of a new convention in April 1992. The 1992 Helsinki Convention, which after entry into force replaces the 1974 Convention, is much broader in scope. The main theme is restoration of the Baltic Sea Area and the preservation of its ecological balance. Unlike the 1974 Convention, the purpose is not to abate pollution, but to eliminate it (art. 3, para.1). Internal waters are now included in the area of application. The 1992 Convention makes a distinction between a harmful substance and a hazardous substance, which is persistent, toxic or liable to bio-accumulation (art. 2). In this way, a greater variety of substances falls under the regulations of the Convention. In article 3, under the title of fundamental principles and obligations, the precautionary principle, polluter-pays principle, Best Available Technology (BAT) [for point sources] and Best Environmental Practice (BEP) [for all sources] are mentioned. Moreover, duties of notification and consultation on pollution incidents (art. 13), co-operation in combating marine pollution (art. 14), nature conservation and biodiversity (art. 15), reporting and exchange of information (art. 16), and information to the public (art. 17) are all new provisions in this convention. The EC, which actively participated in the negotiations for the new Convention and will be a party to it, has joined the 1974 Convention pending the entry into force of the 1992 Convention. There is no change in unanimous decision-making scheme of the HELCOM, and each Member State has one vote. The HELCOM's structure and competence is more or less the same as before.

[37] "Restoration" in this context means a return to the relatively clean state of the Baltic Sea in 1950. That objective has been coined as "Forward to 1950". Achieving that goal is estimated to take some sixty years. That is due to the natural conditions such as low temperature and long residence time which make the recovery process slow. " 'Forward to 1950' ": Policy Considerations for the Baltic Environment", Ambio, Special Report 7, September 1990, pp. 21–4, at p. 22.

[38] They are: World Bank, European Investment Bank, Nordic Investment Bank and European Bank of Reconstruction and Development.

Since the major source of concern in the Baltic in recent years has been agricul-tural run-offs and the discharge of nutrients with ensuing eutrophication problems, and this type of environmental stress was not regulated by the 1974 Convention, the 1992 Convention, in Annex III, deals with this as well as a range of other land-based sources of pollution. One may say that although the 1992 Convention is by far a more comprehensive Convention and the duties of the parties are more clearly spelled out, its institutional organ – the Helsinki Commission – has gained no more power, and the effective implementation of the Convention still depends on the will of the Member Stats.

### c. The North Sea

Unlike the Baltic Sea, where the disparities in financial and technical feasibilities constitute a major obstacle to the effective protection of the marine environment, the problem in the North Sea is the difference in priorities of the coastal states – caused mainly by economic considerations – for combating marine pollution. The net result is that the stricter regulations of some states may be offset by perhaps milder rules and less active enforcement in other states. Under these circumstances, international legal arrangements become indispensable tools for persuading reluctant states to harmonize their national efforts with those of the states with stronger demands for the protection of the marine environment as a whole.

The 1972 Oslo Convention, which applies to the high seas and territorial seas of the north-east Atlantic Ocean including the North Sea, regulates the prevention of dumping from ships and aircraft. It contains three annexes listing the substances whose dumping is regulated. All North Sea states are parties to this convention. In 1983, a new annex concerning incineration at sea was appended to the Oslo Convention. Its institutional body, the OSCOM, has no mandate to take legally binding decisions for the states parties. However, it may recommend amendments, additions and deletions in the annexes which shall enter into force after unanimous approval of the governments of the contracting states. All the decisions of the OSCOM shall be taken by consensus. Due to the fact that dumping of industrial wastes, sewage sludge and incineration at the North Sea have almost terminated, the continuous existence of the OSCOM has been questioned.

The Paris Convention regulates the prevention of marine pollution from land-based sources.[39] The membership is more or less the same as for the Oslo Conven-tion.[40] The important exception is the EC, which is party to the Paris Convention. Atmospheric pollution, which was not originally covered by the Convention, was added to its mandate through the adoption of a protocol in 1986. The Paris Convention is different from the Oslo Convention in that it includes the power to

---

[39] The Paris Convention, according to article 3(a), applies to "the high seas, the territorial seas of Contracting Parties and water on the landward side of the baselines from which the breadth of the territorial sea is measured, extending, in the case of watercourses up to the freshwater limit ..."

[40] Finland, a member of the OSCOM, holds an observer status at the PARCOM. Finland does not cause any land-based pollution in the North Sea, and thereby is not a party to Paris Convention.

draw up programmes and measures for the reduction or elimination of the pollution by the substances listed in its annexes. The implementation of these programmes and measures becomes obligatory for the contracting parties two hundred days after their adoption by the PARCOM.[41] Decisions are taken by consensus. However, if consensus cannot be obtained, resort can be had to three-quarters majority voting, and a decision so taken becomes mandatory for the parties which have voted for it. There is a close organizational cooperation between the OSCOM and the PARCOM, with a joint secretariat located in London, which at the same time functions as the secretariat for the Bonn Agreement. Both the PARCOM and the OSCOM have, within the limits of their mandates, performed important functions. However, the continued deterioration of the marine ecosystem of the North Sea gave rise in the early 1980s to the need for a fresh political impetus to achieve concrete, comprehensive and coordinated measures.

In response to the above-mentioned need, three International North Sea Conferences (INSCs) at the ministerial level have so far been held in Bremen (1984), London (1987) and the Hague (1990). At the end of each conference, a declaration has been issued. The most important statement in the first declaration was the acceptance by all participants of joint responsibility for the protection of the North Sea. The declaration of the second conference contains the commitments of the responsible ministers to reduce all harmful inputs from the land, and to terminate disposal of wastes at sea. The London conference also noted the need for establishing a closer link between science and policy. It therefore created a scientific task force in order to organize a coordinated programme of research and monitoring on the North Sea. The third conference in the Hague was even more successful, in that it did not confine itself to water quality like the first two conferences but broadened the scope of its work to include questions of coastal state jurisdiction, salvage of sunken ships and/or hazardous cargo, protection of habitats and species and fisheries. The Precautionary and Best Available Technology principles have been mentioned in these declarations as two of the guiding principles.

Although the Conference declarations are political in nature, they have nevertheless clear legal repercussions. The participants in the third INSC, for example, declared their intention to implement the declaration in national or EEC legislation.

Developments such as the consolidation of the Precautionary Principle as a dominant principle, repeated references to Best Available Technology as the prevailing method, considerable change in the sources and patterns of pollution, and, above all, the inefficiency of the present regional arrangements, have given rise to the need to revise the Oslo and Paris Conventions in order to replace them with a more effective legal system. Adoption of a single convention and assimilation of the OSCOM and the PARCOM to create one institutional organ is the expected result of such revision. Although there seems to be no substantial disagreement among the Member States of the Paris and Oslo Conventions with respect to adoption of a model similar to that of the Baltic Sea, certain Member States have resisted efforts to give

[41] Article 18(3).

more power to a commission to control the protection of the marine environment in the North Sea. This is partly due to the constitutional restraints of some of those States with respect to a broader legal competence of an institutional organ and partly the result of national environmental policies.

The European Community's specific engagement in the protection of the North Sea is a rather recent development. In the four EC Action Programmes for the protection of environment, problems of the North Sea have got some attention in only the Third and the Fourth Programmes from 1983 and 1987. The Fourth Action Programme did set, as one of its objectives improvement of the aquatic environment, notably that of the North Sea. However, since the 1970s, general Community acts on different aspects of environmental protection have had repercussions for the North Sea.

Many EC environmental acts, both before 1987 and since adoption of the Single European Act, contribute to the environmental protection of the North Sea, although not expressly addressing it. Mention in this respect should be made of framework directives on discharges of hazardous substances,[42] directives on the quality of marine water,[43] directives on polluting industries on the coast,[44] and decisions concerning the establishment of an information system in relation to the spillage of hydrocarbons and other harmful substances at sea.[45] All these instruments were adopted before 1987. Pursuant to the declaration of the second INSC in 1987, several legislative proposals have been put forward which are clearly inspired by the decisions at the INSC.[46]

The EC, in addition to activities at the internal level, participates in different international legal fora for the environmental protection of the North Sea and, since the beginning of 1992, of the Baltic Sea. The EC is a party to the Paris Convention, the 1983 Bonn Agreement, and the 1974 Helsinki Convention. Moreover, the EC participates in the INSCs and in the meetings of the OSCOM and IMO. The independent membership in these regional arrangements enables the EC to put into effect the decisions adopted in those fora without having resort to supranational powers and solutions.

### d. Present Trends and a View of the Future

The relatively long history of the legal protection of the marine environment in the Baltic and the North Sea bears witness to the difficulties that exist in co-ordinating national laws and reconciling national interests of the countries surrounding these two marine areas. Since inherent discrepancies between the legal, political and economic perceptions of states are not prone to change easily, it may be expected that, despite intensive efforts to revise old and inadequate national laws, they will

---

[42] Council Directive 76/464/EEC, 4 May 1976; Council Directive 86/278/EEC, 12 June 1986.

[43] Council Directive 79/923/EEC, 30 October 1979.

[44] Council Directive 78/176, 20 February 1978.

[45] Council Decision 86/85 EEC, 6 March 1986 as amended by Council Decision of 16 June 1988.

[46] A recent example is Commission proposal [COM(89)544] concerning the limit of the nutrient level in certain vulnerable agricultural zones which was approved by the EC environment ministers on 14 June 1991.

continue to remain insufficient for safeguarding the Baltic and the North Sea against pollution and deterioration.[47]

The move to render the existing regional inter-governmental organizations more efficient is a response to the need for further international measures. Revision of the Oslo and Paris Conventions for the protection of the North Sea, to create a single regional legal framework with more comprehensive competence and better structured machinery, should be seen in this light. The adoption of a new convention for the protection of the Baltic Sea Area, in order to include new protective assignments in its mandate is another example. It is true that these international instruments and their institutional organs generally lack the necessary power to impose binding decisions upon a recalcitrant member state; they will, however, fulfil a very significant purpose by serving as a forum to negotiate and convince all participants of the benefits of concerted actions for the protection of the marine environment.

The role of the EC in this respect has become more important in recent years. Being aware of its significant role, the EC has intensified its efforts to protect the environment of the Baltic and the North Sea. A further concrete step is a Commission proposal for a Council Regulation on specific action to protect the environment in the coastal areas and coastal waters of the Irish Sea, North Sea, Baltic Sea and North East Atlantic Ocean (Norspa).[48] This programme is modelled on a similar scheme for the protection of the Mediterranean (Medspa). What is particularly interesting with Norspa is that its objectives should be incorporated into the proposed EC financial instrument for the environment (LIFE).[49] The independent membership and participation in several international legal arrangements for the protection of the Baltic and the North Sea enables the EC to act on two levels: coordination and enforcement of decisions already agreed upon within the regional organizations, and enactment of legislation in its supranational capacity where the required legislation for a specific activity is missing.

This second function can have significant dimensions if the EC Council frequently avails itself of qualified-majority voting schemes. As long as decisions on environmental matters are taken by consensus, it is foreseeable that disparities in national environmental policies will not permit adoption of stringent rules. It may be noted that the expected membership of Sweden and Finland in the EC as from January 1995[50] will enhance the possibilities of the EC to establish a more unified legal system for the protection of the Baltic and the North Sea. The membership of Sweden alone will bring almost half of the Baltic Sea under the EC legislative competence.

It seems that stronger regional cooperation and a more powerful central

[47] National laws, particularly those of the North Sea states, have been constantly revised or amended in order to remain consistent with the decisions at the regional or EC level. Two recent examples are the laws amending the Swedish environmental legislation, adopted in June 1991 (SFS 1991: 650-683, 17 June 1991 – Collection of Swedish legislation, laws no. 1991: 650–83) and the UK's Environmental Protection Act, which became law on 1 November 1990.

[48] COM(90)498.

[49] The establishment of such an instrument has been put forward in a Commission proposal for a Council regulation, COM(91)28.

[50] Sweden and Finland have already submitted their applications for membership.

enforcement mechanism will govern the North Sea and the Baltic. Enforcement at the national level is expected to be enhanced in different ways. One measure should be the promotion of environmental education. Another could be a gradual reversal of the approach to activities with possible risks for the environment. To date the burden of proof as to the existence of such risks rests, in the majority of the cases, with the authorities or interest groups. A better approach is to require all those who are planning to engage in such activities not only to carry out an environment impact assessment but also to assume eventual responsibility for all damage.

The undeniable shift in policy from prevention on the basis of conclusive scientific evidence of deleterious effects to prevention based on plausible detrimental impacts had been borne out by repeated statements in the declarations of the INSCs, PARCOM decisions and EC documents. The Precautionary Principle thus seems to dominate the legal developments, be it in the form of amending present conventions, enacting new laws, or adopting new EC legislation. Likewise, it may be expected that an overall application of Best Available Technology will become an inseparable component of the precautionary approach.

Finally, mention should be made of another development which will certainly have some impact on the preservation of the marine environment both in the Baltic and in the North Sea, namely, the establishment of exclusive economic zones (EEZ). In the North Sea, Norway and France have established such zones. The question of establishing EEZ by other North Sea states has been under consideration. In the Baltic Sea, Estonia, Latvia, Lithuania and Poland already have EEZ and Sweden has prepared a bill to that effect. The establishment of the EEZ will enhance the protection of the marine environment specifically against dumping and vessel source pollution in the areas beyond the territorial seas. At present these areas are mainly governed by international conventions such as MARPOL 73/78 and the 1972 London Dumping Convention.

## 3. Maria Teresa Mosquete Pol, *The Protection of the Sea in Spain*

### Introduction

The importance of the sea for mankind has been constant throughout history, for economic as well as cultural and social reasons. The sea has been a source of fishing and energy resources, a means of communication among distant continents, and an ideal environment for recreational and sports activities. Until recently, there was little concern expressed for the quality of waters of the marine environment and of the resources contained therein.

The Stockholm Conference of 1972 was of prime importance in creating public awareness and inspiring environmental protection legislation. The Conference Declaration asserted the fundamental right to an environment suitable to enjoy a certain quality of life and the obligation of preserving and protecting the environment for current and future generations. With regard to the marine environment, the Stockholm Declaration provides that "States shall take all possible steps to prevent pollution of the seas by substances that are liable to create hazards to human health, to harm living resources and marine life, to damage amenities or to interfere with other legitimate uses of the sea".

This international awareness of the need to protect the marine environment led to many legislative efforts in European countries and in international bodies. Because some navigational waters are located near and others far from the shoreline and concentrated areas of pollution stem from highly varied origins, different legal approaches have been adopted. All countries have national legal regulations to protect their territorial waters, coexisting with international treaties and agreements that aim to protect international waters. Between 1972 and 1976, most international agreements to protect marine waters were signed, the first directive of the EEC on protection of the aquatic environment issued, and new national legislation was adopted in Spain.

Many international treaties exist that aim to protect the sea from different types of pollution; some of them have special significance for Spain. The 1972 London Anti-Dumping Convention, ratified by a large number of countries, has adopted resolutions that set restrictions on the burning of waste at sea, prohibit dumping industrial wastes as of 31 December 1995 and temporarily prohibit the dumping of radioactive waste in the Atlantic trench. A working group was created in November 1992 to propose amendments to the treaty and add the prohibitions agreed to in the different resolutions.

To the London Convention must be added the MARPOL agreement, the 1971 Oslo Convention for the Prevention of Marine Pollution by Dumping from Ships and Aircraft, the 1974 Paris Convention for the Prevention of Marine Pollution from Land-Based Sources, and the 1992 Paris Convention for the Protection of the North East Atlantic Marine Environment. The last named agreement was signed on 22 September 1992 with the purpose of fully protecting the marine environment, replacing the Oslo and Paris Conventions. The new treaty attempts to reduce or eliminate the sources of pollution that can affect the sea either directly or indirectly by way of rivers or the atmosphere. The treaty was inspired by the UNCED meeting held in Rio de Janeiro in June 1992 and thus incorporates the precautionary and polluter pays principles.

Compared to the earlier agreements, the new Paris Treaty contains important innovations: it provides the possibility of making legally binding decisions and it includes an obligation to provide information to the public on the status of the marine environment, the activities which may affect it and the measures taken to comply with the treaty. Four annexes regulate land-based pollution (annex I), dumping and incineration of wastes from ships (annex II),[51] prevention and elimination of pollution caused by exploration and exploitation of the seabed (annex III) and monitoring the quality of the marine environment (annex IV). The regional seas agreements for the protection of the Mediterranean also have significant impact on Spain. Finally, the two Brussels Conventions on Civil Liability and Compensation for Oil Pollution Damage must be mentioned.

---

[51] The treaty generally prohibits the dumping of low and medium grade radioactive wastes, with a fifteen-year transition period accorded the United Kingdom and France as of 1 January 1993.

Evaluation of the implementation of international maritime agreements indicates that the treaties aimed at combating accidental oil pollution have had some success in reducing the number of oil tanker accidents. Similarly, treaties prohibiting dumping from ships have been useful in convincing states to halt using this traditional method to eliminate industrial wastes. On the other hand, treaties and protocols on land-based pollution have had a negligible effect. The last conclusion indicates the need for devising national measures to combat this form of marine pollution.

### Spanish Law

Spain is a country surrounded by the sea, comprised of a peninsula and islands. Its culture, its tradition of seafaring trade dating back to the Phoenicians, and its seafood cuisine, make the sea an essential factor in its life. Many legal provisions thus seek to protect the sea and its resources from the harmful consequences of human activities.

The Spanish Constitution, approved in 1978, establishes in Article 45 the right of all persons to have the benefit of an environment suitable for their development as individuals and, as a counterpart thereto, the obligation to preserve the environment. Unlike some European constitutions, there is little detail on the factors comprising the concept of the environment, although it is obvious that the sea and its resources are included.

The second paragraph of Article 45 states that the public authorities shall see to the rational use of all natural resources for the purpose of protecting and restoring the environment. The task that is entrusted to the public authorities is reinforced in the third section of the same Article, which calls for criminal or administrative penalties for those who violate the obligation set forth in the preceding paragraph, as well as for violation of the obligation to repair environmental damage caused.

The Constitution thus authorizes criminal, civil and administrative legislation to correct, repair and penalize assaults on the marine environment. This is logical because the Constitution prevents access to the Constitutional Court to citizens to enforce Article 45 directly. The right to the environment can only be invoked in the Courts of Common Pleas when implementing laws and regulations have been violated.

The reference to the sea implied in Article 45 is coupled with express mention in Article 132 of the Constitution. The latter provision includes the marine environment in its mention of state-owned properties in the public domain, specifically the coastal waters, beaches, territorial waters, the natural resources of the commercial fishing area, and the continental shelf.

The concept of offences against the environment was first included in the Spanish Penal Code in 1983. It is included in Article 347(a) under the heading "hazardous offences in general". The article sets forth the penalty of close arrest, from one to six months in prison, and a fine of up to five million pesetas, for anyone who, violating the laws and regulations protecting the environment, gives rise to or carries out emissions or releases into the atmosphere, soil or inland or sea waters that seriously endanger the public health or can seriously endanger the living conditions of plants or animals.

The maximum penalty shall be imposed when any of the following circumstances takes place:

— clandestine operation of an industry;

— disobeying express orders from the administrative authority to correct or cease the polluting activity;

— presentation of false data regarding the environmental aspects of the industry;

— hindrance of the inspection activity of the Administration;

— when the acts previously described were to give rise to a risk of a deterioration of catastrophic proportions.

Reference to laws and regulations protecting the environment makes this principle a standard penal provision.

Article 347(a) does not in itself determine the criminal nature of an activity. In cases in which serious harm is caused to the environment, it is necessary to prove that one or more provisions of different environmental laws and the regulations developing them have not been followed.

The coexistence of penal and administrative penalties for punishing the same conduct and the impossibility of imposing them jointly based on the principle *non bis in idem* makes it necessary to determine the boundaries of penal law and administrative law. The Constitutional Court has repeatedly stated its opinion that the enforcement of one or another of these sets of laws shall be based on the seriousness of the conduct in question.

In spite of the fact that dumping of pollutants at sea is one of the most important environmental problems for Spain, there are a minimal number of sentences handed down in enforcement of Article 347(a), based on failure to comply with administrative regulations restricting or prohibiting such dumping.

## The Coastal Law 22/1988 of 28 July 1988

The need to devise national measures in conjunction with international treaties, to control land-based threats to the marine environment, was the motive for the Spanish Coastal Law 22/1988 and the regulations developing the law.

Spain has almost eight thousand kilometres of coastline, a quarter of which are beaches. The coasts are the most densely populated areas of the country. Thirty-five per cent of the inhabitants live on the coast, and this proportion increases considerably in summer, particularly on the Mediterranean coast. Most basic industries are also located in this area.

Spanish coastal waters receive two thousand direct industrial dumps and almost five hundred municipal dumps. The diversity of origins of marine pollution and the variety of geographic conditions require legislative solutions to protect the marine environment.

The Coastal Law is aimed at protecting the seas and land properties in the public domain, a concept which takes in the coastline and the estuaries, the territorial waters, the inland waters, the natural resources of the commercial fishing area and the continental shelf. The Act combines coastal planning principles and water quality protection principles, although it concerns mainly the land environment. Nevertheless, it is evident that adequate protection of the coastline involves an improvement in the marine environment.

On public lands, the Act creates a mandatory protection area of one hundred metres calculated from the seashore, in which all housing construction, intercity roads, activities entailing the destruction of sandy areas and the dumping of raw sewage is prohibited. This represents a major step forward compared to prior legislation which restricted this area to twenty metres, and under which a variety of environmental damage was committed, especially in the form of construction of immense blocks of apartments and buildings which overshadow the beaches, block the wind and airborne shifts of sand, and which generate a flow of intensive and polluting motor traffic around them.

In the protected area, dumping of both solid waste and debris and of untreated sewage is prohibited. This is not the case for dumping carried out in the area of public lands. Although sea dumping of solid waste and debris is prohibited, the dumping of other products is not expressly banned, but must be submitted for prior authorization from the administration. The authorization will be granted only when specific requirements are met:

— the applicant must prove the impossibility of using any alternative solution for the elimination or treatment of the material to be dumped;

— the materials to be dumped must not contain any substances which may represent a greater than admissible harm or hazard to human health and to the natural environment;

— they should not cause any significant alteration in the receiving medium; and

— an assessment of the effects of the dumped products on the environment should be performed.

To ensure efficient protection of the seas, the administration has the power:

— to prohibit, in specific areas, certain industrial processes which can give off waste that risks more than acceptable levels of pollution;

— to modify dumping permits when the circumstances change that gave rise to their approval.

The law contains the "polluter pays" principle. Actually, a tax is charged on the dumping of pollutants, the amount of which is set in terms of the amount of pollutants. This is collected by the administration which granted the authorization and is put toward operations for cleaning and improving the quality of the waters.

Monitoring and control of both illegal and authorized dumping is the responsibility of the Regional Government Administrations, although there may be some exceptions to this general rule, in which case responsibility lies with the State Administration. In conjunction with preventive measures, which are directly aimed at the protection of the sea, there are sanctions which have an indirect deterrent effect, changing behaviour through the fear of punishment.

Unauthorized dumping of sewage in the sea may be sanctioned in two ways, either under the administrative code or the penal code. The Coastal Act categorizes the unauthorized dumping of sewage as a serious offence, and sanctions the infraction with a monetary fine of up to fifty million pesetas.

Finally, the Coastal Act imposes an obligation on the polluter to replace and restore things to their previous state, and when this is not possible, which is obvious in the case of dumping, those responsible for the violation must pay the compensation set by the administration in accordance with the law.

### The National Ports and Merchant Marine Law 27/1992 of 24 November 1992.

According to data from 1990, 86 per cent of all Spanish imports and 69 per cent of all Spanish exports, in tons, passed through mercantile ports in Spain. More than one quarter (27.6 per cent of the importing and 12.8 per cent of the exporting) was done by private shippers. This indicates the importance of the merchant marine and sea transport to the country's economic development. At the same time, the heavy seaport traffic makes it necessary to devise means of protecting the marine environment.

The National Ports and Merchant Marine Law does not explicitly mention environmental protection among the objectives of the law; however, many of its provisions have this aim, both with regard to port activities and those carried out by the merchant marine.

The law is solely applicable to the ports relevant to the public interest, which are those managed by the State and in which trading activities are carried out. Thus, pleasure boat harbours, havens of refuge and other ports not of a mercantile nature, the management of which falls to regional authorities, are not within its scope.

Under the law, the dumping of pollutants of any type from ships or from platform vessels is prohibited. All potentially polluting waste accumulated on board must be unloaded on land and deposited in containers, facilities or tanks set aside for this purpose by the port authorities. In turn, the dumping of pollutants from ships or platform vessels of any type in waters over which Spain has authority, outside ports, must meet the requirements of international agreements.

All dumping into the sea from land requires a permit from the competent administration. Permits are to be granted in accordance to the provisions of the Coastal law. For the purpose of preventing and combating possible spills, the obligation is set forth for oil refineries, chemical plants and chemical storage and distribution facilities having oil compound loading or unloading terminals in port areas to possess the suitable facilities for collecting and treating polluting oil waste.

As for Merchant Marine policy, the law sets forth protection of the marine environment as one of its objectives. Spanish shipping companies are obligated to have civil liability insurance to cover any liability with which they may be charged in their shipping operations, in the terms which are set by the government in keeping with regulations according to the normal coverage in this sector on the international market.

Likewise the Government is to determine the cases in which foreign ships sailing through the restricted commercial fishing area (EEZ), the contiguous zone, the territorial waters or inland waters in Spain must have civil liability insurance coverage for any civil liability which may be imputed thereto in the course of the sailing thereof, as well as the extent of the coverage.

# C. Documents

*1. Convention for the Prevention of Marine Pollution by Dumping from Ships and Aircraft,*
Oslo, 15 February 1972.

...

### Article 3

The Contracting Parties agree to apply the measures which they adopt in such a way as to prevent the diversion of dumping of harmful substances into seas outside the area to which this Convention applies.

### Article 4

The Contracting Parties shall harmonize their policies and introduce, individually and in common, measures to prevent the pollution of the sea by dumping by or from ships and aircraft.

### Article 5

The dumping of the substances listed in Annex I to this Convention is prohibited.

### Article 6

No waste containing such quantities of the substances and materials listed in Annex II to this Convention as the Commission established under the provisions of Article 16, hereinafter referred to as "the Commission" shall define as significant, shall be dumped without a specific permit in each case from the appropriate national authority or authorities. When such permits are issued, the provisions of Annexes II and III to this Convention shall be applied.

...

### Article 10

The composition of the waste shall be ascertained by the appropriate national authority or authorities in accordance with the provisions of Annex III to this Convention before any permit or approval for the dumping of waste at sea is issued.

...

### Article 15

1. Each Contracting Party undertakes to ensure compliance with the provisions of this Convention:

    a. by ships and aircraft registered in its territory;

    b. by ships and aircraft loading in its territory the substances and materials which are to be dumped;

    c. by ships and aircraft believed to be engaged in dumping within its territorial sea.

2. [as amended by the Protocol of 5 December 1989] Each Contracting Party undertakes to issue instructions to its maritime inspection vessels and aircraft and to other appropriate services to report to its authorities any incidents or conditions on the high seas [or in that part of the sea beyond and adjacent to the territorial sea under its jurisdiction in accordance with international law] which give rise to suspicions that dumping in contravention of the provisions of the present Convention has occurred or is about to occur. That Contracting Party shall, if it considers it appropriate, report accordingly to any other Contracting Party concerned.

3.  Each Contracting Party shall take in its territory appropriate measures to prevent and punish conduct in contravention of the provisions of this Convention.

...

### Article 17

It shall be the duty of the Commission

a.  To exercise overall supervision over the implementation of this Convention;

b.  To receive and consider the records of permits and approvals issued and of dumping which has taken place, as provided for in Articles 8, 9 and 11 of this Convention, and to define the standard procedure to be adopted for this purpose;

c.  To review generally the condition of the seas within the area to which this Convention applies, the efficacy of the control measures being adopted, and the need for any additional or different measures;

d.  To keep under review the contents of the Annexes to this Convention, and to recommend such amendments, additions or deletions as may be agreed;

e.  To discharge such other functions as may be appropriate under the terms of this Convention.

### Article 18

1.  The Commission shall draw up its own Rules of Procedure which shall be adopted by unanimous vote. The Government of Norway shall call the first meeting of the Commission as soon as practicable after the coming into force of this Convention.

2.  Recommendations for modifications of the Annexes to this Convention in accordance with Article 17(d) shall be adopted by a unanimous vote in the Commission, and the modifications contained therein shall enter into force after unanimous approval by the Governments of the Contracting Parties.

## 2. OSCOM Decision 89/1 of 14 June 1989 on the Reductions and Cessation of Dumping Industrial Wastes at Sea

The Contracting Parties to the Oslo Convention agree:

1.  that the dumping of industrial wastes in the North Sea shall cease by 31 December 1989, and in other parts of Convention waters by 31 December 1995, except for inert materials of natural origin, and except for those industrial wastes for which it can be shown to the Commission through the Prior Justification Procedure (PJP) both that there are no practical alternatives and that the materials cause no harm in the marine environment.

...

4.  to take measures to encourage and promote:
    — the modification of industrial processes in such a way as to reduce and eliminate the amount of waste generated;
    — the recycling of wastes or the re-use of them in other industries;
    — the treatment of wastes on land;
    — the further development of alternative and environmentally sound means of disposal (e.g. by promoting appropriate scientific and technical research; by economic incentives); ...

## 3. Convention for the Prevention of Marine Pollution from Land-Based Sources, Paris, 4 June 1974

### Article 1

1. The Contracting Parties pledge themselves to take all possible steps to prevent pollution of the sea, by which is meant the introduction by man, directly or indirectly, of substances or energy into the marine environment (including estuaries) resulting in such deleterious effects as hazards to human health, harm to living resources and to marine ecosystems, damage to amenities or interference with other legitimate uses of the sea.

...

### Article 3

For the purpose of the present Convention:

a. "Maritime area" means the high seas, the territorial seas of Contracting Parties and waters on the landward side of the base lines from which the breadth of the territorial sea is measured, extending, in the case of watercourses up to the freshwater limit unless otherwise decided under Article 16 of the present Convention;

b. "Freshwater limit" means the place in the watercourse where, low tide and in period of low freshwater flow, there is an appreciable increase in salinity due to the presence of sea-water.

c. "Pollution from land-based sources" means the pollution of the maritime area:

    i. through watercourses,

    ii. from the coast, including introduction through underwater or other pipelines,

    iii. from man-made structures placed under the jurisdiction of a Contracting Party within the limits of the area to which the present Convention applies.

### Article 4

1. The Contracting Parties undertake:

    a. to eliminate, if necessary by stages, pollution of the maritime area from land-based sources of substances listed in Part I of Annex A to the present Convention.

    b. to limit strictly pollution of the maritime area from land-based sources of the substances listed in part II of Annex A to the present Convention.

...

### Article 5

1. The Contracting Parties undertake to adopt measures to forestall and, as appropriate, eliminate pollution of the maritime area from land-based sources by radioactive substances referred to in Part III of Annex A of the present Convention.

...

### Article 8

No provision of the present Convention may be interpreted as preventing the Contracting Parties from taking more stringent measures to combat marine pollution from land-based sources.

...

## Article 11

The Contracting Parties agree to set up progressively, and to operate within the area covered by the present Convention, a permanent monitoring system allowing of:
— the earliest possible assessment of the existing level of marine pollution;
— the assessment of the effectiveness of measures for the reduction of marine pollution from land-based sources taken under the terms of the present Convention.

...

## Article 15

A Commission made of representatives of each of the Contracting Parties is hereby established. The Commission shall meet at regular intervals and at any time, when due to special circumstances it is so decided in accordance with the rules of procedure.

...

## Article 17

The Contracting Parties, in accordance with a standard procedure, shall transmit to the Commission:

a. the results of monitoring pursuant to Article 11.

b. the most detailed information available on the substances listed in the Annexes to the present Convention and liable to find their way into the maritime area.

The Contracting Parties shall endeavour to improve progressively techniques for gathering such information which can contribute to the revision of the pollution reduction programmes adopted in accordance with Article 4.

## Article 18

...

3. The Commission shall adopt, by unanimous vote, programmes and measures for the reduction or elimination of pollution from land-based sources as provided for in Article 4, and for scientific research and monitoring as provided for in Articles 10 and 11 and the decisions under Article 16c.

Such programmes and measures shall commence for, and be applied by, all Contracting Parties two hundred days after adoption, unless the Commission specifies another date.

Should unanimity not be attainable, the Commission may nonetheless adopt a programme or measures by a three-quarters majority vote of its members. Such programmes or measures shall commence for those Contracting Parties which voted for them two hundred days after their adoption, unless the Commission specifies another date, and for any other Contracting Party after it has explicitly accepted the programme or measures which it may do at any time.

...

## Article 19

Within its competences, the European Economic Community is entitled to a number of votes equal to the number of its member States which are Contracting Parties to the present Convention.

The European Economic Community shall not exercise its right to vote in cases where its member States exercise theirs and conversely.

*4. Convention on the Protection of the Marine Environment of the Baltic Sea Area,* Helsinki, 11 March 1992.

...

### Article 3

1.  The Contracting Parties shall individually or jointly take all appropriate legislative, administrative or other relevant measures to prevent and eliminate pollution in order to promote the ecological restoration of the Baltic Sea Area and the preservation of its ecological balance.

2.  The Contracting Parties shall apply the precautionary principle, i.e., to take preventive measures when there is reason to assume that substances or energy introduced, directly or indirectly, into the marine environment may create hazards to human health, harm living resources and marine ecosystems, damage amenities or interfere with other legitimate uses of the sea even when there is no conclusive evidence of a causal relationship between inputs and their alleged effects.

3.  [Use of best environmental practice and best available technology]

4.  The Contracting Parties shall apply the polluter-pays principle.

...

### Article 7

1.  Whenever an environmental impact assessment of a proposed activity that is likely to cause a significant adverse impact on the marine environment of the Baltic Sea Area is required by international law or supra-national regulations applicable to the Contracting Party of origin, that Contracting Party shall notify the Commission and any Contracting Party which may be affected by a transboundary impact on the Baltic Sea Area.

2.  The Contracting Party of origin shall enter into consultations with any Contracting Party which is likely to be affected by such transboundary impact, whenever consultations are required by international law or supra-national regulations applicable to the Contracting Party of origin.

3.  Where two or more Contracting Parties share transboundary waters within the catchment area of the Baltic Sea, these parties shall cooperate to ensure that potential impacts on the marine environment of the Baltic Sea Area are fully investigated within the environmental impact assessment referred to in paragraph 1 of this Article. The Contracting Parties concerned shall jointly take appropriate measures in order to prevent and eliminate pollution including cumulative deleterious effects.

...

### Article 13

1.  Whenever a pollution incident in the territory of a Contracting Party is likely to cause pollution to the marine environment of the Baltic Sea outside its territory and adjacent maritime area in which it exercises sovereign rights and jurisdiction according to international law, this Contracting Party shall notify without delay such Contracting Parties whose interests are affected or likely to be affected.

2.  Whenever deemed necessary by the Contracting Parties referred to in paragraph 1, consultations should take place with a view to preventing, reducing and controlling such pollution.

3. Paragraphs 1 and 2 shall also apply in cases where a Contracting Party has sustained such pollution from the territory of a third state.

## Article 14

The Contracting Parties shall individually and jointly take, as set out in Annex VII, all appropriate measures to maintain adequate ability and to respond to pollution incidents in order to eliminate or minimize the consequences of these incidents to the marine environment of the Baltic Sea Area.

## Article 15

The Contracting Parties shall individually and jointly take all appropriate measures with respect to the Baltic Sea Area and its coastal ecosystems influenced by the Baltic Sea to conserve natural habitats and biological diversity and to protect ecological processes. Such measures shall also be taken in order to ensure the sustainable use of natural resources within the Baltic Sea Area. To this end, the Contracting Parties shall aim at adopting subsequent instruments containing appropriate guidelines and criteria.

## Article 16

1. The Contracting Parties shall report to the Commission at regular intervals on:

    a. the legal, regulatory, or other measures taken for the implementation of the provisions of this Convention, of its Annexes and of recommendations adopted thereunder;

    b. the effectiveness of the measures taken to implement the provisions referred to in sub-paragraph a of this paragraph;

    c. problems encountered in the implementation of the provisions referred to in sub-paragraph a of this paragraph.

2. On the request of a Contracting Party or of the Commission, the Contracting Parties shall provide information on discharge permits, emission data or data on environmental quality, as far as available.

## Article 17

1. The Contracting Parties shall ensure that information is made available to the public on the condition of the Baltic Sea and the waters in its catchment area, measures taken or planned to be taken to prevent and eliminate pollution and the effectiveness of those measures. For this purpose, the Contracting Parties shall ensure that the following information is made available to the public:

    a. permits issued and the conditions required to be met;

    b. results of water and effluent sampling carried out for the purposes of monitoring and assessment, as well as results of checking compliance with water-quality objectives or permit conditions;

    c. water-quality objectives.

2. Each Contracting Party shall ensure that this information shall be available to the public at all reasonable times and shall provide members of the public with reasonable facilities for obtaining, on payment of reasonable charges, copies of entries in its registers.

...

## Article 19

1. The Baltic Marine Environment Protection Commission, referred to as "the Commission", is established for the purposes of this Convention.

2. The Baltic Marine Environment Protection Commission, established pursuant to the Convention on the Protection of the Marine Environment of the Baltic Sea Area of 1974, shall be the Commission.

3. The chairmanship of the Commission shall be given to each Contracting Party in turn in alphabetical order of the names of the Contracting Parties in the English language. The Chairman shall serve for a period of two years, and cannot during the period of chairmanship serve as a representative of the Contracting Party holding the chairmanship.

   Should the chairman fail to complete his term, the Contracting Party holding the chairmanship shall nominate a successor to remain in office until the term of that Contracting Party expires.

4. Meetings of the Commission shall be held at least once a year upon convocation by the Chairman. Extraordinary meetings shall, upon the request of any Contracting Party endorsed by another Contracting Party, be convened by the Chairman to be held as soon as possible, however, not later than ninety days after the date of submission of the request.

5. Unless otherwise provided under this Convention, the Commission shall take its decisions unanimously.

···

### Article 23

1. Except as provided for in Paragraph 2 of this Article, each Contracting Party shall have one vote in the Commission.

2. The European Economic Community and any other regional economic integration organization, in matters within their competence, shall exercise their right to vote with a number of votes equal to the number of their member states which are Contracting parties to this Convention. Such organizations shall not exercise their right to vote if their member states exercise theirs, and vice versa.

···

### Article 26

1. In case of a dispute between Contracting Parties as to the interpretation or application of this Convention, they should seek a solution by negotiation. If the Parties concerned cannot reach agreement they should seek the good offices of or jointly request mediation by a third Contracting Party, a qualified international organization or a qualified person.

2. If the Parties concerned have not been able to resolve their dispute through negotiation or have been unable to agree on measures as described above, such disputes shall be, upon common agreement, submitted to an *ad hoc* arbitration tribunal, to a permanent arbitration tribunal, or to the International Court of Justice.


*5. Act on Prohibition of Dumping of Wastes in Water,*
17 December 1971. SFS 1971:1154 (Swedish Collection of Law, 1971, no. 1154) (Excerpts)

1. Within the Swedish territorial sea, wastes, either solid, liquid or gas, may not be discharged (dumped) from ships, aircraft or other transport means. Dumping may not occur from the Swedish ships or aircraft in the high seas either. Wastes which are intended to be dumped in the high seas may not be transported out of the country.

3. The Government or the authority which the Government appoints may grant dispensation from section 1 if dumping can be carried out without causing nuisance from the environmental protection point of view. Dispensation may be conditional.

4. The authority which the Government appoints shall be responsible for the enforcement of the law and of the conditions and regulations which will be adopted according to the law. The said authority has the right to get, upon request, those information and documents which are required for the enforcement of the law.

   In order to enforce the law, the authority has the right to enter the transport means, the place or the area which are used in connection with dumping, and has the right to make investigation on the place.

5. The one who has wilfully or through negligence

   1. breaches against requirements in section 1;

   2. disregard conditions or regulations which will be announced in accordance to section 3 will be convicted to fines or prison up to one year.

## 6. Act on Measures against Vessel Source Pollution, 5 June 1980 SFS 1980:424 (Swedish Collection of Laws, 1980, no. 424) (Excerpts)

### Chapter 1. Introductory provisions

1. This law contains provisions concerning prohibition of vessel source pollution, reception of harmful substances from vessels, vessel design as well as supervision and other measures in order to prevent or limit vessel source pollution.

### Chapter 2. Prohibition of Vessel Source Pollution

1. Provisions in this chapter apply to those discharges of harmful substances from the vessel which is originated from or has connection to the normal operation of the vessel.

2. Within the Swedish territorial seas and the Baltic Sea Area outside those seas, oil may not be discharged but should be kept on board or be delivered to the oil-reception facilities.

3. The Government or the authority that the Government appoints adopts regulations concerning prohibition of discharge of other harmful substances from vessels.

4. If, as a result of an accident, harmful substances discharge of which is prohibited will be emitted from a vessel, the discharge shall be limited as far as it is possible.

### Chapter 3. Reception of Polluted Balance Water or Tank Waste Water

1. Facilities for reception and management of oily balance water or tank waste water shall exist in those places within the Swedish territory where oil is unloaded or oil tankers are repaired. The ones who unload the oil or carry out the reparation shall see to it that there exist necessary reception and management facilities.

2. No fee shall be charged for the facilities concerning reception and management of oily balance water or tank waste water.

### Chapter 4. Vessel's Design

1. The Government or the authority that the Government appoints adopts regulations

concerning the vessel's design, equipments and operation in order to prevent or limit water pollution and issue certificates which demonstrate that these regulations have been observed.

### Chapter 9. Liability, etc.

1.  The one who has violated the provisions of Chapter 2, sections 2 and 4 or violated the regulations which are adopted in accordance with Chapter 2, sections 2 and 3, shall be convicted to fines or a prison of up to 2 years if the penal code has not provided for higher sanctions.

### Chapter 10. Miscellaneous

1.  This law is applicable to Government ships operated for non-commercial purposes only to the extent that the Government decides.


## 7. Greece, Law 743/1977 on Protection of the Marine Environment, 13 October 1977

### Article 1

### Definitions

For the implementation of the provisions of the present law, the terms set forth have the following meaning:

(a)  "Waste" The thrown away liquids, either by shore installations or by industries, containing or not residue of the substances used or produced by them.

(b)  "Discharge" Residues of any nature either solid or semi-liquid thrown away by vessels, tankers, or shore installations.

(c)  "Disposal" The emission or spillage of any substance into the sea.

(d)  "Authority" Central Port Authorities, Port Authorities, Sub-Port Authorities.

(e)  "Dispersants" Every chemical substance properly approved as fit to neutralize pollution.

(f)  "Installations" Oil refineries, oil companies, shipyards, ship-repairing units, industries, and plants of any kind situated near the coast and using those substances for their functional needs or having an important and direct influence to the marine environment.

(g)  "Reception facilities" The shore or floating installations of any kind used or to be used for the reception and further disposal from vessels and tankers of residue, oil mixtures, toxic and poisonous substances, cargo residues, sewages, and generally every substance or object either thrown away or spilled into the sea which may cause pollution, according to the meaning of paragraphs (p) and (q) of this article.

(j)  "Sewages" The liquids thrown away in general through the draining system of vessels, tankers, and installations.

(i)  "Mile" Nautical mile consisting of one thousand eight hundred and fifty-two metres.

(k)  "Oil" Any type of petroleum including crude oil, fuel oil, solid oil residue, oily discharge products of distillation, as well as any other type, notwithstanding its chemical composition, is specially defined by the Convention as oil.

(l)  "Oily mixture" Any mixture containing oil as same is defined by the present law or the "Convention".

(m) "Vessel" Any craft or floating craft excluding tankers, self propelled or towed.

(o) "Tanker" Any craft or floating craft in general which is specially defined by the "convention" as tanker, or notwithstanding the definitions of same, it is used in its bigger part for the transportation of oil either self propelled or towed, or for the storage of same.

(p) "Pollution" The presence in the sea water of any substance which adulterates the physical condition of sea water or renders same dangerous for human health or for live animals and flora of the sea and in general being inconsistent to the purported uses.

(q) "Conventions" All conventions ratified by Greece and being in force together with their Protocols, Annexes, and Addenda which refer to marine pollution and in general regarding the protection of the marine environment.

(r) "Recommendations" The recommendations addressed by the International Organization to the Governments of their State Members to take measures for the protection of the marine environment.

### Article 2

### Scope of application of the law

1. The present law applies in case of pollution of:

   (a) the ports and coasts of the country and the Greek territory waters by installations or vessels and tankers under Greek or foreign flag.

   (b) the open seas by vessels and tankers under Greek or foreign flag, without prejudice to the provisions of the Conventions in force.

2. War vessels and auxiliary vessels used by the war fleet, as well as state vessels in general, excluding those used for commercial purposes, without taking into consideration their flag, must, while they are within the Greek jurisdiction, apply the same measures as to the ones provided for in the provisions of the present law in order to avoid the pollution of the sea.

### Article 3

### Prohibiting provisions

1. It is prohibited:

   (a) the disposal in ports, coasts, and territorial waters of waste of any nature, sewages, and discharge which may cause pollution of the sea.

   (b) the discharge into the open seas of oily and other pollutant substances which may cause pollution as provided for in the "conventions".

2. The discharging into the sea of any substances by coastal or other installations is only allowed following a permission accorded pursuant to the provisions in force and if there is no danger of pollution.

### Article 4

### Obligations of vessels and tankers

1. Vessels and tankers, arriving at Greek ports or calling at anchorages or bays for loading must:

   (a) deliver the oily mixtures and waste of any nature to the reception facilities indicated by the authority.

   (b) deliver the residue of the carried poisonous and toxic substances according to the instructions of the authority. An index of the substances which are prohibited to be thrown into the sea is fixed by a Ministerial Decision taking always into consideration the International Conventions in force.

2. Such compliance is certified according to the provisions contained in specific Ministerial decisions.

3. Tankers, in addition to the obligations contained in para. 1, must, before loading, proceed to gas freeing, unless they are going to load a similar to the previous cargo.

4. Vessels or tankers which have disposed their residue of any nature as indicated by the authority are exempted from the requirement of para. 1, and tankers, even if they have not proceeded to such disposal, if they are equipped by sufficient means of process and separation or load top system, according to the provisions of the "convention".

5. The Authority prohibits vessels and tankers to sail until the disposal of waste and their oily mixtures, as well as the poisonous residues and toxic substances and discharges, if they are bound to sail for ports where disposal facilities do not exist. Vessels and tankers which, due to the nature of their voyages, are expected to call soon at Greek ports and their Captain undertakes the obligation to dispose the waste and mixture immediately after their arrival.

6. Presidential decrees issued following a Ministerial proposal may impose that tankers calling at Greek ports, anchorages, or bays must be equipped with the means and materials provided in art. 6 para. 1 of the present law and at a quantity specially indicated for this case. They may also provide for the discharge of this obligation if a special institution is established and which will undertake to combat possible pollution during their passage or their stay at a Greek port, anchorage, or bay and for any reasons whatsoever.

## Article 5

### Obligations of installations

1. Installations used for oil transfusions or for ship repairs must dispose oil reception facilities, residue and oily mixtures, non clean ballast, and of other pollutant substances.

2. The capacity and the power of said reception facilities must be such as to cover the needs of the vessels serviced by them and without any delay.

3. The installations must, during their operation, take all necessary measures to avoid pollution.

4. The establishment, expansion, or modification of sea baths installations is only allowed following the permission of the Authority and following the consent of the Health Services which will be granted after the checking of the sea water and only if, under the responsibility and care of the installation, these installations have the means to combat incidents of pollution of a small importance. The so required means will be defined by a Ministerial decision.

5. Sea-baths installations which operate pursuant to the existing regulations must, within six months as from the entering into force of the present law, obtain the permission provided for in the preceding paragraph. They must also have such equipment in order to provide in every case sufficient cleaning of the produced sewages, as well as to neutralize pollution incidents of a small importance, as may be defined by the authority.

6. If from the inspections carried by the Health Services it is proved that pollution of the waters of an area has been increased to a dangerous level for the public health, the licence of the sea-baths installation is revoked and its further use for swimming is prohibited by the Authority. The prohibition is recalled and the permission is granted again if, following a

new inspection by the Health Authority, it is ascertained that pollution of waters dangerous to the public health has disappeared.

## Article 6

### Oil transfer process

1. During the loading or discharge of oil or fueling at an installation of a capacity over 150 tons, the following measures must be taken either under the care and responsibility of the vessel or by the installations.

    (a) a floating barrier of an approved Ministry type is extended within the area so that the possible oil leakage during the above works is safely limited within the barrier.

    (b) to exist in readiness appropriate means for the sucking up suction and in general for the collection of the effused portion of oil.

    (c) the required portion of dispersants of an approved by the Ministry type is disposed according to the needs, in order to confront oil leakage or its derivatives.

2. Persons liable to the obligations of the preceding paragraph may be discharged from same following a decision of the Authority, if the observation of these obligations has been undertaken by a state or private institution which is deemed appropriate for the confrontation of the risks from oil pollution.

3. In case that the works provided for in para. 1 are taking place at installations of a capacity less than 150 tons, then the measures to be taken are fixed by a decision of the Authority.

4. In case that a ship is going to call from abroad at a Greek port in order to load or to discharge oil, then she must, under the supervision of the captain or the agent of the vessel, advise the local Port Authority at least 24 hours before the arrival regarding:

    (a) her last port of call abroad

    (b) the portion and the nature of the cargo to load or to discharge

    (c) the portion of oily residue or non clean ballast.

...

## Article 8

### Additional obligations for tankers

Ministerial Decisions published in the Government Gazette may impose:

(a) the smallest distances of passage of loaded or unloaded tankers from the nearest coast, the compulsory route of same, and, in general, measures referring to the sea passage of tankers in order to avoid pollution of areas of a major interest of the national economy.

(b) the prohibition of calling of a tanker for loading or discharge at a Greek port or bay the subdivision of which or its construction does not comply with the provisions of the "Convention" or other international Conventions ratified by Greece.

(c) the prohibition of calling of large tankers within areas if, due to their tonnage, the manoeuvres may become difficult, or if danger to cause pollution due to accident is increased, as well as the obligatory pilotage of tankers during their passage from the above areas for a better security.

## Article 9

### Reception facilities

1. The terms and conditions to approve floating reception facilities are determined by Ministerial decisions.

## Article 10

### Existing and new installations

1. Installations which exist and operate when the present law will come into force are subject to the provisions contained herein and to the Presidential decrees and Ministerial decisions to be issued pursuant to the present law, as well as the provisions in force regarding the disposal of waste and discharge.

2. In order that new installations are established or for the expansion or amendment of the existing ones, a prior permission for the disposal of waste and discharge is required, according to the relevant provisions in force.

3. If, due to the size, nature, or activity of the installations, a general danger for the change of the marine environment exists, then a special report is submitted by the interested persons to the competent authority regarding the unfavourable effect for the environment.

## Article 11

### Obligations of persons liable for pollution

1. In case of pollution or of an obvious or imminent danger of same, the captain of the vessel, the person in charge, or the manager of the installation, as well as any authorized persons, are obliged to take all the appropriate measures to avert, to limit, or offset said pollution, reporting forthwith the event to the competent Authority or the Ministry.

2. The Authority, as soon as will be informed for an incident of pollution or an obvious or imminent danger of same, takes any adequate measures to limit and to avert the consequences deriving therefrom, informing at the same time the captain or the shipowner or his legal representative and, in their absence, his agent or other competent person, and, in case of installations, the owner or the person having the financial control of same.

    The Authority may use and coordinate private facilities and apply for the help of other similar Organizations or private enterprises which dispose the necessary means and the required practice in order to confront incidents of the sort.

...

4. The use of the facilities belonging to Organizations or to individuals is effected under the supervision of the Authority, and all pertinent expenses are borne either by the vessel or the installation, as well as anyone who instigates the pollution.

## Article 12

### Securing of claims

1. The person who has negligently caused pollution is liable to restore damage due to pollution, as well as for the expenses incurred to avert or minimize same, jointly with the above person they are liable in whole.

    (a) In case of vessels and tankers, the captain, the shipowner, the charterer, the manager of the vessel in Greece, and, for vessels and tankers owned by companies (*sociétés anonymes*), also the president of the board of directors, as well as the managing director.

    (b) In case of installations, the owners or the beneficial owner and, if this is owned by a company, the president of the board of directors and the managing director, and in general the person representing such installation.

2. The Courts of the place where the pollution occurred or one of the ports where the vessel arrived and, in case of pollution of the open sea and of non calling of the vessel at a Greek port, the Courts of Piraeus have the jurisdiction to hear the claims deriving from para. 1.

Article 13

Sanctions

1. Offenders of the present Law, the "Convention", as well as of the Presidential decrees and ministerial decisions, are subject to the following penal, administrative, and disciplinary sentences:

(a) Penal sanctions

(1) Persons willfully causing pollution are liable to imprisonment of at least 3 months. If from their act danger of damage may be caused to persons or property, then they are sentenced to imprisonment of 1 year at least.

(2) Persons negligently causing the above acts are subject to imprisonment. These may be relieved from any sentence if they willfully minimize the pollution and avert every possible damage or if, due to the early announcement to the Authorities, they might contribute to the neutralization of the pollution, bearing in the same time all relevant expenses.

(b) Administrative sanctions

(1) Persons liable for pollution of the sea or coasts are, following a decision of the competent Authority, sentenced to a fine which may amount up to eight hundred thousand drachmas (800.000).
In case of continuation of the pollution, the Authority may impose a fine of three hundred thousand drachmas (300.000) for every day of that exceeding the fixed period for restoration.
In case of considerable pollution, the Minister of Mercantile Marine imposes a fine up to fifty million drachmas (50.000.000).

(c) Disciplinary sanctions

If the persons liable for the pollution are Greek seamen, these are also liable to the disciplinary proceedings pursuant to the provisions of the Fifth Part of the L.D. 187/73 "Re: Code of Public Maritime Law", being sentenced to a temporary disqualification to exercise their job.

2. The above sanctions, if the case may be, are cumulatively imposed.

. . .

Article 15

Establishment of regional anti-pollution stations

1. Regional preventive and anti-pollution stations are established in the ports of Piraeus, Thessaloniki, Patra, Elefsis, Kavala, and Chania.

2. The duties of these stations are to supervise the vessels when oil loading and discharge is taking place, the checking of delivery of the oily mixtures and other polluting substances, to the existing reception facilities.
Further, they have the duty to inspect either by floating or shore means the sea environment, by special troops all pollution incidents as well as every service vested to them pursuant to the Ministerial decisions provided for in para. 5 of this article.

## 8. Bulgaria, Act of 8 July 1987 Governing the Ocean Space of the People's Republic of Bulgaria

### ARTICLE 3

The aims of the present Act are: to protect the rights and legitimate interests of the People's Republic of Bulgaria in the ocean space, as well as its sovereignty and security; to use the Black Sea for peaceful purposes and in the interest of co-operation with coastal and other States; to facilitate maritime communications and guarantee the safety of navigation; to develop scientific research, exploit marine resources, protect the marine environment and maintain the ecological balance.

...

### ARTICLE 16

(1) The territorial sea of the People's Republic of Bulgaria includes the zone contiguous to the coast and internal waters having a breadth of 12 nautical miles, measured from the baselines.

...

### ARTICLE 19

(1) Ships of all States shall enjoy the right of innocent passage through the territorial sea in accordance with the provisions of the Act and international law.

### ARTICLE 20

Passage of a foreign ship through the territorial sea shall be prejudicial to the peace, good order and security of the People's Republic of Bulgaria when the ship engages in any of the following activities:

...

8. Any act of wilful and serious pollution of the marine environment.

...

### ARTICLE 23

(1) Foreign ships exercising the right of innocent passage through the territorial sea and stopped in internal waters, ports and roadsteads shall be required to respect the rules of navigation as well as immigration, customs, financial, health, phytosanitary, veterinary and port regulations and any regulations relating to protection of the environment.

### ARTICLE 24

Foreign nuclear-powered ships and ships carrying nuclear, radioactive, toxic or other dangerous substances shall, when passing through the territorial sea, carry the necessary documents and observe precautionary measures established for such ships by international agreements.

...

### ARTICLE 31

(1) In the case of damage caused by an act of quasi delict occurring in internal waters or in the territorial sea as well as in the case of damage resulting from a violation of the rights and jurisdiction of the People's Republic of Bulgaria in the contiguous zone, on the continental shelf or in the exclusive economic zone, national jurisdiction shall be applicable and the Bulgarian courts shall be competent in matters of litigation.

...

## ARTICLE 46

The exclusive economic zone of the People's Republic of Bulgaria shall extend beyond the limits of the territorial sea to a distance not greater than 200 nautical miles from the baselines from which the breadth of the territorial sea is measured.

...

## ARTICLE 48

In the exclusive economic zone, the People's Republic of Bulgaria shall exercise:

2. Its exclusive rights and its jurisdiction with regard to:

   (a) The construction and use of artificial islands, installations and structures;

   (b) Marine scientific research;

   (c) The protection of the marine environment.

...

## ARTICLE 51

When it is reported that a foreign non-military ship situated within the limits of the exclusive economic zone has violated or intends to violate the sovereign rights and jurisdiction of the People's Republic of Bulgaria, the relevant provisions of article 45 shall be applicable.

...

## ARTICLE 58

(1) The discharge, introduction and dumping of any kind of solid or liquid waste and of substances harmful to human health or to the living resources of the sea by vessels, aircraft, platforms or other artificial structures, or from land-based sources, shall be forbidden, as shall any other pollution of the marine environment in the internal waters and the territorial standards recognized by the People's Republic of Bulgaria.

## ARTICLE 59

(1) If there are clear grounds for believing that a non-military vessel navigating through the internal waters, territorial sea and exclusive economic zone has violated the provisions of this Act, or any other regulation or international agreement concerning the prevention of pollution of the marine environment, the relevant sections of the Environmental Protection Committee, the Ministry of Transport and the Committee on the Peaceful Utilization of Atomic Energy may take appropriate steps, including:

   1. Requesting the master of the vessel to provide necessary information for purposes of investigating the incident;

   2. Inspecting the vessel, if there is reason to believe that the information was incomplete;

   3. Seizing the vessel for purposes of prosecution.

(2) The bodies referred to in the preceding paragraph may, if necessary, request the collaboration of the services of the Ministry of the Interior and the Ministry of Defence.

## ARTICLE 60

(1) In the event of serious pollution of the marine environment in the internal waters, territorial sea or exclusive economic zone of another State, the People's Republic of Bulgaria shall provide legal assistance at the request of that other State by undertaking interrogations and inspecting the documents or technical condition of the vessel responsible for the pollution

when it is lying in a port or in the internal waters of that country. Such assistance shall also be provided at the request of the flag State.

(2) The legal assistance referred to in the preceding paragraph shall be provided on the basis of reciprocity.

## ARTICLE 61

In the event of a breakdown, damage or other maritime casualty in the ocean space of the People's Republic of Bulgaria which presents a danger of pollution of the marine environment or coastline or which might harm related interests, the Ministry of Transport, in collaboration with the organization concerned, shall take all necessary steps to prevent, reduce or eliminate the danger.

## ARTICLE 62

The services of the ministry of transport shall prohibit a vessel lying in internal waters, in a port or roadstead from sailing if the vessel's technical condition is such that compliance with the standards for the prevention and reduction of pollution of the marine environment adopted by the people's republic of Bulgaria cannot be guaranteed.

## ARTICLE 63

In the course of drilling operations, exploratory work or other activities relating to the development and exploitation of natural resources in the ocean space of the People's Republic of Bulgaria, the Environmental Protection Committee and the Ministry of Transport shall monitor compliance with the measures adopted for the prevention of damage or release of oil or other pollutants and for the immediate elimination of their effects.

## ARTICLE 64

Where there is a real danger that pollution in the ocean space of the People's Republic of Bulgaria might spread into the waters of another coastal State on the Black Sea, that State shall be informed thereof through the diplomatic channel.

...

## ARTICLE 67

The disposal of loads of earth and of sediment in ocean space shall be authorized solely in places designated by the Ministry of National Defence in coordination with the Ministry of Transport and the Environmental Protection Committee.

...

## ARTICLE 76

(1) A fine of between 500 and 100,000 ... shall be imposed on:

1. Anyone committing or permitting a violation of the provisions of article 58, paragraph 2;

2. The master of a foreign non-military vessel who orders or permits commercial fishing in the exclusive economic zone.

(2) The penalty provided for in the preceding paragraph shall be imposed on the master of a foreign non-military nuclear-powered vessel or of a foreign non-military vessel transporting nuclear or radioactive substances or other hazardous or toxic substances who enters into internal waters without authorization or does not submit to the inspection of documents, to dosimetric inspection or to any other inspection on board the vessel in connection with protection of the environment.

# Questions and Problems

1. What are the advantages and drawbacks of regional arrangements for protection of marine environment in northern Europe?

2. Given the fact that institutional organs for the protection of the North Sea and the Baltic Sea lack the necessary powers to effectively implement related conventions, what other measures can be taken to enhance the implementation at a national level?

3. In what way does protection of marine environment in northern Europe differ from the marine protection in other parts of Europe? Can similar legal arrangements be devised for different European seas?

4. Can the increased influence of the EC in the protection of the North Sea and the Baltic ultimately lead to the weakening of the role of the regional conventions?

5. Is compensation for ecological damage excluded from liability conventions? The definition given in Art. I(5) of the 1969 Convention provides that "pollution damage means loss or damage caused outside the ship carrying oil by contamination resulting from the escape or discharge of oil from the ship, wherever such escape or discharge may occur, and includes the costs of preventive measures and further loss or damage caused by preventive measures". Why is it so difficult to get agreement on international liability for pollution damage?

6. Why is the legal technique of framework conventions so often used for international regulation concerning protection of the marine environment?

7. How extensive are the measures necessary to control land-based pollution?

8. Can pollution of the marine environment be controlled only by prohibitions? What is the role of norms concerning:
   — the construction of ships
   — qualifications and training of personnel
   — rules of navigation
   — loading and unloading of cargo
   — packaging and storage of cargo?

9. Analyze and comment on the definition of pollution given in UNCLOS article 1(4).

10. Are states obliged to assist another state which is the victim of a major accident polluting the marine environment?

11. Can Spain dictate the type of insurance policy required of ships navigating in its exclusive economic zone? What other measures may it take to protect the marine environment of this region?

# Bibliography

Dupuy, R. J. & Vignes, *Traité du Nouveau Droit de la Mer* (Paris, 1985).

Freestone, D. & Ijlstra, T. (eds.), *The North Sea: Perspectives on Regional Environmental Cooperation* (1990).

Freestone, D. & Ijlstra, T. (eds.), *The North Sea: Basic Legal Documents on Regional Environmental Cooperation* (1991).

Fitzmaurice, M., *International Legal Problems of the Environmental Protection of the Baltic Sea* (1992).

Kindt, *Marine Pollution and the Law of the Sea* (1988).

Lebullenger and Le Morvan, *Le Communauté Européenne et la Mer* (1990).

Soni, R., *Control of Marine Pollution in International Law* (1985).

Starace, *Diritto Internazionale e Protezione Dell'ambiente Marino* (1983).

CHAPTER IX

# ATMOSPHERIC POLLUTION

## A. Overview

Air pollution has been defined as "the introduction by man, directly or indirectly, of substances or energy into the air, resulting in deleterious effects of such a nature as to endanger human health, harm living resources and ecosystems and material property, and impair or interfere with amenities and other legitimate uses of the environment".[1] This definition adapts the general concept of pollution, focusing on risk or harm from changes in the environment.

The introduction of pollutants into the atmosphere creates multiple effects. The air is essentially a place of transit: gases or particles remain there temporarily and often manifest their impact only after returning to soil, plants, the oceans, lakes or rivers. However, poisonous air also can directly damage living creatures and objects. The two most serious known ecological catastrophes – Bhopal, India, and Chernobyl, Ukraine – produced the greatest number of victims as a result of direct contact with polluting elements in the atmosphere. Finally, it is significant that air pollutants move quickly and cover greater distances than do pollutants in watercourses or the marine environment.

Air pollution has long been considered a threat to human health. Public authorities acted to limit the emission of fumes and to sanction abusive releases well before physical or chemical analyses of gas or particulates were possible. As early as the fourteenth century measures to combat air pollution were enacted. King Charles VI of France forbid in Paris "bad-smelling and nauseating fumes" while in 1306 England's King Edward I issued a royal decree forbidding the use of coal in open furnaces in London. The English law punished first violators by fine, demolished the furnace for a second infraction, and imposed capital punishment in the third instance.

The industrial revolution greatly exacerbated air pollution, motivating, at least in part, the French legislation on dangerous, unhealthy and noxious establishments, regulated by an imperial decree of 15 October 1810. A similar measure was adopted in the English Act of 1921 Concerning Steam Engines.

Air pollution also created problems relatively early in international relations. From the end of the nineteenth century, fumes emitted by a zinc and lead smelter situated in Trail, Canada, some dozen kilometres from the United States border, posed the problem of transfrontier pollution and reparation for the damages it caused. Slightly more than forty years later, an arbitral decision rendered in the *Trail*

---

[1] Article 1(a), Convention on Long-Range Transboundary Air Pollution (Geneva, 13 November 1979).

*Smelter* case became the first and, until now, the only major decision of international jurisprudence announcing the obligation of each State not to cause or allow to be caused transfrontier pollution damage to other states.

With intensification of industrial production, growth in the size of urban communities, and the multiplication of vehicles emitting exhaust fumes, air pollution has taken on serious, even disquieting, proportions. To combat it, initial measures sought to disperse the pollutants through increasing the height of factory smokestacks. The "solution" proved mistaken: emissions taken to higher atmospheric levels were carried considerable distances by air currents, causing long-range pollution damage. As a result, in the 1970s it became clear that air pollution was no longer solely a local phenomenon concerning large cities and industrial zones, but one that affected non-industrial countries and agricultural areas often far from the source. The proportion of atmospheric pollutants of foreign origin grew through the 1980s to reach 92 per cent in Norway, 90 per cent in Switzerland, 82 per cent in Sweden, 77 per cent in the Netherlands, 64 per cent in Denmark. The sources of this pollution lay in the Ruhr, England, Poland, and Czechoslovakia.

Current knowledge of air pollution, in particular its geographic scope, has thus considerably evolved over the decades. It also has undergone transformation in regard to polluting elements and their effects. During the 1970s acidification of Scandinavian lakes by sulphuric rain originating from afar was at the heart of discussions. By 1980, public opinion in Central and Eastern Europe and in Canada turned to the disappearance of forests (Waldsterben) due to pollution. Finally, during the middle of the 1980s concern grew about depletion of the ozone layer. Towards the end of the decade, a new preoccupation arose about changes in the global climate caused by human activities modifying the composition of the atmosphere.

It is evident that this extension, both objective and subjective, in the scope of air pollution has had a major impact on the framework of legal regulation. In particular, the relative importance of national regulations and international norms has altered considerably from that observed twenty years ago. The emphasis increasingly is placed on continental or even global dimensions of the problem of atmospheric pollution. This calls for a deviation from the method used to present other topics, in order to discuss first the principal legal methods found in national legislation. Community law on air pollution has become so integrated into the national laws of member states that the two topics will be treated together. Subsequently, international norms will be presented.

## 1. *National and Community Regulation*

The legal norms applied by the different European States to combat air pollution contain significant variations from one country to another. Emphasis can be placed on emission controls or on air quality, on particularly polluted zones or on those that demand special protection, on local pollution, or on medium- and long-distance impacts.

There also exist parallels, particularly in fixing norms mandated by the EC or inter-governmental organizations, or under the influence or in execution of international treaties. It is thus useful to compare schematically the different legal techniques and mechanisms developed in environmental law to combat air pollution.

*a. Legislation Concerning the Protection of the Environment in General, Applicable to Air Pollution*

As has been discussed above, one of the most widely adopted legal techniques for combating pollution and nuisances consists in submitting all pollution-causing activities to prior authorization. Existing licensing regimes have played a great role in the prevention of air pollution.[2] The titles of these different legislative instruments by themselves demonstrate the diversity of concepts and methods utilized to address comparable if not identical situations. However, these texts have similarities, notably concerning the definition of the activities covered. These are generally enumerated in a list, although the criteria of classification – such as size of the installation, the nature and quality of the emissions and their effect on the environment, the feasibility of preventing pollution by using an alternative production process, and the likely risk of a major accident – are not always the same.

The provisions of general EC directives have brought a certain harmonization, at least concerning some procedural aspects. In particular, Directive 85/337/EEC of 27 June 1985[3] concerning assessment of the effects of certain public and private projects, generally requires impact assessment. Similarly, the "Seveso" directive,[4] relating to the risks of major accidents of certain industrial activities, applies to activities which risk causing major air pollution in case of accident.

*b. Special Measures Concerning Air Pollution*

In addition to general regulations, most European countries have specific legislative instruments concerning air pollution. If there is a conflict between the two types of dispositions, the specialized texts take precedence over general provisions, according to a well-established principle of law.

Framework laws are frequently used for this subject.[5] They involve a law of general scope, defining the concepts and the fundamental principles of action to be

---

[2] Austria: Industrial Code of 1973; Belgium: General Regulation for the Protection of Work, of 11 February 1946; Denmark: Environmental Protection Act of 13 June 1973 [Act 372/1973]; France: Law on Classified Installations of 19 July 1976 modified 3 July 1985; Greece: Framework Act for the Environment 1650/86 [GG 160/A/16.10.86]; Ireland: Public Health (Ireland Act) 1878, the Alkali Works Regulation Act 1906, the Local Government (Sanitary Services) Act 1962, and the Local Government (Planning and Development) Acts of 1963 and 1976; Italy: National Health Act of 27 July 1934 [Royal Decree 27 July 1934, no. 1265]; Netherlands: Nuisance Act [Stb. 1986, 374]; United Kingdom: Alkali Works Regulation Act 1906, Health and Safety at Work Act 1974.

[3] O.J. no. L 175 of 5 July 1985. See the text, *supra*, p. 86.

[4] 82/501/EEC of 24 March 1982, O.J. no. L 230 of 5 August 1982, modified 19 March 1987, O.J. no. L. 85 of 28 March 1987). See the text, *infra*, p. 442.

[5] Austria: Law on industrial combustion plants, in force 31 March 1981; Belgium: Law of 28 December 1964 relating to combating air pollution; France: Law of 2 August 1961 concerning combating air pollution and odors (the "anti-smog" law) and Presidential decree of 23 November 1967; Germany: Federal Air Pollution Control Act of 1974; Ireland: Air Pollution Act 1987; Luxembourg: Law of 21 June 1976 to combat air pollution; Netherlands: Air Pollution Act of 1970; Spain: Air Protection Act (38/72); United Kingdom: Clean Air Act of 1956 and 1968.

undertaken, as well as designating the areas in which more detailed regulation should be adopted. The Belgian Act of 28 December 1964 on combating air pollution provides an example. Article 1 of the Act states:

> The Crown is empowered to take all appropriate measures to prevent or combat air pollution, especially:
> 1. to prohibit specified forms of pollution;
> 2. to regulate or prohibit the use of appliances or installations which can cause pollution;
> 3. to stimulate or regulate the use of appliances or installations intended to prevent or combat pollution.

Framework laws are completed and implemented by laws or decrees of application that detail the scope in the determined fields. Most often, the detailed regulation which completes these texts is elaborated by the executive or by local authorities. Such is the case, generally, with emission standards and air quality objectives and for establishing special regulations applicable to special zones. This fashion of proceeding streamlines the process of adapting norms in light of needs that vary according to place and pollution levels. The latter, in particular, can evolve rapidly for better or worse.

### c. Special Regulations Aimed at Particular Activities or Installations

There are fundamental differences in regulations directed at fixed sources and those aimed at movable pollution sources (e.g. automobiles). The first type of regulation is the most important.

Most frequently, fixed sources above certain dimensions are submitted to authorization or licensing according to precise criteria and are subject to regular monitoring. In addition to fixing emission standards, which can be general or specific, different rules can be established for different installations or different types of installations. Thus, in Italy, a distinction is made between industrial installations, which should be equipped with pollution-reducing mechanisms and be situated outside inhabited zones, and non-industrial installations – commercial enterprises, workshops, and homes – which can be placed in inhabited areas but whose activities are strictly regulated. Such regulations may concern, in particular, gas and particulate emissions, the kind and amount of fuels, and the height of chimneys. In France, a distinction is made between heating installations on one hand and industrial installations on the other. For the latter, limit values on pollutants are the object of technical circulars from the central administration, aimed at harmonizing the prefectorial decisions authorizing these activities. The solutions adopted are particular to each branch of industry, within the minimum standards established by Community law. Similarly, in Belgium a royal decree of 8 August 1975, imposes on industrial combustion facilities emission standards for sulphur oxides and for dust, foresees measures concerning the utilization of certain fuels and regulates the height of chimneys. Other distinctions can be made between pollution coming from domestic heating and other sources (Luxembourg), between large and small installations (Germany) and between already existing enterprises and new ones, it being understood that the first should have a specific time period to comply with pollution controls (Germany).

Several Community directives have been adopted in order to harmonize the applicable methods. The first, 84/360 of 28 June 1984[6] concerns pollution coming from industrial installations. It makes obligatory for certain categories of installations a system of prior authorization by competent national authorities. These industries include: energy (mines, oil refineries), production and working of metals and minerals, chemical industries, waste treatment, and certain paper mills. Licences are not to be delivered unless the enterprise has adopted appropriate measures to prevent air pollution and the limit values for emissions and air quality are respected. Specially protected zones can be established. Demands for authorization and decisions of competent authorities should be placed before the affected public and environmental impact statements can be required. When pollution is capable of affecting other EC states, they should be informed and can request consultations.

A subsequent regulation, adopted 24 November 1988, relates to limiting emissions into the air of certain pollutants coming from large fuel-burning installations[7]. Energy producing industries are covered, if their thermal power is equal to or greater than fifty megawatts. Emission levels and the corresponding percentages of reduction also have been fixed for sulphur dioxide and for nitrous oxide: each State should establish programmes for their application. Any licence to operate a new installation must assure strict respect for emission standards for these two substances, as well as for dust. States undertake to assure surveillance of the implementation of these measures, including at the cost of the operator, and should submit to the EC Commission periodic reports on the results of implementing national programmes to reduce polluting emissions.

Air pollution caused by waste incinerators has attracted the attention of the EC. Directive 89/369 of 8 June 1989[8] concerns the prevention of air pollution from new municipal waste incinerators. It establishes technical parameters which should be applied prior to delivery of an operating licence. The scope of this directive will be gradually extended to cover existing installations, with all regulated by 1 December 2000.

Motor vehicles using hydrocarbons are the primary movable source of air pollution. Their exhaust fumes contribute in large measure to urban air pollution, but also, in reduced percentages, to the destruction of forests. Specific rules are necessary that differ from those applicable to fixed installations, rules that are easy to identify and monitor. Two methods are in widespread use: the first establishes technical requirements for motor vehicles themselves; the other establishes standards for petrol.

The first motor vehicle requirements were those adopted by the Economic Commission for Europe of the United Nations and were not specifically aimed at air pollution. In 1958 the Commission sought to facilitate international trade by establishing uniform standards for automobile equipment and parts, today accepted in all

[6] O.J. no. L 188 of 16 July 1984.
[7] 88/609/EEC, O.J. no. L 336 of 7 December 1988.
[8] O.J. no. L 163 of 14 June 1989.

European countries. Among the measures adopted were several aimed at creating "cleaner" exhaust by imposing engine standards concerning carbon monoxide (CO), nitrous oxides, and unburned petrol emissions.[9]

In the framework thus established, national legislatures have introduced different measures, such as the adoption of emission norms and regular monitoring of automobiles (Austria: 1967 Motor Vehicle Law). Means of transportation not demanding the use of fossil fuels are under investigation, in some cases subsidized by public funds: e.g. the development of electric cars or, more long term, engines utilizing hydrogen.

The second method of combating air pollution caused by vehicles with combustion engines consists of improving the quality of fuels they use. During the 1980s there was considerable opposition between those concerned with environmental protection and those representing industrial interests, along with advocates of fast cars, over requiring drivers to utilize lead-free petrol, with the technical modifications of automobiles that this required. Within the EC, several stages have been foreseen for the gradual reduction in the amount of lead in petrol; the most recent directive establishes a limit of 0.013 grams of lead per litre of petrol, with older cars permitted to continue using leaded petrol.

Finally, in addition to the two direct methods already discussed to combat air pollution from movable sources, less direct methods are sometimes used. Reducing speed limits on freeways to 130 or 120 kilometres per hour, adopted in all European countries except Germany, plays an important role because pollution levels rise with increased speed. The utilization of local forms of mass transit, as well as increasing access to and use of long distance trains, are also among important measures to keep in mind.

### d. Provisions Relating to the Emission of Specific Pollutants

Among European countries important differences exist in the regulation of emissions causing air pollution. Certain states have practically no rules in this field (Ireland, Luxembourg) and rely upon EC norms. In other countries, norms apply only in certain regions or to certain installations (Italy).

In contrast, some states have elaborated complete regulations based on limiting polluting emissions. For example, in Germany, the thirteenth federal order on emissions determines limit values for sulphur dioxide ($SO_2$), nitrous oxide ($NO_x$), carbon monoxide (CO), dust, and heavy metals, as well as fluoride and chloride compounds emitted by industrial heating plants of more than fifty megawatts. A transition period extending to 1 April 1993 has been granted to older facilities. For all licensed industrial and commercial facilities, "technical instructions relating to pure air" dating from 1986 establish emission limits for inorganic substances and for those of some one hundred organic substances. England has regulated the emissions of a large series of pollutants such as sulphur gases, particulates and dust, nitrogen oxide, vinyl chloride, heavy metals (zinc, arsenic, lead, mercury and its compounds,

---

[9] Regulations 15, 20, 24, 47, and 49 annexed to the Geneva Accord of 20 March 1958; affirmed by EC Directive 70/220 of 20 March 1970, O.J. no. L 76 of 6 April 1970.

cadmium, beryllium, fluoride and its compounds) (Health and Safety, Industrial Air Pollution Regulation, 1983.)

## e. Establishment of Air Quality Standards

Air quality standards establish the maximum allowable limits for substances in the atmosphere, rather than controlling emissions directly. It is the method most widely adopted by the EC. Community air quality standards have been established for sulphur,[10] lead[11] and for nitrogen dioxide.[12]

While implementing Community directives, not all states favour defining air quality objectives (Belgium, France, Luxembourg). Among countries that have from the beginning utilized this method, different techniques are adopted. In Ireland, basic air quality is sought through dispersion of pollutants using high smokestacks. This is also the case in Italy, but there are few uniform norms enacted for the entire country; in general, regional authorities set the height of smokestacks for industrial installations, taking into account local circumstances.

In Germany the Technical Instructions regarding Clean Air (TA–Luft) contain air quality standards for thirteen pollutants. Some norms apply to administrations, who can impose them on industries through the licensing process. Other norms establish levels of dangerousness and are recommendatory. The persistence of the pollutant in the atmosphere is equally taken into account. In all cases, air quality standards require the existence of procedures to determine air quality.

## f. Zoning

Often, regulatory measures to combat air pollution are taken locally or regionally, due to particular conditions. These rules can differ considerably from one area to another. Legislative instruments may establish zones in general laws (e.g. Danish law no. 372 of 13 June 1973 concerning the protection of nature and the environment, art. 61–2, revised by law no. 288 of 26 June 1975, art. 4). Most often, however, zones are foreseen in special norms. The objective is always to adapt standards, as much as possible, to geographic realities. Two tendencies can be observed. First, activities causing the greatest pollution are forbidden or limited in determined zones: protected nature sites (Luxembourg, Law of 11 August 1982), dense population zones (as governed by a series of rules established in France for Paris, Marseille and regions of the north and the Rhone area). Second, special rules establish particular zones where the air is particularly polluted; in these zones, stricter emission standards or air quality standards may be set (e.g. zones in Belgium for Antwerp, Brussels, Charleroi, Ghent, and Liege; zones "A" and "B" in Italy; "smoke control areas" in England).

In the Belgian zones, for example, fuel for heating purposes is subject to special conditions: peat, lignite, non-smokeless coal and waste materials cannot be burned;

---

[10] Directive 80/779/EEC of 15 July 1980, O.J. no. L 229 of 30 August 1980.
[11] Directive 82/884/EEC of 3 December 1982, O.J. no. L 378 of 31 December 1982.
[12] Directive 85/203/EEC of 7 March 1985, O.J. no. L 87 of 27 March 1985.

the sulphur content of liquid fuels and the volatile sulphur content of solid fuels may not exceed 1 per cent by weight. Other dispositions can call for the preparation of plans to combat certain forms of pollution, measures of surveillance and monitoring, measures to take during emergencies, and limitations on polluting emissions, including halting certain activities in case of massive pollution.

## 2. *The International Dimensions of Air Pollution*

It has been noted earlier that the most important jurisprudential precedent in the field of transfrontier pollution concerns a case of air pollution, decided well before the ecological era. The Trail smelter in Canada caused damage to agricultural lands in the United States by releasing into the air up to 350 tons daily of sulphurous smoke beginning in 1896. Some arrangements for indemnification of victims were made, but in 1925 it became necessary to undertake a collective action. In 1927 the United States government officially began negotiations with Canada, resulting in an agreement to submit the dispute to an international arbitral tribunal. The latter delivered its final judgment on 11 March 1941, concluding that

> under the principles of international law ... no State has the right to use or permit the use of its territory in such a manner as to cause injury by fumes in or to the territory of another or the properties or persons therein, when the case is of serious consequence and the injury is established by clear and convincing evidence.[13]

It is on analogous bases, especially those announced in the Stockholm Declaration, that a body of norms has been created that can be considered as customary international law, or, at least for some of them, as emerging customary law. These have been discussed above in regard to freshwaters but they also are applicable to transfrontier air pollution.

The first multilateral international instrument concerning air pollution appeared only in 1979. Air pollution was long considered as essentially a local phenomenon; the acidification of Scandinavian lakes made evident the necessity of multilateral action and led to the Convention on Long-Range Transboundary Air Pollution, adopted in Geneva on 13 November 1979, by European states, the United States and Canada.

The Convention is based on traditional international law but opens new avenues for the construction of international environmental law. Even in the initial definitional section, certain legal difficulties are apparent:

> long-range transboundary air pollution: means air pollution whose physical origin is situated wholly or in part within the area under the national jurisdiction of one State and which has adverse effects in the area under the jurisdiction of another state at such a distance that it is not generally possible to distinguish the contribution of individual emission sources or groups of sources.[14]

[13] Trail Smelter Arbitration, 3 U.N.R.I.A.A. 1911, p. 1965.
[14] Article 1, para. 1(b).

It is evident that law, which usually seeks to discover the link of causality between acts causing pollution and the resulting damage, must evolve to deal with this phenomenon where the author of the pollution cannot be identified. The only solution is to seek a global reduction in polluting emissions. To arrive at this point, it is necessary to stimulate inter-state cooperation. For this reason, the Convention obliges states parties to endeavour to limit and, as far as possible, gradually reduce and prevent air pollution, including long-range transboundary pollution. In addition, the contracting parties agree to collaborate in research on air pollution and in the monitoring and study of pollution. They also must consult if a state is suspected of significant pollution to the detriment of other states.

This treaty, which contains few immediately restricting elements for states parties, has had important impact, due to the willingness of a number of parties to improve air quality in Europe. In a relatively short time, a network of ninety air quality monitoring stations has been established, with the participation of twenty-four countries. In addition, some states have agreed to not await the transition period established by the treaty to reduce their emissions. Finally, three protocols have been adopted to complete the terms of the Geneva Convention: the first aims to reduce sulphur emissions by at least 30 per cent as rapidly as possible and at the latest before 1993,[15] the second to stabilize emissions of nitrogen oxide at their 1987 levels,[16] and the third to reduce, also in principle by 30 per cent, emissions of volatile organic compounds or their transboundary fluxes.[17]

This collection of treaty instruments has innovations in substance and in form. The substantive innovation was the adoption of a framework convention with very few obligations, announcing fundamental principles on the subject and inviting states to cooperate to fill in the framework with more precise norms. The other innovation, even more important, derives from the first: states parties initiated a process of continuous negotiations, based on an agreed point of departure, the Geneva Convention. The willingness of some states to accelerate the process and implement their obligations before the time limits also constitutes a new phenomenon in international life.

These new techniques have been utilized to confront a planetary extension of the problem of air pollution, stemming from the need to protect the stratospheric ozone layer. Studies undertaken since the 1970s led to the conclusion in Vienna, 22 March 1985, of a framework treaty providing for systematic cooperation between states, especially in research on the factors which modify or could modify the ozone layer. Little more than two years later, the well-known Montreal Protocol was adopted 16 September 1987. The Protocol designated certain chlorofluorocarbons and halons as responsible, at least in part, for the reduction of stratospheric ozone. Reduction of their production and their consumption was called for by stages, leading to a reduction of 50 per cent by 1999. Immediately after the Protocol was signed, new

[15] Helsinki Protocol of 8 July 1985.
[16] Sofia Protocol of 1 November 1988.
[17] Geneva Protocol of 18 November 1991. The volatile organic compounds are defined as including "all artificial organic compounds, other than methane, that can produce photochemical oxidants by reaction with nitrogen oxides in the presence of sunlight", Art. 1, para. 9.

research discovered the summer "hole" in the ozone layer over Antarctica. Negotiations thus continued and led to the adoption of amendments in June 1990 and November 1992, according to which in the year 1995 all production and consumption of CFCs and certain other substances should cease. Halons should be progressively reduced before 1997. A further innovation saw Northern countries accepting for the first time to financially aid Southern states to comply with the obligations of the Montreal Protocol.

The same techniques appear in the Framework Convention on Global Climate Change, which was signed by 153 states at the 1992 United Nations Conference on Development and the Environment (UNCED). The Convention's objective is to stabilize the concentrations of warming gases in the air, particularly carbon dioxide, methane, and chlorofluorocarbons, at levels that will prevent any dangerous disruption by human agents of the global climate. The Convention announces fundamental principles to govern the matter: some common responsibilities for all countries; other duties that vary according to the level of national development; elaboration of inventories and national programmes to reduce climate changes; transfer of technologies; aid in research, etc. Negotiations should continue to detail the obligations and the charges on different categories of countries of the North as well as of the South. It could eventually lead to the institution of an energy tax.

With these developments, air pollution, the "Cinderella" of environmental law initially limited to local action, has emerged to address the planetary aspects of environmental protection.

# B. Case Studies

1. Jose Juste, *Protection of the Atmospheric Environment by International Law*

The atmosphere constitutes the least stable milieu of the planet. It is also the element of the environment with which the Earth's inhabitants have the closest contact, yet its transparency makes it seem less physically real and more remote than other environmental sectors. The atmosphere is both the most individual and at the same time the most collective possession we have; it could be said to be the singularly genuine "Global Common".

Internationally, protection of the atmosphere has been characterized by intermittent action. It was the subject of one of the rare judicial decisions in the environmental field: the Canada/USA arbitral award of 11 March 1941 in the Trail Smelter case.[18] The decision set a precedent both because of its pioneering character and because of the content of the award. In 1968, the Council of Europe adopted a Declaration of Principles on Air Pollution Control, laying down the broad guidelines for all future action in this area.[19] The Stockholm Declaration, adopted at the United Nations Conference on the Human Environment in 1972, regarded air pollution as one

[18] USA/Canada, ONU. *Reports of International Arbitral Awards*, vol., III, p. 1965.
[19] Resolution 68(4). Text in Rüster, B. Simma, B. *International Protection of the Environment*, New York (Oceana) 1979, vol. XV, p. 7522.

among several forms of pollution and failed to lay down any specific rules concerning it. The subject returned to the international scene with the Convention on the Prohibition of Military or any Other Hostile Use of Environmental Modification Techniques, of 18 May 1977,[20] and above all the Convention on Long-Range Transboundary Air Pollution of 13 November 1979.[21] It was indirectly addressed in the United Nations Law of the Sea Convention of 1982, which considered it one of the sources of marine pollution.[22] Finally, as part of the preparations for the United Nations Conference on Environment and Development (UNCED), a Framework Convention on Climate Change was adopted in New York on 9 May 1992 and opened for signature at UNCED. Protection of the atmosphere also constitutes one of the chapters in Agenda 21, the programme of action adopted at UNCED.

In recent years, the fight against atmospheric pollution has been characterized both by its accelerating tempo and its spread to include all parts of the earth: thus Professor Kiss looks upon atmospheric protection as one example of the globalization of problems in the environmental field.[23] Three problems in particular demonstrate the global concerns: acid rain, depletion of the stratospheric ozone layer, and global climate change threatened by the greenhouse effect.

## 1. Acid Rain

In the mid-1970s people began to become aware of a very serious phenomenon, referred to as "acid rain", that was having serious ecological and economic consequences. Various types of sulphur-containing precipitation caused the acidification of lakes, corrosion of metals and damage to buildings (especially to historic monuments) as well as the destruction of forests.[24]

The main victims of this precipitation, which came principally from other countries and often made its effects felt at a long distance, were the Scandinavian countries. Acidification also was experienced in European countries as a whole, in North America, and in Japan. The substances causing the pollution were mainly sulphuric gases ($SO_2$), but also nitrogen dioxide ($NO_2$) and ozone ($O_3$) resulting from the combustion of hydrocarbons during sunny periods.[25] These pollutants were produced by the activities of industries burning fossil fuels and exhaust gases from vehicles.

---

[20] Fischer, G. "La Convention sur l'interdiction d'utiliser des techniques de modification de l'environnement à des fins hostiles", *AFDI* 1987, pp. 820–36. Sanchez Rodriguez, L. I. "United Nations Convention on the Prohibition of Military or any Other Hostile Use of Environmental Modification Techniques", in Ronzitti, N. *The Law of Naval Warfare. A Collection of Agreements and Documents with Commentaries*, Dordrecht (Nijhoff) 1988, pp. 661–72.

[21] *See infra*, note 27.

[22] UNCLOS, arts. 212, 222.

[23] Kiss, A. Ch. "La protection de l'atmosphère: un exemple de la mondialisation des problèmes", *AFDI*, 1988, pp. 701–8.

[24] Kiss, A. Ch. "Du nouveau dans l'air: des 'pluies acides' à la couche d'ozone", *AFDI* 1985, pp. 814–15.

[25] Fossil-fuel combustion produces carbon dioxide directly, and ozone indirectly, as a result of the interaction of nitrogen oxides and carbon monoxide with sunlight.

### a. The Geneva Convention of 13 November 1979

On 13 November 1979 the Convention on Long-Range Transboundary Air Pollution was signed at Geneva. It entered into force on 16 March 1983.[26] This regional convention, which was promoted by the Conference on Security and Cooperation in Europe (widely referred to as the Helsinki process), and elaborated under the auspices of the United Nations Economic Commission for Europe, is binding on practically every industrialized state in both western and eastern Europe, in addition to Canada, the United States, and the European Community.

The Convention – the normative content of which is rather weak, with a text which is highly flexible – mainly establishes an international framework for research and development issues (Art. 7), the exchange of information (Art. 8), monitoring and evaluation (Art. 9), and the coordination of national policies and strategies designed to combat, as much as possible, the discharge of substances liable to cause long-range transboundary air pollution (Arts. 2 to 4). Each Contracting Party commits itself to working out systems compatible with balanced development for the management and control of air pollution originating in particular from new or rebuilt installations, by using the best available technology which is economically feasible, as well as low and non-waste technologies (Art. 6). In the case of actual or threatened significant risk of long-range transboundary air pollution, the Parties involved agree to hold consultations promptly (Art. 5); nevertheless, the Convention formally excludes (in a footnote to Art. 8) drawing up any rule on State liability for damage.

At the institutional level the Convention establishes an Executive Body, which meets at least once a year, and a small Secretariat. It also puts into effect the "Cooperative Programme for Monitoring and Evaluation of the Long-Range Transmission of Air Pollutants in Europe" (EMEP), which has developed a standardized international network for continuous monitoring and periodic exchange of information on the agreed-upon long-range air pollutants (beginning with sulphur dioxide). At the present time, the network has more than eighty monitoring stations in twenty-two countries.

### b. The four Protocols to the Geneva Convention

One and a half years after the entry into force of the Geneva Convention, a first Protocol was adopted in Geneva on 28 September 1984.[27] It ensured the long term financing of EMEP.

Progress in the reduction of emissions was somewhat slower. On 21–22 March 1984, ten States Parties to the Convention met at Ottawa and adopted a Declaration concerning, in particular, their commitment to reduce $SO_2$ emissions by at least 30

---

[26] Text in 18 *I.L.M.*, 1442 (1979). Kiss, A.Ch. "La Convention sur la pollution atmosphérique transfrontière à longue distance", *Revue juridique de l'environnement*, 1981, pp. 30–5.

[27] Protocol to the 1979 Convention on Long-Range Transboundary Air Pollution on Long-Term Financing of the Cooperative Programme for Monitoring and Evaluation of the Long-Range Transmission of Air Pollutants in Europe. 24 *I.L.M.* 484 (1985).

per cent by the year 1990 as compared with 1980 emission levels. After several preparatory meetings, a second Protocol was signed in Helsinki on 8 July 1985[28] during the third session of the Executive Body. It calls for a reduction by 30 per cent of transboundary sulphur emissions as rapidly as possible and, at the very latest, by 1993. The Helsinki Protocol entered into force in 1987 for eighteen States; unfortunately, it has not yet been ratified by three of the main "exporters" of $SO_2$: Poland, the United Kingdom and the United States.

The problem of nitrogen oxides has been more difficult to solve, not only because – as Russia has pointed out – these substances originally were not mentioned by the Convention, but also because a particularly sensitive source of pollution was targeted in their reduction, namely motor vehicles. Nevertheless, in the wake of Community directives and alarming reports of EMEP, a Protocol was signed on 31 October 1988 in Sofia[29] calling for the reduction of emissions and transboundary fluxes of nitrogen oxides ($NO_x$) from fixed or mobile sources, with the aim of stabilizing them at the 1987 level by the year 1995. Of the twenty-five States signing the Protocol, twelve also made a Declaration stressing their commitment to reduce $NO_x$ emissions by at least 30 per cent by 1988, as compared with any year between 1980 and 1986.

A fourth Protocol combating the emissions of volatile organic compounds (VOC) or their transboundary fluxes was signed in Geneva on 18 November 1991, but was not in force as of June 1992.[30] In the presence of sunlight, VOCs form ground-level ozone, an important element in "smog". The protocol aims to reduce emissions through providing options for states to freeze or reduce their VOC emissions and by requiring the adoption of technology controls for stationary sources, motor vehicles, and products that emit VOCs.

## 2. Depletion of the Ozone Layer

Ozone is an unstable gas composed of three-atom oxygen molecules. Ultraviolet radiation creates ozone by breaking apart the two-atom oxygen that we breathe, although over time ozone naturally tends to return to the more stable two-atom oxygen. This constant process of atmospheric change produces a thin stratospheric ozone layer which acts as a shield protecting all life on earth from ultraviolet radiation.

A disturbing environmental problem was discovered recently when a "hole" in the ozone layer became apparent over the Antarctic region. Based on scientific studies,[31] WMO identified certain halogens derived from carbon, nitrogen and,

---

[28] Protocol to the 1979 Convention on Long-Range Transboundary Air Pollution on the Reduction of Sulphur Emissions or their Transboundary Fluxes by at least 30 per cent. 27 *I.L.M.* 707 (1988).

[29] Protocol to the 1979 Convention on Long-Range Transboundary Air Pollution Concerning the Control of Emissions of Nitrogen Oxides or their Transboundary Fluxes. 28 *I.L.M.*, 214 (1989).

[30] Protocol to the 1979 Convention on Long-Range Transboundary Air Pollution Concerning the Control of Emissions of Volatile Organic Compounds or Their Transboundary Fluxes, Geneva, 18 November 1991, 31 *I.L.M.* 568 (1992).

[31] The first findings about the disturbing effects of CFCs on the ozone layer were made by two scientists from the University of California (Irvine) in 1974: *see* "Molina and Rowland Report", *Nature* 1974, p. 810.

above all, chlorine and bromine, as agents involved in the depletion of the ozone in the stratosphere; in particular, chlorofluorocarbons (CFCs) and halons. The emissions of these substances result from the use of vaporizers (aerosols, foams and sprays), solvents and refrigerants, and perhaps from the use of fertilizers in agriculture (but not from the flight of supersonic commercial aircraft, as was thought at first). Although twenty-five countries manufacture CFCs, they are mainly produced by three large company groups: Du Pont de Nemours (United States), ICI (United Kingdom) and ATOCHEM (France). The search for solutions to this problem could be made easier by such a concentration of production but, according to all indications, some time will elapse before the replacement products already developed can substitute for the CFCs. The principal consumers are the United States (30 per cent), the European Community (30 per cent), Japan (11–12 per cent) and Russia (8 per cent). However, developing countries are becoming more and more dependent on the use of CFCs, especially in the refrigeration chains of which they have need.

### a. The Vienna Convention of 22 March 1985

At the end of the 1970s, UNEP included the issue of ozone depletion in its legal plan of action, considering that it was necessary to have some international regulation in this matter. After five years of preparation and negotiations, which were at times difficult, a diplomatic Conference convened in Vienna adopted the Convention on the Protection of the Ozone Layer, 22 March 1985.[32] The Convention, which entered into force on 22 September 1988, is binding today on forty States in addition to the EC, including most of the producers of CFCs, but not including South Africa, Argentina, Brazil, India, Poland, Romania and former Czechoslovakia.

As with the 1979 Geneva Convention, the Vienna Convention is a framework agreement of international scope, with only slight normative content. Its main purpose is to lay the groundwork for systematic cooperation. It establishes general obligations for Parties, in accordance with the means and capabilities open to each one of them, to take appropriate measures designed to control, limit, reduce or prevent human activities which have or are likely to have adverse effects on the ozone layer (Article 2). This should be done through cooperation in research and systematic observation (Article 3 and Annex I) as well as through an exchange of legal, scientific and technical information (including information of a socio-economic and commercial nature) and the promotion of development and transfer of technology and knowledge (Article 4). Information on the measures adopted should be communicated through the Secretariat to the Conference of the Parties in accordance with the ways and means prescribed thereto (Article 5 and Annex II).

In order to give a more precise content to the action taken for the protection of the ozone layer, the Convention stipulates that the Conference of the Parties shall make provisions for its implementation including the adoption of recommendations for minimizing the release of ozone depleting substances as well as "programmes" for research, systematic observations, scientific and technological cooperation, the

---

[32] Vienna Convention for the Protection of the Ozone Layer. 26 *I.L.M.*, 1529 (1987).

exchange of information and the transfer of technology and knowledge (Article 6). The Conference of the Parties may also adopt additional protocols (Article 8) which will become binding for those Parties to the Convention expressing their consent thereto (Article 17).[33]

### b. The Montreal Protocol of 16 September 1987

In accordance with the provisions of a resolution contained in the Final Act of the Vienna Conference, a Protocol on Substances that Deplete the Ozone Layer was signed in Montreal on 16 September 1987.[34] It entered into force on 1 January 1989. With the aim of combating the harmful global effects of the substances subject to regulation (namely, CFCs 11, 12, 113, 114 and 115 and halons 1211, 1301 and 2402), the Protocol calls for precautionary measures to be taken in order to regulate such emissions in an equitable manner, with the ultimate objective of their elimination on the basis of developments in scientific knowledge, taking into account technical and economical considerations (preambular paragraph 6).

As far as production and consumption are concerned, the Protocol established rather precise measures according to a detailed time schedule which is, however, written in a somewhat cabalistic manner. Taking as a point of reference the 1986 levels, the production and consumption of CFCs was to be frozen by 1 July 1990 and to reduce progressively to 50 per cent of the levels of 1986 by 1999. However, the Protocol did not call for subsequent reductions.

Some exceptions were allowed: developing States which consume less than 0.3 kg of CFCs *per capita* annually were granted a moratorium of ten years in order to conform to the restrictions on production and consumption established by the Protocol (Article 5); the Member States of a regional economic integration organization could jointly satisfy their allocations concerning consumption (case of the EC) (Article 2, para. 8); periods of grace were also allowed to Parties having factories in the course of construction, provided that such facilities were completed before the end of 1990 and that the calculated annual level of consumption of the beneficiary country does not raise above 0.5 kgs *per capita* (case of the USSR) (Article 2, para. 6).

The Protocol also regulated trade between the Parties and with other States. As far as trade with non-Parties is concerned, each Party had to prohibit all imports of controlled substances from non-Party States before 1 January 1990; the Protocol even foresees the possibility of banning the import of products "containing" these substances or "produced with, but not containing" them (Article 4, paras. 1, 3 and 4). From 1 January 1993 on, developing countries with low consumption are no longer permitted to export controlled substances to non-Party States (Article 4, para. 2); as of the same date, the Parties will no longer be allowed to subtract their exports to non-Parties in calculating their levels of consumption (Article 3 (c) in fine).

---

[33] Article 16 of the Convention makes explicit that: "A State or regional economic integration organization may not become a party to a protocol unless it is, or becomes at the same time, a Party to the Convention".

[34] Montreal Protocol on Substances that Deplete the Ozone Layer. 26 *I.L.M.*, 1550 (1987).

States Parties must provide the Secretariat with statistical information on their production, import and export of the controlled substances (Article 7) and cooperate in research, development, public awareness, the exchange of information, and technical assistance (Articles 9–10). The effectiveness of the measures taken by each Party will be evaluated at least once every four years (Article 6). Procedures and institutional mechanisms for determining non-compliance with the provisions of the Protocol and for treatment of Parties found to be in non-compliance (Article 8) are also provided.

Certain Parties to the Montreal Protocol have sought to accelerate their efforts to minimize and prevent the use of ozone reducing substances. On 2 March 1989, the Ministers of the Environment of the European Community decided to reduce as soon as possible, by at least 85 per cent, the level of production and consumption of CFCs.[35] The Canadian Government also announced its decision to eliminate the CFCs within the next ten years, and proposed to the other countries that the target be established of reducing CFCs by at least 85 per cent by 1999. A World Conference on the Ozone Layer which met in London from 5 to 7 March 1989, attended by representatives of 124 States, proposed an accelerated reduction of the use of CFCs (even their total abolition by the year 2000) as well as a new international assistance programme for developing countries. Then, the first meeting of Parties to the Montreal Protocol adopted the Helsinki Declaration of 2 May 1989, stating the agreement to phase out CFCs before the year 2000 as well as halons and other ozone-depleting substances as soon as feasible.[36]

Finally, during the second meeting of the Parties to the Montreal Protocol, held in London from 27 to 29 June 1990, a series of decisions and amendments were adopted with the aim of eliminating the use of CFCs and halons by the year 2001, and reducing methylchloroform and carbon tetrachloride by 100 per cent as compared with the 1989 levels, by the year 2006. It was also agreed to set up a Fund for the protection of the ozone layer, the initial amount of which would be increased once India and China become Parties to the Protocol.

### 3. *The Greenhouse Effect and Climate Change*

The most recent threat to the atmosphere is also the most enigmatic one, because even its reality is sometimes doubted. However, it is certainly the most serious with regard to its potential catastrophic consequences. The phenomenon referred to is the so-called "greenhouse effect", said to be the cause of global warming and climate change.

Throughout the centuries the Earth's climate has been shaped by cosmic forces. The atmosphere, acting in a way like a greenhouse, helps to maintain the stability of the Earth's temperature. At the same time, it absorbs part of the microwave radiation emitted by the Earth and reflects the rest, in this way producing supplementary irradiation. This natural greenhouse effect is possibly increased considerably by human activity which, as a result of the agricultural, industrial and technological

---

[35] *See* text at note 29.
[36] Text in 28 *I.L.M.*, 1335 (1989).

revolutions, is in the process of changing the composition of the atmosphere. The temperatures on the face of the Earth, which have not fluctuated by more than one or two degrees over the past ten thousand years, might in this way be increased in global average by as much as four degrees by the middle of the twenty-first century.[37] If this should happen, we would face the gravest ecological catastrophe in the history of the world.[38]

Although it is not certain that the global warming we are already experiencing is nothing more than a natural climatic fluctuation,[39] scientists are in a position to state that, on the one hand, the emission of certain gases, and on the other hand deforestation, undoubtedly help to produce the redoubtable greenhouse effect. Carbon dioxide $(CO_2)$ contributes to 55 per cent of the global warming, CFCs 24 per cent, methane $(CH_4)$ and nitrogen oxide (NO) 15 per cent, and other gases, the rest. The gases at issue result mainly from the burning of fossil fuels (coal, petrol and natural gas), coming from fixed sources (industry, domestic heating) as well as from mobile sources (aircraft, trains and automotive vehicles). It suffices to recall that these fossil fuels remain today the source of 90 per cent of the energy consumed in the world, in order to understand that the issues at stake have both an ecological dimension and very deep economic and political implications on a global scale. The problem of deforestation, especially if we focus on Amazonia and the other tropical forests, also has important aspects connected with disparities in development and equity among nations.

The first signs of concern over this new problem led to a series of international Conferences on $CO_2$ between 1985 and 1987.[40] The results of these meetings were rather disappointing and led to an international Conference on the Atmosphere in Evolution and its Implications for the Safety of the Globe, held in Toronto from 27 to 30 June 1988.[41] At that time, the United Nations Environment Programme joined its efforts with those of WMO and ICSU in order to study the scientific aspects of the problem. In November 1988, an Inter-governmental Panel on Climatic Change (IPCC) was created, made up of scientific and political experts, and given the task of exploring possible measures to be taken in order to protect the atmosphere.

The United Nations General Assembly adopted, on 6 December 1988, Resolution 43/53 on the Conservation of the global climate for present and future generations of mankind.[42] Although the Resolution did not use the expression "common heritage

[37] Inter-governmental Panel on Climate Change, "Policy-makers Summary on the Scientific Assessment of Climate Change", WMO/UNEP, June 1990.

[38] *See* Kiss, A. Ch. "La protection de l'atmosphère ..." *op. cit.*, p. 706. The risks resulting from sea level rise have been specially feared by small, insular and low-lying coastal States: *Vide* Malta Declaration of 18 November 1989, *Environmental Policy and Law*, 20/1/2 1990, p. 58 and GA Resolution 42/206 of 22 December 1989.

[39] The four warmest years in the last century each occurred in the 1980s, and global warmth in 1988 increased at a record-setting rate. Nanda, V. "Global Warming and International Environmental Law: A Preliminary Inquiry", 30 *Harvard I.L.J.*, 375 (1989).

[40] Villach Conference (PNUE/OMM/ICSU) 1985, Brussels Symposium (CEE) 1986, Bellagio and Villach Seminars 1987.

[41] *See* WMO/OMM, no. 70, 1989.

[42] Text in 28 *I.L.M.*, 1326 (1989).

of mankind" (contained in the original proposal of Malta), its text did state in particular that climate change was a "common concern of mankind" and that it was necessary to adopt promptly the necessary measures to deal with climate change within a global framework. The Resolution approved the setting up by UNEP, in collaboration with WMO and ICSU, of a World Climatological Programme, and it supported the work of the Inter-governmental Panel on Climate Change (IPCC). It requested these institutions to carry out an overall study on the matter and to examine in particular those aspects which might be covered in a possible international convention on the climate.

On 20–22 February 1989, an International Assembly of Political and Legal Experts was held in Ottawa, charged with working out elements to be used in an international agreement for the protection of the atmosphere. The Hague Conference of 10 and 11 March 1989, convened by France, Norway and the Netherlands, went still further: the Final Declaration, adopted by twenty-four States, proclaimed in particular the fundamental duty to do all that can be done in order to preserve the quality of the atmosphere for present and future generations; it also called for the development of new principles of international law including new and more effective decision-making and enforcement mechanisms, such as the developing of a new institutional authority within the framework of the United Nations which would be responsible for defining protection standards, the respect for which would be under the control of the International Court of Justice.[43]

Resolution 15/36, adopted by the UNEP Executive Council on 25 May 1989 reaffirmed the idea of working out a framework convention on the climate.[44] The Council of the European Communities adopted, on 21 June 1989, a Resolution on the greenhouse effect and the Community, declaring the need to conclude an international agreement on climate change issues as well as to reduce the current levels of CFCs by at least 85 per cent as soon as possible, and to promote action with a view to reducing emissions of other greenhouse gases ($CO_2$ in particular) as well as the need to protect forests and the need for reforestation.[45] On 22 December 1989 the UN General Assembly adopted a new resolution on the subject, emphasizing the urgent need to work out a general convention on climate change issues as well as the need to set up international mechanisms for financing and to guarantee access of developing countries to the technologies required.

The Second World Climate Conference was held in Geneva from 29 October to 7 November 1990, attended by delegations from more than one hundred States, in some cases led by their Heads of State or Government (Mrs Thatcher and M. Rocard). The Conference had before it the IPCC report which, although less dramatic than some had imagined, was explicit regarding the need to adopt immediate precautionary

---

[43] Text in 28 *I.L.M.*, 1308 (1989). On 5–6 June 1990, an international Round-table of legal experts in environmental law was held at La Roche-Dieu to consider what further measures should be taken to give effect to the Hague Declaration. See the conclusions of the Round-table drawn up by professor P.M. Dupuy in *Environmental Policy and Law*, vol. 21, number 2, 1991, pp. 61–3.

[44] Text in 28 *I.L.M.*, 1330 (1989).

[45] Text in 28 *I.L.M.*, 1306 (1989).

measures in order to reduce emissions of gases having a greenhouse effect, as well as other measures aimed at stabilizing the climate (reforestation). During the ministerial phase of the Conference, certain Governments (Saudi Arabia, USSR and United States) showed reluctance to adopt concrete measures which would require the establishment of reductions expressed in figures. Nonetheless, other countries, such as Norway, proposed that the example of the EC be followed in deciding to stabilize carbon dioxide emissions before the year 2000 and reduce them by 20 per cent before 2010. The Final Declaration of the Conference contained a compromise solution requesting developed countries to establish either reduction objectives by specific dates, or "feasible national programmes and strategies", which should have a significant effect on the limitation of emissions of $CO_2$ and other gases having a greenhouse effect.

### a. The Framework Convention on Climate Change

The UN General Assembly, in its Resolution 42/282 of 22 December 1987, called a Conference on Environment and Development (UNCED), held in Rio de Janeiro in June 1992. By its Resolution 44/288 of 22 December 1989, it created a Preparatory Committee charged with establishing the agenda, adopting directives on the organization of the Conference and preparing projects which would be reviewed and possibly adopted by the participating States. At the Organization Session (New York, 5–16 March 1990), the Committee elected Mr Tommy Koh (Singapore) as President and decided to establish two working groups. Group I dealt with the protection of the atmosphere, soil management, conservation of biological diversity and promotion of a biotechnology friendly to the environment. Group II was concerned with the protection of the oceans, freshwater and the management of wastes. A third working group, charged with legal and institutional matters, was subsequently established.

As far as the protection of the atmosphere (working Group I) is concerned, States opinion divided. Some showed themselves favourable to drafting a convention of general scope covering all aspects connected with the protection of the atmosphere (transboundary air pollution, depletion of the ozone layer, emissions of gases contributing to modification of the global climate). Other States, whose views have prevailed, preferred to adopt a convention restricted to the problem of climate.

On 21 December 1990 the UN General Assembly adopted a new resolution on the protection of the world climate for present and future generations.[46] The Resolution reflected a desire to carry to conclusion a single process by means of an Inter-governmental Negotiating Committee (INC), in order to prepare a general and effective convention on climate change.

The sought-after convention was adopted on 8 May 1992 in New York and opened for signature during UNCED. Its stated purpose is to stabilize greenhouse gas concentrations in the atmosphere at a level that prevents dangerous anthropogenic interference with the climate system (article 2). The time frame for change should be sufficient to allow ecosystem adaptation, food production and sustainable economic development. States parties must inventory greenhouse gas emissions, formulate

[46] Text in *Environmental Policy and Law*, vol. 21, number 2, p. 76.

development. States parties must inventory greenhouse gas emissions, formulate measures to mitigate climate change, promote and cooperate in the development of new technologies, and take other similar action (article 4). Partly due to the technical dimensions of the problems being discussed, and partly due to their economic, social and political implications, implementation of the Climate Convention will test severely the will of the States to cooperate, especially the most developed among them.

## 4. Conclusions

Atmospheric protection confronts the jurist with problems which in many respects are new. Indeed, the urgent need for an international regulation to protect and save the atmosphere does not find justification in the certainty of the risks but rather in the catastrophic nature of its presumptive effects. International environmental law, which has in the past tended primarily to be "reactive" to issues and problems facing decision makers, should in this case act not only in the name of prevention and precaution but also in the name of anticipation. The accelerated foreseeable rate of atmospheric change (coming about in decades instead of in the course of the ages), as well as the undefined and indiscriminate nature of the damage that can result, help to bring out the urgent need for solutions.

Nevertheless, although the physical phenomena affecting the atmosphere continue to be poorly known as far as their origins and manifestations are concerned, the same cannot be said of the principal activities of man which are at their root, namely the use of fossil fuels, the use of CFCs and halons, and deforestation. Furthermore, most of these activities are interrelated and can produce combined damage through a multiplier effect. Notwithstanding this, where activities which touch the heart of State economic activity and the life styles of the citizens are concerned, the theoretically simplest and the most drastic solutions (reduction of activities causing pollution) are not the easiest to adopt in practice. Thus it will be necessary to consider the application of less radical but more imaginative measures such as gradual recourse to alternative energy sources, incentives to clean production, or – as some fatalist opinions would suggest – adaptation to the transformation of the planet by climate changes.

From the strictly legal point of view, the road that lies ahead is also long. To begin with, it will be necessary wisely to combine techniques of soft law (even ultrasoft law) with strictness in the application of standards which reflect the fundamental interests of the international community as a whole. The protection of the atmosphere which, like the evolution of the climate, is a "common concern of mankind" (GA Resolution 45/53), should be looked upon more and more as a rule of *ius cogens*, obligatorily *erga omnes*. On the other hand, the grave and massive violation of international rules protecting the atmosphere could constitute an international crime on the part of the State responsible (e.g. the case of the intentional setting fire to the oil wells by Iraq).[47] The time-honoured principles of sovereignty,

---

[47] Kirgis Jr, F. L. "Standing to Challenge Human Endeavors That can Change the Climate", 84 *AJIL*, 525–30 (1990).

territoriality and equitable use should undergo extensive revision (even be abandoned) as far as their application to the atmosphere is concerned. To replace them it will be necessary to consider applying new rules which are more adapted to the situation that needs to be controlled. Above all, it will be necessary either to set up a new institutional authority or to strengthen existing institutions if we are to find an effective answer to the challenge of survival which is involved.[48]

## 2. Ludwig Krämer, *The European Community and Atmospheric Pollution*

The terms "environment", "environmental policy" and "protection of the environment" do not appear in the 1957 Treaty of Rome establishing the European Community. Given that the Community has only the limited competence given to it by these treaties, it is not surprising that the first Community measures taken to combat or reduce air pollution arose in the context of the aims of article 100 of the Treaty. This article calls for harmonizing the national legislation of Member States to assure the establishment and functioning of the common market for products and services. For example, Directive 70/220,[49] concerning polluting emissions from automobiles, was adopted in 1970 in the context of a programme to eliminate technical barriers to commercial exchanges between Member States.

This absence of specific competence in the field of the environment led the Community, when it decided in 1972 to develop a Community environmental policy, to adopt Community action programmes which set forth the body of measures, actions and normative texts that the Community institutions proposed to adopt during the four or five years of the programme. With the concern of assuring a free circulation of products, a directive of 1975 fixed the limit of sulphur in diesel fuel,[50] another directive limited the amount of lead in petrol,[51] while directive 70/220 has been modified several times. These directives establish the principle of uniform rules. However, the directive relative to the sulphur content of diesel introduces already the principle according to which Member States should establish zones, in which the amount of sulphur differs taking into account diverse geographic conditions. Directive 78/611 permits Ireland to market petrol whose lead content is greater than that in the rest of the Community. Moreover, it permits Member States to lower the level of lead to 0.15 g per litre, although the Community limit is 0.40 g per litre. These two directives demonstrate the difficulty of establishing uniform rules for the entire Community due to economic variations on the one hand, and environmental considerations on the other hand.

Environmental directives aimed at air pollution establish quality objectives for the entire Community. Such objectives are fixed for sulphur dioxide and particulates,[52]

[48] Kiss, A. Ch. "Environnement et développement ou environnement et survie?", *Journal de Droit International*, 1991, pp. 263–82.

[49] Directive 70/220 of 20 March 1970, O.J. no. L 76, 6 Apr. 1970.

[50] Directive 75/116 of 24 Nov. 1975, O.J. no. L 307, 27 Nov. 1975.

[51] Directive 78/611 of 29 June 1978, O.J. no. L 197, 27 July 1978.

[52] Directive 80/779 of 15 July 1980, O.J. no. L 229, 30 Aug. 1980.

lead,[53] and nitrogen dioxide.[54] Other directives fixing limits have been announced but not formally proposed.

These three directives require the establishment of measuring stations in areas where the concentration of pollutants is considered to be the most heavy. However, they leave to Member States the choice of the precise location where these stations are to be installed. Given that they indicate only in a vague way the criteria determining the number of these stations, there is great variation in the number installed from one state to another. To this must be added the fact that the measuring instruments and the methodology are such that small changes lead to very different results.

Member States have the possibility, in sensitive zones, not to adhere to the limit values fixed by the directives. Such zones should be designated and communicated to the Commission within a certain period following adoption of the directive in question. At the same time, Member States should submit clean-up programmes with a time-table which assures that air pollution is reduced as rapidly as possible and in any case before 1989 (lead), 1993 (sulphur dioxide and particulates) or 1994 (nitrogen dioxide).

Subsequently, it seems apparent that Member States have designated the appropriate zones, but have not established the corresponding programmes designed to assure a progressive improvement in air quality within these zones. As the regular reports on the implementation of the directives and asserted violations are not always transmitted in the time required, supervision of the effective application of the directives remains very difficult. In other words, it is not clear whether the limits set by the directives are exceeded nor, in such cases, where the violations occur.

The "discovery" at the beginning of the 1980s of damage to the forests of central Europe led to a change of direction in environmental policy towards air pollution. As a result, a general directive relating to air pollution produced by industrial installations was adopted.[55] This directive introduces the obligation to obtain specific authorization for new industrial installations which emit pollutants into the air. Any licence should require utilization of the best available technology not involving excessive costs and, in addition, take into account existing value limits. Member States also are required to develop strategies and programmes progressively to adapt existing industrial facilities to the requirements of the best available technology.

In following the lead of this directive, the Council adopted, in 1988, a directive on installations of combustion of fifty megawatts or more.[56] Each new installation must respect the emission norms fixed by the directive for sulphur dioxide, particulates and nitrogen oxides. For existing plants, Member States create and implement programmes aimed at progressively reducing their annual emissions of these elements. The reductions in relation to 1980 and up to the year 2003 are indicated in absolute quantities and in percentages.

53 Directive 82/884 of 3 Dec. 1982, O.J. no. L 378, 31 Dec. 1982.
54 Directive 85/203 of 7 March 1985, O.J. no. L 87, 27 March 1985.
55 Directive 84/360 of 28 June 1984, O.J. no. L 188, 16 July 1984.
56 Directive 88/609 of 24 Nov. 1988, O.J. no. L 336, 7 Dec. 1988.

Two 1989 directives concern air pollution coming from incinerators of household wastes.[57] New installations must respect emission standards, while existing installations have until 1996 to achieve the same result.

In addition to efforts to reduce air pollution coming from industrial plants, there are measures aimed at reducing product emissions. The content of sulphur in diesel fuel has substantially decreased.[58] A Community regulation giving effect to international treaties aimed at protecting the stratospheric ozone layer limits and progressively reduces the production and consumption of CFCs in the Community.[59] The adoption and contents of this regulation demonstrate that air pollution has become a global phenomenon.

The introduction of catalytic converters in the Community has attracted much public attention. Due to the damage caused to its forests, Germany has insisted since 1983 on the adoption of more restrictive emission standards for automobiles. However, in a 1985 political compromise, it did not insist on Community norms mandating catalytic converters. This compromise could not be implemented however, because of Danish opposition. Denmark argued that the emission standards set by the compromise were not sufficiently strict. This opposition was only overcome after amendment of the Community treaty in 1987 and the introduction of decisions by qualified majority. A first directive made the catalytic converter obligatory for large automobiles.[60] Subsequently, a favourable political climate resulted from elections to the European Parliament. Its strong pressure led, in 1989, to the requirement of converters on all new cars beginning in 1992/1993. Older cars do not have to be retrofitted.[61] As a parallel measure, Member States are required to assure the general availability of unleaded petrol throughout the territory.[62] They also obtained the power to prohibit normal leaded petrol.[63]

These legislative developments lead to the following observations:

The texts regulating products are based in particular on article 100a – before 1987: article 100 of the Treaty – which foresees uniform rules for all Member States. This is explained by the need to establish provisions aimed at the free circulation of products throughout the Community, independently of national boundaries.

Derogating from this principle, the norm concerning the production and consumption of substances affecting the ozone layer, has been based upon article 130S of the Treaty, which is not the correct legal basis, but which has as a consequence that Member States can adopt, at the national level, stricter measures. Even in the case where the legal basis requires the elaboration of uniform provisions, legal norms were established to permit a differentiation in national provisions. Thus, Member States retain the ability to give economic incentives to buy cars equipped with catalytic

---

[57] Directive 89/369 of 8 June 1989, O.J. no. L 163, 14 June 1989; Directive 89/429 of 21 June 1989, O.J. no. L 203, 15 July 1989.

[58] Directive 87/219 of 30 March 1987, O.J. no. L 91, 30 March 1987.

[59] Regulation 3322/88 of 14 Oct. 1988, O.J. no. L 297, 31 Oct. 1988.

[60] Directive 88/76, O.J. no. L 36.

[61] Directive 89/458, O.J. no. L 226; Directive 89/491, O.J. no. L 238.

[62] Directive 85/210 of 20 March 1985, O.J. no. L 96, 3 Apr. 1985.

[63] Directive 87/416, O.J. no. L 225.

converters. As for sulphur in diesel fuel, Member States gained the right to derogate from the uniform norm of 0.3 g/litre and to fix the level at 0.2 g/litre when environmental circumstances so require. In the case of leaded petrol, a specific directive permits prohibiting normal petrol containing lead.

The directive on major combustion installations based on article 130S of the Treaty has implications that vary for the Member States and even foresees the possibility for certain economically disadvantaged States to increase their emissions in comparison with 1980 levels. The directive on incinerators of household wastes foresees minimal uniform rules, leaving to Member States the option of deciding if they wish to adopt stricter regulations. Because such an approach can result in distortions of competition, the Commission has the intention of proposing uniform rules for incinerators of dangerous wastes and to base this proposition on article 100a of the Treaty.

The result of these different provisions concerning air pollution is that Member States are not prohibited from adopting stricter measures on the national level. Obviously, this observation is more important for emissions produced by industrial plants than for those coming from cars or other products. However, as for automobile emissions, this also concerns the economic self-interest of States to preserve the unity of the common market for cars and to not resort to unilateral measures. This is particularly important for Germany which is the largest producer and exporter of cars among the Member States and whose interest is obviously in avoiding barriers to exportation toward other Member States. The possibilities offered by economic incentives have been sufficient to accelerate the introduction of the catalytic converter, in particular in Germany, the Netherlands and Denmark.

Directives establishing quality objectives also permit Member States to establish, for particularly sensitive zones, stricter standards. However, no Member State has acted upon this power.

The evolution of Community legislation reveals that the Community has abandoned recourse to quality objectives, no doubt because adequate environmental protection cannot be attained by this method. In its place, the Community has imposed an "end-of-the-pipe" technology which limits polluting emissions. This approach also has its limits, given that the notion of the "best available technology not involving excessive costs" is viewed in a different manner from one Member State to another. Thus, the different directives utilizing this notion require continuous management on the national level, permitting adaptation of installations to technological innovations; at the same time, a permanent coordination at the Community level is required to assure harmonized implementation. These two conditions are not everywhere fulfilled for the moment.

The problem of management of directives at the national level is also evident in the elaboration and implementation of clean-up programmes foreseen in different Community texts. Such programmes exist only in certain Member States.

The Community has not yet imposed on installations the requirement of specific technology or a detailed specification for products, as for example, an automobile motor which does not consume fuel above a certain quantity, in order to reduce air pollution. It is difficult to foresee today if such measures will be elaborated in the future.

One of the means permitting reduction of air pollution, not only in the Community but also on the global level, is the increase in fuel prices. This necessitates a more rational utilization as well as other means to diminish the costs of consumption. In order to contribute to the global efforts against global warming, the Commission has proposed the introduction of a tax on carbon dioxide on the one hand, on the consumption of energy on the other. It is difficult to predict if this tax will be finally introduced on the Community level.

In the Community, there has been little reduction in sulphur dioxide emissions to the present, a light reduction in nitrogen oxides and a growth in carbon dioxide. Obviously, this summary does not take into account the concentrations of air pollution in urban centres. At present, it can only be stated that national and Community measures are sufficient to slow the death of forests and other ecological damage caused by air pollution.

The application of legislative measures adopted at the Community level falls upon Member States. The Commission should ensure that this implementation takes place. Given that the legal provisions are relatively general and that the measuring methods and instruments are not always completely in harmony, such a control by the Commission is particularly difficult, especially because the different reports Member States are required to transmit to the Commission on the application of different Community texts are not always regularly transmitted nor transmitted by all Member States.

## 3. Owen Lomas, *Air Pollution Control in the United Kingdom*

United Kingdom law and policy on air pollution operates within the framework of international and European Community law and policy. In particular, the United Kingdom is party to the Geneva Convention on Long-Range Transboundary Air Pollution and its Protocols and the Vienna Convention for the Protection of the Ozone Layer with the Montreal Protocol. It has implemented Community Directive 84/360/EEC on combating air pollution from industrial plants; Directive 88/609/EEC on limiting emissions of certain pollutants into the air from large combustion plants; and Community legislation on the control of exhaust gas emissions from motor vehicles and related Directives.

United Kingdom law and policy on air pollution is undergoing substantial reform. The changes being implemented represent a response to international and Community developments and the growth of global environmental concerns. There has, until recently, been remarkably little evidence or awareness of new domestic air pollution problems, either from traditional pollutants or from acid precipitation or from other recently discovered forms of atmospheric pollution, such as ozone depletion and global warming.

There can be pointed out a number of inadequacies of existing law in delivering compliance with international obligations and addressing new environmental problems.

### a. Industrial Plants:

— No provision exists for licensing industrial plants. The only obligation is that complex, more polluting and generally larger processes, approximately two thousand in number, are required to register before operating (Alkali Act 1906).

— There are very few uniform statutory emission standards and an absence of powers to create them. The pollution control system relies instead on an obligation imposed on registered processes to use "the best practicable means" (Health and Safety at Work Act 1974) to avoid or minimize and render harmless atmospheric emissions.

— Enforcement agencies lack resources, leading to lax standards and under-enforcement.

— The system is characterized by pragmatism and flexibility which places a premium upon avoiding "unreasonable" and "excessive" costs to industry. It takes advantage of "the natural capacity of the environment to absorb pollutants" and the philosophy of "dilute and disperse". Standards are fixed locally, plant by plant, focusing on local conditions and individual financial circumstances when determining the "best practicable means". The approach to regulation and enforcement is based upon cooperation, education and encouragement rather than rigorous imposition of standards and regular resort to prosecution and punishment, i.e., the regulator is the "guiding friend" rather than "demanding policeman".

### b. Vehicle Emissions

There is a low-key, *laissez-faire* approach to the control of vehicle emissions based, as in other European countries, upon voluntary emission controls agreed to by the UN Economic Commission for Europe and ratified by the EC. These standards could not be made more stringent and were designed mainly to facilitate a common market in motor vehicles. The British system is increasingly out of step with international and Community obligations, and with the challenges posed by new evidence of cumulative, long-term and often long-range and global environmental degradation.

UK policy on vehicle emissions has passed through a painful transition from a market led to an environmentally led approach, largely because of intense pressure from the European Commission and other Member States of the European Community. After fighting against controls which would require the use of catalytic converters, rather than lean burn engines in which British car manufacturers had invested heavily,[64] the UK has now fallen in with Community policy and, in some respects, begun to lead the debate concerning future steps which might be taken.

---

[64] Lomas, "Environmental Protection, Economic Conflict and the European Community", 33 *McGill L.J.* 506.

Notably, the UK government has pressed for more stringent controls for diesel engines and fuels and there has been some support for substituting an additional tax on petrol and diesel for the tax revenue raised from vehicle excise duties. Proposals have also been made to the Competition division (DGIII) in the European Commission for the introduction of "tradeable credits" for vehicle emissions, under which there would be an average emission level from vehicles which, if bettered by manufacturers, would enable them to sell credits and, if not achieved, would oblige them to buy such credits from others.

In terms of domestic legislation, however, the UK has done little to move beyond the implementation of international and community obligations relating to emission standards, the exception being introduction of a fiscal incentive for the use of unleaded petrol. Thus, there have been no incentives to encourage greater use of cars with catalytic converters or with diesel engines and there have been only limited efforts to encourage discrimination in public procurement in favour of vehicles with lower emissions.

Reforms in UK law and practice are most notable in relation to the control of industrial emissions. Under Part I of the Environmental Protection Act 1990, a new regime for the control of air pollution from "prescribed processes" is introduced. While these provisions represent the UK's response to new demands for the control of air pollution, they also herald the introduction of a new approach to pollution control to all three environmental media (air, water and land), known as "Integrated Pollution Control" (IPC).

The basic elements of the new system are as follows:

— a requirement of prior authorization for prescribed processes with review of authorizations at not more than four yearly intervals;

— provision for authorizations to incorporate a wide variety of conditions, reflecting a mix of some old practices and a number of new ones.

Among the new provisions are those enabling uniform emission standards and environmental quality standards to be established, and for statutory plans to be developed for the progressive reduction of national discharges of specified pollutants. While these provisions, at a minimum, implement obligations under community directives, including the Large Combustion Plants Directive controlling sulphur dioxide and nitrogen oxides, they are drafted so as to enable their use in any other appropriate circumstances. Elements of the traditional "British approach" to air pollution control which were reflected in the concept of "best practicable means" are to be found in the flexibility and concern for cost present in the new obligation to use the "best available techniques not entailing excessive costs" (BATNEEC) which is still ultimately to be determined on a plant by plant basis. However, there are a number of respects in which the approach to the fixing of standards and their enforcement is likely to be more rigorous:

(i) standards are to be set and general duties complied with, which will prevent "pollution of the environment", a term which is defined very widely indeed;

(ii) guidance notes for individual industrial processes are to be more specific, clear and persuasive, with departure from their terms being the exception rather than the rule. They are also to contain timetables for the upgrading of existing plants to new standards;

(iii) the traditional cooperative and informal approach to standard-setting and enforcement by the regulatory agencies is being replaced by a more "arms length", formal approach, involving a greater willingness to take formal steps to ensure compliance;

(iv) details of authorizations, conditions and monitoring data on discharges, as well as details of any enforcement actions, are to be recorded in public registers,

(v) consistent with the 1984 Air Framework Directive, the determination of what constitutes "excessive costs" for existing processes is to be made largely on an industry-wide, rather than plant-by-plant, basis;

(vi) authorizations are to be reviewed at least every four years and up-dated in the light of developments in technology and evidence of environmental impact; and

(vii) local environmental conditions and circumstances are no longer to be of relevance in determining discharge limits for prescribed substances under the new concept of BATNEEC. The philosophy of "dilute and disperse" for prescribed substances is, therefore, effectively brought to an end.

The new approach is technology based in a more meaningful way than was the case under best practicable means. However, the determination of what constitutes "excessive costs" remains an area of significant difficulty and uncertainty in the United Kingdom, as it does in other parts of the European Community.

The other element of the new regime under Part I of the Environmental Protection Act to be noted is the introduction of Integrated Pollution Control and the associated concept of "best practicable environmental option" (BPEO) for approximately five thousand of the more complex and potentially more polluting industrial processes. For these processes, authorizations, conditions and the requirement to use BAT-NEEC will apply not only to emissions to the atmosphere but to discharges of trade effluent to water and waste to land. In addition to achieving BATNEEC for discharges to each environmental medium, conditions must be set with the objective of ensuring that BATNEEC will also be used for "minimizing the pollution which may be caused to the environment taken as a whole by the releases having regard to the best practicable environmental option available ..." The concept of BPEO has been the subject of much discussion and analysis in the United Kingdom, notably by the Royal Commission on Environmental Pollution.[65] However, the concept remains fraught with difficulty, demanding, as it does, extensive scientific evidence as to the impact of pollutants in each of the environmental media and, in some cases, subjective evaluation of whether one facet of the environment is more deserving of protection than another. In this latter respect, the concept could even draw regulators into a debate about environmental values and ethics, although this is not, one suspects, what the legislator intended.

Discharge by motor vehicles and industrial plants of carbon dioxide and other

---

[65] 11th Report CM. 310.

greenhouse gases which contribute to global warming have not so far been mentioned. This is because UK law does not currently address this problem, nor are there firm proposals to do so. The UK government has been reluctant to set arbitrary targets for $CO_2$ emission reductions, although it is now conditionally committed to return emissions to the level in 1990 by the year 2005. The condition is that other countries do likewise. The UK remains reluctant to act in this area, except together with economic competitors. It is still very susceptible to UK business pressure, even where joint action is envisaged. The UK is likely to maintain opposition to the Community's proposals for energy and carbon taxes.

## Analysis and Conclusions

British policy on air pollution control has traditionally been characterized by the subordination of environmental goals to the economic imperative of minimizing production costs and remaining competitive. This approach has favoured scientific "proof" before action, pragmatic case by case imposition of controls and heavy reliance on the perceived capacity of the environment to absorb and render harmless pollutants. The subordinate status of environmental objectives, and the concomitant approaches to pollution control which have been followed, have militated against the development of an intellectually coherent framework and objectives for environmental policy and rendered the UK particularly ill-equipped to engineer a timely and effective response to recent changes in the nature and scale of environmental problems.

The process of change which is now underway will not, of itself, produce a coherent policy. Traditionally, British policy-making has eschewed coherence and principle in favour of pragmatism and gradual adaptation of existing practices to new circumstances. Moreover, given that the pressure for reform has been largely external and legal in character, there has been a tendency for the economic imperative to be replaced, not by an environmental one, but by the minimal requirement of compliance with international and European Community obligations.

There are now signs, however, that some intellectual coherence may be emerging. This is partly because as Britain has been locked into the Community's environmental policy framework, it has adopted some of the Community's ideological baggage as its own. Thus, for example, the "precautionary approach" to pollution control is now heralded (whether accurately or not) as one of the cornerstones of British policy and technology-based pollution controls are in growing use, mitigated only by considerations of excessive cost, rather than perceived environmental necessity as well.

In some respects, there is now also evidence of largely "homegrown" coherence in environmental strategy and in the setting of objectives. The Environmental Protection Act 1990 is notable, both for the atypical inclusion of relevant definitions of, for example, "environment" and "pollution of the environment" and for the remarkably wide terms in which these expressions have been defined. These definitions now underpin both the specific controls on discharges and the general duties to avoid pollution which are found in the Act.

The Act also incorporates a significant commitment to greater freedom of access to environmental information. Despite being in some respects less than will be necessary to comply with the recent EC directive on the subject, this is nonetheless indicative of a new strategic approach, under which public and pressure group vigilance and agitation is intended to be employed in making both industry and the regulators more accountable for their actions.

The introduction in Part I of EPA of IPC, although mirrored to some degree by developments in other western industrialized countries, is a departure which has the potential to bring clarity and consistency of direction and organizational coherence in the pursuit of environmental protection, as well as facilitating the pursuit of defined environmental objectives. It is too early to tell how far this potential will be realized. In this regard, the inclusion of an obligation on those discharging to more than one environmental medium to use the "best practicable environmental option" for minimizing the pollution which may be caused to the environment taken as a whole, could be of great significance. However, as has been noted, application of the BPEO principle is fraught with difficulty and there is consequently a danger that only lip service will come to be paid to it as an environmental objective. If this occurs, then IPC is likely to lose much of its appeal as a strategy for environmental improvement, with its effective function reduced to providing a more efficient "one stop" licensing system for industry.

Finally, policy makers in the United Kingdom recently have shown interest in "environmental economics", the internalizing of the "true" economic cost of industrial activities in terms of their impact on the environment, and the use of fiscal incentives and penalties to promote less damaging products and productions methods. Concrete measures in this area have, so far, been conspicuous by their absence and it is unclear how, if at all, Government sees such market mechanisms integrating with other more conventional regulatory approaches to form a coherent overall strategy. One explanation for the Government's reticence may be that it is understandably reluctant to intervene in the market in advance of the UK's major industrial competitors. There is an underlying suspicion, however, that rather than using market mechanisms to ensure environmental protection, the intention is to let a "perfected" market determine whether, and if so to what extent, there will *be* effective environmental protection.

# C. Documents

*1.* Council of Europe, Council of Ministers, *Declaration of Principles of Air Pollution Control*
Res. (68)4, adopted 8 March 1968.

## PART I

### Preamble

As air is essential to life, its natural quality must be maintained in order to safeguard man's health and well-being and to protect his environment.

This natural quality of air may be affected by the introduction of a foreign substance or by a significant variation in the proportion of its components.

Air is deemed to be polluted when the presence of a foreign substance or a variation in the proportion of its components is liable to have a harmful effect or to cause nuisance.

The Member States of the Council of Europe will take the necessary legislative and administrative action to prevent or abate air pollution from all sources in accordance with the principles set out below.

## PART II

### Principles

1. Liability of those causing pollution

    Legislation should provide that whoever causes or adds to air pollution must, even where there is no proof of damage, keep such pollution to a minimum and ensure that impurities emitted are properly dispersed.

2. Basis of regulations

    Legislation on air pollution control must be based on the principle of prevention.

    In each particular case where the circumstances so require, the competent authorities should be in a position to enforce appropriate practicable technical measures, having due regard to the degree and frequency of pollution, the geographical situation, present and future population density and all other relevant factors.

    Prevention may be regulated differently according to the nature of the source of the pollution:

    (a) where the setting up of new installations or the alteration of old installations is likely to contribute significantly to air pollution, they should be subject to individual authorization laying down specifications for siting, construction and operation designed to limit emissions; special regulations might be issued for existing installations;

    (b) installations which individually contribute less significantly to air pollution may nevertheless be subject to general operating specifications if, for example, their proximity to each other might lead to a significant concentration of pollutants in the neighbourhood;

    (c) motor vehicles and mass-produced fuel-burning appliances should be subject to general provisions; since motor vehicles circulate across frontiers, uniform European standards for their construction and operation should be established as soon as possible; such standards might also be envisaged for mass-produced fuel-burning appliances which are subject of international trade.

3.  Supervision and implementation
    Member States should set up or cause to be set up administrative machinery:

    (a)  to ascertain the nature and extent of pollution;

    (b)  to check compliance with regulations governing installations, motor vehicles and fuel-burning appliances;

    (c)  to take such action as may be required to bring about the necessary improvements.

4.  Adjustment to technical and scientific progress
    Legislation should be so conceived that due account can be taken of new processes, technical improvements and scientific advances.

5.  Special measures
    Apart from measures applicable to all areas, there should be legislative provision for special measures to be applied to zones requiring special protection, to heavily polluted areas and in cases of emergency.

6.  Financing
    The cost incurred in preventing or abating pollution should be borne by whoever causes the pollution. This does not preclude aid from Public Authorities.

7.  Pollution in frontier areas
    Pollution in frontier areas should be the subject of joint study by the countries concerned, in accordance with a procedure to be laid down.

8.  Town and country planning
    The planning of urban and industrial development should take into account the effects of such development on air pollution; adequate consideration should be given by Planning Authorities to the maintenance and creation of green spaces.

## PART III

### Government aid for research

In order to make air pollution control more effective, Governments must encourage study and research, at national and international level, on the technical means of preventing or abating air pollution, on the dispersal of pollutants and on their effects on man and his environment.

*2. Convention on Long-Range Transboundary Air Pollution,*
13 November 1979, U.K.T.S. 57 (1983), Cmd. 9034; T.I.A.S. No. 1054; 18 I.L.M. 1442 (1979).

The Parties to the present Convention,

...

*Cognizant* of the references in the chapter on environment of the Final Act of the Conference on Security and Cooperation in Europe calling for cooperation to control air pollution and its effects, including long-range transport of air pollutants, and to the development through international cooperation of an extensive programme for the monitoring and evaluation of long-range transport of air pollutants, starting with sulphur dioxide and with possible extension to other pollutants,

*Considering* the pertinent provisions of the Declaration of the United Nations Conference on the Human Environment, and in particular principle 21, which expresses the common conviction that States have, in accordance with the Charter of the United Nations and the principles of international law, the sovereign right to exploit their own resources pursuant to their own environmental policies, and the responsibility to ensure that activities within their jurisdiction or control do not cause damage to the environment of other States or of areas beyond the limits of national jurisdiction,

*Recognizing* the existence of possible adverse effects, in the short and long term, of air pollution including transboundary air pollution,

...

*Affirming* their willingness to reinforce active international cooperation to develop appropriate national policies and by means of exchange of information, consultation, research and monitoring, to coordinate national action for combating air pollution including long-range transboundary air pollution,

Have agreed as follows:

### Definitions

### Article 1

For the purposes of the present Convention:

(a) "air pollution" means the introduction by man, directly or indirectly of substances or energy into the air resulting in deleterious effects of such a nature as to endanger human health, harm living resources and ecosystems and material property and impair or interfere with amenities and other legitimate uses of the environment, and "air pollutants" shall be construed accordingly,

(b) "long-range transboundary air pollution" means air pollution whose physical origin is situated wholly or in part within the area under the national jurisdiction of one State and which has adverse effects in the area under the jurisdiction of another State at such a distance that it is not generally possible to distinguish the contribution of individual emission sources or groups of sources.

### Fundamental principles

### Article 2

The Contracting Parties, taking due account of the facts and problems involved, are determined to protect man and his environment against air pollution and shall endeavour to limit and, as far as possible, gradually reduce and prevent air pollution including long-range transboundary air pollution.

### Article 3

The Contracting Parties, within the framework of the present Convention shall by means of exchanges of information, consultation, research and monitoring, develop without undue delay policies and strategies which shall serve as a means of combating the discharge of air pollutants, taking into account efforts already made at national and international levels.

### Article 4

The Contracting Parties shall exchange information on and review their policies, scientific activities and technical measures aimed at combating, as far as possible, the discharge of air pollutants which may have adverse effects, thereby contributing to the reduction of air pollution including long-range transboundary air pollution.

Article 5

Consultations shall be held, upon request, at an early stage between, on the one hand, Contracting Parties which are actually affected by or exposed to a significant risk of long-range transboundary air pollution and, on the other hand, Contracting Parties within which and subject to whose jurisdiction a significant contribution to long-range transboundary air pollution originates, or could originate, in connection with activities carried on or contemplated therein.

Air quality management

Article 6

Taking into account Articles 2 to 5, the ongoing research, exchange of information and monitoring and the results thereof, the cost and effectiveness of local and other remedies and, in order to combat air pollution, in particular that originating from new or rebuilt installations, each Contracting Party undertakes to develop the best policies and strategies including air quality management systems and, as part of them, control measures compatible with balanced development, in particular by using the best available technology which is economically feasible and low-and non-waste technology.

Research and development

Article 7

The Contracting Parties, as appropriate to their needs, shall initiate and cooperate in the conduct of research into and/or development of:

(a) existing and proposed technologies for reducing emissions of sulphur compounds and other major air pollutants, including technical and economic feasibility, and environmental consequences;

(b) instrumentation and other techniques for monitoring and measuring emission rates and ambient concentrations of air pollutants,

(c) improved models for a better understanding of the transmission of long-range transboundary air pollutants;

(d) the effects of sulphur compounds and other major air pollutants on human health and the environment, including agriculture, forestry, materials, aquatic and other natural ecosystems and visibility, with a view to establishing a scientific basis for dose-effect relationships designed to protect the environment;

(e) the economic, social and environmental assessment of alternative measures for attaining environmental objectives including the reduction of long-range transboundary air pollution;

(f) education and training programmes related to the environmental aspects of pollution by sulphur compounds and other major air pollutants.

Exchange of information

Article 8

The Contracting Parties, within the framework of the Executive Body referred to in Article 10 and bilaterally, shall, in their common interests, exchange available information on:

(a) data on emissions at periods of time to be agreed upon, of agreed air pollutants, starting with sulphur dioxide, coming from grid units of agreed size; or on the fluxes of agreed air pollutants, starting with sulphur dioxide, across national borders, at distances and at periods of time to be agreed upon;

(b) major changes in national policies and in general industrial development, and their potential impact, which would be likely to cause significant changes in long-range transboundary air pollution;

(c) control technologies for reducing air pollution relevant to long-range transboundary air pollution;

(d) the projected cost of the emission control of sulphur compounds and other major air pollutants on a national scale;

(e) meteorological and physico-chemical data relating to the processes during transmission;

(f) physico-chemical and biological data relating to the effects of long-range transboundary air pollution and the extent of the damage[66] which these data indicate can be attributed to long-range transboundary air pollution;

(g) national, subregional and regional policies and strategies for the control of sulphur compounds and other major air pollutants.

Implementation and further development of the cooperative programme for the monitoring and evaluation of the long-range transmissions of air pollutants in Europe

### Article 9

The Contracting Parties stress the need for the implementation of the existing "Cooperative programme for the monitoring and evaluation of the long-range transmission of air pollutants in Europe" (hereinafter referred to as EMEP) and with regard to the further development of this programme, agree to emphasize:

(a) the desirability of Contracting Parties joining in and fully implementing EMEP which, as a first step, is based on the monitoring of sulphur dioxide and related substances;

(b) the need to use comparable or standardized procedures for monitoring whenever possible;

(c) the desirability of basing the monitoring programme on the framework of both national and international programmes. The establishment of monitoring stations and the collection of data shall be carried out under the national jurisdiction of the country in which the monitoring stations are located;

(d) the desirability of establishing a framework for a cooperative environmental monitoring programme, based on and taking into account present and future national, subregional, regional and other international programmes;

(e) the need to exchange data on emissions at periods of time to be agreed upon, of agreed air pollutants, starting with sulphur dioxide, coming from grid-units of agreed size; or on the fluxes of agreed air pollutants, starting with sulphur dioxide, across national borders, at distances and at periods of time to be agreed upon. The method, including the model, used to determine the fluxes, as well as the method, including the model, used to determine the transmission of air pollutants based on the emissions per grid-unit, shall be made available and periodically reviewed, in order to improve the methods and the models;

(f) their willingness to continue the exchange and periodic updating of national data on total emissions of agreed air pollutants, starting with sulphur dioxide;

---

[66] The present Convention does not contain a rule on State liability as to damage.

(g)  the need to provide meteorological and physico-chemical data relating to processes during transmission;

(h)  the need to monitor chemical components in other media such as water, soil and vegetation, as well as a similar monitoring programme to record effects on health and environment;

(i)  the desirability of extending the national EMEP networks to make them operational for control and surveillance purposes.

Executive Body

Article 10

1.  The representatives of the Contracting Parties shall, within the framework of the Senior Advisers to ECE Governments on Environmental Problems, constitute the Executive Body of the present Convention, and shall meet at least annually in that capacity.

2.  The Executive Body shall:

(a)  review the implementation of the present Convention;

(b)  establish, as appropriate, working groups to consider matters related to the implementation and development of the present Convention and to this end to prepare appropriate studies and other documentation and to submit recommendations to be considered by the Executive Body;

(c)  fulfil such other functions as may be appropriate under the provisions of the present Convention.

3.  The Executive Body shall utilize the Steering Body for the EMEP to play an integral part in the operation of the present Convention, in particular with regard to data collection and scientific cooperation.

4.  The Executive Body, in discharging its functions, shall, when it deems appropriate, also make use of information from other relevant international organizations.

Secretariat

Article 11

The Executive Secretary of the Economic Commission for Europe shall carry out, for the Executive Body, the following secretariat functions:

(a)  to convene and prepare the meetings of the Executive Body;

(b)  to transmit to the Contracting Parties reports and other information received in accordance with the provisions of the present Convention;

(c)  to discharge the functions assigned by the Executive Body.

Amendments to the Convention

Article 12

1.  Any Contracting Party may propose amendments to the present Convention.

2.  The text of proposed amendments shall be submitted in writing to the Executive Secretary of the Economic Commission for Europe, who shall communicate them to all Contracting Parties. The Executive Body shall discuss proposed amendments at its next annual meeting provided that such proposals have been circulated by the Executive Secretary of the Economic Commission for Europe to the Contracting Parties at least ninety days in advance.

3.  An amendment to the present Convention shall be adopted by consensus of the repre-

sentatives of the Contracting Parties, and shall enter into force for the Contracting Parties which have accepted it on the ninetieth day after the date on which two-thirds of the Contracting Parties have deposited their instruments of acceptance with the depositary. Thereafter, the amendment shall enter into force for any other Contracting Party on the ninetieth day after the date on which that Contracting Party deposits its instrument of acceptance of the amendment.

...

## 3. Vienna Convention for the Protection of the Ozone Layer, 22 March 1985.

Preamble

The Parties to this Convention,

*Aware* of the potentially harmful impact on human health and the environment through modification of the ozone layer,

*Recalling* the pertinent provisions of the Declaration of the United Nations Conference on the Human Environment, and in particular principle 21, which provides that "States have, in accordance with the Charter of the United Nations and the principles of international law, the sovereign right to exploit their own resources pursuant to their own environmental policies, and the responsibility to ensure that activities within their jurisdiction or control do not cause damage to the environment of other States or of areas beyond the limits of national jurisdiction",

*Taking into account* the circumstances and particular requirements of developing countries,

...

*Aware* that measures to protect the ozone layer from modifications due to human activities require international cooperation and action, and should be based on relevant scientific and technical considerations,

*Aware also* of the need for further research and systematic observations to further develop scientific knowledge of the ozone layer and possible adverse effects resulting from its modification,

*Determined* to protect human health and the environment against adverse effects resulting from modifications of the ozone layer,

Have agreed as follows:

### Article 1

### Definitions

For the purposes of this Convention:

1.  "The ozone layer" means the layer of atmospheric ozone above the planetary boundary layer.

2.  "Adverse effects" means changes in the physical environment or biota, including changes in climate, which have significant deleterious effects on human health or on the composition, resilience and productivity of natural and managed ecosystems, or on materials useful to mankind.

3.  "Alternative technologies or equipment" means technologies or equipment the use of which makes it possible to reduce or effectively eliminate emissions of substances which have or are likely to have adverse effects on the ozone layer.

4.  "Alternative substances" means substances which reduce, eliminate or avoid adverse effects on the ozone layer.

5.  "Parties" means, unless the text otherwise indicates, Parties to this Convention.

6.  "Regional economic integration organization" means an organization constituted by sovereign States of a given region which has competence in respect of matters governed by this Convention or its protocols and has been duly authorized, in accordance with its internal procedures, to sign, ratify, accept, approve or accede to the instruments concerned.

7.  "Protocols" means protocols to this Convention.

## Article 2

### General obligations

1.  The Parties shall take appropriate measures in accordance with the provisions of this Convention and of those protocols in force to which they are party to protect human health and the environment against adverse effects resulting or likely to result from human activities which modify or are likely to modify the ozone layer.

2.  To this end the Parties shall, in accordance with the means at their disposal and their capabilities;

    (a)  Cooperate by means of systematic observations, research and information exchange in order to better understand and assess the effects of human activities on the ozone layer and the effects on human health and the environment from modification of the ozone layer;

    (b)  Adopt appropriate legislative or administrative measures and cooperate in harmonizing appropriate policies to control, limit, reduce or prevent human activities under their jurisdiction or control should it be found that these activities have or are likely to have adverse effects resulting from modification or likely modification of the ozone layer;

    (c)  Cooperate in the formulation of agreed measures, procedures and standards for the implementation of this Convention, with a view to the adoption of protocols and annexes.

    (d)  Cooperate with competent international bodies to implement effectively this Convention and protocols to which they are party.

3.  The provisions of this Convention shall in no way affect the right of Parties to adopt, in accordance with international law, domestic measures additional to those referred to in paragraphs 1 and 2 above, nor shall they affect additional domestic measures already taken by a Party, provided that those measures are not incompatible with their obligations under this Convention.

4.  The application of this article shall be based on relevant scientific and technical considerations.

## Article 3

### Research and systematic observations

1.  The Parties undertake, as appropriate, to initiate and cooperate in, directly or through competent international bodies, the conduct of research and scientific assessments on:

    (a)  The physical and chemical processes that may affect the ozone layer;

    (b)  The human health and other biological effects deriving from any modifications of the ozone layer, particularly those resulting from changes in ultra-violet solar radiation having biological effects (UV-B);

(c) Climatic effects deriving from any modifications of the ozone layer;

(d) Effects deriving from any modifications of the ozone layer and any consequent change in UV-B radiation on natural and synthetic materials useful to mankind;

(e) Substances, practices, processes and activities that may affect the ozone layer, and their cumulative effects;

(f) Alternative substances and technologies;

(g) Related socio-economic matters;

and as further elaborated in annexes I and II.

2. The Parties undertake to promote or establish, as appropriate, directly or through competent international bodies and taking fully into account national legislation and relevant ongoing activities at both the national and international levels, joint or complementary programmes for systematic observation of the state of the ozone layer and other relevant parameters, as elaborated in annex I.

3. The Parties undertake to cooperate, directly or through competent international bodies, in ensuring the collection, validation and transmission of research and observational data through appropriate world data centres in a regular and timely fashion.

Article 4

Cooperation in the legal, scientific and technical fields

1. The Parties shall facilitate and encourage the exchange of scientific, technical, socio-economic, commercial and legal information relevant to this Convention as further elaborated in annex II. Such information shall be supplied to bodies agreed upon by the Parties. Any such body receiving information regarded as confidential by the supplying Party shall ensure that such information is not disclosed and shall aggregate it to protect its confidentiality before it is made available to all Parties.

2. The Parties shall cooperate, consistent with their national laws, regulations and practices and taking into account in particular the needs of the developing countries, in promoting, directly or through competent international bodies, the development and transfer of technology and knowledge. Such cooperation shall be carried out particularly through:

(a) Facilitation of the acquisition of alternative technologies by other Parties;

(b) Provision of information on alternative technologies and equipment, and supply of special manuals or guides to them;

(c) The supply of necessary equipment and facilities for research and systematic observations;

(d) Appropriate training of scientific and technical personnel.

Article 5

Transmission of information

The Parties shall transmit, through the secretariat, to the Conference of the Parties established under article 6 information on the measures adopted by them in implementation of this Convention and of protocols to which they are party in such form and at such intervals as the meetings of the parties to the relevant instruments may determine.

...

## Article 8

### Adoption of protocols

1. The Conference of the Parties may at a meeting adopt protocols pursuant to article 2.

2. The text of any proposed protocol shall be communicated to the Parties by the secretariat at least six months before such a meeting.

## Article 9

### Amendment of the Convention or protocols

1. Any Party may propose amendments to this Convention or to any protocol. Such amendments shall take due account, *inter alia*, of relevant scientific and technical considerations.

2. Amendments to this Convention shall be adopted at a meeting of the Conference of the Parties. Amendments to any protocol shall be adopted at a meeting of the Parties to the protocol in question. The text of any proposed amendment to this Convention or to any protocol, except as may otherwise be provided in such protocol, shall be communicated to the Parties by the secretariat at least six months before the meeting at which it is proposed for adoption. The Secretariat shall also communicate proposed amendments to the signatories to this Convention for information.

3. The Parties shall make every effort to reach agreement on any proposed amendment to this Convention by consensus. If all efforts at consensus have been exhausted, and no agreement reached, the amendment shall as a last resort be adopted by a three-fourths majority vote of the Parties present and voting at the meeting, and shall be submitted by the Depositary to all Parties for ratification, approval or acceptance.

4. The procedure mentioned in paragraph 3 above shall apply to amendments to any protocol, except that a two-thirds majority of the parties to that protocol present and voting at the meeting shall suffice for their adoption.

5. Ratification, approval or acceptance of amendments shall be notified to the Depositary in writing. Amendments adopted in accordance with paragraphs 3 or 4 above shall enter into force between parties having accepted them on the ninetieth day after the receipt by the Depositary or notification of their ratification, approval or acceptance by at least three-fourths of the Parties to this Convention or by at least two-thirds of the parties to the protocol concerned, except as may otherwise be provided in such protocol. Thereafter the amendments shall enter into force for any other Party on the ninetieth day after that Party deposits its instrument of ratification, approval or acceptance of the amendments.

6. For the purposes of this article, "Parties present and voting" means Parties present and casting an affirmative or negative vote.

## Article 10

### Adoption and amendment of annexes

1. The annexes to this Convention or to any protocol shall form an integral part of this Convention or of such protocol, as the case may be, and, unless expressly provided otherwise, a reference to this Convention or its protocols constitutes at the same time a reference to any annexes thereto. Such annexes shall be restricted to scientific, technical and administrative matters.

2. Except as may be otherwise provided in any protocol with respect to its annexes, the following procedure shall apply to the proposal, adoption and entry into force of additional annexes to this Convention or of annexes to a protocol:

(a) Annexes to this Convention shall be proposed and adopted according to the procedure laid down in article 9, paragraphs 2 and 3, while annexes to any protocol shall be proposed and adopted according to the procedure laid down in article 9, paragraphs 2 and 4;

(b) Any party that is unable to approve an additional annex to this Convention or an annex to any protocol to which it is party shall so notify the Depositary, in writing, within six months from the date of the communication of the adoption by the Depositary. The Depositary shall without delay notify all Parties of any such notification received. A Party may at any time substitute an acceptance for a previous declaration of objection and the annexes shall thereupon enter into force for that Party;

(c) On the expiry of six months from the date of the circulation of the communication by the Depositary, the annex shall become effective for all Parties to this Convention or to any protocol concerned which have not submitted a notification in accordance with the provision of subparagraph (b) above.

3. The proposal, adoption and entry into force of amendments to annexes to this Convention or to any protocol shall be subject to the same procedure as for the proposal, adoption and entry into force of annexes to the Convention or annexes to a protocol. Annexes and amendments thereto shall take due account, *inter alia*, of relevant scientific and technical considerations.

4. If an additional annex or an amendment to an annex involves an amendment to this Convention or to any protocol, the additional annex or amended annex shall not enter into force until such time as the amendment to this Convention or to the protocol concerned enters into force.

...

## 4. United Nations Framework Convention on Climate Change, 8 May 1992.

The Parties to this Convention,

*Acknowledging* that change in the Earth's climate and its adverse effects are a common concern of humankind.

*Concerned* that human activities have been substantially increasing the atmospheric concentrations of greenhouse gases, and that these increases enhance the natural greenhouse effect, and that this will result on average in an additional warming of the Earth's surface and atmosphere and may adversely affect natural ecosystems and humankind,

*Noting* that the largest share of historical and current global emissions of greenhouse gases has originated in developed countries, that *per capita* emissions in developing countries are still relatively low and that the share of global emissions originating in developing countries will grow to meet their social and development needs.

*Aware* of the role and importance in terrestrial and marine ecosystems of sinks and reservoirs of greenhouse gases.

*Noting* that there are many uncertainties in predictions of climate change, particularly with regard to the timing, magnitude and regional patterns thereof,

*Acknowledging* that the global nature of climate change calls for the widest possible cooperation by all countries and their participation in an effective and appropriate international response, in accordance with their common but differentiated responsibilities and respective capabilities and their social and economic conditions,

*Recalling* the pertinent provisions of the Declaration of the United Nations Conference on the Human Environment, adopted at Stockholm on 16 June 1972,

*Recalling also* that States have, in accordance with the Charter of the United Nations and the principles of international law, the sovereign right to exploit their own resources pursuant to their own environmental and developmental policies, and the responsibility to ensure that activities within their jurisdiction or control do not cause damage to the environment of other States or of areas beyond the limits of national jurisdiction,

*Reaffirming* the principle of sovereignty of States in international cooperation to address climate change,

*Recognizing* that States should enact effective environmental legislation, that environmental standards, management objectives and priorities should reflect the environmental and developmental context to which they apply, and that standards applied by some countries may be inappropriate and of unwarranted economic and social cost to other counties, in particular developing countries,

...

## Article 1

### Definitions

For the purposes of this Convention:

1. "Adverse effects of climate change" means changes in the physical environment or biota resulting from climate change which have significant deleterious effects on the composition, resilience or productivity of natural and managed ecosystems or on the operation of socio-economic systems or on human health and welfare.

2. "Climate change" means a change of climate which is attributed directly or indirectly to human activity that alters the composition of the global atmosphere and which is in addition to natural climate variability observed over comparable time periods.

3. "Climate system" means the totality of the atmosphere, hydrosphere, biosphere and geosphere and their interactions.

4. "Emissions" means the release of greenhouse gases and/or their precursors into the atmosphere over a specified area and period of time.

5. "Greenhouse gases" means those gaseous constituents of the atmosphere, both natural and anthropogenic, that absorb and re-emit infrared radiation.

6. "Regional economic integration organization" means an organization constituted by sovereign States of a given region which has competence in respect of matters governed by this Convention or its protocols and has been duly authorized, in accordance with its internal procedures, to sign, ratify, accept, approve or accede to the instruments concerned.

7. "Reservoir" means a component or components of the climate system where a greenhouse gas or a precursor of a greenhouse gas is stored.

8. "Sink" means any process, activity or mechanism which removes a greenhouse gas, an aerosol or a precursor of a greenhouse gas from the atmosphere.

9. "Source" means any process or activity which releases a greenhouse gas, an aerosol or a precursor of a greenhouse gas into the atmosphere.

## Article 2

### Objective

The ultimate objective of this Convention and any related legal instruments that the Conference of the Parties may adopt is to achieve, in accordance with the relevant provisions of the Convention, stabilization of greenhouse gas concentrations in the atmosphere at a level that would prevent dangerous anthropogenic interference with the climate system. Such a level should be achieved within a time frame sufficient to allow ecosystems to adapt naturally to climate change, to ensure that food production is not threatened and to enable economic development to proceed in a sustainable manner.

## Article 3

### Principles

In their actions to achieve the objective of the Convention and to implement its provisions, the Parties shall be guided, *inter alia*, by the following:

1. The Parties should protect the climate system for the benefit of present and future generations of humankind, on the basis of equity and in accordance with their common but differentiated responsibilities and respective capabilities. Accordingly, the developed country Parties should take the lead in combating climate change and the adverse effects thereof.

2. The specific needs and special circumstances of developing country Parties, especially those that are particularly vulnerable to the adverse effects of climate change, and of those Parties, especially developing country Parties, that would have to bear a disproportionate or abnormal burden under the Convention, should be given full consideration.

3. The Parties should take precautionary measures to anticipate, prevent or minimize the causes of climate change and mitigate its adverse effects. Where there are threats of serious or irreversible damage, lack of full scientific certainty should not be used as a reason for postponing such measures, taking into account that policies and measures to deal with climate change should be cost-effective so as to ensure global benefits at the lowest possible cost. To achieve this, such policies and measures should take into account different socio-economic contexts, be comprehensive, cover all relevant sources, sinks and reservoirs of greenhouse gases and adaptation, and comprise all economic sectors. Efforts to address climate change may be carried out cooperatively by interested Parties.

4. The Parties have a right to, and should, promote sustainable development. Policies and measures to protect the climate system against human-induced change should be appropriate for the specific conditions of each Party and should be integrated with national development programmes, taking into account that economic development is essential for adopting measures to address climate change.

5. The Parties should cooperate to promote a supportive and open international economic system that would lead to sustainable economic growth and development in all Parties, particularly developing country Parties, thus enabling them better to address the problems of climate change. Measures taken to combat climate change, including unilateral ones, should not constitute a means of arbitrary or unjustifiable discrimination or a disguised restriction on international trade.

## Article 4

## Commitments

1.　All Parties, taking into account their common but differentiated responsibilities and their specific national and regional development priorities, objectives and circumstances, shall:

(a)　Develop, periodically update, publish and make available to the Conference of the Parties, in accordance with Article 12, national inventories of anthropogenic emissions by sources and removals by sinks of all greenhouse gases not controlled by the Montreal Protocol, using comparable methodologies to be agreed upon by the Conference of the Parties;

(b)　Formulate, implement, publish and regularly update national and, where appropriate, regional programmes containing measures to mitigate climate change by addressing anthropogenic emissions by sources and removals by sinks of all greenhouse gases not controlled by the Montreal Protocol, and measures to facilitate adequate adaptation to climate change;

(c)　Promote and cooperate in the development, application and diffusion, including transfer, of technologies, practices and processes that control, reduce or prevent anthropogenic emissions of greenhouse gases not controlled by the Montreal Protocol in all relevant sectors, including the energy, transport, industry, agriculture, forestry and waste management sectors;

(d)　Promote sustainable management, and promote and cooperate in the conservation and enhancement, as appropriate, of sinks and reservoirs of all greenhouse gases not controlled by the Montreal Protocol, including biomass, forests and oceans as well as other terrestrial, coastal and marine ecosystems;

(e)　Cooperate in preparing for adaptation to the impacts of climate change; develop and elaborate appropriate and integrated plans for coastal zone management, water resources and agriculture, and for the protection and rehabilitation of areas, particularly in Africa, affected by drought and desertification, as well as floods;

(f)　Take climate change considerations into account, to the extent feasible, in their relevant social, economic and environmental policies and actions, and employ appropriate methods, for example impact assessments, formulated and determined nationally, with a view to minimizing adverse effects on the economy, on public health and on the quality of the environment, of projects or measures undertaken by them to mitigate or adapt to climate change;

(g)　Promote and cooperate in scientific, technological, technical, socio-economic and other research, systematic observation and development of data archives related to the climate system and intended to further the understanding and to reduce or eliminate the remaining uncertainties regarding the causes, effects, magnitude and timing of climate change and the economic and social consequences of various response strategies;

(h)　Promote and cooperate in the full, open and prompt exchange of relevant scientific, technological, technical, socio-economic and legal information related to the climate system and climate change, and to the economic and social consequences of various response strategies;

(i)　Promote and cooperate in education, training and public awareness related to climate change and encourage the widest participation in this process, including that of non-governmental organizations; and

    (j)    Communicate to the Conference of the Parties information related to implementation, in accordance with Article 12.

2.    The developed country Parties and other Parties included in annex I commit themselves specifically as provided for in the following:

    (a)    Each of these Parties shall adopt national[67] policies and take corresponding measures on the mitigation of climate change, by limiting its anthropogenic emissions of greenhouse gases and protecting and enhancing its greenhouse gas sinks and reservoirs. These policies and measures will demonstrate that developed countries are taking the lead in modifying longer-term trends in anthropogenic emissions consistent with the objective of the Convention, recognizing that the return by the end of the present decade to earlier levels of anthropogenic emissions of carbon dioxide and other greenhouse gases not controlled by the Montreal Protocol would contribute to such modification, and taking into account the differences in these Parties' starting points and approaches, economic structures and resource bases, the need to maintain strong and sustainable economic growth, available technologies and other individual circumstances, as well as the need for equitable and appropriate contributions by each of these Parties to the global effort regarding that objective. These Parties may implement such policies and measures jointly with other Parties and may assist other Parties in contributing to the achievement of the objective of the Convention and, in particular, that of this subparagraph;

    (b)    In order to promote progress to this end, each of these Parties shall communicate, within six months of the entry into force of the Convention for it and periodically thereafter, and in accordance with Article 12, detailed information on its policies and measures referred to in subparagraph (a) above, as well as on its resulting projected anthropogenic emissions by sources and removals by sinks of greenhouse gases not controlled by the Montreal Protocol for the period referred to in subparagraph (a), with the aim of returning individually or jointly to their 1990 levels of these anthropogenic emissions of carbon dioxide and other greenhouse gases not controlled by the Montreal Protocol. This information will be reviewed by the Conference of the Parties, at its first session and periodically thereafter, in accordance with Article 7;

    (c)    Calculations of emissions by sources and removals by sinks of greenhouse gases for the purposes of subparagraph (b) above should take into account the best available scientific knowledge, including of the effective capacity of sinks and the respective contributions of such gases to climate change. The Conference of the Parties shall consider and agree on methodologies for these calculations at its first session and review them regularly thereafter;

    (d)    The Conference of the Parties shall, at its first session, review the adequacy of subparagraphs (a) and (b) above. Such review shall be carried out in the light of the best available scientific information and assessment on climate change and its impacts, as well as relevant technical, social and economic information. Based on this review, the Conference of the Parties shall take appropriate action, which may include the adoption of amendments to the commitments in subparagraphs (a) and

---

[67] This includes policies and measures adopted by regional economic integration organizations.

(b) above. The Conference of the Parties, at its first session, shall also take decisions regarding criteria for joint implementation as indicated in subparagraph (a) above. A second review of subparagraphs (a) and (b) shall take place not later than 31 December 1998, and thereafter at regular intervals determined by the Conference and the Parties, until the objective of the Convention is met;

(e)　Each of these Parties shall:

(i) coordinate as appropriate with other such Parties, relevant economic and administrative instruments developed to achieve the objective of the Conventions; and

(ii) identify and periodically review its own policies and practices which encourage activities that lead to greater levels of anthropogenic emissions of greenhouse gases not controlled by the Montreal Protocol than would otherwise occur;

(f)　The Conference of the Parties shall review, not later than 31 December 1998, available information with a view to taking decisions regarding such amendments to the lists in annexes I and II as may be appropriate, with the approval of the Party concerned;

(g)　Any Party not included in annex I may, in its instrument of ratification, acceptance, approval or accession, or at any time thereafter, notify the Depositary that it intends to be bound by subparagraphs (a) and (b) above. The Depositary shall inform the other signatories and Parties of any such notification.

3.　The developed country Parties and other developed Parties included in annex II shall provide new and additional financial resources to meet the agreed full costs incurred by developing country Parties in complying with their obligations under Article 12, paragraph 1. They shall also provide such financial resources, including for the transfer of technology, needed by the developing country Parties to meet the agreed full incremental costs of implementing measures that are covered by paragraph 1 of this Article and that are agreed between a developing country Party and the international entity or entities referred to in Article 11, in accordance with that Article. The implementation of these commitments shall take into account the need for adequacy and predictability in the flow of funds and the importance of appropriate burden sharing among the developed country Parties.

4.　The developed country Parties and other developed Parties included in annex II shall also assist the developing country Parties that are particularly vulnerable to the adverse effects of climate change in meeting costs of adaptation to those adverse effects.

5.　The developed country Parties and other developed Parties included in annex II shall take all practicable steps to promote, facilitate and finance, as appropriate, the transfer of, or access to, environmentally sound technologies and know-how to other Parties, particularly developing country Parties, to enable them to implement the provisions of the Convention. In this process, the developed country Parties shall support the development and enhancement of endogenous capacities and technologies of developing country Parties. Other Parties and organizations in a position to do so may also assist in facilitating the transfer of such technologies.

6.　In the implementation of their commitments under paragraph 2 above, a certain degree of flexibility shall be allowed by the Conference of the Parties to the Parties included in annex I undergoing the process of transition to a market economy, in order to enhance the ability of these Parties to address climate change, including with regard to the historical level of anthropogenic emissions of greenhouse gases not controlled by the Montreal Protocol chosen as a reference.

7. The extent to which developing country Parties will effectively implement their commitments under the Convention will depend on the effective implementation by developed country Parties of their commitments under the Convention related to financial resources and transfer of technology and will take fully into account that economic and social development and poverty eradication are the first and overriding priorities of the developing country Parties.

8. In the implementation of the commitments in this Article, the Parties shall give full consideration to what actions are necessary under the Convention, including actions related to funding, insurance and the transfer of technology, to meet the specific needs and concerns of developing country Parties arising from the adverse effects of climate change and/or the impact of the implementation of response measures, especially on:

(a) Small island countries;

(b) Countries with low-lying coastal areas;

(c) Countries with arid and semi-arid areas, forested areas and areas liable to forest decay;

(d) Countries with areas prone to natural disasters;

(e) Countries with areas liable to drought and desertification;

(f) Countries with areas of high urban atmospheric pollution;

(g) Countries with areas with fragile ecosystems, including mountainous ecosystems;

(h) Countries whose economies are highly dependent on income generated from the production, processing and export, and/or on consumption of fossil fuels and associated energy-intensive products; and

(i) Land-locked and transit countries.

Further, the Conference of the Parties may take actions, as appropriate, with respect to this paragraph.

9. The Parties shall take full account of the specific needs and special situations of the least developed countries in their actions with regard to funding and transfer of technology.

10. The Parties shall, in accordance with Article 10, take into consideration in the implementation of the commitments of the Convention the situation of Parties, particularly developing country Parties, with economies that are vulnerable to the adverse effects of the implementation of measures to respond to climate change. This applies notably to Parties with economies that are highly dependent on income generated from the production, processing and export, and/or consumption of fossil fuels and associated energy-intensive products and/or the use of fossil fuels for which such Parties have serious difficulties in switching to alternatives.

Article 5

Research and systematic observation

...

Article 6

Education, training and public awareness

...

Article 7

Conference of the Parties

1. A Conference of the Parties is hereby established.

2. The Conference of the Parties, as the supreme body of this Convention, shall keep under regular review the implementation of the Convention and any related legal instruments that the Conference of the Parties may adopt, and shall make, within its mandate, the decisions necessary to promote the effective implementation of the Convention....

Article 9

Subsidiary body for scientific and technological advice

1. A subsidiary body for scientific and technological advice is hereby established to provide the Conference of the Parties and, as appropriate, its other subsidiary bodies with timely information and advice on scientific and technological matters relating to the Convention. This body shall be open to participation by all Parties and shall be multidisciplinary. It shall comprise government representatives competent in the relevant field of expertise. It shall report regularly to the Conference of the Parties on all aspects of its work.

2. Under the guidance of the Conference of the Parties, and drawing upon existing competent international bodies, this body shall:

   (a) Provide assessments of the state of scientific knowledge relating to climate change and its effects;

   (b) Prepare scientific assessments on the effects of measures taken in the implementation of the Convention;

   (c) Identify innovative, efficient and state-of-the-art technologies and know-how and advise on the ways and means of promoting development and/or transferring such technologies;

   (d) Provide advice on scientific programmes, international cooperation in research and development related to climate change as well as on ways and means of supporting endogenous capacity-building in developing countries; and

   (e) Respond to scientific, technological and methodological questions that the Conference of the Parties and its subsidiary bodies may put to the body.

3. The functions and terms of reference of this body may be further elaborated by the Conference of the Parties.

Article 10

Subsidiary body for implementation

1. A subsidiary body for implementation is hereby established to assist the Conference of the Parties in the assessment and review of the effective implementation of the Convention. This body shall be open to participation by all Parties and comprise government

representatives who are experts on matters related to climate change. It shall report regularly to the Conference of the Parties on all aspects of its work.

2. Under the guidance of the Conference of the Parties, this body shall:

   (a) Consider the information communicated in accordance with Article 12, paragraph 1, to assess the overall aggregated effect of the steps taken by the Parties in the light of the latest scientific assessments concerning climate change;

   (b) Consider the information communicated in accordance with Article 12, paragraph 2, in order to assist the Conference of the Parties in carrying out the reviews required by Article 4, paragraph 2(d); and

   (c) Assist the Conference of the Parties, as appropriate, in the preparation and implementation of its decisions.

Article 11

Financial mechanism

1. A mechanism for the provision of financial resources on a grant or concessional basis, including for the transfer of technology is hereby defined. It shall function under the guidance of and be accountable to the Conference of the Parties, which shall decide on its policies, programme priorities and eligibility criteria related to this Convention. Its operation shall be entrusted to one or more existing international entities.

2. The financial mechanism shall have an equitable and balanced representation of all Parties within a transparent system of governance.

3. The Conference of the Parties and the entity or entities entrusted with the operation of the financial mechanism shall agree upon arrangements to give effect to the above paragraphs ...

Article 13

Resolution of questions regarding implementation

The Conference of the Parties shall, at its first session, consider the establishment of a multilateral consultative process, available to Parties on their request, for the resolution of questions regarding the implementation of the Convention.
...

*5.* European Communities, *Council Directive 84/360 of 28 June 1984 on the Combating of Air Pollution from Industrial Plants,* O.J. No. L 188, 16 July 1984, p. 20.

The Council of the European Communities,
...
Has adopted this Directive:

Article 1

The purpose of this Directive is to provide for further measures and procedures designed to prevent or reduce air pollution from industrial plants within the Community, particularly those belonging to the categories set out in Annex I.

### Article 2

For the purposes of this Directive:

1. "Air pollution" means the introduction by man, directly or indirectly, of substances or energy into the air resulting in deleterious effects of such a nature as to endanger human health, harm living resources and ecosystems and material property and impair or interfere with amenities and other legitimate uses of the environment.

2. "Plant" means any establishment or other stationary plant used for industrial or public utility purposes which is likely to cause air pollution.

3. "Existing plant" means a plant in operation before 1 July 1987 or built or authorized before that date.

4. "Air quality limit values" means the concentration and/or mass of polluting substances in emissions from plants during a specified period which is not to be exceeded.

### Article 3

1. Member States shall take the necessary measures to ensure that the operation of plants belonging to the categories listed in Annex I requires prior authorization by the competent authorities. The necessity to meet the requirements prescribed for such authorization must be taken into account at the plant's design stage.

2. Authorization is also required in the case of substantial alteration of all plants which belong to the categories listed in Annex I or which, as a result of the alteration, will fall within those categories.

3. Member States may require other categories of plants to be subject to authorization or, where national legislation so provides, prior notification.

### Article 4

Without prejudice to the requirements laid down by national and Community provisions with a purpose other than that of this Directive, an authorization may be issued only when the competent authority is satisfied that:

1. all appropriate preventive measures against air pollution have been taken, including the application of the best available technology, provided that the application of such measures does not entail excessive costs;

2. the use of plant will not cause significant air pollution particularly from the emission of substances referred to in Annex II;

3. none of the emission limit values applicable will be exceeded;

4. all the air quality limit values applicable will be taken into account.

### Article 5

Member States may
   — define particularly polluted areas for which emission limit values more stringent than those referred to in Article 4 may be fixed,
   — define areas to be specially protected for which air quality limit values and emission limit values more stringent than those referred to in Article 4 may be fixed,
   — decide that, within the abovementioned areas, specified categories of plants set out in Annex I may not be built or operated unless special conditions are complied with.

### Article 6

Applications for authorization shall include a description of the plant containing the necessary information for the purposes of the decision whether to grant authorization in accordance with Articles 3 and 4.

## Article 7

Subject to the provisions regarding commercial secrecy, Member States shall exchange information among themselves and with the Commission regarding their experience and knowledge of measures for prevention and reduction of air pollution, as well as technical processes and equipment and air quality and emission limit values.

## Article 8

1. The Council, acting unanimously on a proposal from the Commission, shall if necessary fix emission limit values based on the best available technology not entailing excessive costs, and taking into account the nature, quantities and harmfulness of the emissions concerned.

2. The Council, acting unanimously on a proposal from the Commission, shall stipulate suitable measurement and assessment techniques and methods.

## Article 9

1. Member States shall take the necessary measures to ensure that applications for authorization and the decisions of the competent authorities are made available to the public concerned in accordance with procedures provided for in the national law.

2. Paragraph 1 shall apply without prejudice to specific national or Community provisions concerning the assessment of the environmental effects of public and private projects and subject to observance of the provisions regarding commercial secrecy.

## Article 10

The Member States shall make available to the other Member States concerned, as a basis for all necessary consultation within the framework of their bilateral relations, the same information as is furnished to their own nationals.

## Article 11

The Member States shall take the necessary measures to ensure that emissions from plants are determined for the purpose of monitoring compliance with the obligations referred to in Article 4. The determination methods must be approved by the competent authorities.

## Article 12

The Member States shall follow developments as regards the best available technology and the environmental situation.

In the light of this examination they shall, if necessary, impose appropriate conditions on plants authorized in accordance with this Directive, on the basis both of those developments and of the desirability of avoiding excessive costs for the plants in question, having regard in particular to the economic situation of the plants belonging to the category concerned.

## Article 13

In the light of an examination of developments as regards the best available technology and the environmental situation, the Member States shall implement policies and strategies, including appropriate measures, for the gradual adaptation of existing plants belonging to the categories given in Annex I to the best available technology, taking into account in particular:

— the plant's technical characteristics,
— its rate of utilization and length of its remaining life,
— the nature and volume of polluting emissions from it,
— the desirability of not entailing excessive costs for the plant concerned, having regard

in particular to the economic situation of undertakings belonging to the category in question.

## Article 14

Member States may, in order to protect public health and the environment, adopt provisions stricter than those provided for in this Directive.

## Article 15

The Directive does not apply to industrial plants serving national defence purposes.

## Article 16

1. Member States shall bring into force the laws, regulations and administrative provisions necessary to comply with this Directive not later than 30 June 1987.

2. Member States shall communicate to the Commission the texts of the provisions of national laws which they adopt in the field governed by this Directive.

...

## Annex I. Categories of Plants Covered by Article 3

1.  Energy industry

    1.1. Coke ovens

    1.2. Oil refineries (excluding undertakings manufacturing only lubricants from crude oil)

    1.3. Coal gasification and liquefaction plants

    1.4. Thermal power stations (excluding nuclear power stations) and other combustion installations with a nominal heat output of more than 50 MW.

2.  Production and processing of metals

    2.1. Roasting and sintering plants with a capacity of more than 1,000 tons of metal ore per year

    2.2. Integrated plants for the production of pig iron and crude steel

    2.3. Ferrous metal foundries having melting installations with a total capacity of over 5 tons

    2.4. Plants for the production and melting of non-ferrous metals having installations with a total capacity of over 1 ton for heavy metals or 0.5 ton for light metals.

3.  Manufacture of non-metallic mineral products

    3.1. Plants for the production of cement and rotary kiln lime production

    3.2. Plants for the production and processing of asbestos and manufacture of asbestos-based products

    3.3. Plants for the manufacture of glass fibre or mineral fibre

    3.4. Plants for the production of glass (ordinary and special) with a capacity of more than 5,000 tons per year

    3.5. Plants for the manufacture of coarse ceramics notably refractory bricks, stoneware, pipes, facing and floor bricks and roof tiles

4.  Chemical industry

    4.1. Chemical plants for the production of olefins, derivatives of olefins, monomers and polymers

4.2. Chemical plants for the manufacture of other organic intermediate products

4.3. Plants for the manufacture of basic inorganic chemicals

5. Waste disposal

5.1. Plants for the disposal of toxic and dangerous waste by incineration

5.2. Plants for the treatment by incineration of other solid and liquid waste

6. Other industries

Plants for the manufacture of paper pulp by chemical methods with a production capacity of 25,000 tons or more per year.

Annex II. List of Most Important Polluting Substances (within the meaning of Article 4(2))

1. Sulphur dioxide and other sulphur compounds

2. Oxides of nitrogen and other nitrogen compounds

3. Carbon monoxide

4. Organic compounds, in particular hydrocarbons (except methane)

5. Heavy metals and their compounds

6. Dust; asbestos (suspended particulates and fibres), glass and mineral fibres

7. Chlorine and its compounds

8. Fluorine and its compounds

## 6. United Kingdom, *Environmental Protection Act, 1990.*

### PART I
Integrated pollution control and air pollution
control by local authorities

1. (1) The following provisions have effect for the interpretation of this Part.

(2) The "environment" consists of all, or any, of the following media, namely, the air, water and land; and the medium of air includes the air within buildings and the air within other natural or man-made structures above or below ground.

(3) "Pollution of the environment" means pollution of the environment due to the release into any environmental medium from any process of substances which are capable of causing harm to man or any other living organisms supported by the environment.

(4) "Harm" means harm to the health of living organisms or other interference with the ecological systems of which they form part and, in the case of man, includes offence caused to any of his senses or harm to his property; and "harmless" has a corresponding meaning.

(5) "Process" means any activities carried on in Great Britain, whether on premises or by means of mobile plant, which are capable of causing pollution of the environment and "prescribed process" means a process prescribed under section 2(1) below.

...

6.   (1)   No person shall carry on a prescribed process after the date prescribed or determined for that description of process ... except under an authorization granted by the enforcing authority and in accordance with the conditions to which it is subject.

...

7.   (1)   There shall be included in an authorization –

      (a)  subject to paragraph (b) below, such specific conditions as the enforcing authority considers appropriate, when taken with the general condition implied by sub-section (4) below, for achieving the objectives specified in subsection (2) below;

      (b)  such conditions as are specified in directions given by the Secretary of State under subsection (3) below; and

      (c)  such other conditions (if any) as appear to the enforcing authority to be appropriate; but no conditions shall be imposed for the purpose only of securing the health of persons at work [...].

   (2)   Those objectives are –

      (a)  ensuring that, in carrying on a prescribed process, the best available techniques not entailing excessive cost will be used –

         (i)  for preventing the release of substances prescribed for any environmental medium into that medium or, where that is not practicable by such means, for reducing the release of such substances to a minimum and for rendering harmless any such substances which are so released; and

        (ii)  for rendering harmless any other substances which might cause harm if released into any environmental medium;

      (b)  compliance with any directions by the Secretary of State given for the implementation of any obligations of the United Kingdom under the Community Treaties or international law relating to environmental protection;

      (c)  compliance with any limits or requirements and achievement of any quality standards or quality objectives prescribed by the Secretary of State under any of the relevant enactments.

   ...

   (7)   The objectives referred to in subsection (2) above shall, where the process –

      (a)  is one designated for central control; and

      (b)  is likely to involve the release of substances into more than one environmental medium;
include the objective of ensuring that the best available techniques not entailing excessive cost will be used for minimizing the pollution which may be caused to the environment taken as a whole by the releases having regard to the best practicable environmental option available as respects the substances which may be released.

   (8)   An authorization for carrying on a prescribed process may, without prejudice to the generality of subsection (1) above, include conditions –

      (a)  imposing limits on the amount or composition of any substance produced by or utilized in the process in any period; and

   (b)  requiring advance notification of any proposed change in the manner of carrying on the process.

...

(10)  References to the best available techniques not entailing excessive cost, in relation to a process, include (in addition to references to any technical means and technology) references to the number, qualifications, training and supervision of persons employed in the process and the design, construction, lay-out and maintenance of the buildings in which it is carried on.

## 7. Netherlands, *Act of 26 November 1970 Containing Regulations for the Prevention and Limitation of Air Pollution (Air Pollution Act)*

### Chapter I

### Definitions

### Article 1

For the purposes of this Act and its implementation, the following definitions shall apply:

   * air pollution: the presence in the atmosphere of pollutants;

   * pollutants: solid, liquid or gaseous substances, other than fissionable matter, ores or radioactive matter as referred to in the Nuclear Energy Act, which, when present in the air either alone or together with or in combination with other substances, can constitute a danger to public health or a nuisance to the public, or can cause damage to animals, plants or goods;

   ...

   * act causing pollution: an act which may cause one or more pollutants to be emitted into the atmosphere and which does not result from the normal use of a machine or fuel and is not performed in an establishment with respect to which either Article 20 of this Act or Article 2 of the Nuisance Act is applicable.

### Chapter II

### The Air Pollution Council

### Article 2

There shall be an Air Pollution Council.

### Article 3

(1)  It shall be the duty of the Council to advise Our Minister, either at his request or of its own volition, on the implementation of this Act and on all other matters relating to air pollution.

(2)  Each year the Council shall publish a report containing among other things an account of the situation with regard to air pollution in the Netherlands and of any developments therein. The report shall be forwarded to Our Minister and to the States-General.

...

### Chapter III

### Machines, fuels and acts causing pollution

### Article 13

(1)  To prevent and limit air pollution, regulations governing machines, fuels and acts causing pollution may be made by General Administrative Order.

(2) These may include regulations which:

(a) prohibit the use, manufacture, importation, storage with a view to sale, offering for sale, sale, delivery or transportation of a machine or fuel belonging to a category designated by the Order, in so far as the advantages of allowing the same would not, in Our opinion, outweigh the disadvantages from the point of view of air pollution;

(b) prohibit doing the same without a licence granted by a body designated by the Order;

(c) prohibit doing the same if the machine or fuel does not satisfy the requirements prescribed by the Order;

(d) prohibit doing the same if the machine does not belong to a type approved at an inspection carried out in accordance with the provisions laid down for that purpose by or under the Order;

(e) prohibit the use of a machine belonging to a category designated by the Order if no proof can be produced that it was approved at an inspection carried out within a preceding period specified by the Order and in accordance with the provisions laid down for that purpose by or under the Order;

(f) prohibit the provision of a fuel belonging to a category designated by the order for a machine or a dwelling or other building when the fuel is intended for use therein;

(g) prohibit the use of a machine or fuel belonging to a category designated by the Order at places specified by the Order, in a manner specified by the Order or in circumstances specified by the Order;

(h) impose an obligation on the user of a machine belonging to a category designated by the order to measure the emission of pollutants from that machine in a manner specified by or under the Order;

(i) impose an obligation to give notice of the use of a machine or fuel in the cases specified by the Order and in the manner specified by the Order.

## Article 14

A General Administrative Order as referred to in Article 13 may also impose an obligation on the person concerned to comply with further requirements, concerning subjects dealt with in the Order, set by government bodies designated by the Order. When such a requirement is set, the time at which the obligation in respect of that requirement shall commence, shall also be determined.

## Article 15

In a General Administrative Order in which regulations of the type referred to in Article 13, paragraph 2(a), (b), (c) or (d), were made in respect of machines, a period shall also be specified upon whose expiry those regulations become applicable to machines which have already been manufactured and are present in the Netherlands when the Order comes into force.

...

Chapter IV
Establishments
Part 2
General Provisions
Article 19

(1) Categories of establishments capable of causing a significant amount of air pollution shall be designated by General Administrative Order.

(2) In areas where there is considerable air pollution, categories of establishments capable of causing air pollution may also be designated by General Administrative Order.

...

## Article 20

(1) An establishment belonging to a category designated under paragraphs (1) and (2) of Article 19 shall not:

    a.  be set up or operated, or

    b.  be altered or extended, nor shall any method employed in the establishment be changed, without a licence issued by the Executive of the province in which the establishment is or will be situated, either wholly or mainly.

(2) A licence shall be valid for both the person to whom it has been issued and his successors in title.

...

## Article 27

(1) A licence may only be refused for the purpose of preventing or limiting air pollution.

(2) A licence may stipulate that it shall lapse if that to which it relates has not been put into operation within a period specified in the licence, such period to be reckoned from the time at which the licence becomes irrevocable.

## Article 28

(1) A licence shall be issued subject to the conditions necessary for the prevention and limitation of air pollution. The conditions attaching to a licence may include:

    (a)  the obligation to apply methods for the prevention and limitation of air pollution as specified therein;

    (b)  the proviso that the amount of pollutants which may be emitted from the establishment or the concentration of pollutants emitted from the establishment in the surrounding area must not exceed a stated limit;

    (c)  the obligation to measure the emission of pollutants and to measure the concentration of pollutants in the surrounding area;

    (d)  the obligation to made the results of the measurements referred to under (c) available to the government bodies designated by the condition.

...

(3) The conditions attaching to a licence may contain the obligation to satisfy further requirements set by government bodies designated in the condition. When such a requirement is set, the time at which the obligation is to commence with regard to that requirement shall be stated.

## Article 29

A condition may also be attached to a licence under which the holder of the licence is obligated to furnish all the persons employed in his establishment with instructions in writing intended to preclude any actions on their part which might result in the establishment being set up or run in a manner that is inconsistent with the licence, or in a provision attaching to the licence being contravened.

...

Part 3
Closure of the establishment
Article 39

(1) If anything is done in relation to an establishment in breach of the prohibitions imposed in Article 20, the Provincial Executive may order the person concerned to close the establishment or a part thereof, or to put out of service a machine employed therein.

...

Chapter VI
Measurement of air pollution
Article 59

(1) It may be provided by General Administrative Order that:

(a) when a government body is taking measurements of air pollution, the regulations prescribed by the Order are to be observed;

(b) the provincial and municipal authorities, bodies having legal personality ... and other public bodies, designated by the Order, shall be bound within the area of their jurisdiction to take measurements as referred to under (a) or to cooperate with any government bodies taking such measurements, thereby observing the regulations prescribed by the Order.

(2) Regulations as referred to in paragraph (1)(a) and (b) hereof may relate *inter alia* to:

(a) the density of the network of measuring stations;

(b) the frequency with which the measurements are to be taken;

(c) the methods to be applied in taking the measurements;

(d) the making of meteorological observations;

(e) the processing and recording of the results of the measurements;

(f) the making available of the results and the transmission of information thereon to the government bodies designated by the Order.

...

# Questions and problems

a) *International law*

1. Make separate diagrams indicating producing activities, polluting substances and damaging effects of (a) acid rain; (b) ozone-layer depletion and (c) greenhouse gases.

2. What human activities and air pollutants could have a cumulative effect on acidification, ozone layer depletion and global warming? Can the 1979 Geneva Convention on Long-Range Transboundary Air Pollution be instrumental in controlling emissions of ozone depleting substances and/or greenhouse gases?

3. Is the atmosphere a "common heritage of mankind"? What is the meaning and the legal consequence of such a characterization?

4. What institutional mechanisms should be developed at the international level for better protection of the atmosphere?

5. Is adaptation/evolution a reasonable solution to the problems raised by climate change? Would global warming have positive consequences at least for some countries? Evaluate the answer given to Bangladesh by one US delegate in the IPCC Working Group on Response Strategies when affirming that sea level rise was not a disadvantage, but merely a "change in resources – instead of cows there would be fish".

6. Is it possible to achieve a worldwide policy of clean production, renewable energy and energy efficiency? What could be the social, economic, and environmental advantages and disadvantages of such a global strategy? Do we need a non-fossil-fuel dependent industrial world?

7. Can the territorial sources of acid rain always be identified? How can environmental law react to the problem of diffuse sources of air pollution?

8. The 1979 Geneva Convention on Long-Range Transboundary Air Pollution is generally described as a "weak" normative instrument. What legal features of the Convention do you identify as expressing "soft law"? Can you find some stronger legal elements of a protective or controlling nature? What are the arguments for taking either a "soft" or "hard" approach to the regulation of transboundary air pollution through an international convention? Are your answers the same for efforts to protect against global climate change?

9. How could the Geneva Convention be improved in order to be more effective? How can acid rain be more efficiently combated on a global scale?

10. What are the basic legal obligations of the parties to the Vienna Convention and the Montreal Protocol? In particular, what is the meaning of "appropriate measures"? Are these measures required to be taken by all states on an equal and reciprocal basis? Is international regulation of ozone-depleting substances stronger than that concerning substances producing acid rain? What evidence supports your conclusion and reasons?

11. What decision-making, control and enforcement mechanisms are set forth in the Vienna Convention? Can the Conference of the Parties to the Convention adopt legally binding resolutions? To what extent do the obligations, control and enforcement mechanisms set forth by the Vienna Convention and the Montreal Protocol affect also non-party States?

12. What is the role of a protocol or annex to the Vienna Convention on the Protection of the Ozone Layer? What are the "pros" and "cons" of a legal structure that consists of a framework convention and additional protocols? What alternative legal formats might be appropriate or effective?

13. Describe the evidence and uncertainties that exist regarding the state of present scientific knowledge on the greenhouse effect and climate change issues. Is there enough evidence of actual and potential damage to demand immediate legal action to control emissions of greenhouse gases? What should be the goal: stabilization, reduction or elimination?

14. What are the present obligations of states parties to the United Nations Convention

on Climate Change? Is North–South equity preserved concerning both the stabilization/reduction of emissions of greenhouse gases and the need to control deforestation and to improve reforestation? What types of financial instruments and technology transfer systems are or should be established at the international level to assist developing States in their efforts to minimize emissions of greenhouse gases and to prevent deforestation? Can intergenerational equity be preserved as well?

15. Is an act such as the voluntary burning of oil-wells by Iraq during the Gulf war an international crime of the state according to the following International Law Commission Draft Articles on State Responsibility?

Article 19

...

2.     An internationally wrongful act which results from the breach by a State of an international obligation so essential for the protection of fundamental interests of the international community that its breach is recognized as a crime by that community as a whole, constitutes an international crime.

3.     Subject to paragraph 2, and on the basis of the rules of international law in force, an international crime may result, *inter alia*, from

    ...

    (d)   a serious breach of an international obligation of essential importance for the safeguarding and preservation of the human environment, such as those prohibiting massive pollution of the atmosphere or of the seas.

## b) *Community law*

1. How much variation in regulation of air pollution is permitted from one state to another? How much should be permitted?

2. Are Community norms given retroactive effect? Under what circumstances are industries required to retrofit to comply with new environmental standards? Compare the Netherlands legislation.

3. Why does the Community not impose specific technology on installations?

4. What are the obstacles to implementing Community norms on air pollution?

5. What explains the greater amount of Community action on industrial air pollution compared to that on motor vehicle emissions?

6. How does Community law implement or react to international law? In particular, what is its relation to the Geneva Convention on Long-Range Transboundary Air Pollution?

7. What are the advantages and disadvantages of controlling air pollution through (a) emission standards, or (b) air quality standards?

## c) *National law*

1. Is the definition of pollution and of air pollution the same in international, Community and national legal texts?

2. What are the advantages and disadvantages of integrated pollution control compared to a law solely and specifically addressed to air pollution?

3. Should regulators be concerned with environmental values and ethics?

4. How does UK legislation compare to Community standards and to the Netherlands law on air pollution?

5. What is the philosophy of "dilute and disperse"? Why is it considered inappropriate as an approach to environmental protection?

6. What are the advantages and disadvantages to local environmental control compared to integrated (national or industry-wide) regulation?

7. What are "environmental economics"? Do they favour environmental protection?

8. To what extent does UK law reflect the influence of international and Community law? To what extent does UK law and policy impact upon the development of international and Community law? Are the answers the same for your State?

## Bibliography

Benedict, R. E., *Ozone Diplomacy: New Directions in Safeguarding the Planet* (1991).

Bennett, G. (ed.), *Air Pollution Control in the European Community* (1991).

Caron, D., "Protection of the Stratospheric Ozone Layer and the Structure of International Environmental Lawmaking", 14 *Hastings Int'l & Comp. L.Rev.* 755–77 (1991).

Castillo Daudi, M., "La protección internacional del medio ambiente atmosférico: Estado de la cuestión", 6 *Revista De Derecho Ambiental,* 9–27 (1990).

Christol, C. Q., "Stratospheric Ozone, Space Objects and International Environmental Law", 4 *J. Space L.* 23–31 (1976).

Churchill (eds.): *Law, Policy and the Environment* (Blackwell, 1991).

Elrifi, I., "Protection of the Ozone Layer: A Comment on the Montreal Protocol", 35 *McGill L. J.* 387–424 (1990).

Flinterman, C. Kwiatkowska, B. and Lammers, J., *Transboundary Air Pollution,* Dordrecht (Nijhoff, 1986).

Kindt, J. W., and S. P. Menefee, "The Vexing Problem of Ozone Depletion in International Environmental Law and Policy", 24 *Tex. Int'l L. J.* 262–93 (1989).

Kiss, A. Ch., "Du nouveau dans l'air: des "pluies acides" à la couche d'ozone", *AFDI,* 812–22 (1985).

Kiss, A. Ch., "La protection de l'atmosphère: un exemple de la mondialisation des problèmes", *AFDI,* 1988, pp. 701–8

Lomas, O. and Adams, T., "The Environmental Protection Act 1990: Integrated Pollution Control and Air Pollution Controls by Local Authorities", 2 *Util. Rev.* 44 (1991).

Mintz, J. A., "Keeping Pandora's Box Shut: A Critical Assessment of the Montreal Protocol on Substances that Deplete the Ozone Layer", 20 *U. Miami Inter-Am. L. Rev.* 565–78 (1989).

Nagle, O. E., "Stratospheric Ozone: United States Regulation of Chlorofluorocarbons", 16 *B.C. Envt'l Aff. L. Rev.* 531–80 (1989).

Nanda, V., "Stratospheric Ozone Depletion: A Challenge for International Environmental Law and Policy", 10 *Mich. J. Int'l L.* 482 (1989).

Noble-Allgire, A. M., "Depletion of the Ozone Layer: Global Dimensions", 25 *Trial* 92–100 (1989).

Roan, S., *Ozone Crisis: The 15-year Evolution of a Sudden Global Emergency* (1989).

*This Common Inheritance: Britain's Environmental Law and Strategy* (1990). Cm 1200.

*This Common Inheritance: The First Year Report* (1991). Cm 1655.

Tromans, S., *The Environmental Protection Act 1990: Text and Commentary* (Sweet & Maxwell, 1991).

Wexler, P., "Protecting the Global Atmosphere: Beyond the Montreal Protocol", 14 *Md. J. Int'l L. & Trade* 1–19 (1990).

# PART III

# TRANSSECTORAL ISSUES

## CHAPTER X

# REGULATING SOURCES OF ENVIRONMENTAL HARM

## A. Overview

The environmental laws of many countries, as well as regional and international measures, often are adopted piecemeal. Such laws can aim to provide environmental protection for a single sector, for example the air, or even a single resource, such as a river or lake. The problem is that many products and processes threaten most or all sectors and pose particular dangers of transsectoral or cross-media environmental harm. In turn, law can regulate these products and processes directly at the source rather than through protection of the target sectors. In addition, special measures can be taken to minimize the damage from accidents and emergencies that threaten cross-media environmental harm.

Regulation of potential sources of environmental damage must take into account four stages of activity: production, transport and distribution, utilization, and elimination. Production includes both the primary components and the production processes. Particular problems are posed by nuclear power plants and radioactivity. Other concerns are created by products that separately are not hazardous, but become so when combined with other products or when misused. These in turn may create complex issues of waste disposal.

Most pollution, particularly water pollution, owes its origin to dangerous primary components, products, and processes. Water quality standards often include lists of components or products whose discharge is either forbidden or is subject to prior authorization. Special legal regimes also have been developed to regulate hazardous products, including chemicals and pesticides, radioactivity, and the wastes they produce. These measures primarily rely upon licensing, monitoring and inspections of facilities or processes utilizing hazardous products. In addition, a number of substances are regulated or banned for all or some uses. Finally, special liability rules often apply to hazardous products and processes, as reflected in the European Convention on Civil Responsibility for Damages Resulting from the Exercise of Activities Dangerous for the Environment.

### 1. *Hazardous Substances*

The number of chemical products commercially sold at present is estimated at 70,000 to 80,000, with nearly 66,000 chemical substances utilized in their production. Each year 1,000 to 2,000 new products arrive on the market, in some cases without testing or evaluation of their potentially harmful effects. According to one estimate, facts concerning the effects on human health are available for only 10 per cent of the pesticides and 18 per cent of the medicines sold. Moreover, the testing done is generally limited to direct effects on human health, not on plant life, soil, or other environmental sectors.

Such products can be dangerous to human health or to the environment. One problem for legal regulation is defining the term "dangerous". EC Directive 67/548[1] defines dangerous in an inclusive, detailed fashion. It means substances or products that are explosive, oxidizing, flammable, toxic, harmful, corrosive, irritant, dangerous for the environment, carcinogenic, teratogenic, or metagenic.

Agriculture can be an important source of soil and groundwater contamination coming from pesticides and fertilizers. The latter may lead to leaching of nitrates, potassium and phosphate into ground and surface water and contribute to the accumulation of heavy metals in the soil and to acidification. High intensity farming has exacerbated the problem. Farmers in the EC annually spend over 12 billion ECUs on artificial fertilizers, with an estimated 65 per cent of soils exceeding EC target rates for nitrate concentration. As for pesticides – disinfectants, fungicides, herbicides and insecticides – Europe is the largest agrochemical user in the world and six of the individual countries are among the top ten global consumers. Although the amount used during the past five years seems to have stabilized, this may result from the use of more powerful pesticides. As a consequence, the groundwater of all European states is threatened with contamination and soils risk loss of sustainability for crop growth. On approximately one-quarter of all European agricultural land, pesticide use is ten times the EC standard, causing health problems particularly among children.

*a. Production Controls*

Prior evaluation is required of the potential effects of chemical substances and products on humans and on the environment. Internationally, a 1974 OECD recommendation envisages coordinated methods of assessing the potential environmental effects of chemical compounds (ecotoxicity).[2] A second recommendation establishes procedural guidelines and requirements for anticipating the potential effects of chemical products on man and the environment.[3] OECD also has adopted decisions on mutual acceptance of data in the assessment of chemical products and principles of good laboratory practice (C/81/30, 12 May 1981), minimum pre-marketing data requirements regarding the assessment of chemicals (8 December 1982),

---

[1]  67/548/EEC of 27 June 1967, on the approximation of laws, regulations and administrative provisions relating to the classification, packaging and labelling of dangerous substances (O.J. no. L 196 of 16 August 1967), often amended.

[2]  OECD Recommendation C(74)215 of 14 November 1974.

[3]  OECD Recommendation C(77)97 of 7 July 1977.

and a recommendation for recognizing implementation of good laboratory practices (C/83/95, 26 July 1983).

Several texts have been adopted for the protection of worker health and safety and amelioration of the working environment. For example, International Labour Convention 155, concerning occupational safety and health and the working environment requires member states to take steps to implement and periodically review a national policy on occupational safety, occupational health and the working environment. In particular, the competent authority in each state shall determine conditions governing the design, construction and layout of undertakings, operations, alterations, safety of technical equipment, and procedures; work processes and substances and agents the exposure to which is to be prohibited, limited or made subject to authorization or control; and health hazards due to the simultaneous exposure to several substances or agents. Additional measures are required to establish notification procedures concerning occupational diseases and to compile statistics on this topic, with annual publication of information on worker health and safety and on measures taken in pursuance of the national policy. Enforcement of laws and regulations must be secured by an adequate and appropriate system of inspection. Finally, states should introduce or extend testing or other systems to examine chemical, physical and biological agents in respect of the risk to the health of workers. Application of the Convention is limited by opt-out clauses in articles 1(2) and 2(2); these provide that a ratifying state may, after consultation with employers and workers, exclude from coverage in part or in whole, limited categories of economic activity, such as maritime shipping or fishing, in respect of which special problems of a substantial nature arise, or categories of workers in respect of which there are particular difficulties. Any cases of exclusion must be reported to the ILO, together with reasons for the exclusion and indications of progress towards wider application of the treaty. The requirements of this Convention are supplemented by a 1990 Convention on Chemicals in the Workplace.

The European Community also has several directives aimed at protecting the working environment. Council Directive 78/610/EEC of 29 June 1978[4] calls for the approximation of laws, regulations and administrative provisions of Member States on the protection of the health of workers exposed to vinyl chloride monomer, a substance that can produce skin and liver diseases through prolonged and/or repeated exposure. Protection is required through technical preventive measures, the establishment of limit values for the atmospheric concentration of vinyl chloride monomer in the working area, the definition of measuring methods and fixing of provisions for monitoring the atmospheric concentrations of the substance in the working area, personal protection measures, information for workers, registration of workers according to type and duration of work and type of exposure, and medical surveillance provisions. Overall the aim is to reduce to the lowest possible levels the concentrations of vinyl chloride monomer to which workers are exposed. Monitoring and measurements must be undertaken. Similarly, Directive 83/477[5] establishes

[4]  O.J. no. L 197, 22 July 1978, p. 12.
[5]  O.J. no. L 263 of 24 September 1983, p. 25.

provisions for the protection of workers against the risk of exposure to asbestos in the workplace, while Council Directive 87/217 of 19 March 1987, concerns the prevention and reduction of pollution by asbestos.

National legislation also can focus on worker safety. In Great Britain, the Health and Safety at Work Act 1974 places a duty on any person manufacturing, importing or supplying any substance for use at work (a) to ensure that the substance is safe, (b) to have the substance tested as may be necessary and (c) to ensure adequate information about such tests. The Control of Substances Hazardous to Health Regulations 1988 impose strong obligations on employers and sometimes employees with respect to substances at work that are hazardous to health. It requires all employers to assess the risks to the health of employees and other persons arising from hazardous substances in the workplace and the steps that need to be taken to meet the requirements, as a precondition to commencing the work activity. The wide definition given to "substances hazardous to health" goes well beyond the chemical industry to affect most businesses.

The Health and Safety at Work Act 1974 also attempts to protect persons other than those at work against risks to their health and safety arising out of or deriving from the activities of persons at work. It controls the keeping and use of explosive or highly flammable or otherwise dangerous substances and generally prevents the unlawful acquisition and use of such substances. The Notification of Installations Handling Hazardous Substances Regulations 1982 require any person who undertakes any activity in which there is liable to be a notifiable quantity or more of a hazardous substance on any site or in any pipeline to notify the Health and Safety Executive in writing of the particulars at least three months before commencing the activity and of any changes thereafter. Renotification is due when the amount of the hazardous substance increases to three or more times the amount originally notified. If the substance is categorized as dangerous, 1990 regulations require the person in charge of a site to ensure that there is not present at any one time a total of 25 tons or more unless written notification with specified particulars has been given to the fire authority and to the Health and Safety Executive or local authority. Specified safety signs must be posted and maintained to warn firefighters of the presence of large amounts (more than 25 tons) of dangerous substances.

British law regulates numerous other aspects of the working environment: sanitation, hygiene, temperature and ventilation, overcrowding and accommodation, drinking water, protective clothing, the age of employees, and enclosing machinery. Regulations from 1985 require employers in certain dangerous enterprises, e.g. mines, quarries, pipelines, etc., to report major injuries, specified diseases, and dangerous occurrences to the Health and Safety Executive.

Apart from worker safety, national legislation commonly requires licences for the production of potentially hazardous products, or products containing hazardous components. In Hungary there are three kinds of licences: testing, temporary (for at least three years) and final. No final licence may be given until the temporary licence has been issued and expired. The United Kingdom, France, and Germany also have special regimes that deal with the production, distribution, marketing and application of hazardous substances, including pesticides. These measures are discussed further below.

In many countries, implementation and enforcement of production regulations is done through licensing and the requirement that all relevant information be furnished to government regulators. In addition, production often must be undertaken only in approved facilities subject to inspection. When there is reason to suspect that a product is unsafe or being used without regard to safety, manufacturers are required to comply with restrictions imposed by appropriate regulatory agencies. The laws give many agencies administrative powers to stop the sale, use or production of unsafe products, to suspend or cancel registrations, or to direct the recall of products.

Criminal laws can be invoked for deliberate or reckless conduct that leads to serious endangerment or actual harm. However, law enforcement is directed primarily toward compliance with agency orders rather than toward punishment for injuries to humans and the environment.

### b. Marketing and Use

The Community has regulated marketing of chemical products since the end of the 1960s. EC Directive 79/831[6] sets out procedures for classifying dangerous substances according to the degree of hazard and the nature of the risks entailed as well as provisions for packaging and labelling. It and its parent directive, 67/548 of 27 June 1967, as amended, aim to harmonize the legislative, regulatory and administrative measures in force in member states in regard to the classification, packaging and handling of substances dangerous to man and the environment, placed on the market in member states.

The directive has been modified sixteen times since it was adopted. Eleven of these modifications remain in force. The sixth amendment in 1979 (Council directive 79/831/EEC) introduced a system of control and prior notification before placing new chemical substances on the Community market.

As amended, Directive 67/548 establishes methods for determining the physico-chemical properties as well as the toxicity and ecotoxicity of substances and preparations and the characteristics that should be taken into account in evaluating the real or potential dangers the substances pose to the environment. The substances should be packaged and handled according to the provisions of the directive. Substances may be introduced to the market forty-five days after notification to the competent national authority. The notification should include a technical file with details regarding the new substance, as well as certain other elements. The state immediately transmits a copy to the European Commission, later joining its own comments, and the Commission in turn transmits these documents to other member states. The latter can directly consult with the national authority that received the original notification, if they desire further information on particular points.

On the basis of the information thus furnished by the member states, the Commission has established an inventory of substances found in the Community. A

---

[6]  79/831/EEC, O.J. no. L 259 of 15 October 1979, amending for the sixth time Directive 67/548/EEC on the approximation of laws, regulations and administrative provisions relating to the classification, packaging and labelling of dangerous substances.

distinction is made between new substances, and those existing on the market before 18 September 1981 listed in a European inventory of commercial chemical products. The Commission has submitted to the European Court of Justice a case against Germany concerning the right of member states to decide for themselves the labelling and classification of a substance falling within the scope of Directive 67/548/EEC. Other directives contain specific regulations for particular products: solvents;[7] paints, varnishes, printing inks, glues and related products;[8] pesticides;[9] phytopharmaceutical products;[10] polychlorinated biphenyls (PCBs) and polychlorinated terphenyls (PCTs);[11] mercury; and chlorofluorocarbons.[12] In some cases, the directives provide limit values for the contents of certain hazardous substances in products. For example, Directive 85/581 of 20 December 1985[13] establishes limits for lead and benzene in petrol. Similarly, Directive 73/404, as amended,[14] prohibits placing on the market and use of detergents containing more than specified levels of non-biodegradable substances. Two Community directives concern fertilizers. The first regulates labelling and packaging[15] while the second seeks to approximate the laws of member states relating to straight ammonium nitrate fertilizers of high nitrogen content.[16]

Many of the standards involve strict bans on certain products. For example, the pesticide directive, 79/117, provides that member states shall ban pesticides containing active ingredients listed in an Annex (mercury and its compounds and persistent organo-chlorine compounds such as DDT). Some of the restrictions do not apply to exports of hazardous products to countries outside the EC, notably the regulations concerning mercury and organochlorides. Thus, certain products harmful to human health can be and are exported, with possible consequences to health in Europe when agricultural products contaminated with these substances are subsequently imported.

Implementation of EC directives can be seen in legislation of the United Kingdom, France and Germany, among others. These laws establish the toxicity tests necessary to classify each substance, based on the Community directive on approximation of laws of member states on the classification, packaging, and labelling of dangerous substances. The regulations also specify packaging and labelling requirements. In the United Kingdom, pesticide manufacturers in particular are required to notify the

[7] 73/173/EEC, of 4 June 1973, O.J. no. L 189 (11 July 1973) (modified 82/473/EEC, O.J. L 213 (21 July 1982).

[8] 77/728/EEC of 7 November 1977, O.J. no. L 303 (28 November 1977), modified by 82/265/EEC of 16 May 1983, O.J. no. L 147 (6 June 1983).

[9] 78/631/EEC of 26 June 1978, O.J. no. L 106 (29 July 1978), modified 81/187/EEC of 26 March 1981, O.J. L 77 (2 April 1981).

[10] 79/117/EEC of 21 December 1978, O.J. no. L 33 (8 February 1979).

[11] 76/769/EEC of 27 July 1976, O.J. no. L 262 (27 September 1976) and L 197 (3 August 1979).

[12] 80/372/EEC of 26 March 1980, O.J. no. L 90 (3 April 1980).

[13] O.J. no. L 372 (31 December 1985).

[14] 73/404/EEC of 22 November 1973 (O.J. no. L 347 of 17 December 1973, p. 1), as amended by 82/242/EEC of 31 March 1982 (O.J. no. L 109, 22 April 1982, p. 1) and 86/94/EEC of 10 March 1986 (O.J. no. L. 80, 25 March 1986, p. 51).

[15] 76/116/EEC of 18 December 1975 (O.J. no. L 24, of 30 January 1976, p. 21).

[16] 80/876/EEC of 15 July 1980 (O.J. no. L 250 of 23 September 1980, p. 7).

government prior to marketing a new pesticide or suggesting new uses of an old one; to provide sufficient data to enable the government to assess dangers; to include warnings, precautions, and the names of active ingredients on product labels; and to withdraw unsafe products at the government's request. In all three countries, the government also is authorized to specify maximum pesticide residues on crops, foods, and livestock feed. In France this is done by decree. Germany includes exports among the matters regulated.

Because of their danger to the food supply and to nature, pesticides often come under particularly strict regulation. Belgium prohibits all placing on the market, acquisition, offering, exposing or placing for sale, retention, preparation, transportation, sale, importation or utilization of pesticides without prior authorization of the Minister of the Agriculture. No authorization is given without an opinion of an authorization committee, composed of seven persons chosen from the Ministries of Agriculture, Public Health and Environment, Employment and Work. The Minister of Public Health must approve all pesticides designed for non-agricultural use, based on an opinion of a council on public health. The maximum period of authorization is ten years, with possible renewals. Testing, classification according to toxicity, labelling and packaging requirements are imposed, as well as measures to avoid environmental harm. The appropriate minister keeps a register of authorized products, while there also are lists of restricted and banned products. On the international level, the UN Food and Agricultural Organization has adopted an International Code of Conduct on the Distribution and Use of Pesticides (adopted as Resolution 10/85, amended November 1989). The code is voluntary, but is intended to serve as a reference standard for entities and countries that have not yet established adequate regulatory infrastructures for pesticides. The Code establishes that governments are responsible and should take action, as a high priority, to regulate the distribution and use of pesticides in their countries, as well as the export to other countries. This includes establishing a pesticide registration and control system and a process to decide or review decisions on the pesticides to be marketed in the country, their acceptable uses and their availability to each segment of the public. Even where there are no regulations, manufacturers and traders should ensure proper testing according to good laboratory practice, quality control and that pesticides are properly packaged and labelled. Information on safe and effective use should be included in each package. Government officials should be able to see testing reports for assessment, with evaluation of data referred to qualified experts. The use and effects of pesticides should be monitored under field conditions.

In addition to the notification measures already cited, an OECD resolution of 18 May 1971 provides for all member countries to receive notification in advance of proposed measures in other member states concerning substances having an impact on man or the environment, in cases where these measures could have significant effects on their economies and commerce. The concerned countries also can consult at their request with any state that claims it is or will be affected by the proposed measures of protection. Several recommendations concern industrial secrets and property rights.[17]

---

[17] OECD Resolutions C(83)96, C(83)97 and C(83)98 of 26 July 1983.

### c. Transport and Import/Export Controls

In general hazardous products and substances can only be shipped and distributed through approved trade channels. In some cases transboundary shipment may be prohibited or subject to strict controls. In the Bulgarian Environmental Protection Act of 1990, the importation of dangerous substances into Bulgaria for storage, as well as technologies with negative environmental impacts, are prohibited. Transit of dangerous substances across the territory and the territorial sea requires authorization of the Minister of Environment, based upon international treaties to which Bulgaria is a party, with strict observance of safety measures. In Sweden, the Parliament banned in 1988 the manufacture and use of CFCs and adopted an Ordinance banning the importation of aerosol sprays containing this substance. The government followed with a prohibition, effective 1 January 1991, on importation of most plastic products, especially polyurethane, manufactured with CFCs. It covers raw materials, semi-finished goods, packaging materials, building materials, mattresses and furniture. In exceptional cases, it is possible to apply to the Swedish Environmental Protection Agency for exemption. The Agency cannot grant exemptions for products for which substitutes manufactured without CFCs exist. If a product is exempted, an environmental levy will be imposed on it. Note that for EC member states, the Treaty of Maastricht permits interim import restrictions taken for environmental reasons, subject to Community review.

British law contains two sets of regulations on transport of hazardous substances. The Dangerous Substances (Conveyance by Road in Road Tankers and Tank Containers) Regulations 1981 and the Road Traffic (Carriage of Dangerous Substances and Packages etc.) Regulations 1986 impose duties on the operator of vehicles used for the carriage of dangerous substances concerning vehicle design, materials, construction and suitability, having regard to the nature of the journey to be undertaken and the quantity and characteristics of the dangerous substances being carried. A duty also is imposed on the consignor to provide correct and sufficiently detailed information about the hazards relating to the substances, to enable the operator to comply with the Regulations.

The FAO Code of Conduct on Pesticides, discussed above, provides that the government of any country taking action to ban or severely restrict the use or handling of a pesticide to protect health or the environment should notify FAO as soon as possible and FAO will notify the national authorities of other countries. Minimum identifying information and the reasons for the control or ban should be included. Pesticides that are banned or severely restricted for reasons of health or the environment are subject to a requirement of prior informed consent. In other words, no pesticide in these categories should be exported to an importing country without that country's prior informed consent.

## 2. *Nuclear Radiation*

Concern with protecting humans and the environment from the harmful consequences of radiation began almost immediately in the aftermath of the first nuclear explosions. These concerns have grown with the use of nuclear fuels to produce energy, leading to conflicting national policies. Nuclear power plants have become significant sources of energy. In Europe, there are some 222 nuclear power plants in operation, 68 of which are in Central and Eastern European countries. Thirty-six more plants are under construction as of May 1992, twenty-nine of which are in Eastern Europe. In 1988, nuclear plants accounted for nearly 40 per cent of the electricity generated in Germany and 45 per cent in Sweden.

Nuclear power plants are the most significant man-made source of radiation. All steps of the fuel cycle are involved: mining, enrichment, energy production, reprocessing, waste disposal, and deactivation of the nuclear plant. During normal conditions, the average annual dose of radiation to the public as a result of nuclear power production is estimated to be 0.01 per cent of the dose resulting from natural background radiation. Thus under normal conditions, the risk is small. However, nuclear radiation is, by nature, harmful to life. Cancer and genetic damage are the most important effects of low-level radiation exposure for humans, as well as other animals and plants. The lack of agreement among scientists on the assessment of such risks – one of the most important examples of scientific uncertainty – has led to the adoption of different regulations and safety devices in different countries. This has generated widespread public debate over the propriety and safety of nuclear energy. The issue of nuclear safety contributed to bringing down two national governments in Sweden; a 1978 national referendum produced a thirty-year moratorium on nuclear development, with a complete phase-out by 2010.

Because of the hazards involved in the use of nuclear materials, legal controls are in place both nationally and internationally, primarily regulating the production of nuclear energy. An inter-governmental organization, the International Atomic Energy Agency, based in Vienna, recommends safety standards for protection of health and minimization of danger "to life and to property".

Nationally, nuclear energy plants generally are subject to stringent licensing requirements. In Germany, these licences set strict standards for reactor safety and require the reactor operator to guarantee provision for the management of spent fuel for at least six years. Formally, the power to grant and revoke licences lies with the designated ministries in the Länder. Their primary function, however, is to coordinate the licensing process, ensure that procedural rules have been followed, and take licensing decisions on the basis of technical and other advice. Conformity of norms is ensured through regulatory intervention of federal agencies, because final regulatory authority for nuclear safety lies with the federal government. The licensing procedure of nuclear facilities is primarily concerned with establishing whether a plant represents the "state of science and technology". The definition of this is regulated by ordinances and technical bulletins issued by the responsible federal ministry and by a system of expert review.

In the United Kingdom, a distinction is made between licensed and non-licensed sites (mainly industrial users). The latter come under the Radioactive Substances Act and must be registered with the Secretary of State responsible for the environment. Small users also must hold authorizations to accumulate and discharge radioactive substances. Authorizations are enforced through inspections. Nuclear facilities are operated pursuant to the Nuclear Installations Act under licences issued by the Nuclear Installations Inspectorate.

Although France is among the countries that most heavily rely on nuclear power, the situation is more complicated, there being no single law applicable to nuclear installations. Authorization to create a "basic nuclear installation" is regulated by several decrees.[18] None of them require special authorization as far as the choice of site for a nuclear power plant is concerned. The creation of a nuclear plant is authorized by decree of the Council of Ministers, after approval by the Minister of Health or after three months if no consent is given. Since 1988, the Minister of the Environment also must approve construction of a new plant. The decision must be preceded by a consultation among various ministries, a public investigation based on presentation of an impact statement, an examination of a preliminary safety report, and an opinion of the interministerial Commission on Basic Nuclear Installations.

Nuclear safety in France is regulated by a decree of 13 March 1973, which includes measures to be taken at each stage from conception, to construction, functioning and shutting down of installations. In addition, non-nuclear establishments situated within a perimeter zone around a nuclear installation are subject to special regulation. The 1973 decree takes "basic" nuclear installations out of the normal regulation of classified installations. However, there are other installations utilizing radioactive substances that are not "basic" nuclear plants and thus would seem to fall within the normal regulations.

The provisions of the 1973 decree are designed to prevent accidents and limit the effects of any that occur. Supervision is a matter for engineers and falls within the competence of the Ministry of Industry. A Council on Nuclear Safety makes recommendations to the Ministry on nuclear safety and provides public information in case of accidents or incidents. The Council is multidisciplinary and represents various interest groups: one member each from the National Assembly and the Senate, six representatives of trade unions, twelve independent scientists, and three representatives of environmental organizations. There is also a central service for nuclear safety that manages authorization procedures and monitors installations through specially qualified inspectors chosen from among inspectors of classified installations. The inspectors verify compliance with technical mandates, but cannot enjoin nor cite violations. The latter controls are undertaken by the central service of nuclear safety with the aid of engineers or technicians from the Institute for the Protection of Nuclear Safety attached to the Commissioner for Atomic Energy. Only the Minister of Industry can take measures in emergencies to assure security, such as suspending the functioning of the installation, on proposition of the Minister of Health. Decree

18 Decree no. 63–1228 of 11 December 1963, modified by decree no. 73/405 of 27 March 1973, 85/449 of 23 April 1985 and 90/78 of 19 January 1990.

90/78 of 19 January 1990, requires that the Minister of the Environment be informed without delay of any incident or accident. The Minister can request, jointly with the Minister of Industry, that the operator reexamine the safety of the installation. It is not a model designed for quick action.

Finally, the European Community has taken action to protect the public and workers from radiation. Several Euratom Council Directives, most recently 76/579/ Euratom and 80/836/Euratom,[19] establish radiation safety standards for the health protection of the general public and workers. Both directives apply to the production, processing, handling, use, holding, storage, transport and disposal of natural and artificial radioactive substances and to any other activity that involves a hazard arising from ionizing radiation. All such activities are subject to prior authorization, reporting, surveillance, and inspections, with certain exceptions. In addition, maximum dose limits are established for the public and workers, with provisions for monitoring and assessments. Directive 80/836 added as a fundamental principle "operational protection of the population" meaning "all arrangements and surveys for detecting and eliminating the factors which, in the production and use of ionizing radiation or in the course of any operation involving exposure to its effects, are liable to create an unjustifiable risk of exposure for the population". The extent of precautions depends upon the magnitude of the risk of exposure, especially in the event of an accident, and upon demographic data. Measures must include the examination and testing of protective arrangements and dose determinations carried out for the protection of the population. Also included are examination and approval of proposed installations involving an exposure hazard and of the proposed siting of installations within the territory, as well as checks on safety equipment and measuring devices. Other provisions apply to preventing and limiting the consequences of accidents.

## 3. Hazardous Processes and Activities

According to prevailing views, major accidents and their consequences are within the scope of environmental law to the extent that they are caused by human activities. As with pollution in general, natural events, however great their consequences, are excluded from consideration. The most serious industrial accident in the history of the EC occurred on 10 July 1976, at Seveso, Italy. On 24 June 1982, the EC adopted the directive now known as the Seveso directive. It aims at risks of serious accidents from listed industrial activities undertaken in particular installations and those employing or stockpiling one or several dangerous substances. Accidents include an emission, a fire, or an explosion of major importance with regard to the industrial activity, entailing serious, imminent or long-term danger for humans inside or outside the establishment and/or for the environment.[20] Annex I to the Seveso directive enumerates the industrial activities to which it applies, including production, proc-

---

[19] 76/579/Euratom of 1 June 1976 (O.J. no. L 187, 12 July 1976, p. 1) and 80/836/Euratom of 15 July 1980 (O.J. no. L 246, 17 September 1980, p. 1).

[20] Article 1, Directive 82/501, O.J. no. L 230 of 5 August 1982, modified by directive 87/216 of 19 March 1987, O.J. no. L 85 of 28 March 1987.

essing or treatment of substances using specific procedures (e.g. hydrolysis, oxidation, polymerization). Annex III lists some 180 substances whose presence can create a presumption of danger.

Major accident hazards sometimes are not covered by general legislation. Accidents at sea, for example, are regulated by specific texts. In other cases, provisions appear in particular treaties: the two Bonn Conventions of 3 December 1976, one of which concerns protection of the Rhine against chemical pollution, the other pollution by chlorides, establish a warning system in case of a sudden increase of polluting substances in the river, or if a government has knowledge of an accident capable of seriously threatening Rhine water quality (article 11 of each treaty). Unfortunately, the system did not operate as foreseen when toxic substances were discharged in massive quantities into the Rhine following a November 1986 fire at the Sandoz factories near Basel, Switzerland. Subsequently, the agreements were revised and improved. Switzerland has integrated into its national legislation the principles of the Seveso directive.

Finally, as is the case throughout environmental law, regulations relating to major hazards treat separately those arising from nuclear activities.

*a. Regulation*

It is clear in the framework outlined by international instruments and by Community directives, that the establishment and implementation of standards fall to individual states. Regulation begins with the designation of installations presenting major risks.

Rules concerning major hazards generally respond to two needs: first, adoption of preparatory measures to be taken in advance of an eventual accident and its consequences; second, defining the actions to take when the accident occurs.

A certain number of precautionary measures should be observed. First, the risk of accident should be taken into account in deciding whether to grant a licence to an installation and, if so, under what operating conditions. The intervention of different competent authorities is important in this regard, as is the public, who should be informed and participate in any decision authorizing the activity or limiting or refusing such authorization.

Several accidents, notably Bhopal, India, which caused more than 2,500 deaths and the evacuation of some 20,000 persons in December 1984, demonstrate the importance of surrounding hazardous operations with an adequate security perimeter and of forbidding the construction of homes within the zone. Such measures can entail significant economic consequences, including depreciating land values in the surrounding areas.

For functioning installations, any effective response in case of an accident is dependent upon the acquisition and dissemination of basic information to the authorities and the public. Authorities must know the geographic location and dominant meteorological conditions, as well as the potential sources of danger from the site, the maximum number of persons working on the site and those exposed to risk. A general description of technical processes, elements of the installation important to security, a list of substances stockpiled or employed, products manufactured, by-products and residues is also necessary. Installations should inform the authorities of measures taken to assure the proper functioning of machinery in secure conditions, emergency plans, as well as services and persons competent to handle security matters (article 5 of the Seveso directive).

The public also should be informed and acquire some information during the public hearings preceding licensing. However, this is generally insufficient. According to the Seveso directive, all those potentially affected must be given the name and address of the enterprise that could be the origin of sudden pollution, the name of the person responsible for safety, the nature of the activities that could be the cause, the principal potential dangers, the nature of the accident hazard, the means by which the population will be alerted in case of accident, and, of course, the actions they should take.

In nuclear matters, governmental measures should be based, at least in principle, on the non-obligatory texts of the International Atomic Energy Agency. Its codes of good practices and guides relating to safety of nuclear facilities contain standards relating to choice of sites, taking into account atmospheric conditions and water as well as population density; the organization and construction of nuclear facilities; the qualification of personnel; general principles of safety and emergency systems, as well as the definitive shutdown of the facility.

If a major accident occurs, the operator is obliged immediately to inform the competent authorities, communicating all useful information on the circumstances of the accident, the dangerous substances which are involved, and the emergency measures to take. It should also make known all the facts available to evaluate the impact of the accident on humans and on the environment. The competent authorities should assure that the emergency measures and measures necessary in both the medium and long term are taken. They should also gather, as much as possible, necessary information to complete the analysis of the accident and eventually to make recommendations (Seveso directive, article 10).

The International Atomic Energy Agency also has elaborated directives. However, these texts have not been taken into consideration by all states as they should have been. Upon the occurrence of the Chernobyl nuclear reactor accident on 26 April 1986, the former Soviet Union did not respect the norms regarding immediate notification of the population, especially those in foreign countries. As a result, two new international conventions were adopted on 26 September of the same year. Most European States are parties to the conventions. The first imposes an obligation on a state party to provide notification without delay of any nuclear accident and rapidly to furnish pertinent available information. The information should include, to the extent known, the exact time, location and nature of the accident, the installation or activity concerned, the presumed or known cause, the likely evolution of the accident, the general characteristics of the radioactive discharge, and current meteorological conditions, and protective measures taken or projected outside the site. The information should be supplemented as new data become available. States affected can demand further information or consultations in order to limit as much as possible the radioactive consequences within the limits of their jurisdictions. The obligation to notify applies to all accidents from any nuclear reactor, any nuclear fuel cycle facility, radioactive waste management facility, the transport and storage of nuclear fuels, as well as any operation involving the manufacture, storage, disposal or transport of radioisotopes. The follow-up to the Chernobyl accident has shown that the different states act differently based on such information, especially in evaluating the consequences of the accident, that is, the applicable standards concerning contamination levels.

A second convention, also adopted at Vienna on 26 September 1986, concerns assistance to foreign states in case of a nuclear accident or urgent radiological situation. It provides details of two types of measures to aid states that are victims of nuclear catastrophes: those to be taken prior to potential accidents and those which should be undertaken when the situation is actually presented. Assistance, which should be requested by the State where the accident occurs is not obligatory. The State Party requiring assistance should indicate the scope and type of assistance required and should furnish all necessary information. Requests may include medical treatment or the temporary relocation of persons involved in a nuclear accident or radiological emergency into the territory of another state. Direction, control, coordination and supervision of assistance falls on the requesting State.

### b. Liability

Originally, the norms of responsibility applied by European states to damage caused to the environment by accidents were scarcely different from those of common law. The conclusion of the European Convention on Civil Responsibility for Damage Resulting from the Exercise of Activities Dangerous for the Environment will likely modify this situation, in introducing specific uniform rules.

There also exist special international conventions concerning certain sectors, where the damage caused by accidents can be particularly important. This is the case for damage caused by pollution of the sea by oil (Brussels Civil Liability Convention of 29 November 1969, completed and modified in 1971, 1977 and 1984) and for pollution damage resulting from exploration and exploitation of mineral resources of the marine sea-bed (London Convention of 1 May 1977). There are two conventions relating to civil liability for nuclear damage (Paris Convention of 29 July 1960 and the Vienna Convention of 21 May 1963). These instruments impute liability automatically to the operator of a nuclear installation, without the necessity of demonstrating fault.

### 4. Wastes

Waste has been defined as any substance or object that the holder disposes of or is required to dispose of pursuant to the provisions of legislation.[21] This definition is parallel to that contained in various national laws; article 1 of the French law no. 75/960 of 15 July 1975 speaks of "any object that is abandoned or that its holder

---

[21] Directive 75/442/EEC of 15 July 1975, article 1a, O.J. no. L 194 of 25 July 1975.

seeks to abandon". The definitions both contain a subjective element of intention to dispose of something.

The current scope of the waste problem is relatively new, having appeared with the industrial age and human population explosion. Non-industrial, rural areas experience few of the problems of waste disposal. In pre-industrial Europe, domestic animals consumed some wastes, another part was utilized as agricultural fertilizer, and most metal was recycled. Today, the constant increase in wastes has become a major concern. In 1989, non-communist European countries "produced" 136 million tons of domestic wastes and more than 300 tons of industrial wastes, 10–15 per cent of which was considered dangerous. When the countries of central and eastern Europe are added, with nearly 36 million tons, there are close to 50 million tons of dangerous waste produced each year in Europe.

In addition to domestic and industrial wastes, if one adds agriculture, mines, and dredging, Europe produces more than 2 billion tons of waste each year; that is, 65 tons a second. The amounts produced have continued to grow: between 1980 and 1985, household wastes increased by 1.3 per cent a year; from 1985 to the end of the decade the increase was 2.8 per cent a year. Relatively developed economies produce the greatest amounts of wastes. Germany, France, the United Kingdom and Italy produce 85 per cent of the total volume of wastes and 78 per cent of dangerous substances within the Community, while Ireland, Denmark, Portugal, Greece and Spain together count for about 5 per cent of the total volume and 4 per cent of the dangerous substances.

It should be added that the wastes mentioned above do not include those emitted into the air or into water. A complete picture must include all polluting emissions. These, too, are substances that the owner seeks to abandon. Thus, wastes as they are classically thought of, can be transformed into smoke, by incineration, or into liquid discharges by dissolving in water. However, common usage generally restricts the term waste to solid wastes, not including liquid or gas emissions.

The origin of wastes can determine their treatment. Normally, a distinction is made between household wastes collected in neighbourhoods, industrial wastes, agricultural wastes, and medical wastes. In all cases, wastes can be dangerous or not. The definition of dangerousness depends upon several criteria: activities from which the wastes come (e.g. medical wastes, companies producing pharmaceuticals and herbicides); substances contained in the wastes (e.g. arsenic, mercury, cadmium, lead, and their compounds); and characteristics of the wastes (flammability, toxicity, corrosiveness, etc).[22]

Solid wastes can be eliminated by different methods: discharge such as deposit into dumps, burial in the earth, submersion into the ocean or lakes, incineration. All these operations risk raising objections coming either from neighbours or from authorities charged with protecting the environment, or both. From this the term NIMBY has arisen: "not in my back yard", meaning each person agrees that wastes

---

[22] See annexes 1 and 3 of the Basel Convention of 22 March 1989 on transfrontier movements of dangerous wastes and their elimination.

should be disposed of, but not in any proximate location. Similar objections have been raised to incinerators.

Fortunately, more ecological disposal methods exist: re-utilization, recycling, as well as reduction in the quantity of wastes produced. However, recourse to these methods presupposes substantial material means and both organization and substantial discipline.

Some management rules can be extracted from European legislation. It is useful to examine them before analyzing different methods of waste disposal.

### a. Management Rules

The objective of management rules has been defined by EC Directive 75/442, adopted 15 July 1975: dispose of wastes without endangering human health, without threatening harm to the environment through creating risks for water, air, or soil, flora or fauna, without establishing nuisances due to noise or odours, and without endangering sites or countrysides.[23]

In several countries, the disposal of wastes is the object of framework legislation, promulgated at the national level (e.g. the German law of 1972 on wastes modified in 1977; French law of 15 July 1975; Italian law of 10 September 1982; Luxembourg law of 26 June 1980; Dutch law of 1977). In other cases, legal principles regulating wastes form part of the general law on environmental protection (Swiss federal law on environmental protection, in force since 1 January 1985, articles 30–32), completed by special instruments (Swiss ordinances of 12 November 1986 on movements of wastes; of 10 December 1990 on the treatment of wastes; of 22 August 1990 on drink packaging). The fundamental provisions concerning wastes also can be incorporated in a law specially concerned with pollution (United Kingdom, Control of Pollution Act of 1974, first part).

As far as management itself is concerned, most European legislation reveals a strong tendency to decentralization. The UK law of 1974 on pollution requires local authorities, the county councils in England, district councils in Wales and Scotland, to prepare plans for the disposal of all wastes, from whatever source; the Dutch law of 1977 on wastes delegates coordination of disposal procedures to the provinces, while waste collection itself is the responsibility of municipal authorities. These provisions are in conformity with article 5 of EC Directive 75/442 on wastes, according to which member states should establish or designate one or several competent authorities responsible within a given zone to plan, organize, authorize and supervise the operations of waste disposal.[24]

The fundamental principle is that wastes should be permanently under the control of designated authorities. These authorities must establish plans covering the types and quantities of wastes to discharge, appropriate sites for discharge, and conditions to impose. Anyone holding wastes should either assure the elimination of the wastes, or deliver them to a public or private collector or to a waste treatment plant (articles

---

[23] Article 4, Directive 75/442/EEC of 15 July 1975, O.J. no. L 194, of 25 July 1975.
[24] *Op. cit.*

6 and 7). Waste treatment plants, as well as those for storage and dumping, should obtain prior authorization specifying the types and quantities of wastes to be treated, as well as precautions to be taken and general technical requirements. At the request of the competent authority, the installation should provide information on the types and quantities of wastes as well as their origin, intended destination and planned disposition. In addition, a periodic inspection should be undertaken, principally in compliance with the conditions of the licence (articles 8 and 9).

Directive 75/442 was the first Community directive invoking the "polluter pays" principle. According to article 11, the cost of eliminating wastes should be borne first by the holder who delivers wastes to a collector or an enterprise and then, when appropriate, by the former holders or the producer of the product generating the wastes.

All European regulations, those of the Community as well as those of national legislation, establish especially strict treatment for toxic and dangerous wastes. According to a Community directive of 20 March 1978, replaced on 12 December 1991,[25] these wastes should be stocked, treated and/or disposed of, only by installations, establishments or enterprises having obtained a special authorization. Operations of elimination should be supervised by authorities designated for this purpose. A register of wastes should be maintained by the operators and a document of identification should accompany any transport of wastes.

Certain countries have anticipated these norms. In Germany, the terms of a federal ordinance of 1977 require the producers of "special" wastes to maintain a register of these wastes. The transport of such wastes must be authorized and documents permitting identification of wastes (their nature, composition, volume, etc) should accompany the transport. These last provisions are found also in the British regulations elaborated in application of the Control of Pollution Act of 1974.

The elimination of radioactive wastes is generally regulated by special texts, outside of texts governing wastes in general, or even toxic or dangerous wastes. The reason is, no doubt, that these substances can be particularly hazardous because of their effects as well as because of their persistence. Nuclear waste regulation is based in large part on international texts concerned particularly with transnational movements (see, e.g. the Code of Good Conduct elaborated by the International Atomic Energy Agency in June 1990).

The management, storage, and discharge of radioactive wastes on the territory of states also are regulated by national legislation. The French law of 30 December 1991, concerning research on the management of radioactive wastes, is particularly interesting in this regard. Its significant fundamental principle is announced in the first article: the management of highly active and persistent radioactive wastes must be assured with respect for the protection of nature, the environment, and health, taking into consideration the rights of future generations. This last affirmation places the problem in its true, long-term perspective. The resulting standards establish both an administrative licensing system and the conditions for authorization. The latter

[25] No. 91/689, O.J. no. L 377 of 31 December 1991, giving a new definition of toxic or dangerous wastes.

cannot be granted or prolonged except for limited periods. Radioactive products must be disposed of at the expiration of the licence. Stocking of imported radioactive wastes in France is prohibited, even if they have been treated within the country, beyond the time necessary for treatment. The law also defines the conditions for studying the possibility of stocking persistent, highly active radioactive wastes in deep underground areas; in general, such research requires a licence issued by decree after an impact study, permission of the competent authorities, and public hearings. Finally, the law creates a National Agency for the Management of Radioactive Wastes, with a mandate to manage the long-term disposal of radioactive wastes. In addition, a local information and monitoring committee is established for each site on which subterranean research will be conducted.

### b. Methods of Waste Discharge

The different methods utilized to discharge wastes can have widely varying effects on the environment, necessitating elaboration of specific rules.

### i. Dumping sites

This form of waste elimination is the oldest and also the most widespread. An average of 60 per cent of household garbage is discharged into dump sites. In numerous European regions, having particularly dense populations, landfills have reached their limits, so that other regions are being sought to receive waste deposits.

Dumps and waste landfills can be particularly dangerous for the aquatic milieu. Rainwater or flooding can cause toxic material to enter surface waters. The origin of the Sandoz factory accident in Basel in November 1986 was a fire in a chemical waste dump; the utilization of large quantities of water by firefighters transported these substances into the Rhine, causing serious pollution. Toxic substances can seep into subterranean water sources where they will persist for many years.

The first condition for waste installations is comprehensive knowledge of the site to choose, hence the importance of the licensing procedure and a detailed impact study taking into account all the particularities, hydrographic and geological, of the site. In this regard a French ministerial circular of 22 January 1980, establishes three categories of sites that can receive wastes: the first category has impermeable ground and does not permit underground infiltration of substances, the second has limited permeability, and the third is entirely permeable. The licence to accept wastes details in each case the substances that can be deposited in a site belonging to a particular category.

Similarly, an Italian governmental decree of 27 July 1984 establishes several categories and sub-categories of wastes, according to the nature of wastes which can be deposited and according to the presence of certain matter. The norms which govern, notably for the construction and functioning of waste disposal, are inscribed in the licence delivered to the operator. Another, stricter method, is utilized in the Netherlands whose territory is extremely limited in proportion to its population; the law of 1976 on chemical wastes forbids the disposal of wastes containing more than a certain proportion of any of eighty-three specified substances, as well as those coming from nine categories of activities. It also is generally forbidden to discharge or place on the soil used oil.[26] Similarly, special rules are adopted for motor vehicles whose proprietors wish to dispose of them; they must be delivered to a recognized demolition enterprise.

In several countries, the past has left a heavy burden in this field: waste disposal sites, primarily industrial, contain toxic and dangerous substances that have been abandoned, often in unknown areas. It is important to uncover these sites; inventories can be prepared and a regular inspection conducted by authorities. The cleanup of polluted sites is very expensive. The Netherlands had to demolish areas constructed on toxic disposal sites, notably in Lekkerkerk; 870 persons were evacuated, one hundred houses demolished. The operation cost some $70 million. The Council of Europe Convention on Civil Responsibility for Damage Resulting from the Exercise of Activities Dangerous for the Environment, adopted in September 1992, contains important provisions on this subject. It declares that the operator of a site is responsible for damages caused by wastes placed in permanent disposal, at the moment when the damage occurs (articles 5–7).

## ii. Incineration

Incineration is used to dispose of either household wastes or "special wastes", that is, certain chemical substances. In the first case the advantage of the operation is to reduce considerably the volume of wastes and to produce energy. The negative aspect is that there remain residues that often contain potentially toxic material to dispose of and for which significant investment may be necessary to avoid toxic and foul-smelling emissions. For "special wastes", like dioxin, incineration is sometimes the only method of elimination. The main problem this poses is the resulting air pollution. Preventing the latter requires very advanced technology, therefore considerable economic investment, and a rigorous monitoring of the functioning of installations.

In spite of the problems, European states have increased their use of incineration as a method for disposing of wastes, above all for toxic and dangerous substances. The alternatives are landfill, which presents too many dangers, export towards a less-developed country or another region of the same country – now prohibited – or other means that may be impractical where the territory of the State is already overutilized. It is also clear that incineration technology is progressing. Nonetheless, maritime shipboard incineration is prohibited by the 2 March 1983 Protocol to the Oslo Convention for the Prevention of Marine Pollution by Dumping from Ships and Aircraft (15 February 1972).

Incineration levels are different for household wastes and special wastes. For the first, the scope has remained the same since 1985: approximately 20–25 per cent of organic wastes are burned. In contrast, the amount of incineration of toxic or dangerous substances has continued to grow. Currently, approximately 1.5 million

[26] Conforming to article 4 of Directive 75/439/EEC of 16 June 1975, on the disposal of waste oils O.J. no. L 194 of 25 July 1975.

tons of toxic or dangerous wastes are incinerated each year in Western Europe. Germany leads in this field with nearly 740,000 tons.

All major waste incinerators are licensed. The norms aimed at preventing air pollution are applicable to these installations with, sometimes, additional specifications deemed necessary by the nature of the substances burned.

### iii. Immersion in water

The immersion of wastes in the sea is regulated by the international conventions previously discussed. The immersion of radioactive wastes in the sea is forbidden by the London Convention of 29 December 1972 (article IV and annex I). An international organization created by western industrialized States, the Nuclear Energy Agency, controls the immersion of other radioactive material.

The immersion of wastes in lakes and rivers is regulated by Community instruments and national legislation regarding water pollution. Special mention can be made, however, of international treaties relating to protection of the Rhine against pollution and especially chloride pollution.

### iv. Re-utilization of wastes

Recommendations of international organizations, such as the OECD, were among the first legal texts to mention re-utilization of certain wastes, such as drink containers.[27] Some countries have introduced obligatory recycling or reusable packaging and which are clearly identifiable as such (Swiss decree of 22 August 1990 on drink packaging; Danish law of 1978 on reutilization of wastes). These containers are consigned to the seller who is required to accept them on return (Swiss decree, art. 5). Containers made of PVC (plastics) are prohibited and the maximum quantities of non-recyclable containers are fixed by material: thus the maximum quantity of aluminium coming from packaging that should appear in urban waste is eight hundred tons per year (Swiss decree, art. 6). Re-utilization is most common for glass, which constitutes above 7 per cent of household wastes.

Of course, the main instruments encouraging re-use of wastes combine obligations imposed on manufacturers and retailers with reimbursement to consumers of container deposits.

### v. Recycling

The difference between re-use and recycling of wastes is that in principle reuse does not change the nature of the object, while recycling transforms the waste into new products. Here again, the basic texts come from international or Community action. Two examples are particularly interesting: old paper and used oil.

Each ton of paper manufactured from recycled paper rather than new wood reduces by one-quarter to three-fifths the energy utilized and almost 75 per cent of

---

[27] OECD Recommendation C(78)8 of 3 February 1978.

the air pollution, without adding the additional waste produced by new paper. OECD recommends the collection of old papers.[28] The primary method utilized in Europe for increasing recycling is persuasion. Numbers show that it can be effective: with an average annual consumption by Western Europeans of 170–180 kilograms per year, 40–45 per cent of the papers are recycled, the national averages varying from 20 to 65 per cent.

Another example, very different from the case of paper, is the recuperation and recycling of used oils. In the past these oils were burned, creating air pollution, in particular by lead. In addition, significant quantities of motor oil were discharged into the ground or into water. A Community directive of 16 June 1975[29] invites Member States to give priority to treatment of used oil by regeneration, in forbidding any discharge into water, any disposal in the soil and any treatment that enhances air pollution above limit values established by the directive. Collection of used oil should be organized by licensed or, at least, registered companies. In application of these provisions, a French decree of 21 November 1979 established a system imposing on those holding used oil the requirement to keep it until collection or disposal. They should either give it to a recognized collection agency, or assure for themselves the transport or elimination after having obtained a permit. The collection is systematically organized throughout the territory and reserved to an agency licensed by each department, with two for Paris. The actual disposal can be carried out only by a licensed operator. To assist in financing these operations, a tax has been imposed on synthetic and mineral oils. The protection of regenerated oil has allowed an appreciable reduction in imported fuel, up to 25 per cent of new oil.

## c. Reducing the Volume of Wastes

Of course, the best method of resolving the problem of wastes is to produce the least amount possible. Several European states have moved in this direction. The primary focus has been packaging materials. In Western Europe, 30–35 per cent of the mass of household garbage, and nearly half the volume, comes from packaging. In member states of the Community, these materials and those coming from offices totalled forty million tons in 1990, of which only five million were recycled.

The most important action has been taken in this field by Germany, in the framework of its strategy to reduce wastes, adopted in 1986. One of the fundamental principles is that those who produce packaging are obliged to take it back, an application of the "polluter pays" principle: the producers pay the cost of eliminating wastes, not the public treasury. However, the real objective is to reduce the volume of wastes and to collect up to eight million tons of packing materials for recycling. The application of these measures is progressive: the collection should reach 80 per cent of packing materials by July 1995.

Packaging industries foresee a reaction through increasing the costs of packaging for customers, a supplement of perhaps 0.1 ECUs by package. Companies participating

---

[28] OECD Recommendation C(79)218 of 30 January 1980.
[29] No 75/439, O.J. no. L 194 of 25 July 1975, modified 23 December 1986.

in the system are obliged to recycle or eliminate under the best conditions packaging collected in this framework. This system could cost up to a million ECUs.

Among other methods intended to reduce the volume of wastes are encouragements, especially by financial incentives, to industries utilizing new technologies that produce less waste (Denmark, Germany, Italy).

### d. Transfrontier Movement of Wastes

One of the most difficult problems in environmental law is the movement of wastes, in particular dangerous wastes, across borders. Many states are finding it difficult to locate new sites for waste disposal and it is not easy to construct new treatment facilities. The easy solution and sometimes the least costly is to send the wastes to a foreign country. In some cases, both for economic and technological reasons, the treatment of specific kinds of wastes by a foreign country is appropriate.

Environmental law has sought a solution that permits identifying the wastes whose movements across borders should be subject to special realistic and effective regulation. Several international institutions have attempted this task: OECD, the European Community and UNEP. UNEP sponsored the adoption of an international Convention on Transboundary Movements of Hazardous Wastes. The treaty, the result of efforts among several organizations, was adopted in Basel on 22 March 1989. The Convention includes a definition of toxic or dangerous wastes, founded on several criteria: activity having engendered the wastes, categories of wastes, characteristics of dangerousness. The major principles applicable are those of prior consent of the importing country for any import of dangerous wastes, the obligation to reimport wastes from another state that declines to receive them, the obligation to not export wastes to a country that lacks adequate means to dispose of them.

These rules apply to the Community, contracting party to the Basel Convention. However, even before this, the problem of wastes circulating within the Community was attacked by two directives adopted to monitor and control transboundary transfers of dangerous wastes.[30] Two principles are basic to Community regulation. First, the receiving state must accept transport of wastes on its territory. Second, the wastes must be accompanied by a document giving indications of their origin and composition, the itinerary and insurance covering eventual damages, measures of security during transport, and, finally, the technical capacity to proceed in conditions which do not present a danger for human health or for the environment.

### 5. Noise

Noise is an essentially subjective phenomenon, both quantitatively and qualitatively. "Disco" music can be as loud as the sound of a jackhammer; however, adherents of the former will readily perceive distinctions between the two. The subjective element is reflected in complaints to police concerning neighbourhood

---

[30] Directive 84/631 of 6 December 1984, O.J. no. L 326 of 13 December 1984, modified several times, in particular by Directive 87/112 of 23 December 1986, O.J. no. L 48 of 17 February 1987.

noise; it appears that most originate in other disputes and are linked to long-standing resentments.

Studies on noise have established three categories for sound:

— 55–60 decibels (disturbs sleep);

— 60–65 decibels (seriously disrupts the hearer);

— above 65 decibels (can cause behaviour modification).

According to estimates of the OECD, by the beginning of the 1980s more than 130 million persons in Western industrial countries regularly were exposed to noise levels above 65 decibels. The sounds come primarily from motor vehicles, meaning that efforts to regulate noise must take into account such factors as population density, the level of urbanization and the number of cars relative to the number of inhabitants.

Noise can be combated in several ways: reducing the source, separating the sound sources from population centres, or from certain buildings (schools, hospitals) frequented by the public, isolating houses, or constructing anti-noise barriers, for example along auto routes. The different techniques can be adapted to different types of noise; they also can be combined.

As with many other areas of environmental protection, the forms and structures of legislation differ from one country to another. Some states have collected provisions concerning noise into a principal law, such as the 1979 Dutch Noise Nuisance Act (Wet Geluidhinder) and the 1973 Belgian Noise Control Act of 1973, implemented by a series of royal decrees. Other states insert into a general environmental protection law provisions relating to combating noise pollution (Swiss Federal law of 1983 on Environmental Protection, articles 11–18 and 19–25, supplemented by ordinance of 15 December 1986 on protection against noise). But the most usual method of regulating noise is through dispersed provisions found in several instruments concerning different types of activities (France, Italy, Portugal, Spain, United Kingdom). However, many sources of neighbourhood noise may be unregulated.

### a. Industrial Noise

Noise caused by industrial installations is taken into account when it produces effects outside the perimeter of the installation. During the licensing process for proposed establishments, the various sound sources can be evaluated and considered, if necessary, with conditions imposed in order to limit them. Distinctions are often made between sounds emitted during the day and those issuing during the night. Measures concerning land use or zoning are often used to restrict such installations to locations away from inhabited areas or public places; in the Netherlands, for example, all municipal administrations must create "noise zones" around particularly loud installations. Acoustical limits for industrial processes may be set by legal texts (Belgium, Italy). In Germany, if the costs of meeting the maximum standards are prohibitive, the company may ask for an exemption and pay compensation to those in the neighbourhood.

Protection of workers against noise within factories or workplaces is generally guaranteed by legislation relating to the safety of such places. EC directives provide that employers must provide protection for their employees for sounds in excess of 90 decibels. The UK has implemented this norm by the Noise at Work Regulation, which entered into force 1 January 1990. It should be noted that workers generally do not seem to favour this measure, instead preferring a reduction in noise sources.

### b. Transportation Noise

The constant growth in the number of motor vehicles, especially in the industrialized world, has made them an increasingly important source of acoustical nuisance. Road traffic now heads the list of noise sources, being the most widespread.

Several types of measures can be taken to reduce the impact of road noise. At the international level, a series of texts issued by the United Nations Economic Commission for Europe, and by the Community, limit motor noise emissions.[31] To this can be added limitations on the use of horns and other warning noises, found, for example, in the French decree of 5 February 1969. Belgium issued a motor vehicle racing decree in 1976, modified in 1987. It prohibits racing outside specified zones and requires authorizations for all races.

Other more general measures can be taken: regulation of traffic, including prohibiting trucks from certain roads or during certain hours, creation of pedestrian zones, and urban traffic plans. Measures that support public transport can encourage drivers to use these means rather than private automobiles; this approach also seeks to reduce air pollution and traffic congestion on the streets of cities.

The sound of trains has been less of a preoccupation for legislatures. However, train noise can be significant near railway stations, reaching 90 to 100 decibels, and in densely populated areas: in Switzerland more than 36 per cent of the population is exposed to at least 55 decibels from this source. With the multiplication of high speed trains, this noise source could become more important. Germany and the Netherlands are among the few states that regulate train noise.

Airplanes have become less noisy as a result of technical improvements, due at least in part to international regulations contained in annex 16, chapters 2 and 3 of the Chicago Convention on International Civil Aviation. The majority of western countries do not permit landing of airplanes without certificates demonstrating that they are in conformity with these standards. On the other hand, the increase in air traffic, close to 10 per cent per year, risks cancelling out this improvement. In many states, buffer zones are created around airports. In Germany, there are zones around more than 50 airports. The German Act of 1971 on Aircraft Noise, amended in 1986, requires all operators to conduct their activities with minimum adverse effect on the environment. There must be continuous monitoring and an airport noise committee is required to supervise compliance with noise laws.

Besides the imposition of norms, particularly for landing and take-off, taxes can

---

31 See, for example, Directive 70/157/EEC of 6 February 1970, O.J. no. L 42 of 23 February 1970, modified in 1973 and 1984 and adapted several times to technical progress, O.J. no. L 231 of 22 November 1973; L 66 of 12 March 1977; L 131 of 18 May 1981; L 196 of 26 July 1984, and L 238 of 6 September 1984.

be imposed on airplanes according to size and level of noise emitted by their engines (French decree of 23 December 1983). The regulation of air traffic can also be an effective mechanism: prohibiting landings and take-offs during the night, restricting flight paths over residential areas and national parks or flight levels below a certain altitude.

Those in the neighbourhood of airports may receive assistance to sound-proof their houses or take measures against vibrations. In some cases, individuals have invoked human rights protections in order to combat noise pollution, although without much success. In *Power and Rayner*,[32] English homeowners near London's Heathrow airport contended that noise from operations at the airport impaired the right to privacy guaranteed in article 8 of the European Convention on Human Rights. The European Court of Human Rights rejected their complaint, holding that European states have a certain amount of discretion (margin of appreciation) on decisions as to the proper scope of noise abatement for aircraft arriving and departing from their airports.

*c. Neighbourhood Sounds*

Within this category are noises from which most people claim to suffer. In the Netherlands, among 66 per cent who assert they are bothered, between 15 and 26 per cent say that such sounds are difficult to support. The problem grows with the increasing number of noise-making objects, from stereos to motorized lawn-mowers, toys and home appliances.

Regulations can impose noise emission limits on certain engines; for example, a framework directive of the EC[33] established harmonizing measures for materials utilized in construction. A French decree of 17 October 1975, establishes source noise limits for machinery used in repairs and cleaning, air conditioning, elevators (lifts), etc. Labels also can be issued for equipment or instruments respecting certain norms. Other measures impose fixed hours for utilization of noisy equipment or forbid their utilization during the night and on holidays, as well as encouraging contractors to ensure sound-proofing of homes and apartments, particularly in areas exposed to sound from airports or roads (French decree of 14 June 1969). Some local communities may ban petrol engine lawnmowers, to combat both noise and air pollution and to improve the health of the persons mowing lawns. A Belgian decree establishes acoustical standards for music in public and private areas. Inside buildings the limit is 90 decibels; outside it is 35 decibels. In addition, the government provides subsidies for local governments to purchase sound meters, one for every 50,000 inhabitants. Finally, the police or the courts can be called on to intervene when noise levels can no longer be tolerated. Here again, the best means of combating environmental deterioration may be public education.

---

[32] European Court of Human Rights, Judgment of 21 February 1990, Ser. A, no. 172.
[33] 84/532/EEC of 17 September 1984, O.J. of 19 November 1984.

# B. Case Studies

## 1. Mary Sancy, *International Environmental Law, Industrial and Radioactive Wastes*

Wastes, whether industrial or household, toxic or non-toxic, are one of the blights of our civilization. How can we rid ourselves of the residues of the consumer society?

It is estimated that each year more than three million tons of wastes are transferred from the northern to the southern part of our planet. The problem is local, regional, national and international in scope. It is estimated that for the OECD countries, production at the beginning of the 1980s amounted to 1 billion tons. By the middle of the 1980s it was 1 billion 300 million tons.[34] Within this category an increasing proportion must be considered as hazardous. It is estimated that current production for the continent of North America is in excess of 280 million tons and that of the EEC, between 20 and 35 million tons.[35] OECD admits that close to 10 per cent of the hazardous wastes produced in Europe are eliminated outside national frontiers.[36] Among the methods of elimination, incineration on land has often been chosen since the prohibition of incineration of wastes at sea.[37] Most incineration is of household wastes; however, industrial wastes are being incinerated with increasing frequency. The EEC capacity to incinerate hazardous wastes is estimated at about two million tons per year, an amount the European Commission considers to be adequate.

Radioactive wastes are covered by a large body of international regulations designed to manage the peaceful use of nuclear energy. Some countries have begun to exploit nuclear power without having previously introduced regulations applying specifically to wastes. On the other hand, techniques to neutralize such wastes are far from having proved their effectiveness.

Nuclear wastes are seldom treated on national soil. They are the object of international movements of three types:

— immersion in the sea of wastes of weak and medium radioactivity; such movements are now prohibited;

— retreatment of irradiated fuel elements of foreign origin, followed by retransfer to the country of origin following a period of storage and stabilization;

— international movements of used radio-isotopes sent back to the suppliers by countries unable to treat them.

---

[34] See "1992 et les déchets", J. P. Hannequart and Th. Lavaux, IBGE document.

[35] Belgium produces about 27 million tons per year of industrial wastes, of which 440,800 tons are hazardous. IBGE document, *op. cit.* World production is estimated at about 325 million tons.

[36] Ireland and Luxembourg export all their hazardous wastes, Switzerland and Austria close to half, Denmark and Germany 15 per cent. Belgium, on the other hand, imported six times more wastes in 1988 than it exported.

[37] This will go into force on 31 December 1994.

Aside from the retreatment of fuel, which is done in only some countries,[38] wastes are usually stored. Some are now being buried in the ground.

Finally, just as the barrels of wastes in Seveso[39] favourably influenced international regulations in the field of hazardous wastes, the accident at Chernobyl has demonstrated the risks and weaknesses of the instruments set up to manage nuclear material, whatever its status.

### a. Definitions: Hazardous, Toxic, and Nuclear Wastes

The present analysis concerns hazardous wastes rather than toxic wastes, because the latter are covered by specific international regulations and lend themselves to a comparison with radioactive wastes. Finally, the toxicity of a particular waste product is only one aspect of the danger which it represents.

The definition of waste has been a problem since the first rules were adopted in this respect. The EEC framework directive of 15 July 1975[40] states that a waste is any substance or any object which its possessor gets rid of or is obliged to get rid of due to national regulations in force. The framework directive was amended by a directive of 16 March 1991.[41]

The new directive states in Article 1 that a waste is any substance or any object which falls within the categories set out in Annex I and which the possessor gets rid of or which he has the intent or obligation to get rid of. Excluded from the definition are radioactive wastes (which are the subject of a special regulation), gaseous effluents, mining wastes, agricultural wastes, wastewater and downgraded explosives. The new definition was largely inspired by the work of the OECD. On 27 May 1988 the OECD clarified the basic notions[42] which were later embodied in the Basel Convention and have largely influenced the new directive 91/156.[43]

The current Community definition of toxic or hazardous waste is contained in Directive 78/319.[44] This definition contains a descriptive part and a list of substances in an annex. The approach is not very practical and often makes implementation impossible since the appropriate quantities and concentrations are not mentioned. The new directive on hazardous wastes which replaces Directive 78/319 has a definition closer to that of the Basel Convention on transboundary movements of hazardous wastes, discussed below. A list of these wastes will be drawn up by the

---

[38] Including the Hague centre in France.

[39] An accident occurred at Seveso, Italy, in 1976, after which 41 barrels containing earth contaminated by dioxin were sent wandering aimlessly and without control in Europe. In 1982 they were found in France and finally sent back to the producer, the Hoffmann-La Roche Company in Switzerland.

[40] 75/442, O.J. no. L 194 of 25 July 1975.

[41] 91/156, O.J. no. L 78 of 26 March 1991.

[42] Decision C (88) 90.

[43] For a more detailed study of this question see "La notion de 'déchets' at de 'déchets dangereux': les définitions proposées par la Commission des C.E.", Carel de Villeneuve in *Aménagement-Environnement*, special number on "Les Déchets", 1990, pp. 14 *et seq.*

[44] Directive 78/319/EEC on toxic or hazardous wastes of 20 March 1978, O.J. no. L 84, 31 March 1978.

Commission on the basis of distinct criteria.[45] In addition a consensus has been reached that henceforth reference will be made only to hazardous wastes, since toxicity is only one of several dangerous characteristics.[46] When a waste exhibits one of the characteristics of danger set out in Annex III, it will be considered hazardous unless there is proof to the contrary.

The definition of radioactive wastes is, on the other hand, simpler and often found in national legal texts: "all those materials which contain or are contaminated by radionucleides in concentrations higher than the values which competent authorities consider to be admissible in materials which can be discarded without control and with respect to which no use has been foreseen".[47] It should be noted that the values admissible have been modified and that substances which a few years ago were not considered to be wastes have sometimes come to be so today.[48]

At the international level, OECD initiated the important conventions and the procedures adopted for the immersion of radioactive wastes. Depending on the radioactivity they emit, such wastes will be stored temporarily until the most stable emissions have been reduced. Wastes for which radioactivity can be considered as eternal on the human scale will be stored, protected by security barriers which require particular institutional controls.

More than 80 per cent, by weight, of the radioactive wastes which result from nuclear activity consist of paper, clothing, laboratory equipment and slightly contaminated gravel and soil. All the rest is the result of the irradiation of fuel and is often exported for retreatment.

### b. Management of Hazardous Wastes

Two international organizations have been working in this area, namely OECD and UNEP. The United Nations Environment Programme (UNEP) included the elimination and transport of toxic and hazardous wastes among the priority subjects for discussion at the Montevideo Conference in November 1981. Directives were issued by the UNEP Governing Council on 17 January 1987.[49] The text is very general; however it insists on the prevention, planning and monitoring of wastes, as well as personnel training and education.

[45] Generic categories characterized by their nature or by the activity of which they are a product, provided they exhibit one of the danger characteristics.

[46] As in the case of corrosivity, inflammability, ecotoxicity, etc.

[47] Belgium: Royal decree of 30 March 1981 determining the missions and establishing the ways and means of functioning of the government organization for the management of radioactive wastes and fissionable materials, published in the "Moniteur Belge" of 5 May 1981, Article 1.

[48] See the definition given by Evdokia Moëse in the article "La réglementation internationale en matiére de déchets radioactifs", I.B.G.E. document 1991: "Toute matiére contenant ou contaminée par des radionucléides en concentrations supérieures aux valeurs que les autorités compétentes considéreraient comme admissibles dans des matériaux propres à une utilisation sans contrôle ou au rejet, et pour laquelle aucun usage n'est prévu." ("Any substance containing or contaminated by radionucleides in concentrations higher than the values which the competent authorities would consider to be admissible in substances suitable for being used or discarded without control and for which no use has been foreseen.")

[49] For a more detailed study, see A. C. Kiss and D. Shelton "International Environmental Law", p. 314.

OECD has been very active in this field for many years. In particular, it issued a general recommendation for an overall approach to the management of wastes[50] in order to protect the environment, with the wastes being reduced at the source through application of the "polluter pays" principle.

Recommendations on the re-use and recycling of beverage containers[51] as well as the recuperation of paper[52] implement the general recommendation. A recent decision of the OECD stresses the need for ecological management of wastes in order to reduce those which should be eliminated.[53]

The most important international event of recent years was the signing of the Basel Convention[54] concerning the movements of wastes. It places emphasis on the possibility of a state barring access to its territory of hazardous wastes of foreign origin, and on promoting their elimination in the State where they are produced. The term "ecologically rational and effective management" is used in the Convention, but without describing the contents in further detail.[55] Finally, the Convention prohibits the export of wastes to:

— the Antarctic;

— States parties which have announced such prohibition;

— States parties which have not expressed their consent in writing;

— States which are not parties to the Convention.

Article 11 nevertheless permits Parties to conclude regional and bilateral or multi-lateral agreements with any country or countries whatsoever, provided such agreements are ecologically sound. The field of application is determined by reference to a list of categories, characteristics, hazards and operations designed to eliminate wastes.

EEC measures to manage hazardous wastes began with a directive on wastes of 15 July 1975,[56] which established a general legislative framework, now amended by a directive of 16 March 1991.[57] The amended directive establishes a hierarchy of objectives to be attained: its priority is to encourage prevention and recycling, resorting to elimination and storage only when it is not possible to do otherwise. The new directive is inspired by a desire to promote cleaner technologies and recycling techniques protective of the environment. Annexes II and III itemize the elimination processes and the various possibilities of recuperation.

A directive of 20 March 1978[58] is more specifically concerned with hazardous

---

[50] Recommendation dated 28 September 1976 C (76)155.

[51] 3 February 1978 C (78)8.

[52] 30 January 1980 C (79)218.

[53] C (90)178. See also OECD, Environment Monographs No. 34, Follow-up and control of transboundary movements of hazardous wastes, May 1990.

[54] Signed on 22 March 1989 by some thirty countries.

[55] Article 4, §8.

[56] 75/442, O.J. no. L 194 of 25 July 1975.

[57] 1/156, O.J. no. L 78 of 26 March 1991.

[58] 78/319, O.J. no. L 84, 31 March 1978. This directive applies to wastes which contain, or which are contaminated by, substances contained in a list, and which are concentrated to a degree which makes them a health and environmental risk. Twenty-seven "toxic and hazardous" substances are mentioned. The latter include, in particular, asbestos, cadmium, pharmaceutical solvents and products, ether, mercury and tar.

wastes, providing for their collection, transport, processing, conversion, recycling and deposit. A certain number of specific, highly technical directives also have been adopted on particular substances.

On 14 September 1989 the Commission adopted a new policy on wastes. Wastes are henceforth considered to be "secondary" raw materials. The Commission has put forward five strategies designed to avoid abuse due to competition and intended to promote environmental protection. The principles of prevention, integration and subsidiarity are recognized, developing the idea that action can be more appropriate at the Community level than at the level of the Member States.

The strategies that have been developed are based on:

— prevention;

— upgrading;

— optimization of elimination;

— control of transport;

— remedial action.

Prevention must begin with the design of the products and technological processes. Recycling and re-use will be introduced through economic incentives, the creation of markets for reusable raw materials, and research and development. Elimination will be optimized by the harmonization of technologies, depending on the laws in force, and due to the suspension of the practice of incineration and discharge of wastes into the sea. Finally, remedial action will concentrate on the cleaning up of contaminated sites.

This new programme is accompanied by a great many proposals which must now be allowed to follow their respective courses. It is regrettable, however, that the priority objectives (prevention and recycling) were established without more effective instruments and that the member states are not formally obliged to give priority to the implementation of these strategies.

Among the problems of waste management are the control of wastes at source, self-sufficiency in elimination, the transport of hazardous wastes and civil responsibility for damage caused by such wastes.

Today there is general international agreement that the guiding principle underlying the management of wastes should be that of minimizing the volume of hazardous wastes through the development of clean technologies. This is reflected in the Basel Convention[59] as well as in the preamble of Directive 91/156. The Community had already made explicit reference to the principle of prevention in the Directive on containers for beverages dated 7 June 1985.[60] The Single European Act and the Maastricht Treaty are also fundamentally concerned with prevention.

On ethical grounds, it is necessary that all hazardous wastes be eliminated wherever possible at the place where they are produced. Any transport of hazardous wastes is highly undesirable for social and security reasons.

---

59 See art. 4 §2(a) of the Basel Convention.
60 Directive 85/339 of 7 June 1985, O.J. no. L of 27 June 1985.

Beginning in 1984, the OECD recommended that its member states promote the setting up of appropriate installations for the elimination of wastes within the limits of their jurisdiction. The European strategy adopted in 1989 also declares one of its goals to be the elimination of wastes throughout the EEC. The strategy places emphasis on a harmonization of technical standards with respect to installations for waste elimination, which must take into account a high level of protection.

The Basel Convention on the one hand, and Community law on the other, forbid the export of hazardous wastes without prior consent of the importing country. In order to obtain this consent, prior details concerning the plan to ship such wastes must be provided. The exporting country must deliver an authorization and follow up on the shipment.[61] The written consent of the importing country is absolutely required; its absence is tantamount to a tacit refusal.

The transfer is governed by other specific rules, such as those that apply to chemicals and transboundary pollution, as well as the rules applying to international transport.

International movements of wastes call for the establishment of an effective control system, the wastes being accompanied by a uniform shipping document. The case of transit countries is more difficult. While notification of the movement must be made, authorization from the exporting country does not apparently have to wait for receipt of consent from the country of transit. According to OECD regulations and the Basel Convention, the exporting country is responsible for the ecologically rational management of the wastes and of the proper carrying out of international movements. If the wastes do not reach the places of elimination, the exporting country must accept them back into its own territory. In the case of illicit traffic, the exporting country must be responsible for re-importing them if the exporter is unable to carry out the operation himself. The European Community prohibits export of hazardous and radioactive wastes to ACP countries.[62]

On 6 December 1984,[63] the Council adopted a directive concerning the monitoring and control within the Community of transboundary transfers of hazardous wastes. This directive was amended by directives 85/469, 86/121 and 86/479.[64] The procedure, which excludes wastes that can be recycled, controls transfers by means of a shipping document or bill which must always accompany the wastes as a means of general notification. The directive also sets forth the technical conditions for transport. The system imposed is based on the granting of authorization. Notification made by the possessor of wastes must contain information on their origin and composition, the measures which have been taken concerning the itinerary and insurance, security measures and a demonstration of the technical capacity of the

---

[61] See EEC Directive 84/631 of 6 December 1984, O.J. no. L 326 of 13 December 1984 and the Basel Convention, Article 4, 57c.

[62] Lomé IV Convention between the EEC and the African, Caribbean and Pacific States (ACP), signed 15 December 1989.

[63] Directive 84/631, O.J. no. L 326, 13 December 1984, p. 31.

[64] Respectively: O.J. no. L 272, 12 October 1985, p.1; O.J. no. L 100, 16 April 1986, p. 20; O.J. no. L 181, 4 August 1986, p. 13.

eliminating agent or installation. Prior approval from the country of destination must be obtained. The competent authorities of the importing country must acknowledge receipt and make known any objections which they may have. To avoid disturbing trade among member states, such objections must be based on the laws and regulations in force concerning protection of the environment, public order and public health. Packaging and labelling are subject to special regulations.

On 19 September 1990 the Commission approved the text of a regulation on the monitoring and control of the transfer of wastes entering and leaving the Community. Its aim is to incorporate the provisions of the Basel and Lomé IV Conventions and the Community strategy into the existing rules and regulations. This proposal covers all wastes except those destined for re-use, reprocessing and recycling. This regulation is intended to apply to any movement inside the EEC. Management must be ecological and rational. It will be necessary to establish the points of transit into and out of the EEC, and self-sufficiency of the Community with regard to the elimination of wastes is necessary. In addition, the shipments must be bonded.

### c. Civil responsibility for damage caused by wastes

The Commission published a proposed directive on 4 October 1989[65] which was amended in July 1991[66] following review by the Parliament.[67] The proposal has its source in Article 11§3 of Directive 84/631 on the transboundary transfers of hazardous wastes. Like other directives that have to do with wastes, it is based on the polluter pays principle. Producers of wastes will be held responsible all along the line for any damage caused, until transfer to the eliminating agent or installation. The liability is objective or strict, without regard to fault. Application of the directive is limited to liability for wastes, which caused a reaction in Parliament. Indeed, a directive on the overall problem of liability for environmental damage is necessary.[68] To this, the Commission replied that it was engaged in the preparation of a "green book" on the entire problem of "environmental responsibility" and that another proposed directive had been submitted on the overall question.[69]

The following principles underlie the two proposals:

— channelling of liability towards the producer;

— an obvious causal relationship;

— the absence of a limit to liability;

— proportionality between the damage and the cost of its compensation.

In the draft proposal on wastes, wherever the producer cannot be identified, the

[65] O.J. no. C 251 of 4 Oct. 1989, p. 3. See in this connection M. Sancy, "Quelques remarques et observations sur la directive du Conseil de la CEE concernant la responsabilité civile pour les dommages causés par les déchets", Proceedings of the Colloquium Euroforum Altlasten, 11–13 June 1990.

[66] O.J. no. C 192/6 of 23 July 1991.

[67] O.J. no. C 324/248 of 24 December 1990.

[68] See, for example, "Waste management policy in the internal market", Dr. J. Bongaerts, Institute for European Environmental Policy, Bonn, May 1991, pp. 40 et seq.

[69] O.J. no. C 190/1 of 22 July 1991.

person currently in control of the wastes will be liable. Public interest groups can sue for damages[70] and reimbursement of clean-up costs.[71] The right to act is also granted to government authorities. The directive will apply only to damage which occurs after it enters into force; nevertheless the wastes which caused the damage may have been produced years before. The "incident" which provokes the damage is not defined.

Damages and injuries which cannot be remedied (Article 11) will be compensated, according to the Commission.[72] Although consideration is being given to setting up a compensation fund, there is still disagreement about whether the fund should be made to cover all environmental damage.[73]

In conclusion, it should be said that this proposed directive does not offera complete solution. Still open are questions of the definition of the incident, compulsory insurance, and the retroactivity of the directive.

### d. Thoughts on the Evolution of International Law in Respect of Hazardous Wastes

Whether it be through the work of OECD, of the Basel Convention or of Community law, important principles are in the process of being adopted. Among these, prevention appears to be one of the most important over the long term. Nevertheless, Community directives have thus far shown a lack of concreteness. Recuperation and optimization of the final elimination process represents an area in which the Community has made proposals, the objective of which is clearly set forth in the new directive 75/442 as amended on 16 March 1991. Optimization of final elimination should lead to stricter regulations governing the use of improved and more advanced techniques and processes on behalf of the environment. It is a matter of giving expression to current thinking on "the best available technologies at an acceptable cost". Lists of wastes and prohibited elimination processes will undoubtedly be established.

## 2. Zdenek Madar, Laws and Regulations on Industrial and Radioactive Waste in Former Czechoslovakia

The codification of waste management has long been the weakest point in the whole system of environmental law in the Czech and Slovak Federal Republic (CSFR). Until very recently, the CSFR had no comprehensive law on waste management and

---

[70] Nevertheless national law must offer them an opportunity for legal recourse; in addition to putting an end to the situation which caused the pollution, groups may also obtain reimbursement of the costs incurred for prevention and re-establishment of the environment.

[71] For a more complete analysis see "Environmental Law and Policy", Deskbook; "The European Community Environmental Law System", Turner Smith and Roszell Hunter, Hunton & Williams, Brussels, 16 July 1991, pp. 90 et seq. and "The revised European Community Civil Liability for Waste proposal", Turner Smith and Roszell Hunter, Hunton & Williams, Brussels, 5 August 1991.

[72] Theoretically this should be before 31 Dec. 1992.

[73] See "Proposition dé directive concernant la responsabilité civile pour les dommages causés par les déchets", Philippe Renaudière, in Aménagement et Environnement, numéro spécial; Les Déchets, 1990.

disposal of unusable wastes. The only adequately codified field is that of radioactive waste disposal.

The main public health aspects of waste disposal were covered by Law No. 20/1945 on public health and implementing regulation No. 45/1966 on the establishment and safeguard of healthy living conditions (both of them still in force). These, however, lay down only the basic principles of waste management from the public health point of view, formulated in very general terms. In addition, several regulations of less legal force have been issued since the beginning of the 1960s, codifying aspects of the management of some types of waste which can be exploited further economically (such as Government Order No. 68/196 on the management of metal wastes and salvaged raw materials and Decrees Nos. 118/1971 and 12/1972 on the management of salvaged raw materials). These have been revised several times.

The completely unsatisfactory state of affairs in the field of waste management legislation has been criticized again and again since the beginning of the 1970s by advocates of environmental protection (at that time a small minority). The only result of this criticism was the drafting of a new law in the 1980s. However, this law covered only industrial wastes. Moreover, the work proceeded extremely slowly and conceptually was very poor.

Only with the introduction of democratic reforms in Czechoslovakia were the necessary conditions established for adequate and up-to-date waste management legislation. In the relatively short time that has elapsed since then, draft legislation has been elaborated which will undoubtedly help to provide a basis for future environmental protection laws. All the legal rules underlying waste management in Czechoslovakia have not yet been worked out; nevertheless, it is possible to give a sufficiently reliable account on the basis of already existing regulations.

### a. Contemporary Waste Management Codification

On 22 May 1991 the Federal Assembly of the Czech and Slovak Federal Republic enacted Law No. 238/1991 concerning wastes. It is the basis of contemporary waste management codification in the country. This law was modified from European Community legislation in order to respond to the specific situation of the Czech and Slovak Federal Republic arising from the past and from the present transition to a market economy. The envisaged accession of the CSFR to the Basel Convention on the Transboundary Movements of Hazardous Wastes was also taken into account.

The principal aims of the law mentioned are to protect the environment against the negative effects of wastes and to promote a planned and rational exploitation of natural resources, not only from the economic point of view, but also from that of the environment. The law is not limited in scope to certain violators but generally applies to all legal entities and natural persons handling wastes in one way or another. In Section II, the law defines such key notions as "waste", "special waste", "hazardous waste" and "secondary raw materials". The definitions of these terms generally correspond to definitions contained in the legislation of advanced European countries.

The Act establishes the responsibility of legal and natural persons for the management of wastes, as well as their duty to reduce to a minimum the very sources and causes of wastes. Further, it lays down the duty of every legal and natural person to protect public health and the environment when handling wastes and to create the prerequisites for the proper handling and disposal of wastes. Wastes may be dumped and disposed of only in spaces, buildings and facilities set aside for that purpose.

The Act further contains a general prohibition of waste import into the territory of the Czech and Slovak Federal Republic. Only four specific exceptions are allowed to this rule:

a) if the import of wastes is done in accordance with a treaty covering the supply of an officially recognized technology for the disposal of such wastes, corresponding to generally accepted world standards of science and technology, to which Czechoslovakia is a party;

b) the technology in question must have been adopted for permanent use within the territory of Czechoslovakia;

c) all the wastes that have been imported must be intended for disposal; further, the quantity of such wastes and the degree of danger incurred by analogous wastes originating within the territory of the CSFR are to be substantially reduced; and

d) the responsible authorities in the Government must have authorized the import, transport and storage of such wastes.

Furthermore, it is forbidden to export hazardous wastes without prior written consent from the importing or transit state to the import or transit of such wastes. The expression "hazardous waste" is used to refer to such special wastes as are, or may be, dangerous for the health of the population and the environment by virtue of properties such as toxicity infectiousness, irritability, explosiveness, inflammability, chemical, carcinogenic, teratogenic or mutagenic properties.

Prior authorization from the competent CSFR government authorities is required for the operation of waste disposal facilities, the handling of hazardous wastes, business operations in the field of waste handling and management, the export of hazardous wastes, the transport of wastes within or across the territory of the CSFR and some other operations.

The responsibility and liability of waste producers, forwarders and carriers are laid down very clearly.

The waste originator, i.e. the legal or natural person authorized by the firm or enterprise whose operations generate wastes (in respect of local community wastes, the waste originator is deemed to be the local government) is bound by the law to take the following measures:

a) draft a programme of waste management and submit the same to the appropriate government authority for approval;

b) collect the wastes that have been produced, classify them according to type and protect them from deterioration, theft or any other undesirable manner of disposal;

c) collect and separate hazardous wastes according to type, labelling them in the prescribed manner and managing them strictly in accordance with the laws and regulations in force;

d) report the origin, quantity, nature and method of exploitation or disposal of "special wastes" to the competent government authority;

e) exploit wherever possible the waste that has been generated as the source of secondary raw materials or energy – if at all possible in the operations of the enterprise itself or, failing this, offer the wastes that have not been thus exploited to other parties;

f) ensure proper waste disposal in all cases where exploitation proves to be impossible;

g) keep records on the types, quantities, storage, exploitation and/or disposal of all wastes generated by the enterprise;

h) allow access by the control authorities to the buildings, areas and facilities and furnish documentation and true and complete information on waste management to these authorities upon their request.

In addition, every manufacturer is bound to specify in the documentation accompanying his product or on the outside of the package or container, or in the instructions for use of the product, just how the unused parts of the product or packaging can be used as the source of secondary raw materials or energy, and/or recommend methods for the disposal of the residues together with all necessary information on how the latter should be done.

Furthermore, carriers and forwarders also have specific duties, as follows:

a) ensure the transport of wastes in accordance with road transport and national forwarding regulations in accordance with Law No. 68/1979 CoL;

b) keep up-to-date records of the transported hazardous wastes;

c) report to the local responsible government authorities the quantity and type of hazardous wastes and the manner of their transport;

d) allow control organs access to the waste for inspection purposes during transport.

Before hazardous wastes may be transported, authorization of the competent government officials is required.

The consent of the appropriate government authority is also required for the collection, acquisition and modification of wastes and for the operation of waste disposal facilities.

The operator of the waste disposal facility is bound in particular to dispose of wastes in accordance with the previously approved operating rules and to ensure that such wastes are not stolen, nor liable to be disposed of in some other undesirable way; he is obliged to publish a list and description of the items of waste which he has been authorized to dispose of; also, he must keep records on the quantity, type and origin of wastes transmitted for disposal, report the quantity, nature and method of disposal of hazardous wastes to the competent local authorities, depending on the location or place of business of the waste disposal facility operator, etc. Should the operator of such facility fail to comply with the above-mentioned rules and regulations, the government authorities may forbid his continued operation of the said facility.

Legal and physical persons must pay a fee for the dumping of wastes. The amount of such a fee and the conditions under which it can be imposed will be specified in orders issued by the Czech National Council and the Slovak National Council.

The non-observance of the provisions of the Wastes Act is punishable by fines running from 10,000 Kcs to 10 million Kcs. These fines are imposed on legal and natural persons in accordance with the gravity of the offence. The imposition of a fine in no way prejudices the right to obtain compensation for damages. The government agency or authority which has imposed the fine must specify the conditions under which it will be paid and the deadlines for payment.

Should a legal or natural person again violate the provisions of the law for which a fine has been imposed, and if this should occur within one year from the day on which the decision on the imposition of the fine has acquired legal force, that person or persons will be subject to the imposition of an additional fine, double the amount of the previously-imposed fine.

The Federal Wastes Act provides that detailed codification of some of the problems regulated under its provisions will be contained in specific regulations to be issued subsequently. Among the aspects to be regulated in this way are the procedures and conditions for reporting the origin, quantity, nature and manner of exploitation or disposal of wastes of a special kind, the content and method of reporting and recording wastes, problems encountered in recording and reporting hazardous wastes, reporting of the transport of hazardous wastes, the records of wastes taken over or transmitted for disposal and the reporting of the disposal of hazardous wastes.

As previously mentioned, the Czech National Council and the Slovak National Council will enact detailed regulations establishing fines and penalties for the dumping of wastes.

Under the Federal Wastes Act, the governments of the Czech Republic and the Slovak Republic are authorized to issue orders on the records of wastes, including records of waste dumps which came into existence prior to the enactment of the Waste Act. The orders will also cover the details of waste management.

The Czech National Council and Slovak National Council will also issue regulations on waste management by state authorities. At the time of writing the Czech National Council has adopted Law No. 311/1991 of 8 July 1991, on state administration in waste management, and the Slovak National Council an analogous law No. 494/1991 of 5 November 1991, on state administration in waste management.

These laws provide that waste management is a shared responsibility of the Ministry of the Environment, the Czech Environmental Inspection Agency, district authorities and local governmental authorities in the Czech Republic, and a shared responsibility of the Slovak Commission of Environment, Slovak Environmental Inspection Agency and Offices for Environmental Protection in the Slovak Republic.

The Ministry of the Environment of the Czech Republic, and the Slovak Commission for Environment in the Slovak Republic, are the supreme authorities for waste management supervision. They determine the waste management programme of the Czech and Slovak Republics, give consent to the import, transport and storage of wastes earmarked for disposal, give consent to the import of wastes for purposes other than disposal, including their exploitation as secondary raw materials, their transport and storage, approve the export of hazardous wastes, approve the transit of wastes across the territory of the Czech or Slovak Republic, etc.

The Czech and the Slovak Environmental Inspection Agencies control the observance of laws and regulations in matters of waste management. They impose fines upon legal and natural persons for the violation of legal obligations under Sections 11 and 12 of Law No. 238/1991 on wastes, and establish the conditions and periods for corrective action.

The district authorities of the Czech Republic and the Offices for Environmental protection in the Slovak Republic enact waste management programmes in their respective districts, approve the waste management programmes of waste originators and keep records of reports received from legal and natural persons on the origin, quantity, nature and manner of exploitation or disposal of special wastes; they also keep records of the reports of carriers and forwarders on the quantity and types of hazardous wastes being transported, including the methods of their transport, and records received from waste disposal facilities on the quantity, nature and method of disposal of hazardous wastes.

These authorities also have power to authorize the setting up and operation of waste disposal facilities, the handling of hazardous wastes, enterprises in the field of wastes management, etc. They may withdraw such authorization in case of failure to abide by the regulations.

They are charged with the overall responsibility for ensuring that the law is complied with. They can forbid operations causing or liable to cause the production of wastes posing a serious threat to the environment.

### b. Regulation of Radioactive Wastes Management

This subject is covered by Decree No. 67/1987 of the Czechoslovak Atomic Energy Commission regulating safety measures in the handling of radioactive wastes. This decree was issued on the basis of Section 21 of Law No. 28/1984 CoL on state control over safety in installations producing or concerned with nuclear energy.

This decree lays down technical and organizational standards required in the prevention of escape of radioactive substances into the air, water or soil and in the handling of radioactive wastes originating in nuclear energy installations.

The term "radioactive wastes" is defined in Section 13 of the Decree as being unusable wastes and unusable objects which are liable to contain radionucleides and which are liable to be introduced into the environment.

Radioactive wastes management is based on the principle that nuclear energy installations must be designed, built, operated and also dismantled or put out of operation in such a way as to ensure that "the amount of radioactive wastes produced [by the installation] is as low as possible in view of economic and social criteria" (Section 4, para. 1). Nuclear installations and facilities must be designed in such a way as to permit an analysis of the composition and quantity of radioactive wastes produced during operations and liable to be produced under emergency conditions. The design must also make it possible to evaluate and control the methods used in the collection, sorting, modification, processing, storage and transport to final dumping sites of the radioactive wastes as well as, as applicable, the manner and degree of their inadvertent release into the environment.

Any system for the handling of radioactive wastes must be designed and constructed so as to be able to: (a) reliably collect and store radioactive wastes originating from the operation of nuclear facilities, as well as radioactive wastes originating under emergency conditions; (b) permit ready access to the installation for purposes of repair, maintenance and decontamination; (c) permit rapid action to prevent clogging and facilitate easy removal of any possible deposits or sediments; and (d) prevent the escape of radioactive waste into the surrounding area.

During the operation of radioactive wastes handling systems, the quantities and values used as a basis for determining whether or not such systems are functioning correctly must be continuously measured. The implementation of standards limiting the introduction of wastes to the environment must be controlled without interruption and the results of the measurements must be recorded.

The radioactive wastes and their mixtures with other substances must be collected at the place of origin and, wherever technically feasible and justifiable, sorted out and safely conveyed to the site where treatment, modification and disposal is to be carried out. Radioactive wastes are not allowed to come into contact with the environment during their collection and storage, and it is particularly important that they be prevented from penetrating into the surface or groundwater.

Radioactive wastes and their mixtures with other substances must be classified by category in order to facilitate further handling in accordance with nuclear safety regulations. In particular, their physical and mechanical properties and the manner of their further treatment and modification must be taken into account.

Radioactive wastes must be processed in such a way as to permit the recovery and reintroduction into the production process of separable and exploitable materials wherever possible.

If modified radioactive wastes cannot be transported immediately to the dumping site, they must be stored safely within the nuclear facility in which they have been modified. The modified radioactive wastes must be stored in such a way as to prevent any change in their properties which could make their final dumping impossible.

Radioactive wastes which are within the limits and meet the conditions imposed for final dumping, must be dumped at the dumping site by the organization authorized to do so. Dumping grounds are considered to be a nuclear facility. They must be designed, built and operated in such a way as to separate safely the dumped radioactive wastes from the environment for as long a period as is required for their radioactivity to drop below the required level. In locating and designing the dumping ground, it is also necessary to allow for the possibility of final dumping of radioactive wastes originating under exceptional conditions or during the period immediately following the termination of operations of such nuclear facilities. In addition, it is necessary to ensure that the dumping ground will continue to remain under surveillance and control even after it has been put out of operation.

Further provisions concerning radioactive wastes are contained in the Decree of the Ministry of Health of the Czech Republic No. 59/1971 CoL on public health protection against ionizing radiation, and in an analogous Decree of the Ministry of Health of the Slovak Republic No. 65/1972 CoL.

These decrees codify the conditions of transport of radioactive emitters and lay down special conditions for the disposal of radioactive emitters and wastes. Organizations may dump radioactive emitters and radioactive wastes (i.e. wastes in solid, liquid or gaseous state, originating during the use of radiation sources or during the extraction and processing of raw materials containing radioactive substances or contaminated by the same) in the soil, or they may discharge them into the atmosphere, but only with the consent of the public health authorities.

The public health authorities are empowered to grant permission to bury such emitters and wastes in the ground after having received the approval of the water management authorities, and to grant permission to discharge these wastes in the atmosphere with the concurrence of the environmental inspection services. The disposal of radioactive wastes through their discharge into waterways may be done only with the permission of the water management authorities and with approval from the public health authorities.

### c. Conclusions

It is a cause of great satisfaction that within the short time that has elapsed since the demise of the totalitarian system in Czechoslovakia, a Waste Act has been enacted which will serve as a basis for the entire body of legal rules to codify this important field.

No doubt it is too early to judge the impact of the Federal Waste Act and the Czech National Council Law on state administration in the field of waste management. Nevertheless, several preliminary conclusions can be drawn, as follows:

1. As regards industrial wastes, the legislation now being prepared will represent a very great improvement over the previous laws and regulations, particularly in view of the transition of the Czech and Slovak Federal Republics to a market economy. Economic forces will probably work in favour of compliance with the provisions of this law.

2. As regards radioactive wastes, the previous codification can be considered satisfactory. It will probably require no important changes in the immediate future.

3. The new Waste Act also covers special and hazardous wastes – a field which has not been codified at all previously. In this respect, too, it represents an important step forward.

4. The drafting of the respective implementing regulations is proceeding rapidly and their submission to the respective state authorities for approval is foreseen for the end of 1991. With their adoption, the system of codification of waste handling and management in the CSFR will be more or less operational.

5. All the new legislation and regulations in this field in the Czech and Slovak Federal republic have been modelled after the experience and guidelines available from the European Community. Hence, it is reasonable to suppose that major revisions will not be required in the immediate future.

### 3. C. P. Naish, *The Policy of Waste Disposal in the Chemical Industry*

In the late 1970s and early 1980s, most European countries introduced legislation on the management of industrial wastes. In general such legislation defined special or hazardous wastes, and concerned the tracking of such wastes from the generator to disposal facility using waste manifests or tickets, and the licensing of disposal facilities.

About the same time, Ciba–Geigy and some other chemical companies developed their own, company-specific policies and procedures for the management of their wastes. These policies and procedures were designed, not only to meet local legislative requirements, but also to ensure proper on-site management of wastes.

CEFIC, the European Chemical Industries Federation based in Brussels, established a working party of waste disposal experts from some major chemical companies in Europe to develop a unified approach to industrial waste management. CEFIC represents fifteen national chemical federations of Western Europe and has as corporate associate members most of the major chemical companies with headquarters in Europe. CEFIC thus represents an industry which employs two million people and accounts for approximately 30 per cent of world chemical production.

The ten Principles for the Management of Special Wastes were published in 1985 (revised in 1989) to assist chemical companies in complying with the "CEFIC Guidelines for the Protection of the Environment".

#### a. The CEFIC Principles

The CEFIC principles for the management of special waste define waste as any unavoidable material resulting from an industrial operation for which there is no economic demand and which must be disposed of. Discharge of liquid effluents to watercourses and gaseous emissions to atmosphere are not included in the definition. The principles demand

1. *Waste minimization: Take all economically and technically justifiable measures to minimize generation of waste, through process optimisation or re-design.*

   All chemical processes inevitably generate a certain amount of residue. Those residues, which cannot be recovered or recycled, are wastes which have to be disposed of. For economic as well as environmental reasons it is in the waste generator's interest to minimize these.

2. *Residue recovery: Seek every opportunity for the economic recovery of residues, as feedstock, for energy production, or any other purpose.*

   As not all residues may be treated for recovery or re-use under acceptable attractive economic conditions and recovered materials often have a value much lower than the primary products of the process, deliberate steps need to be taken to identify the possibilities for recovery. Generally speaking, the recovery of residues must be economically favourable or at least reach a "break-even" situation. Recovery processes usually result in the production of residues or wastes which must in turn be properly managed.

3. *Characterization: Obtain an adequate knowledge of the composition and characteristics of the wastes generated.*

   The majority of wastes are usually highly complex mixtures and it is often impracticable or even impossible to determine their precise composition or characteristics. A broad assessment of the chemical, physical and toxicological properties is necessary

   — to protect the health of people handling the waste;

   — to select the best method of disposal;

   — to ensure correct classification of the wastes according to the legislative requirements.

4. *Disposal methods: Select a disposal method that is appropriate, considering the characteristics of the waste.*

   As a general rule the waste generator is responsible for the selection of the disposal method – unless the use of a specific means of waste disposal is obligatory or forbidden by legislation. A manager who has access to sound technical knowledge and is fully aware of the legislative requirements should be in charge of the safe and environmentally acceptable disposal of the wastes generated by the site.

5. *On-site management: Take appropriate steps to ensure proper management of wastes at production sites.*

   The responsibilities, administrative procedures and documentation should be defined and established for all steps of the disposal chain from source up to final disposal. In other words, wastes should be handled in the same way as raw materials or products.

6. *Use of contractors: When outside transport or disposal contractors are employed, satisfy oneself that they can deal with waste materials safely, effectively and legally, and confirm that waste consignments reach the specified final disposal site and are disposed of in the agreed environmentally safe manner. Regular assessment or audits of outside contractors should be carried out to ensure continuing acceptability.*

7. *Management plans: Establish waste management plans in order to ensure that the provisions of these principles are efficiently implemented; management plans should be reviewed frequently to take into account changes in production processes, waste generated and suitability and availability of disposal options.*

8. *External relationships: Ensure adequate and open dialogue with the public and good working relationship with the controlling authorities.*

   Reputation of a solid compliance with the regulations and demonstrated efficiency in the handling of wastes helps the company establish its credibility.

9. *Information to customers: Provide customers or processors with adequate information about potential hazards in disposing of the products they buy or handle.*

10. *Research and development: Foster the exchange of technical, scientific and economic information*

*about safe disposal of wastes and, where appropriate, support studies to find more effective methods.*

This includes the development of low-waste technologies, improved recovery and recycling processes as well as improved disposal methods.

### b. Implementation of the Principles in Ciba–Geigy

The principles laid down by CEFIC are endorsed by Ciba–Geigy; indeed the company played a major role in their preparation. The principles have, however, been formulated to cover the wide range of chemical industries and companies operating in Europe. The systems each company installs to ensure adherence to the principles will depend on company culture, type of products and processes, national practices and regulatory regimes, to name but a few factors.

Ciba–Geigy has issued corporate and site-specific guidelines and directives which describe the management systems which must be implemented to ensure compliance with the CEFIC principles. The management systems define responsibilities, documentation and procedures for all phases of waste management.

When required, individual sites can obtain advice and assistance from corporate staff on waste management, for example standardized forms and computer programmes for the characterization and tracking of wastes from production to final disposal have been developed, also specialized engineering staff assist in design, installation and commissioning of special waste incineration plant.

Training courses have been carried out for management staff from our world-wide sites. These ensure the introduction of effective waste management systems in all our sites and have also formed the basis for training of all site employees on their responsibilities for waste management.

Since 1981 Ciba–Geigy has had an Environmental Audit function, one task of which is to assess compliance of each production site with company waste disposal policies, to recommend improvements in waste management and to assess the suitability of both company-owned and third-party waste transport and disposal facilities. Further the audit group has prepared checklists to assist production sites in making more frequent assessments of these facilities.

### c. Harmonization of Legislation

Ciba–Geigy welcomes all efforts to harmonize legislation dealing with waste disposal and indeed all environmental legislation. This should reduce distortion of competition and lead to an improvement in the environment. We are, however, very concerned about what appears to be developing into an international competition to introduce the lowest possible limits for discharges into the environment. Discharge limits should have a scientific basis, i.e., they should be measurable and wherever possible should be based on a scientific assessment of the effects of an emission. They should not be subject to continual lowering for emotional or political reasons, as this latter leads to wasteful use of resources and is thus incompatible with sustainable development.

# C. Documents

## 1. Council Directive 91/156/EEC of 16 March 1991 on Waste, O.J. No. L. 78 of 26 March 1991.

The Council of the European Communities

...

Has adopted this Directive:

[Article 1]

For the purposes of this Directive:

(a) "waste" shall mean any substance or object in the categories set out in Annex I which the holder discards or intends or is required to discard. The Commission, acting in accordance with the procedure laid down in Article 18, will draw up, not later than 1 April 1993, a list of wastes belonging to the categories listed in Annex I. This list will be periodically reviewed and, if necessary, revised by the same procedure;

(b) "producer" shall mean anyone whose activities produce waste ("original producer") and/or anyone who carries out pre-processing, mixing or other operations resulting in a change in the nature or composition of this waste;

(c) "holder" shall mean the producer of the waste or the natural or legal person who is in possession of it;

(d) "management" shall mean the collection, transport, recovery and disposal of waste, including the supervision of such operations and after-care of disposal sites;

(e) "disposal" shall mean any of the operations provided for in Annex II, A;

(f) "recovery" shall mean any of the operations provided for in Annex II, B;

(g) "collection" shall mean the gathering, sorting and/or mixing of waste for the purpose of transport.

### Article 2

1. The following shall be excluded from the scope of this Directive:

    (a) gaseous effluents emitted into the atmosphere;

    (b) where they are already covered by other legislation:

        (i) radioactive waste;

        (ii) waste resulting from prospecting, extraction, treatment and storage of mineral resources and the working of quarries;

        (iii) animal carcasses and the following agricultural waste: faecal matter and other natural, non-dangerous substances used in farming;

        (iv) waste waters, with the exception of waste in liquid form;

        (v) decommissioned explosives.

2. Specific rules for particular instances or supplementing those of this Directive on the management of particular categories of waste may be laid down by means of individual directives.

## Article 3

1. Member States shall take appropriate measures to encourage:

   (a) firstly, the prevention or reduction of waste production and its harmfulness, in particular by:
   — the development of clean technologies more sparing in their use of natural resources,
   — the technical development and marketing of products designed so as to make no contribution or to make the smallest possible contribution, by the nature of their manufacture, use or final disposal, to increasing the amount or harmfulness of waste and pollution hazards,
   — the development of appropriate techniques for the final disposal of dangerous substances contained in waste destined for recovery;

   (b) secondly:

   (i) the recovery of waste by means of recycling, re-use or reclamation or any other process with a view to extracting secondary raw materials, or

   (ii) the use of waste as a source of energy.

2. Except where Council Directive 83/189/EEC of 28 March 1983 laying down a procedure for the provision of information in the field of technical standards and regulations applies, Member States shall inform the Commission of any measures they intend to take to achieve the aims set out in paragraph 1. The Commission shall inform the other Member States and the committee referred to in Article 18 of such measures.

## Article 4

Member States shall take the necessary measures to ensure that waste is recovered or disposed of without endangering human health and without using processes or methods which could harm the environment, and in particular:
— without risk to water, air, soil and plants and animals,
— without causing a nuisance through noise or odours,
— without adversely affecting the countryside or places of special interest.
Member States shall also take the necessary measures to prohibit the abandonment, dumping or uncontrolled disposal of waste.

## Article 5

1. Member States shall take appropriate measures, in cooperation with other Member States where this is necessary or advisable, to establish an integrated and adequate network of disposal installations, taking account of the best available technology not involving excessive costs. The network must enable the Community as a whole to become self-sufficient in waste disposal and the Member States to move towards that aim individually, taking into account geographical circumstances or the need for specialized installations for certain types of waste.

2. The network must also enable waste to be disposed of in one of the nearest appropriate installations, by means of the most appropriate methods and technologies in order to ensure a high level of protection for the environment and public health.

## Article 6

Member States shall establish or designate the competent authority or authorities to be responsible for the implementation of this Directive.

## Article 7

1. In order to attain the objectives referred to in Articles 3, 4 and 5, the competent authority or authorities referred to in Article 6 shall be required to draw up as soon as possible one or more waste management plans. Such plans shall relate in particular to:
   — the type, quantity and origin of waste to be recovered or disposed of;
   — general technical requirements;
   — any special arrangements for particular wastes;
   — suitable disposal sites or installations.
   Such plans may, for example, cover:
   — the natural or legal persons empowered to carry out the management of waste;
   — the estimated costs of the recovery and disposal operations;
   — appropriate measures to encourage rationalization of the collection, sorting and treatment of waste.

2. Member States shall collaborate as appropriate with the other Member States concerned and the Commission to draw up such plans. They shall notify the Commission thereof.

3. Member States may take the measures necessary to prevent movements of waste which are not in accordance with their waste management plans. They shall inform the Commission and the Member States of any such measures.

## Article 8

Member States shall take the necessary measures to ensure that any holder of waste:
   — has it handled by a private or public waste collector or by an undertaking which carries out the operations listed in Annex II A or B, or
   — recovers or disposes of it himself in accordance with the provisions of this Directive.

## Article 9

1. For the purposes of implementing Articles 4, 5 and 7, any establishment or undertaking which carries out the operations specified in Annex II A must obtain a permit from the competent authority referred to in Article 6. Such permit shall cover:
   — the types and quantities of waste,
   — the technical requirements,
   — the security precautions to be taken,
   — the disposal site,
   — the treatment method.

2. Permits may be granted for a specified period, they may be renewable, they may be subject to conditions and obligations, or, notably, if the intended method of disposal is unacceptable from the point of view of environmental protection, they may be refused.

## Article 10

For the purposes of implementing Article 4, any establishment or undertaking which carries out the operations referred to in Annex II B must obtain a permit.

## Article 11

1. Without prejudice to Council Directive 78/319/EEC of 20 March 1978 on toxic and dangerous waste, as last amended by the Act of Accession of Spain and Portugal, the following may be exempted from the permit requirement imposed in Article 9 or Article 10:

   (a) establishments or undertakings carrying out their own waste disposal at the place of production; and

(b) establishments or undertakings that carry out waste recovery. This exemption may apply only:

— if the competent authorities have adopted general rules for each type of activity laying down the types and quantities of waste and the conditions under which the activity in question may be exempted from the permit requirements, and

— if the types or quantities of waste and methods of disposal or recovery are such that the conditions imposed in Article 4 are complied with.

2. The establishments or undertakings referred to in paragraph 1 shall be registered with the competent authorities.

3. Member States shall inform the Commission of the general rules adopted pursuant to paragraph 1.

### Article 12

Establishments or undertakings which collect or transport waste on a professional basis or which arrange for the disposal or recovery of waste on behalf of others (dealers or brokers), where not subject to authorization, shall be registered with the competent authorities.

### Article 13

Establishments or undertakings which carry out the operations referred to in Articles 9 to 12 shall be subject to appropriate periodic inspections by the competent authorities.

### Article 14

All establishments or undertakings referred to in Articles 9 and 10 shall:

— keep a record of the quantity, nature, origin, and, where relevant, the destination, frequency of collection, mode of transport and treatment method in respect of the waste referred to in Annex I and the operations referred to in Annex II A or B;

— make this information available, on request, to the competent authorities referred to in Article 6. Member States may also require producers to comply with the provisions of this Article.

### Article 15

In accordance with the "polluter pays" principle, the cost of disposing of waste must be borne by:

— the holder who has waste handled by a waste collector or by an undertaking as referred to in Article 9, and/or

— the previous holders or the producer of the product from which the waste came.

### Article 16

1. Every three years, and for the first time on 1 April 1995, Member States shall send the Commission a report on the measures taken to implement this Directive. This report shall be based on a questionnaire, drawn up in accordance with the procedure referred to in Article 18, which the Commission shall send to the Member States six months before the above date.

2. On the basis of the reports referred to in paragraph 1, the Commission shall publish a consolidated report every three years, and for the first time on 1 April 1996.

### Article 17

The amendments necessary for adapting the Annexes to this Directive to scientific and technical progress shall be adopted in accordance with the procedure laid down in Article 18.

### Article 18

The Commission shall be assisted by a committee composed of the representatives of the

Member States and chaired by the representative of the Commission. The representative of the Commission shall submit to the committee a draft of the measures to be taken. The committee shall deliver its opinion on the draft within a time limit which the chairman may lay down according to the urgency of the matter. The opinion shall be delivered by the majority laid down in Article 148 (2) of the EEC Treaty in the case of decisions which the Council is required to adopt on a proposal from the Commission. The votes of the representatives of the Member States within the committee shall be weighted in the manner set out in that Article. The chairman shall not vote. The Commission shall adopt the measures envisaged if they are in accordance with the opinion of the committee. If the measures envisaged are not in accordance with the opinion of the committee, or if no opinion is delivered, the Commission shall, without delay, submit to the Council a proposal relating to the measures to be taken. The Council shall act by a qualified majority. If, on the expiry of a period of three months from the date of referral to the Council, the Council has not acted, the proposed measures shall be adopted by the Commission.

## 2. Council Directive 82/501/EEC of 24 June 1982 on the Major Accident Hazards of Certain Industrial Activities, O.J. No. L 230, of 5 August 1982 p. 1.

The Council of the European Communities,
has adopted this directive:

### Article 1

1. This directive is concerned with the prevention of major accidents which might result from certain industrial activities and with the limitation of their consequences for man and the environment. It is directed in particular towards the approximation of the measures taken by Member States in this field.

2. For the purposes of this directive:

   (a) industrial activity means:
       — any operation carried out in an industrial installation referred to in annex i involving, or possibly involving, one or more dangerous substances and capable of presenting major accident hazards, and also transport carried out within the establishment for internal reasons and the storage associated with this operation within the establishment,
       — any other storage in accordance with the conditions specified in annex ii;

   (b) manufacturer means:
       — any person in charge of an industrial activity;

   (c) major accident means:
       — an occurrence such as a major emission, fire or explosion resulting from uncontrolled developments in the course of an industrial activity, leading to a serious danger to man, immediate or delayed, inside or outside the establishment, and/or to the environment, and involving one or more dangerous substances;

   (d) dangerous substances means:
       — for the purposes of articles 3 and 4, substances generally considered to fulfil the criteria laid down in annex iv,

— for the purposes of article 5, substances in the lists in annex iii and annex ii in the quantities referred to in the second column.

## Article 2

This directive does not apply to the following:

1. Nuclear installations and plants for the processing of radioactive substances and material;

2. Military installations;

3. The manufacture and separate storage of explosives, gunpowder and munitions;

4. Extraction and other mining operations;

5. Installations for the disposal of toxic and dangerous waste which are covered by Community acts in so far as the purpose of those acts is the prevention of major accidents.

## Article 3

Member States shall adopt the provisions necessary to ensure that, in the case of any of the industrial activities specified in article 1, the manufacturer is obliged to take all the measures necessary to prevent major accidents and to limit their consequences for man and the environment.

## Article 4

Member States shall take the measures necessary to ensure that all manufacturers are required to prove to the competent authority at any time, for the purposes of the controls referred to in article 7 (2), that they have identified existing major accident hazards, adopted the appropriate safety measures, and provided the persons working on the site with information, training and equipment in order to ensure their safety.

## Article 5

1. Without prejudice to article 4, Member States shall introduce the necessary measures to require the manufacturer to notify the competent authorities specified in article 7:

   — if, in an industrial activity as defined in article 1 (2) (a), first indent, one or more of the dangerous substances listed in annex iii are involved, or it is recognized that they may be involved, in the quantities laid down in the said annex, such as:

   — substances stored or used in connection with the industrial activity concerned,
   — products of manufacture,
   — by-products, or
   — residues,

   — or if, in an industrial activity as defined in article 1 (2) (a), second indent, one or more of the dangerous substances listed in annex ii are stored in the quantities laid down in the second column of the same annex.

   The notification shall contain the following:

   (a) information relating to substances listed, respectively, in annex ii and annex iii, that is to say :

   — the data and information listed in annex v,
   — the stage of the activity in which the substances are involved or may be involved,
   — the quantity (order of magnitude),
   — the chemical and/or physical behaviour under normal conditions of use during the process,
   — the forms in which the substances may occur or into which they may be transformed in the case of abnormal conditions which can be foreseen,

— if necessary, other dangerous substances whose presence could have an effect on the potential hazard presented by the relevant industrial activity;

(b) information relating to the installations, that is to say :
— the geographical location of the installations and predominant meteorological conditions and sources of danger arising from the location of the site,
— the maximum number of persons working on the site of the establishment and particularly of those persons exposed to the hazard,
— a general description of the technological processes,
— a description of the sections of the establishment which are important from the safety point of view, the sources of hazard and the conditions under which a major accident could occur, together with a description of the preventive measures planned,
— the arrangements made to ensure that the technical means necessary for the safe operation of plant and to deal with any malfunctions that arise are available at all times;

(c) information relating to possible major accident situations, that is to say:
— emergency plans, including safety equipment, alarm systems and resources available for use inside the establishments in dealing with a major accident,
— any information necessary to the competent authorities to enable them to prepare emergency plans for use outside the establishment in accordance with article 7 (1),
— the names of the person and his deputies or the qualified body responsible for safety and authorized to set the emergency plans in motion and to alert the competent authorities specified in article 7.

2. In the case of new installations, the notification referred to in paragraph 1 must reach the competent authorities a reasonable length of time before the industrial activity commences.

3. The notification specified in paragraph 1 shall be updated periodically to take account of new technical knowledge relative to safety and of developments in knowledge concerning the assessment of hazards.

4. In the case of industrial activities for which the quantities, by substance, laid down in annex ii or iii, as appropriate, are exceeded in a group of installations belonging to the same manufacturer which are less than 500 metres apart, the Member States shall take the necessary steps to ensure that the manufacturer supplies the amount of information required for the notification referred to in paragraph 1, without prejudice to article 7, having regard to the fact that the installations are a short distance apart and that any major accident hazards may therefore be aggravated.

### Article 6

In the event of modification of an industrial activity which could have significant consequences as regards major accident hazards, the Member States shall take appropriate measures to ensure that the manufacturer:
— revises the measures specified in articles 3 and 4,
— informs the competent authorities referred to in article 7 in advance, if necessary, of such modification in so far as it affects the information contained in the notification specified in article 5.

### Article 7

1. The Member States shall set up or appoint the competent authority or authorities who, account being taken of the responsibility of the manufacturer, are responsible for:

— receiving the notification referred to in article 5 and the information referred to in the second indent of article 6,

— examining the information provided,

— ensuring that an emergency plan is drawn up for action outside the establishment in respect of whose industrial activity notification has been given, and, if necessary,

— requesting supplementary information,

— ascertaining that the manufacturer takes the most appropriate measures, in connection with the various operations involved in the industrial activity for which notification has been given, to prevent major accidents and to provide the means for limiting the consequences thereof.

2.  The competent authorities shall organize inspections or other measures of control proper to the type of activity concerned, in accordance with national regulations.

### Article 8
(as amended by directive 88/610/EEC O.J. no. L 336, 07/12/88 p. 14)

1.  Member States shall ensure that information on safety measures and on the correct behaviour to adopt in the case of an accident is supplied in an appropriate manner, and without their having to request it, to persons liable to be affected by a major accident originating in a notified industrial activity within the meaning of article 5. The information shall be repeated and updated at appropriate intervals. It shall also be made publicly available. Such information shall contain that laid down in annex vii.

### Article 9

1.  This directive shall apply to both new and existing industrial activities.

2.  "New industrial activity" shall also include any modification to an existing industrial activity likely to have important implications for major accident hazards.

3.  In the case of existing industrial activities, this directive shall apply at the latest on 8 January 1985.

    However, as regards the application of article 5 to an existing industrial activity, the Member States shall ensure that the manufacturer shall submit to the competent authority, at the latest on 8 January 1985, a declaration comprising:

    — name or trade name and complete address,

    — registered place of business of the establishment and complete address,

    — name of the director in charge,

    — type of activity,

    — type of production or storage,

    — an indication of the substances or category of substances involved, as listed in annexes ii or iii.

4.  Moreover, Member States shall ensure that the manufacturer shall, at the latest on 8 July 1989, supplement the declaration provided for in paragraph 3, second subparagraph, with the data and information specified in article 5. Manufacturers shall normally be obliged to forward such supplementary declaration to the competent authority; however, Member States may waive the obligation on manufacturers to submit the supplementary declaration; in that event such declaration shall be submitted to the competent authority at the explicit request of the latter.

### Article 10

1.  Member States shall take the necessary measures to ensure that, as soon as a major accident occurs, the manufacturer shall be required:

(a)　to inform the competent authorities specified in article 7 immediately;

(b)　to provide them with the following information as soon as it becomes available:
— the circumstances of the accident,
— the dangerous substances involved within the meaning of article 1(2)(d),
— the data available for assessing the effects of the accident on man and the environment,
— the emergency measures taken;

(c)　to inform them of the steps envisaged:
— to alleviate the medium and long-term effects of the accident,
— to prevent any recurrence of such an accident.

2.　The Member States shall require the competent authorities:

(a)　to ensure that any emergency and medium and long-term measures which may prove necessary are taken;

(b)　to collect, where possible, the information necessary for a full analysis of the major accident and possibly to make recommendations.

### Article 11

1.　Member States shall inform the Commission as soon as possible of major accidents which have occurred within their territory and shall provide it with the information specified in annex vi as soon as it becomes available.

2.　Member States shall inform the Commission of the name of the organization which might have relevant information on major accidents and which is able to advise the competent authorities of the other Member States which have to intervene in the event of such an accident.

3.　Member States may notify the Commission of any substance which in their view should be added to annexes ii and iii and of any measures they may have taken concerning such substances. The Commission shall forward this information to the other Member States.

### Article 12

The Commission shall set up and keep at the disposal of the Member States a register containing a summary of the major accidents which have occurred within the territory of the Member States, including an analysis of the causes of such accidents, experience gained and measures taken, to enable the Member States to use this information for prevention purposes.

### Article 13

1.　Information obtained by the competent authorities in pursuance of articles 5, 6, 7, 9, 10 and 12 and by the Commission in pursuance of article 11 may not be used for any purpose other than that for which it was requested.

2.　However this directive shall not preclude the conclusion by a Member State of agreements with third countries concerning the exchange of information to which it is privy at internal level other than that obtained through the Community machinery for the exchange of information set up by the directive.

3.　The Commission and its officials and employees shall not divulge the information obtained in pursuance of this directive. The same requirement shall apply to officials and employees of the competent authorities of the Member States as regards any information they obtain from the Commission. Nevertheless, such information may be supplied:
— in the case of articles 12 and 18,

— when a Member State carries out or authorizes the publication of information concerning that Member State itself.

4. Paragraphs 1, 2 and 3 shall not preclude the publication by the Commission of general statistical data or information on matters of safety containing no specific details regarding particular undertakings or groups of undertakings and not jeopardizing industrial secrecy.

...

### Article 17

This directive shall not restrict the right of the Member States to apply or to adopt administrative or legislative measures ensuring greater protection of man and the environment than that which derives from the provisions of this directive.

### Article 18

Member States and the Commission shall exchange information on the experience acquired with regard to the prevention of major accidents and the limitation of their consequences; this information shall concern, in particular, the functioning of the measures provided for in this directive. Five years after notification of this directive, the Commission shall forward to the Council and the European Parliament a report on its application which it shall draw up on the basis of this exchange of information.

...

*3. OECD, Guidelines in respect of Procedures and Requirements for Anticipating the Effects of Chemicals on Man and in the Environment,* Recommendation adopted on 7 July, 1977, C(77)97(Final)

...

11. For the purpose of these Guidelines, chemical substances are: chemical elements and their compounds as they occur in the natural state or as produced by industry. Formulations should usually be excluded from any requirements for systematic assessment, except where a new chemical substance enters the country as a component of such formulations.

### II Approach and data requirements

12. The principal purpose of any assessment procedure is to identify the hazard of a chemical substance in order to determine the conditions of its use, thereby minimizing the risk of exposing man as well as the environment to hazard. For the purpose of assessing the potential effects of a chemical substance and the likelihood that man and/or the environment may be exposed to such a substance, a phased approach should be applied:

a) an initial assessment to determine the likelihood of

   i) health hazard from the substance;

   ii) environmental hazard from the substance;

b) further assessment to elucidate, for selected chemical substances, their effects on man and/or the environment.

13. The initial assessment is intended to segregate

a) those chemical substances which are least likely to create hazard and for which no further studies are deemed necessary at the time;

b)   those chemical substances which may create health hazard but are unlikely to reach the environment, and for which further studies are needed mainly on human health effects;

c)   those chemical substances (with or without health hazard) which reach the environment and for which detailed studies are needed of effects on the natural environment.

14. The initial assessment consists of two steps:
STEP I to determine, for the chemical substance under investigation, its

a)   physical and chemical properties (to indicate its likely behaviour);

b)   potential human health hazard (in the first instance for worker protection; in addition to indicate the need for further health studies);

c)   potential for access to the natural environment (to indicate the need for an assessment of environmental hazard).

STEP II to determine, for the chemical substances that could reach the environment in quantities which are significant with regard to toxicity, other effects and properties, their

d)   potential environmental hazard (to indicate the need for further studies of effects on the natural environment).

15. Where human health hazard has been indicated through Step I of the initial assessment, detailed studies should be made for further assessment of human health effects.

16. Where environmental hazard has been indicated through Step II of the initial assessment, detailed studies should be made for further assessment of effects on the natural environment.

17. Certain groups of chemicals are already subject to special procedures for detailed assessment of either human health effects or environmental effects. Such procedures should be extended to ensure that the chemicals are considered in terms of both human and environmental hazard.

18. Chemical substances presenting unreasonable hazard to health and the environment, should – unless prohibited – be allowed only for supervised use, and only when less hazardous substitutes are not available.

### III. Administrative requirements

19. Responsibility for generating and assessing the data necessary to determine the potential effects and the safe use of chemical substances with respect to man and the environment must be part of the overall function and liability of industry.

20. In respect of administrative requirements, several options are available to the authorities. Progressive options are:

a)   an obligation on the manufacturer to maintain the results of his assessment for examination by the authorities upon request.

This option should be followed by the gradual implementation of a notification system for new chemical substances;

b)   an obligation on manufacturers and importers to notify their authorities of all new chemical substances, with a declaration of, for example,

    i) nomenclature (identification),

    ii) projected quantities to be manufactured or imported during a calendar year,

iii) intended usage.

This option should be followed by the selection of priority substances for examination by the authorities:

c)  an obligation on manufacturers and importers to submit to their authorities a dossier for the chemical substance under investigation including the information required for an initial assessment.

This option should be followed automatically by an examination of the dossier resulting in

i) no action, or

ii) the establishment of testing programmes, or

iii) regulations for use.

Requirements for notification or submission of dossiers will be dependent upon the resources available to the national authorities.

21. Provision should be made to ensure protection of confidential information.

## 4. OECD, *Noise Prevention and Abatement*, Recommendation adopted on 14 November 1974, C(74)217.

The Council,

recommends:

That Member Governments strengthen their noise prevention and abatement efforts through advance planning and through the application of the best available technology, taking into account the cost of implementation.

That these efforts include the following elements:

a)  the promulgation of noise emission standards for products which are major sources of noise, and in particular, transportation equipment, construction equipment, and internal combustion engines of all kinds;

b)  the requirements to consider the impact of noise and the desirability of reducing existing noise levels and of avoiding the creation of new noise conditions in the planning, design, approval, construction and operation of all major facilities including housing, highways, public transportation systems, airports, industrial developments, etc.;

c)  adequate education programmes and information campaigns designed to make the public more aware of the need to behave in such a manner as to avoid producing unnecessary noise.

I. Recommends that Member countries:

1.  Develop comprehensive noise abatement programmes and co-ordinate existing regulations and actions. In particular Member countries should develop comprehensive laws to cover all noise sources and means of action.

2.  In their noise control policies give utmost priority to abatement at source through emission standards on noisy products and activities.

3.  Strengthen their noise abatement policies by adopting a progressive approach using dynamic standards (i.e. a progressive lowering of noise limits over time according to a predetermined and announced schedule).

4.  Support this dynamic approach to noise abatement by using, as appropriate, economic

incentives. These incentives could consist of noise related charges for certain noise producing equipment. When this is not in conflict with the national fiscal system, the resulting proceeds should be devoted to the financing and promotion of noise abatement measures.

5.  Encourage the production and use of quieter equipment by restricting the use of the noisier ones. Inducements such as exemptions or liberalization of times of use might be envisaged for any equipment considered exceptionally quiet.

6.  Consider the provision for compensation procedures in cases of damages resulting from unacceptable noise levels due to new facilities or from a significant increase in the use of existing facilities as a result of their modification. Such compensation should only be considered when a severe noise nuisance still prevails although all practicable noise abatement measures have been taken.

7.  Ensure that land-use planning, including transport planning, incorporates noise abatement requirements and that noise abatement be considered at the outset of public and private projects. Ensure that no new noise sensitive activities (such as new residences) are placed in areas that have high noise levels; include noise abatement measures when rehabilitating housing in urban areas with high noise levels.

8.  Combine noise insulation of buildings with thermal insulation required for energy conservation.

9.  Introduce measures, which are often at low cost and can be rapidly implemented, as part of a comprehensive noise abatement strategy and as a complement to regulatory procedures, such as: noise abatement campaigns, information, education, product labels showing the level of noise the product will produce, traffic management, periodic evaluations of the effectiveness of enforcement programmes.

10. Encourage the harmonization of noise measurement methods and test procedures designed to protect the environment and to establish a close link between procedures for measuring noise emission and immission.

*5. Court of Justice of the European Communities, Re Disposable Beer Cans: EC Commission (United Kingdom intervening) v. Denmark* (Case 302/86) [1988] ECR 4607, [1989] 1 CMLR 619.

DECISION: By an application received at the Court Registry on 1 December 1986 the EC Commission brought an action pursuant to Article 169 for a declaration that, by introducing by Order 397 of 2 July 1981 a system under which all containers for beer and soft drinks must be returnable, the Kingdom of Denmark has failed to fulfil its obligations under Article 30 EEC.

The system alleged by the Commission to be incompatible with Community law is characterised by an obligation on producers to market beer and soft drinks only in containers which can be re-used. The containers must be approved by the National Agency for the Protection of the Environment, which may refuse approval for a new type of container, especially if it considers that the container is not technically adapted to a system of return, that the system of return set up by those concerned does not ensure actual re-use of a sufficient proportion of containers, or if a container of equal capacity which is both available and suited to the intended use has already been approved.

The above rules were amended by Order 95 of 16 March 1984 which allowed the use, provided that a deposit-and-return system had been set up, of non-approved containers, but excluding metal containers, within a limit of 3,000 hl per producer per year, and also in connection with operations by foreign manufacturers in order to test the market.

...

For the purpose of deciding the present case it should be observed that, firstly, in accordance with settled case law (Case 120/78, REWE ([1979] ECR 649, [1979] 3 CMLR 494); Case 261/81, RAU ([1982] ECR 3961, [1983] 2 CMLR 496) ), in the absence of common rules relating to the marketing of the products concerned, obstacles to movement within the Community resulting from disparities between the national laws must be accepted in so far as such rules, applicable to domestic and imported products without distinction, may be recognised as being necessary in order to satisfy mandatory requirements of Community law. It is also necessary for such rules to be proportionate to the aim in view. If a Member State has a choice between various measures to attain the same objective, it should choose the means which least restrict the free movement of goods.

In the present case the Danish Government contends that the compulsory system for the return of beer and soft drink containers in force in Denmark is justified by a mandatory requirement for the protection of the environment.

The protection of the environment has already been considered by the Court in Case 240/83, ASSOCIATION DE DEFENSE DES BRULEURS D'HUILES USAGEES ([1985] ECR 531), as 'one of the essential objectives of the Community' which may, as such, justify certain restrictions on the principle of the free movement of goods. Furthermore this assessment is confirmed by the Single European Act.

In view of what has been said it must be concluded that protection of the environment is a mandatory requirement which may limit the application of Article 30 of the Treaty.

The Commission argues that the Danish regulations infringe the principle of proportionality because the objective of protecting the environment could be attained by means which are less restrictive of trade within the Community.

On this point it should be borne in mind that, in Case 240/83 cited above, the Court stated that measures adopted to safeguard the environment should not exceed the inevitable restrictions justified by an objective for the general good such as the protection of the environment.

Under these circumstances it is necessary to determine whether all the restrictions which the legislation in question imposes on the free movement of goods are necessary to attain the objectives of these regulations.

Firstly, with regard to the obligation to set up a deposit-and-return system for empty containers, it should be noted that this obligation is an essential element of a system aiming to secure the re-use of containers and therefore appears to be necessary to attain the objectives of the disputed regulations. In view of this finding, the restrictions which they impose on the free movement of goods should not be considered as disproportionate.

Secondly it is necessary to consider the obligation on manufacturers or importers to use only the containers approved by the National Agency for the Protection of the Environment.

During the procedure before the Court the Danish Government indicated that the operation of the present deposit-and-return system would be affected if the number of approved containers were to exceed thirty because retailers who had joined the system would not be prepared to accept too many types of bottles owing to increased handling costs and the greater storage space which this would entail. This is said to be the reason why the Agency has hitherto arranged matters so that new approvals are normally accompanied by the withdrawal of existing approvals.

Even if these are cogent arguments, it must nevertheless be said that the system at present in force in Denmark enables the Danish authorities to refuse approval to a foreign producer even if he is prepared to ensure that returned containers are used again.

In such a situation a foreign producer who nevertheless wishes to sell in Denmark would be compelled to manufacture or purchase containers of a type already approved, which would entail considerable extra cost for him and would therefore make it very difficult to import his products into the country.

To overcome this obstacle, the Danish Government amended the regulations by the abovementioned Order 95 of 16 March 1984 which authorises a producer to market up to 3,000 hl of beer and soft drinks per annum in non-approved containers, provided that he sets up a deposit-and-return system.

The provision of Order 95 limiting to 3,000 hl the quantity of beer and soft drinks which can be marketed by each producer per annum in non-approved containers is disputed by the Commission on the ground that it is not necessary for attaining the objectives of the system.

On this point it should be observed that certainly the existing system of return for approved containers guarantees a maximum percentage of re-use and therefore gives considerable protection to the environment because the empty containers can be returned to any retailer of beverages, whereas non-approved containers can only be returned to the retailer who sold the beverage because of the impossibility of setting up such a complete organisation for such containers also.

However, the system for returning non-approved containers is intended to protect the environment and, so far as imports are concerned, covers only limited quantities of beverages by comparison with the quantity consumed in the country because of the restrictive effect of the compulsory return of containers on imports. Under these conditions, limiting the quantity of products which can be marketed by importers is disproportionate to the objective.

Therefore it must be concluded that by restricting, by Order 95 of 16 March 1984, to 3,000 hl per producer per annum the quantity of beer and soft drinks which may be marketed in non-approved containers, the Kingdom of Denmark has failed, in relation to imports of those products from other Member States, to fulfil its obligations under Article 30 EEC.

*6.* United Kingdom, *Environmental Protection (Controls on Injurious Substances) Regulations 1992,*
SI 1992 No. 31, in force 28 February 1992.

The Secretary of State for the Environment, as respects England, the Secretary of State for Wales, as respects Wales, and the Secretary of State for Scotland, as respects Scotland —

...

in exercise of the powers conferred on them by section 140(1), (2)(b) and (9) of the Environmental Protection Act 1990, and of all other powers enabling them in that behalf, hereby make the following Regulations

...

(2) In these Regulations —

"CAS Number" means a number described in the CAS Registry Handbook, ISSN 0093–058X, published in instalments from 1965 to 1971 with supplements for 1972 to 1976, 1977 to 1981, 1982 to 1986 and 1987 to 1991 by the Chemical Abstracts Service, American Chemical Society, Columbus, Ohio, USA;

"historic building" means —

(a) a listed building (within the meaning of section 1(5) of the Planning (Listed Buildings and Conservation Areas) Act 1990 or section 52(7) of the Town and Country Planning (Scotland) Act 1972) which when last notified to a local planning authority by the Secretary of State as a building of special architectural or historic interest was classified as a Grade I or Grade II (starred) or, in Scotland, as a category A listed building, or

(b) a building which is a scheduled monument within the meaning of section 1(11) of the Ancient Monuments and Archaeological Areas Act 1979.

...

## SECTION: 3 Lead carbonate and sulphate in paint

(1) Subject to paragraphs (2) and (3), no person shall –

(a) supply by way of sale for any purpose, or

(b) use in connection with any trade or business or manufacturing process, lead carbonate or lead sulphate which is intended for use as paint, or any substance so intended of which lead carbonate or lead sulphate forms a constituent.

(2) Paragraph (1)(a) shall not apply to the supply of paste or paint which is ready for use and –

(a) is supplied for use in the restoration or maintenance of an historic building, or of a fine or decorative work of art, where it is required to restore or maintain historic textures or finishes,

(b) is supplied not earlier than three weeks after the supplier has given the competent authority a completed declaration made in the form set out in the Schedule to these Regulations, and

(c) is supplied in accordance with that declaration.

(3) Paragraph (1)(b) shall not apply to the use of paste or paint which is ready for use and –

(a) was supplied to the user before these Regulations came into force, or

(b) was supplied to the user in accordance with these Regulations, and

(i) is used in accordance with the declaration in accordance with which they were so supplied, or

(ii) is used, not earlier than three weeks after the user has given to the competent authority a further completed declaration made in the form set out in the Schedule to these Regulations, in accordance with that further declaration.

## SECTION: 4 Mercury compounds in heavy duty textiles

No person shall supply by way of sale, or use in connection with any trade or business or manufacturing process –

(a) mercury compounds which are intended for use in the impregnation of heavy-duty industrial textiles, or of yarn intended for the manufacture of such textiles, or

(b) any substance so intended of which mercury compounds are a constituent.

## SECTION: 5 Mercury, arsenic and organostannic compounds in industrial waters

No person shall supply by way of sale, or use in connection with any trade or business or manufacturing process –

(a) mercury, arsenic or organostannic compounds intended for use in the treatment of industrial waters, irrespective of the use of those waters, or

(b) any substance so intended of which mercury, arsenic or organostannic compounds are a constituent.

SECTION: 6 DBB

(1) Subject to paragraph (2), no person shall supply by way of sale for any purpose, or use in connection with any trade or business or manufacturing process DBB, or any substance containing DBB, in a concentration equal to or greater than 0.1 per cent by weight.

(2) Paragraph (1) shall not apply to DBB or any substance containing DBB if that substance is intended solely for conversion into finished products in which the concentration of DBB will be less than 0.1 per cent by weight.

SECTION: 7 Offences and penalties

A person who contravenes regulation 3, 4, 5 or 6 or causes or permits another person to contravene one of those regulations shall be guilty of an offence and shall be liable, on summary conviction, to a fine not exceeding level 5 on the standard scale and, on conviction on indictment, to imprisonment for a term not exceeding two years, or a fine, or both.

## 7. Turkey, *The Environment Law*, No. 2872 of 9 August 1983.

Article 13: The principle of environment protection shall be taken into consideration in the production, importation, transportation, storage and use of chemical substances which produce permanent effects on air, water or soil or which upset the ecological balance. Restrictions regarding the production, importation, transportation, storage and use of such substances shall be stipulated by special regulations.

Article 14: Producing noise above the standards specified by the regulations in such a way as to destroy the repose and peace of mind and the physical and mental health of human beings shall be prohibited. The necessary measures shall be taken to reduce to a minimum the noise in factories, workshops, places of work, place of entertainment, service buildings, dwellings and transport vehicles.

## 8. Sweden, *Environment Protection Act (1969: 387)*.

### Section 1

This Act applies to

1. discharge of waste water, solid matter or gas from land, buildings or installations into a watercourse, lake or other water area;

2. use of land, buildings or installations in a manner that may entail a disturbance to the surrounding environment owing to air pollution, noise, vibration, light or other such means, unless the disturbance is wholly temporary.

Any action or use which, in accordance with the above provisions, is covered by the Act is termed environmentally hazardous activity.

...

### Section 4

The site chosen for environmentally hazardous activity shall be such that the purpose is attainable with the least possible encroachment and detriment, without unreasonable expense.

## Section 4a

A permit under this Act may not be granted in contravention of a detailed plan or area regulations. However, minor deviations may be allowed, provided that they do not contravene the purpose of the plan or of the regulations.

When environmentally hazardous activity is examined, the Natural Resources Act (1987:12) shall be applied.

## Section 5

Anyone performing or intending to perform environmentally hazardous activity shall take such protective action, tolerate such restriction of the activity and take such other precautionary measures as may reasonably be demanded for preventing or remedying detriment. The duty to remedy detrimental effects remains after the activity has ceased.

The extent of the obligations imposed by the provisions of paragraph one above is to be assessed on the basis of what is technically feasible for the activity in question, and taking both public and private interests into consideration.

In assigning priorities between various interests, particular attention shall be paid, on the one hand, to the nature of the area that may be subjected to disturbance and the severity of the effects of the disturbance and, on the other hand, to the usefulness of the activity, the cost of protective action and other financial implications of the precautionary measures concerned.

## Section 6

Should an environmentally hazardous activity be feared to cause substantial detriment even if the precautionary measures referred to in Section 5 above are taken, the activity may be carried out only on special grounds.

Should the feared detriment entail a substantial deterioration in the living conditions of a large number of persons, a significant loss from the viewpoint of nature conservation or considerable damage to a similar public interest, the activity may not be performed. However, the Government can issue a permit under this Act if the activity is of particular importance to the economy or the local community, or otherwise serves the public interest.

The provisions contained in paragraphs one and two above do not apply to an installation or activity whose permissibility has been examined under Section 4 of the Natural Resources Act (1987:12), or to piping the laying or use of which has been examined under the Act (1987:160) on certain piping. Neither paragraph one nor the first sentence of paragraph two above precludes the use of an airport, a road or a railway for the purpose intended when its construction is examined under special regulations.

...

## Section 9

The government may issue directives stating that

1. factories or establishments of certain kinds may not be constructed;

2. waste water of a certain quantity, type or composition may not be discharged;

3. solid waste or other solid matter may not be discharged or stored in such a manner that land, a watercourse, lake or other water area or groundwater can be polluted;

4. establishments of certain kinds, or their uses, may not be modified in a manner that can cause increased or new detriment, or that in any other respect causes substantial disturbance, unless the Licensing Board has issued a permit under this Act or an application has been made to the authority appointed by the Government.

...

Section 11

The Licensing Board comprises a chairman and three other members. When preparatory action is to be taken, when the question of whether to reject an application or dismiss a case is to be examined, and when an appeal against the Board's decision is to be dealt with, the Board may consist of the chairman alone.

*Environmental Protection Ordinance (1989:364)*
Section 1

This Ordinance applies to activities and measures covered by the Environment Protection Act (1969:387).

...

Section 3

It is prohibited, without a permit, according to the Environment Protection Act (1969:387), to

1.  erect a factory or any other establishment,

2.  discharge waste water or

3.  discharge or store solid waste or other solid material, if the action concerned is designated A or B in the Annex to this Ordinance.

Paragraph one above also applies to a modification of an establishment or activity, if the action concerned means that a discharge or a disturbance may change in character or extent in such a way that significant detriment from the viewpoint of public health or environmental protection may arise.

...

Section 5

Matters relating to permits of the kind referred to in Section 3 are examined by the Licensing Board with respect to any environmentally hazardous activity that, in the Annex to this Ordinance, is designated A, and by the county administrative board with respect to any environmentally hazardous activity designated B in the Annex.

A question relating to a permit that, according to paragraph one above, shall be examined by the county administrative board shall, instead, be examined by the Licensing Board if

1.  the Government shall examine the question pursuant to Chap. 4 of the Natural Resources Act (1987:12);

2.  the question is connected with another application that is being examined by the Licensing Board, or

3.  the county administrative board finds that the question should, for special reasons, be referred to the Licensing Board.

Section 6

An application for a permit for an environmentally hazardous activity that is not covered by the permit obligation according to Section 3 shall be examined by the county administrative board.

Paragraph one above does not apply if the Licensing Board, in connection with the activity referred to in a permit application, handles a case according to Section 41 of the Environment Protection Act (1969:387), or if a permit application is connected in any other way with a case being dealt with by the Board.

The county administrative board may refer a case of the kind referred to in paragraph one above to the Licensing Board, if there are special reasons for doing so.

...

## Section 9

Anyone planning to erect an establishment or take an action for which a permit is compulsory shall, in good time before applying for a permit, obtain advice and information from the county administrative board as to how the obligation of consultation defined in Section 12 a of the Environment Protection Act (1969:387) should appropriately be fulfilled.

## Section 10

A permit-issuing authority decides of its own accord whether an application or request shall be considered by the authority itself, or whether the case shall be submitted to another supervisory authority for examination. No appeal may be lodged against such a decision.

### *Environmental Damage Act (1986):225*
## Section 1

Compensation for damage pursuant to this Act shall be payable for personal injury damage to property and pure financial loss caused to the surroundings by operations performed on real property.

Compensation for pure financial loss which is not caused by an offence shall, however, only be payable if the loss is significant.

Compensation for damage or injury which is not caused wilfully or through negligence shall only be payable if the disturbance that is the cause of the damage or injury is not admissible with regard to local conditions or to its occurrence generally in similar conditions.

## Section 2

The Act shall not be applicable to damage or injury caused by ionizing radiation or the effect of electric current from an electrical installation in cases which are subject to special regulations.

## Section 3

Compensation shall be payable for damage or injury caused by:

1. pollution of watercourses, lakes or other water areas;

2. pollution of groundwater;

3. changes in the groundwater level;

4. air pollution;

5. soil pollution;

6. noise;

7. vibration; or

8. other similar disturbances.

Points 1–3 above do not apply to damage or injury caused by activities carried on with permission pursuant to the Water Act (1983:291).

Damage shall be considered to have been caused by a disturbance as referred to in paragraph one above if, in view of the nature of the disturbance and the damage, of other possible causes of the damage, and of other circumstances, there is substantial probability of a causal connection.

...

## Section 6

Those liable to pay compensation pursuant to this Act are persons who carry on or cause to be carried on the aforementioned deleterious activities in their capacity of owners of real property or site leasehold rights. The same liability pertains to others who carry on or cause to be carried on such deleterious activities and who use such a property in their business or in public service activities.

If another person who uses the property carries on or causes to be carrried on such deleterious activities, he is liable to pay compensation pursuant to this Act only if he has caused the damage wilfully or through negligence.

## Section 7

Any person who, without being the owner of property or site leasehold rights or otherwise a user of the property, carries out or causes to be carried out work on the same in his own business shall also be liable to pay compensation pursuant to this Act.

## Section 8

If two or more persons are liable to pay compensation pursuant to this Act, they shall be jointly and severally responsible for the payment thereof, unless a limitation in the liability of any of the persons requires otherwise.

The payment made by those jointly and severally liable shall, unless otherwise agreed upon, be divided between them according to what is reasonable with regard to the grounds of their liability, the possibility of preventing the damage or injury and other circumstances.

## Section 9

If, with respect to damage to property, the amount of compensation payable can appropriately be estimated in advance, compensation shall be determined for future damage if one of the persons so requests.

If there is good reason for it, a certain annual amount of compensation may be determined. If circumstances change after this amount has so been determined, the amount of compensation may be adjusted in accordance with what is reasonable in view of the change in circumstances.

## Section 10

With respect to deposition, division and payment of compensation which is determined as a lump sum payable to the owner of real property or of a site leasehold right is the same for future damage to the property, the Expropriation Act (1971:719) shall be applicable. This Act shall also be applicable with respect to the effect of such deposition, division and payment of compensation.

If a creditor with a mortgage in the property suffers loss on account of underestimation of the compensation pursuant to the first paragraph, and the compensation has not, by reason of the agreement between the person liable to payment thereof and the person entitled to compensation, or for other reasons, been tried by a court of law, the creditor shall be entitled to claim compensation from the person liable thereto subject to his claim in this respect being written off on the instrument of debt.

## Section 11

If, as a result of an activity referred to in this Act, a property loses its usefulness to its owner, partly or in whole, or if use of it causes great detriment, the property shall at the owner's request be bought by the person who carries on the activity.

The Expropriation Act (1972:719) is applicable to such payments for real property. With respect to the appreciation in value that has occurred during the period from ten years to the day prior to the filing of a suit chapter 4, section 3 of the same Act is applicable.

## Section 12

Any person who wishes to present a claim for compensation pursuant to this Act shall bring an action at the district court in whose area the deleterious activity is or has been mainly carried on.

If the compensation relates to real property or to a building or other installation on another person's land the action shall, however, be brought at the real property court in whose area the activity is or has been mainly carried on. The same shall apply if anyone wishes to claim compensation pursuant to section 10 second paragraph or payment for a property pursuant to section 11. The real property court may, if it is appropriate with regard to the investigation or other circumstances, consider other cases involving the same or other parties in conjunction with a case to which the provisions of the first and second sentences of this paragraph relate.

Section 13

Any person who carries on or proposes to carry on an activity which may cause such damage or injury as is referred to in section 3 may apply to the real property court in whose area the activity is or will be mainly carried on for consideration of the question of compensation.

## Questions and Problems

1. What is the primary aim of existing regulations concerning hazardous substances:
   — the protection of workers;
   — the protection of the public;
   — the protection of the environment?

   Can these aims be combined without excessive cost for the producer and/or for the user?

2. What is the best method for regulating hazardous substances:
   a) obligatory texts issued by
   — an international body
   — a state authority
   — an association of producers
   b) non-obligatory codes of conduct issued by
   — an international body
   — a state authority
   — an association of producers
   — non-governmental organizations of consumers or environmentalists?

3. During which phase of the life cycle of hazardous substances can regulation be the most effective:
   — production;
   — marketing;
   — use?

4. Discuss the role of public information on the chemical substances used in products. To what extent can access to industry information be restricted?

5. Should foreign state authorities or the EEC have access to industry information? If so, what conditions should be imposed?

6. To what extent should radioactive materials be subject to special legal rules? Why?

7. Why is the definition of wastes difficult?

8. Should reference be made to "toxic and hazardous" or only to "hazardous"?

9. Draft a permit for a waste incineration plant, including all the necessary restrictions and requirements.

10. Discuss the different methods of preventing waste production.

11. Which of the following costs should be covered by insurance:
    — deposit of wastes;
    — incineration;
    — transport;
    — pollution of underground water by wastes;
    — clean-up of contaminated sites?

12. According to certain authors, noise is essentially a subjective nuisance. Can objective criteria be adopted?

13. What type of environmental standards would you recommend for reducing road traffic noise:
    — limitations on use of motor vehicles;
    — product standards, e.g. engine size, restrictions on horns;
    — noise emission standards;
    — anti-noise protections, e.g. walls, trees, buffer zones along freeways?

14. How can damage caused by the noise of a nearby airport be measured and compensated?

15. What is the role of liability in regulating transsectoral harm? How comprehensive is the Swedish law in this regard?

## Bibliography

Berkhoat, F., *Radioactive Waste, Politics and Technology*.

Denison, R. A. and Ruston, J. (eds) *Recycling and Incineration: Evaluating the Choices* (1990).

Government of the Netherlands, Ministry of Housing, Physical Planning, and Environment, *Memorandum on the Prevention and Recycling of Waste* (The Hague, 1988).

Haigh, L. *et al.*, *EC Environmental Policy in Practice (4 Vols.): Comparative Report on Water and Waste in Four Countries*.

Handl, G., Lutz, R., "An International Policy Perspective on the Trade of Hazardous Materials and Technologies", 30 *Harv. L. J.* 351 (1985).

Hill, R., "Problems and Policy for Pesticide Exports to Less Developed Countries", 28 *Nat. Res. J.* 699 (1988).

Martin, G., "La responsabilité civile du fait de déchets en droit français", *Revue Internationale de Droit Comparé* (1992), p. 65.

OECD, *Fighting Noise in the 1990s*.

## CHAPTER XI

# INTEGRATED ENVIRONMENTAL PROTECTION

## A. Overview

### 1. *Urban and Rural Planning*

Environmental problems vary according to factors that include population density, the nature of human activities, and the physical characteristics of the surrounding area. During the growth of environmental law over the past three decades, the demographics of Europe have changed. Cities have become larger and there are more of them. Urban concentrations of five thousand persons per square kilometre have become common, while rural population density now stands at approximately twenty persons per square kilometre. The steady decline in rural population has been accompanied by an increase in industrialized agriculture.

As their populations have grown, the functions and compositions of cities have changed. In northern cities, the traditional manufacturing sector has declined while light industry and services have expanded. New economic activities often prefer locations in the suburbs or small urban zones, leaving high population concentrations in poorer parts of cities. Populations shifts into new areas or changes in activities can exacerbate environmental problems. The primary tool of integrated environmental protection for various areas is land use planning. It can make a significant contribution to environmental protection. It involves government development of a comprehensive plan for regulating population density and activities.

Generally, planning and land use controls regulate public or private construction and works, quarries, and mines. Based on plans, anyone seeking to construct a new building, renovate an old one, engage in mining, locate an industrial facility, or make major changes in the use of land or buildings needs permission. Legislation on planning often excludes forest and agricultural activities.

Denmark's 1969 law on land management provides an example of a general planning law; it governs the development of towns while protecting agriculture, by establishing zones for urbanization. A subsequent law of 1983, on national and regional planning, seeks balanced development and creates an agency for the management of the territory, to coordinate national and regional planning. The agency presents annual reports to the Minister of the Environment and Parliament on the state of the environment.

Similarly, since 1947, all development proposals in the United Kingdom have required a grant of planning permission, now contained in the Planning and Compensation Act, 1990. Grants must be in accordance with development plans prepared by various levels of planning authorities, who have wide discretion. Development plans must include policies on "the conservation of natural beauty and amenity of land" and consideration of traffic disturbances.

Particular protection is often given certain buildings and areas. Apart from sites protected under international or EC texts like the Unesco Convention on Cultural and Natural Heritage, the Ramsar Convention, and the Community directive on habitats, national legislation may provide stricter protection for buildings of historic or architectural interest, areas of archaeological importance, sites of special scientific interest, and conservation areas.[1] Conversely, when the government seeks to encourage development and job creation, other areas, known as Simplified Planning Zones or Enterprise Zones, may benefit from relaxed controls.

Laws vary on who must develop plans. In the UK, under the Town and Country Planning Act 1990, local planning authorities must balance development and change against the need to protect the countryside and character of villages, towns and cities. Attempts to decentralize decision-making can result in small units controlling various areas, sometimes in conflicting ways. In London, for example, there are more than thirty local planning authorities, none with overall authority for the city as a whole. Each agent may generally issue permission for most types of development, except waste disposal and mineral extraction.

### a. The Urban Environment

Some 40 per cent of the European population lives in cities of more than 50,000 inhabitants and almost 20 per cent in cities of more than 500,000. The strong concentration results in particularly high levels of air and water pollution, with resulting health impacts to which traffic, domestic heating and local industry all contribute. In Berlin 60 to 80 per cent of the air pollution stems from industrial smokestacks. Indoor pollution is superimposed and varies according to building style, ventilation, heating practice and activities. In addition, human physical and mental health is directly affected by the existence or absence of green spaces and the location of industry.

Urban plans increasingly rely on development and protection of green spaces to improve the environment. The planning of open areas or green spaces serves several purposes. The first is biophysical: plants purify the air and absorb urban noise. Second, open green areas fulfil an aesthetic purpose in providing a more pleasing environment. Third, a social function is served by permitting human interaction.

Studies in France showed that urban dwellers were nearly unanimous in finding green spaces contribute the most to the quality of life in an urban setting. In Paris, where traffic is notoriously congested, more than 80 per cent of the population judged that green spaces were as important as parking spaces. The decision to develop city

---

1 See, for example, the Planning Act (Listed Buildings and Conservation Areas) Act 1990 of the United Kingdom.

"green spaces open to the public" is relatively recent. French jurisprudence long considered gardens as within the private jurisdiction of communities and not as part of public services. In 1960 the Conseil d'Etat determined that open spaces should figure in urban planning for public hygiene in the public interest. Article 65 of the law of 23 December 1960 (No. 60–1384) included in the public domain land acquired by the départements in France for creation and management of green spaces.

In France, urban planning documents include classification of areas as "wooded areas to be protected". Within such areas, prior authorization is required for the cutting of any trees or other activities that would change the nature of the area. Servitudes also can be imposed on areas alongside green spaces to restrict private building or public works.

The planning of open spaces varies considerably throughout Europe, from Toulouse (0 square metres per inhabitant) to Vienna (25 square metres per inhabitant). Vienna has over 900 public gardens, 445 school grounds, and over 550 playgrounds for two million inhabitants. Fewer areas can lead to overuse of green spaces; near Berlin, close to 300,000 people may visit the shores of rivers and lakes on a given Sunday.

Most land use planning systems are complex. In France the laws of January 1983 and 22 July 1983, completed by decrees, form the Planning Code. The fundamental principle is that any commune undergoing development must plan this development by means of a land-use plan. In the absence of a plan, development cannot take place beyond the limits of areas already urbanized. In regions of substantial growth due to tourism, urbanization, industrial activity or major projects, plans governing several communes must be undertaken and approved.

Denmark has a typical urban planning structure. Municipal authorities must establish a comprehensive plan for the various elements of the urban environment. This includes dwellings and working places, the size and location of holiday cottage districts, traffic facilities, institutions, public supply services and technical facilities. Activities which, because of the need to prevent pollution, require that special regard be paid to their location, must be included in the plans. The size and location of areas reserved for agricultural purposes and the use of areas in accordance with the purpose of the Nature Conservation Act must also be determined. The same rule applies to areas used for exploitation of stone, gravel and other natural resources in the ground.

The plan must indicate the distribution of buildings according to their kind and use; areas in which specific methods of heating must be given a preferential use; institutions and technical plants; the supply of public services; the traffic system; green areas, allotment garden areas, etc. Building conditions must include the maximum density and height of residential and other buildings, what buildings should be conserved, and whether urban renewal is needed. It also must be decided what areas should be transferred to urban zones or holiday cottage districts. The municipal plan must be accompanied by information about the national planning directions and regional planning, plus the goals of the municipality in terms of demographic and economic development. Municipal plans require public information campaigns to provoke public debate and must allow a time period of no less than four months for the submission of objections.

The regional planning authority must ensure that the municipal plan is in accord with regional and national planning guidelines. The municipal authorities must amend the plan if incompatibilities are found.

An International Society of City and Regional Planners is drawing up an international manual of planning practice. In this regard, most systems, established to consider urban problems, are now are under review for their ability to control rural change.

### b. Rural Planning

Rural environment plans can concern activities (agriculture, forestry, recreation) or issues (pollution, access, conservation), taking into account natural factors (wildlife, landscape, natural resources) as well as economic and social ones (employment, revenues). Technology and individual decision-making over privately owned land also must be taken into account. Rural planning is often contained in provisions for nature protection. For example, in the UK the National Parks and Access to the Countryside Act 1949 (UK) and the Wildlife and Countryside Act 1981 protect rural sites.

Denmark has about fifty planning systems relevant to land use. In addition to municipal action, planning occurs at the national and regional levels. Regional plans must contain general guidelines for the distribution of future urban growth in the county and must indicate where major centres, traffic facilities, other technical installations, public institutions etc. should be located. The locations of factories and other polluting installations must be noted. The size and location of areas reserved for agricultural purposes, the use of land for the utilization of stone, gravel, and other natural resources in the ground, and the size and the location of holiday cottage districts and other areas for recreational purposes must be indicated. The regional plan must be accompanied by an account of the considerations on which it is based, including the anticipated timetable for implementation of the plan.

The procedure begins with proposals from the municipal councils of the region and negotiations between the region and them. The regional planning authority then publishes alternative outlines of the proposed regional plan. At the same time it is sent to municipal councils and the Minister. After six months, final negotiations between the municipal councils and the region result in adoption of the final plan, which is published with a four-month period for objections. The final report is then sent to the Minister for approval. Subsequent developments and municipal plans and investments must not be contrary to the regional plan. The plan also has an impact on private property, as it is the duty of the regional planning authority and the municipal council to promote implementation of the plan and to use, if necessary, their discretionary powers under the land use law in individual cases.

Plans must be kept up to date, with mandatory reports submitted to the Minister every two years after approval of the plan, indicating what development has taken place in respect of the region and assessment of the regional planning authority on conformity of development and planning with the plan.

Under the provisions of the Danish Agricultural Land Act, the regional planning authority also must provide an agricultural land plan for the protection of specially valuable agricultural areas. The plan, which constitutes part of the regional and municipal planning, must be submitted to the Minister of Agriculture for approval.

### c. Integrated Planning

There is a dualism between comprehensive planning and specialized planning, for example, plans for conservation of nature and landscape or agriculture. Germany has a variety of land-use plans, some comprehensive, some specialized with reference to land use. The legal basis for planning is formulated by the federal government, but implementation is done by the Länder and their administrations. The Raumord-nungegesetz 1965 (law of regional policy) requires comprehensive planning on three levels: state (Land), regional (parts of the Länder) and local. Land use is mostly integrated in the regional plan with landscape and at the local level with town planning.

In Switzerland, the federal law of 22 June 1979, aims to support efforts undertaken to protect the natural bases of life. Within the principle of land management, the protection of the countryside, including forests, plays a large role. One of the principles is that inhabited places should be preserved as much as possible from harm. Cantons establish their plans on the basis of the criterion of ecological function (article 6, para. 2(b) ). Zones are established: protected zones, including waters and their banks, countrysides of value from all points of view, and biotopes of animals and plants (article 17, para. 1). Without special permission, it is forbidden to construct or modify construction or installations outside construction zones (art. 22, para. 2(a) and article 24). An ordinance of 2 October 1989 on approval of land use plans now requires the authority who establishes a plan to send it to the competent authority for approval, together with a report demonstrating its conformity with the provisions of legislation on protection of the environment (art. 26).

Land use plans are subject to legislative measures that create a national park or construct a national motorway. The French Planning Code stipulates what must be included within a land-use plan and the procedures for its development. Planning Code article 121–10 states that land-use plans must both preserve agricultural land, afforested areas, natural sites and landscapes, and provide for a reasonable degree of urbanization. Legislation in 1985 and 1986 adopted specific measures for areas, such as the coastline and mountains, that need special protection. The coastline may no longer be built upon within a 100-metre band stretching from the high-water mark in areas not yet urbanized. Local land use plans must comply with this requirement. In mountain regions, legislation protects hay meadows and alpine pastures necessary to maintain certain types of farming activities.

Land use plans consist normally of a written presentation, a zoning regulation, and local by-laws. The written presentation must describe the impacts foreseen on the environment. Zoning can be simple or complex, depending upon the size of the commune and the nature of its problems. By-laws concern the entire plan and each zone. They determine the rules concerning density or architecture. In France, provisions are made for public hearings.

In addition to direct planning measures, land use can be considerably affected by economic measures. Tax and grant incentives, building regulations and investment decisions can establish biases in favour of particular kinds of development or urban renewal.

## 2. Environment and Development

Since the end of decolonization during the 1960s, the term "development" has been understood as economic growth of relatively young countries, primarily in the southern hemisphere. The developing countries, also known as the Third World after the Third State of the French Revolution, constitute a category including more than 120 States. The South has become a point of comparison with the North, where most of the developed countries of the world are found. Within regions, or even within states, the same economic disparity often can be found. The necessity to ensure development for all countries and regions has become one of the principal foundations of global policies, both political and economic.

With the liberalization in Central and Eastern Europe, it is clear that development also concerns the Northern Hemisphere, especially those countries where industrialization has been considerably slower and its consequences more severe than in areas of Western Europe.

When concern with environmental protection intensified at the end of the 1960s, it was frequently contrasted with development. Representatives of the Third World themselves considered that environmental protection was essentially a battle against pollution, produced primarily if not exclusively by industry. It was therefore a question of an "illness of the rich" that did not concern poor countries, deprived of industrial growth. Later, a better comprehension of the many aspects of environmental deterioration demonstrated that desertification, lack of clean water in many areas, erosion, deforestation, touch Southern countries as much as or more than they harm Northern ones. Moreover, the exportation of pollution from industrialized zones to developing countries provoked reactions after chemical products prohibited in their countries of origin, toxic wastes, and especially polluting activities, were transferred into Southern states to maximize profits. On their side, industrialized countries began to realize that planetary environmental problems such as protection of the ozone layer, stabilization of the global climate and protection of biological diversity, could not be regulated without the cooperation of all countries. The increased linking of environment and development is expressed in the term "sustainable development". It refers to development seeking to satisfy the needs of the present generation while respecting the environment for the needs of future generations. Formulated and elaborated by a United Nations Commission, the Brundtland Commission, it was the basis of the Rio de Janeiro Conference on Environment and Development.

European countries recognized rather early the need to assist development in poorer countries. Many were colonial powers whose colonies needed assistance upon becoming independent. In addition to bilateral aid transferred from one European state to one developing country, various forms of multilateral cooperation have arisen, in particular through the European Community. The preamble of the Treaty of Rome of 1957 already raised this question in affirming the solidarity that links Europe to countries overseas. A first agreement of cooperation was signed at Yaounde on 20 July 1963, between the EEC and states of Africa. The agreement was updated in 1969. The subsequent doubling in the number of Community member states and increased foreign policy concerns required a complete reformulation of cooperation, accomplished with the signature on 28 February 1975, of the first Lomé agreement. This treaty associated not only African states with the Community, but also many Caribbean and Pacific countries. Together these are referred to as the ACP states.

The most recent Lome agreement was adopted on 15 December 1989 between the Community and the now 68 African, Caribbean and Pacific states. The agreement contains important provisions concerning environmental protection. Among the principal objectives of cooperation are included rational management of natural resources, priority accorded to environmental protection and to the conservation of natural resources, described as "essential conditions for a sustainable and balanced development on both the economic and human levels" (article 6). In the second part of the treaty, defining the areas of cooperation, the first title is devoted to environment. It details the precise undertakings of states in this field, including the explicit mention of the need for a long-term policy, the preventive approach, an integrated approach including social and cultural dimensions, the preparation of impact studies, control of international movements of hazardous and radioactive wastes, common studies on major ecological risks, such as the effect of acid rain, the depletion of the ozone layer, and the evolution of tropical forests.

The Treaty of Maastricht on European union, adopted on 7 February 1992, also refers to cooperation for development. Its articles, beginning with 130 U, proclaim that the policy of the Community in this field supports economically and socially sustainable development in developing countries, particularly the least developed, the harmonious and progressive integration of these countries into the global economy and the battle against poverty.

As for countries of Central and Eastern Europe which have undergone democratization since 1989, investment policies and the transfer of technology have been launched both by the European Investment Bank and by the Community. Bilateral and private actions also play an important role.

# B. Case Studies

## 1. H. Williams, *The Environment in Europe's Cities – Whose Responsibility?*

As the European Community moves towards a more integrated and unified future, one of the most vigorous debates concerns the balance of powers and responsibility between European, national and local authorities. At first, it would seem obvious that responsibility and powers for urban environment should lie with towns themselves. Such decentralization would help to sustain the rich diversity of environments, cultures and values that is one of Europe's strengths; and which is nowhere more clearly expressed than in the variety of its towns and cities. Furthermore, the re-emergence of cities – almost as city states – can lead them to play an important political, cultural and economic role at the European and even world scale. However, our major towns are not independent. Actions taken by city administrations affect other levels of government and people far beyond their boundaries. European towns are subject to common problems and all are affected by international and national policies. Furthermore, many, if not most, are dependent upon public finance from "higher" levels of government.

How can a balance be struck between the needs and benefits of integration on the one hand, and the strength of diversity on the other? How should responsibility and powers for the urban environment be divided between the different levels of government? The ugly word "subsidiarity" is used to encapsulate the principle that powers and responsibilities should remain at the most decentralized level possible and appropriate. In order to address this, it is helpful to look briefly at the nature and causes of urban environmental problems, at some of the general lessons learnt concerning successful responses and at the city in its wider context. While the focus of the discussion is primarily upon the physical environment, it is important to recognize that environmental issues are but one aspect of urban life and that a comprehensive approach must include social, cultural, housing and economic aspects. Any measures of the "success" of a city must include progress on all of these fronts. To some degree the lessons and views presented here are relevant to these wider issues.

### a. The nature and causes of urban environmental problems

Throughout the Community, citizens complain of a common set of urban environmental problems which affect almost all our major towns and cities. Clearly there are variations. For example, certain towns subject to rapid urbanization have difficulties in providing adequate infrastructure for waste disposal or sewage treatment. Older towns in decline have severe problems of obsolescence of such infrastructures and the need to upgrade sewers and treatment plants. Underused and derelict land may be most prevalent in some of the older, declining industrial cities yet vacant and underused sites may be found in even the rapidly growing cities of Southern Europe. Nevertheless, these are small variations within a common set of environmental problems which have a striking similarity from city to city across the Community regardless of whether they are in the North or South, are large or small, or at different stages in the cycle of urbanization. The key or common problems of the urban environment in Europe are:

  i) air pollution – primarily from traffic and energy sources;
 ii) problems of waste management and disposal;
iii) problems of waste water treatment in some areas;
 iv) the destruction of amenity:
   — through increased traffic, congestion and particularly traffic noise,
   — the loss of heritage and public spaces in towns to new developments, roads or traffic,

— the loss of ecological resources in towns and in their surrounding areas,
— the increased use of land resources for building/development, both in towns and their surrounding areas;

v) social polarization of cities in which the poor and other less fortunate social groups are concentrated in certain areas and excluded from others.

Whilst we can list and recognize the nature of the environmental problems in our cities, rather less is known about the underlying causes of these problems. Yet it is these causes which need to be addressed if fundamental improvements are to be achieved. There are at least three broad causal processes at work which need to be better understood but which also indicate at what level of government action might need to be taken.

First, an important underlying mechanism is the impact of market forces, in many instances now being strengthened by the impetus of the drive towards the EC internal market. Some of these latter effects are discussed in the recent commission document "1992 – The Environmental Dimension". In general, the impacts of market forces are all-pervasive. Whilst there is a considerable understanding of the technological solutions to, and the causes of, increased pollution and waste from industry and households through economic growth, it is those aspects which relate to the rate and form of development and the growth of demand for transport which are of particular relevance to many of the key urban environmental problems. Examples include: the growth in car ownership and increase in urban traffic, the demands of industry related to access requirements and lower density buildings giving rise to pressures for peripheral development, the increasing importance of just-in-time delivery and the associated demand for distribution centres and easy road and rail access to industrial and retail sites, the impact of the freedom of movement of capital and investment on the location of plant and ownership of land and buildings in major cities.

Finally, in relation to market forces it is also relevant to mention the increasing competition between European cities for economic activity and mobile investment. This is a two-edged sword. It requires cities to offer an increasingly more attractive quality of life and to compete to provide a good environment. On the other hand, cities also have to be more responsive to the demands of particular companies or sectors and hence are under more pressure to conform to the demands for particular sorts of development (peripheral sites, large redevelopment schemes, etc.) which may not always suit the overall scale and shape of the host city.

The second group of important impacts on urban environments arise from the effects of policy actions themselves – primarily through the unintended or unconsidered environmental effects of policies concerned with other sectors, but also through the mistakes or lack of coordination. It must also be recognized that there are indeed "trade-offs" to be made between environmental quality and other objectives or, indeed, between environmental quality in one area as opposed to another (the choice of location of waste disposal sites or of infrastructure with a major environmental impact such as airports are classic examples of the latter).

In the case of an individual city, the impact may arise from policy made at a "higher" government level (regional, national, EC), from the impact of policy in neighbouring municipalities, or as a result of uncoordinated sectoral policies in the city itself. Of the latter kind, transport policies are classic examples. In many cities, transportation planning gives greater emphasis to individual and private car mobility at the expense of the environmental impact. Environmental externalities affecting neighbouring municipalities can arise from such decisions as the location of a municipal airport or the quality of treated waste water returned to a shared river. In addition, the "top down" sectoral policy context within which cities operate can have profound and sometimes unforeseen effects. A striking example of this is in the impact of the new European Community agreements to increase allowable sizes of heavy goods vehicles. In environmental terms this will result in a requirement for larger turning circles (and hence larger junctions) with considerable implications for requirements to widen streets, demolish buildings and place under pressure older more historic centres and street forms. Other examples are, of course, the impact of the policy of the single market, although here we see the first steps in a preventive and more integrated approach being developed through the Commission's study to assess the potential environmental impact.

Finally, in considering the causes of environmental deterioration, it is important to remember that these market, and indeed policy, forces are often related to the conflicting demands of consumers and residents. For example, much of the pressure for suburbanization and decentralization to the rural areas around major conurbations comes from demands from residents seeking lower density, more rural locations and what they perceive as an improved quality of life. Similarly, pressures for traffic growth are not purely commercial – many people still want the freedom and flexibility afforded to them by the use of the private car. Yet these, too, are the residents who are affected by the environmental impact of traffic and the loss of vitality of urban centres.

### b. Successful responses to urban problems

There have been, over recent years, many conferences and studies reporting experience of solutions to urban environmental problems at the city scale. Indeed, the OECD has recently completed a major review of urban policy experience in many countries. Two important lessons emerge from all this experience. Firstly, despite the similarity of urban environmental problems there is no single set of solutions, urban design responses, etc., that can be universally applied. Rather, the diversity of European urban culture means that solutions have to be tailored to the particular needs of each town or city. This does not deny the value of exchanging experience and learning from examples. It merely emphasizes that such experience cannot be transferred as a model to be blindly copied from one town to another.

Nevertheless it is possible to identify the features which characterize successful solutions to urban environmental problems:

   i) integrate environmental and other sectoral issues;

   ii) involve the local community in developing and implementing solutions through encouraging partnership between city government, the private sector, the voluntary or not-for-profit sector, and residents;

iii) identify the local features of problems and build upon the strengths and opportunities of the local town or city.

Solutions of this kind can most easily be developed at the local or city scale. It is clearly only possible to make the links between the different groups at the local scale or indeed to identify the opportunities upon which to build. The urban system is highly complex and a large number of inter-relationships exist between the urban environment and other aspects of urban policy. It is therefore easier to recognize, handle and understand the complexity at a local or city scale.

Furthermore, there are, in many cases, choices to be made in detail, and in terms of broad objectives, between levels of environmental quality, quantitative and qualitative aspects of the local environment and, possibly, other objectives (related to costs, other sectoral policies, such as tourism development, access policy, etc.). In many cases, the value judgments, trade-offs and reconciliation of competing objectives and views can most legitimately be made at the local level by local citizens through their channels of communication and their democratic structures in municipalities and local authorities.

### c. Economies of Scale in Solving Environmental Problems

The local nature of solutions to environmental problems should not obscure the fact that urban areas are the major concentrations of people and economic activity in Europe and hence are major sources of air and water pollution and of waste. Indeed, urban areas offer opportunities for "economies of scale" in solving some types of environmental problems. That is to say there are a number of important environmental problems that can be solved at the city scale because the density of activity and development in urban areas lends itself to suitable solutions. This is of major significance in the context of a European Community policy on urban environments since many of the problems which might be addressed in this way are of international or global significance. Three examples highlight this. The city of Berlin has made energy savings by an integrated approach to energy planning for industrial users and by the use of district heating and associated energy planning for residential areas. In addition to these approaches, the Swedes have pioneered designs for residential districts which, through control of micro-climates, reduce heat loss. In the more southern climates there is experience also of using building layout and tree planting to create micro-climates that reduce heat gain and hence reduce energy demand for air conditioning. In all of these cases, it is the proximity of many potential users and of buildings which make the solutions viable and hence only appropriate in urban areas.

The effects of such solutions are, of course, to reduce energy demand and hence in those Member States where energy is produced from fossil fuels, to reduce the generation of "greenhouse gases" and the contribution to acidic air pollution ($CO_2$, $NO_x$, $SO_2$, etc.). Transportation and, in particular, motor-vehicles are also major contributors to the pollution load of greenhouse and acidic air pollution. It is only in urban areas where there is a high density of population and activity that mass transit systems – which are more energy efficient – can provide viable alternative transport solutions.

It is also in towns or densely settled areas that the opportunities arise to collect, process and recycle or otherwise re-use waste. The recycling of materials becomes more viable where the density of population makes the collection process easier. Similarly, in major areas where there are very large volumes of municipal solid waste it becomes more feasible to build sophisticated plants for the treatment, sorting, recycling and energy recovery from waste. These solutions reduce resource use, can contribute to reduced energy demand and help reduce disposal to landfill with its resulting production of methane – another "greenhouse gas".

It is thus clear that urban areas and cities because of their very nature can adopt policies and projects which can make a significant contribution towards the solution of major global environmental problems and help to move us towards more sustainable development.

So far in this discussion we have defined the symptoms of environmental problems at an urban scale and also pointed towards some of the solutions that can be designed and implemented at the city level. However, cities cannot be addressed solely as if they were independent of wider national and international concerns.

### d. "No City is an Island"

Although it is true that there is something of a renaissance in the international role and importance of the individual city, it is also the case that cities, whether they like it or not, cannot operate independently from their regional, national and international context. This is so for a number of reasons:

(i)  The environmental impact of an urban area is widespread. In the section above, mention was made of the global significance of air-polluting emissions from energy and transport sources to which cities make the major contributions. Another example relates to the great rivers of Europe where the abstraction policies of urban areas and quality of waste water returned to rivers must be addressed within a wider national or international context. On a more local scale development decisions, for example, for the choice of location for a municipal airport, can have environmental consequences for neighbouring municipalities. Even the apparently local choices related to the conservation of historic monuments and "patrimony" have wider consequences. This may be particularly so with regard to major monuments, since there may be a legitimate interest by all Europeans in the preservation of what can be seen as a common cultural heritage. This is especially so in a context where there are Community actions in place providing support for economic and social cohesion and convergence between regions which could, if not carefully handled, damage such cultural resources.

(ii)  Certain solutions to environmental problems are not available for cities to develop at the urban level. For example, controls over the design of standards of vehicles (lorry size, noise limits on vehicle engines) can only be negotiated and imposed at an international level. In many other situations, urban areas have to develop their environmental policies within the framework of a wider national policy, for example, on waste disposal or allowable emission levels, etc. Again, for reasons of harmonization, national competition control or competence, these frameworks have to be developed and applied at regional, river basin, national or international levels. Finally, urban areas may well find environmental control imposed upon them as a result of international action and conventions designed to resolve global or international problems (e.g. North Sea, transfrontier pollution, etc.).

(iii) Cities and urban areas are subjected to the effects, including the environmental consequences, of sectoral policies that are the responsibility of higher tiers of government – energy pricing, transport policy, etc.

(iv) Cities and urban areas are also interdependent in other ways. Increasingly, urban areas act within a wider international and global economy, having direct links with markets in other countries and being part of a network of multinational influences. This raises again the need to understand the environmental consequences of certain aspects of market forces mentioned above. It is also within this context that the economic competition between cities arises. It may be that cities need to coordinate their actions if they see a need to make a concerted response to economic pressures for environmental reasons or they may need some ground rules for competition if they are not to undermine each other.

(v) Finally, but of great significance, municipal governments throughout the Community rely on their state and central governments (and to some extent the European Commission) for major financial support from the tax base. To the degree that resources come from higher levels of government, there will always be a degree of control over how municipalities spend these resources because of the need to retain accountability.

Thus, whilst the city scale may be the ideal level of administration for designing and implementing a very wide range of integrated environmental urban policies, there is an important need for coordination between authorities. This coordination has to be both "horizontal" between cities and local authorities and "vertical" between local areas, cities, regions, Member States and the European Community.

Furthermore, higher levels of government have to set the framework within which municipalities can have the flexibility and freedom to develop and implement sensitive and successful integrated environmental policies at the local scale. This is not simple or even primarily an issue of the devolution of power downwards (the competence of different levels of government varies markedly between Member States). It is a recognition that many of the frameworks within which city councils operate (legal, economic, agreements on standards, etc.) are set at a higher governmental level. Moreover, as indicated above, some solutions to urban environmental problems can only be initiated and implemented at national/international scales.

Many aspects of the details of urban environments can be and are adequately addressed by legislation/control at the city level – particularly with respect to those aspects that relate to the cultural or welfare element of environment – planning controls, layout of cities, etc. However, those aspects that relate to the potential impact on health (building standards and control, air quality standards, water standards) are rightly an issue for national governments and – increasingly, the European Community – given the issues of harmonization and competition. However, as outlined in the paper, there is a much more complex web of interrelations that influence and affect urban environments and help to define the application of the principle of subsidiarity.

## 2. Marianne Sillen, *Toward Integrated Environmental Protection in Sweden*

Swedish environmental law today is a mixture of private and public law approaches, resulting in a mosaic of many acts and regulations, in which many pieces do not fit. The purposes and background of the laws are different, many overlap or are inconsistent. To a large extent, environmental laws are based on balancing protection and conservation against other societal interests. Considerable inconveniences may be accepted if the "benefits" are deemed to outweigh the damages. The large number of different rules makes implementation difficult and there is an urgent need for coordination of the laws.

The legal system may be divided into four parts: land and planning legislation, environmental protection legislation (air, water, ecology, etc.), legislation on the utilization of natural resources, and legislation on controlling certain types of installations (roads, pipelines, etc.). A brief description is given below of some of the most important laws concerning the urban environment. Also discussed are current problems of the work that is being done to improve the legal framework. Finally, a few ideas are presented regarding expected developments in the field.

### a. Use of Natural Resources

The use of natural resources in Sweden is based on the Natural Resources Act (1987). The purpose of the Act is to obtain a long-term efficient management of natural resources: and thus it contains certain "Resource Management Principles". The Natural Resources Act is intended to be an "umbrella law". The standards of the Act are applied by local municipalities when adopting plans for the use of land and water areas in accordance with the Planning and Building Act, and also by all Government authorities and water courts when examining applications under special acts, e.g., the Environmental Protection Act, the Water Act. Another object of the Natural Resources Act is to lay down strict rules in order to prohibit the exploitation of certain rivers and river sections that are identified as being of "national interest". Finally, certain types of activities of vital importance for the conservation of the country's total land and water resources are subject to Government approval. Other installations or activities also may be subject to Government approval if they are expected to cause considerable environmental damage, e.g., the Oresund bridge project. In principle, the Government examines the geographical location of these activities. However, in most cases no permit may be issued without approval of the concerned municipality; in effect, the municipality has a veto in these cases.

The use of land and water resources in general is regulated in the Planning and

Building Act. According to this Act, the local authority has the exclusive privilege of planning the land and water resource use, based upon a fairly new approach of decentralization. Sweden is divided into 24 counties and 284 municipalities. In the early 1970s, environmental law and policy were implemented and enforced by the central Government and county administrations. Increasing authority was delegated to municipalities, eventually resulting in entry into force of the Planning and Building Act on 1 July 1987.

Each municipality is required to adopt a comprehensive plan for the municipality, a so-called *overview plan*. However, for constitutional reasons, the plan has no legal force, but serves instead as an information source for further decisions. When considered necessary, municipalities are entitled to adopt more detailed, still comprehensive plans for certain areas within the municipality: *small area plans*. These may be given legal force as regulations. Finally, before building new housing, the municipality should have adopted a *detailed plan*.

In line with decentralization, all plans in Sweden are decided upon by the municipality. According to the previous Building Act of 1947, the adoption of plans had to be confirmed by the County Administration to carry legal force. This is no longer the case, and municipal decisions are sufficient to enact regulations and detailed plans.

### b. Industrial Environmental Protection

Industrial environmental protection focuses on one of the most important environmental acts, the Environmental Protection Act (1969). This Act applies to all land or water uses which may cause pollution of surface or groundwater, as well as noise and non-temporary air pollution.

A permit is required for the construction, expansion or alteration of certain types of stationary sources of major and medium size, while a notification will suffice for other minor sources. Thus, the central governmental administrative body, the Franchise Board for Environmental Protection, is responsible for licensing the potentially most-polluting plants, for example pulp and paper mills, iron and steel works, refineries, etc., in total some 770 industrial plants (List A). The 24 county administrations are responsible for licensing another 10,000 industrial plants (List B). Notification authority has recently been given to the Local Environmental and Health Protection Boards for a further 5,100 plants (List C).

When issuing permits, the authorities must be confident that certain "general requirements" set out in the Act are complied with. There are no quality standards in the Act, and no criteria for balancing inconveniences against benefits. This means that the clean air policy is carried out mainly by means of individual examination of each major source applying for a permit to operate. The basic criterion is that disturbances should be prevented as far as possible. The requirements lay down a duty to choose the reasonably best location. Environmental protection measures should be considered on the basis of what is technically feasible using the best available technology within reasonable expenditures. The requirement is, in short, that the authorities in their decisions find a proper balance between what is technically feasible, economically possible and environmentally motivated.

A permit in accordance with the Environmental Protection Act specifies the conditions for future activities, e.g., the location and the total amount of different pollutants allowed to be discharged into air or water. As long as these conditions are complied with, the supervising authorities may not require further protection. The Act provides, however, for a reconsideration of the permit, by the Franchise Board or the County Board, normally after ten years.

### c. Use of Hazardous Products

Control of hazardous products with respect to different activities such as import, manufacturing, marketing, storage, use of fertilizers and pesticides, waste management, etc., is regulated in the Act of Chemical Products (1985). Chemical products are "materials" and "mixtures". As regards "goods", e.g. car batteries, a control is provided for only in some situations. The Act specifies basic requirements, and several regulations contain detailed requirements concerning specific issues. Transport and final management of hazardous waste, for instance, can in principle only be handled by municipalities and state authorities (Hazardous Waste Regulations). Certain types of batteries must be separated from other waste (Hazardous Batteries Regulations). Pesticides must be registered before marketing (Pesticides Regulations). PCB and cadmium are, with a few exceptions, prohibited (PCB Regulations, Cadmium Regulations).

The basic programme for control of chemicals can be summarized in the following four points:

— All substances and products that are handled in society have to be sufficiently examined with regard to their effect on man and the environment.

— Anyone handling a chemical product should make sure that he has enough information on the risks and on precautionary measures to handle the product in a safe way.

— Chemical products should be handled in such a way that injury to man and the environment is avoided.

— If two products are available, the less hazardous one must be chosen, within reasonable additional costs.

There are certain specific laws as regards control of chemicals, besides the Hazardous Products Act and connected regulations. One of these is the Transportation of Hazardous Goods Act (1982), which requires marking of products and similar precautionary measures in order to avoid accidents. Another law is the Sulphur Discharges Act (1976), which determines the maximum amount of sulphur permitted to be discharged from plants. Finally, certain economic incentives exist, e.g., benefits for leaving used cars with junk dealers.

### d. Automobile Pollution

The problem of motor vehicle pollution has two aspects: the location and building of roads and streets, and the control of motor vehicles.

According to the Planning and Building Act, roads and streets in urban areas are included in the detailed plans. Municipalities must pay attention to the risks for air and water pollution, but also to other interests such as well-functioning communications. These priorities are primarily established by the municipalities. Before building a road, a permit must be issued by the Roads Authority according to the Roads Act (1971). The road must be "located and built so as to achieve as little inconvenience as possible within reasonable costs". The Roads Authority must consider environmental protection and nature conservation interests and since 1987 an Environmental Impact Assessment (EIA) is requested in the application for a permit.

The Environmental Protection Act applies to pollution, noise and other disturbances from roads and streets. No permit is required according to this legislation. Supervising authorities, and the Franchise Board, may, in specific cases, decide upon precautionary measures, e.g. speed limits or direction of traffic from one part of the traffic system to another. In practice, however, such decisions are rare.

The Traffic Regulations authorize the County Board and Municipalities to decide upon speed limits for the purpose of environmental protection. Such decisions are made from time to time as regards certain highways, in order to reduce the discharge of nitrogen.

The requirements for motor vehicles are stated in the Car Pollution Act (1986), in which limits are set for certain pollutants from new cars. In practice, this necessitates catalytic converters.

Several kinds of taxes exist for cars and fuels. The purpose of some of these is to stimulate the use of less hazardous cars and fuels and to support public transport.

### e. Recent Legislative Enactments

Environmental impact assessments have been introduced in a number of laws up to 1 July 1991. From an international perspective, these requirements are not as far-reaching as in certain EC states. The laws do not directly require that alternatives, e.g. different possible locations, be considered. Neither is there a formal legal procedure for the EIA; it is integrated in the usual permit procedure. However, the Swedish requirements fulfil the minimum standards of the EC directives.

During 1990 and 1991, several taxes and fees on pollutants from factories and energy production plants, as well as on cars, airplanes and fertilizers, have been introduced in Sweden. These economic incentives are complementary to the traditional administrative legal instruments.

### f. Is Swedish Environmental Law Effective?

From one point of view it may seem that the Natural Resources Act is a useful instrument for environmental protection. Several principles certainly aim at protection and conservation, but other principles provide for exploitation, e.g. of energy production plants, roads, factories, mines, etc. In this manner, the same area may be considered important both for protection and exploitation purposes. The Act does not provide any clear guidance on how to solve such conflicts.

The conflict between different interests is also clearly shown in the urban planning done by municipalities. As was pointed out above, municipalities must not only consider the risk of pollution, but also the need for efficient means of communication and energy demands. In conflicting situations, and those are indeed frequent in practice, the law does not provide a clear-cut solution, so that the choice is left in practice to urban communities.

In sum, a conflict of interests has always existed in Swedish environmental law. Environmental protection and conservation issues have been balanced against other interests in society, and the result of this balance is laid down in the environmental legislation. Another problem is that the Swedish environmental legal system of today consists of several overlapping and inconsistent laws. The large number of rules makes implementation difficult as well.

### g. Review of Swedish Environmental Law

A parliamentary committee was appointed in May 1989 to review environmental law. The committee was given the task of drawing up proposals which would include consideration of the environment in all sectors of society. The work delegated to the committee was presented in the Government Bill on Environmental Policy 1990/91:90. In this, it was stated that the various Swedish environmental laws should be brought together in one integrated Environmental Code. The Government emphasized that provisions corresponding to the Natural Resources Act would be in the Code. This would provide a natural connection between different interests in terms of environmental awareness on the one hand and exploitation on the other.

Traffic legislation is to be harmonized with other legislation, and the possibility of increasing the influence of local bodies on the traffic environment is to be looked into by the committee.

Regulations stating permissible levels are intended to be made more strict in the new environmental legislation in order to make it quite clear that all activities which may affect the environment should be assessed in terms of their effect on health and on the environment. More emphasis is to be placed on environmental awareness. The committee is also to look into the way in which environmental quality standards may be taken into account in legislation. The committee is also asked to consider whether the regulations for permit reviews need to be changed.

The possibility of issuing regulations of a general nature is very limited under today's Environmental Protection Act. However, this legislative method characterizes the Act on Chemical Products and other related laws and regulations in the legislation on chemicals. The Government proposes that in the new, comprehensive Environmental Code, a considerable amount of additional space should be given to general regulations. The introduction of general regulations should serve a useful purpose, particularly for activities which exist in large numbers and are technically similar. General regulations concerning protective measures should be used mainly for activities for which permits are not required. The general regulations represent minimum requirements which may be tightened up in individual cases in conjunction with the consideration of permit applications. In certain cases, it should be possible to issue general regulations for operations whose permits have already been granted.

When drawing up proposals for an Environmental Code, particular attention will be paid to how the proposals relate to environmental legislation in other countries, as well as to current product requirements in other Nordic countries and the EC.

In certain countries, an international agreement automatically becomes a part of the internal legal system as soon as it comes into force. A different procedure is used in Sweden and other Nordic countries, however, requiring that a national law be passed before the provisions of the agreement can be incorporated into the internal legal system and thus be applicable at a national level. This also applies to the area of environmental policies. The review of the legislation should therefore examine whether the Swedish Bill 1990/91:90 embraces the whole content of conventions in the field of environmental law to which Sweden is a party.

The relationship between Swedish environmental law and international undertakings is also highlighted in the context of the harmonization of laws which will result from closer ties to the EC. Even if the level of environmental requirements should remain unchanged, certain adaptation of law will be necessary. The Government has declared its intention to continue to work on a new Environment Code. In the Government Declaration, the need for explicit environmental goals and the importance of economic incentives were stated.

## h. Expected Developments

Laws are to a large extent based on the idea of balancing protection and conservation against other interests. Even major inconveniences are accepted if the seen "benefits" are deemed to outweigh the drawbacks. Perhaps a new principle should be adopted, starting from the current state of nature, a "non-deterioration" principle. Quality standards are no doubt instruments which could implement such a principle by determining the maximum of certain pollutants allowed in the environment.

As mentioned above, there is a clear trend towards decentralization in Sweden. Many legal decisions of vital importance are taken by local politicians. There are almost three hundred municipalities in Sweden, and there is a great difference between their competence, political majority and economic resources. Is it possible to fulfil the national environmental goals in an effective manner? The connection between national environmental goals on the one hand, and regional and local planning and decision-making on the other should be clarified.

Environmental control has focused traditionally on factories, plants and other stationary sources. It is more or less accepted that, for some of these sources, it will no longer be possible to achieve more efficient purification, without extraordinary costs. It would perhaps be more efficient to direct the efforts towards pollution from agriculture, cars and other non-stationary sources, by making use of economic incentives. Economic incentives such as taxes and fees already exist in Sweden, but could be more frequent and varied, such as adopting a system of emission trading rights.

The system of sanctions has been debated from time to time. It is probably true that supervising authorities in many places lack economic resources. It is true that prosecutors run into different kinds of problems when facing environmental legislation. A continued investment in training qualified prosecutors to deal with environmental offences would be a highly desirable development. Penalties for environmental crimes are lenient; most cases are regarded no more than shop-lifting. The attitude towards these types of offences should be changed.

Should the possibilities of bringing civil law suits against polluters be expanded? This right is often not exercised because of the legal effect of permits according to the Environmental Protection Act. Should the law provide for groups of people to bring a common law-suit (class action)? Some nature conservation organizations are likely to include competent environmental expertise. Why not give these organizations the legal rights to bring law suits and to appeal?

## 3. Tamás Prajczer, *An Introduction to Landscape Protection*

No system of law can by itself create an attractive landscape or distribute control over land so as to satisfy everyone in society. The more that legislators try to trap elusive qualities, such as beauty or amenity, in a framework of rules, the less clear the law becomes, and the more initiative is stifled (Harte,1985).

In traditional societies, a visual harmony between human activities and their context has been reached by local people who know the landscape. The detailed knowledge of these people preserves and sustains landscapes. In other areas, the rapid growth of urbanization and technical development have produced an explosion in the nature and scale of visual impacts on landscapes.

### a. Landscape

The word "landscape" has its origins in the Dutch language; it now has two different meanings in English. The first meaning refers to the surface features of an area, including both natural elements (landform, water, soil, flora and fauna etc.) and artificial objects (settlements, roads, dams, irrigation canals etc.) shaped by natural processes and human activities. In its other sense, landscape is the group of visible features of an area from an observer's viewpoint, defined by forms, lines, colours and textures.

Landscape elements can stimulate other senses, but the visual is the most important; it provides about ninety per cent of human sensory input. Other senses are less understood and manipulable (sound, smell, taste, touch), but they are also indispensable to holistic perception and study of the tangible world. Landscape aesthetics provide a wide framework for the complete interpretation and assessment of sensations awakened by natural and cultural elements (Porteous,1982). This section will focus on the second meaning of "landscape" and will emphasize visual sensation. In this regard "landscape features" is defined as those natural and artificial elements which can be potentially viewed.

## b. Landscape Protection

Landscape protection is provided by technical and landscape architectural measures adopted by law in order to preserve and improve the aesthetic quality of landscapes. To define landscape protection in detail some questions should be answered.

Landscape protection requires the application of knowledge obtained from studying of aesthetics, landscape and management.

The aims of landscape protection are to preserve and to improve the aesthetic resources of landscape.

There are three interested groups in this field:

— the users of the amenity of landscape;

— the owners, both public and private, of the aesthetic resources;

— the professionals, whose task is to achieve the aims of landscape protection.

Landscape protection is founded upon an understanding of:

— landscape and its natural and artificial elements and their mutual relationship;

— the visual effects of the changing landscape;

— the measures used in landscape protection;

— the effect of time.

The main tasks of landscape protection are:

— to recognize and to preserve the threatened aesthetic resources;

— to diminish the negative effects of human development;

— to improve aesthetic quality, where it is possible;

These tasks include several activities:

— execution of visual impact assessment;

— advising interested groups and organizations;

— formulating policy for protected areas etc.;

— managing experts' work;

— application of technical, landscape architectural and legal means.

Technical and administrative measures and landscape architectural techniques can be used in order to achieve the aims and tasks mentioned above.

The main application of technical measures are:

— to fit structures into their context;

— to apply natural building materials (quarry stone, timber, etc.) instead of artificial ones (concrete, steel, plastics, etc.);

— to use the rules of the natural sciences in designing structures (bridges, utility poles, water towers);

— to mitigate visible public utilities (transmission lines);

— to reclaim strip mines.

Landscape architectural techniques are used in order:

— to mitigate scenic ills by afforestation;

— to protect traditional land use and building style in special area (for example vineyards);

— to protect hedgerows and wetlands around agricultural areas;

— to use native species in case of afforestation;

— to avoid too much excavation;

— to protect historically important buildings and sites.

The functions of law in landscape protection are:

— to set building, zoning and view protection regulations;

— to designate areas for protection;

— to formulate policies;

— to require Environmental Impact Assessments.

The treatment of visual problems by biological and physical approaches is better than a merely aesthetic solution. Controlling runoff and erosion, restoration of native vegetation and preserving floodplains provide not only acceptable environmental quality, but also enhance visual appeal of the landscape (McCloskey,1979; Thorne,1991).

### c. Legislation and Aesthetics

To analyze regulations in landscape protection several approaches can be used. In relation to their connection with aesthetics, regulations which deal with the appearance of the landscape can be divided into two groups:

— those laws and other regulations which contain direct references to aesthetics,

— those which do not, but regulate activities having an effect on visual appeal.

Some of the regulations deal with details (in the case of the National Building Act, this means the size and height of buildings, etc.), while others only give a framework for protection (the Nature Conservation Act only lists reasons for designation).

During the 1960s and 1970s awareness of environmental problems grew. Visual resources management procedures were developed in the United States to integrate scenic or visual values, among others, into the decision-making process. These systems were developed by government agencies in response to legislative mandates (Zube,1982; Smardon,1986).

River channel management is a good example of the recognition of scenic values and appreciation of them by legislation (Brookes,1988). The Niagara Falls and River is an appropriate precedent for a transboundary scenic value possessed and managed by two countries.

Landscape protection problems can be handled with good results by taking environmentally sound sustainable development into consideration and only if the active persons are sensitive to the problem, understand environmentally conscious design, and are skilled in its application.

# C. Documents

*1. Council Directive 90/660 of 4 December 1990 on the Transitional Measures Applicable in Germany with Regard to Certain Community Provisions Relating to the Protection of the Environment, in Connection with the Internal Market,* O.J. No. L 353, 17 December 1990 p. 79.

### Article 1

1.  By way of derogation from Council Directive 67/548/EEC of 27 June 1967 on the approximation of laws, regulations and administrative provisions relating to the classification, packaging and labelling of dangerous substances as last amended by Directive 90/517/EEC, the Federal Republic of Germany is authorized to take the measures necessary to ensure compliance with the provisions of that Directive in the territory of the former German Democratic Republic by 31 December 1992 at the latest.

2.  The Federal Republic of Germany shall take the measures necesary to ensure that substances and preparations which do not comply with Directive 67/548/EEC are not placed on the territory of the Community other than the territory of the former German Democratic Republic. These measures must be compatible with the Treaty, and in particular with the objectives of Article 8a thereof, and must not create checks and formalities at the borders between the Member States. Any substance which does not appear on the Einecs list provided for in Article 13 of Directive 67/548/EEC must be notified in accordance with the provisions of that Directive. The conditions governing the notification of substances existing on the market of the former German Democratic Republic prior to 18 September 1981 which do not appear on the Einecs list shall be laid down by the Commission.

### Article 2

1.  By way of derogation from Article 2 (1) of Council Directive 75/716/EEC of 24 November 1975 on the approximation of the laws of the Member States relating to the sulphur content of certain liquid fuels, as amended by Directive 87/219/EEC, the Federal Republic of Germany shall be authorized, in respect of the territory of the former German Democratic Republic, to exempt producers established in that territory on the date of unification from the obligation to comply with the limit value for the sulphur content of gas oil. The German authorities may grant such authorization only in cases where compliance with the limit value for the sulphur content of gas oil would be an unreasonable requirement for the producer concerned. Authorization cannot be granted for values exceeding the limit of 0.5 per cent sulphur content limit. All such authorizations must have a cut-off date and terminate by 31 December 1994 at the latest.

2.  The Federal Republic of Germany shall take the necessary measures to ensure that gas oil which does not comply with Directive 75/716/EEC is excluded from Community territory other than the territory referred to in paragraph 1. These measures must be compatible with the Treaty, and in particular with the objectives of Article 8a thereof, and must not create checks and formalities at the borders between the Member States.

Article 3

The Federal Republic of Germany shall forthwith inform the Commission of the measures taken pursuant to Articles 1 and 2, which the Commission shall communicate to the other Member States and to the European Parliament.

Article 4

1. Adjusting measures to fill obvious loopholes and to make technical adjustments to those provided for in this Directive may be adopted in accordance with the procedure laid down in Article 21 of Directive 67/548/EEC.

2. Adjusting measures must be designed to ensure coherent application of the Directives referred to in Articles 1 and 2 in the territory of the former German Democratic Republic, with due regard for the specific circumstances in that territory and the special difficulties involved in the application of those Directives. They must be consistent with the principles of those Directives and be closely related to one of the derogations provided for by this Directive.

3. The measures referred to in paragraph 1 may be adopted not later than 31 December 1992. Their applicability shall be limited to the same date; however, as regards the Directive referred to in Article 2, that date shall be 31 December 1994.

4. Any Member State may refer any difficulties to the Commission. The Commission shall, as a matter of urgency, examine the question and submit its conclusions, possibly accompanied by appropriate measures.

## 2. Turkey, *The Environment Law*, Law 2872 of 9 August 1983.

Article 9: The protected areas established in conformity with the decision regarding land use in rural and urban areas and the principles of use and protection to be implemented in these areas shall be stipulated by special regulations.

Within the framework of these principles, the following are prohibited by law: overuse and misuse of resources, upsetting of the balance of the country's basic ecological systems as a result of waste or garbage of any kind imported from abroad, endangering of the life or propagation of any species of plant or animal, and destruction of natural assets. ·

The Council of Ministers is authorized to identify and declare "Special Environment Protection Regions" with the purpose of being able to provide the necessary arrangements to ensure that areas of world ecological importance sensitive to environmental pollution and destruction shall remain intact for future generations, and to stipulate by which Ministries plans and projects may be prepared and undertaken in such areas based on the principles of protection and use to be implemented.

*3. Agreement between the European Community and the group of African, Caribbean and Pacific States (ACP),*
15 December 1989 (Lomé IV), 29 I.L.M. 809 (1990).

## CHAPTER 1
Objectives and principles of cooperation
### Article 1

The Community and its Member States, of the one part, and the ACP States, of the other part (hereinafter referred to as the Contracting Parties), hereby conclude this cooperation Convention in order to promote and expedite the economic, cultural and social development of the ACP States and to consolidate and diversify their relations in a spirit of solidarity and mutual interest.

...

The Contracting Parties hereby express their resolve to intensify their effort to create, with a view to a more just and balanced international economic order, a model for relations between developed and developing states and to work together to affirm in the international context the principles underlying their cooperation.

### Article 2

ACP–EEC cooperation, underpinned by a legally binding system and the existence of joint institutions, shall be exercised on the basis of the following fundamental principles:

— equality between partners, respect for their sovereignty, mutual interest and interdependence;

— the right of each State to determine its own political social, cultural and economic policy options;

— security of their relations based on their system of cooperation.

### Article 3

The ACP States shall determine the development principles, strategies and models for their economies and societies in all sovereignty.

### Article 4

Support shall be provided in ACP–EEC cooperation for the ACP States' efforts to achieve comprehensive self-reliant and self-sustained development based on their cultural and social values, their human capacities, their natural resources and their economic potential in order to promote the ACP States' social, cultural and economic progress and the well-being of their populations through the satisfaction of their basic needs, the recognition of the role of women and the enhancement of people's capacities, with respect for their dignity.

Such development shall be based on a sustainable balance between its economic objectives, the rational management of the environment and the enhancement of natural and human resources.

...

### Article 6

1. With a view to attaining more balanced and self-reliant economic development in the ACP States, special efforts shall be made under this Convention to promote rural development, food security for the people, rational management of natural resources, and the preservation, revival and strengthening of agricultural production potential in the ACP States.

2. The Contracting Parties recognize that priority must be given to environmental protection

and the conservation of natural resources, which are essential conditions for sustainable and balanced development from both the economic and human viewpoints.

...

## Article 8

The Contracting Parties acknowledge the need to accord special treatment to the least-developed ACP States and to take account of the specific difficulties confronting the landlocked and island ACP States. They shall pay special attention to improving the living conditions of the poorest sections of the population.

Cooperation shall comprise, *inter alia*, special treatment when determining the volume of financial resources and the conditions attached thereto in order to enable the least-developed ACP States to overcome structural and other obstacles to their development.

For the landlocked and island ACP States, cooperation shall be aimed at devising and encouraging specific operations to deal with development problems caused by their geographical situations.

## Article 9

In order to step up the effectiveness of the instruments of this Convention, the Contracting Parties shall adopt, in the framework of their respective responsibilities, guidelines, priorities and measures conducive to attaining the objectives set out in this Convention and agree to pursue, in accordance with the principles set out in Article 2, the dialogue within joint institutions and in the coordinated implementation of development finance cooperation and the other cooperation instruments.

## Article 10

The Contracting Parties shall, each as far as it is concerned in the framework of this Convention, take all appropriate measures, whether general or particular, to ensure the fulfilment of the obligations arising from this Convention and to facilitate the pursuit of its objectives. They shall refrain from any measures liable to jeopardize the attainment of the objectives of this Convention.

...

## Article 12

Where the Community intends, in the exercise of its powers, to take a measure which might affect the interests of the ACP States as far as this Convention's objectives are concerned, it shall inform in good time the said States of its intentions. Towards this end, the Commission shall communicate regularly to the Secretariat of the ACP States any proposals for such measures. Where necessary, a request for information may also take place on the initiative of the ACP States.

At their request, consultations shall be held in good time so that account may be taken of their concerns as to the impact of those measures before any final decision is made.

After such consultations have taken place, the ACP States shall also be provided with adequate information on the entry into force of such decisions, in advance whenever possible.

## CHAPTER 2
### Objectives and guidelines of the Convention in the main areas of cooperation

## Article 13

Cooperation shall be aimed at supporting development in the ACP States, a process centred on man himself and rooted in each people's culture. It shall back up the policies and measures adopted by those States to enhance their human resources, increase their own creative capacities and promote their cultural identities. Cooperation shall also encourage participation by the population in the design and execution of development operations.

Account shall be taken, in the various fields of cooperation, and at all the different stages of the operations executed, of the cultural dimension and social implications of such operations and of the need for both men and women to participate and benefit on equal terms.

## Article 14

Cooperation shall entail mutual responsibility for preservation of the natural heritage. In particular, it shall attach special importance to environmental protection and the preservation and restoration of natural equilibria in the ACP States. Cooperation schemes in all areas shall therefore be designed to make the objectives of economic growth compatible with development that respects natural equilibria and brings about lasting results in the service of man.

In the framework of efforts to protect the environment and restore natural balances, cooperation shall help promote specific operations concerning the conservation of natural resources, renewable and non-renewable, the protection of ecosystems and the control of drought, desertification and deforestation; other operations on specific themes shall also be undertaken (notably locust control, the protection and utilization of water resources, the preservation of tropical forests and biological diversity, the promotion of a better balance between urban and rural areas, and the urban environment).

## Article 15

Agricultural cooperation shall be aimed at the pursuit of food self-sufficiency and food security in the ACP States, developing and organizing their productive systems, improving the living standards and conditions and the life styles of the rural population and achieving the balanced development of rural areas.

Operations in this field shall be designed and executed to support the agricultural and food policies or strategies adopted by the ACP States.

## Article 16

Cooperation in the field of mining and energy shall be directed at promoting and expediting, in the mutual interest, diversified economic development, deriving full benefit from the ACP States' human potential and natural resources, and at fostering better integration of these and other sectors and their complementarity with the rest of the economy.

Cooperation shall be aimed at creating and consolidating the cultural, social and economic environment and the infrastructure required to achieve that objective.

Support shall be provided for the ACP States' efforts to devise and implement energy policies suited to their situation, notably the gradual reduction of the dependence of the majority of them on imported petroleum products and the development of new and renewable sources of energy.

Cooperation shall be aimed at encouraging improved exploitation of energy and mining resources by taking account of the energy component in the development of the different economic and social sectors and thus helping to improve living conditions and the environment, leading to the better conservation of biomass resources, particularly fuelwood.

## Article 17

The Community and the ACP States acknowledge that industrialization is a driving force – complementary to agricultural and rural development – in promoting the economic transformation of the ACP States in order to achieve self-sustained growth and balanced and diversified development. Industrial development is needed to enhance the productivity of the ACP economies so that they can meet basic human needs and step up the competitive participation of the ACP States in world trade by way of selling more value-added products.

...

## Article 19

The aim of cooperation in fisheries shall be to help the ACP States to develop their fishery resources in order to expand production for domestic consumption as part of their efforts to achieve increased food security and increase production for export. Such cooperation shall be designed to serve the mutual interests of the Parties, in accordance with their fishery policies.

...

## PART TWO
### The areas of ACP–EEC cooperation
### TITLE I   Environment
### Article 33

In the framework of this Convention, the protection and the enhancement of the environment and natural resources, the halting of the deterioration of land and forests, the restoration of ecological balances, the preservation of natural resources and their rational exploitation are basic objectives that the ACP States concerned shall strive to achieve with Community support with a view to bringing an immediate improvement in the living conditions of their populations and to safeguarding those of future generations.

### Article 34

The ACP States and the Community recognize that the existence of some ACP States is under threat as a result of a rapid deterioration of the environment that hinders any development efforts, in particular those aimed at achieving the priority objectives of food self-sufficiency and food security. For many ACP States efforts to halt this deterioration of the environment and conserve natural resources are imperative and call for the preparation and implementation of coherent modes of development that have due regard for ecological balances.

### Article 35

The dimension of the environmental problem and of the means to be deployed mean that operations will have to be carried out in the context of overall, long-term policies, drawn up and implemented by the ACP States at national, regional and international level with international support.

To this end, the Parties agree to give priority in their activities to:

— a preventive approach aimed at avoiding harmful effects on the environment as a result of any programme or operation;

— a systematic approach that will ensure ecological viability at all stages, from identification to implementation;

— a transsectoral approach that takes into account not only the direct but also the indirect consequences of the operations undertaken.

### Article 36

The protection of the environment and natural resources requires a comprehensive approach embracing the social and cultural dimensions.

In order to ensure that this specific dimension shall be taken into account, attention shall be given to incorporating suitable educational, training, information and research schemes in projects and programmes.

### Article 37

Cooperation instruments appropriate to environmental needs shall be designed and implemented. Where necessary, both qualitative and quantitative criteria may be used.

Jointly approved check-lists shall be used to help estimate the environmental viability of proposed operations, whatever their scale.

Environmental impact assessment will be carried out as appropriate in the case of large-scale projects and those posing a significant threat to the environment.

For the proper integration of environmental considerations, physical inventories, where possible translated into accounting terms, shall be drawn up.

The implementation of these instruments has to ensure that, should an adverse environmental impact be foreseen, the necessary corrective measures are formulated in the early stage of the preparation of the proposed project or programme so that it can go ahead in accordance with the planned timetable though improved in terms of environmental and natural resource protection.

## Article 38

The Parties, desirous of bringing real protection and effective management to the environment and natural resources, consider that the areas of ACP–EEC cooperation covered in Part Two of this Convention shall be systematically examined and appraised in this light.

In this spirit the Community shall support efforts made by the ACP States at national, regional and international level and also operations mounted by inter-governmental and non-governmental organizations in furtherance of national and inter-governmental policies and priorities.

## Article 39

1.  The Contracting Parties undertake, for their part, to make every effort to ensure that international movements of hazardous waste and radioactive waste are generally controlled, and they emphasize the importance of efficient international cooperation in this area.

    With this in view, the Community shall prohibit all direct or indirect export of such waste to the ACP States while at the same time the ACP States shall prohibit the direct or indirect import into their territory of such waste from the Community or from any other country, without prejudice to specific international undertakings to which the Contracting Parties have subscribed or may subscribe in the future in these two areas within the competent international fora.

    These provisions do not prevent a Member State to which an ACP State has chosen to export waste for processing from returning the processed waste to the ACP State of origin. The Contracting Parties shall expedite adoption of the necessary internal legislation and administrative regulations to implement this undertaking. At the request of one of the Parties, consultations may be held if delays are encountered. At the conclusion of such consultations each Party may take appropriate steps in the light of the situation.

2.  The Parties undertake to monitor strictly the implementation of the prohibition measures referred to in the second paragraph of paragraph 1. Should difficulties arise in this respect, consultations may be held subject to the same conditions as those provided for in the second paragraph of paragraph 1 and with the same effect.

3.  The term "hazardous waste" within the meaning of this Article shall cover categories of products listed in Annexes 1 and 2 to the Basel Convention on the Control of Transboundary Movements of Hazardous Wastes and their Disposal.

As regards radioactive waste, the applicable definitions and thresholds shall be those which will be laid down in the framework of the IAEA. In the meantime, the said definitions and thresholds shall be those specified in the declaration in Annex VIII to this Convention.

## Article 40

At the request of the ACP States, the Community shall provide available technical information on pesticides and other chemical products with a view to helping them develop or reinforce a suitable and safe use of these products. Where necessary and in accordance with the provisions for development finance cooperation, technical assistance can be given in order to ensure conditions of safety at all stages, from production to disposal of such products.

## Article 41

The Parties recognize the value of exchanging views, using existing consultation mechanisms under this Convention, on major ecological hazards, whether on a planetary scale (such as the greenhouse effect, the deterioration of the ozone layer, tropical forests, etc.), or of a more specific scope resulting from the application of industrial technology. Such consultations may be requested by either Party, insofar as these hazards may in practice affect the Contracting Parties, and will be aimed at assessing the scope for joint action to be undertaken within the terms of this Convention. If necessary, the consultations will also provide for an exchange of views prior to discussions conducted on these subjects in the appropriate international fora.

...

## Drought and desertification control
## Article 54

The ACP States and the Community recognize that certain ACP States are facing considerable difficulties as a result of endemic drought and growing desertification, which hold back all efforts at development, in particular those aimed at achieving the priority objective of food self-sufficiency and food security.

The two Parties agree that in a number of ACP States control of drought and desertification constitutes a major challenge on which depends the success of their development policy.

## Article 55

The correction of this situation and the sustainable development of the countries affected or threatened by such disasters require a policy encouraging the restoration of the natural environment and of the balance between resources and the human and animal population, in particular through such means as improved harnessing and management of water resources, appropriate agriculture, agroforestry and reafforestation schemes and control of the causes of desertification as well as of practices that engender it.

## Article 56

If a return to the natural balance is to be expedited, a drought and desertification control component in particular must be incorporated into all agricultural and rural development operations, such as:

1.   — the extension of agroforestry systems combining farming and forestry, research and development activities to produce plant species that are more adapted to local conditions;

    — the introduction of suitable techniques aimed at increasing and maintaining the productivity of agricultural land, arable land and natural pastureland with a view to controlling the various forms of erosion;

    — the reclamation of land that has deteriorated, by means of reafforestation or agricultural land improvement, combined with maintenance schemes involving, as far as possible, the people and authorities concerned in order to safeguard the progress made;

2.   the encouragement of measures to economize on wood as an energy source by stepping up

research into, application of and information on new and renewable sources of energy such as wind, solar and biomass energy, and by the use of improved stoves with a greater heat yield;

3. the rational development and management of forestry resources by setting up at national or regional level, forestry management plans aimed at optimizing the exploitation of forestry resources;

4. the pursuit of ongoing campaigns to educate the people concerned to be aware of the phenomena of drought and desertification and to train them in the possible ways of controlling them;

5. an overall coordinated approach which, as a result of schemes such as those referred to in points 1 to 4, seeks to ensure the restoration of a suitable ecological balance between natural resources and the human and animal population, without prejudicing the objective of harmonious economic and social development.

### Article 57

The operations to be undertaken, where necessary with research backing, shall cover, *inter alia*:

1. improving man's knowledge of, and ability to forecast, desertification phenomena by observing developments in the field, by means, *inter alia*, of modern technologies such as remote sensing, by making use of results achieved and gaining a better understanding of the changes to the human environment in time and space;

2. making an inventory of water-tables and of their replenishment capacity with a view to better predictability of water supplies, using surface and ground water and improving management of these resources, in particular by means of dams or other appropriate developments for the purpose of satisfying the needs of people and animals, and improving weather forecasting;

3. establishing a system for the prevention and control of bush fires and deforestation.

## Questions and Problems

1. What could be the content of the "non-deterioration principle" in Swedish law?

2. Is integrated environmental protection mainly based on
   — planning for the use of space
   — regulation of determined human activities
   — the use of determined substances?

3. Can integrated environmental protection best be assured at the national, regional, local or other level? In case of a conflict between standards on the different levels, which should prevail?

4. Why is it necessary for Europe to help developing countries to protect the environment? Should there be different standards for developing regions of Europe? Consider the application of EC law to the eastern region of Germany.

5. If you were asked to create a commission for urban planning, what specialists would you invite to participate in it?

6. What is the impact of road traffic on the environment? What actions are the most appropriate to reduce such impact?

7. Should environmental law be codified? Discuss the advantages and disadvantages of codification.

8. What is the definition of "landscape"?

9. If you were charged with reducing advertising billboards alongside roads, what measures would you take? On what authority?

10. What is the impact of tourism on environmental protection?

## Bibliography

Brookes, A., *Channelized Rivers: Perspectives for Environmental Management* (1988).

EEC, "The Future of Rural Society", COM(88)501 final/2.

EEC, "Green Paper on the Urban Environment", CCE, DG XI.

EEC, "Migration Patterns in the European Community During the 1980s and the Outlook for the 1990s", CCE, DG XVI (1991).

EEC, "Urbanization and the Functions of Cities in the European Community" (Centre for Urban Studies, University of Liverpool), CCE, DG XVI (1991).

Harte, J. D. C., *Landscape, Land Use and the Law* (1985).

McCloskey, M., "Legislation and Landscape Aesthetics", in: *Our National Landscapes* (Smardon, R. C. and Elsner, G. H., eds.) U.S. Forest Service (1979).

Newman, P. and Kenworthy, J., *Cities and Automobile Dependence* (1981).

Porteous, D., "Approaches to Environmental Aesthetics", 2 *J. Envtl Psych.*, 53–66 (1982).

Thorne, J. F. and Huang, C. S., "Toward a Landscape Ecological Aesthetic: Methodologies for Designers and Planners", 21 *Landscape Urban Plann.*, 61–79 (1991).

Smardon, R. C., "Review of Agency Methodology for Visual Project Analysis" in *Foundations for Visual Project Analysis* (Smardon, R. C., Palmer, J. E., Felleman, J. P., eds.) (1986), pp. 141–6

## CHAPTER XII

# THE ROLE OF THE PUBLIC AND NON-GOVERNMENTAL ORGANIZATIONS

## A. Overview

Unlike many areas of law, environmental protection directly affects every individual. Regulations, or the lack of them, can implicate not only health and well-being, but also economic standards and the general quality of life. To protect themselves against environmental harm and make judgments about the proper measures to take, individuals must be informed about and be able to participate in decisions that affect them. Guarantees of information and participation are basic to the concept of environmental rights and have been incorporated into many national, Community and international laws. In addition, legal measures often recognize a particular role for non-governmental associations interested or expert in environmental matters. This final chapter examines the role of individuals and non-governmental organizations in the development and implementation of European environmental law.

### 1. *The Role of the Public*

Environmental law is characterized by the elaboration of comprehensive rights and duties. Constitutional texts that proclaim the state's obligation to conserve the environment or a right to a clean or healthy environment often also contain individual or societal obligations in this regard. In such circumstances, each person has the right to have his or her environment protected, but is obliged to contribute to the effort.

The fulfilment of this obligation necessitates community education, information and action. State or local government not only must ensure its citizens receive information concerning any measure that could menace their environment, but should provide means for the participation of individuals or groups in environmental decision-making. In addition, education is required that will allow all persons to make the best use of the information they receive.

#### a. *The Right to Information*

Access to environmental information is a prerequisite to public participation in decision-making and to monitoring governmental and private sector activities. Access to information also can assist enterprises in planning and utilization of the best available technology. The nature of environmental deterioration, which often arises only long after a project is completed and is often irreversible, also compels early and complete data, to make informed choices. Transboundary impacts raise the new problem of providing information across borders.

The elaboration of legal norms guaranteeing environmental information poses several problems concerning the scope of such a right. The "right to information" can mean, narrowly, freedom to seek information, or, more broadly, a right to access to information, or even a right to receive it. Corresponding duties of the state can be limited to abstaining from interfering with public efforts to obtain information from the state or from private entities, to requiring the state to obtain and disseminate all relevant information concerning both public and private projects. If the government duty is limited to abstaining from interfering with the ability of public representatives to seek information from those willing to share it, without a right of access, then little may actually be obtained. A governmental obligation to release information about its own projects can increase public knowledge, but fails to provide access to the numerous industrial, private-sector activities that can affect the environment. Information about the latter may be obtained by the government through licensing or environmental impact requirements. Imposing upon the state a duty to disseminate this information in addition to details of its own projects provides the public with the broadest basis for informed decision-making.

European legal texts contain various formulations of a right to information or a corresponding state duty. Article 10 of the European Convention on Human Rights guarantees "the freedom to receive information" in general. This has been interpreted to mean that a state is prohibited from restricting the right of a person to receive information that others are willing to give.[1] In general, the right to information in the Community means that the individual has the right to be informed about the environmental impacts of products, manufacturing processes and their effects on the environment, and industrial installations. Directive 76/160, on bathing water quality, states that "Public interest in the environment and in the improvement of its quality is increasing; the public should therefore receive objective information on the quality of bathing water".[2] Article 13 requires Member States to submit regularly to the Commission a "comprehensive report on the bathing water and most significant characteristics thereof". The Commission publishes the information "after prior consent from the Member State concerned". However, the consent may limit the information provided, undermining its "objective" nature. Other water quality directives contain no provisions on publication of information[3] and Directive 80/778 has no reporting obligation for Member States.[4]

Air pollution directives also vary in regard to public rights to information. The

---

[1] See, Stefan Weber, "Environmental Information and the European Convention on Human Rights", 12 *Human Rights Law Journal* 177 (1991).

[2] Directive 76/160 of 8 Dec. 1975, O.J. no. L 31/1, 5 Feb. 1976.

[3] For example, Directive 76/464 of 4 May 1976 on water pollution caused by certain dangerous substances discharged into the aquatic environment of the Community, O.J. 1976, no. L 129/23, 10 May 1976; Directive 80/68 of 17 Dec. 1979 on the protection of groundwater, O.J. no. L 229/11, 26 Jan. 1980.

[4] Directive 80/778 of 15 July 1980 on the quality of water for human consumption, O.J. no. L 20/43, 30 Aug. 1979.

Directives that establish limit values for sulphur dioxide and suspended particulates, for lead and for carbon dioxide, require Member States to submit reports to the Commission, but make no reference to public information.[5] In contrast, article 9 of Directive 84/360 on combating air pollution by industrial installations,[6] provides that "applications for authorization to operate an installation which is air-polluting shall be made available to the public concerned in accordance with the procedures provided for by national law". The same applies to decisions by the competent authorities on such applications.

Member States are required to establish, maintain, and publish plans for the disposal of toxic and dangerous wastes.[7] Directive 85/339 on containers of liquids for human consumption[8] requires that a Member State which introduces a system of refillable containers take steps to ensure that the containers are clearly marked that they are refillable.

The "Seveso" directive concerning major accident hazards of certain industrial activities states that

Member States shall ensure that information on safety measures and on the correct behavior to adopt in the case of an accident is supplied in an appropriate manner, and without their having to request it, to persons liable to be affected by a major accident ... The information shall be repeated and updated at appropriate intervals. It shall also be made publicly available.[9]

The Directive was amended in 1988 to strengthen the information requirements.

Linked to the Seveso Directive are other measures that seek to enhance safety in the workplace, guaranteeing workers information on hazardous products and processes. Framework Directive 89/391[10] on the protection of workers against risks at the workplace includes provisions for employee information and consultation. Implementing directives include a directive on the minimum safety and health requirements for the workplace,[11] Directive 90/679,[12] protecting workers from risks related to exposure to biological agents at work, and Directive 80/1107, covering all chemical, physical and biological agents at work.[13] The last, general, directive has been supplemented with a series of individual directives concerning particular substances, such as lead[14] and asbestos.[15] Other directives apply to specific industries,

[5] Directives: 80/779/EEC, O.J. no. L 229/30; 82/884/EEC, O.J. no. L 378/15; 85/203/EEC, O.J. no. L 87/1.

[6] O.J. no. L 188/20.

[7] Directive 78/319/EEC, Article 9, O.J. no. L 84/43.

[8] O.J. no. L 176/18.

[9] Article 8, Directive 82/501/EEC O.J. no. L 230/1, amended by Directive 88/610/EEC, O.J. no. L 336/14.

[10] O.J. no. L 183.

[11] O.J. no. L 393.

[12] O.J. no. L 374. The Commission submitted a proposed amendment on 15 July 1992 to supplement the list of biological agents and their classification. O.J. no. C 217.

[13] O.J. no. L 327, amended by Directive 88/642, O.J. no. L 356.

[14] E.g. 82/605, O.J. no. L 247.

[15] E.g. 83/477, O.J. no. L 263, amended June 1991, O.J. no. L 206.

such as mining and fishing. In all cases, the directives require that information be given to workers about the risks they face.

Two general directives address rights of information. The duty to provide information in connection with mandatory environmental assessment projects is made explicit in Council Directive 85/337 concerning the assessment of the effects of certain public and private projects on the environment.[16] States must adopt measures to ensure that the project developer provides the information necessary for the assessment. Listed in Annex III, the information includes a description of the project, in particular its site, its concept, its dimensions, the principal characteristics of its production processes; an estimate of the expected types and quantities of residues and emissions; a description of the alternatives to the project studied by the developer; a description of the elements of the environment likely to be significantly affected by the project and the likely effects which will result, including a description of the developer's assessment methodology; and a description of measures envisaged to prevent, reduce, and where possible offset any significant adverse effect on the environment. Article 6 provides that "States should make public all requests for authorization of a public or private project which might significantly affect the environment".[17] States also should ensure that opportunity is given to concerned members of the public to express an opinion before the project is approved. Member States should establish the means to provide this information and consultation. Based on the particular characteristics of the projects or sites concerned, the State may determine what sector of the public is concerned, decide on the location where the information can be consulted and establish the particular methods of information (poster, newspapers, displays). States also may determine the manner according to which the public should be consulted (written submission, public inquiry) and fix the appropriate time limits for the various stages of the procedure.

On 7 June 1990, the European Community adopted a Directive on Freedom of Access to Information on the Environment.[18] Public authorities are required to make available information relating to the environment to any person upon request without the person having to prove an interest. Exceptions are provided to protect commercial and industrial confidentiality and personal data. If a request for information is refused, the applicant may seek a judicial or administrative review of the decision. Community work on adopting the Directive began in July 1985,[19] with attention increasing after the April 1986 accident at the nuclear power plant in Chernobyl, Ukraine.

Access to information covers information held by public authorities which relates to the state of the environment; activities or measures adversely affecting or likely so to affect the environment; activities or measures designed to protect the environment (article 2(a)). The provision thus includes virtually all environmental data. The term

---

[16] Council Directive 85/337/EEC of 27 June 1985, O.J. no. L 175/40, 7 July 1985.

[17] Op. cit.

[18] Council Directive 90/313/EEC of 7 June 1990 on the freedom of access to information on the environment, O.J. no. L 158, 23 June 1990.

[19] European Parliament, document B2–736/85 of 16 July 1985.

public authorities means all administrations with responsibilities relating to the environment (article 2(b)). In addition, article 6 extends the directive's coverage to all bodies which have responsibilities for the environment which derive from public authorities; thus anyone delegated environmental functions is included. Judicial and legislative bodies are excluded provided they act "in a judicial or legislative capacity".

Access to information is available to any "natural or legal person". (Article 3(1)). No specific form is required and there is no distinction according to geographic origin. Thus, persons in another Member State or even those from outside the Community may have access to information. The applicant need not "prove an interest" in order to obtain the information.

The directive allows Member States to refuse a request for information when it affects the confidentiality of proceedings of public authorities, international relations and national defense; public security; matters which are or have been in litigation or under inquiry, or which are the subject of preliminary investigation proceedings; commercial and industrial confidentiality, including intellectual property; the confidentiality of personal date and/or files; material supplied by a third party without that party being under a legal obligation to do so; material the disclosure of which would make it more likely that the environment to which such material relates would be damaged; where it involves a supply of unfinished documents or data or internal communications, or where the request is manifestly unreasonable or formulated in too general a manner. The state may, but is not obliged to, refuse information in the cases listed. It is unclear if the scope of the grounds for refusal, e.g. public security, is subject to review by the European Court of Justice or remains within the discretion of Member States.

Procedural guarantees in the directive include requiring a response within two months to any request for information. Reasons must be given for any refusal. A judicial or administrative review of the decision is allowed in accordance with the relevant national legal system. Requests for information must be fulfilled or responded to as quickly as possible, at least within the period of two months.[20] All Member States were required to adopt necessary measures to comply with its mandates by December 1992.

Among other organizations, the World Health Organization's European Charter on the Environment and Health states that "every individual is entitled to information and consultation on the state of the environment". Finally, within the Helsinki process, the States involved have confirmed the right of individuals, groups, and organizations to obtain, publish and distribute information on environmental issues.

Where transboundary environmental consequences are foreseen, international texts may establish a duty to inform the citizens of the potentially affected state. As early as 1977, the OECD recommended that authorities of the country of origin take appropriate measures to provide persons exposed to a significant risk of transfrontier pollution with sufficient information to enable them to exercise their rights in a timely manner. This information should be equivalent to that provided in the country of

[20] *Id.* at art. 3(4).

origin in cases of comparable domestic pollution. Exposed countries should designate one or more authorities who have the duty to receive the information and disseminate it.[21] The principle of prior information also is contained in bilateral treaties[22] and in regional agreements. In the Nordic Environmental Protection Convention,[23] it is provided that information about any activity which could cause harm in another state must be communicated to a special authority in the latter state, appointed to safeguard the general environmental interests. Article 7 provides that communications relating to the projects shall be published in the local newspaper or made public in some other appropriate manner.

On a national level, European states have widely different laws concerning access to environmental information. In the United Kingdom there is no general right to information. However, local authorities and water authorities have a duty to maintain registers open to the public of planning applications and decisions. The Environment and Safety Information Act 1988 provides limited public access to information on a register about suspected breaches of environmental standards. There is a right of appeal against inclusion on the register.

In contrast, Luxembourg introduced Directive 90/313 on freedom of access into national law in virtually identical terms. Denmark gives organizations a limited right to information from the files of administrative authorities and major public companies. County councils are obliged to publish plans and alternative ideas. Sweden and the Netherlands provide more expansive rights of information. In Sweden a government act protects freedom to obtain and receive information, allowing any Swedish subject to see any documents of a state or municipal agency whether or not the document concerns them personally. Officials in most cases may not ask who wants the information or why. Most documents written by the authorities are available to the public on demand. In addition, the Freedom of the Press Act gives a right to seek and receive information from the government. In the Netherlands, constitutional and environmental legislation gives individuals, private organizations and governmental bodies, including those in other countries, the right to information regarding licenses, environmental quality standards, emissions and product standards and the content of environmental impact statements during the decision-making process.

Bulgaria enacted a 1991 law that gives physical and legal persons, state and local authorities, access to environmental information. The information may include data concerning the state of the environmental components, data about the results of activities that bring or may bring about pollution or damage to the environment or its components, and data concerning activities and actions undertaken for protection and restoration of the environment. The Ministry of the Environment, the Ministry of Public Health and the Ministry of Agriculture are obligated to collect this information.

Legislation in most states provides exceptions to the type of information that may be released. For example, Sweden limits access to information in order to protect

---

[21] OECD Council Recommendation C(777)28(Final), 17 May 1977.

[22] See, for example, the French–Belgian agreement on protection from radioactivity concerning construction of the nuclear power station at Ardennes, 23 September 1966, art. 2.

[23] Stockholm, 19 February 1974.

national security, the integrity of individuals, to ensure safety and order, to facilitate the prevention and prosecution of crime and "where particularly important reasons so warrant". There is a right to know the reason a request is refused and there is a right to appeal a refusal. In 1989, the Swedish government also enacted a Trade Secrets Act specifying criminal sanctions for employees who reveal secrets about their employers, excepting serious or illegal activities.

### b. Public Participation

Obtaining information is a prerequisite for the major role played by the public, which is participating in decision-making. OECD has adopted several texts recommending that its member states encourage public participation when preparing decisions having significant consequences on the environment. Principle 23 of the 1982 World Charter for Nature provides most explicitly:

> All persons, in accordance with their national legislation, shall have the opportunity to participate, individually or with others, in the formulation of decisions of direct concern to their environment, and shall have access to means of redress when their environment has suffered damage or degradation.

This principle is repeated in binding texts. Community Council Directive 85/337 on environmental assessment provides in article 6 that not only any demand for authorization of a public or private project which could have effect on the environment, as well as information received on this subject should be made public, but the public also should be afforded an opportunity to express an opinion before the project is approved.

Public participation is based on the right of those who may be affected to have a say in the determination of their environmental future. This may include foreign citizens and residents. The 1991 Espoo Convention on Environmental Impact Assessment in a Transboundary Context requires states to notify the public and to provide an opportunity for public participation in relevant environmental impact assessment procedures regarding proposed activities in any area likely to be affected by trans-boundary environmental harm. In a final decision on the proposed activities, the state must take due account of the environmental impact assessment, including the opinions of the individuals in the affected area.

Many states that provide wide rights of access to information, also establish a right to participate in environmental decision-making. In the Netherlands, individuals, private organizations and governmental bodies may express their views during the decision-making processes on licenses, environmental quality standards, emissions and product standards and the content of environmental impact statements. In Denmark, industry confederations, agricultural organizations, consumer groups, and workers' unions are consulted about new legislation. More specifically, all inhabitants of a county are entitled to participate in regional planning.

The primary device of public participation is hearings or views submitted in connection with licensing or permits, or review of environmental impact assessments. In Bulgaria, article 20, section 1, of the Environmental Protection Act provides that all physical and legal persons concerned have the right to take part in the discussion of the results of an environmental impact assessment. They must be informed through the national and local media or in another appropriate way not less than one month prior to the review procedure. The public does not have the right to make the final decision, but public opinion must be taken into consideration by the authorities.

Public participation also may take the form of organized efforts to promote adoption of stricter environmental standards, litigation to challenge environmental decisions already made or to seek remedies for harm that has occurred.

## 2. The Role of Non-Governmental Organizations

Non-governmental organizations and associations (NGOs) are an organized means of public participation in environmental decision-making. Like individual members of the public, NGOs may compile data, seek to influence legislation, intervene in decisions on licensing or permitting projects, and monitor compliance with environmental laws. In some countries, standing to sue to enforce environmental norms has been afforded NGOs under certain circumstances (Netherlands, France). With these roles and because of their greater means, expertise, and organized efforts, NGOs often can more effectively assert public rights of information and participation. Their greater power is often necessary to counterbalance powerful industrial interests. Because of their importance, the Brundtland Commission recommended that governments establish official consultation with NGOs to share information, strategies and resources, and to permit meaningful participation in all aspects of environmental matters.[24] Indeed, NGO representatives played a major role before and during the Rio Conference.

### a. Delegating Management Functions to NGOs

In some circumstances and countries, NGOs may undertake activities which are traditionally the competence of governmental agencies. For example, the Bulgarian Hunting and Fisheries Union controls the national reserves, imposes sanctions on offenders and carries out some economic activities to develop the reserves, pursuant to the Reserve Act of 1982 and the Fish Industry Act of 1982.

### b. Using NGO Expertise

Governments may call upon NGO members or the organization in its entirety to provide scientific or other expertise to state authorities. In this regard, international non-governmental organizations are particularly important. The World Conservation Union, for example, publishes Red Data Books that describe threatened species of mammals, amphibians, reptiles, invertebrates, plants and papilionides. In addition, each year it publishes a list of threatened species, national parks and protected areas. The Union has played a strong role in the elaboration of some major international

---

[24] Our Common Future, supra, p. 213.

environmental treaties and prepared the first draft of the World Charter for Nature. The Union consults with governments on conservation, collection and analysis of information, and provides technical support.

### c. Complaining of Violations

Every resident or organization normally may complain to public authorities if environmental violations occur. In some cases, as noted above, NGOs may become involved in litigation to enforce environmental protection. In the Reinwater case in the Netherlands, the Dutch highest court gave environmental organizations standing to sue where the stated purpose of an organization has been affected; the interests in the lawsuit lend themselves to grouping; and the interests served by the litigation are protected by civil law. In Austria, the World Wildlife Fund intervened in a case concerning the construction of a hydroelectric dam on the Danube. The dam would have caused the destruction of an ancient forest unique in Europe. The government abandoned the project following two decisions of the Austrian High Court in January 1985 and September 1986.

Luxembourg recently increased the role of non-governmental organizations, amending its law of 11 August 1982 which gave certain groups the right of access to court in regard to nature protection. Under the new law, dated 10 August 1992, the same societies may act in court on laws regarding the elimination of waste, pollution of the atmosphere, noise pollution, and fishing.

### d. Participation in Licensing and Permit Procedures

As discussed above, public participation is generally guaranteed as part of the environmental impact assessment procedure, a necessary prerequisite to licensing in most states. NGOs often take a lead in commenting on impact statements.

### e. Funding Environmental Projects

Some NGOs are in a position to fund conservation measures or projects of environmental protection. Indeed, NGOs have been the principal source of debt-for-nature swaps with primarily Third World debtor countries.

Governments may require the registration of NGOs and establish certain requirements for their recognition. For example, in Hungary, an NGO must have a board of directors, at least ten members and a statement of purpose. Although most non-governmental organizations rely upon membership fees and other private fund-raising, in some cases public interest NGOs may be subsidized by the government (France).

In general, it is hard to overstate the importance of environmental non-governmental organizations. Their publications and other efforts ensure an informed and active citizenry and contribute to long-term environmental protection.

# B. Case Study

## Cyril de Klemm, *The Work of the World Conservation Union*

The protection of nature seems even today to occupy a narrow and somewhat neglected place in environmental law. At the same time, increasingly serious threats weigh upon species, ecosystems and biological processes. If no measures are taken, a massive wave of extinction can be expected in the coming decades. The consequences of this eventual ecological catastrophe are for the most part unforeseeable. It is, however, impossible to deny that the destruction of biological diversity will mean the disappearance of a scientific capital of inestimable value, as yet poorly known, and will significantly alter the course of evolution.

In response to growing scientific concern about the disappearance of species and numerous natural milieus, concern now shared by public opinion in numerous countries, a consensus in favour of the conservation of nature gradually has emerged. It remains for the consensus to be transformed by the adoption of and respect for concrete and effective measures of conservation. For this to happen a catalyst often seems necessary. Such a role has fallen to the World Conservation Union (IUCN).

IUCN has become a model for international non-governmental organizations and has contributed to promoting conservation of nature at the international level. The decision to create the organization was taken during a conference held in Brunnen, Switzerland, in 1947, with the aid of UNESCO. The government of France and UNESCO organized a further conference in Fontainebleau in 1948 for the official establishment of IUCN, a non-governmental organization to which States also have the ability to adhere.

## 1. *Institutional Structure of IUCN*

The IUCN is a union, that is, an association of other groups. It presents a composite nature, because its statute permits its membership to include: states, whose number now exceeds sixty; public organizations; and more than four hundred national and international non-governmental organizations. The IUCN is, in this regard, the only world organization in which these various groups cooperate to defend the cause of conservation. From the legal point of view, the statute of the IUCN is that of a private association under Swiss law.

The institutional structure of the IUCN is organized classically around three principal organs:

(a) *The General Assembly* is the directive organ of the IUCN; it is charged with establishing the general policy of the organization during triennial reunions of all its members. The Assembly is divided into two colleges, composed on one side of governmental delegates and on the other of representatives of NGOs. The adoption of a decision requires majority approval by both colleges. Since 1948, the Assembly has met 19 times.

(b) *The Council* is charged with execution of the decisions of the General Assembly and assuring continuity in IUCN actions. It is composed of: (a) 36 members elected by the General Assembly on a geographic basis of three councillors each for eight regions: Africa, Central and South America, North America and the Caribbean, Eastern Asia, Western Asia, Oceana, Eastern Europe, and Western Europe; (b) five invited councillors; (c) the president of IUCN as well as the presidents of six commissions, elected by the Assembly General.

The IUCN, with the aim of understanding all aspects relevant to the conservation of nature, has in effect formed a reserve of experts divided into commissions concerning:

— survival of species;

— national parks and protected zones;

— environmental law;

— strategies and environmental planning;

— education and communication.

Each president chooses and solicits experts forming the commission that he or she directs. The experts, appointed in their individual capacities because of their competence, cannot therefore represent the interests of organizations of which they are members. The functions assured by the commissions are multiple: they include giving advice, undertaking research and directing field operations.

(c) *The Secretariat* is the permanent organ of the Union. It is located in Gland, Switzerland, between Geneva and Lausanne. The Director General is named by the Council and is responsible to it. The Director appoints the members of the Secretariat, who now number two hundred. They are divided between the headquarters (eighty persons), the Centre for Environmental Law in Bonn, the specialized unit for plants in London, and a certain number of regional bureaux established in Nairobi, Kenya; Dakar, Senegal; Harare, Zimbabwe; Karachi, Pakistan; San Jose, Costa Rica; and Washington, DC, United States. In addition, there exists at Cambridge, England, a continuous environmental monitoring centre charged with compiling all information related to endangered species, protected zones, and trade in wild flora and fauna.

The centre, initially attached exclusively to IUCN, became a financial burden and it was decided to offer its services simultaneously to the IUCN, UNEP, and the Worldwide Fund for Nature (WWF). It benefits, in turn, from financial support from the three organizations.

The financing of IUCN is provided from different sources, principally coming from membership fees. Certain States contribute supplementary amounts. In addition, IUCN, in the framework of contracts negotiated with international organizations or states, is paid for its preparation of reports, impact studies, and other work. The budget of the Union has risen considerably in a short time: from 4 million Swiss francs in 1980, it is now more than 30 million Swiss francs annually.

## 2. Vocation and Role of IUCN

### (a) Action of IUCN

The first goal of IUCN is to promote an alliance between ecological science and a policy of conservation. It expresses a global ecological consciousness based upon solid scientific evidence.

The Union is a source of information for governments and equally aims to influence them in order to, on the one hand, prevent the extinction of species and disappearance of ecosystems, and, on the other hand, to support the adoption of positive conservation measures such as the creation of protected zones.

IUCN is at the origin of several important developments. Aware that the preservation of species threatened with extinction requires their prior identification, it launched a vast "census" enterprise, beginning in 1966 with the publication of the "red data books". The books form a unique international register listing a large number of species threatened with extinction. It constitutes a reference work for states for the adoption of conservation measures.

The IUCN was also the principal architect of a document of major importance: the World Conservation Strategy. The Strategy is founded on three fundamental principles:

— maintenance of essential ecological processes;

— preservation of genetic diversity;

— sustainable exploitation of species and ecosystems.

Requested by UNEP, which financed its elaboration with WWF, sponsored by FAO and UNESCO, this document was published in 1980. In integrating conservation of natural resources with economic development, it has profoundly influenced national conservation strategies. A new version of this Strategy was launched in October 1991 under the name "Caring for the Earth".

In the field of conservation law, the IUCN has played a considerable role. It actively contributed to drafting the World Charter for Nature, which was subsequently adopted and proclaimed in 1982 by the United Nations General Assembly. The initiative for this Charter came from the president of Zaire, who proposed the elaboration to the IUCN General Assembly meeting in Kinshasa in 1975. The original text was drafted by a group of members of the legal Commission of IUCN and was then examined by the Union Assembly before being transmitted to the United Nations.

The Charter, which is a fundamental document in the development of international conservation law, even if it is only "soft law" sets out a certain number of principles directly inspired by the World Conservation Strategy which constitutes, as it emphasizes, a moral code of action for humans.

IUCN also has participated in the drafting of most international conventions on nature conservation. In certain cases, IUCN itself initiated preparation of a treaty. This is the case, for example, with the Convention on International Trade in

Endangered Species (CITES), which was the object of a resolution of the General Assembly of the Union in 1963, before being concluded in Washington in 1973. Similarly, the Convention on Biological Diversity, opened for signature at the UNCED meeting in 1993, has its origin in a resolution of the Assembly in 1981. In the two cases, the first drafts of the treaties were prepared by IUCN.

For other treaties, IUCN has been directly involved in the elaboration of preparatory texts: the African Convention for the Conservation of Nature (Convention of Algiers, 1968), the Convention on Wetlands of International Importance (Ramsar, 1971), the Convention on the Protection of Nature in the South Pacific (Appia, 1976), the Convention on the Conservation of Migratory Species (Bonn, 1979), and the Agreement on the Conservation of Nature and Natural Resources in the ASEAN Region (Kuala Lumpur, 1985). Finally, even when IUCN has not actively participated in the elaboration of a text, it has been nearly always consulted on its contents.

One other recent initiative of IUCN is the draft of a world agreement on the conservation of the environment and sustainable development of natural resources. This document, which has the form of a treaty, establishes general principles covering all aspects of the problem.

The IUCN also plays an important role in the application of certain international conventions. It provided the secretariat for CITES until this was taken over by UNEP. It continues to act in this way for the Ramsar Convention, according to the provisions of the treaty itself. The Convention on the Protection of the World Heritage provides expressly, for its part, that a representative of IUCN assists at meetings of the World Heritage Committee, with consultative status, that the Committee can call upon IUCN to implement its programmes and projects, and that the Director General of UNESCO should utilize to the maximum the services of IUCN to prepare documentation for the Committee and the execution of its decisions. These provisions have resulted in IUCN presenting communications on all requests for inscription of new items on the World Heritage List.

The IUCN is, finally, one of the international organizations which is seated in the Group on the Conservation of Ecosystems, beside UNEP, UNESCO and the FAO. This group aims to coordinate international action in the field of nature conservation. In law, as in other fields, IUCN can place at the disposition of states who so request the service of experts to assist in particular projects. Thus, members of the IUCN legal Commission have assisted certain countries to elaborate or improve their laws on conservation of species or natural spaces.

*(b) IUCN Assets*

To perform its tasks well, IUCN has numerous assets. The first consists of its universality. Present in nearly all countries of the world, IUCN has succeeded in escaping political divisions, whether east–west or north–south, and has therefore always been considered as an apolitical organization where all the problems of conservation can be freely debated.

Its credible scientific basis, its capacity to intervene wisely, its cautious positions, have assured it a vast audience and undoubted prestige. The recommendations of the Assembly General have an impact and are often followed with concrete action. IUCN has therefore gradually become somewhat the global ecological conscience. It was towards it that the national non-governmental organizations have turned to better understand their respective governments. It is to it also that governments turn to obtain assistance to solve certain of their problems. Proof of its prestige can be found in the large number of countries that have elaborated national conservation strategies directly inspired by the global strategy. Further, the three primary objectives of the global strategy are now included in numerous national laws and even sometimes in constitutions, such as that of Brazil.

The third major asset of IUCN is the network that it has established around the globe, thanks to its member organizations and to the members of its Commissions, who are in general academics or civil servants of national administrations for the protection of nature. It can thus be easily informed of the situation in numerous countries and it can intervene in turn, often efficiently, when important problems of conservation appear on a national level.

In spite of its undeniable assets, IUCN often has encountered difficulties. Its statute and mixed structure, governmental and non-governmental, presents difficulties as well as advantages. Careful, as is called for by its goals, to integrate the needs of conservation with the imperatives of development, IUCN can find itself divided. Of course, it aims to show in each case that, as the World Conservation Strategy underlined, only conservation guarantees sustainable development. Nonetheless, there are sometimes uncomfortable situations where development projects undertaken by Member States menace ecosystems and species whose preservation is important.

Another problem is that of financing the Union. There have been serious financial crises since the Union's founding. Dues paid by members are completely inadequate and it is not possible, for many reasons, to increase them substantially. Financing by external sources: subventions by organizations such as UNEP and the WWF, practiced in the past, voluntary contributions of certain members, grants coming from foundations like the Ford Foundation in the 1970s, or contracts for services, remain scattered and can undermine the independence of the organization. In addition, such funds generally are contributed for particular projects and not to the functioning of the Union.

The overview of more than forty years of activity of IUCN is on the whole very positive. The Union has succeeded in stimulating a global consensus on the need to conserve the natural habitats of wild species and in turn has benefited from the consensus to lobby effectively.

However, the dangers threatening nature and the environment in general continue to grow. The problems are increasingly taking on a global dimension: acid rain, reduction of the ozone layer, eventual climate changes, and the general destruction of biological diversity. These problems are not only of an ecological nature. They are equally political, economic and social and all the factors must be taken into account if a global consensus is to be achieved to resolve them. The great achievement of IUCN is to have strongly contributed to a consciousness-raising regarding the importance of ecology and in this sense it should continue, while being aware of the importance of other factors and the significance they have.

From a small institution functioning almost exclusively with volunteers, IUCN has become a prestigious organization with a professional personnel and substantial means, but these remain inadequate. It is consulted, heard and often understood. Before the growing threats to our planet, its role can only gain in importance, on condition that the necessary means for it are not lacking.

## C. Documents

*1. The Rio Declaration on Environment and Development,* adopted 14 June 1992 at Rio de Janeiro, A/CONF.151/5/Rev.1, 31 I.L.M. 874 (1992).

### Principle 10

Environmental issues are best handled with the participation of all concerned citizens, at the relevant level. At the national level, each individual shall have appropriate access to information concerning the environment that is held by public authorities, including information on hazardous materials and activities in their communities, and the opportunity to participate in decision-making processes. States shall facilitate and encourage public awareness and participation by making information widely available. Effective access to judicial and administrative proceedings, including redress and remedy, shall be provided.

*2. Council Directive of 7 June 1990 on the Freedom of Access to Information on the Environment (90/313/EEC),* O.J. No. L 158, 23 June 1990 p. 56.

### Article 1

The object of this directive is to ensure freedom of access to, and dissemination of, information on the environment held by public authorities and to set out the basic terms and conditions on which such information should be made available.

### Article 2

For the purposes of this directive:

(a) "information relating to the environment" shall mean any available information in written, visual, aural or data-base form on the state of water, air, soil, fauna, flora, land and natural sites, and on activities (including those which give rise to nuisances such as noise) or measures adversely affecting, or likely so to affect these, and on activities or measures designed to protect these, including administrative measures and environmental management programmes;

(b) "public authorities" shall mean any public administration at national, regional or local level with responsibilities, and possessing information, relating to the environment with the exception of bodies acting in a judicial or legislative capacity.

## Article 3

1. Save as provided in this article, Member States shall ensure that public authorities are required to make available information relating to the environment to any natural or legal person at his request and without his having to prove an interest. Member States shall define the practical arrangements under which such information is effectively made available.

2. Member States may provide for a request for such information to be refused where it affects:
   — the confidentiality of the proceedings of public authorities, international relations and national defence,
   — public security,
   — matters which are, or have been, *sub judice*, or under enquiry (including disciplinary enquiries), or which are the subject of preliminary investigation proceedings,
   — commercial and industrial confidentiality, including intellectual property,
   — the confidentiality of personal data and/or files,
   — material supplied by a third party without that party being under a legal obligation to do so,
   — material, the disclosure of which would make it more likely that the environment to which such material related would be damaged.

   Information held by public authorities shall be supplied in part where it is possible to separate out information on items concerning the interests referred to above.

3. A request for information may be refused where it would involve the supply of unfinished documents or data or internal communications, or where the request is manifestly unreasonable or formulated in too general a manner.

4. A public authority shall respond to a person requesting information as soon as possible and at the latest within two months. The reasons for a refusal to provide the information requested must be given.

## Article 4

A person who considers that his request for information has been unreasonably refused or ignored, or has been inadequately answered by a public authority, may seek a judicial or administrative review of the decision in accordance with the relevant national legal system.

## Article 5

Member States may make a charge for supplying the information, but such charge may not exceed a reasonable cost.

## Article 6

Member States shall take the necessary steps to ensure that information relating to the environment held by bodies with public responsibilities for the environment and under the control of public authorities is made available on the same terms and conditions as those set out in articles 3, 4 and 5 either via the competent public authority or directly by the body itself.

## Article 7

Member States shall take the necessary steps to provide general information to the public on the state of environment by such means as the periodic publication of descriptive reports.

## Article 8

Four years after the date referred to in article 9 (1), the Member States shall report to the Commission on the experience gained in the light of which the Commission shall make a report to the European Parliament and the Council together with any proposal for revision which it may consider appropriate.

## 3. Bulgaria, *Environmental Protection Act,* Law No. 86 of 18 October 1991.

### Information Concerning the State of the Environment
### Article 8

The information about the state of the environment consists of:

1. data concerning the state of the environment components;

2. data about the results of activities that bring or may bring about pollution or damage to the environment or its components;

3. data concerning activities and action undertaken for protection and restoration of the environment.

### Article 9

All persons and the state and municipal authorities shall have the right of access to the available information concerning the state of the environment.

### Article 10

Published and submitted information shall be supplemented by explanations of the possible consequences for human health and the environment and by recommendations for the conduct of the citizens in case of expected negative influence.

### Article 11

(1) Information concerning the state of environment shall be collected by the Ministry of Environment, the Ministry of Health and the Ministry of Agriculture and Food Industry, by the persons authorized by them and by the municipal authorities.

(2) The corporate and physical persons producing goods and services shall submit the data under Article 8, Item 2 to the authorities under Paragraph 1.

(3) The authorities under Paragraph 1 shall furnish and announce information through the mass media or in another way in a comprehensive form and, if possible, constantly when it contains data on negative changes in the state of the environment.

...

### Article 13

The [state and municipal] authorities, [the corporate and physical persons and the producers of goods and services] ... shall inform the population without delay when pollution or damage of the environment occur, including natural disasters, industrial accidents and fires, and shall provide information about the changes in the environment that have taken place, the measures for their restriction and elimination and the requirements for the conduct of the citizens with a view to ensure their health and safety.

### Article 14

The producers of goods and services, their middlemen and the merchants, including those dealing with agricultural and food products, shall be obliged simultaneously with the sale or performance of the service to give customers information in writing, and, in flagrantly unimportant cases, in oral form, about the harmful ingredients of the goods and services, as well as about the possible negative effects of the performed services.

Article 15

An authority or a person under Article 9 who considers their request for access to information unjustifiably rejected or unlawfully restricted, or that the obtained information is unreliable, shall have the right to request protection of their rights through administrative channels or through the court.

*4.* Belgium, Court of Cassation, *Castle John and Nederlandse Stichting Sirius* v. *NV Mabeco and NV Parfin,*
Judgment of 16 December 1986 (European Transport Law, 1985, p. 536).

This is an appeal against the judgment rendered on 19 July 1985 by the Court of Appeal of Antwerp.

The Court has considered the report of President of the Section Janssens and the submissions of Advocate General D'Hoore.

On the ground of appeal based on violation of Articles 6(1),15(1) and 19 of the Geneva Convention of 29 April 1958 on the High Seas, ratified by the Law of 29 July 1971

The Court of Appeal found as follows:

The action taken by the applicants, with a view to alerting public opinion to the dangers inherent in the discharge into the sea of waste products which are harmful to the environment, remains subject to existing laws and decrees. The object, in itself laudable, pursued by the applicants cannot serve to justify the illegal means which they used.

(...) The judge at first instance was wrong in holding that he had no jurisdiction to prohibit action designed to prevent or impede in whatever manner discharge operations on the high seas because the vessels in question, being on the high seas, were exclusively subject to the jurisdiction of the flag State, in this case the State of the Netherlands. This principle (exception to the exclusive jurisdiction of the flag State) applies in the main in relation to policing powers with regard to navigation on the high seas, which States enjoy for the suppression of violations of treaty provisions or customary rules. States exercise these powers by allocating warships or other vessels to the service of the public authorities.

Furthermore the fundamental principle of the exclusive jurisdiction of the flag State is subject to numerous exceptions based on both custom and treaty.

In this case the applicants committed acts on the high seas which fall within the application of the notion of "piracy", for which they cannot claim application of the law of the State whose flag they are flying. (...) It appears from the facts available that, at the time of their action against the Wadsy Tanker and the Falco, the applicants resorted to "violence". (...) The acts in question were committed for personal ends, in furtherance of the second applicant's objects. Furthermore, more personal motivation such as hatred, the desire for vengeance and the wish to take justice into their own hands are not excluded in this case. There is no provision of municipal or international law which imposes restrictions on the competence of the Belgian courts, in relation to their own nationals, to take measures to protect their free right of passage and their lawful activities and even if necessary to pronounce a civil sanction to ensure respect for the freedoms granted to all persons.

The Court of Appeal found that the action in question had been taken by the applicants ... in order to alert public opinion to the dangers inherent in the discharge at sea of waste products harmful to the environment was a goal which was laudable in itself but that in this case the action committed on the high seas by the applicants fell under the application of the notion of "piracy" for which they could not seek to rely on the law of the State whose flag they were flying, since those acts were committed "for personal ends". This decision was deduced simply "from the pursuit by the applicant of the objects set out in its articles of association". The Court of Appeal concluded that in fact personal motives such as hatred, the desire for vengeance or the wish to take justice into their own hands are not excluded in this case and there is no provision of municipal or international law imposing any restriction on the competence of the Belgian courts to take "with regard to their own nationals" measures to protect their free right of passage and their lawful activities and even if necessary to pronounce a civil sanction to ensure respect for the freedoms granted to all persons. [The appellant therefore considers] that the Court of Appeal has failed to provide a proper legal justification for its decision (violation of the provisions of the Geneva Convention cited in the grounds of appeal).

[This Court considers] that Article 15 of the Geneva Convention of 29 April 1958 on the High Seas, ratified by the Law of 29 July 1971 provides

Piracy consists of any of the following acts

(1) Any illegal acts of violence, detention or any act of depredation committed for private ends by the crew or the passengers of a private ship ...

In the judgment under appeal it was held that the applicants committed on the high seas acts falling under the application of the notion of "piracy", from which it follows that they are not entitled to invoke the law of the State whose flag they are flying.

That decision is based on the consideration that the acts in question were committed for personal ends, in particular the pursuit by the applicant of the objects set out in its articles of association.

It is held in the judgment

that the action was taken by the applicants with a view to alerting public opinion to the dangers inherent in the discharge at sea of waste products harmful to the environment.

The applicants do not argue that the acts at issue were committed in the interest or to the detriment of a State or a State system rather than purely in support of a personal point of view concerning a particular problem, even if they reflected a political perspective.

On the basis of these considerations the Court of Appeal was entitled to decide that the acts at issue were committed for personal ends within the meaning of Article 15(1) of the Convention. The ground of appeal is therefore unfounded in law.

# Questions and Problems

1. Could a Japanese environmental protection association ask for information on a project affecting the environment in Denmark under EC Directive 90/313?

2. Can Directive 90/313 be used for obtaining information directly from an industrial company? How would you proceed if you wanted to get such information?

3. How does Directive 90/313 compare to the right to information contained in the European Convention on Human Rights? To the Bulgarian Environmental Protection law?

4. What persons or associations should be offered the opportunity to participate in the prior assessment of an activity or project? Should there be criteria based on:
    — geographic proximity;
    — personal interest;

— representation of collective interests?

5. Where a non-governmental organization brings a court action for reparations for environmental harm, what remedies might be available:
— cancellation of an authorization or license to proceed;
— injunction against further action;
— moral satisfaction (a symbolic sum of money);
— monetary compensation;
— restitution or restoration of the damaged environment?

6. Discuss the view that in a democracy, the elected representatives embody the public interest and there is therefore no need to give non-governmental organizations the right to express public concerns before administrative or judicial bodies.

Does the judgment in the *Castle John* case have any bearing on this issue?

# Bibliography

Fuhr, M. and Roller, G. (eds), *Participation and Litigation Rights of Environmental Associations in Europe: Current Legal Situation and Practical Experience* (1991).

Krämer, L., *Focus on European Environmental Law* (1992).

Kromarek, P. (ed.), *Environnement et Droits de l'Homme* (1987).

van der Lek, B., "Democracy and the Right to Know" in *Associacao Portuguesa Para O Direito Do Ambiente* (1988).

Weber, S., "Environmental Information and the European Convention on Human Rights", 12 *Hum. Rts. L. J.* 177 (1991).

# LIST OF CONTRIBUTORS

Dr Stefano Burchi received his law degree from Rome University and an LL.M. from Harvard Law School (1977). He also holds a M.Sc. from the School of Natural Resources of the University of Michigan. From 1979–83 he was in charge of water resources legislation activities in the United Nations Department of Technical Cooperation for Development. Since 1983 he has been in charge of land and water legislation for the Development Law Service of UN Food and Agriculture Organisation (Rome, Italy). He has authored more than twenty legal articles.

Dr Malcolm Forster is Head of the International Section of the Environment Group at Freshfields, a major international law firm based in London. He has written and lectured widely in environmental law matters and is vice-chairman of the Environmental Law Commission of the IUCN.

Dr Jean Gottesmann undertook forestry studies at the Swiss Federal Institute of Technology in Zurich. In 1969 he became a certified engineer based on his work on soil physics. In 1985 he received his doctor iuris degree with a thesis on energy law. He works in Switzerland as an independent consultant for environmental law matters.

Professor F. A. M. de Haan is professor of Soil Hygiene and Soil Pollution in the Department of Soil Science and Plant Nutrition of the Agricultural State University, Wageningen, Netherlands. His major areas of research concern waste management, soil mixing, soil compaction and other issues concerning soil pollution. He has written over 100 scientific publications.

Mr Antti Haapanen is a Counsellor in the Division of Nature Conservation, Ministry of Environment, Helsinki, Finland.

Mr Hector Hacourt serves as Administrateur principal for the Division on the Conservation of Nature, Council of Europe, Strasbourg, France.

Professor Jose Juste Ruiz is professor of public international law at the University of Valencia, Spain. He studied in Valencia, Paris and California. He received a masters degree in comparative law from the University of California, Berkeley, in 1975. He also holds the diploma of the Hague Academy of International Law. He has been a consultant to the Minister of Foreign Affairs and the Minister of Public Works and Transport in regard to Conventions on the protection of the marine environment. He has been a member of various Spanish delegations to conferences on marine pollution. He is the author of several books and numerous articles.

Professor Cyril de Klemm received law degrees from the Universities of Aix-en-Provence and Paris. He is a consultant to UNESCO, the Council of Europe and IUCN. He is a member of the IUCN Commissions on Environmental Planning and on Policy, Law and Administration.

Dr Ludwig Krämer is the Director of Legal Affairs and Application of Community Law for DG XI of the Commission of the European Communities, the directorate responsible for environmental matters. He is the author of several works, most recently *Focus on European Environmental Law* (1992).

Professor Owen Lomas, Solicitor, is a lecturer in environmental law at the University of Warwick and convenor of the University's Legal Research Institute expert group on

Environmental and Housing Law. He is Editor of the UK Environmental Law Association Journal of Environmental Law. He has been an advisor to both the UN and the Council of Europe on environmental issues. He is the author of *Environmental Protection by Criminal Law in England and Wales* (1988) and is a regular contributor to leading journals and conferences on environmental law and practice.

Professor Alberto Lucarelli is a professor of regional law at the Centro Nazionale della Ricerca, Instituto Giuridico, in Naples, Italy, and a lawyer.

Professor Zdenek Madar is at the Institute of Law of the Czech Academy of Sciences, Prague, The Czech Republic.

Dr Said Mahmoudi received his LL.M. from the University of Tehran (1973) and his LL.D. from Stockholm University (1987). Since 1988 he has been Associate Professor of international law at the Faculty of Law, Stockholm University. He has published on the subjects of law of the sea and the environment.

Ms. Maria Teresa Mosquete Pol is at the Ministry of Public Works and Transport, Madrid, Spain.

Mr Peter Naish works as an Environmental Auditor for Ciba–Geigy, Basel, Switzerland.

Professor Tamas Prajczer is in the department of landscape planning at the University of Horticulture, Budapest.

Professor Michel Prieur is the Dean of the Faculty of Law and Economic Sciences at Limoges. He is also a director with the French National Centre for Scientific Research and President of the International Centre for Comparative Environmental Law. He is the author of *Droit de l'Environnement* (1984).

Professor Harald Rossmann has been an assistant professor at the Institute for State and Administrative Law of the University of Vienna. From 1974–7 he served on the Supreme Water Authority and from 1977–91 he was deputy ombudsman. Since 1991 he has acted as an environmental attorney in Vienna, Austria.

Professor Mary Sancy is a professor of environmental law at the Fondation University Luxembourgeoise (Arlon). She is vice-president of the Belgian Environmental Law Association and member of the International Centre of Comparative Environmental Law.

Professor Meinhard Schröder received his doctorate from the University of Bonn. In 1978 he became a professor of national and foreign public law, international and EEC law at the University of Trier. Since 1985 he has been the director of the Institut für Umwelt & Technikrecht in Trier.

Professor Tullio Scovazzi is a professor of Public International Law at the University of Genoa, Italy. He has also taught at the Universities of Milan, Turin, and Parma. He is the author of numerous publications concerning law of the sea, international environmental law and Antarctica.

Professor Marianne Sillen is an Assistant Professor in the Department of Business Law at Lund University, Sweden. Her research concerns the effect of environmental protection measures on enterprises.

Mr Hugh Williams is Joint Managing Director of Ecotec Research & Consulting Ltd, Birmingham, England. Mr Williams assisted the European Commission in the development of the 'Green Book' on urban environments and is responsible for Ecotec's economic/environment work throughout Europe.

Dr A. N. van der Zande received his doctorate from Leiden University in 1976. He has worked as a nature conservation officer and in management for the State Forestry Service, as well as on national nature conservation policy. He is now head of the Section on Nature Conservation of the Ministry of Agriculture, Nature Management and Fisheries, The Hague, Netherlands.

# INDEX